The World of Theatre
Tradition and Innovation

Mira Felner, *Hunter College*
of The City University of New York

Claudia Orenstein, *Hunter College*
of The City University of New York

PEARSON

Boston • New York • San Francisco
Mexico City • Montreal • Toronto • London • Madrid • Munich • Paris
Hong Kong • Singapore • Tokyo • Cape Town • Sydney

Series Editor: *Molly Taylor*
Editorial Assistant: *Suzanne Stradley*
Development Editor: *Ellen Darion*
Senior Marketing Manager: *Mandee Eckersley*
Senior Production Administrator: *Donna Simons*
Cover Administrator: *Linda Knowles*
Composition and Prepress Buyer: *Linda Cox*
Manufacturing Buyer: *Megan Cochran*
Editorial Production Service: *WordCraft, LLC*
Electronic Composition: *Modern Graphics, Inc.*
Interior Designer: *Joyce Weston*
Photo Researchers: *Laurie Frankenthaler; Rachel Lucas*
Cover Designer: *Studio Nine*

For related titles and support materials, visit our online catalog at www.ablongman.com

Between the time website information is gathered and then published it is not unusual for some sites to have closed. Also, the transcription of URLs can result in typographical errors.

Library of Congress Cataloging-in-Publication Data

Felner, Mira
    The world of theatre : tradition and innovation / Mira Felner, Claudia Orenstein.
        p. cm.
    Includes bibliographical references and index.
    ISBN 0-205-36063-7
        1. Theater. 2. Drama. I. Orenstein, Claudia. II. Title.
PN1655.F45 2006
792—dc22

                                                                    2005048757

Cover Photo Credits:

Front cover: *Top row left:* © Stephanie Berger; *Top row right:* © Michal Daniel, 2004; *Middle row left;* © Hideo Haga/HAGA/The Image Works; *Middle row middle:* © Joan Marcus; *Middle row right:* © Bob Krist/CORBIS; *Bottom row:* © Free Agents/CORBIS

Back cover: Photo by Gianfranco Fainello, Fondazione Arena di Verona. All rights are exclusively reserved.

Printed in the United States of America
10 9 8 7 6 5 4 3 2 1 VHP 09 08 07 06 05

To our husbands,
Richard and Taylor,
and our children,
Joshua, Caleb, and Sophie;

and for

Vera Mowry Roberts,
who paved the way for women scholars of the theatre.

Brief Contents

Contents

Part Two. Encountering Traditions   49

3   Understanding Plays   53

4 The European Written Tradition and Its Genres 85

5 Performance Traditions: Legacy and Renewal 113

6 *Alternative Paths to Performance* 149

Part Three. Shaping the Performance 179

7 The Actor: Theatre's Living Presence 181

8 The Director: The Invisible Presence 215

13 *Lighting and Sound Design*   339

14 *Technology and Theatrical Innovation*   363

Part Five. Understanding Today's Theatre 387

15 The Critical Response 389

Features at a Glance

Artists IN PERSPECTIVE

History IN PERSPECTIVE

Performance IN PERSPECTIVE

Texts IN PERSPECTIVE

Preface

Theatre: A Contemporary Global View

How can we understand theatre, an art form whose roots go back more than 2500 years, from the perspective of today's rapidly changing world? *The World of Theatre: Tradition and Innovation* responds to this question by presenting theatre as a diverse and global art in which traditional and experimental forms adapt to the forces of multiculturalism, interculturalism, globalization, and new technologies. While American and European forms are central to the text, international and alternative theatres are placed beside these forms for comparison and contrast throughout. From this global perspective, we see how theatre continues to reinvent itself and remain a vibrant, living art.

Developing technology expands the possibilities of theatrical forms and daily brings distant and diverse cultures into close contact, challenging long-held notions of culture and community, and even our concept of the nature of theatre itself. The theatre naturally responds to these new circumstances. Taking the student on a journey to performances of a *Kathakali King Lear*, a *Zulu Macbeth*, a female *kabuki*, a Singapore musical, and then out into cyberspace where actors can perform with their counterparts thousands of miles away and be present with audiences around the world, this text explores the very boundaries of theatrical art and challenges the reader to think critically about the aesthetic and sociopolitical issues raised by contemporary performance of both traditional and innovative forms.

To trace a single history of theatre's evolution is a questionable task in an era that recognizes the subjectivity and multiplicity of historical accounts. We have chosen to intersperse history throughout the text, where relevant, rather than isolating historical material in separate chapters or using history as an overall framework. Readers can discover the evolution of particular theatrical elements or unique traditions as they encounter them within a larger, global context.

Organization and Content

The text is divided into five parts:

- **Part One, "Navigating the World of Theatre,"** orients the reader to the global forces that are shaping today's theatre and the many ways audiences encounter and respond to theatrical events in different cultural contexts.
- **Part Two, "Encountering Traditions,"** examines the various bases for performance. Chapters on play analysis and genre present the Western play tradition. A chapter on traditions based on performance texts and codes that are passed down from generation to generation presents a multiplicity of such forms from around the world. The final chapter in this section explores alternative methods of creating performances and texts across the international scene.

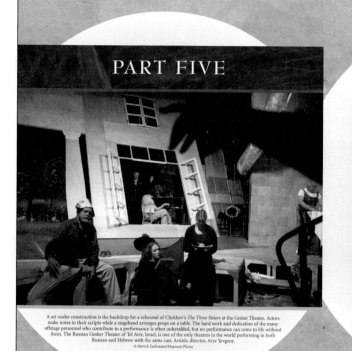

PART FIVE

Understanding Today's Theatre

E
very theatrical production, whether it be the smallest community show, an ancient traditional performance, the Broadway mega-production, or the college show, begins with a daring leap of faith that an empty space can be transformed into a place of magic and illusion in the enactment of an artistic vision. Although the first step is an act of spirit, the process of realization is a tangible one. It sets in motion a system of collaboration requiring the contributions of many people. It will require hard work, commitment, sacrifice, and, however lofty the goals, money and publicity.

Like every act of faith, theatre has its risks, because every performance is subject to critical reaction from the general audience and from the critics who help shape the public's perception of a theatrical production. In fact, theatre artists toil in anticipation of the critical reception, knowing full well that theatre comes alive in the moment it provokes a response. Theatre is a public event and subject to public reaction. Without this vital response, it would cease to have a reason for being.

How we make theatre and how we learn to respond to it is the subject of our final chapters. The hope is that you will become knowledgeable theatregoers and perhaps even be inspired to become theatre makers. Theatre is an art form that draws upon many different kinds of talent, and there is a place for everyone who wants to join the creative community.

A set under construction is the backdrop for a rehearsal of Chekhov's *The Three Sisters* at the Gesher Theatre. Actors make notes in their scripts while a stagehand arranges props on a table. The hard work and dedication of the many offstage personnel who contribute to a performance is often unheralded, but no performance can come to life without them. The Russian Gesher Theater of Tel Aviv, Israel, is one of the only theatres in the world performing in both Russian and Hebrew with the same cast. Artistic director, Arye Yevgeny.
© Patrick Zackmann/Magnum Photos

387

- **Part Three, "Shaping the Performance,"** examines the elements that regulate performance—the actor, the director, and the space. Again, each of these elements is placed in a global perspective. An interview with an American actor is presented side by side with an interview with a Japanese *noh* master. International training systems are compared and contrasted. Profiled directors come from various nations and traditions. Traditional and nontraditional theatre spaces from around the world are examined for their cultural meaning.

- **Part Four, "Art and Technology: Design for the Theatre,"** is devoted to the technical and visual aspects of theatre. The lead chapter examines how design elements are passed down in various performance traditions. Chapters on set, costume, lighting, and sound design in the Western tradition follow. We believe the last chapter in this section is unique to this text in its exploration of the relationship between theatre and technology. It traces both historical technical innovations and the effect of computerization and cyberspace on today's theatre, demonstrating how technology has always shaped the theatre. The chapter raises important questions about how far innovation can go before it transforms the very nature of the theatre itself.

- **Part Five, "Understanding Today's Theatre,"** focuses on the interaction between creating theatre in different contexts and the critical response. In Chapter 15, we introduce the various faces of the critic and the many roles criticism plays in the creation and interpretation of theatre. We provide students with guidance for their own initial attempts at critical writing. Chapter 16 demonstrates to students how artistic vision, talent, and passion intersect with social, political, and eco-

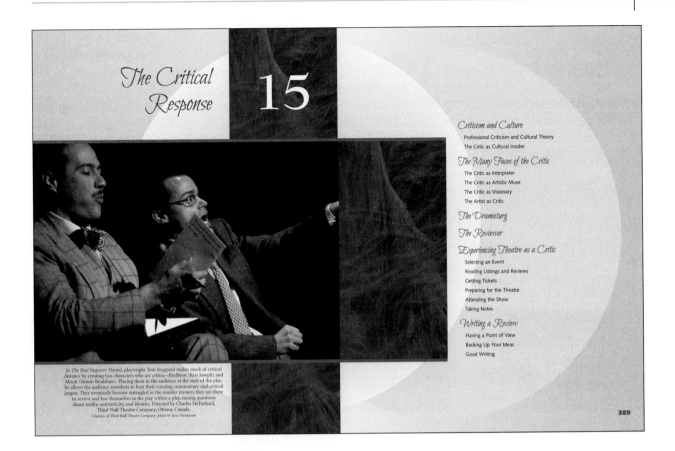

The Critical Response **15**

In *The Real Inspector Hound*, playwright Tom Stoppard makes mock of critical distance by creating two characters who are critics—Birdboot (Kris Joseph) and Moon (Simon Bradshaw). Placing them in the audience at the start of the play, he allows the audience members to bear their running commentary and critical jargon. They eventually become entangled in the murder mystery they are there to review and lose themselves in the play within a play, raising questions about reality, authenticity, and identity. Directed by Charles McFarland, Third Wall Theatre Company, Ottawa, Canada.
Courtesy of Third Wall Theatre Company; photo by Jesse Henderson

389

History IN PERSPECTIVE

THE RECONSTRUCTION OF THE GLOBE THEATRE

William Shakespeare was one of six original shareholders in the first Globe Theatre built in 1599 to house the performances of the Lord Chamberlain's Men, the acting company responsible for the premiers of the great writer's most significant works. Here it was that Hamlet, Macbeth, Lear, and Othello first strutted across the stage in a disreputable district just outside the then city limits of London.

Burned down in 1613 when an ember from a stage cannon set the thatched roof on fire, the Globe Theatre was rebuilt a year later only to be torn down by the Puritans in the 1640s because they condemned the immorality of theatrical activity. For centuries the Globe existed as a theatre of legend, living only in panoramic London drawings, maps, building contracts, and written accounts of Elizabethan theatre-goers.

All this was to change when American actor and film director Sam Wanamaker came to London in search of the Globe, only to discover that there was no lasting monument to the theatre's greatest writer. In 1970 he created the Shakespeare Globe Trust to raise money for a reconstruction of the original theatre based on the existing records, drawings, and accounts, as well as archeological excavations and extant structures from the period. From 1987 to 1997, construction proceeded on a site two hundred yards from the original building. Using materials such as oak timbers, handmade bricks, thatched roof, bright paints, and lime-washed walls, the builders of the new theatre approximated as closely as possible the first Globe. The painting of the heavens is recreated on the roof of the stage. Unfortunately, Wanamaker died in 1993 and never saw the completion of his dream.

Since 1997, summer performances at the Globe of period plays have been produced with attention to historical accuracy in costume, props, set pieces, music, and sound. Musicians are placed on the stage itself or on the stage balcony. No recorded sound is ever used. An all-male cast performs the plays as in Shakespeare's time, and **groundlings**, lower class spectators who could not afford seats, still stand for the duration of the performance, rain or shine, in the open pit area in front of the stage. There are still many unknowns about the acting and pronunciation of the period as we have no tangible evidence to reproduce.

The limited backstage dressing room and storage areas pose challenges to the actors and theatre personnel, but the only concession to today's needs has been in issues of safety. There are twice the number of entrances, illuminated exit signs, and a sprinkler system, lest the fire of 1613 be repeated. The contemporary audience need only cast off their modern attitudes and expectations to experience history.

The New Globe Theatre in London tries to reproduce the feeling of Shakespeare's original Globe with audience members sitting in three tiers of galleries and standing in the pit up to the very edge of the stage itself. The roofed playing area, supported by pillars, follows scholarly assumptions about what Shakespeare's original playing space was like. This photo captures the circular theatre interior, the three galleries of seating around the perimeter, and the general atmosphere in the pit.
© Andrea Pistolesi/Getty Images

The Elizabethan Globe Theatre The ground plan of Shakespeare's Globe theatre. Audience members stood in the pit or sat in three tiers of galleries, surrounding the action on three sides. Actors made their entrances from the tiring house. The discovery space and trap door on the stage allowed for special effects and revelations.

257

nomic reality in the making of theatre everywhere, in all its forms and variety. We examine the various ways theatre is created and celebrate the many unsung heroes whose offstage work helps produce and stage theatrical events around the world. We acknowledge the commitments and sacrifices people make to create theatre today.

Features

Each chapter contains an unusual boxed feature program that gives students historical background and new perspectives on particular topics to provoke critical thinking. Through rich, detailed examples of particular cases, these boxes help explain how theatre is made and discuss its potential for social and political impact.

■ **"History in Perspective"** boxes focus on important historical events and trends relevant to the chapter topic. These boxes introduce students to real-life applications of the concepts presented.

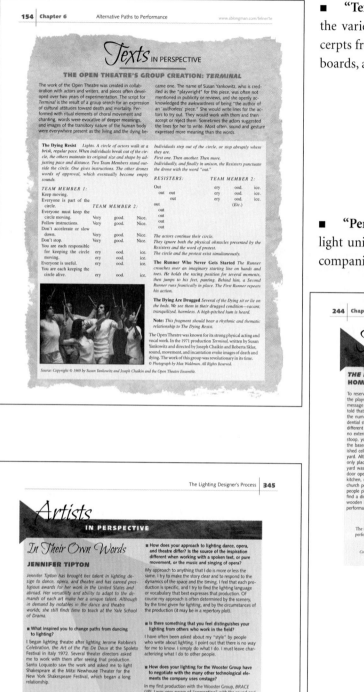

Photo Essays in Chapters 1, 10, and 11 demonstrate global and multicultural influences in all types of theatre. The essay in Chapter 1 focuses on multiculturalism, those in Chapter 10 focus on design traditions and modernism, and the essay in Chapter 11 focuses on visualizing the character's world.

Dispersed throughout the text are **"Challenges and Choices"** margin questions that challenge beliefs and raise important issues in today's theatre. These questions appear adjacent to discussions of pertinent information in the body of the text. They can be used by instructors to prompt class discussion and debate or to stimulate response papers.

Photo Essay

Multiculturalism

Groups not fully represented in the majority culture have a long tradition of forming theatre companies to produce works that speak to the particular needs of their communities. These productions are often a source of pride in identity and can reshape public perceptions. Pictured here are theatres that address ethnicity, race, sexual orientation, and disability.

EAST WEST PLAYERS

Sab Shimono and Jodi Long in *The Wind Cries Mary* by Philip Kan Gotanda, directed by Lisa Peterson at East West Players, Los Angeles. Established in 1965, this important Asian American Theatre organization gives voice to the Asian Pacific American experience. *Courtesy of East West Players; photo by Michael Lamont*

SPLIT BRITCHES

Performances by the lesbian-feminist group Split Britches cause us to question our perceptions of gender. Lois Weaver and Peggy Shaw are seen here in the gender-bending piece "Adultery" at a benefit performance in New York City. *© Dixie Sheridan*

16

Contemporary Design: Collaboration and Evolution | **289**

Photo 10.8
East meets West in Heisei Nakamura-za's production of the traditional *kabuki* play *Natsumatsuri Naniwa Kagami (The Summer Festival: A Mirror of Osaka)*. Here, in a twist on the play's traditional ending, actors dressed as New York City policemen arrest Danshichi Kurobei (Nakamura Kankuro, right) for the murder of his father-in-law, and Issun Tokubei (Nakamura Hashinosuke) for helping his friend escape. This innovative plot turn connected the performance with the contemporary world of the New York audience, reviving the popular spirit of the early *kabuki* tradition. *© Jack Vartoogian/FrontRowPhotos*

Contemporary Design: Collaboration and Evolution

Today designers are free to borrow, combine, and juxtapose elements from various conceptual movements, traditions, and cultures. Stylistic eclecticism is the hallmark of postmodernism and defines a shift in sensibility from earlier periods. With access to images from every culture past and present and the benefit of global cultural exchanges, designers have a varied palette of visual vocabularies and stage techniques from which to draw. These can merge and cross-fertilize or remain distinct. Designers are called on to realize a written play text as well as alternative forms of performance. The result is productions with their own visual styles, unique unto themselves and the designer's imagination.

KEY IDEAS

- Theatre captivates the audience through sound and spectacle. Performance traditions inherit design conventions, while designers in the interpretive tradition imagine the world of the stage afresh for each new production.
- Each performance tradition is associated with particular visual and aural elements that have become emblematic of the form.
- In actor-centered traditions, colorful dress, masks, and makeup convey important information about character through a visual, symbolic language. Set elements tend to be sparse.
- In performance traditions master craftspeople build the sets, masks, and costumes. The skillful execution of established designs is often of greater value than originality.
- In Europe, in the late nineteenth and early twentieth centuries, naturalistic plays and the emergence of the director gave rise to the interpretive design tradition.
- In realistic stage design, all that we see and hear on stage closely resembles the natural world.
- Symbolism, expressionism, futurism, and constructivism were reactions against realism's search for truth in everyday reality. The impact of these European movements was expressed in the United States in the *new stagecraft*.
- Today designers borrow, combine, and juxtapose elements from various conceptual movements, traditions, and cultures. They work in a collaborative process to create the world the characters will inhabit.

In addition to the Challenges and Choices, pedagogical support is furnished by part introductions that provide an overview of the topics and core concepts covered in each section. **Key Ideas** at the end of each chapter summarize major chapter concepts. An end-of-book **Glossary** of terms, which appear in boldface in the text, lists key terms in alphabetical order. A chapter-by-chapter **Bibliography** at the end of the book includes articles, books, videos, and websites students may consult for further reference.

A Note on Usage

The global nature of this text often presented difficulties of nomenclature, spelling, and word order for foreign terms and names. We have chosen to write the names of theatre artists mentioned in the text according to the customs of their home countries. Thus the names of Japanese- and Chinese-born theatre artists appear last name first, as is the custom in Japan and China. For artists whose work is widely discussed in the United States, we made judgment calls to use the Western order of first name first.

Foreign words, such as *mudra* and *kimono,* are pluralized as *mudras* and *kimonos,* as in English, to facilitate reading, even if such words would remain unchanged in the plural in their native language. All foreign genres and theatrical forms are shown in lowercase italics. For words with multiple English spellings—

kutiyattam, kudiyattam, or *kutiyaattam*—we have chosen one consistent spelling for all appearances of the word.

Supplemental Resources

We have prepared a package of resources to accompany *The World of Theatre.* The Instructor's Manual/Test Bank provides suggested syllabi, a course outline, and suggestions for using the book in an introduction to theatre course. The test questions include multiple-choice and short essay questions for each chapter and are available as a computerized test bank in TestGen as well as in printed format. A series of PowerPoint lectures are available online at www.ablongman.com/irc. A Companion Website, found at www.ablongman.com/felner1e, contains an array of electronic materials for students and instructors, including objectives, flashcards, weblinks, and practice tests.

In addition, Allyn and Bacon offers *Explore Theatre: A Backstage Pass,* a peer-to-peer interactive DVD learning tool (available in a package with the text at no additional cost) developed by students for students under the direction of Michael O'Hara, an award-winning teacher of theatre at Ball State University. Seventeen major content areas (director, actor, costume designer, etc.) are covered, with an eye toward introducing students to the people and processes that make much of American theatre happen.

Acknowledgments

The number of people who have helped us in this endeavor is large and global, like this book. We must first thank the wonderful artists around the world who gave generously of their time for interviews: Jane Alexander, Linda Cho, Judith Dolan, Pamela Howard, Tina Howe, Stanley Kauffmann, Robert Kaplowitz, Elizabeth LeCompte, Matsui Akira, Claudio Pinhanez, Lloyd Richards, Stanley Sherman, Alisa Solomon, Ruth Sternberg, Bill Talen, and Jennifer Tipton. Louisa Thompson also advised us on our chapters on set and costume design.

The list of colleagues who have been of special support is long. Thanks to Richard Emmert for his labor conducting and translating from the Japanese the interview with Matsui Akira; Samuel Leiter for his consultations on Japanese theatre; David Saltz for his information on new technology; James P. Taylor for his assistance with materials for the lighting section; Maggie Morgan for her material on costuming; Phillip Zarrilli for his aid with photographic material; and Mark Ringer for his writings on opera and for stimulating conversation.

Other colleagues who have offered advice and assistance include John Bell, Betty Bernhard, Robert Brenner, Claire Conceison, Jutka Devenyi, Breffny Flynn, Kathy Foley, Dan Hurlin, Susan Jain, Tom Leabhart, Haiyan Lee, Jim Moore, Alice Rayner, Farley Richmond, Jonah Salz, Carol Sorgenfrei, Elizabeth Wichmann-Walczak, Ruth Wikler, Yuewai Wong, and Neguin Yavary. Thanks to David Howe at the Hudson Scenic studios for the informational tour, and to Mei-Chen Lu and the Dance Notation Bureau.

Our many colleagues at Hunter College and the Graduate Center of the City University of New York supported us emotionally and intellectually in this endeavor. Special appreciation goes to Barbara Bosch, Joel Bassin, Jean Graham-Jones, Marvin

Carlson, Jonathan Kalb, Tamara Green, and Ian Calderon. Thanks to David Bean and Pam Snyder for technical assistance. To our department administrative assistant, Bettie Haigler, the backstage hero who saves computer files, fixes glitches, downloads photos, and listens to our plaintive wails, how could any of us function without you?

We are privileged at Hunter College to teach the most diverse group of students to be found at an American university. Current and former students have taught us much about their native traditions and have enlightened us as we wrote this book. Some have gone on to prominence in their own right. They have been translators, go-betweens, researchers, and scholars. We are indebted to: Deirdre O'Leary, for her careful preparation of the instructors' manual; Debra Hilborn, for her research and help preparing the manuscript and bibliography; Nara Lee, for her expertise on the Korean theatre; Eileen Hawkins, for information on the American musical; Nancy Guevara, for her research on Central America; Ibuki Kaori, for her translating skills; Osnat Greenbaum, for her thoughts on makeup; and Pattara Danutra, Maria Duarte, Ana Martinez, Yuki Yokote, Jung Hyun Park, and Ikeda Yoko. Barbara Knowles, now the Chief Curator of the Billy Rose Theatre Collection of the New York Public Library for the Performing Arts, gave us invaluable research tips, and Brian Hurley contributed to our understanding of sound design.

We also extend our appreciation to the manuscript reviewers. Their many thoughtful suggestions enhanced this book: Dennis C. Beck, Bradley University; Michael L. Counts, Lyon College; Marilyn De Simone, Florida Community College at Jacksonville; Richard E. Donnelly, University of Notre Dame; Mary K. Foley, University of California Santa Cruz; Desmond Gallant, Florida Atlantic University; Alber C. Gordon, Washington & Lee University; Richard Hansen, Middle Tennessee State University; Leslie A. Hindercykx, Northeastern University; Robert Homer-Drummond, Parkland College; Susan Kattwinkel, College of Charleston; Craig Latrell, Hamilton College; Nina LeNoir, Minnesota State University, Mankato; and Susan Mason, California State University, Los Angeles.

We were fortunate to have the support of Allyn and Bacon as this project expanded from its original conception. This book would never have achieved the coherence of its current organization without the skills of our wonderful project editor, Ellen Darion. Her careful reading and insightful comments were a guiding light. To Molly Taylor, who let us fly with this new idea, and Donna Simons, who is responsible for its production, our appreciation for your efforts. The photos that grace this book are the result of the tireless efforts of Laurie Frankenthaler and Rachel Lucas, whom we sent to the remote reaches of the planet to find the right image of obscure performance forms; how can we ever say thank you enough? We must also acknowledge Susanne Forman, who encouraged us to bring this project to our publisher.

Personal gratitude to Gloria Orenstein, Nadine Orenstein, Stephen Orenstein, and Susan Fox for their constant support, and to Sharon Brown and Priscilla Flores for their dependable childcare. The years spent in creation of this book required sacrifices by our husbands and children. Very special thanks to Taylor Carman, Caleb, and Sophie for their love and endless patience; to Joshua Cutler who served—mostly willingly—as our test college student reader, fact checker, and preliminary copyeditor; and to Richard Cutler whose advice, open ear, and steadfast devotion gird this book.

PART ONE

European and American Admirals, portrayed as buffoons with comic wigs and noses, ensnare the Japanese Shogun in their flags in this Japanese revival of Stephen Sondheim's *Pacific Overtures*, a musical about Western imperialism. The Japanese production later opened on Broadway with an Asian American cast. Director, Miyamoto Amon; Ben Hura as "Abe the Shogun." The Lincoln Center Festival, New York.

© *Jack Vartoogian/FrontRowPhotos*

Navigating the World of Theatre

In tribal villages and temples, in schools and opera houses, parks and playhouses, people come together all over the world to witness a singular event we call theatre. The impulse that draws people to these places of performance is universal and fundamental to the human spirit, but what they see is as varied as the human social experience.

Theatre is a living, vital art where live actors engage the audience through the energy of their physical presence. Performance traditions evolve and are renewed through the work of innovative theatre artists who seek new ways to express changing social concerns. No form can be permanent in theatre, the most evanescent of art forms. Each performance lives on only in memory, leaving us free to create again.

The great diversity of theatrical forms that coexist today is a reflection of the complex, global world in which we live. They challenge us to reach beyond the traditions of our own society to embrace the artistic forms of other cultures. Although we hold deep inside of us the values and prejudices of our own social experience, we can learn to appreciate the way people in other times and places have told and continue to tell their stories on the stage.

Theatre: A Global Experience

1

The plays of Shakespeare have formed the basis of many intercultural productions around the globe. The Johannesburg Civic Theatre's *Umbatha: The Zulu Macbeth,* adapted and directed by Welcome Msomi, draws parallels between the story of King Shaka and Shakespeare's Scottish Thane and stages the tale with African masks, costuming, and drumming. This Zulu-language production toured the world.

The need to make sense of our world is the driving force behind all theatrical forms, and every culture has developed some form of theatrical presentation through which to examine the mysteries of life and the most pressing concerns of its society. Because the actor on the stage is a live human being like us, the theatre mirrors our lives more directly than any other art form. It is a glimpse into the meaning of our existence with its aspirations and disappointments, crises and triumphs, as well as a reflection of our social values.

The mirror is an apt metaphor for the stage. In it we are ourselves and not ourselves, real and an illusion, true and yet false. When we look in the mirror, we stand outside ourselves, looking at ourselves, searching for an objective understanding of who and what we are, and this is what we do in the theatre. In the theatre we are always aware that we are watching real people play fictions that have a greater reality than our own lives for the duration of the performance. So the image we see on the stage is not passive, but rather one that stimulates us to consider our lives more deeply. It can be a spur to social consciousness and political action, and sometimes performance itself can be an act of protest or conscience. No electronic form can excite and unsettle us in this way. Despite the accessibility and easy consumption of film and television, the theatre continues to be the stage for examination of the deepest questions surrounding human existence.

To say the theatre is a mirror of life does not mean that all theatre is always realistic or must create a replica of the real world on stage. Sometimes it is more like a fun house mirror distorting, refocusing, exaggerating to make us see ourselves in a different light. Although theatrical expression is a universal human activity, each society, culture, and time has its own lens through which it looks at and creates the mirror of the stage. For that reason, theatres in different places and times have presented different images to their audiences.

How can we understand how other people portray themselves and tell their stories in performance? How do we balance time-honored theatrical traditions with the need for innovations that reflect who we are at any given moment? The journey through this book is an examination of what is universal to all theatre and what is specific to a given time, place, and culture. No book can look at every form of theatre that has ever existed, but we can begin to develop a way to approach the unfamiliar. Though we may always feel more at ease with our own forms, we can develop an understanding of difference that can lead to respect for, and hopefully admiration of, other traditions. We achieve this by examining the changing conventions of the theatre as a reflection of our values and beliefs.

Theatrical Conventions and Culture

Every society develops rules of behavior that define the way individuals conduct themselves and transmit thoughts, and we tacitly accept and internalize these rules, or norms. We learn how to read the significance of a touch, a kiss, a handshake, or a stare. In exchange, we receive tools for communication and conduct that help us cope with life's interactions without conscious thought. These behavioral norms are not static, but ever-evolving reflections of social values. They can vary from era to era and from place to place, even within a specific culture. Theatre, as the most social of all the arts—human beings coming together in the same space to share an event—also has its rules of conduct and understood communication codes. We call these codes **theatrical conventions**, and just as we use social conventions to navigate in the larger world, so do we navigate in the world of the theatre according to the conventions of the stage.

Accustomed to the theatre of our own society, we do not realize how odd our own practices might appear in other cultures or eras. Imagine that you are from another planet sent to observe people on earth. You watch many people approach a building,

Performance
IN PERSPECTIVE

THE IRANIAN *TA'ZIYEH* AND ITS CONVENTIONS

The *Ta'ziyeh*, or tragic play, performed in Shi'a communities in Iraq, Lebanon, Pakistan, and even Jamaica, enacts the 680 C.E. martyrdom of Imam Hoseyn, the grandson of the Prophet Mohammad. Hoseyn, his male children, and male followers were massacred and the women were captured at Karbala by the followers of Yazid, who sought to head the Islamic community. These events mark the start of the historic division between Sunni and Shiite Muslims. *Ta'ziyeh* audiences regard the performance as a religious event and view it as a form of communal, ritual mourning for Shiite martyrs.

Ta'ziyeh performances take place at both indoor and outdoor venues during the month of Muharram. A performance may occur at a single location, or episodes may be enacted throughout the town. These are community events that involve dozens of actors, musicians, and live animals. They may be performed by professional actors, but most commonly they are performed by local amateurs. The performance indulges in emotion, arouses pity, stimulates religious fervor, and is heightened by dramatic singing. The director is called *mo'in-al-boka*, "the one who helps bring tears."

Ta'ziyeh is governed by a set of specific conventions that reflect the ritual nature of the performance and make the action clear to people familiar with the tradition. For those unfamiliar with the performance, its many theatrical conventions need explanation. Hoseyn

and those who support him wear green and sing their lines, while those who are against him wear red and recite their text. Women are played by men who veil their faces. When an actor dons a white shirt, it signifies that the character will soon be martyred. Circling the playing area on foot or horseback indicates that a character has traveled a long distance to another location, while a diagonal walk across the stage represents a shorter journey. Turning around in place indicates a change of character or locale. Straw is used to place the action in the desert; a tub of water represents the Euphrates River, and a single tree branch stands in for a palm grove. The performers, called "readers," carry strips of paper with their lines to which they may refer rather than relying on memorization. The director is visible throughout the performance, handing lines to actors, giving them entrance cues, and placing or removing stage props. *Ta'ziyeh*'s traditional audiences also act according to a unique set of conventions. Caught up in the emotion of the event, they wail, weep, and beat their breasts in sorrow. An actor playing one of the villains, transported by the crowd, may himself be moved to tears before slaying one of the martyrs.

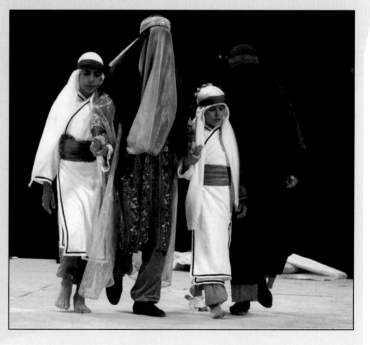

This is a play about the martyrdom of the children of one of Hoseyn's followers. As seen in this picture, the children are first shielded by women before their eventual slaughter. Following the conventions of *ta'ziyeh*, the women's roles are performed by men in veils. The green of the children's garments shows that they are followers of Hoseyn and the white shows that they will be martyred. The red in the women's clothes shows them to be members of the opposing camp. From *The Ta'ziyeh of the Children of Moslem* performed at the Lincoln Center Festival.
© *Michael Nagle*

and each one hands a person standing at the door a small piece of paper that is torn in half. These people are then directed to seats in a large hall and are handed larger papers to read. They talk with one another naturally, but when the lights begin to dim, they all grow silent at once and sit expectantly in the dark. Now some new people enter a lit portion of the room and explain their most intimate feelings in loud voices; these new people live in rooms where all the furniture faces in one direction, and they don't seem to know that a thousand people are watching them even if they stand stark naked. The people in the seats, after remaining silent for two hours, bang their hands together, while the people who were talking in loud voices bend at the waist. What is going on? How could you possibly explain this behavior? These are some of our accepted theatrical conventions that allow us to share a common theatre experience. Thinking about the strangeness of our own conventions allows us to understand and accept those of other eras and cultures.

Conventions affect every aspect of a performance; they dictate how actors will move, speak, and be clothed, as well as the form and content of the event, how and where it will be staged and designed, and how the audience should respond. Some of these conventions reflect centuries of cultural tradition, and others are recent innovations; some transcend cultural borders, others are culturally specific, and some change in different circumstances within the same culture. The combined effect of these conventions working together is **style**—the manner in which a performance depicts the world. For a style to be successful, its particular audience must find it authentic and meaningful so they can, through the power of the imagination, engage in what British poet Samuel Taylor Coleridge (1772–1834) called the "willing suspension of disbelief"—believing in the reality of theatrical make-believe. As you will learn, theatrical styles vary widely in different eras and from one culture to another, so what is considered theatrically true embraces many forms.

Just as knowing your own society's theatrical conventions enables you to feel comfortable in the theatre and to better understand the embedded values in the performance, learning about theatrical conventions in other cultures and eras enables you to feel at home in the global world of the theatre. Go to the Concert Party Theatre in West Africa and you will find audience members talking back to the actors, coaching and encouraging them to take action, warning them of danger, while an American audience would sit silently watching the events unfold and would be annoyed if others spoke out loud. At the Chinese opera, the audience is in constant chatter, while in Bali spectators may sometimes enter a performance-induced trance, absorbing the events through a semiconscious state. In India you might find actors using stylized hand movements and positions as an encoded language of signs; throughout Africa, drama tends to incorporate drumming and dance, and a *t'alch'um* performance in Korea uses masks that are sometimes burned in a postperformance ritual fire.

The Evolution of Conventions

Because theatre is a reflection of society, its values, and the way it views and judges human behavior, it follows that in other historical periods and in other places, we would find theatrical forms and conventions different from those we experience today. In fact, the history of the theatre is really a history of evolving conventions. A good example of this is the exclusion of women from the theatre. In ancient Greece, the so-called "golden age" of Greek theatre during the fifth century B.C.E. was not so golden for women, who were not considered worthy of participation in theatrical performance. Scholars even debate whether women were allowed in the audience. Women were also excluded from performing in Shakespeare's time (imagine the young lover Juliet played by a boy), and today, in certain societies, women continue to be locked out. The Japanese *noh* and the Indian *kathakali* are examples of centuries-old theatre forms that continued to exclude women from professional performance to the present day. Imagine trying to pass a law in the United States today excluding women from theatrical activity. What do you think would happen? Can you see the protests? Who would vote for it? This could not happen in the American theatre today because it would not reflect our value system and the role of women in our culture.

Artists
IN PERSPECTIVE

IRA ALDRIDGE (1807–1867)

Ira Aldridge, known as the African Roscius, for the great Roman actor, was an internationally acclaimed American-born tragedian who garnered honors and awards from heads of state throughout Europe and from the Republic of Haiti. Many facts of his biography and background are a matter of debate. By some accounts, Aldridge's father, Daniel, was a descendent of princes of the Fulah tribe from Senegal, Africa, and was brought to New York by a missionary to study. By other accounts Daniel was a slave born in New York, or a "free Negro." In either case, his son Ira developed a taste for theatre as a young boy studying at the African Free School in New York. The school's proximity to the Park Theatre afforded the young Aldridge the opportunity to see many of the illustrious actors of his day, including the Englishman Edmund Kean performing Hamlet and Lear, but only from the balcony, the section reserved for black spectators.

Aldridge began his own acting career with the African Theatre in New York, the first black theatre company in the United States, which was founded in 1820. Dissatisfied with the career opportunities for blacks and the general reception of black performers by American audiences at a time when slavery was legal in the United States, he emigrated to England. In 1825, he debuted in London as Prince Oroonoko of Africa in the melodrama *The Revolt of Surinam, or A Slave's Revenge* and later went on to play leading Shakespearean roles including Othello, Shylock, Macbeth, and Richard II. Although he had some detractors, his performances were generally well received by the public, and his work was praised by the great British actor Edmund Kean himself.

Some of the positive statements about Aldridge in the British press would appear blatantly racist today. The audience was exhorted to subdue their repugnance to his "thick lipped" Othello as his "labial peculiarity" did not interfere with his pronunciation and elocution. Whether critics praised or maligned his acting, they could not take for granted the unusual fact of a black man performing Shakespeare on stage.

Aldridge toured continental Europe, where he received his greatest honors. He was knighted by the Duke Bernhard of Saxe-Meiningen and given the first-class medal of arts and sciences by the king of Prussia and the White Cross in Switzerland, among many other accolades. He returned triumphantly to the London stage.

Aldridge was married twice, to Margaret Gill, an Englishwoman, in 1825, and to the Countess Amanda von Brandt of Sweden in 1865 after Margaret's death in 1864. During his lifetime he contributed to campaigns in support of emancipation, and his impressive stage presence and powerful acting lent weight to the abolitionist cause. While performing on a theatrical tour in 1867, Aldridge died in Lodz, Poland, where he is buried. Just a few weeks before his death, he received an invitation to perform in New York.

Ira Aldridge projects dignity and the tragic dimensions of his character in the role of Aaron from Shakespeare's *Titus Andronicus*, Act IV, Scene 2. In such performances, Aldridge reached beyond the limited roles available to black actors in his time.
Photo by Hulton Archive/Getty Images

In the United States, there was a long period during which actors of different races did not perform together. This reflected the social reality that kept blacks and whites apart. The great African American actor Ira Aldridge (1807–1867) had to go to Europe in 1825 to perform in venues where his talent could be recognized. In fact, equal opportunity in the American theatre is a relatively recent phenomenon, and some would argue that it has yet to arrive.

In societies that have sustained and maintained performance traditions, theatrical conventions evolve more slowly, and ancient forms continue to exist. The *noh* theatre of Japan is an example of a theatrical form that began in the fourteenth century and continues today with many of its original conventions unchanged. But even these long-lived traditions evolve, and there have been changes in training, design, and performance over the centuries, despite the remarkable stability of the form. For example, many traditional Asian forms such as the Indian *kathakali* had performances that may have lasted an entire night, from sundown to sunrise; today, although these performance traditions continue, most have abbreviated performance time to three or four hours to accommodate contemporary lifestyles and new audiences.

Universals of the Theatre

Although theatrical conventions are specific to time, place, and culture, certain universals apply to all theatre everywhere.

- Theatre is *live in the present moment* and requires the presence of a *live actor* and an *audience.*
- Theatre is *ephemeral* in that no performance can ever be totally duplicated or captured.
- Theatre is *collaborative*: it requires the efforts of many people working together.
- Theatre is a *synthesis* of many arts.

Theatre Is Live

A quickening of the heart, a surge of anticipatory excitement—these are the feelings that course through us at the start of a performance. Even experienced theatre-goers feel this awakening each time they are in the audience for live theatre. In the movies, we merely reach for more popcorn, sit back, and relax. What is it about the theatre that continues to thrill?

The performer on the stage is alive and vital. We sense the inherent daring and danger as we watch a human being take emotional and physical risks before our eyes. An unexpected event can strip away the mask and reveal the man or woman beneath the role. A missed line, a fall, a malfunctioning prop, and suddenly we are aware of the person we have forgotten under the character. We know that each performance is a triumph over the odds. To go to the theatre is to believe in miracles. We watch in awe as the actor physically transforms and flexes the emotions. Every performance is a journey through time and space with infinite opportunity for mishap, and yet, each evening and matinee, all over the world, actors walk the tightrope without a safety net and return to repeat the feat. Virtuoso performances take our breath away.

We in the audience are a part of the event and are challenged by it. We can alter it by our presence, our actions and reactions, and we may even be invited to actively participate. We must be vigilant and ready to play our part.

Without these two elements—the live actor risking all and the live audience responding and creating invisible lines of communication—theatre cannot exist. Today, as we spend more and more time alone, confined to rooms with televisions and computers, the theatre has become one of the few places where we must come together, form a community, and become live witnesses to acts of daring.

Theatre Is Ephemeral

If the theatre is live, in the moment, then no element can be exactly replicated because it depends on the interaction of live actors and audience and what they bring to a fleeting, uncapturable moment in time and space. Theatre's time is the present. If you record it or film it, the reproduction is not a theatrical event; it is film or video, an archival record. It is not what the audience experienced. The theatrical event is specific to a set time, place, audience, and performers. Move a production to a larger theatre and the entire dynamic changes. See the same production on a different night and the actors will have made infinite small adjustments to the new audience. Have the understudy step in and the entire cast must accommodate the change. Actors must also deal with physical and emotional stresses in their daily lives that affect each performance. Although the basic outlines of a production remain the same, you will never see the exact same event twice.

Theatre Is Collaborative

How is it that lines are so seldom flubbed, props are rarely out of place, scenery almost never falls, the light and sound cues go off on time, costumes fit flawlessly, and actors appear on cue? The success of the theatrical event is the result of a community of people working toward a common goal. It requires putting trust in a company of individuals to create a seamless imaginary reality with no opportunity for retakes. Everyone in this collaborative effort is a valued contributor to the total effect. Some are part of the creative team; others are support staff—stage managers, crew, and technicians. But all are equally necessary if the production is to be a success. A bonding occurs among members of a theatre company. This sense of family is what draws many people to the theatre. Shared creation is a joyous activity, and we take pleasure in it.

One often overlooked part of the collaborative process of theatre is the one that occurs between the audience and the performers; the spectators' responses help shape the rhythm of a theatrical event. This is why, in communities, schools, and universities all over the world, wherever neighbors can come together, people make theatre. This book will examine the roles of all the various contributors to better understand how theatre happens.

Theatre Is a Synthesis of Many Arts

So many people are involved in theatrical creation because theatre uses so many artistic materials for a combined effect. Actors give life to a text or an idea through movement, dance, speech, and song with the aid of directors, playwrights, musicians, and choreographers; and they do this in a space that must be determined and designed. Theatre uses the spatial arts. The stage set must be painted or sculpted. The set must be lit to enhance the environment for the performance and so the actor can be seen, and the lighting designer will sculpt and paint with light. The actor must wear something or not; even the decision for nudity is an artistic choice that a costumer and director must make. Masks may be made. Faces may be painted. There may be music and sound effects, and each element must be composed or designed and executed by artists and technicians. All of these elements must unite to form a single vision of another world that is organized by the director, or someone serving in that function. The theatrical form is therefore a synthesis of other arts and the work of many artists. It uses language, painting, sculpture, costume, music, dance, mime, movement, light, and sound to create its effects. Theatre is a complex, composite art form.

Tradition and Innovation

These universal aspects of theatre do not mean that it is a static art. Its forms change over time, and even long-revered performance traditions can accommodate innovation. Theatre practitioners reach out to their public inventing new forms, borrowing techniques from other cultures, reinterpreting plays, and integrating new technologies to reinvigorate their art. With the ease of global exchange today, tradition and innovation encounter and transform each other, or coexist, around the world. In the United States, where innovation and reinvention is a way of life, theatrical forms transform and evolve rapidly. American theatre reflects our changing population, demographics, economics, and politics. To understand today's theatre, we must look at the forces that are altering contemporary performance.

Postmodernism

Postmodernism, which evolved with the worldwide political and social changes of the late twentieth century, is a complicated concept without a single definition. It encompasses a variety of ideas and trends in different disciplines and has had an enormous impact on the theatre. In contrast to the view of a world with fundamental truths, postmodernism poses a world of contradiction and instability, with no grand scheme of meanings or universals. The "truths" of the past are seen as constructions of those in political power. What seems true to the master might not seem true to the slave; what seems true to a man might not seem true to a woman; what seems true to a heterosexual might not seem true to a homosexual. For centuries the world was dominated by a Eurocentric, white, male, heterosexual establishment that excluded and invalidated the perspective of groups outside the power structure, which it defined as "other." Today we realize that the cultural dominance of some groups can lead to the exploitation and even obliteration of others.

Challenges and Choices

How would you define what constitutes a work of art? Must it meet a set of objective criteria? Must it be aesthetically pleasing? Can it be utilitarian? Must it be created with artistic consciousness?

Postmodernism has invited those whose views were not included in the old world order to construct their own histories, philosophies, and art forms and has considered all constructions of equal validity. This has called into question divisions between what used to be labeled "high art"—that for which there were established formal aesthetic standards—and "low art"—the vernacular culture that surrounds us. Defying these divisions is also a political act that brings the artistic expressions and voices of previously marginalized or disenfranchised groups to general attention. Needless to say, this has cast the long-standing question of what constitutes "art" in a new light. It has also engendered debate as to what happens to aesthetic criticism in a world without absolute values: Can anyone say that a work of art is "good" or "bad" without being accused of cultural bias? Once there was an acknowledged canon, a list of unquestioned great works; today we question whether any such canon exists, and if it does, what it should include. What should be the place of the old traditional canon in today's education, and what time-honored works should be replaced by new ones? If postmodernism is to truly embrace a multiplicity of viewpoints, it must allow the great works of the old traditions to stand as important objects of study, even as we make room for new voices to be heard.

Relinquishing fixed forms or traditional styles, postmodernists feel free to mix styles and genres to create new forms. This can be seen clearly in many recent theatre productions. It is not unusual today to see film and video mixed with live action in a work by Canadian director Robert Lepage (b. 1957) or in a play by Chilean Ramón Griffero (b. 1953); puppets on the Broadway stage with live actors as in *Avenue Q*; or a mélange of acting, gymnastics, martial arts, drumming, slide projections, religious ritual, and dancing, as in *Cookin'* from Korea. Now there is also a free borrowing of styles from other cultures that were once seen as inferior, but are now valued for their difference, as seen in the 1999 *Kathakali King Lear* at London's Globe Theatre, which incorporated stylized Indian theatrical movement, costumes, makeup, and songs with Shakespearean text. South Africa's *Umbatha: The Zulu Macbeth* demonstrated that borrowing has become a two-way street when playwright Welcome Msomi appropriated a Shakespearean text and substituted characters from Zulu history while replacing some of Shakespeare's lines with tribal drumming and dancing (see photo at opening of chapter). Along with these new styles have come new organizational systems and new ways of creating and collaborating to make theatre.

Although much of theatre today continues older traditions, postmodernism has changed the way we look at the world by creating an openness to other cultures and an awareness of how older structures impeded the development of particular ideas and forms. Aided by globalization, we live in an era of awareness that prizes the cultural contributions of all people.

Globalization

The expression "the global village" captures the reality of contemporary life and the impossibility of living in cultural isolation in a world where time and space are compressed through modern transportation and communication. People travel from place to place bringing their cultural traditions with them, so we are all exposed to diverse theatrical forms in a way unheard of in past generations. Yet despite this constant contact, we still encounter forms that seem strange to us, that perplex us and defy comprehension. The theatre as a direct reflection of cultural values is often the most enigmatic of the arts, and today, more than ever, we need to understand and appreciate difference.

Globalization has often had a significant negative impact on less modernized societies that were held together by an ancient cultural glue of community values and ritual performance and are now threatened by new socioeconomic structures and exposure to "modern" lifestyles. Much traditional theatre, born in the premodern era, was part of the fabric of community life on which it depended for its sustenance. Today, as fewer and fewer people live in isolated communities, a new generation questions the contemporary significance of traditional values and the ancient theatre forms that embody them. As a result, traditional performance may lose its place as an integral part of daily existence and an expression of communal values. These forms are often relegated to museum status in state-run or university theatres, used as cultural symbols and assertions of identity, or presented to attract tourists. Unlike other art forms that can be preserved in museums and libraries or on CDs, theatre lives only in the moment of active exchange with a live audience. Once a performance form fails to engage its public, its survival is threatened, and many ancient forms have been forced to adapt to changing times in order to continue.

Ironically, while some societies are abandoning their traditional forms, globalization has awakened others to the beauty and interest of these forms. One culture may be borrowing or appropriating what another culture is rejecting or forsaking. Sometimes this brings increased communication, but many fear it will dilute or destroy many traditional theatrical forms whose very survival may now depend on their ability to adapt to the contemporary world.

Once all politics was local; today all politics is global. We are united in shared problems, tensions, dilemmas, and fears. As the contemporary theatre seeks to address these concerns, it is engaging similar themes and bringing similar forms to urban audiences the world over. In Tokyo, New York, Paris, Seoul, or Sydney, a largely educated, middle-class audience can see much of the same commercial theatre—big, corporate-sponsored productions that tour worldwide, or performances of the established avant-garde that travel a circuit of international theatre festivals and centers. When today's theatre moves away from its intimate communal roots, much of the community-based audience for traditional theatre may be excluded.

In a world without boundaries, where we watch each other's films, eat each other's food, and use each other's goods, we also see an increasing homogenization of culture. Those who value cultural difference fear the eradication of many performance forms in favor of globally disseminated mass popular entertainment. Theatre itself may be an endangered art in the global electronic era.

Challenges and Choices

What do you think are the benefits and disadvantages of globally disseminated mass entertainment?

IN PERSPECTIVE

PERSONAL STORIES, GLOBAL EFFECTS: EVE ENSLER AND V-DAY

Eve Ensler's 1996 solo performance piece *The Vagina Monologues* was assembled from more than two hundred interviews with women around the world who discussed their relationship to the most intimate part of their bodies, and in so doing revealed thoughts about gender, orgasm, love, marriage, sexuality, and experiences of rape, incest, abuse, and mutilation. By simply breaking the social taboo against uttering any word for the female genitalia in a public forum, Ensler unveiled some of the most pressing issues of our time for examination. The monologues range from the hilarious to the tragic. The work is ultimately a poignant reminder that women suffer the consequences of world events, social repression, and domestic dysfunction in the most private places of their being. Women, long taught to think of their bodies as obscene and even not as their own, were empowered by the performance to take back this forbidden identity with pride. Men in the audience responded with interest to all they had not known or considered.

Ensler has used the piece as the inspiration for a crusade to stop violence against women and girls around the world. In 1998, V-Day, a grassroots movement, was organized as a global effort. Funds raised through performances have helped start organizations in seventy-six countries to protect women from the different threats to their well-being in particular cultures. Initiatives have been launched in Africa, the Middle East, and parts of Asia and the Caribbean. The V-Day team is currently working in partnership with women's groups in Egypt, Jordan, Palestine, Israel, Pakistan, India, Kenya, and Afghanistan to end bride burnings, female genital mutilation, honor killings, sexual assault, rape, and many other forms of gender-based violence. In the United States, the organization has worked to raise awareness of the abuse of Native American women, who suffer more than any other group in the country from domestic violence. Their global efforts reach across all religious and ethnic divisions. Student groups at universities and colleges around the world are invited to sponsor productions of *The Vagina Monologues* to raise money for the cause, and funds are donated directly to local organizations.

This amazing story of the work of an avant-garde solo performer spawning a global movement is testimony to the continuing power of theatre to transform our lives. In the era of globalization, the most private story can reverberate around the world.

Eve Ensler's outrageous, in-your-face performance style parallels the ground she has broken in taking up formerly taboo subject matter. The Vagina Monologues, King's Head Theatre, London.
© Robbie Jack/CORBIS

Multiculturalism

Multiculturalism calls for a respect for neighboring cultures living under the same political system. Multiculturalism grew out of the social and political awakening of the 1960s and 1970s when the civil rights movement, the women's movement, and the protests against the war in Vietnam were the source of political and social upheavals that raised the consciousness of marginalized groups. The last few decades have been an era of identity politics, and minority populations in North America have felt increasingly empowered. Parallel political trends spread across Europe, Asia, South America, and Australia. Many of the tenets of postmodernism are expressed in multiculturalism.

This pride in identity found expression in the theatre because it enabled particular communities to represent and "re-present" themselves to establish a public cultural identity. Multiculturalism is linked to postmodernism because those whose viewpoints were overlooked or marginalized by mainstream theatre—women, the elderly, the disabled, African Americans, Native Americans, Asian Americans, Latinos, and gays and lesbians, for example—now create theatre pieces that speak to their concerns. In turn, as you will see, theatrical forms have been reconfigured to best give voice to the needs of particular communities. Detractors of multiculturalism claim it has often led to a separation of various communities rather than fostering a deeper cultural exchange. On the whole, multicultural theatre has provided a valuable forum to affirm, explore, or challenge a group's identity, beliefs, and practices and has allowed us to hear new voices in the theatre.

Theatre is a place to explore who we are. The very nature of "identity" has been questioned by multicultural artists. What does it mean to be American? Female? Gay? Disabled? Latino? Of color? Don't we all possess multiple identities and belong to several defining groups? Is identity something we carry inside or something projected onto us by others? How do we express our identity in theatrical performance? This has been the subject matter of many contemporary theatre works and new theatrical forms and texts explore these and other multicultural issues. Sarah Jones's performance pieces explore the perception of identity as she seamlessly slips in and out of Middle Eastern, Chinese, Black, Jewish, Latino, Caribbean, and gay characters among a host of others. She challenges her audiences to question what constitutes a racial or ethnic identity if it can be taken on as a role. Other artists have explored the identity inherent in their own groups, as playwright Hanay Geiogamah does for Native Americans and Cherrie Moraga does for Chicanos.

In the early twentieth century, before the era of radio and television, the United States and Canada had ethnic theatres that provided entertainment to immigrant groups in their native languages. These theatres served as cultural hubs and meeting places and presented the aspirations and idealism of new Americans at a time when assimilation and abandoning of old traditions was expected. These early ethnic theatres used either the theatrical forms of the dominant theatre culture in the United States and Canada or forms the groups brought with them from their homelands. Few of these original ethnic theatres continue today because the next generation of actors was assimilated into mainstream American culture and lured by Broadway and Hollywood. Today new immigrant groups bring with them the theatre traditions of their native countries but, unlike the generations that preceded them, they come to an America that now celebrates difference. They have developed new kinds of multicultural performance in which they can celebrate their own traditions within an American context and still attract audiences outside the immigrant community. Thriving multicultural theatres now exist in many major cities.

Interculturalism

The blending of traditions from various cultures is called **interculturalism**. It goes beyond multiculturalism in that it not only values but also promotes an exchange and interaction among various cultures that may ignite interest or friction. Fascination with other cultures is not a new phenomenon. Travelers to other lands from as far back as we have documentation marveled at the traditions they discovered, and many artists have acknowledged the influence of foreign forms and ideas on their work. Globalization has intensified our exposure. What was once haphazard and crude cultural tourism has now become a conscious borrowing, blending, absorption, and appropriating of other cultures' art forms into new hybrid forms. Interculturalism is not without its dangers. There is the risk of stereotyping, of misusing and denigrating cultural symbols, and of engaging in a kind of cultural colonialism. Once we are exposed to new forms, they permeate and alter our consciousness.

Photo Essay

Multiculturalism

Groups not fully represented in the majority culture have a long tradition of forming theatre companies to produce works that speak to the particular needs of their communities. These productions are often a source of pride in identity and can reshape public perceptions. Pictured here are theatres that address ethnicity, race, sexual orientation, and disability.

EAST WEST PLAYERS

Sab Shimono and Jodi Long in *The Wind Cries Mary* by Philip Kan Gotanda, directed by Lisa Peterson at East West Players, Los Angeles. Established in 1965, this important Asian American Theatre organization gives voice to the Asian Pacific American experience.

Courtesy of East West Players; photo by Michael Lamont

SPLIT BRITCHES

Performances by the lesbian-feminist group Split Britches cause us to question our perceptions of gender. Lois Weaver and Peggy Shaw are seen here in the gender-bending piece "Adultery" at a benefit performance in New York City.
© *Dixie Sheridan*

TEATRO HUMANIDAD

In Austin, Texas, Teatro Humanidad's mission is to nurture emerging Latino artists. Their award-winning sketch comedy troupe, the Latino Comedy Project, performs irreverent cultural parody for Latino and mainstream audiences.

Courtesy of Teatro Humanidad; photo by Ike Taylor

SAINT LOUIS BLACK REPERTORY COMPANY

The Saint Louis Black Repertory Company provides theatre from the African American perspective to heighten the political and social awareness of its audience. Shown here is a scene from Sherry Shephard-Massat's *Waiting to Be Invited*, a play about three middle-aged black women who attempt to integrate a department store lunch counter during the civil rights movement. Directed by Ron Himes. Left to right: Marjorie Johnson, Sally Eaton, and Marguerite Hannah.

Courtesy of St. Louis Black Repertory Company; photo by Stewart Goldstein

NATIONAL THEATRE WORKSHOP OF THE HANDICAPPED

Since 1977, this group has provided education and produced works that deal with the subject of disability. Under the guidance of Brother Rick Curry, S.J., members of the National Theatre Workshop of the Handicapped find self-expression and enhance their opportunities on stage and in the workplace through rigorous professional training in all areas of theatre. Here students perform at the school's residential campus in Balfast, Maine.

Courtesy of National Theatre Workshop of the Handicapped (NTWH)

17

Early explorations in intercultural theatre began at the start of the twentieth century by European avant-garde artists who were intrigued by the theatricality of Asian performance that had begun touring the continent. During the 1920s in France, director-critic Jacques Copeau (1879–1949) used Asian movement techniques to train French actors, and director Vsevolod Meyerhold (1874–1940) did the same in Russia. Etienne Decroux (1898–1991) developed modern statuary mime in the 1930s, inspired by the stillness of the Japanese *noh*. While these borrowings often occurred without understanding, even the misinterpretation of other cultures' forms can sometimes be a vital source of artistic renewal. Bertolt Brecht's inadequate knowledge of Chinese opera helped him shape his concept of *epic theatre*, which we will discuss in the next chapter. Antonin Artaud's misreading of Balinese dance formed his ideas for the *theatre of cruelty*. The term "**Orientalism**" refers to this kind of exoticizing of Asian arts, and now implies an imposition of a Western perspective on Asian forms.

In Europe, we see interculturalism represented by the works of Peter Brook (b. 1925) with his Centre Internationale de Recherche Théâtrales and Ariane Mnouchkine (b. 1939) and her Théâtre du Soleil. Brook's production of *The Mahabharata* in 1985, based on the great ancient Indian religious epic, was hailed in performances the world over while sparking controversy and anger in those who felt he disrespectfully appropriated a cultural property of the people of India in a neocolonial act of plunder. Mnouchkine's production of *Les Atrides*, an adaptation of the ancient Greek *Oresteia* tragedies, also toured the world. Although her company is based in France, Asian musical instruments, movement, and costumes gave the piece a sense of belonging to a time-honored Asian tradition, although the plays hailed from ancient Athens—a different time and place from the staging. The piece truly belonged to no specific culture.

Even Broadway has become home to intercultural work. On the large commercial scale, Julie Taymor (b. 1952) in *The Lion King* used theatrical forms from various traditions. Masks and puppets borrowed from Asian traditions appear on stage with more usual forms of American musical theatre. Her earlier production of *Juan Darien* used shadow puppets, masks, and circus forms taken from Asian, African, and European styles.

Postcolonialism

If multiculturalism opens up the exploration of the identities of groups living within a single culture, postcolonialism explores identity within the geographic boundaries of formerly colonized states in Latin America, Asia, and Africa. Where once an imposed imperial power sought to eradicate or exploit indigenous cultural forms, formerly subjugated populations now seek to understand their own cultural heritage and the impact of colonial rule on their traditions and self-image. Former colonies that lived under such oppression are still reacting to its legacy.

Generations of theatre artists were taught that their homegrown forms were inferior and that they should emulate European models. The educated class was steeped in Western traditions. Today artists find themselves in a position of contradiction—while now free to celebrate native culture, many choose by habit or education to use the very European forms they reject to expose the hypocrisy and moral bankruptcy of imperialist rule. The result has been a tension between the imposed culture and native traditions that often plays out in the political arena as publicly funded arts centers debate which tradition to support. Many artists find that both forms live within them and that they are actually *hybrid* cultural beings. Try as they may to throw off the influence of the European theatrical tradition in favor of local performance styles, the imposed colonial forms have a hold on their consciousness that is reinforced by the idea of progress in today's global world. For this reason, when we look at the theatre in former colonies, especially in Africa, we often see the two traditions either mingling or standing side by side.

Challenges and Choices

Can traditional forms ever be used simply for their artistic expression with artists borrowing freely from other cultures, or must the political and historical implications of borrowing always be taken into account?

Performance

IN PERSPECTIVE

PETER BROOK'S *MAHABHARATA* AND INTERCULTURAL THEATRE PRACTICE

The controversy that erupted over English director Peter Brook's 1985 production of *The Mahabharata*, the foundational Hindu epic, crystalizes many issues surrounding intercultural performance. Already well known for his innovative productions of Shakespeare and Peter Weiss's *Marat/Sade* at the Royal Shakespeare Company in England, Brook began a new period of theatrical exploration in 1970 when he founded the Centre Internationale de Recherche Théâtrales in Paris. With an international company of actors, Brook sought a universal form of theatrical expression and communication. The company's 1971 production *Orghast*, first performed in Iran, was a verse-drama in an invented and attempted universal language written by poet Ted Hughes.

The nine-hour *Mahabharata* premiered at the Avignon Festival in France in 1985, the product of a long research process, three years of script work by playwright Jean-Claude Carrière, and more than six months of rehearsal. The production whittled the enormous epic down to events leading up to and including the monumental battle between the Pandavas and Kauravas and focused on the theme of war and destruction. The piece toured Europe, the United States, Australia, and Japan. In Avignon and Australia, the performance took place in stone quarries where the resonating sounds and the natural, open air environment lent the production a primal intensity. The natural elements of fire, earth, and water were used to astonishing effect, with a real river on stage and, in one scene, a wall of flames. The Indian-inspired costuming was generally simple. Stage properties were few: mats and banners used to help set the scene; actors' gestures replaced elaborate stage devices. Scenes of dynamic action in which arrows and spears flew across the stage alternated with quieter, moving moments. Japanese composer Tsuchitori Toshi united international musical effects using eastern horns, Aboriginal didjeridus, conches, Japanese *kodo* drums, Indian *tabla* drums, gongs, and other instruments, for a score that was partly improvised in performance. Brook again created an exceptional theatrical experience.

Many Indian critics and South Asian scholars, familiar with performances and oral tellings of this epic in its home country, although affected by Brook's theatricality, found his presentation a superficial "orientalist" view of the profound Hindu epic. By eradicating subplots and complicated Indian philosophical ideas to accommodate an Aristotelian, linear form, and diluting important Hindu beliefs in reincarnation, a strict caste system, polytheism, and the importance of *dharma*, or duty, critics claimed Brook had sacrificed philosophical complexity for easy accessibility. The result was a piece that was not universal, but Western and un-Indian.

Stories about Brook's disrespect for the indigenous tradition while doing research in India—his slighting of Indian village performers and his demands for performances at times and in ways out of sync with ritual and artistic considerations—compounded the feeling that Brook had stolen a central piece of Indian cultural heritage for his own purposes—oblivious to the culture, religion, or people who gave it birth and for whom it remained an important and living tradition. The history of British colonization of India served as backdrop to this cultural exchange, which seemed to replay that earlier exploitation and domination.

The production did provoke interest in Hindu philosophy and the *Mahabharata* text and raised consciousness of this ancient tradition. The production inspired much debate about intercultural practices. Is it unethical to decontextualize great works from their culture? Is some exposure to other traditions, even filtered through an artistic lens, better than none at all? Can and should we seek a universal message in the works of other cultures? Whose interests should a theatre artist serve? The text? A particular culture? The larger world artistic community?

Peter Brook's international cast recreate the epic battle to restore righteous action in *The Mahabharata* by Jean-Claude Carriere. Note the minimalist set that puts the focus on the work of the actor.
© *Gilles Abegg*

Challenges and Choices

Using the cultural forms imposed by an oppressive colonial power, can an artist ever find an authentic voice?

Most African performance was not text based and many dialects had no written language, so the very use of written plays and the language of the colonizer creates a hybrid form. Many want to promote an independent African identity by reviving ancient languages and performance traditions. Others view African theater pieces that mix indigenous performance with the written word as a way of taking control of the instruments of oppression to construct one's own narrative, writing in the stories of those peoples who were written out, or written off, by European history. Nobel Prize–winning playwright Wole Soyinka is an example of an African writer who uses European forms infused with African ritual elements. There is no easy way to decide the best path to establishing cultural identity through the arts.

Performance Studies

The scope of theatre studies has been widened by the new field of **performance studies**, which views theatre as only one of a continuum of events that possess "performative" elements. Other activities such as religious rituals, story-telling, sports events, games, striptease, parades, lectures, and political conventions also have a set space, a set duration, actors, audience, and the awareness that something outside the ordinary is occurring. The field of performance studies has given us a vocabulary with which to discuss these forms.

Performance studies has enabled us to move beyond a narrow view of what constitutes a theatrical event to examine performance in cultures using forms outside the typical European and American experience, as well as unusual forms within the Western tradition. An example of this might be the study of an African festival or a Balinese clown ritual in a theatre class. We might look at how a World Wrestling Entertainment match uses elements of theatre: it is live; it has actors playing roles before an audience; it is scripted, of set duration, and in a particular space; there is an interaction between the actors and the audience; and it cannot be exactly repeated.

Performance studies can provide a basis for understanding human behavior and social interaction. We are actually "performing," acting with a conscious awareness that we are in a role, a good deal of the time. In fact, we prepare ourselves for various roles every day as we choose appropriate clothes, hairstyles, and demeanors for particular activities. To think we are "performing" our own lives at first seems contrary to our sense of having a stable, fixed identity. But when we consider how we "act" in different situations, it becomes clear that we don we different masks for different occasions and interactions. The idea that we construct our identities—even things as basic as our gender and sexuality—has, in turn, influenced the contemporary theatre. Many plays such as Caryl Churchill's *Cloud Nine* have taken this concept as subject matter. Constructing and deconstructing identity has become a recurrent theme in contemporary theater, dissolving traditional notions of character. However, while theatre is an interesting metaphor

Photo 1.1
Protestors at the World Economic Forum in New York use elements of performance—music, costume, and processional puppets—to convey their anti–global-capitalism message. The growing use of theatrical elements in political activism reinforces the perceived connection between theatre and other performative acts.
© Paul J. Richards/AFP/
Getty Images

Artists

IN PERSPECTIVE

WOLE SOYINKA

The theatre work of Nigerian playwright, poet, novelist, essayist, and Nobel laureate Wole Soyinka (b. 1934) marries African and Western European influences as it addresses Nigeria's evolving political conditions, its legacy of colonialism, and the power of its rituals. Soyinka's life and works embody the conflicts and dilemmas faced by many postcolonial artists.

Born in Western Nigeria in 1934, Soyinka's early years were marked by a missionary education at schools where his father and uncle taught, and by time spent steeped in Yoruba culture and traditions. He received his college education in two countries, from 1952 to 1954 attending University College at Ibadan, in Nigeria, and then completing a degree in drama at Leeds, in England, in 1957. After graduation he worked at London's Royal Court Theatre as a play reader while writing his own early plays, *The Swamp Dwellers* and *The Lion and the Jewel*, both successfully produced in London and Ibadan.

Nigeria's struggle for independence from British rule framed Soyinka's early experiences. In 1960, when the battle was won, Soyinka returned to Nigeria, where he founded a theatre company that produced his first major play, *A Dance of the Forests*, as part of the country's celebration of independence. The play warned of coming political corruption if Nigerians did not develop the wisdom necessary to exercise self-rule. His use of European forms, which some called an elitist aesthetic, and his rebuke of Nigerian politics garnered criticism on many fronts.

The following years were prolific ones for Soyinka. He wrote and directed *The Trials of Brother Jero* (1960), *The Lion and the Jewel* (1964), *Kongi's Harvest* (1967), *The Strong Breed* (1967), and *The Road* (1969), and also published his first novel, *The Interpreters* (1965) and a book of poems. These plays integrated the routines of Nigerian daily life into a European dramaturgical framework, and many examined the inevitable tension between ancient traditions and changing political and social realities.

European and African belief systems clash as Sergeant Amusa, an agent of the colonial government, confronts the Yoruba women in an effort to stop a ritual death. The Sergeant wears the European uniform of his office, while the women display their connection to African heritage in their traditional dress in Wole Soyinka's *Death and the King's Horseman* at Philadelphia's Lantern Theatre.
Courtesy of Lantern Theater Company; photo by Nick Embree

Arrested for his political activism in 1965, and again in 1967, during Nigeria's civil war, Soyinka spent much of his two-year imprisonment in solitary confinement. He describes this period in his 1972 memoir *The Man Died: Prison Notes of Wole Soyinka*. On his release, Soyinka left Nigeria and went into voluntary exile in England, where he completed his doctoral degree. He wrote his most important plays in this period. *The Bacchae of Euripides* (1973), presented at England's National Theatre, integrated Yoruba ritual with classical Greek tragedy. *Madmen and Specialists* (1970) and *Death and the King's Horsemen* (1975) continued his exploration of ritual in African consciousness. A series of critical essays on literature collected in *Myth, Literature and the African World* (1976), as well as essays on politics, followed.

Soyinka's critical writings on theatre point to ritual as a powerful healing force and define the three worlds of Yoruba cosmology: the world of the ancestors, the world of the living, and the world of the unborn. His theatre embodies the flow between past and present, between the world of the spirits and the world of the living. The surreal style embodied in the movement between these worlds often challenges his audiences.

In 1986 Soyinka was awarded the Nobel Prize for Literature. In 1994 he again went into exile, fleeing Nigeria and General Sani Abacha's violent and corrupt regime, and has been living in California since 1998. He continues to write plays that are performed throughout the world and to speak out on political issues through his works. He was briefly detained by police in Lagos as recently as May 2004, while visiting Nigeria and attending a pro-democracy rally.

for life, life is not theatre. Theatre is heightened, objectified, aestheticized, delimited, and controlled.

Theatre in Changing Times

Changing times are changing the theatre. Technological advances are expanding creative possibilities and forcing theatre practitioners and theorists to rethink the limits of theatrical performance and to find new innovative forms. At the same time that technology is opening up new possibilities for the theatre, it is also a potent reminder of the living and immediate essence of theatre and what it can and must provide in an increasingly depersonalized world.

Television, radio, and film are instantly and easily accessible forms of entertainment. We will probably soon be able to access thousands of movies on our computers. Yet people continue to be drawn to the ancient art of the theatre, whose basic elements—the actor and audience—have remained unchanged through the centuries.

Nothing can replace the vitality and thrill of live performance. MTV will not stop the lines of people trying to buy tickets to hear Madonna live. In fact, electronic media feed our desire to be present in the same space with the performer we long to touch. When stars perform on Broadway, they attract crowds of theatre-goers who could more easily rent a video to see them. Theatre is about the immediacy and presence found in that communication between the actor and the audience. All electronic forms of entertainment, on the other hand, are one-way streets; we receive, but we do not return our feelings. The great cycle of human communication is incomplete, and there is a fundamental yearning to respond and be felt.

Why Theatre Today?

Why does every community and school continue to do theatre? It is easier to walk around with a videocamera and make a movie—no weeks of rehearsal, no risks before a live audience. What drives so many people all over the world to create theatre despite the hard work and risk? There is great joy in working with others toward a shared goal, and theatre is always collaborative. Anyone who has ever participated in a theatre production will tell you how close members of the cast and crew become. Facing the danger of opening night together and triumphing together is a bonding experience. It is almost like having a surrogate family. This sense of belonging that comes from working on a production is especially pleasurable in a world in which our sense of community is increasingly eroded.

For the individual, theatre also provides a form of self-expression, a full use of every part of one's being. It is a way to test your limits and your courage. It is a place to explore your inspirations, ideas, and values. Because theater is an art in time and space and can be created with limited funds for small audiences, it permits experimentation in a way not permitted in more commercial forms of mass media. It provides an opportunity to step outside yourself and to feel empathy for others. And it is a place to find appreciation, emotional reinforcement, and applause.

As you begin your study of theatre, you will see the history of civilization reflected in theatrical forms and find our own social concerns illuminated. You will learn how theatre is created, the potential of the art form, and what kind of theatre appeals to you most. You may even decide to participate. But, assuredly, you will become what every theatre artist desires most—an informed and passionate audience member.

KEY IDEAS

- The theatre is a mirror of life because it allows us to look at ourselves with an objective understanding of who and what we are, but it is not necessarily a replica of the real world.
- Theatrical conventions govern every aspect of the art form and establish its boundaries. They vary from one culture and historical period to another and evolve along with social values.
- Throughout the world all theatre is live; it requires the presence of an actor and an audience; it is ephemeral, collaborative, and a synthesis of many arts.
- Tradition and innovation exist in a dynamic tension in the theatre as artists adapt to changing times and audiences.
- The diversity of today's theatre is the product of many forces, including postmodernism, globalization, multiculturalism, interculturalism, and postcolonialism.
- Performance studies is an academic field that looks at theatre as one kind of performance on a continuum with other kinds of performance such as ritual and sports events. It helps us understand and discuss today's varied theatrical forms.
- Despite the ready availability of easily consumable popular culture and electronic entertainment, theatre continues to draw audiences because of its immediacy and liveness, and the thrill of direct contact with the performer.
- Theatre remains an art that binds a community of people in a collaborative effort in an increasingly depersonalized world.

The Audience
Partners in Performance

More intimate than many modern theatres, Heisei Nakamura-za's reconstructed Edo period *kabuki* theatre brings audience members seated near the rampway close enough to reach out and touch the actor making his way to the stage. From his vantage point, the actor can take in the entire audience. *The Summer Festival: A Mirror of Osaka*, performed at the Lincoln Center Festival, New York.

© Kayte Deioma

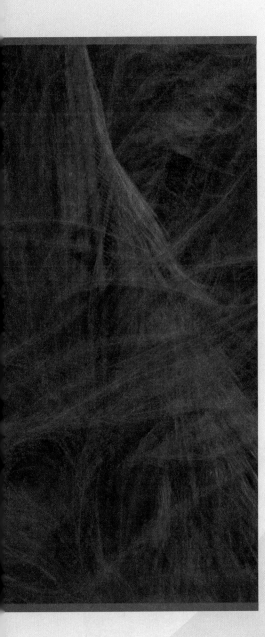

To go to the theatre is to experience the special excitement of live performance and to enter into a new set of relationships with actors, a performance, and the spectators that surround you. As you wait for the event to begin, in all likelihood it has not entered your head that the actors have also been waiting for you. All of their work has been in anticipation of your response. The performers *need* you to be there, and if you and everyone in the audience suddenly vanished leaving an empty theatre, there would be no performance. Your presence is vital to the theatre experience itself, for the most essential component of the theatre is the live actor–audience interaction with all its stimulation and surprise.

History IN PERSPECTIVE

THE ORIGINS OF THEATRE

The need to tell a story, to imitate, to play, and to perform repeated acts that ensure the continuation of a community are so vital to the human psyche that cultures everywhere have developed some form of enactment. Since these activities predate recorded history and leave no tangible trace, the precise origins of theatre are cloaked in mystery. Theatre most likely evolved over time as a form of cultural expression and has no specific moment of creation.

The use of music, dance, costumes, props, and masks are common to ritual and theatrical performances, so theorists have speculated that many forms of theatre evolved from rituals. The earliest rituals were performed to please or appease the gods who were the intended audience, and some extant traditions today remind us that ritual and theatre can coexist in the same form. Consider performance traditions such as the *kutiyattam* from the Kerala region in India that uses special sacred places for performance. Actors face the shrine and the temple deity. Attendance at a performance is also an act of worship. In Japan at the Ise Shrine, the most sacred spot in Japan, priestesses of the indige-

nous Shinto religion perform special dance ceremonies. Here too, audiences may come to watch, but the performers face away from them because the dances are meant primarily for the pleasure of the divine spectators, the Shinto gods. As the human audience takes on increased importance, we see the movement from sacred ritual to secular theatre.

We have evidence that ancient Greek tragedy evolved from **dithyrambs**, hymns sung and danced in praise of the god Dionysus, the god of wine and fertility, and early Greek theatres contained an altar. From the ancient Egyptian Abydos ritual performance that hieroglyphs date to 2500 B.C.E. to the Christian passion plays of medieval Europe, many of the rituals associated with performance tell tales of resurrection and renewal often connected to fertility and rites of spring. This indicates that theatrical

In Metlakatla, Alaska, audience members join in the dancing of this Tsimshian dance troupe at a potlatch, a ceremony that includes feasting, music, speeches, singing, dancing, and gifts for the guests. Such events are held to bear witness to and celebrate a wide variety of occasions including the payment of a debt, a wedding, a funeral, or the building of a house. Performance here builds and cements community relations.
© *Lawrence Migdale/Pix*

The Audience and the Actor: The Invisible Bond

Unlike a television or movie audience, the live theatre audience always participates in some way in a performance. In fact, the level of audience participation can be anywhere on a continuum from community creation and participation to total separation of audience and performer.

activity is linked with the continuation of community and the affirmation of the beliefs that sustain a culture's well-being.

In some cultures **shamans**, priests or priestesses, are charged with communicating with the spirit world on behalf of the community to bring peace and prosperity to the populace, or healing to the sick. They may induce spirits to possess them as part of this communication, providing their own bodies as vessels through which spirits manifest themselves to the group. Donning a mask or costume or holding a particular object associated with a spirit often serves as a path to possession. Shamans in a state of possession may move, speak, and in every way act like the spirit that possesses them, an image that parallels the work of the actor. While some shamans give themselves over to irrational powers and enter a paranormal state, others carefully plan the elements of their performance. It can be argued that this aesthetic consciousness turns the performance into both a theatrical and a religious event. Such developments can be found in Native American shamanistic rites and throughout Asia, Australia, and Africa. The Buryat people of Siberia and Mongolia have incorporated shamanistic elements into contemporary theatre forms, demonstrating the coexistence of the sacred and secular in performance.

In many cultures religious events offer an opportunity to enact stories from a group's mytho-historical past. Such presentations may be necessary to ensure the health of the community and its members or to effect a particular transition—an individual's passage from childhood to adulthood, such as the Apache puberty drama, or a seasonal shift from winter to spring. They may serve as a means of passing on oral heritage or perpetuating values and beliefs, and as a form of communal and sacred entertainment.

Some scholars believe that the roots of theatre lie in storytelling, a universal cultural activity that passes on a community's shared cultural experiences and knowledge. Entertaining narrators naturally embellish their tales by taking on the voices, facial expressions, and mannerisms of different characters, and may even add props, costume pieces, and physical movement to help bring the action to life. Through these additions, storytelling blossoms into theatrical presentation.

Some suggest that the origins of theatre lie in dance, where physical movement and mimed action gave expression to ideas before developed language. Early expressive movement in imitation of animals and people may have led to further transformations and elaborations, and later to dramatic content. The presence of dance in ritual links it to the development of theatre.

It is unlikely that any single practice gave birth to the theatre, which embraces all of these elements and is influenced by so many traditions. It is more constructive to understand the development of theatrical activity as a movement along a continuum in response to the needs of communities to express their deepest concerns, to teach their members, and to ensure the community's survival through performance.

At this Buddhist Tsam festival in Himachal Pradesh, India, monks wearing papier mâché masks and ornate costumes represent Guru Padmasambhava and his Eight Emanations. In India, Tibet, Nepal, and Mongolia, monks perform masked dances as part of their sacred duties.
© *Lindsay Hebberd/CORBIS*

Scholars believe that many forms of theatre evolved from religious ritual in which everyone present was a participant and the intended audience was the invisible divinity. When one member of the group first steps out of a communal role to perform for the others, theatre appears in its embryonic form. By claiming the role of the actor, the performer also creates the audience. Over time, as the roles become more clearly divided by function—audience, performer, playwright—we have the development of the theatrical form. In this model, theatre is deeply tied to its communal roots, with the actor and the audience emerging from the same tightly knit group and held together by an invisible bond. In some ways, the theatre is always about community—the community of artists that create it, the community of spectators that observe it, and the union of both groups in the moment of performance.

Even today, when the roles of actor and audience feel so distinct, they are still codependent in the creation of theatre. Actors on stage can feel the audience's reactions and consciously or unconsciously adjust the performance accordingly. If the audience is laughing, an actor will wait until the laughter has died down to speak the next line. If the audience is quiet and unresponsive, an actor might unconsciously push or work harder to get the audience to react. An unexpected noise such as the ring of a cellphone or a sneeze might cause an actor to lose focus for a moment. In many performance traditions in which participation of the community is required, actors may direct all their energy toward heightening the audience involvement. Theatre performers are always playing in relation to the audience as its members laugh, cry, sigh, and breathe together. The live actor–audience interaction is one of the special thrills of the theatre for both performers and spectators, and it pulls actors back to the theatre despite lucrative film careers.

The Audience Is a Community

In some places around the world, the audience still comes from a tightly knit community linked by shared values and history outside the theatre. In other places, when you take a seat in a theatre auditorium, or gather around street performers, or join a dancing crowd, you become part of a temporary community tied together only for the duration of the performance. Either way, this assimilation into a group empowers you. You can influence the actions of others around you, and they can influence yours. We all have felt how much easier it is to be openly responsive when we are part of a crowd than when we are alone. Imagine screaming at a sporting event if you were the only spectator. You are more likely to laugh out loud when others are laughing as well. There is a special freedom that comes from being an audience member, just as there are special constraints.

Many factors can affect the degree of interaction among audience members. The spacial configuration of the theatre and lighting can contribute to a heightened awareness of other people's responses. Performances outdoors in daylight tend to make us feel part of a crowd. But even in darkened theatres with the audience all facing the stage, we can sense an atmosphere in "the **house**"—the term theatre people use for the collective audience—that sets an emotional mood of the spectators. It is so palpable that performers can feel the audience even before a performance begins. Stage managers often report backstage before curtain that it feels like "a good house" tonight, commenting on the invisible currents of energy circulating among the audience members. Actors can sense the audience as a group from the stage immediately, and they adjust their performances accordingly. The audience is the one thing that changes completely every night, and because of the interplay between actor and audience, no two performances are ever exactly alike.

Audience Members Construct Meaning as Individuals

Although the audience is usually addressed as a group by theatre artists, an audience, like any community, is made up of individuals with varying backgrounds and points of view. In close-knit societies, with shared values and histories, the differences among audience members may be less marked, but nonetheless, no two people bring the same set of life experiences to a performance, and each audience member perceives a theatrical event through a personal lens. Because audiences are collections of individuals with different pasts, every audience will respond in a unique way.

Our personal histories always influence how we react as audience members in many ways. If you are watching a performance from a culture outside of your own, you may not understand its nuances, or point of view, or performance style. If you have recently gone through a traumatic event such as the death of a parent, you might have a particularly strong or empathetic reaction to a play addressing this subject. If you are seeing a play or a performance tradition you have studied, you will measure this production against how you imagined it. If you are an experienced theatre-goer, you might not be as impressed by a lavish set or spectacular scenic change as a novice would. If you are attending a play that you have already seen, you may find yourself comparing the interpretations, directing, acting, and design. All of these individual experiences will affect your response, just as taking this class will probably make you a very different audience member in the future.

Personal Identity and the Construction of Meaning

Our personal histories, including our age, culture, race, religion, ethnicity, gender, sexuality, education, and economic or social class, play a part in our response to a performance. Usually theatre attempts to bridge the space between audience members' personal experience and the content of a performance through the creation of **empathy**, the capacity to identify emotionally with the characters on stage. Sometimes theatre artists

Photo 2.1
In this production of *The Blacks: A Clown Show* by Jean Genet, levels of reality were confused as the black–white political conflict that is the subject of this play is realized through the direct confrontation of white audience members by black actors. This action reversed the traditional power structure between blacks and and whites. At some performances white spectators were traumatized by the psychological assault of the drama. Directed by Christopher McElroen for the Classical Theatre of Harlem.
Courtesy of The Classical Theatre of Harlem, Inc.; photo by Richard Termine

choose to exploit these differences for social or political reasons. Whether through empathy or distance, the goal is always to increase our understanding of others like or unlike ourselves.

The Free Southern Theater's 1968 production of *Slave Ship* by Amiri Baraka (b. 1934; also known as Leroi Jones), enacted a history of African Americans in the United States and deliberately divided its audience along racial lines. A symbolic slave ship was constructed in the middle of the large playing area, with close seating on all sides. The hold of the ship, where slave bodies were piled in cramped quarters, was eye level with the audience, magnifying the inhuman conditions on board. During an enacted slave auction, female slaves were stripped topless and thrust at white men in the audience, who were asked what they thought the women were worth. Many white audience members were so disturbed by this aggressive confrontation with history that they left at midpoint; others wished they had. At the end of the piece, cast members, invoking black power movements, invited black audience members to join them in encircling the white audience, while shouting for violent revolution. At many performances, black audience members, feeling empowered by the performance, joined the cast in shouting and intimidating white spectators. Many white audience members felt threatened and angry that they had paid to be abused, or felt helpless to express their sympathy with the blacks in an atmosphere of hostility. This play was meant to provoke different responses from different audience members to teach the lessons of history, and racial background could not help but influence the audience's experience of the play. A 2003 production of Jean Genet's *The Blacks* by the Classical Theatre of Harlem used the same techniques to polarize the audience along racial lines and drive home similar points (see Photo 2.1). Once again, many white audience members were visibly shaken by the direct confrontation.

Chicana playwright Cherrie Moraga (b. 1952) focuses on the problems of the community of Mexican American migrant farmworkers in California. In her play *Heroes and Saints*, the bodiless central character Cerezita represents Chicano children with birth defects from pesticides used in the fields (see Photo 2.2). The play's treatment of homosexuality within the Chicano community interweaves sexuality with religious symbolism and seeks to expose the oppressive aspects of Catholicism. Moraga liberally mixes English and Spanish dialogue, reflecting the actual speech patterns of the Chicano community. The play draws heavily on Chicano cultural images, and audience members unfamiliar with Spanish or with the social world Moraga depicts might feel lost or unable to appreciate her reworking of cultural symbols. Those familiar with that community might feel deeply touched by the play. These charged themes provoke different responses based on sexual preference and religiosity, even within the Chicano community.

Eve Ensler's popular play *Vagina Monologues* (see Chapter 1), dealing with such an intimate part of the female anatomy, elicits different responses from audience members based on their gender, even creating a sisterhood among women in the

Challenges and Choices

Should there be limits on how actors treat unsuspecting audience members, especially when the action is confrontational?

Photo 2.2
Note the images and symbols of Chicano culture in Cherrie Moraga's *Heroes and Saints* at Brava! for Women in the Arts, San Francisco, directed by Albert Takazauckas. Actors: Hector Correa and Jaime Lujan.
Courtesy of Brava Theater Center; photo by David M. Allen

audience. Tim Miller's work (discussed in Chapter 6) speaks directly to issues of concern to the gay community.

Theatre experiences that address race, ethnicity, religion, sexual preference, and gender seek to create awareness of the life conditions of people both like and unlike ourselves. What we take away from such provocative performances and what meaning we construct depends on how we filter the staged events through our personal histories. Theatre, the most public of all the arts, is also a private act with personal meaning.

Audience Members Choose Focus

At a theatrical event, individual audience members possess a certain amount of autonomy to choose their focus and to control their personal experience of a performance. A theatre spectator sees the entire playing space and can choose to look anywhere. Lighting effects and other staging techniques can draw the audience's attention to one area or another, but spectators can still decide whether they want to watch the actor who is speaking or see the reaction of the actor who is listening. Where spectators choose to focus will affect their interpretation of a performance. This puts a burden on stage actors and directors to create a center of compelling dramatic action, which explains the heightened theatricality of stage acting. Compare this to film or television in which the director, through the camera lens, and the editor, with a cut, preselect what they want the audience to see and from what perspective.

Some stage directors take advantage of the audience's visual autonomy. They create productions with many stages and many events occurring at the same time and ask the audience to choose its own focus time and again. In Richard Schechner's (b. 1934) work with environmental theatre during the 1960s and 1970s, there was no demarcation between the audience space and the performance space, and simultaneous action occurred in many places. Actors engaged individual audience members, sometimes whispering dialogue in their ears. This required each member of the audience to actually construct the drama based on a completely individual experience.

Photo 2.3
Note the platform stages reminiscent of fairground booths. The audience can watch different scenes from various sides and angles. Some audience members stand to get a better view of action taking place at the opposite side of the playing area. The Théâtre du Soleil performing *1789* directed by Ariane Mnouchkine. Scenery by Roberto Moscoso and costumes by Françoise Tournafond. Cartoucherie de Vincennes, Paris, 1970.
© Martine Franck/Magnum Photos

In 1970–1971 the French troupe the Théâtre du Soleil created *1789* in the company's huge old ammunition factory on the outskirts of Paris. Its scenes from the French Revolution took place on five stages surrounding the audience creating a fairground atmosphere with multiple focuses. The audience chose where to look just as they might at an outdoor fair (see Photo 2.3). One particularly poignant moment used two stages at opposite ends of the space to represent the physical and cultural distance that separated Louis XVI, the French king, from the illiterate peasants in the countryside. While the king proclaimed that he wanted to respond to his subjects' needs, the peasants had no means of communicating with him.

Conventions of Audience Response

When you attend the theatre, most likely you are not aware that you have entered into a silent contract determining how you will behave during the performance and what your relationship will be to the theatrical event and the performers. You are unaware of this agreement because, in general, audiences conduct themselves according to time-honored traditions that are observed by spectators and actors alike. When these rules are broken, on purpose or by accident, as when an actor planted in the audience interrupts the stage action or an audience member leaps uninvited onto the stage, it can be exciting or disturbing, but it is always provocative, because it is a violation of the prevalent theatrical conventions and audience expectations. A performance constructs its conventions of audience response through cues given by the actors, the spatial arrangement, directorial concept, lighting, and set design. In the chapters ahead, we will look at how each of these elements determines the role of the audience.

Although the audience's presence is a vital part of theatrical performance, the nature of the audience's participation may vary from place to place, society to society, era to era, and even at different kinds of events or in different venues within the same culture. At evening performances of the opera in the Roman arena in Verona, Italy, during the overture, the audience lights small candles and the entire arena is lit up like a giant birthday cake (see Photo 2.4). The locals in the upper tiers picnic during the performance, passing around chicken legs, salami, and wine. Those in the high-priced seats, however, behave more like opera house audiences in New York, London, or Paris, where people come to be seen in their designer best and await intermission to sip champagne. Although eating is taboo during most performances inside opera houses and can disturb the performers and other audience members, when the New York Metropolitan Opera performs in Central Park, audience members feel free to behave more like the audience in Verona, picnicking on the grass and drinking wine. We see that expected audience behavior can be different for the same kind of performance in different settings.

Around the world today, in countries outside of Western Europe and America, most theatrical traditions expect vocal audience response of one kind or another during the show. In the Japanese *kabuki* theatre, at the climactic moments of a play, the fans yell out phrases such as "I've been waiting for this my whole life!" or "Do it the way your father did it!" Through this yelling they support their favorite actors, cheering them on to masterful execution the way a baseball fan in America might yell "strike him out" to a pitcher during a game. At performances of Chinese opera, whenever a performer does something praiseworthy, members of the audience will applaud and shout *"Hao, hao"* (Good, good). They do not feel compelled to hold their applause until the end. In African concert party theatre, audience participation is expected, and spectators are invited, even drawn, into the performance by the actors who encourage them to hiss the villains and warn them of danger. Actors may engage in a call and response with the audience by repeating simple questions about the plot for the audience to answer. When these kinds of performances are

Photo 2.4
At the Roman Arena in Verona, Italy, audience members play their part in the operatic spectacle by lighting small candles during the overture. The entire arena is aglow in an audience-created lighting effect.
Photo by Gianfranco Fainello, Fondazione Arena di Verona. All rights are exclusively reserved.

played to spectators unfamiliar with their expected role, it can feel like a rock band performing for a classical music audience. The performances can seem lifeless without the expected audience response, and actors who have come to rely on the vocal support of their admirers can feel let down. If you are unfamiliar with these customs, you will surely not be able to fully appreciate a performance that depends on your interaction. You may feel out of place or unsure how to conduct yourself. One of the most important things to learn about the theatre is how to be an appropriate audience member.

Audience Conventions in Western Theatre History

In Europe and America today, and in theatres in the Western tradition around the world, most often we expect to be silent during a performance and to hold our applause until the end. Sometime after we take our seats, the lights dim and a hush settles over the crowd as we become quiet and attentive listeners. Although this is the prevalent convention in Western theatre today, it was not always the case.

The Once-Active Audience

The outdoor daylight performances in ancient Greece took place in a festive atmosphere in which social interaction, eating, and drinking were all part of a daylong theatre event. In ancient Rome, theatre was performed at religious festivals that offered an enormous array of entertainments. Both sacred and secular, performances were meant to please the gods as much as the human spectators. Because theatre had to compete with chariot races and wild animal fights for its audience's attention, it was common for spectators to walk out in the middle of a play if they thought that something more interesting might be happening at another venue. The prologues of ancient Roman comedies often admonish the audience to pay attention to the show.

Throughout the Middle Ages, theatre was very much a community affair. Audiences would gather around wandering players in town squares and interact with each other and the performers. The Christian cycle plays that began in the fourteenth century and depicted stories from the Old and New Testaments were projects that engaged the entire town in preparation. The audience who had shared in the creation of the piece, providing sets, costumes, props, and other needs, attended in an open spirit of camaraderie to watch their fellow townsmen perform.

An open exchange between actors and the public was part of the spirit of the theatre even as performances became more formal events performed by professional actors in theatre buildings during the sixteenth century. In his own time, Shakespeare's plays were performed before a rowdy audience who booed, hissed, cheered, conversed, ate, drank, and even threw food at the performers, offering one explanation for the rat infestation in theatres of the period. Many believe that the open roof of the Elizabethan playhouse was a means to let the stench of food, drink, and unwashed bodies escape. If we remember that Shakespeare wrote for a popular audience, we can appreciate the earthy humor, double entendres, and theatrical devices that made him a crowd pleaser.

In late seventeenth-century Europe, as theatre moved increasingly indoors, the behavior of the audience was somewhat tempered, but spectators were still actively engaged in the event. Indoor theatre in this period was a social event for an elite audience. Candelabra lit up the audience as well as the stage, and the horseshoe-shaped auditorium made it as easy to be seen by others as to see the show. Those seated on the long sides of the horseshoe actually had to turn their heads to the side to see the stage; when they looked straight ahead or down, they looked at each other and could easily observe who else was in the audience, what they were wearing, and who were their escorts, feeding the social gossip of the time. Some spectators even sat on the stage when additional seats were added to raise revenues, bringing them even more attention.

Photo 2.5
In 1830, audience riots followed the first performance of Victor Hugo's *Hernani*, pictured here in a painting by Albert Besnard. Hugo's romantic play broke with the stage conventions of neoclassical tragedy, and the romantics and the classicists drew battle lines as to which form should dominate. The horseshoe shape of the theatre enabled those in the circular balconies to communicate with the spectators in the orchestra, facilitating the shouting match.
© *Erich Lessing/Art Resource, NY*

History IN PERSPECTIVE

THE ASTOR PLACE RIOTS

During the nineteenth century in Europe and the United States, theatre was the people's art. Passionate audiences protested vociferously over issues of concern from ticket prices to theatrical forms and the treatment of stars. Some of the public outrage addressed at controversial films today would seem tame in contrast.

Lingering American antagonism against the British and the "highbrow" Americans who identified with them may have been at the root of the violent Astor Place Riots that erupted on May 10, 1849, at the Astor Place Opera House in New York City, ostensibly the result of a professional rivalry between the American actor Edwin Forrest (1806–1872), and the English actor William Charles Macready (1793–1873). Macready's subtle and intellectual style contrasted with Forrest's vigorous acting and muscular bearing that many felt embodied American democratic ideals. Forrest's portrayal of common heroes like the Roman Spartacus were widely admired by popular American audiences. The bad blood between the two actors began in 1845 during one of Forrest's tours in England when, blaming Macready for his lack of success, Forrest openly hissed Macready during a performance. Their simultaneous performances in New York transplanted their animosity to the United States and translated into a call to arms for homegrown American culture.

Forrest's admirers assailed Macready with critical newspaper articles and threw objects at him during performances. After a disastrous opening night in New York, when audience members threw chairs at the stage along with the usual vegetables and fruit, Macready was ready to return home. Persuaded by a group of powerful New Yorkers, he continued his run in defiance of the treatment received. On hearing that Macready would continue on, Forrest's supporters drummed up a nationalist fury against the production. At the next performance the house was full to capacity, and policemen and crowds of thousands gathered outside the theatre in protest. When Macready walked on stage, the gathering erupted beyond the control of the police. The crowd outside threw paving stones at the building and pushed to get in, and Macready barely escaped with his life. The national guard was called in from a nearby armory, and total mayhem ensued when soldiers shot at the crowd. According to various accounts, the Astor Place Riots left between twenty and thirty-one dead, over one hundred wounded, and the theatre in ruins.

In an attempt to restore order, National Guardsmen at Astor Place shoot at rioters throwing stones at the theatre where the English actor William Charles Macready performs.
© Bettmann/CORBIS

In eighteenth-century London, spectators often arrived early and entertained each other before the show began. In his *London Journal*, James Boswell recounts how on one such occasion he imitated a cow to the delight of other audience members, although they were not as taken with his imitation of a chicken. The plays of the Restoration and early eighteenth century, with their depiction of an artificial social world with pretentious manners and behavior, can be seen as mirrors of the audience in the theatre.

European plays of the sixteenth through the nineteenth centuries were punctuated with dramatic devices addressed directly to the audience such as **asides**—short comments that revealed a character's inner thoughts often to comic effect, **soliloquies**—lengthy speeches through which a character revealed state of mind, and dazzling poetic **monologues** or speeches. The audience might erupt in appreciative applause after a monologue or soliloquy, much the way they do today at the opera after an aria.

The eighteenth- and nineteenth-century theatre, reflecting the democratic revolutions occurring in the outside world, increasingly included popular entertainments and easily accessible drama. American audiences were some of the rowdiest of all. They exercised their democratic freedom at theatre events and brought tomatoes, cabbages, and rotten eggs with them to throw at the actors if they didn't like the performance. Sometimes they tore up the seats, throwing those as well, and on occasion they were moved to riot. At a good performance they cheered ecstatically and cried out for encores; an actor would have to repeat a speech as many times as the crowd demanded.

The Rise of the Passive Audience

With this long history of involved audiences, how did it come to pass that today, in Western Europe and the Americas, the audience is generally more passive? In fact, the quiet, passive spectator is a relatively recent historical phenomenon and dates only from the late nineteenth century, as a result of a theatrical style known as **realism**. In realistic theatre, the audience is asked to accept the stage world as a believable alternate reality where things happen much as they would in life, and people behave in seemingly natural ways. This is achieved when the actors conduct the lives of their characters as though the audience were not watching, in spaces designed to look like their counterparts in the real world; in turn, the audience, representing a different reality, agrees not to intrude on the imaginary world on the stage to preserve its perfect illusion. This creates the convention of an invisible **fourth wall** separating the stage from the audience.

We should remember that realism is not any more *real* than any other style of theatre. In fact, actors are not talking in their everyday voices or volumes; they are not any more like their characters than actors in nonrealistic plays; the sets and costumes are just as artificial as those that present an abstract or poeticized style. What realism provides is the *illusion of the real*, and that is as much an illusion as every other stage world. Because realism came to dominate the American theatre, we refer to the nonrealistic theatre as stylized; but realism is as much a style—a manner of presenting the world through accepted conventions—as any other approach to the theatre.

Realism as a style resulted from a confluence of forces: the ideas of Darwin that presented human beings as objects of scientific study; the birth of sociology and psychology that sought to objectively observe human behavior on every social rung; a surge of playwrights interested in applying these ideas to the theatre; and advances in stage lighting—first gas and later electric—that permitted the darkening of an auditorium to separate the audience while simultaneously shining a focused light on the stage to illuminate human behavior as though it were under the lens of a microscope. The advances in lighting enabled the actors to move away from the front of the stage and behind the proscenium arch (see Chapter 9).

As more and more playwrights chose to write in this realistic style, it came to dominate the Western theatre, and its impact on acting, directing, and design can be seen to this day. Theatre architecture altered to reflect social change and to facilitate this new approach. The horseshoe shape for theatres was abandoned in favor of a theatre in which all the seats faced forward, focusing the audience on the stage and altering its relationship to the performance. Economic motives pushed theatre managers to place upholstered armchair seating in front of the stage in the pit, in what we now call the orchestra section. Where rowdy lower class spectators once stood or sat on backless benches, wealthier audiences now sat in expensive reserved seating, changing the atmosphere in the theatre.

Aesthetic Distance

Peculiarly, the more the conventions of realism separated the audience from the actors, and the more passively the audience watched, the more they lost their **aesthetic distance**, the ability to observe a work of art with a degree of detachment and objectivity. Realism drew audiences into the performance. The presentation of a world so like their own, inhabited by characters whose concerns and problems so closely paralleled their own experience, heightened the level of audience identification and emotional involvement with the characters on the stage. Styles other than realism still provide a constant reminder of the fiction before us, and this awareness enables us to separate psychologically from the work.

Every theatrical experience sets up an emotional relationship with the audience that is regulated by theatrical convention. This can range from icy dispassion to overwhelming emotional involvement. Some amount of distance is always necessary; without it, we would be unable to discern that the events unfolding on the stage are a fiction and that the actors are really playing characters who live only for the duration of the performance. Distance maintains the audience's sanity, or else we would all be leaping onto the stage to stop Romeo from killing himself. Theatre critics from Plato (circa 427–347 B.C.E.) to the present have debated the importance of aesthetic distance and its moral implications. Many have feared that exposing the audience to violent or sexually explicit acts and offensive language can foster such behavior. Others have argued that aesthetic distance permits a purging of our aggressive desires through art and enactment. Aristotle (384–322 B.C.E.) referred to this emotional release as **catharsis**. These concerns are echoed in today's discussions of violence in the media.

Challenges and Choices

Is the witnessing of violent and disturbing images and language on stage so provocative that it requires government regulation, or should audience members be left to regulate their own aesthetic distance?

Rebelling against Realism's Passive Audience

As soon as realism became an accepted convention, the continuing cycle of tradition giving way to innovation produced experimental artists on a divergent course. From the turn of the twentieth century on, theatre practitioners have been seeking ways to tear down realism's fourth wall and reengage the audience in performance, creating new sets of conventions in the process. Some have simply sought ways to reinvigorate the stage, such as Thornton Wilder's use of a character called the Stage Manager who speaks directly to the audience as he sets the scene, narrates events, and introduces the characters of *Our Town*. Other theatre practitioners manipulate aesthetic distance for their own political or aesthetic ends. Avant-garde theatre artists have even toyed with the audience's aesthetic distance, confusing them as to what is *real* and what is *pretend*, which is an unsettling experience. In *The Last Supper* (2002), Ed Schmidt invited the audience into his home, promising them a wonderful dinner as part of the event. Bantering with the audience in seemingly unscripted remarks as he cooks in his kitchen, he realizes he's forgotten to defrost the fish and has run out of ingredients. The audience settles for cheese and crackers while he orders out for pizza. Sitting in the intimacy of the actor's home with real rumbling stomachs, the audience could not distinguish where the real person left off and the role began and were baffled as to what was true and what was false, raising questions about perceptions of reality.

Political Theatre: Moving the Audience to Action

Playwrights have used the theatre for political commentary as far back as the ancient Greek comic playwright Aristophanes (448–c. 380 B.C.E.), who satirized the people and institutions of ancient Athens. However, in the early twentieth century, a different kind

Photo 2.6
Banda Calavera drums up an audience for a Teatro Campesino performance in Fresno, circa 1969. Pictured: Feliz Alvarez, Chale Martinez, Manuel Pickett, Lupe Valdez, Phil Esparza.
Courtesy of El Teatro Campesino

of political theatre aimed at activating audiences for social change in the real world took root. Such political theatre places special demands on its audience, as its goal is to spur them to real action. Practitioners experiment with strategies for audience activation adapted to specific circumstances and political goals.

Agit-Prop: Activating the Audience

Agit-prop (from *agitation* and *propaganda*) was an early form of political theatre developed during the 1920s in Russia and later adopted abroad. Born in the Marxist fervor of the Russian Revolution, it supported the workers' struggle for political, social, and economic justice. In the spirit of the ancient town criers, agit-prop brought the day's news to illiterate peasants and factory workers to enlist their support for the massive economic and social changes in the aftermath of the revolution. As songs and skits on relevant issues were added, these presentations grew into "living newspapers." Agit-prop reached out to its audiences, playing where ordinary people gathered, in workers' cafes and community halls, expressing important information in a short, simple, explicit, and entertaining way.

Agit-prop became a model for political theatre in many countries. German troupes such as the Red Megaphone incorporated group declamatory speeches and cabaret-style skits into their performances. During the Spanish Civil War (1936–1939), players used agit-prop to inspire the people to fight against fascism. The Federal Theatre Project, organized to provide jobs for unemployed theatre artists during the Great Depression in the United States, performed *Living Newspapers* from 1935 to 1939. These used documentary material to inform the American public of pressing social concerns. In the 1960s, groups such as the San Francisco Mime Troupe and El Teatro Campesino used agit-prop techniques to fight for civil rights, for immigrants' rights, and against the Vietnam War. The Mime Troupe mixed the didacticism of agit-prop with popular American and European theatrical forms like vaudeville, *commedia dell'arte*, and circus clowning to create extended outdoor plays that brought home a political message and urged the audience to adopt a position. Teatro Campesino, a Chicano group founded by Luis Valdez (b. 1940), brought theatre to immigrant farmworkers by performing in churches and on the back of a flat-bed truck in crop fields in short plays called *actos*, improvised skits that explained to California's immigrant farmworkers why they should join the Farm Worker's Union and demand better conditions. Many *actos* ended with the actors exhorting the audience to call for "*La Huelga*" (a strike). The performances were accompanied by Chicano songs that served to disseminate information, much like the early Russian living newspapers.

Bertolt Brecht: Challenging the Audience

Throughout the world, theatre artists look to the work of the German playwright and director Bertolt Brecht (1898–1956) for a model of how to engage the audience. Brecht wanted to turn his audience members into critical viewers who, like fans at a sporting event, would think about what they were seeing, take sides, comment on the action, and come up with alternative courses of action.

Brecht built on the work of German director Erwin Piscator (1893–1966), an early pioneer in political theatre who developed a series of stage devices that increased the audience's aesthetic distance and prevented them from becoming emotionally absorbed in the play, so they could see the political issues more clearly. Piscator abolished fourth wall realistic stage sets that had come to be the standard, and replaced them with slide projections, film, and placards naming time and location, often providing a historical backdrop for contemporary issues.

Brecht extended these ideas. Mood lighting was replaced by utilitarian illumination to provide visibility. He revealed the means of creating theatrical illusion, such as light fixtures, ropes, and pulleys to keep the audience fully aware that they were watching a theatrical event. Brecht wrote plays (which we will discuss in the next chapter) that could utilize these staging techniques. The action is interrupted by narratives, projections, and songs that comment on the situation and whose music and content are frequently jarringly dissonant. The finales of his plays often leave the situation unresolved or directly ask the audience to come up with a resolution. Brecht worked with a troupe to develop a style of acting that could enable the actor to comment on the character, not become the character.

Photo 2.7
The map that serves as backdrop and the puppet-like figure of Hitler are both devices that create a distancing effect in this production of Bertolt Brecht's *Schweyk in the Second World War* directed by Richard Eyre at the Olivier Theatre, London.
© *ArenaPal/Topham/The Image Works*

Through these and other techniques, Brecht hoped to achieve what he called the *verfremdungseffekt*, translated as **distancing** or **alienation effect**, a separation of the audience emotionally from the dramatic action. The audience is thus an observer, able to decide the best course of action to resolve social ills. As politically motivated theatre practitioners around the world adopted Brecht's methods, these devices became a part of our theatrical vocabulary and no longer have the same startling effect on audiences; artists therefore continue to look for new techniques and strategies.

Augusto Boal: Involving the Audience

Brazilian theatre theorist and practitioner Augusto Boal (b. 1930) extended Brecht's ideas in his theatre of the oppressed, a theatrical form in which all barriers between actors and audience are destroyed, returning theatre to its communal roots in which we can all become participants in social drama. He turns passive spectators into active "spect-actors" who don't just think about alternative solutions, but try them out on stage as rehearsals for social revolution.

Under the umbrella of the *Theatre of the Oppressed*, Boal developed different theatrical strategies for different situations and audiences. In *forum theatre*, members of a community create a short piece about shared problems that they perform for other spect-actors who are invited to stop the show at any time, take over roles, and try out new solutions. In his *invisible theatre*, provocative dramas about burning issues are enacted in normal everyday settings like subway cars or restaurants, as if they were happening in real life. The unsuspecting public, unaware that the action is rehearsed and planned, unwittingly join the debate or action and become actors themselves. In one piece performed on a boat in Sweden, a young woman pretended to be pregnant and in labor to catalyze a discussion about the shortcomings of the health care system. During a term spent as a city councilman in Brazil, Boal worked on *legislative theatre*, a form of *forum theatre* designed to reveal issues of primary concern to the community to guide political policy.

Boal's *Theatre of the Oppressed* was originally designed to reach the poor of Brazil, but now there are centers for the dissemination of his methods all over the world. Local practitioners throughout South America, Asia, Australia, and Africa have adapted his methods to their pressing social problems and audiences. In the more bourgeois cultures of the United States, Europe, and Canada, Boal's ideas have been used psychotherapeutically to address the oppressive forces within our psyches, drawing on a collection of techniques called *The Rainbow of Desire*.

The Living Theatre: Confronting the Audience

During the 1960s many theatrical groups in the United States and abroad spoke out against the Vietnam War and sought new ways to galvanize their audiences against the war and the political-industrial complex that supported it. One of the most innovative and influential groups was The Living Theatre, founded by Judith Malina (b. 1926) and Julien Beck (1925–1985). The company has a long history of important productions, beginning with their staging of Jack Gelber's drama about drug addiction, *The Connection* in 1959, and Kenneth Brown's *The Brig* in 1963, which placed a mesh fence between the audience and the dehumanizing action of military prisons depicted on stage. The group lived out their anarchist politics by moving to Europe and living as a nomadic collective. They created *Paradise Now* in 1968 to make audiences aware of the restraints social and political institutions imposed on individual freedom and to conscript spectators into renouncing these structures in favor of building an alternative "paradise" community. Goading audience members to shake them from their complacency, the group used

Performance
IN PERSPECTIVE

ADAPTING POLITICAL STRATEGIES TO LOCAL AUDIENCES

In countries the world over, political theatre groups develop strategies and find theatrical forms that can speak to local audiences and issues. When the Peruvian troupe Yuyachkani discovered that its early pieces about land reform and miners' strikes did not connect with its audiences, its director Miguel Rubio incorporated traditional celebrations, masks, songs, dances, and costumes from the communities of miners and peasants they sought to activate. They now begin a show with a fiesta that is interrupted by a dramatic conflict.

The Parivartan Theatre Project in the tribal area of Khedbrahma in Gujarat, India, uses local villagers as performers and incorporates traditional songs and folk theatre conventions to address tribal attitudes toward women and issues of domestic violence, dowry death, and infanticide, which plague the region. The first part of a presentation enacts a well-known folk tale related to the treatment of women, and the second part retells the story in a contemporary context. The players go from house to house to announce the show and after the presentation disperse into the crowd to discuss the play with the villagers in small groups.

Sistern, a theatre collective in Jamaica, presents plays in Creole by and for working-class women on topics such as women's work, incest, poverty, and violence against women. In their workshops they use improvisation, oral histories, traditional ring games, folk tales, and other techniques to address problems, find solutions, and turn the women's experiences into educational performances. Their 1978 production *Bellywoman Bangarang*, about teenage pregnancy, was staged in the audience as a further means of reaching out to spectators.

In times of political repression and censorship, a special bond can form between theatres and their audiences as artists seek to be the community's mouthpiece. Under President Suharto's oppressive dictatorship, Indonesia's N. Riantiarno and his group, Teater Koma, addressed Jakarta's urban middle class and critiqued contemporary society and politics in a blend of Western-style structured scripts, Brechtian aesthetics, and musical theatre with influences from Indonesia's indigenous and more improvisational folk forms. In *Time Bomb* (*Bom Waktu*, 1982), audiences watched the struggles of Jakarta's urban slum dwellers play out underneath a fancy restaurant where wealthy diners eat a sumptuous meal. In the Philippines under Ferdinand Marcos's martial law and severe theatrical censorship (1972–1986), amateur groups, student groups, and professional urban and rural theatres all took an active role in denouncing the regime's corruption and use of torture. In 1979 PETA (The Philippine Educational Theatre Association) transformed the folk *pannuluyan*, a Christmastime street procession in which Joseph and Mary search for an inn. In their version, seeing the slum conditions, Joseph and Mary join forces with the down-and-out of the city. In 1984, on Human Rights Day, students and faculty from the University of the Philippines performed *The Nation's Oratorio* (*Ortoroyo Ng Bayan*). While the audience sang and chanted, the actors read out articles from the Universal Declaration of Human Rights, enacting scenes that illustrated its abuse under the current regime.

Yuyachkani grabs the attention of villagers in Quinua, Peru, with festive costumes, musicians, and stiltwalkers.
Courtesy of Casa Yuyachkani, Peru

IN PERSPECTIVE

In Their Own Words

BILL TALEN, AKA REVEREND BILLY

Bill Talen is the author and actor who performs as the televangelist Reverend Billy. He began as a sidewalk preacher in Times Square in the late 1990s, to fight against the "Disneyfication" of the neighborhood. Since then, he and his "Stop Shopping Gospel Choir" have toured a range of transnational chain stores, especially Wal-Mart and Starbucks, to preach against mindless consumerism and the eradication of small local businesses. He was arrested and sentenced to jail for his performance inside a Los Angeles Starbucks in 2004.

■ **How did you come to a form of theatre that involves audience participation?**

Before I began to walk out into the audience to touch people on their heads and hands, I was always fascinated with the sounds and seat shiftings an audience makes. When I was a regular stage actor, and then later a monologuist/storyteller, I would listen to the sounds of the audience as if it was a single body—all those sighs and unconscious chuckles and levels of breathing.

■ **How do you get reluctant audiences to participate?**

The notion of the audience's involvement in our Stop Shopping rituals speaks to a general hunger for a group spirituality that eludes fundamentalism. One mark of fundamentalism, whether from organized religion or the most powerful church of all, The Church of Consumption, is the absence of any humor. If you pretend that you know all the answers to the questions of life and

death, you can't joke about them. In the anarcho-faith that we prefer, serious questions of life and death are just hilarious. The reluctance to shout "Amen!" or "Change-a-lujah!" is difficult to maintain when people all around you are laughing. That is how the community is created, through the ritual sharing of the joke and the defeat of socializing seriousness. In our service nowadays, this "mockery" lasts a few seconds. All we need is the cultural frame, which we then break and get on to more complex matters.

■ **Did art drive your politics or politics drive your art?**

Desperation at the Disneyfication of my neighborhood in Times Square was the driving force. In more recent years, the onslaught of Wal-Mart and Starbucks—and after 9/11, Halliburton, and Bechtel—have aroused whatever we have left for our own defense—all the art or politics we can muster. But no one has time to stop and name one gesture "artful" and one bit of writing "political." Transnational capitalists come at you, so to save your community you have to drop those categories of theater, politics, and religion, and just resist with all you've got.

Now we perform inside stores, in actions that we call "retail interventions." It could be argued that politics drove this decision because going undercover, and inside, is "behind the lines." (And anyway, there's no place to protest outside, anymore.) But it could also be called more artful because there is no theatrical space more charged than a retail store in the Land of Consumption.

■ **Do your performances spawn other grassroots activism efforts?**

There are Stop Shopping churches throughout the world. We stream sermons and songs through the church website, Revbilly.com. We try to "make place" by creating

---

Challenges and Choices

What is the audience's responsibility to the event? Must audience members accept the conventions of a performance, or can they refuse to participate as the show prescribes?

inflammatory political statements that brought spectators to their feet, and sometimes to the top of their seats, screaming back in anger. Company members then invited spectators to join them on stage and in their nomadic, tribal lifestyle.

The work of the Living Theatre became famous and inspired many theatre artists of the 1960s and after to adapt the group's techniques for their own purposes. The Living Theatre is still held up as an important example of engaged theatre and continues to perform today with pieces such as *Not in My Name*, a ritualistic action against the death penalty, enacted in Times Square in New York City on the eve of every state execution. In this piece, performers confront passers-by individually, avowing that they themselves will never kill and asking spectators for the same commitment, continuing their use of direct encounter to motivate an end to violence.

meta-communities through "ritual resistance." We will ask all the church members in Melbourne to go to the 36 Starbucks there and put their hands on the cash registers and videotape themselves while they recite prayerfully the first paragraph of Chapter 3 of Jane Jacobs's *Death and Life of Great American Cities.* Then we stream this through the website to the faithful on other continents, who are watching this on their computers inside Starbucks. Finally, the churchgoers from the rest of the world perform their simultaneous reply. They also enact the Jane Jacobs sacred text, and their hands are also on the cash register, but we have asked them to do so in an Aussie accent if they can, as a signal of fondness. They loved it in Melbourne.

- **What long-term impact do you think your performances have on audience members?**

We have larger live audiences now. People in Barcelona and London and California seem ready for their "credit card exorcism"

when the Stop Shopping Gospel Choir steps off the bus. On the other hand, transnational capital, while so widely discredited, still expands and destroys. Revolution no longer has a Winter Palace to storm, or a Berlin Wall to tear down. Transnational capital, the great displacer, is everywhere and nowhere. It dazzles you and it dulls you. It comes at you in pixels, and secret police, and ten-story-high supermodels. We have to make defending our own neighborhoods, and our own psychological selves, as dramatic as the revolutions that come to us from history.

Reverend Billy with supporters preaching against the evils of transnational capital.
Copyright 2004 Fred Askew Photography.

Source: Used with permission of Bill Talen, aka "Rev. Billy."

Engaging the Audience Today

Today a new breed of activist artists is expanding on the methods of these pioneers to engage spectators in political activism responsive to contemporary issues. The Internet has provided a rapid way to contact large groups of participants and to call them to theatrical political action telling them when and where to show up. Reclaim the Streets, a group boasting participants in New York, London, and around the globe, turns street corners and subway cars into spontaneous parties to reclaim overregulated open spaces for general public use. Some performer-participants get messages via the Internet, while others simply become part of the show by walking down the street. The Surveillance Camera Players raise awareness of the loss of privacy in our daily lives by performing short, silent pieces in public for surveillance cameras. Their performances point out the unobtrusive cameras that watch our every move.

At his "Church of Stop Shopping," Bill Talen performs in the guise of Reverend Billy, a preacher who speaks out against consumer culture. Performances are mock revival meetings with left-wing politics rather than religion as their theme. During the course of his shows, Reverend Billy asks audience members to practice "stop-shopping" techniques such as discarding their credit cards. At the end of every piece, Reverend Billy leads the audience outside the theatre to take action in the real world. His audiences have walked to a community garden under threat by corporate development and planted seeds, and marched with him to picket the local Starbucks that had forced out neighborhood stores. Reverend Billy's audience participation teaches spectators how grassroots activism can help local people take back control of their neighborhoods.

From Provocation to Mainstream: The Evolution of a Convention

Although experimental and political theatre artists in the twentieth century first used audience participation as a form of rebellion against the passive bourgeois audience and other theatrical conventions of realism, tamer forms followed. The idea of the active spectator eventually left the realm of the avant-garde and became a firmly established convention.

Productions such as Off-Off-Broadway's *Tony and Tina's Wedding* (1988) treat audience members as guests at a wedding. They attend the church ceremony and walk as a group to the reception where they sit at tables and eat a full dinner, complete with champagne, as they watch Tony and Tina's family relationships explode around them. A far cry from agit-prop theatre, the event is a fun night out and a novel date for both dinner and

Photo 2.8

Original cast members Rachel Benbow Murdy as Mia and Anna Wilson as Sander, perform among the audience in *The Donkey Show,* club El Flamingo, New York. Note the lively interaction with the involved crowd.

Courtesy of and special thanks to Randy Weiner, Creator and Writer of THE DONKEY SHOW, Diane Paulus, Creator and Director of THE DONKEY SHOW and Keira Fromm, Resident Director of Project 400 Theater Group and THE DONKEY SHOW.

a show that has now become a national franchise with a website, gift certificates, and commercial performances in cities around the United States. The unusual way the production asks the audience to participate in the show continues to attract audiences.

The Donkey Show (1999), a retelling of Shakespeare's *A Midsummer Night's Dream* using disco songs from the 1970s in place of Shakespeare's dialogue, also incorporates the audience into the action. Staged in an old disco club, the action takes place around spectators who are encouraged to buy drinks and dance just as they would at a club. The audience configuration continually changes as actors dance, sing, and perform moving through the crowd on a series of platforms. The dance party in the audience continues throughout the show, and on some nights goes on long after the actors have changed out of their costumes and gone home. The audience in this production hedonistically indulges their own pleasures as they mix with the actors.

Such mainstream performances demonstrate that what was once a defiant radical strategy to overturn prevailing conventions can evolve into a popular and accepted theatrical form. The participatory audience has entered our general culture as well, spawning interactive art in museums, galleries, and on the Internet.

Meeting Theatre's Challenges

Although we often think of the theatre as a place of entertainment, the theatre poses special challenges to its audience. In the theatre, you must be attentive as you decide where to focus, or you will miss significant information. Theatre often depends on language more than a visual medium like film and therefore demands good listening skills. Sometimes you will be confronted by an unexpected theatrical style—difficult language, stylized movement, strange sets, and costumes might seem jarring—and you will need to remain open and try to adjust to the new form and how it communicates. Theatre, unlike television, is often imagistic and metaphorical, so the most important thing to bring to the theatre is your imagination.

Some productions ask spectators to make a special commitment by challenging them physically, emotionally, or intellectually. So-called "marathon performances" may

Photo 2.9
For this production of *Faust,* heavy demands were placed on the audience. Note the audience members standing and surrounding the action and the orange curtains that separate the playing spaces used for alternate scenes. The audience's frequent migrations between the spaces forced them to continually reorganize themselves, fostering social interactions during this marathon event. Goethe's *Faust,* Parts I and II, directed by Peter Stein, Berlin, Germany.
© *Ruth Walz*

Photo 2.10
Members of the Montana Shakespeare in the Parks company bring their performances to remote areas around the state and are housed by local families. Featured here is a performance of *Tartuffe* in Poker Jim Butte. The audience travels long distances to partake of this cultural event.
© *Ted Wood*

be six, eight, or twelve hours long. German director Peter Stein's (b. 1937) 2000 production of Goethe's *Faust* took on the whole work, rarely performed in its entirety, for a twenty-hour event. The audience faced more than the challenge of length. The space was divided into two playing areas. For each scene, the audience was shuffled back and forth between the two spaces, which were reconfigured every twenty to sixty minutes. The seating arrangement changed several times and the audience was even expected to stand for a particular portion (see Photo 2.9). Navigating the performance became one of the demands placed on the audience.

The six-hour *Rwanda 94* (1999), created by the Belgian company Groupov along with artists from Rwanda, also challenged its audience with more than length, by addressing the horrors of the Tutsi genocide and Hutu massacre that took place in Rwanda in 1994. Video images of dead bodies hacked by machetes and an account of events by a woman whose children and husband were murdered were all part of the piece. Audiences were challenged to deal with these emotional presentations as they learned more about the causes of the violence, including the role played by European and American powers.

Sometimes the journey to a production becomes a challenge in and of itself. The Théâtre du Soleil's location in the woods of Vincennes requires a trip to the last stop on the Paris metro and transportation from there to the theatre on a special theatre shuttle bus. Arriving at night, through the woods, to the theatre's courtyard, illuminated with tiny lights that bedeck the trees, is a magical experience in itself that prepares the spectator for the rest. As more and more urban theatre groups are priced out of downtown space, performances are occurring in out-of-the-way places and seedy areas, and making the trip becomes a test of faith in the product. Many who live in remote regions consider a theatrical event worthy of a pilgrimage. The annual tour of Montana Shakespeare in the Parks takes it to remote areas of the state, where ranchers and other locals from as far as one hundred miles make the journey on winding gravel roads to small towns like Poker Jim Butte to participate in a rare opportunity for live theatre. Actors are housed and fed by members of the community, who regard the troupe's arrival as an opportunity for culture and fun.

Attendance at the theatre is demanding, but it is also rewarding. As audience members, you have the power to choose your focus, engage emotionally and intellectually, express your response, and have your presence felt and acknowledged by the artists. These are part of the special thrill of being in a theatre audience. Some theatre pieces affect you deeply and cause you to undergo a transformation that may affect your life. Opening yourself to new theatrical experiences and what they proffer is the true challenge and pleasure of being a member of a theatre audience.

KEY IDEAS

- The audience's presence is vital to the theatrical experience. The immediate interaction between actor and audience is one of the special thrills of live performance.
- The presence and participation of the audience reflects the theatre's communal roots in ritual. When you join the audience, you become part of a unique, temporary community.
- Audience members also respond to the theatre as individuals influenced by their own personal histories. Ethnicity, religion, race, class, or gender can divide or unite an audience.
- Unlike film audiences, theatre audiences choose their focus.
- Conventions of audience response and participation vary from place to place, throughout history, and even from one production to another. These conventions may be inherited through tradition or set up by a production.
- Aesthetic distance is the ability to observe a work of art with a degree of detachment and objectivity. Artists manipulate aesthetic distance for their own ends.
- Political theatre places special demands on its audience, challenging and confronting their beliefs to spur them to real action.
- Over time conventions evolve and radical new relationships between the audience and performers can become traditional arrangements.
- Theatre can challenge its audience physically, emotionally, and intellectually.
- Opening ourselves to new theatrical experiences and what they proffer is the true challenge and pleasure of being a member of a theatre audience.

PART TWO

In *Samritechak*, a Cambodian classical dance-drama based on Shakespeare's *Othello*, the dancers wear the traditional ornate costumes and masks of the *lakhon khol* masked dance-drama. The upward curve of the fingertips is typical of this form's elegant gestures. The production was choreographed by Sophiline Cheam Shapiro, who was among the first to train in classical Cambodian Dance at the School of Fine Arts (now the Royal University of Fine Arts) after Pol Pot's brutal regime left only one in ten dancers alive to carry on this tradition. Shapiro now lives in California, and her position between cultures enabled her to retell *Othello* using the classical dance vocabulary, expanding the reach of the ancient art. The play's theme of taking responsibility for one's actions has deep meaning in her homeland. Royal University of Fine Arts Theatre, Phnom Penh, Cambodia.

© Kayte Deioma

Encountering Traditions

Traveling the global world of theatre today, you might attend the Chinese opera and witness a tradition performed, staged, and sung much the way it was two hundred years ago. In Africa you might participate in a communal performance celebration paying homage to the king and his ancestors. A beautiful child representing the royal spirit is carried high above the dancing crowd, accompanied by a day of endless drumming, a tradition whose origins are so old no one knows when it began. In Phnom Penh, you might see a retelling of Shakespeare's *Othello* performed with the gestures of Cambodian classical dance. You might find an abandoned factory in Paris converted into a theatre where actors rehearse ancient Asian dance movements for their roles in a new production of a 2,500-year-old Greek tragedy. What are we to make of these diverse experiences?

As we study performances around the world, we encounter two basic kinds of theatrical traditions. The first is based on a **performance tradition** whose staging, music, dance, characterization, masks, and acting are passed from generation to generation as a totality of expression. Performance traditions are usually rooted in the values and beliefs of the community, are often linked to religious ritual, and sometimes involve total community participation. The second tradition is based on a written **play text** to be interpreted in performance. Although a play is born out of the values of its community, it is not tied to its original concept, time, or place, and can be passed down for reinterpretation by future generations of performers. The actor is at the center of the performance tradition as the embodier of the performance values and as the transmitter of the performance text to the next generation. Play traditions privilege the writer, because it is the written text that is passed down, so a play's ability to inspire new performance concepts is key to its longevity on the stage.

Europe has provided us with the longest theatrical tradition based on the written play. While popular performance has always existed, it has been valued as secondary to the written text. We now possess a body of dramatic literature in the European tradition that dates back to the fifth century B.C.E., and an accompanying tradition of dramatic criticism that has provided methods for approaching and interpreting these works.

As Europeans colonized the world, they brought their dramatic literary tradition with them. Indigenous performance traditions were often suppressed and feared, or exploited for political purposes. School systems set up by colonial authorities taught the theatre of the dominating country. Shakespeare was mandatory for high school plays in the British colonies, just as Corneille and Molière played in those parts of the world dominated by the French. Latin America adopted the genres of the Spanish Golden Age that flourished at the time of conquest. Often, indigenous playwrights inserted local color, costume, or dialects, as in the *costumbristas* of South America, but the forms of plays remained fundamentally European and were written in the language of conquest. We may now decry the way the European tradition was imposed, but important plays inspired by European genres and structures can now be found the world over.

Vibrant indigenous performance traditions somehow survived the colonial era, and in a peculiar reversal of history, are now prized in Europe and

America for their inherent theatricality and the communal values they embody. Theatre artists, through the twentieth century to the present, have been haunted by the belief that in ancient performance traditions based in ritual lies a theatre that connects to our deeper spiritual nature and can provide a universal human language.

And so we come to the strange place we now find ourselves: Traditions that were once each other's scourge now stand side by side as a source of inspiration to today's theatre artists, who blend, borrow, insert, and interweave each other's theatrical conventions in mutual appreciation. In the chapters ahead we will examine both theatrical traditions and seek to understand the current dialogue among performance traditions, written forms, and the contemporary theatre.

Understanding Plays

3

In a comic mismatch, the bewitched Titania, Queen of the Fairies (Suzanne Bouchard), falls in love with Bottom the Weaver (Geoff Hoyle), who is metamorphosed into an ass in Shakespeare's *A Midsummer Night's Dream* at the Seattle Repertory Theatre, directed by Sharon Ott. Set design, Hugh Landwehr; costume design, Paul Tazewell.

© Chris Bennion Photo

The artistic value of a play lies in its capacity to be imagined and reimagined on stage, for the true mettle of a play is tested in performance. No writer for the theatre ever intends the reading of the dramatic text as an end goal. All playwrights create in the hope of seeing their work realized in a live performance before an audience, so reading a play is not like reading a novel or short story, where reading completes the intended communication. The staging of a play is another step in the interpretive process that begins with the playwright and ends with the audience.

As a reader of a play, you will be challenged to create the performance in your mind's eye by playing the roles of designer, director, and actor in your imagination. When you read a play, you must imagine the characters inhabiting the world of the theatre, not the world of real life. Sometimes the playwright gives you insight into the world of the play through descriptions of setting and character, stage directions, and prefatory comments; often all you have is dialogue, and you must create all the performance elements that are absent—all that you will see and hear. You must envision the setting, the theatre space, the kind of stage, the mood created by the colors of the lights, and the style of the performance. You must imagine what the characters will look like—their costumes and movement. Will there be sound effects, music, dance, or song? How will the actors' voices sound, and how will they read their lines? Each choice you make defines what the play will mean to you. Everything you learn about the theatre will contribute to the power of your dramatic imagination.

Storytelling and Cultural Tradition

We define ourselves and our culture by the stories we tell about ourselves. Others define us by the stories they tell about us. Through stories we create our histories and transmit the lessons we have learned to others. The theatre is not only the place where we tell our stories, it can also be the source of this human narrative.

There are many ways of telling stories in the theatre, and these are determined by culture and convention. Western tradition usually thinks of a play as telling a story through a progression of causally related events transpiring in linear time and enacted in three-dimensional space. Some argue that the idea of "progression" is a reflection of a culture that values progress; as other cultures have other paradigms for dramatic action. Some build stories out of a sense of cosmic time and sacred space in which all events evoke the past and the future, as in the Australian aboriginal tradition, which traces the interrelatedness of the sacred, physical, and human worlds to *dreamtime* when the world took shape. Some cultures focus on the instrumentality of an individual in triggering events; others focus on the role of the community or the ancestral spirits as forwarding the dramatic action. Stories can also be constructed from seemingly unrelated events much the way we attempt to connect the images and happenings of a dream. Today many of us experience the world as a barrage of simultaneously occurring sensory events and seek a form that can capture the multiplicity of experience. Many recent plays present the sounds and images of a fragmented reality.

Whatever the nature of the story, the challenge for the playwright is to find a form through which these events can materialize in the theatre and speak to the audience. The playwright must always keep the performability of the text in mind and construct a bridge between the linearity of the written text on the page and the multidimensionality of the stage where the text is played. How the playwright constructs dramatic action, character, and language to tell a story is as much an expression of culture and convention as the story itself. In this chapter, we will discuss the most common conventions of playwriting in the Western tradition.

The Playwright Shapes the Story

The **story** of a play includes all the events that happen or are mentioned in the text. A play's story may include many incidents that have taken place before the play begins. In Sophocles' play *Oedipus Tyrannos*, in which King Oedipus discovers that he murdered his own father and married his mother, the crimes of patricide and incest that lead to his downfall have taken place many years before the events of the play itself. A play's story may include many things that do not actually occur on stage, but that are only spoken about. In ancient Greek tragedy, for instance, it is a theatrical convention that violent events always take place off stage. Spectators never see these graphic scenes but only see their aftermath or hear about them through the reports of a messenger. Although they don't happen on stage, these events are essential to the story.

The **plot** of a play is the ordering or structuring of the events that actually take place on stage. The plot defines *how* the events unfold for the reader or viewer. Playwrights use the plot to create dramatic tension, usually through developing **conflict** and creating struggles and obstacles for the characters to overcome. Through the choices they make to win this central conflict, characters define themselves. In the modern era, many plays refocused the struggle on forces inside the character, creating dramatic tension through a progression of emotional states of increasing intensity. Plotting the story is calculated for maximum emotional impact on the audience.

Authors can tell the same story through different plots to focus on particular ideas or themes. The interaction between story and plot is one of the ways playwrights shape a play's meaning. Where an author chooses to begin a story, from whose perspective it is told, what events occur on stage, or which characters or facts a playwright includes or highlights all make one telling different from another. You may have listened to someone telling a story of a shared experience and noticed that the person didn't tell it the way you would. You may even have interrupted to add information you considered vital that the other person left out. How one tells a story reflects what the storyteller values. The "how" of storytelling is as important as the tale itself and reflects the identity and perspective of the storyteller.

A good storyteller will capture our attention even if we already know what is to come. The ancient Greek tragic poets drew from a fount of legend and history that was well known to their audiences, so they were judged by how well they told familiar tales. Aeschylus, Sophocles, and Euripides each wrote a play about the murder of Clytemnestra by her children, Electra and Orestes, in revenge for her murder of their father, yet each tells the story in a completely different way, focusing on different characters and offering different accounts of their motivations and moral responsibility.

Playwrights in different eras may pick up the same subject matter and turn it on end through plot. Both Euripides' fifth-century-B.C.E. play *Hippolytus* and Jean Racine's seventeenth-century play *Phèdre* tell the story of Phaedra's incestuous love of her stepson Hippolytus. Each chose to focus on a different character as evidenced in their titles, which alters our perspective on the events. Euripides' Hippolytus is a haughty, prudish young man who rejects love, marriage, and passion and is the favorite of the virgin goddess Artemis. Aphrodite, the goddess of love, punishes him for his allegiance to the chaste Artemis by afflicting Phaedra with the passion that will drive them both to their doom. Racine's version has no gods and focuses instead on the destructive force of Phaedra's unbridled passion, putting her at the center of the drama. Hippolytus is presented as a sympathetic victim and is even given a love interest who does not appear in the ancient play. In fact, this was Euripides' second play about the story, written after his first version was condemned for being too harsh toward Phaedra, so even the same playwright can re-plot the same story. In 1924 Eugene O'Neill (1888–1953) wrote an updated version of the tale in *Desire Under the Elms*, in which he explored repression and desire through the lens

IN PERSPECTIVE

In Their Own Words

TINA HOWE

Tina Howe (b.1937) is the author of The Nest, Birth and After Birth, Museum, The Art of Dining, Painting Churches, Coastal Disturbances, Approaching Zanzibar, One Shoe Off, Pride's Crossing, *and* Rembrandt's Gift. *These plays put center stage the primary personal concerns of women—motherhood, marriage, and menopause—celebrating the courage with which women confront the crises of their daily lives. Influenced by absurdist drama, Howe's style moves the family drama beyond realism where the dark hidden side of everyday relationships can be explored. Her major awards include an Obie for Distinguished Playwriting, the New York Drama Critics' Circle award, a Tony nomination, two NEA fellowships, and two honorary degrees. Her new translation of Ionesco's* The Bald Soprano *and* The Lesson *premiered at the Atlantic Theatre in 2004.*

The English director Max Stafford-Clark said the most amazing thing to me as we were heading into rehearsals for my forty-four-character play *Museum* at the Public Theater in 1977. (Or he might have said it after we'd opened to decidedly mixed reviews. The timing doesn't matter. It was the shock of the idea.) He said, "Tina, this is a great time to be a woman writing for the stage, because women haven't been heard from yet!"

It never occurred to me that my gender could be a boon. He was absolutely right! In theory. But almost thirty years later, I wonder if we'll ever be heard from! Sure, we're praised for our plays about women as victims—plays that show us at the mercy of disease, abuse, and self-doubt. But how much of our work is produced

Tina Howe's *Pride's Crossing* traces the life of a woman determined to be the first to swim from England to France across the English Channel. Cherry Jones as Mabel Tidings transforms on stage from age ten to age ninety in the Mitzi E. Newhouse Theater production at Lincoln Center, New York, directed by Jack O'Brien.
Sara Krulwich/The New York Times

that celebrates strong women? Sexy and canny women? Daughters, sisters, wives, and mothers who move mountains, not just dust rags? It's a tricky balance and one I'm particularly aware of since I have my white glove plays about aging WASPs recalling better times and my bare hands plays about women blasting into the light *now*. Today!

Having been married to the same radiant man for forty-four years, I've always been fascinated with fidelity. It's a subject you rarely see in the theatre. Infidelity is so much more titillating. But there's nothing I enjoy more than showing a household under siege and watching the women transform—grow antlers, fins, and wings as they seek, and ultimately gain, salvation. These plays invariably fail with the critics, or never even find productions, because I pull off my white gloves and all pretense of good breeding along with them. They're as carefully crafted as the WASPy ones, but they deal with panic, not nostalgia—how a mother reacts to her four-year-old child who's played by a large, hairy man, the stages of delirium a wife goes through as her house sinks further and further into the ground, or a woman struggling to avoid eviction due to her husband's obsessive hoarding. Sure, they overreact once in a while, but look at the hijinks the fellas get to put their heroines through! But if we shimmy out of our traces, we're labeled "sentimental," "undisciplined," or worse. We're ladies after all! Look at the restrooms theaters give us. The line stretches for miles because there are only three stalls! Backstage and on stage we deserve more room to take care of our business.

So what is the restless female playwright to do? We all have our strategies. I tend to alternate my WASPy plays with my frisky ones. My last production was neither. It wasn't even my own play! The Atlantic Theatre Company just produced my new translations of Eugène Ionesco's *The Bald Soprano* and *The Lesson*. I was exhilarated for two reasons: (1) because Ionesco has always been my hero—the quintessential mischief maker, and (2) because my work was finally beyond gender. I didn't have to worry whether my gloves were on or off. I was just the dutiful translator. Perhaps some day, people like Max won't even talk about women playwrights. We'll just be part of the mix.

Source: Used with permission of Tina Howe.

of Freudian psychology. Eben, his Hippolytus character, is motivated by an Oedipal complex, lusting for his stepmother and reviling his father.

Today we are aware that in past eras some people were excluded from the storytelling process in the theatre, and others told their tales. Women's voices were rarely heard until the modern era, and in fact, the three Phaedra plays just discussed, which are about a woman's passion, were written by men. Indigenous people and racial and ethnic minorities had few opportunities to express their own narratives on the Western stage. Through multiculturalism and interculturalism we have begun to appreciate the diverse stories told by people of different genders, races, ethnicities, classes, cultures, and sexual orientations, and the many ways they shape their tales in the theatre.

It is not unusual today to see playwrights from disempowered groups reclaiming their own stories. Playwrights may take classical texts and explore them from some unusual perspective that can reveal the point of view of a character who was disenfranchised in the original version. David Henry Hwang's (b. 1957) *M Butterfly* (1986) twisted the plot of Puccini's opera *Madame Butterfly* (1904). In the opera, Butterfly (Cio-cio San), is betrayed in love by an American naval officer for whom she has sacrificed all. In the Hwang play, Song, the Asian "actress" who is really a man, hides his gender and victimizes a French diplomat, Gallimard, upsetting our stereotypes of the "submissive Oriental." Gallimard is easily duped because he has projected his preconceived feminine Asian onto Song. The two stories are conflated through the use of famous music from the opera and Gallimard's donning of Butterfly's traditional costume in his prison cell at the end of the play. Hwang's play not only reflects on the racist values embedded in our cultural myths and projected on others, his replotting of *Madame Butterfly* also asserts an Asian American understanding of Asian identity. Today we are sensitive to the many perspectives people bring to the telling of a story. Understanding how the playwright uses the plot to emphasize particular themes provides audiences and readers with a tool for analyzing a play.

Dramatic Structure

Dramatic structure is the scaffolding on which a playwright plots a tale to frame or shape the action. Different dramatic structures become conventions of playwriting in different times and places. When playwrights find themselves with new ideas to convey, they often need to create new dramatic frames to help express them. If enough artists follow this new structure, it too becomes a convention. The choice of dramatic structure strongly influences the impact of a play and can help convey a play's meaning as expressively as its characters or its dialogue.

Dramatic structure describes the scope and progression of the action. Some plays cover a wide scope of time and a large number of characters and events, while others are more tightly circumscribed. Some plays evolve in a linear fashion so that one action leads inevitably to the next in a causal chain, whereas others may move back and forth between different locations, plots, characters, time periods,

Challenges and Choices

If telling stories is a way of expressing culture and identity, can anyone tell any story? Do only some people have the right to tell certain stories by virtue of their cultural heritage or gender?

Photo 3.1
John Lithgow, as the French diplomat Rene Gallimard, admires the Chinese opera star Song Liling he believes to be the ideal Asian woman for whom he will sacrifice all. Hauntingly played by B. D. Wong, Song conforms to all of Gallimard's romantic stereotypes. The original production of *M Butterfly* by David Henry Hwang was directed by John Dexter at the National Theatre in Washington.
© 1987 Martha Swope

History IN PERSPECTIVE

ARISTOTLE (384–322 B.C.E.)

The ancient Greek philosopher Aristotle was the first person to devise a method of dramatic analysis. In his essay on literary criticism, the *Poetics* (350 B.C.E.), Aristotle lays out a system for critiquing Greek tragedy, which he considered a branch of poetry along with comedy, epic poetry, and lyric poetry. Aristotle broke tragedy into six elements: plot, character, language or diction, ideas, music, and spectacle.

For Aristotle, plot was the most important element, the "soul of tragedy," followed by character, which he saw as defined by the dramatic action. Language addressed the quality of the words chosen by the poet, clearly separate from the manner of delivery by the actor. Music referred to the sounds of the words and the accompanying music of Greek tragedy. Spectacle, the element he associated with the emotional effect of a play achieved through its staging, was the least important, lying outside the realm of poetry. Aristotle spends most of the *Poetics* on the elements of plot, character, and language, saying relatively little about elements of performance.

Aristotle's writings became the foundation of European theatrical criticism, and his prioritizing of elements, with its privileging of the written text over performance values, was the dominant mode of writing and thinking about the theatre for two millennia. The twentieth century saw a revision of these assumptions. Theatre critics now consider performance elements as integral to the total theatrical experience as the written play. Free from Aristotle's prejudices, Western scholars can begin to study performance traditions not rooted in a written text without bias. Explorations of new forms of plays that challenge Aristotle's precepts are common today.

In the next chapter we will take a close look at Aristotle's views on tragedy and how they have molded an understanding of that theatrical genre. Some scholars believe that Aristotle's analysis of tragedy may have had a partner text analyzing comedy as well, but apart from the few comments he makes on comedy in the *Poetics*, his thoughts have not come down to us. Even as we move beyond Aristotle's method of analysis and his particular views on the theatre, which reflect the culture of his times, his work continues to provide an effective breakdown for the study of many conventional plays.

and levels of reality such as dreams and fantasies. Each play will set up its own structural rules, but the few basic structural models outlined in the following sections reflect traditions that have prevailed over time. It is important to remember that how a play does *not* fit into one of these models is often as significant as the ways it does.

Climactic Structure

A play with a **climactic structure** has a tight-knit form that limits the scope of events, the number of characters to whom they happen, and the time in which they transpire. Because the Greek philosopher Aristotle was the first to describe this structure in his famous essay on dramatic criticism, the *Poetics*, it is sometimes referred to as an **Aristotelian plot**. Aristotle's ideas have been so influential in Western theatre that plays that deviate from his descriptions of plot are often called "non-Aristotelian," as if he defined the critical vocabulary and expected norms.

In climactic structure, the **point of attack**, the place in the story where the action begins, is usually late in the story, at the heightened part of the action. **Exposition** reveals events that occurred before the start of the play through some device such as a confidant or a soliloquy that enables a character to speak all the necessary information to the audience to set up the plot. Circumstances build on each other through cause and effect causing **complication** of the dramatic situation leading toward a **climax**—the point of highest emotional intensity—followed by a final resolution. Because Aristotle saw the dramatic tension coiling ever tighter toward the climax, he referred to the rising dramatic action as the tying of the knot, and the falling action as the untying. We usually refer to the resolution by the French word *denouement,* which is a translation of Aristotle's "unknotting." In English we speak of tying up the loose ends. Regardless of the term used, the act of bringing all the parts of the play to a final conclusion is the same.

When the plot cannot easily resolve itself, playwrights often use a convention called a *deus ex machina*—a god from the machine—to resolve the drama. In ancient Greece, this literally was a god figure lowered from a crane to put an ending on a play (see Photo 3.2). Euripides ended many of his plays by bringing in a god to finalize the fates of the mortal characters on stage. Today the term *deus ex machina* refers to any dramatic device, outside of the main action, used to bring the play to a final resolution. The seventeenth-century French playwright Molière (1622–1673) turned King Louis XIV into a metaphorical god at the end of *Tartuffe,* when after a decent family has been ruined by the religious hypocrite Tartuffe, a royal emissary arrives to set everything right so the play can have its happy ending.

Photo 3.2
Medea leaves Corinth on a flying chariot sent by her grandfather, the Sun, taking the bodies of her dead children away from their father, Jason. The device of the chariot puts a neat ending to an otherwise irresolvable situation and is seen here in the Ninagawa Yukio production of *Medea* at the Delacorte Theatre, Central Park, New York.
© Jack Vartoogian/FrontRowPhotos

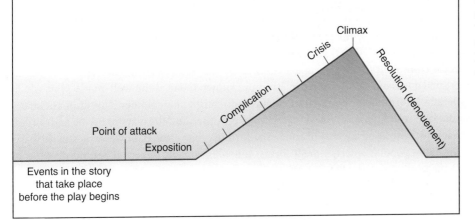

Figure 3.1   Climactic Play Structure   This diagram helps you visualize how events build one upon another to create rising dramatic tension in a climactic structure. Note the late point of attack in the story line and the fall of tension after the climax.

Artists
IN PERSPECTIVE

HENRIK IBSEN (1828–1906)

Norwegian playwright Henrik Ibsen helped establish theatrical realism through a series of controversial plays exposing social ills. Venereal disease, infidelity, failed marriages, corrupt business practices, which were the focus of Ibsen's dramas, were not thought to be appropriate subject matter for the public stage. Ibsen's use of the theatre as a site of intellectual exploration of pressing social questions was at first unwelcome.

Ghosts (1881), the first play ever to deal with congenital syphilis, uses the disease as a metaphor for the moral decay of a society bound by outmoded ideas and conventions that hide and protect immoral behavior. This indictment of middle-class hypocrisy, which was at the heart of much of Ibsen's realism, provoked public resentment as much as the disease in question, which is never actually named in the play. *Ghosts* so shocked the public that it was banned throughout Europe; it premiered in the United States by a Scandinavian company on tour in 1882.

Daring young artists and freethinkers embraced Ibsen's work. Throughout Europe, small theatres, supported by subscription audiences, provided venues for the presentation of this new style of theatrical realism and its investigation of social issues in what became known as the "Independent Theatre Movement." "Private" subscription membership allowed these theatres to skirt censorship laws that applied to public institutions. The Freie Bühne in Berlin and the Independent Theatre in London both produced *Ghosts* as their opening produc-

tions in 1889 and 1891, respectively, and the Théâtre Libre in Paris produced the play in 1890.

Ibsen's Manipulation of the "Well-Made Play" Structure

Ibsen made his stage world "realistic" by doing away with direct address to the audience and other intrusive devices and by creating fully developed characters whose actions are comprehensibly motivated by heredity, environment, and internal psychology. His gripping "realistic" illustrations of social maladies in the context of middle-class Norwegian life owe a great deal to Ibsen's artful exploitation of the "well-made-play" formula, the foundation of much of the popular theatrical fare of his time.

In *A Doll's House* (1879), Ibsen introduces the audience to the plight of Nora, a conventional bourgeois woman who discovers that the measures she took long ago to secure her husband's health could destroy her and her family. Ibsen uses the visit of Nora's old friend, Kristina Linde, as an opportunity to present *exposition* about the past. Another visitor, Mr. Krogstaad, threatens to reveal that Nora once committed the crime of forging her dead father's signature, unless she persuades her husband to give him a job. This provides the *inciting incident* as Nora works vigorously throughout the play to keep these facts from her husband, Torvald. A letter reveals the whole situation to Torvald, bringing about the play's *crisis*. Initially Torvald is furious with his wife, but

The Well-Made Play

In the nineteenth century, Frenchmen Augustin-Eugène Scribe (1791–1861) and Victorien Sardou (1831–1908) wrote for the popular Boulevard Theatre. To keep their audiences coming back, they needed a continuous supply of exciting, successful plays. They created a variation of Aristotelian structure known today as the **well-made play**, which became a formula for producing one successful script after another. This dramatic structure is in reality no more "well made" than any other, and the plays of Scribe and Sardou have not withstood the test of time. The formula they created, however, is still the basis for many popular entertainment forms. You will probably discern it behind the plots of familiar movies and television shows.

The well-made play keeps spectators on the edge of their seats by continually introducing new obstacles and complications. The opening scenes often include **foreshadowing**—hints about events to come that set the audience up. Once the stage is set, the play introduces an **inciting incident**, an event that sets the action into motion. An inciting incident is like a bomb with a lit fuse that keeps the audience watching to see if and when it will explode. The characters work vigorously to keep the real or metaphor-

when Krogstaad vows to keep the crime a secret, Torvald is appeased and forgives her.

In a *well-made-play*, Torvald's forgiveness would move the action toward *resolution*, leading to the *denouement* and a return to the status quo. In this play, however, just when the action should end, Nora undergoes a transformation. Torvald's behavior toward her has opened her eyes to the real nature of their relationship and her subordinate position in the house. She walks out on her husband, leaving her children behind as well, in an extrastructural scene that indicts society and its treatment of women. The original audience was so appalled at this ending, which violated both social custom and theatrical convention, that Ibsen was forced to write a new one for the German production. Ibsen led his audience through a familiar plot struc-

ture, but thwarted their expectations as a means of presenting his social message.

Ibsen's writings were not confined to realism. He wrote twenty-five plays spanning a stylistic scope from early verse dramas such as *Brand* (1866) and *Peer Gynt* (1867) to plays infused with symbolism such as *The Master Builder* (1892), *John Gabriel Borkman* (1896), and *When We Dead Awaken* (1899). Just as his realistic plays set a model for the form, many see his later plays as the inspiration for the rebellion against realism that occurred at the turn of the twentieth century.

This photo captures the growing tension between Torvald (Stephen Caffrey) and his wife Nora (René Augesen) as he discovers the secret she has kept from him during their long years of marriage. Henrik Ibsen's *A Doll's House* at the American Conservatory Theater, San Francisco, California. New translation by A.C.T.; dramaturgy by Paul Walsh; directed by Carey Perloff.
Courtesy of American Conservatory Theater; photo by Ken Friedman

ical explosion from taking place, driving the action forward. Just when a character believes she has prevailed, another bomb goes off, and this pattern is repeated throughout the course of the play to keep the action moving and building. A serious incident is usually placed at the end of an act so the audience is sent off at intermission impatient to find out how this last twist of fate will be resolved. In nineteenth-century melodrama, during intermission audiences anticipated the resolution of what was literally a **cliffhanger**. An act might end with someone in actual physical peril, hanging off a cliff, for instance. Today we use this term to refer to anything that keeps the audience guessing about the outcome during a break in the playing of the action. Television borrows these theatre conventions by placing cliffhangers before commercial breaks or at the end of an episode or season to entice viewers to tune in to the following installment.

The action comes to a head in a **crisis**, after which all elements must be resolved once and for all. The resolution comes in what is called the "obligatory scene." In this scene all questions are answered, all mysteries solved, and all outcomes revealed. We can recognize this type of scene in the common conclusion of many murder mysteries, when at the end all the characters gather together to hear the detective reveal who the murderer is and how the crime was committed.

Artists

IN PERSPECTIVE

BERTOLT BRECHT (1889–1956)

The life and work of German playwright, director, and theorist, Bertolt Brecht, one of the most influential dramatists of the modern era, reflect the social, economic, and political turmoil that marked the first half of the twentieth century. As a young medical student in 1916, Brecht was called up to work as an orderly in a military hospital and saw up close the brutal effects of World War I. His early poems reflect his horror at what he had witnessed, and antiwar plays such as *Mother Courage and Her Children* (1939) are among his greatest works. Brecht's experiences during two world wars undercut any romantic view of militarism, and many of his plays depict the dehumanizing effect of military conflict.

The Russian Revolution of 1917 and its reverberations in a Germany in economic turmoil led Brecht to Marxism. He joined the Independent Social Democratic Party in 1919. Moving to Berlin, Brecht was fortunate in working with director Erwin Piscator, who was developing **epic theatre**, a proletarian theatre directed toward social change through pioneering new approaches to the stage and stage technology. Brecht's work with Piscator from 1927 to 1933 was to shape his dramaturgy and his own brand of epic theatre.

Brecht viewed the world from a Marxist perspective and believed that the inequitable distribution of wealth and power under the capitalist system were the foundations of social and moral problems. He famously summed up this view with "first the grub, then the morals." In *The Threepenny Opera* (1928), Mr. Peachum, a capitalist whose successful business involves licensing and training people to be successful beggars, has a daughter who falls for Mac the Knife, a charming thief who asks the audience whether robbing a bank is really any worse than founding a bank. About to be hanged for his many crimes, Mac receives a pardon with a royal pension and title. *The Caucasian Chalk Circle* (1944–1945) depicts a parental rights dispute over a child of nobility abandoned by his mother and cared for by a kitchen maid to demonstrate by analogy that land should belong to those who work it and make it fruitful, and not just to those who claim hereditary ownership.

The rise of Nazism forced Brecht to flee Germany in 1933; he traveled to Vienna, Switzerland, and France, settling for a time in Denmark, and eventually ended up in California in 1940. Plays such as *Fear and Misery of the Third Reich* (1935–1938), a series of scenes showing the struggles and brutality of life under the Third Reich, and *The Resistable Rise of Arturo Ui* (1941), which uses a Chicago gangster as a stand-in for Hitler and traces his rise to power, provide critical insight into the workings of the Nazi regime.

In exile, Brecht continued his theatre work. His most successful work in the United States was *The Life of Galileo*, performed in Hollywood and New York in 1947 and starring Charles Laughton (see photo on page 384). The play depicts Galileo as a pragmatic compromiser willing to acquiesce to the Catholic Church on scientific matters in order to continue his own pleasurable pursuit of science. Like many German ex-patriots at the time, Brecht became involved with the Hollywood movie scene and worked on Hollywood scripts to make ends meet.

Brecht was called before the Committee on Un-American Activities in Washington in 1947, where he denied having ever espoused communist ideas. Within days of his appearance, Brecht returned to Europe. With his usual pragmatic caution, Brecht had bought his ticket back to Germany before leaving for Washington.

Brecht returned to a Berlin now cut in two, where he was courted by the Communists who offered him a large, fully supported theatre, the Berliner Ensemble. Like the characters in his plays, he made a decision based on rational reflection and necessity, rather than ideology. He chose East Berlin only after being assured that he might travel freely back to West Berlin and after having left his

---

The well-made play became a formula for an endless stream of popular and entertaining plays during the nineteenth century and after. In the hands of Henrik Ibsen, it became more than a contrivance but a form capable of addressing the most pressing social issues of the era.

Episodic Structure

A play with an episodic structure is characterized by an early point of attack in the story and a proliferation of characters and events. The events are not necessarily related through cause and effect, and the dramatic action builds through cumulative tension.

copyrights with a West Berlin publisher to guarantee his financial future. At the Berliner Ensemble, Brecht was finally able to write and direct his plays with financial support. The company's European tours in the 1950s popularized Brecht's plays and his staging techniques throughout Europe.

Episodic Structure in Brecht's Epic Theatre

Brecht used episodic structure for political ends. Believing that the theatre should be used to expose social and economic problems, he rejected climactic structure and the close emotional involvement with the characters it elicited from the audience. Episodic structure, on the other hand, with its constant shifting of time, place, and characters, keeps the audience at an emotional distance from the action so spectators can rationally determine the social conditions that caused the characters' problems and contemplate social change.

Brecht believed that Aristotelian theatre showed characters whose actions are determined by who they are, unlike his epic theatre, in which actions are determined by social and economic circumstances. A person who is rich and powerful will act to safeguard his position, adopting ideas sympathetic to his own con-

cerns, whereas a person who is poor will likewise work for his own advantage. Each may be driven to despicable acts in the name of self-interest, a fact often displayed in Brecht's plays. Brecht points out that in the Aristotelian theatre, people are presented as fundamentally "unalterable," while in the epic theatre, they are capable of change once their social and economic conditions are altered.

The Good Person of Szechuan (1938–1940) describes the plight of the kind young woman Shen Te scraping by in hard times. She is so exploited by scoundrels who take advantage of her good nature that she must transform herself into the evil man Shui Ta to survive. The mask she dons to transform into her fictitious uncle is a theatrical device that both distances the audience and provides a metaphor for the social masks we are obliged to wear to get by. As Shui Ta, she ruthlessly abuses others as they had abused her, demonstrating that behavior is determined by economic need as well as the impossibility of virtue in an unjust world. The play's episodic structure allows us to see the many situations that lead to Shen Te's plight and the way all the characters change according to the situation. Even the gods who come seeking a good soul change their standards for "good" once they have been exposed to the vicissitudes of mortal life. Unlike the *deus ex machina* of the Greeks, these gods abandon Shen Te and the rest of the world at the end of the play and leave us to find our own solution to social ills.

Forced to play the role of her own tyrannical uncle Shui Ta, Shen Te reclaims her tobacco shop from parasites. Note the use of masks by all the actors to create a distance between the actor and the character and the character and the audience. Bertolt Brecht's *The Good Person of Szechuan*, The Berliner Ensemble, Germany.
Courtesy of Stiftung Archiv der Akademie Der Kuenste

Episodic structure is less restricted than a climactic structure and tends to include a longer time frame and multiple locations. An episodic play may also follow many different stories at once. When there is one main plot and another subsidiary plot, the less central action is called the **subplot**. **Parallel plots**, in which the action of the main plot is echoed in a secondary action, often drive home the central meaning through common subjects and themes that comment on the central action.

Dramatists of the Elizabethan era (1558–1603) were influenced by the English medieval tradition in which plays could jump from Jerusalem to Europe, from biblical times to the present, from scene to scene. Shakespeare almost always used an episodic structure; his plays take place across a wide range of locations, moving from palaces, to battlefields, to private chambers, or even from one country or city to another over extended periods of time. The large number of characters, some of whom may appear only once or twice, give an opportunity to present various angles on the events of the play and show the ramifications of actions from different perspectives. *Hamlet* portrays the contrasting behavior of three sons, Hamlet, Laertes, and Fortinbras, each avenging his father's death, enabling one to comment on the other. In Shakespeare's *A Midsummer Night's Dream*, three groups of characters from different worlds—fairies, court nobles, and laborers—follow interweaving plots that provide different perspectives on the vagaries of love. Shakespeare can tell each story with a different sensibility, giving depth and texture to the dramatic action.

Much as Ibsen played with the conventions of climactic structure for his own social goals, the German director and playwright Bertolt Brecht (1898–1956) used episodic structure for political ends, providing a model for politically committed playwrights around the world to use to engage their audiences. Many contemporary dramatists continue to call on episodic structure and the conventions of Brecht's epic theatre to portray their concerns.

Tony Kushner's *Angels in America* is a recent example. It uses episodic structure to present the landscape of American political conservatism as a backdrop for individual struggles and the AIDS epidemic. It links the consequences of public actions to private lives. The play's portrait of the moral crisis in America is personified by the character of Roy Cohn, who made his reputation in the 1950s as Senator Joseph McCarthy's chief aide, hounding supposed communists out of hiding while he himself was hiding his homosexuality. Cohn died of AIDS in 1986, never revealing his secret and remaining faithful to the tenets of the conservative right that would have reviled him. The play creates several parallel plots, each of which reinforces the central ideas. We encounter the staunch Mormons Joe and Harper Pitt, who struggle with the demons of homosexuality and mental illness; we meet a gay couple, Louis and Prior, dealing with the scourge of AIDS; and we watch an unrepentant Roy Cohn in denial as he confronts illness and the ghosts of his past. The play presents their interactions with real and fantasized people in their lives in interweaving plots that frame a portrait of America at the millennium painted by a gay artist. The epic structure allows the play to move from location to loca-

Photo 3.3
The physical action and costuming of this production of *A Midsummer Night's Dream* capture the comic confusions that occur among four young lovers who venture out of their familiar world into a wood where a spell makes them fall in love with the wrong partners. Adapted and directed by Joe Calarco; set by Michael Fagin; costumes by Helen Huang. The Shakespeare Theatre, Washington.
© *Carol Rosegg*

tion, from fantasy to reality, and from character to character to present a sweeping panoramic vision of national hypocrisy in historical context.

Circular Structure

Both episodic and climactic structures move forward to a conclusion. Some plays, however, seem to end where they began. Plays with this structure reflect the ideas of French writer-philosopher Albert Camus (1913–1960), who used the myth of Sisyphus as a metaphor for our existence. Sisyphus was condemned by the gods to endlessly roll a heavy boulder up a hill only for it to roll back to the bottom each time for him to restart the tedious journey up. For Camus, all human activity was like Sisyphus' burden—the exertion of all our energy toward the ultimate accomplishment of nothing. In our delusion that we are actually getting somewhere, when in fact our lives are filled with meaningless routines and daily activities that count for naught, Camus saw the absurdity of existence. This dark view of life captured the loss of a rational framework for understanding human existence that resulted from the events of World War II. Circular structure is an expression of the futility and meaninglessness of human efforts.

One of the best examples of a play with a circular plot is *The Bald Soprano* (1950), subtitled "an anti-play" by Romanian-born Eugène Ionesco (1909–1994). The play presents characters engaged

Photo 3.4
This powerful visual image from Tony Kushner's *Angels in America* captures the sprawling scope of this drama as it paints a panorama of American politics and religion and the intimate effects of the collision of these historical forces on individuals' lives. The production was directed by George C. Wolfe; scenic design by Robin Wagner; costume design by Toni-Leslie James; lighting design by Jules Fisher; sound design by Scott Lehrer; hair design by Jeffrey Frank. Walter Kerr Theatre, New York.
© Joan Marcus

in empty conversation and the seemingly meaningless activities and routines of daily life. The play begins with Mr. and Mrs. Smith, an English couple, sitting in their comfortable middle-class home after supper. Mr. Smith is smoking his "English pipe" and reading an "English newspaper" while Mrs. Smith, darning some "English socks," recounts a series of inane details relating to the evening meal (see Photo 3.5). The scenes do not move in any kind of logical progression, and the play culminates in an explosive exchange of nonsensical and familiar phrases among the four main characters, suggesting that language and the ability to communicate have broken down. At the end of the play the opening lines are repeated, only now the Smiths' friends, Mr. and Mrs. Martin, have taken the couple's place, implying that the characters, their words, and their lives are interchangeable, and the whole series of events just witnessed could proceed again, and is proceeding again and again everywhere.

In Samuel Beckett's (1906–1989) *Waiting for Godot* (1953), we watch two tramps, Vladimir and Estragon, spend their time along a deserted road waiting for Godot, who never comes. Throughout the play, the characters engage in repeated rituals and games to pass the day. The ending of the first act and the last are identical:

> **Vladimir:** Well? Shall we go?
> **Estragon:** Let's go.
> *They do not move.*[1]

---

1. Samuel Beckett, *Waiting for Godot* (New York: Grove Press, 1954), 61.

Photo 3.5
Mrs. Smith (Jan Maxwell) re-
cites a string of banalities to
her husband, who ignores her
behind his newspaper. The repetition of the flower pattern on
the walls, carpets, and furnishings captures the way this play
transforms the ordinary into
the absurd in the Atlantic Theatre Company's New York production of Eugène Ionesco's
The Bald Soprano, a new
translation by Tina Howe
directed by Carl Forsman.
Sets by Loy Arcenas; lighting
by Josh Bradford; costumes
by Theresa Squire; sound
by Obediah Eaves.
© Carol Rosegg

Beckett varies the content of the two acts and adds details that give the false hope that Godot may come, aiding the characters' self-deception. The circular structure and the immobility of the characters underscore the anguish of living in a senseless world without the possibility of self-fulfillment.

Serial Structure

When a play is composed of a series of scenes that don't follow a continuous story or even include the same characters, it possesses a **serial structure**. Each scene may be an independent vignette that could, under other circumstances, stand on its own. The scenes in such plays are often thematically related and give a varied perspective on a sub-ject through the juxtaposition of characters and events, rather than through the pro-gression of a single story. In some plays, scenes may be unrelated like a series of skits in a variety show.

Serial structure has been a format for popular entertainments in many times and places. American vaudeville used a serial format presenting jugglers, singers, dancers, magicians, and actors one after another on the same bill. In the late twentieth century, many postmodern playwrights wrote texts that incorporate the variety show sensibility and yet provide the experience of a single play. We will look at performances that incor-porate this structure in Chapter 6.

Feminist playwright Megan Terry created a serial structure for her feminist plays through the improvisation device of transformations. In *Calm Down Mother* (1965), each scene ends in a physical position for the actors that can be transformed into an en-tirely different context for new characters in the next story. Actors create instantaneous character switches through physical and vocal technique in order to tell the next tale. Each sketch focuses on some aspect of female identity and explores the various women's roles proscribed by our society. Written in a time of social upheaval and change for women, the use of serial structure through transformation actually serves as a metaphor for the thematic material in the play.

The use of a serial format for a single play has become more common, which may be attributed to postmodernism's acceptance of *pastiche*, a mixture of styles and forms

Photo 3.6
Mama (Vicklyn Reynolds) and her daughter Medea (Danitra Vance) in "The Last Mama-on-the-Couch Play" in George C. Wolfe's *The Colored Museum* directed by L. Kenneth Richardson at the Joseph Papp Public Theater.
© 1992 Martha Swope

generally executed in a playful manner that comments ironically on the forms themselves. An excellent example of a play that uses a serial structure as a way of providing a postmodern perspective is George C. Wolfe's (b. 1955) *The Colored Museum* (1986). The eleven scenes, sometimes comic, sometimes serious, and unrelated to any single story, explore issues of identity and the struggle of African Americans to define themselves as individuals. Each scene explores a different cultural myth using a completely different set of characters and a new situation. "Symbiosis" shows a middle-aged black businessman struggling with his younger self over the objects of black power, such as an Afro comb and *dashiki*, that he accumulated in his youth. The older self wants to assimilate into the mainstream middle class, while the younger self still tries to express a revolutionary image of black power. In "The Hairpiece," a woman's two wigs—one an Afro and the other with straightened hair—argue over which one of them she should wear to break up with her boyfriend. The Afro wig claims the advantage of projecting "attitude" and accuses the other of being a "Barbie doll dipped in chocolate," while the straight-haired wig denounces the Afro's black authenticity by revealing that she was made in Taiwan. The woman herself, torn between the two images she desires, is bald. In "The Last Mama-on-the-Couch Play," characters drawn from various Black theatre forms—from Lorraine Hansberry's realism to Ntozake Shange's choreopoems—share the stage. The Mama in this scene satirizes a popular character type. She is so much a cliché of Black middle class aspiration that she literally blends into the setting around her. With its serial structure and pastiche of different dramatic styles, *The Colored Museum* offers a variety of perspectives on how to express racial identity in a world saturated with received cultural definitions.

Structural Variation: Playing with Time

For thematic purposes, playwrights may play with notions of time, breaking with the idea of moving in normal chronological order through a story line. Several American classics use flashbacks to transport us back and forth through time, creating a variation on traditional structure. In Tennessee Williams's (1911–1983) *The Glass Menagerie* (1945), Tom, who is both the narrator and a character in the play, tells us he is going to

IN PERSPECTIVE

SAMUEL BECKETT (1906–1989)

When Samuel Beckett's *Waiting for Godot* premiered in Paris in January of 1953, audiences were confronted with a play that defied the theatrical conventions of the time. Instead of developing to a climax and *denouement*, the plot seemed to go in circles, with act two repeating the events of act one with only slight differences. Instead of psychological characters, the two tramps in this play have no pasts, nor is the audience told how they came to their present circumstances. The tramps speak in succinct, almost mundane sentences, and the only long speech in the play, delivered by Lucky, is a collection of nonsensical phrases. The stagnant action of two tramps, on a near barren stretch of road, passing time as they wait for an elusive character named Godot, who never arrives, unsettled its audience to such a degree that one critic stormed out proclaiming, "I will not wait for Godot!" Since this first disturbing encounter with Beckett's unique dramaturgy, scholars and audiences have come to understand Beckett's work, recognizing him as one of the foremost dramatists of the twentieth century.

Beckett's work has often been characterized by its minimalism—the reduction of theatrical elements to their barest essentials. Language, character, and action are distilled, but each phrase and movement is carefully chosen and weighty with implications. Beckett was deeply critical of directors' attempts to add to his plays through production choices not specified in the text. Beckett, who was Irish but spent most of his adult life in France, wrote most of his works in French and the constraint of writing in a foreign language forced him to be more precise. His later

works, among them *Play* (1964), *Not I* (1973), *Ohio Impromptu* (1981), and *Rockabye* (1981), so condensed dramatic elements that they led some to question whether these were plays at all and others to see Beckett as quintessentially exploiting the theatrical medium by making every gesture, utterance, and light cue expressive.

Beckett's plays search for a notion of how one constitutes an understanding of the self. Characters are often cut off from their physical beings. In *Endgame* (1957) an elderly couple live in garbage cans; only their upper bodies are exposed when they emerge from their bins. Hamm, their son, sits in a wheelchair, unable to move around the small room that encases them all without the help of his servant Clov, who can't sit down. In *Happy Days* (1958), Winnie is half buried in a mound of sand in act one and buried up to her neck in act two. As she disappears, she speaks an endless chatter about herself to her nearly mute husband, Willie. In *Not I*, the only character is just a woman's mouth speaking a long stream-of-consciousness monologue about her life. In her rambling she tells of hearing a buzzing, which she later realizes is her own voice. In the absence of physical presence, language takes on a greater role in the construction of self.

Many characters in Beckett's plays form symbiotic duos dependent on each other for the validation of their own existence. The two tramps and the master–servant duo of Lucky and Pozzo in *Waiting for Godot* are examples. Characters often require others as listeners to the stories they tell about themselves. Hamm makes Clov listen to a story he works on each day, Pozzo uses the tramps as an audience, and Winnie has Willie. Being heard helps affirm that you are there.

take us back in time, and we travel back in almost cinematic terms to an earlier period. Arthur Miller's *Death of a Salesman* (1949) constructs the character of Willy Loman through flashbacks that reveal the formative relationships and moments in his life. The technique enables us to see his past reflected in his present subjective view of reality.

David Henry Hwang's *Golden Child* (1998) is a recent intercultural memory play. By traveling back and forth through time, the characters explain the legacy of traditional Chinese culture and beliefs in the lives of present-day Chinese Americans. The doubling of actors as both modern American and traditional Chinese characters enhances the sense of cultural continuity through time despite the geographic pulling up of roots.

In British playwright Tom Stoppard's deftly plotted play *Arcadia*, the early nineteenth century and the present intersect as characters from both eras inhabit a country estate (see Photo 3.7). Two modern scholars explore competing scholarly theories of mathematics whose origins may lie in the work of the nineteenth-century ingenue. The time shifts provide comment on historical scholarship and contemporary scientific theorizing. Caryl Churchill jumps through time in *Cloud Nine*, in which act one takes place

Beckett develops this theme, and in some plays the individual becomes both speaker and listener as if we were watching the action of consciousness itself. In *Ohio Impromptu*, two identically dressed white-haired figures sit at a table, one listening to the other read from a book, helping out when the reader falters. In *Rockabye*, an old woman sits in a rocking chair listening to a voice, perhaps her own. When the voice stops, she calls for "more," prompting it to start up again.

Beckett demonstrates that the process of constructing a sense of the self through speaking and storytelling is inherently unreliable because both language and memory are flawed visions of reality. In *Krapp's Last Tape* (1958), a sixty-nine-year-old man has celebrated each birthday making and listening to tapes that document his life. A decrepit Krapp replays the tape he made of himself when he was thirty-nine and in his prime. The striking dissonance between

the man on the tape and his present condition records an ever-changing self and makes us question the construction of our identity through memory, while confirming the elusiveness of happiness.

The dwindling down of self and diminished consciousness as a movement toward death is felt in *Play*, where three heads emerge from urns, as if from the grave, and speak one by one when illuminated by an interrogating spotlight. Each tells his or her version of a love triangle involving all three. The whole play is repeated again, only with the light slightly dimmer. For Beckett, life is a kind of dying, a set of repetitions and dimmings, a winding down of memory, language, and consciousness, even as characters use these means to affirm that they are alive.

The barren landscape and withered tree, emblematic of this Beckett play, put the characters in an unspecific location that mirrors their lack of certainty about their pasts, presents, and futures. The rope that Pozzo holds around Lucky's neck is an expression of the interdependence of these characters, who rely on each other's presence to make sense of their own existence. Samuel Beckett's *Waiting for Godot* at the Piccadilly Theatre, London.
© *Robbie Jack/CORBIS*

in 1880 in British colonial Africa, and act two takes place one hundred years later in London. For the characters, however, only twenty-five years have elapsed. By transplanting Victorian characters into the present, Churchill compresses history to comment on the status of women and sexual relationships in the present.

Playing with time, playwrights can even present events in the opposite order of how they would occur in life, starting with the end and moving back in time toward the beginning. As we move backward through events, we discover the origin of situations we've already seen and the motivations for actions already revealed. English playwright Harold Pinter made use of regressive storytelling in his 1978 play *Betrayal* about a love triangle in which Emma has a seven-year affair with her husband Robert's best friend, Jerry. The play begins two years after the liaison has ended and moves back in time to the lovers' breakup, and then further back to the moment the relationship began. The play also explores the relationship between the lover and the husband, who unbeknownst to his wife and friend has been aware of the deception. The characters are attempting to reconstruct how they arrived at the present as the audience tries to construct the story. The regres-

Photo 3.7
Characters living two hundred years apart occupy the same house in a play that delves into chaos theory. Here a character from the present is oblivious to one from the past as she reaches for her computer mouse. Tom Stoppard's *Arcadia,* directed by Trevor Nunn, presented at the Vivian Beaumont Theatre, New York, by arrangement with the Royal National Theatre.
© Joan Marcus

sive structure presents the architecture of betrayal, allowing seemingly insignificant gestures and dialogue to convey their true import because the audience has already witnessed the hidden truths.

Dramatic Characters

Every play expresses its ideas through the actions and words of characters, so it is impossible to completely separate plot from language and character. Meaning in the theatre comes not just from what happens—*story,* or *how* it happens (*plot*), but from *who* makes it happen and to *whom* (*character*). This is the human element that gives the play significance and emotional interest.

Some have argued that characters drive the dramatic action and are the most important element in a play. Others believe that plot is the most significant because it sets up the situation out of which the characters will emerge. This is a bit like the heredity or environment argument in human nature. Just as we are creatures of our genetic predisposition in interaction with the environment, dramatic characters are envisioned by their creators with predispositions, but they are also caught in the web of circumstance, and are shaped by it, and act on it. Characters create action, and action creates character. Our role as audience or reader is to interpret these actions, to give them significance.

You already know how to analyze dramatic characters. You do this all the time when you try to figure people out. *You listen to what they say*, and you ask yourself *what they really mean.* Are they honest, or do they have a hidden agenda? *You observe what they do.* You sense when words and actions don't quite align. *You listen to what others say about them* and make judgments on the value of what is said. *You observe their interactions with others, and watch what others do because of them.* In everyday life, you do much of this unconsciously, so you think you have an intuition about a person. In the theatre, we tend to be more conscious of our observations and conclusions, but the process of analysis is the same.

Playwrights strive to create characters who are compelling and magnetic, who stimulate our interest, provoke our compassion, and sometimes rile our rage and frustration.

With the exception of recent experimental plays, it is almost impossible to think of a truly great play that does not have a memorable character. The character who leaves us passive and unmoved lacks the theatricality to generate dramatic action and provide a presence that fills the stage to claim a hold on our psyches. We may forget the exact order of events in *Hamlet*, or *Tartuffe*, or *A Doll's House*, or *A Streetcar Named Desire*, but we remember Hamlet, Tartuffe, Nora, Blanche, and Stanley in all their pulsating humanity.

Why are these characters so indelibly imprinted on our memory? What makes their brief two-hour lives of interest to us? All characters are presented at moments of difficulty, often at times of great crisis, always confronting obstacles to their desires. This is as true of comedy as it is of serious drama. Ordinary people caught in extraordinary circumstances can rise to the occasion and become extraordinary characters. Life shows us what heights individuals can climb to in times of crisis that test their true mettle, and the essential energy of the theatre lies in capturing these moments of intense struggle against circumstance. It is a universal struggle with which we can all find common cause as we grapple with the difficulties of our own lives. For this reason, we call the lead role the **protagonist** from the Greek word *agonistes*, which means both "actor" and "combatant." Sometimes, another character directly thwarts the desires of the protagonist, we call this role the **antagonist**. Whether the obstacle is internal or circumstantial, or another character, in essence, we start relating to characters by identifying with their struggle. To some extent, then, every drama is a kind of combat, and it draws us the way we would stop to watch a fight on the street or go to an athletic contest. In the magnetism of battle there are winners and losers, and the fight defines character, just as it helps us define ourselves.

Think about yourself. What do you really want in life? To what extremes would you go to attain your goals? The answers to these questions tell us about the values, drives, and temperament that define our character. As readers and audience members, we follow the path of a character's desire to fulfillment or defeat. For this reason, when actors analyze a role, they often start by trying to define the central desire that drives the character and the action throughout the play.

Character and Culture

Every era and culture develops its own view of the human psyche and how we understand people and their motivations. This in turn shapes how dramatists envision characters for the stage. Ancient Greece saw human action in a struggle with the gods. The medieval period viewed life on earth as insignificant in relation to eternal life. Under the influence of Freud, human behavior was viewed as the result of the dark inner forces of repressed desire. Marxist theory sees our actions as the result of economic circumstance. Playwrights of every era reflect the way human action is valued by their culture. It follows that characters are drawn differently in different periods, and that not all characters are equally compelling to us today.

Playwrights must also bring different approaches to character that fit the style and genre in which they are writing. Consider the way painters of different periods have created portraits that reflect the values and styles of their times. Leonardo in the Renaissance and Picasso in the twentieth century present the human face in very different ways, yet each tell us something important about the character's humanity. Just as the visual artist brings these different approaches to character portraits, so does the playwright.

Archetypal Characters

Archetypal characters embody the essence of particular human traits that enable them to speak across cultures and centuries. They are extraordinary people placed in extraordinary conditions, and their actions loom larger than their circumstances. They help to shape the way we think about the world and ourselves. Because of the extreme circumstances presented in most Greek tragedies, they are filled with such characters. Oedipus is the archetype of the man blind to his own flaws who sees within only when he is blind. Medea is the archetype of the wronged woman who seeks revenge at all costs. Modern plays can also present archetypes who have a peculiar hold on our imaginations and whose names stand in for all of us in similar straits. Willy Loman in *Death of a Salesman* became the archetype for the little man with big dreams, delusions, and nothing to show for himself. These types of characters embody the quintessence of particular virtues, vices, and emotions and seem to transcend the specific context of their stories to represent what we can all become and fear. Archetypal characters should not be confused with the allegorical characters found in late medieval drama who embody clear-cut virtues and vices, often with names such as Good Deeds, Beauty, Death, and Mischief, but who do not have the psychological complexity to haunt us.

Psychological Characters

Some playwrights paint portraits so rich in detail and interest that we feel it is possible to understand their characters in depth, to comprehend their motivations and desires, even to fabricate a life for them that preexists their appearance in the play. When characters appear in such complexity, we call them **psychological characters**.

Psychology as a modern science dates only from the 1870s. Before that time, metaphysical or physiological explanations were given for human behavior. Characters written with motivational complexity became common during the twentieth century under the influence of Freudian thought, but in fact, complex characters have been with us for a long time. In his book, *Hamlet and Oedipus* (1949), the Freudian analyst Ernest Jones placed the imaginary character Hamlet on the psychoanalyst's couch to plumb the depths of his psyche. The very idea that an imaginary character could be placed in psychoanalysis to uncover hidden motivations for behavior in the drama presupposes the complexity of the portrait drawn by Shakespeare. This is an example of psychological character predating the notion of psychology, and it also explains our continuing fascination with Hamlet.

Many realistic American plays reflect the deep interest in Freud and psychoanalysis in the United States and present portraits of psychological characters. Eugene O'Neill

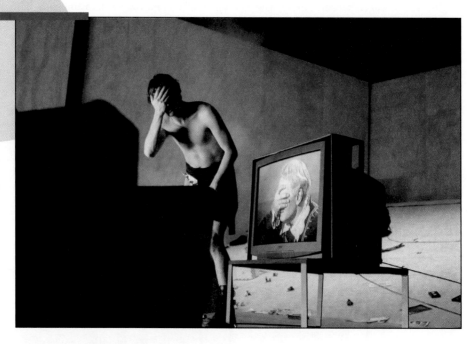

Photo 3.8
In this production of *Hamlet,* the self-dramatizing nature of the character is evident as he watches Laurence Olivier perform his Freudian interpretation of the role on a television screen. Directed by Nicolas Stemann at the Schauspiel Theatre, Hanover, Germany.
© *Thomas Aurin*

was the first important American playwright to directly explore Freudian theories through his characterization. Tennessee Williams and Arthur Miller gave us deep psychological portraits. Blanche DuBois, the fading Southern belle in Williams's *A Streetcar Named Desire* is such a character. Watching her putting on superior airs, cavorting in fancy clothes, and fantasizing about millionaire lovers, we imagine her childhood, and even see that child hiding in her present persona. We begin to get a picture of her life in her former estate, Belle Reve; the behavior in which she engaged; and the depths to which she sank before losing everything and turning up in the play. We feel this character had a past worthy of psychoanalysis, and that to know about it would help us understand her needs and actions as they unfold before us. Miller's use of flashbacks in *Death of a Salesman* to construct the psychological past of Willy gives us the impression of a life lived fully, and we can flesh out relationships between Willy and his brother Ben, his sons growing up, and his wife Linda. We see the false values he passed on to his sons, his lost opportunities, and the lies he tells himself and others. Again, these characters seem able to take on an imaginary life beyond the play itself.

Stock Characters

In many ways, **stock characters** are the opposite of psychological characters. They are representative of a type and are defined by externals—class, occupation, marital status—rather than by their individual characteristics. In Roman comedy, slaves and wily servants, miserly merchants, shrewish wives, braggart soldiers, and innocent lovers were recycled into various comedies. They differed little from play to play and were delineated by their function within the plot more than by anything particular to the individual roles. The villains, damsels in distress, and heroes of melodrama worked in much the same way. Imagine a mask that defines character from the outside. Now imagine an actor wearing this mask moving from play to play to fulfill a designated role whose function is to advance the plot, and you have a sense of the stock character. In fact, stock characters were referred to as "masks."

Today, we most often see this kind of character in television sitcoms that return week after week with the same characters playing their predetermined roles within new stories. Think of the manipulative mother-in-law and her curmudgeon husband in *Everybody Loves Raymond*. These kinds of characters are the soul of accessible popular entertainment and were most often found in the theatrical forms that entertained mass audiences before electronic media. They are immediately accessible and comprehensible, and because their outcome is assured, they provide affirmation for the general public. From Roman times through the nineteenth century, acting companies were organized around an assortment of stock characters who could carry every play. Actors played one "type" of character for their entire mature careers.

Characters with a Dominant Trait

From ancient times, the human body was thought to be composed of four kinds of fluids—blood, phlegm, yellow bile, and black bile—humors that regulated body function and emotional life. An imbalance in one of these fluids could cause extreme physical and mental disorder. Out of this view of biology came the idea of an obsessed personality with a dominant trait. Shakespeare's contemporary, Ben Jonson, created many characters based on the concept of humors during the Elizabethan period, even giving the title *Every Man in His Humour* (1598) to one play in which he exposes the follies of his fellow Londoners. The idea of humors was also reflected in the late-seventeenth-century Restoration era's use of character names indicating particular personality types. The plays of Etherege, Congreve, and Wycherley treat us to Sir Fopling Flutter, Mrs Loveit, Fainall, Petulant, and Old Lady Squeamish, names that indicate a dominant trait of their personalities. In the hands of the French comic genius Molière (1622–1673), this

Challenges and Choices

What should a playwright consider when creating characters outside his or her own culture? Can that character ever be "authentic"? Does art require authenticity?

obsessed personality took on psychological depth. In *The Misanthrope* (1666), originally subtitled *The Black-Biled Lover*, we see Alceste, a character so obsessed with unmasking the truth at all costs that he hurts those he loves, drives away friends, and destroys his own hopes for happiness. Alceste, despite his extreme behavior, is not a two-dimensional cartoon, but a complex human being unable to cope with the dominant traits of his personality, and driven to self-destruction.

Depersonalized Characters

In many modern plays, we encounter characters who speak to us through our empathy with their current conditions of existence. These characters may be searching for meaning, purpose, or relationships in an inhospitable world. They fill their lives with games and rituals that substitute for the deeper connections they seek. Although they appear without a psychological past, they are not stock characters. They possess individuality without complexity. They are creatures of their current circumstances, and their hold on their identities feels tenuous at best. We associate most of these characters with the modernism and postmodernism of the twentieth century, although precursors of this kind of persona appear in earlier periods. They represent the individual caught in an increasingly impersonal and dehumanizing world, isolated, lonely, and alienated from the community.

As the twentieth century unfolded and the horrors of two world wars forced playwrights to question the very possibility of finding meaning and purpose, characters were caught in futile quests for these goals. Characters in the plays of Beckett and Ionesco struggle to find significance and relationships. In *Endgame, Waiting for Godot*, and other Beckett plays, the characters find themselves in a mutual dependency that substitutes for a deeper relationship. Although we learn nothing of their lives before this moment, we are engaged by their struggle to fill their existence. The generic married couples in Ionesco's *The Bald Soprano* can only define their relationship from the coincidence of living in the same apartment and sharing what they think is the same child. However compelling their quest and their present moment, we sense that depersonalized characters are replaceable with the next set of characters who happen along a lonely road, or into a living room. Their relationships are of convenience and circumstance, and they remain essentially unknown to each other and themselves. In the later works of these two writers, characters dematerialize, losing their bodies or their voices, and their fragile identities. Although these characters are not fully realized psychological beings, we identify with their struggle and their isolation.

Most American playwrights of the post–World War II period continued to create psychological characters in search of personal fulfillment, whereas most European writers painted a bleaker, more pessimistic view of the world through their depersonalized characters. Perhaps the devastation of war and mass annihilation on their home soil pushed European writers to question the value of an individual life.

Deconstructed Characters

During the later twentieth century, playwrights sought ways to reveal that all character is a performance of socially proscribed roles, and that identity is often a creation of those in control of the social order. In *Cloud Nine* (1979), Caryl Churchill exposes how prevailing notions of class, sexuality, and politics determine character. The obedient wife who does all to please her husband is played by a man, demonstrating that such a character is a construction of the male ego; the daughter who has no identity until it is conferred on her by a man is played by a dummy; the gay son is played by a woman; and the black servant, who does everything to please his master, is played by a white man, reflecting the servant's self-loathing and the desire to be white. In *True West* (1980), Sam Shepard (b. 1943) explores the American myth that you can be anyone through self-invention by having the two brothers who are the central characters in the play trade identities. In the 2000 New York revival, actors Philip Seymour Hoffman and John C. Reilly traded roles each night, underscoring the flexibility of identity. In David Henry Hwang's *M Butterfly*, we saw how a French diplomat can misperceive identity because of the projection of racial stereotypes of a feminized Asian character. In *Day of Absence*, playwright Douglas Turner Ward (b. 1930) reverses the historic stereotypes of white minstrelsy in which blacks were played by whites in blackface. In his play, black actors play whites in white-face, and white identity is constructed from the African-American point of view, reversing and revealing the roles created by the white power structure in American society.

Under the influence of psychology, we have come to think of character as something formed from within, so at first encounter these deconstructed characters are hard to understand and interpret. As the Freudian view of human behavior and identity is losing favor, deconstructed characters offer another concept of how we form ideas of self. They demonstrate how much of our identity is a result of our external situation and social role. Character is shown as a projection of the way others perceive us.

Dramatic Language

The playwright's basic tool of expression is language, but the language of the theatre cannot be judged for literary values alone. Most writers write for readers, but playwrights write for actors, so language in the theatre must be actable and speakable and inspire physical expression so it can be used by actors to create a vibrant stage character. No matter how beautiful the writing, if the language of a play is not a good vehicle for acting, it fails as dramatic language. This does not mean that dialogue must be written exactly the way we speak in everyday life. Everyday speech would seem uninteresting in the theatre. Language on the stage by its very nature is heightened, intensified, and stylized.

The primary form of language in the theatre is dialogue. Unlike novels, in which long descriptive passages can be used to convey information and explain events, emotion, and setting, the playwright must find a way to reveal all the necessary exposition and story through what the characters say in the present. Magnificent language can fail as theatre if it does not possess the basic requirements of the spoken word on stage. Theatrical language must advance the plot; express character; provoke or embody action; compress emotion; and set the mood, style, and tone.

Advancing the Plot

On the simplest level, dramatic language must help to tell the story and advance the dramatic action. Each line a character utters should give the audience information and move the plot forward. The opening lines of Aeschylus' *Agamemnon*, one of the earliest extant plays, begins:

> Oh you Gods! How I long for an end to all this strain,
>
> For a year now, spending my nights crouched like a dog
>
> On watch on the roof of the House of Atreus.

Look how much information Aeschylus gives us in three short lines. We know who the character is, his situation, and his state of mind. The speech is addressed to the gods as a plea, making it active and theatrical instead of a passive description.

Sometimes language can help tell the story by establishing location and character through dialect and usage as in this passage from Hwang's *Golden Child*:

> **Ahn:** Remember? When you are little boy? You lie on my stomach, and I tell you story of our family. My father, Tieng-Bin, he make this family chosen by God. My father work in Philippine, make money. But like all oversea Chinese, he leave behind most important part of life—his three wife, his children—(Ahn begins to speak in the voice of a ten-year-old girl)—all your future, Papa, you left behind in China.[2]

In this passage, Hwang establishes two locations, the United States and China, and the passage of time by changing the voice in which the character speaks, transforming an eighty-five-year-old woman into a ten-year-old girl.

Dialogue must be shaped rhythmically to build intensifying action or set up a climactic moment, or a comedic punchline. Language patterns can alter in rhythm and intensity at heightened moments in the plot, indicating a change in a character's emotional state.

Expressing Character

Every character possesses a singular voice—a way of using language to express thoughts and emotions. This voice has a rhythm, vocabulary, inflection, dialect, and grammatical structure that reflect education, class, values, personality, age, and emotional outlook.

Note the revelation of character and basic attitude toward life expressed in this short piece of dialogue from Oscar Wilde's *The Importance of Being Ernest*. Note the upperclass speech and smugness of the character present in the lines.

> **Gwendolen:** Do you allude to me, Miss Cardew, as an entanglement? You are presumptuous. On an occasion of this kind it becomes more than a moral duty to speak one's mind. It becomes a pleasure.[3]

The playwright's first burden is to capture these idiosyncratic patterns of speech that define the character. Actors can use these language patterns as clues for how to portray a role.

Language must chart the character's inner emotional journey through the play as well as the character's physical journey through the plot. It is therefore a bridge between a character's inner and outer worlds. In realistic plays, language is always linked to a character's psychological intent. Sometimes it must reveal what a character is thinking and feeling so the audience can make sense of the character's actions. When characters are withholding information, language must be used to disguise intent. The language of the stage can be read on two levels: what is actually said and what is actually meant. We call this level of internal meaning the **subtext**—literally, what lies under the text. Good playwrights craft dialogue capable of meaning on both planes. It is the job of the actor to reveal what the words mean to the character, and the job of the playwright to craft dialogue that can play on two levels. Playwrights must therefore capture not only how characters say what they feel, but also how they use language to hide what they feel.

---

2. Henry David Hwang, *Golden Child.* Used with permission of author in *Understanding Plays,* Allyn and Bacon, 680.

3. Oscar Wilde, *The Importance of Being Ernest,* in *The Genius of the Later English Theater,* ed. Sylvan Barnet, Morton Berman, and William Burfo (New York: Mentor Books, 1962), 289.

Provoking and Embodying Action

Because the theatre is a place of action, implicit in dialogue is the need to act—to give physical expression to the spoken word. For this reason, plays are rarely written in the past tense. Theatrical language is about what is happening now, not what has already occurred. Good playwrights tend to see the play unfolding in their mind's eye, and write dialogue that will support and trigger gesture and strong physical action. When the language leaves actors stationary and immobile with no available choice of action, we say that the text is static and difficult to play.

Feel the call to action in these lines from Paula Vogel's *How I Learned to Drive*, when Li'l Bit discovers her uncle wants to take sexually provocative photographs:

> **Li'l Bit:** I'm never doing anything like that! You'd show other people these—other men—these—what I'm doing.—Why would you do that?! Any boy around here could just pick up, just go to the Stop & Go and buy—why would you ever want to—to share—[4]

It is impossible for an actor to read these lines as the character without feeling a need to express these thoughts physically. Try to read these lines aloud in total stillness.

Compressing Emotion

Because on stage a lifetime of meaning is compressed into a two- to three-hour event, the language of theatre is heightened and emotionally charged. Conversations that might take place over hours in life cover the same ground in five minutes on the stage. The playwright carefully selects words for maximum impact to enable emotions and relationships to build quickly. In this rapid exchange from Pinter's *Homecoming* (1965), the characters progress from conversation to sexually charged language in six short lines:

> **Lenny:** Just give me the glass.
> **Ruth:** No.
> **Lenny:** I'll take it then.
> **Ruth:** If you take the glass . . . I'll take you.
> **Lenny:** How about me taking the glass without you taking me?
> **Ruth:** Why don't I just take you?[5]

Setting Mood, Tone, and Style

The sound of language, its rhythm and structure, sets a mood and tone for a play. During certain eras, playwrights were, by convention, required to use particular kinds of language for certain theatrical forms, so types of language are associated with specific theatrical styles and forms. Classical tragedy was almost always written in verse, the strict metrical patterns giving dignity to the style. Verse was filled with images and metaphors that enabled the drama to play on the literal and the symbolic level. **Meter**— the patterns of stressed and unstressed syllables—could subtly draw attention to sig-

---

4. *The Mammary Plays* by Paula Vogel. Copyright © 1998 by Paula Vogel. Published by Theatre Communications Group. Used by permission of Theatre Communications Group.

5. Harold Pinter, *Homecoming* (New York: Grove Press, 1966), 34.

Photo 3.9
The disparate images brought
together in this staging reflect
the fragmented postmodern
style of Müller's text. Heiner
Müller's *Hamletmachine*,
Berlin, 1990.
© *Sibylle Bergemann*

nificant meanings in the text. Note Juliet's plea for time to pass quickly as she waits for news of her love Romeo: "Gallop a pace, you fiery footed steeds." If you say this line out loud, you will feel the rhythm of galloping horses and the urgency of her desire. Devices such as **onomatopoeia** (the use of words that express the feeling of their meaning through sound), **assonance** (the repetition of vowel sounds), or **alliteration** (the repetition of consonant sounds) were used to directly provoke an emotional response in the audience through their aural sense. The line "Blow, blow, thou winter wind" from *As You Like It* combines all of these devices. Say this line and you will feel the wind in the repeated *w* sound, the sound of the howling in the repeated *o* in *blow*, and a suggestion of explosive force in the repeated *b*s. Verse was used in both comedy and tragedy to dramatic effect. Shakespeare's tragedies in blank verse perfected the use of such poetic clues to meaning. The comedies of Molière, many of which were written in rhyming verse, were constructed to get the laugh on the rhyme. Enjoy these lines from *School for Wives* as Arnolphe rails against his betrayal by a young ignorant girl he tried to keep under his control:

> Women, as all men know, are frailly wrought:
>
> They're foolish and illogical in thought,
>
> Their souls are weak, their characters are bad,
>
> There's nothing quite so silly, quite so mad,
>
> So faithless; yet despite these sorry features,
>
> What won't we do to please the wretched creatures?[6]

---

6. Jean Baptiste Poquelin de Molière, *The School for Wives and the Learned Ladies*, trans. Richard Wilbur (San Diego: Harcourt Brace Jovanovich, 1991), 71.

The Failure of Language

During the course of the twentieth century, the power of language to express truth and communicate was challenged. Freud's theories of the unconscious suggested that there were deeper meanings beyond the literal, and while some playwrights used this idea to create complex characters with hidden motives, others wondered whether we could ever truly read each other's inner thoughts through language. Dictators such as Stalin and Hitler hid their vile intentions in rhetoric, and politicians, advertising, and the media exploited language for obscured ends or reduced their messages to predetermined soundbites. In Ionesco's *The Lesson* we see language disintegrate before our eyes. Pinter wrote plays in which silences were often as important as words, and in some plays, language completely disappeared as in Beckett's *Act Without Words* and Peter Handke's *My Foot, My Tutor*. A new theatre of sounds and images has emerged in which language is used evocatively rather than literally.

Form and Innovation

Playwrights are not necessarily constrained by convention and if necessary will invent new ways to express their ideas. Modernism and postmodernism rejected literal realism and valued the search for alternative forms. Many have found new ways of working within old structures, and others have broken with linear plot, causality, and even conventional notions of story, instead creating meaning as a collage of effects rather than through literal narrative, as in works by German writer Heiner Müller (1929–1995), whose *Hamletmachine* (1978) (see Photo 3.9) became a hallmark of postmodernism. A political playwright and Marxist influenced by Brecht, Müller's life was caught in the web of historical events. His father was imprisoned by the Nazis, he was arrested by the Allies in 1945, and he lived a restricted life in East Germany until fame allowed

Challenges and Choices

If form and content follow each other, does bringing new ideas to the stage necessarily require new dramatic forms?

Photo 3.10
Whoopee Goldberg as Ma Rainey in August Wilson's *Ma Rainey's Black Bottom*, set in a recording studio in Chicago, 1927. Directed by Marion McClinton; musical director, Dwight Andrews; scenic design, David Gallo; costumes, Toni-Leslie James. Royale Theatre, New York.
© Joan Marcus

Texts IN PERSPECTIVE

SUZAN-LORI PARKS

Suzan-Lori Parks (b. 1963) was born in Kansas and spent her childhood on the move in the United States and Germany as an army brat. She received her education at Mount Holyoke College and the Yale School of Drama. Her plays were first produced in experimental venues such as BACA Downtown in Brooklyn, New York; The Actors' Theatre of Louisville, and the Joseph Papp Public Theatre, with *Topdog/Underdog* (2001) moving to Broadway and garnering her a Pulitzer Prize. She is an associate artist at the Yale School of Drama and received a MacArthur "genius grant" in 2001. Her difficult plays are an attempt to find a form that can compress time and memory to fill out an understanding of the lost African American experience.

The following quotations from Parks's essay "Elements of Style" express her views of the relationship between form and content and demonstrate how a fresh personal vision brings a new sense of dramatic structure, character, and language.

On Form and Content

A playwright, as any other artist, should accept the bald fact that content determines form and form determines content; that form and content are interdependent. Form should not be looked at askance and held suspect—form is not something that "gets in the way of the story" but is an integral part of the story. This understanding is important to me and my writing. This is to say that as I write along, the container dictates what sort of substance will fill it and, at the same time, the substance is dictating the size and shape of the container. Also "form" is not a strictly "outside" thing while "content" stays "inside." It is like this: I am an African American woman—this is the form I take; my content predicates this form and this form is inseparable from my content. No way I could be otherwise.

Playwrights are often encouraged to write two-act plays with traditional linear narratives. Those sorts of plays are fine, but we should understand that the form is not merely a docile passive vessel, but an active participant in the sort of play which ultimately inhabits it. Why linear narrative at all? Why choose that shape? If a playwright chooses to tell a dramatic story and realizes that there are essential elements of that story which lead the writing outside the realm of "linear narrative," then the play naturally assumes a new shape.

On Repetition and Revision

"Repetition and Revision" is a concept integral to the Jazz esthetic in which the composer or performer will write a play or a musical phrase once and again and again; etc.—with each revisit the phrase is slightly revised. "Rep&Rev" as I call it is a central element in my work; through its use I'm working to create a dramatic text that departs from the traditional linear narrative style to look and sound more like a musical score. . . . Characters refigure their words and through a refiguring of language show us that they are experiencing their situation anew. . . . In such plays we are not moving from A→B but rather, for example, from

him the freedom to travel. His plays express the dilemma of the individual trapped by the movement of history. He uses figures from the masterpieces of Western theatre and places them in a decaying European civilization that has lost its way, allowing one text to comment on the other. Müller's "texts" (some would argue they are not plays in the traditional sense) are jumping-off points for imaginative visual staging, and a production of a fifteen-page play can take three hours to perform. The difficult-to-comprehend surrealistic montage of images and rambling speeches of his plays were meant to disturb the audience and provoke a response to a world without values.

August Wilson (b. 1945) and Suzan-Lori Parks (b. 1963) are African American playwrights whose plays document the history of the black experience in the United

A→A→A→B→A. Through such movement we refigure. And if we continue to call this movement FORWARD PROGRESSION, which I think it is, then we refigure the idea of forward progression. And if we insist on calling writings structured with this in mind PLAYS, which I think they are, then we've got a different kind of dramatic literature.

math

The equation of some plays.

On Character

They are not *characters*. To call them so could be an injustice. They are *figures, figments, ghosts, roles, lovers* maybe, *speakers* maybe, *shadows, slips, players* maybe, maybe *someone else's pulse.*

On Language

language is a physical act

Language is a physical act—something that

involves yr whole bod.

Write with yr whole bod.

Read with yr whole bod.

Wake up.

Here we see the central figure Saartje Bartman, the "Venus Hottentot," brought from Africa and put on display for white audiences. Her costume displays her large posterior and reflects a fanciful European idea of African dress, for the benefit of the European characters who ogle her. Suzan-Lori Parks's version of Bartman's life story questions traditional notions of representation, oppression, and sexuality. *Venus*, directed by Richard Foreman at the Yale Repertory Theatre.
© *T. Charles Erickson*

Source: From The America Play and Other Works *by Suzan-Lori Parks. Copyright © 1995 by Suzan-Lori Parks. Published by Theatre Communications Group. Used by permission of Theatre Communications Group.*

States. Their different perspectives on that experience are reflected in the forms they choose for their works. In a cycle of plays dramatizing African American life in each decade of the twentieth century—among them *Ma Rainey's Black Bottom* (1982) depicting the 1920s (see Photo 3.10), *Fences* (1985) depicting the 1950s, and *The Piano Lesson* (1987) depicting the 1930s—Wilson uses the traditional models of climactic plot and psychological characters to paint a detailed portrait of the longings and frustrations inherent in black life. His rich imagistic language captures the rhythms and spirit of African American speech and music. By contrast, Parks does not believe history can be captured in discrete snapshots of particular moments. She believes we are the product of the totality of our history, which resides in emotions, the unconscious, and the images, relationships, and stereotypes that continue to reincarnate themselves

Challenges and Choices

Should playwrights strive to make their works accessible to their audiences or seek to challenge them through new dramatic form?

in each new generation. Parks creates a new dramatic form that compresses historical forces into the simultaneity of a moment.

The result of Parks's view of history are difficult plays in a new form that challenges us to look past a linear sequence of cause-and-effect events to an accumulation of images and incidents that have an impact through their collective weight. In plays such as *Imperceptible Mutabilities in the Third Kingdom* (1989), *The America Play* (1994), and *The Death of the Last Black Man in the Whole Entire World* (1990) scenes, characters, and lines appear a number of different times, and each time they are slightly altered, echoing the theme and variation of jazz music. This "revision and repetition" as Parks calls it, works like a musical score, with the refrain playing pertinent themes over and over again. Parks shuns the term *characters*, preferring to talk of her personages as figures, figments, ghosts, or shadows through which we construct the present. In *The Death of the Last Black Man in the Whole Entire World*, the characters have names like "Black Man with Watermelon," "Black Woman with Fried Drumstick," "Lots of Grease and Lots of Pork," and "Before Columbus" reflecting the cultural influences they carry with them. The play, which has no easily discernable story, acts as a kind of ritual whereby the forgotten struggles of all black men are remembered and written into history in an attempt to bring emotional resolution to a past marked by oppression and violence.

Reading the Play

When you read a play, you enter a world created by the playwright. Although you will need to consider the way the writer constructs each element of a text, ultimately, the vision that is projected on stage is the result of the coming together of those elements into a cohesive whole. Understanding how language, character, and structure work to shape meaning unlocks the door to the world of the play.

KEY IDEAS

- Plays are not meant to be read as literature, but performed on the stage. Plays challenge readers to imagine the elements of performance as they read.
- The kinds of stories we tell and how we tell them reflect our culture and our values.
- The story of a play includes all the actions in, or mentioned in, the play. The plot is the ordering or structuring of events as they take place on stage. The interaction between story and plot shapes a play's meaning.
- Dramatic structure describes the scope and progression of the action.
- Climactic or Aristotelian structure begins late in the story, past events are revealed through exposition, and complications lead to a climax followed by a *dénouement*. The action usually covers a relatively short time span and is developed in a linear manner with events linked through cause and effect.
- The "well-made play" formula introduced the elements of foreshadowing, inciting incidents, cliffhangers, and the obligatory scene in a climactic model that kept audiences on the edge of their seats.
- The action in episodic structure usually spans an extended time and several locations and includes many subplots, characters, and short scenes.
- In circular structure, events seem to end where they began, creating a feeling of futility.
- In serial structure the action of each scene is independent of the action in the others.

- Playwrights often play with time and the unfolding of events on stage, using flashbacks, regressive storytelling, and other devices for thematic purposes.
- Every era and culture develops its own view of the human psyche and how we understand people and their motivations. This in turn shapes how dramatists envision characters for the stage.
- The primary form of language in the theatre is dialogue, which must be actable and speakable; advance the plot; express character; provoke or embody action; compress emotions; chart a character's journey; and set the mood, style, and tone.
- Since the twentieth century many plays have used dramatic language that expresses the failure of language to communicate.
- New ideas will often call for new dramatic forms, resulting in unconventional and challenging dramas.
- The dramatic elements of structure, language, and character work together to reveal the world of the play.

The European
Written Tradition
and Its Genres

Tragedy

Comedy

Tragicomedy

Melodrama

Genre Today

Driven to kill her own children, Medea (Fiona Shaw) is both murderer and mourner in this updated staging of an ancient Greek tragedy. Euripides' *Medea* translated by Kenneth McLeish and Frederick Raphael; directed by Deborah Warner; at the Queens' Theatre, London.
© *ArenaPal/Topham/The Image Works*

All of us feel joy and sorrow, love and hate, despair and hope, although we perceive and express these feelings in socially prescribed ways dictated by the traditions and beliefs of our cultures. The theatre is the place we give public expression to these private emotions, so it reflects the values and accepted behavior of particular times and places. The specific forms, or **genres** (categories of drama), the theatre uses to convey the human experience reflect both social context and universal feeling.

A cultural bias is inherent in any system of categorization. To illustrate this, Argentine writer Jorge Luis Borges (1899–1986) imagined "a certain Chinese encyclopaedia" in whose pages animals are divided into categories such as "those that belong to the emperor," "embalmed ones," "suckling pigs," "those that tremble as if they were mad," "those drawn with a very fine camelhair brush," and "stray dogs."[1] We laugh at this list because none of us can imagine grouping animals in this way. The humor reveals something important about categorization—we divide things up according to how we look at the world, our habits, our traditions, and our cultural values. Because genre is a way to categorize theatrical works, it too reflects our worldview, customs, and values, and it becomes instantly problematic when we try to apply dramatic categories cross-culturally.

The European theatrical tradition has been shaped by evolving ideas of comedy and tragedy that have been defined in plays and practice, and also in the legacy of criticism begun by Aristotle's strict distinction between tragic and comic forms. All subsequent discussions of plays have been haunted by this sense of opposing genres. In some societies, a critical tradition is absent, and theatrical categories may evolve from the perspective of the artist, the historical development of the form, or other cultural or religious influences. A tradition may divide works by the nature of the main character such as God, Warrior, or Demon plays, as we see in the *noh* theatre of Japan; by the dominant feeling or mood of a piece such as the erotic, the marvelous, or disgust, as we see in Indian Sanskrit theatre; or by ritual function such as war, healing, or wisdom, as we see in the Congo and in Native American performance. We may encounter types of plays and performance that are unfamiliar when we step outside of our own culture or era, just as our own divisions might seem puzzling to those outside our tradition.

European genres, such as comedy and tragedy, are useful for making sense of a written play's emotional impact and point of view, and imply the kind of attitude the playwright brought to the subject as well as the attitude spectators should bring to the experience. Plays fall into particular categories because they express particular views of existence or elicit similar emotional responses, not because of their form. The kinds of stories that are appropriate to tell, the structure of the plot, whether characters should be noble or lowborn, and the use of poetic or prosaic language are all theatrical conventions that reflect the values and concerns of a given society. They do not define a genre; they only explain a particular period's conventions of genre. For this reason, we can find two tragedies or comedies that use different kinds of plot, language, or character.

European theatre history reveals that traditional categories were more illusion than fact. We often find mixed forms: different categories nesting inside each other as in an Elizabethan tragedy with a comic subplot, a serious drama with a happy ending as in *The Tempest*, or an unresolved comedy such as *The Misanthrope*. The Greek and Roman classical eras and the French and Italian neoclassical periods are notable because their genre designations were so rigid. Playwrights create works because they have something to express, and they will not be held back by arbitrary categories if they impede their message. Artists will play with categories, push the boundaries of delineated forms, and possibly develop something new. We need only look at postcolonial playwrights such as Soyinka

---

1. Jorge Luis Borges. "The Analytical Language of John Wilkins," in *Other Inquisitions 1937–1952*, trans. Ruth L. C. Simms (Austin: University of Texas Press, 1984), 103.

(see Chapter 1), who fused indigenous forms with European genres to create hybrid forms that held an internal discourse between cultures within a play. Nonetheless, studying the European written tradition and its genres helps us understand plays in the Western tradition.

Tragedy

How we struggle and confront our limitations is the subject of tragedy. Our fate may be preordained, but we meet it in individual ways, through acts of will, and ultimately, as the instruments of our own destruction. The choices the tragic hero makes are the trigger of the drama. The nature of the tragic character is therefore of primary interest. The tragic hero is never faint of heart. There is a refusal to accept fate, a protestation against the limits of human power, and a determination to achieve self-fulfillment. Implicit in the tragic view is the inevitable failure of our best efforts to overcome human destiny. We are all doomed to death and defeat in a world ruled by forces beyond our control, yet we live our lives struggling to affirm our essential individual humanity.

Tragedy documents the struggle between our desires and the necessities of conscience. As such, the tragic universe encompasses an accepted value system imposing constraints on our behavior. When the hero's choices lead to failure or disaster, the hero assumes responsibility for the drama's chain of events. This claim of responsibility makes tragedy a personal drama of character and belated self-realization. It is the reason tragic heroes become archetypes who claim a place in our imaginations and become symbols of conscience. Tragedy therefore embodies a moral lesson.

Tragedy in Ancient Greece and Rome

Although the people of fifth- and fourth-century B.C.E. Athens took enormous pride in their cultural accomplishments—they created the first democracy, investigated science and philosophy, developed new styles in art and architecture—they were also acutely aware of what they saw as the limitations imposed on human affairs by divine action. For the ancient Greeks, tragic suffering grew primarily from the conflict between duty to society and duty to the family and self in a world governed by a pantheon of often capricious, wrathful, or unfathomable gods who held enormous power over human destiny. The gods set the tragic action in motion, and then individuals did their part to bring on their inevitable end, often by challenging the gods themselves. *Hubris* is the term used to describe the overwhelming pride that leads a character to believe a triumph over the gods could be possible, and it leads inevitably to disastrous consequences. This conflict between human pride and divine power is at the heart of Greek tragedy, and it couples with a character's internal clash between public obligation and personal feelings or duty. Should Antigone, in Sophocles' tragedy by that name, bury her brother in violation of the law against funeral rites for traitors? Honoring her brother, she loses her future husband, the king's son Haemon, and sentences herself to death; choosing love and survival, she dishonors her family and the gods. Aeschylus, Sophocles, and Euripides all wrote plays about the responsibility of Orestes, the son of Agamemnon. Can Orestes murder his mother, Clytemnestra, because she killed his father? Honoring his duty to his father will require him to commit an egregious act and continue an endless cycle of revenge killings; unavenged, his father's death will have no justice. Such are the dilemmas confronting the tragic hero.

Theatre played a central role in ancient Athens. The government sponsored an annual theatre competition during the City Dionysia, a festival honoring the coming of the god Dionysus to Athens. Three tragic playwrights competed for a prize, with each

Photo 4.1

Oedipus (Peter Macon) tears out his own eyes after recognizing the horrible fate he has lived out in spite of his attempts to outwit the gods. Sophocles' *Oedipus* adapted by Ellen McLaughlin; director, Lisa Peterson; set, Riccardo Hernandez; lighting, Christopher Akerlind; costumes, David Zinn. The Guthrie Theatre, Minneapolis.

© T. Charles Erickson

assigned a day of performance. They submitted three tragedies and a **satyr play**—a burlesque of mythic legends—which provided comic relief after a day of tragedies. The entire citizenry of Athens was expected to attend. The central role accorded the theatre reflects the perceived significance of the moral vision of tragedy in maintaining the order of the state.

Ancient Greek tragedy expressed itself through a particular dramatic form with distinct text and staging conventions. Some of these formal features became intrinsically linked to the very idea of tragedy, including a focus on the downfall of characters of high social status—heroes, kings, and queens who spoke in elevated, rhythmic poetic verse; the presence of a singing and dancing chorus to represent the populous and provide commentary and perspective on the action; and the use of a climactic plot ending with the downfall of the hero. Most tragedies began with a *prologue* that provided exposition, followed by the *parodos* or entrance of the chorus, five episodes punctuated by choral odes, and the *exodus* or exit of the chorus.

Aristotle's *Poetics*, written in the fourth century B.C.E., outlined what he considered the essential qualities of a tragic text. The *Poetics* was descriptive of tragedies from the fifth century B.C.E., yet later, others used it as a prescriptive model of the tragic genre. Aristotle based his analysis on Sophocles' (496–406 B.C.E.) *Oedipus Tyrannus* (c. 430 B.C.E.), the story of the brilliant, proud, and arrogant king who, despite all his best efforts to avoid his decreed fate to kill his father and marry his mother, unknowingly makes every choice that will lead him to this destiny. His actions display the *hubris* of one who believes he can defy the gods. Aristotle believed the tragic character should be prosperous, good, and worthy, yet commit some *tragic miscalculation* resulting from his nature that leads to misfortune. We see Oedipus, an essentially virtuous man, who, blinded by a stubborn nature and overwhelming pride, misjudges his course of action. Prosperity at the outset not only accentuated the eventual fall, but it gave the tragic character something to lose, rendering the inevitable suffering all the greater, and causing *pity and fear* in the public that underscored the moral lesson. Witnessing the tragic events takes the audience on a spiritual and moral journey, and the intense impact must be defused through *catharsis*, an emotional release that purges pity and fear, so the spectator can take in the lesson. The essential goodness of the tragic character is necessary for an ethical dilemma to unfold, and goodness forms the basis for audience empathy as well. The hero's misjudgment not only causes the fall, but also provides the basis for identification with our own frailties and failures. Most significant among Aristotle's principles is the necessity of *recognition*: At the moment of an obligatory *reversal of fortune*, the tragic character must take responsibility for action and move from ignorance to self-knowledge. Oedipus, when he recognizes what he has done, pierces his eyes, ironically blinding himself at the moment he sees within most clearly.

The limiting of tragic characters to the highborn reflects the rigidity of the Greek social order and the view that the actions of the ruler could bring ills to the land and its

History IN PERSPECTIVE

THE EUROPEAN MEDIEVAL THEATRE AND ITS GENRES

The Middle Ages (the ninth to the fifteenth centuries) saw the emergence of a unique set of theatrical genres unrelated to the traditions of tragedy and comedy, but reflecting the preeminence of Christianity. In the fifth century C.E., filling the vacuum of power left by the dissolution of the Roman Empire, the Christian church denounced theatrical activity long associated with pagan religious worship and bloody gladiatorial fights as a violation of Christian piety. The tragic and comic plays of ancient Greece and Rome, already out of fashion in the late Roman period, were almost completely erased from the cultural memory of Western Europe in the medieval period. Some texts remained in monasteries where they might be used for learning Latin or rhetoric, and many were preserved in the Eastern Byzantine Empire, but they were not performed. We know that Hrosvitha of Gandersheim (c. 935–973), a nun from Germany and the first known female playwright, had access to the works of the Roman comic playwright Terence, which she used as models for the six plays she wrote on Christian themes.

Ironically, the church that had banned theatre became the home of spectacle and performance as the mass used costume, music, and visual spectacle to speak to the people. New traditions of theatrical performance emerged from the Catholic liturgy itself, demonstrating theatre's ritual origins. The beginnings of **liturgical drama** are found in the addition of tropes, words sung to musical notes often divided among the chorus to create dialogue. This antiphonal choral singing moved toward theatre when, during the Easter service, a trope known as the *Quem Queritas* was sung antiphonally, representing the voices of the angels and the three Marys at Christ's tomb. It was not long before all the elements of theatrical enactment followed, impersonation, staging, costumes, and additional roles. Liturgical drama illustrated significant stories from the New Testament and brought the liturgy to life for the laypeople of Europe within the church walls. Sung mostly in Latin, with members of the clergy and choirboys serving as actors, they were performed in monasteries, churches, and cathedrals at important holidays such as Easter and Christmas. Eventually they grew to include multiple scenes, and small scenic structures called *mansions* were set along the side of the church nave for each scene. Complex plays might require several mansions placed throughout the church and even flying machinery for angels or the star of Bethlehem to descend from on high (see Fig. 4.2).

These performances were successful in teaching religion, and they grew in scenic complexity. The laity were called on to help, and between the thirteenth and fifteenth centuries performances moved outside the church where they now enacted a cycle of stories from the Creation to the Last Judgment, from the Old and New Testaments. Latin was replaced by the vernacular, and the plays became common throughout Europe. Each scene was sponsored by a guild, a union of workers, merchants, or craftsmen who protected each other and the secrets or mysteries of their trade. For this reason these **cycle plays** are often called **mystery plays.**

After 1264, when Pope Urban IV created the festival of Corpus Christi to commemorate the redemptive power of the Holy Eucharist, the consecrated bread and wine of the Catholic service, it became customary to perform the cycles on this day. This festival was adopted throughout the Christian world by 1350, and Spanish conquerors brought the tradition to the Americas, where indigenous performance traditions incorporated Corpus Christi plays, many of which are performed to this day in Latin America. The popularity of the cycle plays waned in Europe during the sixteenth century and were forbidden in England by a royal edict in 1558.

The sets for the mystery plays were pulled to their performance locations in village squares on **pageant wagons**. Several wagons might be placed side by side for a day of performances and replaced by a new set of wagons and dramatic episodes on the following day, or the wagons might be pulled in parade style from one performance location to another throughout the town. Guild members performed, so spectators saw on stage simultaneously the biblical figures of the dramas and the familiar merchants and craftsmen of the town who portrayed them, adding a personal significance to the religious themes. Cycle plays usually had one setting for heaven and one for hell where characters could be taken to their ultimate fates. The pieces also served to promote the guilds, providing an opportunity for them to show off their skills. The shipwrights were often given the episode of Noah's Ark, for which they could build a moving ship onstage.

Cycle plays could take up to forty days to perform in their entirety, depending on the performance practices of the region. They expressed religious doctrine, but also included local comic references. In *The Second Shepherd's Pageant* from the cycle done in Wakefield, England, the shepherds speak like local farmers about the harsh weather and bad times, and have a sheep stolen from them by Mak, whose wife passes it off as her baby by wrapping it in swaddling clothes. This farcical scene precedes a true nativity scene. Mak is

(continues)

punished for his misdeeds by being dragged off in a sack and misses the birth of the real infant Christ and the redemption it promises.

Variations on the cycle play include **passion plays,** episodic plays depicting events from the passion of Christ, and **saint** or **miracle plays,** depicting events from the lives of saints using nonbiblical materials.

Morality plays used allegorical characters to depict moral lessons. Plays such as *The Castle of Perseverance* (c.1400–1425) and *Mankind* (c.1465) focused on the religious battle between the vices and the virtues for the human soul. In *Everyman* (c.1510) Death comes to take Everyman to the afterlife. Everyman looks desperately for a companion to accompany him. He visits Confession and discovers that only Good Deeds will go with him, showing a Christian view of how to prepare for death. All the plays of this type were meant to teach moral lessons.

Morality plays and their allegorical framework provided the philosophical basis for Elizabethan playwrights who depicted conflicts between virtue and vice with three-dimensional characters. When Shakespeare's *Richard III* murders two sweet young princes as part of his plot to become king, we see the murder of virtue

by vice presented with historical figures in a tale of political intrigue.

These genres continue in new incarnations today. Christmas and Easter pageants played by children and church groups in places of worship around the world are a legacy of liturgical dramas and cycle plays. Since 1975 in San Juan Bautista, California, El Teatro Campesino has been performing *La Pastorela*, a story about the shepherd's journey to the nativity based on Mexican folk plays derived from medieval Spanish practices. The Cathedral of Saint John the Divine in New York has offered Epiphany performances of the story of the three kings in English and Spanish with internationally inspired music by Elizabeth Swados, masks and giant puppets by Hudson Vagabond Puppets, and dancing by the children of the Dance Theatre of Harlem. New York's Ensemble for Early Music has recreated several liturgical dramas including *The Parable of the Wise and Foolish Virgins* performed in the Medieval Hall at the Metropolitan Museum of Art. There have been many full restagings of cycle plays including a 1986 production done at Canterbury Cathedral in England.

This cycle of plays on the passion and resurrection of Jesus Christ performed in Valenciennes, France, in 1547 took twenty-five days, with new mansions brought in for each day. Note the Heaven mansion on the left and the Hell mansion, complete with fire, devils, and Hell mouth, on the right. Each mansion appears as an individual architectural structure, with roof and columns. Documents such as these help us to imagine the staging of theatrical events in the Middle Ages.
© *Giraudon/Art Resource, NY*

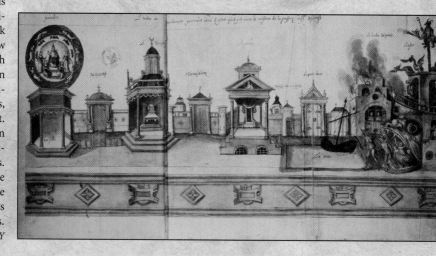

people, just as Oedipus' crimes bring a plague to the land of Thebes and all its citizens. The struggle of the nobility was symbolic—the commoner suffered by proxy. Only the highborn could inspire both pity and fear. When Aristotle wrote that comic characters were inferior, he meant that they allow us to laugh without fear, but interpreters labeled comedy an inferior genre as a result of these words.

The Romans had little interest in serious drama, and by the first century C.E., tragedies ceased to be performed in the public theatre. It is believed the tragedies of Seneca (4 B.C.E.–65 C.E.) were meant to be read. Seneca took his stories from Greek myths, but his plays in no other way resembled Greek tragedy. He extracted from the myths pretexts for violence and bombastic speeches. His plays often have ghosts demanding vengeance for their deaths with murder and mayhem the result. These bloody dramas became known as **revenge plays**. Classical tragedy came to an end as the Catholic Church assumed increasing political control of Europe in the Middle Ages and banned theatrical activity.

Neoclassical Tragedy

Starting in the fourteenth century, as a result of political and economic changes in Europe, there was a renewed interest in classical forms that grew over the next two centuries. This period of rediscovery is called the Renaissance, literally a rebirth. Latin manuscripts had been preserved in monasteries, but now scholars were calling for their collection and preservation. The fall of Constantinople to the Ottoman Turks in 1453 brought fleeing scholars carrying manuscripts of ancient Greek tragedies to Italy. These texts were widely disseminated by the sixteenth century with the invention of the printing press. The rediscovered *Poetics* was interpreted by Italian scholars as a rule book for tragedy, and this and other misinterpretations brought back tragedy in an altered form.

The new neoclassical form required the three unities of time, place, and action that limited tragedies to a single day, in one location, and a single climactic plot, although such restrictions were not required in ancient Greece. The idea of **verisimilitude**—the appearance of truth—not realism but an idealized truth, was introduced. This led to the elimination of soliloquies and the Greek chorus, replacing them with a confidant to whom central characters could speak their inner thoughts in an attempt to be faithful to reality. To reconcile Christianity with classicism, playwrights were also expected to use their tragedies to teach moral lessons. During the seventeenth century, the French took these Italian models to extremes, enforcing strict notions of decorum or proper behavior, strict genre categories, and the three unities. Playwrights often performed plot contortions to conform to these prescriptions.

Pierre Corneille's (1606–1684) tragedy *Le Cid* (1636) depicted a war fought in a day in a single town, a character who within a day of her father's murder agrees to marry his assassin, and a happy ending. This failure to follow the rules provoked a public debate. The moral preoccupation of most French tragedies is with the conflict between love and honor, exemplified by Jean Racine's *Phèdre* discussed in the last chapter. French tragedy is marked by long introspective poetic speeches written in magnificent poetry, in which the hero explores conscience and desire.

Elizabethan and Jacobean Tragedy

Although neoclassicism was studied in universities, its influence was not immediately felt in England's professional theatres. What emerged instead was a dramatic form that combined the Renaissance questioning of the role of human responsibility in an ordered universe with medieval ideas and expansive theatrical forms. A large theatre audience

Photo 4.2
Chimène (Susan Lynch) must call for the death of the man she loves, Rodrigue (Duncan Bell), who killed her father in a duel, in this neoclassic French tragedy where love conflicts with duty and honor. Pierre Corneille's *The Cid*. Translation by Ranjit Bolt; director, Jonathan Kent. The National Theatre, London.
© *Robbie Jack/CORBIS*

demanded new entertainments, and this brought a burgeoning of playwriting during the reign of Elizabeth I (1558–1603) and continued through the Jacobean period under James I (1603–1625). The works of the many great playwrights of the period are still performed today, among them Christopher Marlowe (1564–1593), Ben Jonson (1572–1637), and John Webster (1580–1634). Of course, the undisputed great of the era is William Shakespeare (1564–1616).

The medieval world believed in a chain of being with God presiding over a hierarchy from the angels down to the lowest inanimate objects. The more secular Elizabethan world extended this idea and saw the universe as having parallel systems of order: the cosmic order involving the sun, the planets, and natural phenomena ruled by God; a political order ruled by the monarch functioning metaphorically as a god figure, meting out justice and keeping order over a social order from nobility to commoner; a family order ruled by the household patriarch; and a personal order with our physical and emotional well-being ruled by the mind. The balance of forces within each order led to well-being in the world, and when forces were out of balance on any plane, problems were sure to follow throughout the land. Elizabethan tragedy often traced the effects of vice and corruption in the ruling class, leading to social disruption and the breakdown of society. As the guardians of a divine order on earth, human beings need to purge the kingdom of its debasing forces to reestablish order. Elizabethan tragedy served as a warning to would-be tyrants of what might await them should they abuse their power.

The Elizabethans saw morality from a Christian perspective, and human struggle was directed against vice in all its various forms. The conflict between an ideal of Christian virtue and the corruption of the everyday world are common subjects. Characters who embody greed, ambition, jealousy, vengeance, and unbridled passion, among the range of destructive human motivations, are led to disaster, an admonishment to all of us to keep ourselves in order, reining in harmful human emotions. In a break with medieval thinking, deep questioning of God's will on earth and the place of humankind in the grand scheme haunt the plays of this period. Hamlet's monologues are excellent examples of a character's search for answers to these imponderable questions. Hamlet, Lear, and Macbeth are among the Elizabethan legacy of complex tragic figures who perplex us to this day.

Photo 4.3
King Lear (Nigel Hawthorne) remains in the company of the Earl of Kent (Christopher Benjamin) and the Fool (Sanada Hiroyuki) after dividing his kingdom between the daughters who will betray him. Shakespeare's *King Lear* directed by Ninagawa Yukio at the Barbican Theatre, London.
© *ArenaPal/Topham/ The Image Works*

Like the Greek tragedies before them, Elizabethan and Jacobean tragedies focus on characters of high status. They speak in the elevated poetic language of blank verse. These later plays, however, follow an episodic structure, usually five acts long, with many scenes and subplots. Elizabethan plays do not have a chorus in the Greek sense, but characters reveal their thoughts in soliloquies, and subplots and clowns provide commentary on the central action. Neoclassical rules for decorum were largely ignored by professional playwrights, who catered to a public that loved a share of action and gore. Schools of this period also studied Seneca's tragedies, so revenge motifs and bloody duels and battles are a part of many tragedies. The open panoramic feel of medieval drama remains present, and a resistance to formal rules is everywhere in evidence. Examine the plays of just one playwright, William Shakespeare, and you will find him bending the form to fit the particular needs of each play.

Neoclassicism did eventually come to England after 1660, when King Charles II was restored to the throne after his exile in France. He brought with him a taste for continental drama, and the strict new tragic form took hold for a brief while on British soil.

Bourgeois and Romantic Drama

With the social, political, and economic changes in the eighteenth century brought on by a rising middle class and democratic revolutions, serious drama began to concern itself with the lives of the new rising bourgeoisie. We see vicars, and merchants—people from the ordinary walks of life as subjects of serious drama. Eventually the place of kings and queens is taken by the middle and lower rungs of society as the people of central concern to the theatre. The actions of such figures could not be seen to affect the entire land, removing a central idea in the tragic vision.

George Lillo's *The London Merchant* (1731) was the first true bourgeois domestic tragedy. Based on a character in a popular ballad, George Barnwell, the play is about this young merchant's apprentice who kills his own uncle and betrays his employer under the sway of Milwood, an evil seductress. As he reflects on his evil deed and its consequences in lofty prose, Barnwell rises to the status of tragic hero. He accepts his death at the gallows, hoping it will serve as a warning to others. Lillo claimed that a tragedy about an ordinary individual could teach lessons of virtue to a greater number of people than classical tragedies about noble heroes could, and indeed, young apprentices were sent to see *The London Merchant* during their holidays for years.

Romanticism, which began in the late eighteenth century, revolted against the constraints of neoclassicism and celebrated heroes who pursue their natural impulses and ideals in love or politics. Shakespeare was the inspiration for romantic tragedy with his expansive style and brooding heroes. Johann Wolfgang von Goethe's (1749–1832) early plays of the *Sturm und Drang* or Storm and Stress movement in Germany contributed to the development of German Romanticism. In *Goetz von Berlichingen* (1773), Goetz, the main character, based on an historical figure, is a knight who follows his own mind and whose defiance lands him in jail. The play is almost unstageable with fifty-four scenes and numerous characters. Important events in the life of the main character shape the drama rather than a neatly developed plot, exemplifying the anti-neoclassical impulse of the *Sturm und Drang* movement.

Between 1797 and 1805, Goethe and Fredrich Schiller (1759–1805), who had also been active in the *Sturm und Drang* movement, took German drama in a new direction. Working together at the court theatre in Weimar, they forged a middle path between the rigidity of the French neoclassic model and the freer English form of tragedy using characters who were modeled on the romantic individualist. This style is now called *Weimar classicism.* In Schiller's *Mary Stuart* (1800), the action moves freely between Elizabeth I's palace and Mary's prison and includes a meeting between the two in an open field. The play is a study in contrasts, with Elizabeth nominally free, but weighed down by the

History IN PERSPECTIVE

THE GENRES OF SPANISH GOLDEN AGE DRAMA

The flourishing of Spanish literature, art, and drama during the sixteenth and seventeenth centuries accompanied the rise of Spain as an international political power. Although religious dramas never fell from popularity, a vibrant secular theatre developed out of *entremeses*, the short pieces used as interludes in church plays. The *género chico* included one-act plays of various types from farce to dramatic sketches. These eventually developed into full-length *comedias*, a word that sounds like "comedy" but refers to any secular dramatic work.

Golden Age plays did not keep to the classical distinctions of tragedy and comedy, and in fact *comedias* mixed serious and comic subject matter. The many types of *comedias* included swashbuckling cloak-and-dagger plays (*comedia de capa y espada*) that included intrigue, adventure, and love affairs, comedies of manners (*comedia de costumbres*), honor plays (*comedia pundoñor*), and romantic comedy (*comedias fantasía*). Subject matter could be taken from history, legend, the lives of saints, or current social issues. These plays were generally kept to three acts and catered to the interests and taste of the popular audience. The importance of honor (*pundoñor*) was a central theme, although *comedias* dealt with love, religion, and patriotism as well. The prolific output of Golden Age playwrights was in response to popular demand.

Spain also developed its own version of Christian religious drama called **autos sacramentales** around the sixteenth century, just as religious plays were on the wane in other parts of Europe. These productions, typically staged as part of the Corpus Christi celebrations, combined elements from both the cycle and morality plays, using both biblical and allegorical characters and telling biblical tales and other stories that expressed religious doctrine. They were performed inside churches and in public plazas. These religious dramas held a place of importance, and all playwrights, including the premier dramatists Lope de Vega (1562–1635) and Pedro Calderón de la Barca (1600–1681), wrote *autos* as well as *comedia*, a reminder of the power of the Spanish church.

Lope de Vega was the first Spanish playwright to make a living writing plays, which might account for his enormous output, estimated at around 800 plays, though some have attributed as many as 1,800 titles to him. Although the quality of his writing varies widely, he dominated the theatre of his time and set a model for future playwrights in his attitude toward ancient classics, the scope of his subject matter, and his skill in crafting plots. His many honor plays, a topic he felt most moved the Spanish crowd, contributed to this becoming a predominant theme of Golden Age drama.

In contrast to writers elsewhere in Europe, who looked to classical models, Lope was firmly wedded to pleasing his audience rather than adhering to academic ideals. In *The New Art of Writing Plays for Our Time* (1609), a theoretical work, he listed twenty-eight points for the drama. He allows the mixing of comic and serious elements, but prescribes one central plot. The time limits should be dictated by the story, and language should be suited to the characters. He claimed to lock classical writers like Terence and Plautus out of the room the minute

obligations of her office, and Mary, imprisoned and destined to be beheaded, but free in spirit even as she goes defiantly toward her death.

Modern Tragedy

Challenges and Choices

Do you believe tragedy is possible today? What elements would it contain?

In the modern period, many argued that we were no longer in a world that could accommodate the tragic experience because there were no longer fixed value systems against which to measure human action. Playwright Arthur Miller (1915–2005), and others, proposed a new view of tragedy, which saw tragic experience as independent of universal moral concerns. In this view, tragedy could be expressed as an attitude toward personal experience in plays about the lives of everyday human beings speaking in ordinary language. In his article "Tragedy and the Common Man," Miller argued that what evokes a tragic feeling in us is "the presence of a character who is ready to lay down his

he sat down to write, thinking only of his audience and how to please them.

Lope's best-known work is *The Sheep's Well* (*Fuente Ovejuna*, c. 1614) in which one of the villagers of Fuente Ovejuna, driven to the brink by the actions of a tyrannical lord, kills him. Under torture the townspeople stick together declaring that no individual, but the town as a whole, committed the murder, and in the end they are pardoned by the king. The work has surprisingly modern overtones of revolution, but in the end authority rests with the king and his inquisition, and only the tyrannical actions of the military lord are condemned.

Lope's personal life was as dramatic as some of his plays. He had many love affairs, fought with the Spanish Armada, and in his later years became a priest, while continuing to lead a cavalier life.

Lope's accomplishments were succeeded by those of Pedro Calderón de la Barca, who wrote two hundred plays. Eighty of his surviving works are *autos sacramentales*, a form that he perfected and that took up much of the latter part of his career because, like Lope, he turned to the priesthood in his declining years. Many of his plays were intended for the court, rather than the public audiences Lope favored.

Calderón's most famous work is *Life Is a Dream* (c. 1636) about Prince Segismund imprisoned from infancy by his father to avoid prophecies that he would become a cruel tyrant. When Segismund comes of age, the king brings his son to court to put the prophecies to the test. Segismund's cruel acts lead the king to send him back to prison, where he awakens wondering whether prison life or palace life is the true dream. He eventually learns the truth about his situation and, after battling his own father for the kingdom, becomes a judicious ruler. The play is full of action, places honor over love, and is also a philosophical meditation on the nature of life and illusion.

Spanish *comedias* were presented to a popular audience in outdoor *corrales*, named after the courtyards where plays originally took place. Most of the audience stood in a yard area in front of the stage. Structures surrounding the square yard housed several stories of galleries and boxes for wealthy families, including the *cazuela* or "stewpot," a gallery reserved for women, who were not permitted in the yard. The separation of men and women was a bow to moral authorities who worried about the overall rowdiness of the theatre and the honor of women who attended and performed on stage. The theatres were unruly, with spectators rattling noisemakers, yelling their approval at the players, and calling for refreshments. The *cazuela* could be particularly noisy with as many women as could squeeze onto the benches banging their beads and keys on the guardrails to attract the attention of handsome men down below, and men dressed as women sneaking in and causing a ruckus.

The villagers of Fuente Ovejuna band together to defend their honor by killing their tyrannical lord in this Spanish golden age drama. Lope de Vega's *The Sheep's Well (Fuente Ovejuna)* at the Yale School of Drama.
© *T. Charles Erickson*

life, if need be, to secure one thing—his sense of personal dignity."[2] This attitude can be present in any individual. In his play *Death of a Salesman* (1949), Miller stages a modern tragedy in the struggle of Willy Loman, an ordinary salesman, to make ends meet and achieve self-validation in spite of the economic and social forces acting against him. Measuring himself against the promise of the elusive American dream, he chooses death as his only possible and honorable option. Many have argued against Miller's view, believing that tragedy is impossible in a world of moral relativity. Willy Loman, having lost his moral compass, is either incapable of tragic or heroic status, or is the embodiment of

2. "Tragedy and the Common Man," copyright 1949, renewed © 1977 by Arthur Miller, from *The Theater Essays of Arthur Miller* by Arthur Miller, edited by Robert A. Martin. Used by permission of Viking Penguin, a division of Penguin Group (USA) Inc.

Photo 4.4
Willy Loman, played here by
Brian Dennehy, is an ordinary
salesman who becomes a
tragic figure in Arthur Miller's
Death of a Salesman. Here he
gives flawed advice to his son
Biff (Ron Eldard) on how to
get ahead. Director Robert
Falls; scenic design by Mark
Wendland; costume design by
Birgit Rattenborg Wise; light-
ing design by Michael S.
Philippi. Eugene O'Neill
Theatre, New York.
© Joan Marcus

a new kind of tragic hero. Whether or not you believe that tragedy is possible today, there
is no doubt that all people, including once voiceless populations, can now be the subjects
of serious dramatic exploration.

Comedy

Comedy provides an experience of laughter and exuberance and the merry gloating that
comes from a stolen and momentary triumph over fate. When luck leads us past life's obstacles, comedy celebrates our having prevailed over the odds. This optimistic celebration of our capacity to endure is revealed in the usual happy ending.

It is believed that ancient comedy evolved from rituals that rejoiced in the regeneration of the earth at springtime and the ensuing renewal of hope. These rustic celebrations of fertility explain the sexual humor found in many early comedies. Greek Old
Comedy of the fifth century B.C.E., notably the plays of Aristophanes (448–380 B.C.E.),
were filled with bawdy jokes and choruses of men singing lewd songs and wearing giant
padded phalluses as part of their costumes. Rebirth and renewal are often the culmina-
tion of comic action, and many comedies end with a marriage, or sometimes several,
celebrating those rites that eventually bring a community together and guarantee its
future.

Comedy generally works toward a reknitting of the social fabric by first showing us
its unraveling. It exists in a topsy-turvy world where discord and disturbance have turned
the social order on end. Lost children, lovers, fortunes, and identities must be recovered
in a world manipulated by charlatans, petty family tyrants, and knaves. But the realm of
comedy is also a protected one where we know, no matter how much danger looms, that
there will be no painful consequences, and all will be put right in the end. The trickster
can hold the day for just so long before order is restored. In the meantime, we watch at
a safe comic distance the parade of human foibles before us, see the truth about ourselves, and laugh in relief that we pay no price.

Comedy, unlike tragedy, serves a universal social function. This may be why the
clown, fool, and trickster can be found in almost every culture around the globe. They

exist outside of prescribed social behavior where, free to disrupt the status quo, they can violate taboos and serve as release valves for social repression through laughter. They are free to ridicule even those in power and to put values into question to reestablish their legitimacy. From Native American Navajo and Hopi culture, through the European theatrical tradition, to the Chinese, Balinese, and Indian Sanskrit dramas, these figures appear as forces of nature and renewal.

Comedy is often considered an inferior genre to tragedy, or its polar opposite. In fact, neither is true. While tragedy presents ideals and focuses on the philosophical, comedy is pragmatic and tells it "like it is." But in fact, they both deal with survival, on how we get by, tragedy by helping us define our place in the grand scheme of things, and comedy by showing the way in the here and now. Because comedies deal with the familiar world, they are often topical and remain deeply tied to the particular social concerns from which they emerge.

Ancient Greek comedy was social and political, confronting the issues of its time. Today's comedy is often personal, dealing with the neurotic concerns of individuals. Public or personal, comedy is always a corrective for what ails us. Comedy presupposes a world where norms exist, where social expectations prevail, and where divergence from custom can be immediately recognized. By demonstrating the consequences of deviant behavior, comedy can teach us how to lead our lives.

What Makes Us Laugh: The Tools of Comedy

Human beings need to laugh. Doctors tell us it is good for us and even helps the immune system. We seem to be born with a comic sensibility; even babies will laugh at a funny face, a silly noise, or a pratfall. Simultaneously, some forms of comedy require sophistication and a mature understanding of the world. If a baby can respond to a ridiculous face, and an adult to ridiculous manners or language, the tools of comic expression must range from the broadly physical to the subtle or intellectual. Comedy is created through the serendipitous blending of many elements in front of a receptive audience. The magic formula for making something funny has challenged theatre artists and theorists. The more we try to dissect its components, the further removed we feel from the comic realm and the vitality of its impulsive spontaneity. Nonetheless, writers call on certain devices to portray the deviation that launches comic action on the stage.

■ **Surprise, Contrast, and Incongruity.** Although the unexpected is often a central dramatic element in all kinds of plays, when the element of surprise opposes all normative expectations, contrasts with what we anticipate, or seems incongruous to situation or character, it can turn a serious situation comic.

■ **Exaggeration.** The comic lens exaggerates characters, actions, language, voices, emotions, and situations like a fun house mirror and, ironically, often pulls them into sharper focus. Before the comic magnifying glass, we get a clear picture of human excess that can throw normal social interactions into discord and disarray. **Parody** is the exaggerated imitation of individuals or artistic styles to make them appear ludicrous.

■ **Obsession.** When exaggeration enters the psychological realm, we have obsession, which sends characters out of control in pursuit of a single desire that sets off the comic situation. The miser obsessing over his money, the husband or wife obsessing over a spouse's possible infidelities, the moralist consumed with thoughts of sin are characters we see woven into endless comic plots.

■ **Slapstick.** Slapstick humor is named for the fool's slapstick, two long flat pieces of wood fastened together that created a loud slapping noise when used. The precise origins of this instrument of comic torture are unclear. Today we include knockabout humor—chases, pratfalls, collisions, comic beatings, or semi-acrobatic feats and practical jokes—

under this label. Although slapstick can be considered a form unto itself, slapstick elements may be incorporated into many different kinds of comedy to draw laughter.

■ **Transgression.** Scatological and sexual jokes violate social taboos and offer comic release. Comedy can even violate the moral and religious values of society and court outrage and censorship.

■ **Language.** Humorous language includes puns (plays on words), jokes, understatement, sarcasm, witty repartee, and sometimes nonsensical or rhythmic exchanges. Often comedy is found in the misuse of language—mistakes in pronunciation or grammar, peculiar accents, and *malapropisms*, the ludicrous misuse of words, often by confusing them with similar sounding ones. The term was derived from a character in Richard Sheridan's (1751–1816) play *The Rivals*. Mrs. Malaprop's misuse of terms, such as asking for the "perpendiculars" when she wanted the particulars, was made all the funnier by her exaggerated pretentious behavior.

Comic Forms

There are many forms of comedy that draw on these comic devices in different combinations and degrees. When the device becomes an end in and of itself, it may actually become a form of comedy such as slapstick or parody. Although comic plays can achieve their effect through any number of tactics, certain comic theatrical forms are fairly distinct and represent major divisions in the approach to comic material.

Satire

Sometimes comedy is used as a form of attack on the follies or institutionalized vices of a particular society. Marked by irony and wit, satire can explore pressing social issues and provoke debate. Satire is always topical, and its subjects are immediately recognizable to its audience. It uses ridicule as a corrective and usually has a moral or critical position.

Aristophanes, the first great comic writer in the Western tradition, turned his comic lens on the artists, philosophers, politicians, and even the gods of his time. His plays begin with a prologue addressed to the audience to get them in the comic mood, followed by a debate over some current issue of interest that sets out the comic premise for the play. Many of the comedies of Aristophanes satirized the social and political concerns in an Athenian society stressed by the seemingly endless Peloponnesian war. *The Frogs*, produced in 2004 in New York, updated the play to address contemporary problems and the malaise resulting from the war in Iraq, recognizing the need for topical allusions for satire to get a laugh.

Satirists target figures or ideas that offend a particular group or themselves, so often satire is a way of releasing personal and public emotion. The central character is often shown to be foolish or morally corrupt. The recent London production of *The Madness of George Dubya* was a reaction to war and militarism and presented President Bush in a cowboy hat and Superman T-shirt, a buffoon cud-

Photo 4.5
The Italian Nobel Prize–winning playwright and actor Dario Fo brings an expressive face and physical flexibility to the comic roles he writes, which blend political satire and farce.
© AP/Wide World Photos

IN PERSPECTIVE

TOPICAL SATIRE TODAY: THE *LYSISTRATA* PROJECT

The *Lysistrata* Project galvanized artists throughout the world to turn to this ancient text and its satirical solution to war as a means of protesting America's imminent invasion of Iraq. On March 3, 2003, over one thousand readings and performances of *Lysistrata*, Aristophanes' comedy written in 411 B.C.E., took place in fifty-nine countries and in every state of the United States. Organized by Kathryn Blume and Sharon Bower, readings took place in countries as diverse as Cambodia, Japan, Iceland, Pakistan, and Uruguay. There were some all-star ventures such as the reading with F. Murray Abraham and Kevin Bacon at the Brooklyn Academy of Music in New York. Many churches, colleges, and theatres participated, and one group performed in Lafayette Square, directly in front of the White House in Washington, D.C., bringing this political comedy to the very seat of political power. Readings also raised money for peace and humanitarian organizations around the world.

In Aristophanes' antiwar play *Lysistrata*, written in response to the Peloponnesian War between Athens and Sparta that raged for more than twenty-five years from 431 to 404 B.C.E., the women of Athens deny sex to their husbands until peace is declared. At a time when women of both warring city-states had no say in political affairs, we see men forced to struggle when power and sex become competing drives. The women treat the men as grown-up children, and the boycott eventually proves successful.

Sex and war, constants in human history, allow *Lysistrata* to remain a comedy that speaks to many historical moments. The comparison of Athens, a dominant power at the time, to the United States' position today as a world power, makes an eloquent parallel. As those left at home weigh the cost of war against its benefits, the play's concern with the drain on governmental coffers and the loss of human life that inevitably accompany war remain relevant.

Lysistrata chooses laughter as a means of addressing serious issues. It brings the terms of political debate down to a basic human level, and champions the idea that sex, pleasure, and procreation should win out over war, destitution, and death.

In this church in Japan, non-actors take part in a play reading of Aristophanes' ancient comedy *Lysistrata* in solidarity with groups around the world coordinated by The *Lysistrata* Project's antiwar effort.
Courtesy of the Documentary Film Operation Lysistrata *by Michael Patrick Kelly*

dling a teddy bear while his obsessed military leaders ordered nuclear strikes on Iraq. Satire is often disrespectful and without sympathy for its subjects.

Successful satirists provoke the wrath of individuals and institutions. Nobel prize–winning playwright and actor Dario Fo (b. 1926) has spent a lifetime writing scathing satire attacking religion, family, law enforcement, and politicians, taking most of his topics from current events (see Photo 4.5). His plays expose the hypocrisy and corruption of our times, and they have earned him the scorn of the powerful figures and institutions he attacks. The United States denied him a visa until protests by American artists forced the government to reconsider. His performances have been the victim of protests, bomb threats, police raids, censorship, and lawsuits, but always play to sold-out theatres, proving the power of satire to unsettle its targets and please its audience.

Challenges and Choices

Are some subjects taboo for comic treatment? Is laughter always at someone else's expense?

Situation Comedy

Unlike satire, situation comedies do not rely on topical humor and often revolve around eternal social problems such as business and financial disputes or family conflicts—husband versus wife or mother-in-law, father and son with conflicting goals, rivals competing for an ingenue's hand. As such they are plays for all eras. Such comedies often turn on a ridiculous premise, and chance or accident lead to plot complications. Mistaken identity, hidden lovers, eavesdropping, and misunderstood conversations can make characters behave in absurd ways that create a snowball effect of confusion. The chaos is happily resolved in a comic *denouement* where errors of perception are corrected, true love finds its course, and all is forgiven.

This comic form originated with the Greek Middle and New Comedy during the fourth and third centuries B.C.E., when an Athens destroyed by war turned to safer subjects. Comedy became a popular form, and the public demand for new plays forced writers to rely on these plot formulas. Plautus (c. 254–184 B.C.E.), the popular Roman writer, used these Greek plots with Roman stock characters.

Situation comedies played in every era with writers adding and subtracting elements to appeal to the popular audiences of their times. Today this form is the basis for weekly television sitcoms.

Farce

Despite its high entertainment value, farce is often denigrated as a low form of comedy because of its reliance on broad slapstick humor, extreme situations, and superficial characterization. Intricate, carefully planned plots are woven out of compounded misunderstandings and coincidences, and characters encounter obstacles that become so enormous and accumulate at such a rate that they are sent into ridiculous social and physical contortions to overcome them. The audience suspends its disbelief and accepts the far-fetched premise that sets the plot in motion, usually in some familiar social setting, be it living room, bedroom, or boardroom. Each farce develops an internal logic of its own that keeps the action moving. In fact, the breakneck speed at which farce is played sustains the illogical logic of the plot and prevents characters from untangling the con-

Photo 4.6
Comic mix-ups and sexual escapades lead to embarrassing situations in farce as in this scene from Michael Frayn's *Noises Off,* in which the backstage relationships in a theatrical company intrude on onstage performances. Natalie Walter as Brooke Ashton and Stephen Mangan as Garry Lejeune; director, Jeremy Sams; set design, Rob Jones; lighting, Tim Mitchell; at the Piccadilly Theatre, London.
© HELLESTAD RUNE/CORBIS SYGMA

Photo 4.7
Oscar Wilde's plays satirized the attitudes, fashions, and deportment of the upper classes of his time. In this production of *An Ideal Husband,* the characters' elite social manners are expressed not only through Wilde's witty dialogue but also through the characters' stiff physical bearing, through the frills and feathers of the costumes, and the dainty balancing of teacups. Director, Peter Hall. Ethel Barrymore Theatre, New York.
© *Joan Marcus*

fused web in which they are caught. Because farce's characters are trapped in extreme situations, character is realized as a response to the situation and not from in-depth psychological portraits. The joy of farce is derived from the characters' ability to meet the overwhelming challenges they face and survive. Reading a farce reveals little of its theatrical energy because farce is an actor's medium, relying on physical virtuosity and exquisite timing. It is perhaps the most difficult form of comedy to stage.

Although elements of farce can be seen in Greek comedy, the form developed during the Roman era. In the medieval period, the foolishness of human nature on display in farce provided a respite from religious drama. Although early farces focused on buffoonery, as the form evolved, it developed plot complexities.

Today farce usually centers around the suspected violation of fundamental social taboos. Endless threats to the sanctity of marriage are set out in what we have come to call *bedroom farce.* Several French playwrights—Victorien Sardou, Eugène Labiche (1815–1888), and Georges Feydeau (1862–1921)—were masters of this form. Upright bourgeois families loose their decorum when they are caught in seemingly compromising situations. They struggle through manic scenes in which several characters are hidden under beds or in closets, in order to hold their marriages intact. Because farce releases repressed energy as we chafe under society's rules and obligations, it is harder to write farce as the rules relax. Recent successful farces such as Joe Orton's (1933–1967) *What the Butler Saw* (1969), Michael Frayn's *Noises Off* (1985), and Alan Ayckbourn's *Comic Potential* (2000) are British and reflect the need to escape the tighter structure of that society.

Romantic Comedy

Romantic comedy centers around the relationship between two sympathetic young lovers whose destiny in marriage meets with obstacles to fulfillment. The intervening force can be an overbearing parent, a jealous former lover, or life's adversities. The young pair are always appealing, and we root for the fulfillment of the relationship. These plays always end in consummation of the promised love in marriage. Many of Shakespeare's comedies fall into this category—*As You Like It, Twelfth Night, Much Ado About Nothing,* and *Loves' Labour's Lost* all follow the travails of young love. The form derives from the tradition of the Greek New Comedy and Roman comedy whose plots often turned on thwarted love.

IN PERSPECTIVE

MOLIÈRE (1622–1673): PUSHING THE BOUNDARIES OF COMIC FORMS

Molière, born Jean-Baptiste Poquelin, is the undisputed comic genius of the Western theatre. Comedy, more than other genres, lives in performance, and so it is no accident that Molière was a great actor before he was a great play-wright. He knew what could get a laugh, he knew how to work an audience, and he put his comedian's bag of tricks into his plays, writing himself some great roles along the way. He mastered all the comic forms of his time using every comic device from the broadest slapstick to the sub-tlest wit, and he created a modern concept of comedy that has shaped how we think about the genre to this day.

The improvised Italian *commedia dell'arte* and the medieval French farce were the most popular forms when Molière left the law and a secure bourgeois life for the theatre in 1643. These popular forms relied on formulaic plots and physical humor and had superficial characters who were either pawns in the dramatic ac-tion or stock types for whom the audience had little emotional empathy. Molière's early plays borrowed the plots, but began a search for the essential human ele-ment that could add another dimension to these old forms. The comic buffoon in his hands became the poignant fool at whose foibles we could laugh while simultaneously feeling the pain of his humiliation or defeat. The portraits he drew became increasingly complex. Many of the plays of his later years reversed the plot-driven comic formula that ruled since ancient Greece and were character driven, the plot unfolding as a result of the characters' obsessions. Clumsy resolu-tions mar the plots of many of his plays, but clearly character, not plot, was his focus.

Blind to the ridiculousness of their own behavior, Molière's characters send the world into a spin to fulfill their drives and needs. There are usually moments of comeuppance when characters are forced to confront themselves and the disorder their behavior has caused. Their social masks slip, and we see their suffering and are aware of the pain beneath our laughter. The world is set right in the end, but unlike other forms of comedy, the character may not find happiness unless self-understanding is gained, adding the recognition mo-ment of tragedy to the comic form. Molière revealed his audiences to themselves and often he paid the price of public outrage for making people see too much too well.

Molière was a satirist of his times. In Molière's com-edy of manners, efforts toward conformity with false social values are exposed and ridiculed by first portray-ing these in the extreme. Pretentious bourgeoisie, reli-gious hypocrites, manipulative patriarchs, and arrogant nobles populate his plays, and scandal often followed when portraits were too closely drawn. *Tartuffe*, his play about religious hypocrisy, was banned and set off a five-year public dispute from 1664 to 1669 that em-broiled the archbishop of Paris, the Senate, the papal emissary, and King Louis XIV, his faithful champion, with Molière prevailing in the end at the expense of his finances and his health. This came on the heels of the scandal surrounding *School for Wives*, which de-spite its box office success was deemed a mockery of family, marriage, and religion. Molière answered his critics with another play, *The Critique of School for Wives*, setting off a cycle of outrage.

School for Wives is constructed around the character of Arnolphe, so fearful that he will be a cuckold that he raises a girl from infancy to be his ideal wife. He keeps her locked away and ignorant of all worldly matters so she can never stray from him. Despite Arnolphe's best efforts at

---

Elizabethan comedy also reflected the conventions of medieval courtly love, in which wooing was a ritualized art. These plays are not a laugh a minute like farce, but offer light-hearted fun, usually spoofing courtship rituals or showing them gone awry. Our involve-ment comes from romantic and fantasied identification with the promise of love fulfilled.

Comedy of Manners

Sometimes comedy questions social norms by portraying behavior that reflects those norms in the extreme. Comedy of manners makes fun of ridiculous social mores or prac-tices and the people who engage in them. It holds a magnifying glass to the comportment of the privileged (concern with manners is a luxury not afforded the poor) and derives

complete control, the girl discovers true love elsewhere and turns on him. The play ends as a romantic comedy in marriage between the two young lovers, but the broken Arnolphe is left to face his own foolish quest for domination of another's will, and we see his sullen specter simultaneously with the happy romantic resolution.

In *The Misanthrope*, the central character Alceste turns virtue into a vice, driven by obsessive belief in the rightness of his values. He mocks the hypocrisy of his social world with such insensitivity that he ends isolated and alone, reviled by society and spurned by the woman he loves. We laugh at his excess until his bitter end when

Alceste's character drives the play past the easy comic *denouement* into emotional ambiguity, pushing the limits of the comic form itself.

Running through Molière's plays is the idea that balance is a necessary part of the natural order of the world and must be established in the psyche and society. Attempts to deprive others of their right to self-fulfillment upset this order and will end in disaster, even for men who intervene with women's natural desires, an early feminist principle. His plays pushed comedy past the light entertainment of his day into probing studies of human excess. He created the comedy of character that is the hallmark of most comedy today. His style was imitated in the English Restoration, but not equaled. Molière set the bar higher for all comic playwrights to come.

In this famous scene from Molière's *Tartuffe*, Tartuffe (Henry Goodman), who pretends to be a pious man, tries to seduce Elmire (Kathryn Meisle), the wife of his unsuspecting host Orgon. Unknown to Tartuffe, Elmire has hidden Orgon under the table to witness Tartuffe's lechery and betrayal firsthand. Orgon, refusing to believe his eyes and ears, does not intervene until his wife's honor is almost fully compromised. This comic moment is eclipsed by a near catastrophic outcome for the family. They are saved by the King's intervention. The royal messenger appears as a *deus ex machina* at the end of the play to restore moral order. Directed by Joe Dowling for the Roundabout Theatre Company, New York.
© *Joan Marcus*

its humor from pointed portraits of the contemporary trendy society and the artifices it accepts as a norm. Comedy of manners relies on its audience's familiarity with expected social custom among the elite, or would-be elite. It uses exaggeration and caricature, clever language, wit, and social repartee, and presents the actions and language of people in a social environment that is self-satisfied and distorted in its values. Walk into any New York gallery opening and find the ingredients for a contemporary comedy of manners where a cast of trendy characters fresh from the health club or spa, dressed in black with slightly punk hair, sipping good wine, and discussing the latest independent films and celebrities they know reflects the shallow values behind their behavior. Recent plays such as Yasmina Reza's *Art* (1994) or Douglas Carter Beane's *As Bees in Honey Drown* (1997) focus on this scene and serve as comedies of manners for our times.

The French playwright Molière is usually credited as the inventor of this genre when he depicted the pretentious individuals he encountered in the court of Louis XIV (1638–1717) and the world of the Parisian bourgeoisie who aspired to be like them. *The Learned Ladies* provides a humorous portrait of women of the period whose ultra-refined behavior and intellectual pretensions are belied by their baser instincts. The great comic playwrights of the English Restoration such as William Congreve (1670–1729) and George Wycherly (1640–1715), and later writers such as Richard Brinsley Sheridan, all wrote in this vein. Oscar Wilde (1854–1900) may be the undisputed master of the form (see Photo 4.7). The British upper class and those who aspired to it provided endless fodder for his searing wit. *The Importance of Being Ernest* draws on all the comic devices and is a masterpiece of the form.

The difficulty of fitting all plays into neat categories is apparent as we try to place the work of George Bernard Shaw (1856–1950). Beyond just presenting a portrait of the social excesses he witnessed, Shaw seemed to go further as he questioned the cultural institutions that permitted such behavior. Clearly interested in exposing the social vices of his era, Shaw's plays stand apart from other comedies of manners because of his desire to provide a corrective for social ills and a vision for change. His plays are often referred to as *comedies of ideas.*

Tragicomedy

Experience reveals that we rarely live life through a singular lens. Human existence is marked by loss—loss of youth, loss of health, loss of love and fortune, and eventually, loss of life itself. Yet despite our awareness of this sober fact, we continue on in the hope that we can overcome the inevitable outcome. We celebrate each victory and savor the memory of each triumph, but in the end, every significant moment of our existence, when viewed from a larger perspective, is bittersweet. Tragicomedy is the genre that captures the simultaneity of our anguish and our joy.

To the many generations before us who lived in structured societies with rigid social orders and the human position in the cosmos clearly defined, this simultaneous experience of anguish and joy did not seem so obvious. When an entire society believed that gods controlled fate, or that a better life awaited us in the hereafter, the futility of our optimism and our struggle was not apparent. So tragedy could celebrate our heroism, and comedy could rejoice in our ability to overcome. As societies grew more complex, as more voices were heard in the era following democratic revolutions, the idea of a single worldview and value structure that could give meaning to life became a remnant of the past when gods and kings ruled our lives. The modern era questioned God, religion, and government, repudiating the secure value systems of the past and engaging in the elusive quest for meaning we find in tragicomedy.

The first use of the term *tragicomedy* occurred circa 195 B.C.E. in *Amphitryo,* a comedy by Plautus (254–184 B.C.E.) in which the god Mercury appears in the prologue and addresses the audience:

> Are you disappointed to find it's a tragedy? Well, I can easily change it. I'm a god, after all. I can easily make it a comedy and never alter a line. Is that what you'd like? . . . I'll meet you half way and make it a tragicomedy. It can't be outright comedy, I'm afraid, with all these kings and gods in the cast.[3]

---

3. Plautus, *The Rope and Other Plays,* trans. E. F. Watling (Penguin Classics, 1964), 230. Copyright © E. F. Watling, 1964. Reproduced by permission of Penguin Books Ltd.

Although Plautus is clearly mocking the rigidity of the imposed forms, and the absurdity of tragicomedy, he has captured something significant. He can change a tragedy to a comedy "and never alter a line" because the difference between the genres is not so much what happens, but our perspective on the events.

Plautus anticipated an error in historical discussions of tragicomedy. It has sometimes been viewed as a hybrid form—a cocktail of elements of tragedy and comedy. A tragedy with scenes of comic relief and a comedy with melodrama, or a serious drama with a happy ending and a comedy with sentimentality, are not automatically tragicomedies. This genre is not a little of this and a little of that. It has its own particular ironic perspective on life that simultaneously perceives the opposing elements of comedy and tragedy as coexisting in a dramatic tension at all times.

For centuries, theatrical conventions demanded purity of form. Tragedies and comedies had their proper endings and characters. Yet playwrights always broke the rules. They sensed the fundamental irony of the human condition and from the time of ancient Greece the great dramatists expressed it. Several of Euripides' (480–406 B.C.E.) plays do not fit neatly into the tragic form, and Molière pushed the comic genre in plays like *Tartuffe*, in which villainy threatens permanent harm to family love and order, and for a moment holds control. The play takes us to the brink of tragedy and then rights itself back into comedy. Many of Shakespeare's later plays mixed genres and placed happy endings on plays that in every other way seemed like tragedies. *The Tempest*, which begins as a revenge play, presents a portrait of the evil men can do. Yet Miranda, marooned on a desert island and knowing no man other than her father, proclaims upon first sight of men, "How beauteous mankind is. O brave new world that has such people in't." Her father, Prospero, replies, "T'is new to thee."[4]—a line filled with ironic commentary on her innocent mistaken perception. We laugh at the line, although we know it holds a bitter truth. This perception of dual truths makes these plays feel contemporary to us today. Plays such as *Measure for Measure* and *All's Well that Ends Well*, with happy endings on disturbing tales, were labeled "the problem plays." Serious drama that mixes in comic elements always has some explaining to do.

From the seventeenth century on, increasing numbers of plays broke with neoclassical rules for genre, and labels were sought to describe these forms. *Tearful comedy, sentimental comedy*, the French *drame*, or serious drama, were all proffered as descriptions. Most of these plays were hybrid forms and not tragicomedies in the modern sense, but their burgeoning numbers indicated evolving changes in values and perceptions in the larger society that led to dramatists seeking forms other than the comic and tragic.

Modern Tragicomedy

By the late nineteenth century, two opposing movements converged to create what came to be the dominant genre of the twentieth century, modern tragicomedy. **Naturalism** sought to paint a realistic stage picture of life as it is lived, rejecting tragedy and comedy as inadequate expressions of the experience of daily life, in which purity of genre is never found. **Symbolism**, opposed the naturalists' search for meaning in the concrete objects of the world and felt that truth lay in a metaphysical realm. Tragicomedy offered a form that could unite both visions. Anton Chekhov (1860–1904), the great Russian dramatist of the turn of the twentieth century, creates a synthesis of styles and tragicomedy is realized as a clearly defined genre.

Chekhov's plays puzzled the public of his time. They do not possess the kind of central action we discussed in climactic structure, nor are they episodic. They are dramas of inaction; they dramatize the human condition as Chekhov saw it—lonely,

---

4. William Shakespeare, *The Tempest*, V, 1, 183–184.

Artists

IN PERSPECTIVE

WILLIAM SHAKESPEARE: CROSSING GENRES

William Shakespeare (1564–1616) is undisputedly the greatest dramatist of all times, and his plays, translated into every major language, continue to move audiences around the world and challenge actors and directors of every caliber. Shakespeare wrote over thirty plays, borrowing from many sources including historical chronicles, classical tales, legends, and contemporary ballads. His poetic language, compelling portraits, and deep understanding of human behavior are some of the hallmarks of his creative genius. Yet despite these achievements, he has been assailed by some critics through the ages for his violation of genre categories.

Shakespeare mastered the conventional genres of his era, moving with ease among tragedy, comedy, history, and romance. His plays all combine humor and darkness using one to comment on the other through characters and subplots. The sardonic commentary Hamlet offers in the grave digger scene in which he meditates humorously on the lives once led by those reduced to bones and dust is a comic reminder of our inevitable end and of the tragic finish to the play.

In many of his later plays, starting with *Hamlet*, Shakespeare went beyond the mix of comic and tragic elements of his earlier works into dramas that truly defy categorization. The comic and tragic do not just inhabit the same plays as thematic echoes. They seem to coexist in each moment and to threaten each other's worlds.

Measure for Measure (1604) is an expression of this uncertain universe, and an example of what scholars have labeled the "problem plays." The Duke of Vienna, having reigned poorly over his people and permitted social problems to take root, understands the need for re-

form. Fearing he would lose popularity among his people were he to strictly enforce the laws, he pretends to leave town, putting the authoritarian Angelo in charge. Angelo imposes a moral regime, arresting petty criminals and closing down the brothels. Angelo sentences Claudio to death for impregnating Juliet, Claudio's own fiancée. When Claudio's sister Isabella, a nun, pleads for her brother's life, Angelo, in a moment of passion, demands that she offer her virginity to him as the price of a pardon. Claudio, fearing death, tries to convince his sister to sacrifice her honor in exchange for his life. The Duke, disguised as a monk, plays master puppeteer, substituting another prisoner to be executed in Claudio's place, and another woman, Mariana, once betrothed to Angelo, to go to his bed in place of Isabella. The Duke reveals himself; Angelo confesses and must marry Mariana. Claudio is forgiven and must marry Juliet. Lucio, who committed slander against the Duke, must marry a whore. And the Duke takes Isabella, the novitiate, for his bride. The play in typical comic form ends with four marriages, but atypically for comedy, none brings much cause for celebration.

Unlike medieval allegorical figures of Good and Evil and the Elizabethan embodiment of these ideas in three-dimensional characters, no character in this play can be labeled good or evil. The Duke, a basically good man, does not have the strength of his convictions because of his desire for public adulation. Angelo, the leader of impeccable moral standards, demonstrates that excess of good can lead to bad decisions, and that even he can be overcome by his passion. Isabella, the self-righteous religious figure, is cold and unfeeling and willing to sacrifice another woman in her place. Claudio is a coward and will sacrifice honor rather than his life. The violation of genre distinctions enabled Shakespeare to explore new dimensions of character.

uncomprehending, locked in self-ignorance, and doomed to failure. "Life," said Chekhov, "is an insoluble problem."[5] There can be no facile *denouement*. His first productions led to misunderstandings between him and the great director Constantin Stanislavski (1863–1938), who Chekhov believed did not fully understand the ironic comedy of his plays, but instead saw them as serious drama. Chekhov's work portrays a self-indulgent Russian aristocracy living unaware of the changes that would eventually transform their lives and Russia. There is a palpable clairvoyant vision of the coming Russian Revolution of 1917. These are dramas of disappointment and frustration. No one can find love and artistic fulfillment in *The Seagull*, although all the characters are searching for it. Everyone in *Uncle Vanya* ends in despair or resignation, and the cherry orchard, the central

---

5. Robert Corrigan, *The Theatre in Search of a Fix* (Delacorte Press, 1973), 125–126.

The Elizabethans, accustomed to genre violations, still found these plays perplexing. Many, influenced by the rules of neoclassical decorum, decried the mixing of tragic and comic elements common in the Elizabethan theatre. Philip Sidney, a contemporary of Shakespeare, referred to these mixed genres as "mongrel-tragi-comedy."[1] Continental European critics, accustomed to tragedies that followed the rules, believed Shakespeare was catering to the vulgar tastes of his audience. The French writer Voltaire spoke of "the barbarous irregularities"[2] in *Julius Caesar* and called Shakespeare a full-fledged prolific genius without a shred of good taste or the smallest understanding of the rules [of dramatic genre].[3]

The late eighteenth century and early nineteenth century romantics embraced Shakespeare's rejection of the rules, and saw instead a picture of nature's truth, which does not follow categorization. By the end of the nineteenth century, as the romantic impulse faded, scholars were again questioning these perplexing mixtures of forms, but now the attitude toward mixed genres changes. This is the moment that modern tragicomedy is conceived to address the malaise of life in the twentieth century, so Shakespeare's combining of comic and tragic visions seems to reflect the modern temperament. Critics now attempt to understand the impact of comic resolutions in serious dramas on the content of these plays. Was Shakespeare intentionally mixing genres to shape a play's meaning? Was he questioning the Elizabethan world and its hierarchies? Was he deliberately showing us a world with unclear boundaries and moral ambiguity where the good do evil and the evil can do good?

When we look at the complexity of these later plays, it is hard to believe that Shakespeare was simply writing to popular tastes or was undisciplined. Elizabeth I was dead. The Puritans were banging the drum for moral rectitude. He perhaps foresaw the strict rule of the Puritans that would come in 1642 and beyond that to the moral freedom Charles II would bring to England when restored to the throne in 1660. Perhaps he just saw the essence of human nature. People and their life experiences do not fit in neat categories, and neither do plays about them if the theatre is to present true portraits.

1. *Sir Philip Sidney,* Defense of Poesy, *ed. Lincoln Soens (Lincoln: University of Nebraska Press, 1970), 49.*
2. *Voltaire,* Oeuvres Complètes, *Volume 1 (Paris: Garnier Frères, 1877), 316.*
3. *Ibid., Volume 22,* Lettres Philosophiques, *Letter XVIII, "Sur la Tragédie," 146.*

In this scene from Shakespeare's *Measure for Measure* at the Joseph Papp Public Theater in New York, the novitiate Isabella bemoans her predicament. Directed by Mary Zimmerman.
© *Michal Daniel, 2001*

symbol of the characters' lives in the play by that name, is lost. In the gap between the characters' aspirations and dreams and their futile attempts at realization lies the tragic-comic truth of the self-deception that underlies our existence.

Luigi Pirandello (1867–1936), the great Italian playwright, explored the metaphysical meanings of tragicomedy. Seeing life as a struggle for permanence and meaningful identity in a world governed by time and change, he questioned the very nature of reality as we know it. In his plays, characters are trapped in the social masks they wear to hold onto a sense of stable identity. In the end they are mocked by time and appear comic in their attempt to change their fate. In his famous essay "Umorismo," he describes the old woman who dyes her hair red and cakes on makeup to hold onto a lover or a philandering husband. Her battle against the ravages of time appear both tragic in her desperation and comic in her execution.

Challenges and Choices

Can any subject be treated through any genre? Is it just a matter of point of view, or do some subjects inherently appeal to a particular treatment?

Again and again, throughout the era of modernism in the twentieth century, playwrights brought new perspectives to tragicomedy. Many movements in the visual arts and the development of psychology turned the artist's lens inward. As symbolism reacted to naturalism by exploring the meanings to be found in sensory and metaphysical experiences outside the rational narrative, **expressionism** sought to project characters' inner emotional reality onto the objects of the physical world. **Surrealism**, inspired by Freudian psychology, mined the unconscious for images that expressed the haunting truth of our hidden problems and desires. Following the destruction of World War I, movements such as **dada** and **futurism** questioned old authority systems that gave rise to human devastation and projected a world of randomness without the chain of causality found in traditional stories. Each of these movements expressed the force of the irrational in human affairs, which was captured visually in stage design. (See Chapter 11.)

In the post–World War II era, the Holocaust and the atom bomb seemed to confirm that dark irrational forces were in control of a godless world. Tragicomedy grew increasingly dark and pessimistic, describing a senseless world where human beings could no longer communicate because they were surrounded by a void of meaninglessness, a philosophy summed up in **existentialism**. The plays of this period were logical extensions of the tragicomic vision put forth by Chekhov and Pirandello, shorn of the trappings of realistic stagecraft. In *Waiting for Godot*, discussed in the last chapter, Beckett took Chekhov's drama of inaction a step further. Waiting could now be the subject of a play. Characters wait for Godot all throughout the play, yet simultaneously wonder how they will recognize him even if he should come. This is the tragicomic setup of the play. Gone are the trappings of introspection. These characters are acknowledged clowns caught in the impasse of life. There is no way out, save death, and no way to self-realization in life. We watch and wonder in terror at our own lives, our own illusions. This dramatizes the tragicomic paradox: our laughter at others in our plight only heightens our tragic sense of our own existence.

elodrama

When we watch a melodrama, we root for the hero, we boo the villain, we fear for helpless victims in distress, and in the end we weep for joy at a providential and happy resolution to horrific events. Melodrama speaks directly to our emotions. It stages our deepest, if sometimes unrealistic, anxieties and then appeases them with idealized endings in which vice is always punished and virtue duly rewarded. Melodrama is an easily accessible, popular genre, that finds its roots in the eighteenth century, but is still available to us today in the form of soap operas, westerns, and horror movies. It is characterized primarily by three crowd-pleasing qualities: simplicity, sensationalism, and sentimentality.

In contrast to tragedy, melodrama describes an emotionally satisfying and simplistic moral world. Characters are not complex or conflicted. They are simply good or bad. The disasters that visit good people are the result of outside forces beyond their control—usually the evil machinations of a villain—but do not come from any flaws within themselves. The heroes of melodrama do not bear moral responsibility for the woes that beset them, but are instead victims of circumstance or foul play. Their innately good characteristics, and the generous or noble actions they take in the face of distress, provide motivation enough for the eventual good fortune that comes their way, leaving them blessed with riches, admiration, and other rewards. The villains of melodrama are rarely drawn to elicit sympathy. Motivated by greed, anger, or other vices, they perpetrate wrongdoings on innocent folks. There are few mitigating circumstances here, few insights into character that would serve to justify or pardon their notorious actions.

The struggle of good against evil is cast in extremes of nightmarish horrors and worst-case scenarios. Villains go to unimaginable lengths to terrorize and antagonize their victims, just as natural and economic disasters compound to put characters in the direst of circumstances. Melodrama allows us to experience our worst fears in all their excess with the knowledge that somehow things will be put to rights in the end.

On the nineteenth-century stage, melodrama tapped into the audience's emotions by allowing them to experience disaster in overwhelming and immediate theatrical forms. Masterful special effects—floods, avalanches, and collapsing bridges—all took place right before the audience's eyes. Theatres competed for crowds by developing new technology, just as we see in the movie industry today. Sometimes the ingenious perfection of a new special effect would require the writing of a new play to display it.

In the face of these disasters, simple and heartfelt emotions toward loved ones—family, friends, innocent children—are signs of grace and of human connections that in the end outweigh strife. Melodrama elicits tears, both on stage and in the audience. Typical scenarios include a mother separated from and then reunited with her children, or lovers forced to part only to find each other again. In a morally simple world, tears and deep sentiment help distinguish the virtuous from the duplicitous.

One of the roots of melodrama is found in a device invented by Jean-Jacques Rousseau (1712–1778) around 1762, for a monologue he wrote called "Pygmalion," in which he used music to express the character's emotions. Unlike opera, here music was not sung but underscored silence and reflected the dramatic content and the character's mood at the moment. We can still find this use of music on stage, screen, and television, and few movies today do not use a musical score to augment the emotional impact of dramatic action.

In Germany the term *melodrama* was originally used to designate a passage in opera in which words were spoken and accompanied by music, rather than sung. Rousseau's device influenced other writers, including the German poet and dramatist Friedrich Schiller, who used it in his play *The Robbers*. In the end it was a Frenchman, René Guilbert de Pixérécourt (1773–1844), who popularized a new kind of performance that combined lurid tales from the newspapers with music between the dialogue and came to be called, in French, *mélodie drame* or melodrama. His first success was *Les Petits Auvegnats* in 1797, followed by two more productions that dramatized sensationalist novels of the day. He addressed a popular, uneducated audience, catering to their desire for special effects, emotional extravagance, and moralism.

Melodrama traveled to England and America and became the most popular theatrical form of the nineteenth century. It played to the working-class populations drawn to the cities to meet the needs of the industrial revolution. The simple ideals of melodrama responded to the public's nostalgic longing for the past and a more comprehensible world in the face of widespread social and economic distress caused by displacement and

Challenges and Choices

Must all successful theatre combine emotional appeal with intellectual content, or can good theatre play to either the emotions or the intellect?

Photo 4.9
The slave Eliza and her baby son's daring and dangerous escape to freedom across a frozen river as captured in a lithograph engraved by Charles Bour (1814–1881) from the book *Uncle Tom's Cabin* by Harriet Beecher Stowe (1811–1896). Tense, dramatic, and emotional scenes such as this made Beecher Stowe's book an excellent source of melodrama for the nineteenth-century stage.
© *Historical Picture Archive/CORBIS*

the effects of unregulated capitalism. Melodrama's focus on evil as an external force also helped people feel free from responsibility for the growing social problems around them. The happy endings provided hope to the underclass that flocked to the theatre for these plays.

The urban poverty that resulted from rapid industrialization was an international phenomenon. One of the early popular melodramas, a hit both in America and abroad, was *The Poor of New York*, performed at New York's Wallack's Theatre in 1857. The play depicted the sad plight of urban families living in poverty. Different accounts of the journey of this play exist, but it was probably first performed in Paris as *Les Pauvres de Paris* (*The Poor of Paris*) in 1856, and then was retitled and adapted to fit each city in which it was performed. In 1864 Dion Boucicault (1822–1890) adapted it as *The Poor of Liverpool* and *The Streets of London* incorporating local issues in each version. Melodramas clearly expressed the problems of the poor everywhere.

Easily one of the most popular American melodramas of all time was *Uncle Tom's Cabin, or, Life Among the Lowly*, based on the novel by Harriet Beecher Stowe (1811–1896). The book, and its many theatrical incarnations, gripped the minds of Americans on the eve of the Civil War because of its dramatic plot and critical look at the institution of slavery. The slave Eliza's forced separation from her husband and son, her dangerous escape north to freedom with a babe in her arms (see Photo 4.9), the violence of the villainous slave master Simon Legree, and the simple sincerity of Uncle Tom and Little Eva all provided the excitement, emotion, and sentiment audiences demanded. At this play, white Americans confronted the most pressing issue of their day in a way that was vivid and personal. Its success continued long after the war, and in the 1890s four hundred companies were performing some version of the story of Uncle Tom.

Today the word *melodrama* is often used in a derogatory manner to conjure images of contrived sentimental and emotional stories. Nonetheless, this genre's ability to contact our anxieties and fears, to show us an ideal world where good and bad are easily discerned and in which each is given its due still absorbs us today, and appeals to our deepest urge to feel that the world, even at its worst, is under the control of benevolent forces.

Genre Today

Today traditional genre categories no longer dictate what playwrights create; they may even inspire rebellion or innovation. Nevertheless, genres still give us a convenient framework through which we can approach dramatic material as readers and as theatregoers. Our local video store arranges films by genres taken from the theatre such as drama, romantic comedy, or today's melodramas—horror, sci-fi, and western—to give us some general indication of what kind of emotional experience we will have: whether we will be moved or frightened, whether we will laugh or cry. We still ask before we buy a ticket to the theatre whether we are off to a comedy or a serious drama, a romantic story, or an existential examination of life, and then prepare ourselves for the experience to come.

 ## KEY IDEAS

- Society categorizes theatrical genres or categories of drama according to its habits and cultural values; therefore, the types of plays and performances we encounter outside our own culture may be puzzling to us.
- In the European tradition genre refers to the emotional response a play engenders, rather than to its dramatic form.
- Tragedy is philosophical, while comedy is pragmatic. Tragedy defines our place in the grand scheme of things; comedy shows us how to deal with the here and now.
- Tragedy dramatizes our struggle against the limits of human power. Because the tragic hero assumes responsibility for the drama's chain of events, tragedy embodies a moral lesson.
- Modern tragedy shows that all people, not just characters of nobility, can be the subject of tragedy, and that the essence of the tragic experience lies with an individual's readiness to sacrifice everything to maintain personal dignity.
- Comedy celebrates our ability to overcome life's setbacks. It rejoices in regeneration, with fools and clowns representing the forces of renewal. Comedy is a corrective for social and personal behavior.
- Tragicomedy captures the simultaneity of anguish and joy in the human condition. It gives an ironic perspective on life, perceiving the comic and tragic in a constant dramatic tension.
- The world of melodrama is emotionally satisfying and sentimental. It presents simplistic divisions between good and evil, and vice is always punished and virtue always triumphs.
- Traditional genre categories no longer dictate what playwrights create, but they still provide a framework to help us categorize dramatic material.

Performance Traditions
Legacy and Renewal

In *Shibaraku,* one of the eighteen favorite plays of the Ichikawa *kabuki* family, the hero Kamakura Gongoro Kagemasa (a role created by Ichikawa Danjuro I) arrives to save the day dressed in the largest costume on the *kabuki* stage. Note the actor's rough-style makeup. The stage assistants dressed in black, following convention, are read as invisible as they help unfurl the sleeves in full view of the audience. The white designs on the red *kimono* sleeves, when fully displayed, show the actor's family crest, drawing attention to both the actor and the role.

© Michael S. Yamashita/CORBIS

Indian Sanskrit Theatre

The Theory of *Rasa*

Performance Conventions

Sanskrit Plays

Kutiyattam and *Kathakali*

Mime and the Commedia dell'Arte Tradition

The Mime Tradition in Antiquity

The Birth of *Commedia dell'Arte*

The *Commedia* Form

The Evolution of *Commedia*

Japanese Traditions

The *Noh* Theatre

Kyōgen

Kabuki

Chinese Opera

Makeup and Costume

Movement and Music

The Twentieth Century and Beyond

Carnival Tradition

Carnival's European Origins

African Influence in Colonial Latin America and the Caribbean

Carnival as Political Street Theatre

Carnival Adapts and Evolves

Puppet Traditions around the Globe

Puppets and Ritual

Puppets and the Popular Voice

Puppets and Written Texts

Puppetry in the Twentieth Century and Today

Traditions Evolve

Performance traditions can be found in almost every culture. Some have become attached to written texts; others leave little tangible evidence of their form and live through memory and inherited practice. All performance forms are impermanent and alter through time. Great performers leave their personal mark, and forms adapt to social change and audience demands. A tradition is a living thing, and like everything vital in this world, it must evolve to survive.

Performance traditions tend to present a heightened theatricality through the integration of music, dance, movement, masks, and elaborate makeup and costumes that create a total sensory experience for the audience. Today's theatre artists increasingly turn to ancient forms as a source of inspiration and training. The practice of looking to another age or another place for roots of renewal does not belong to our age alone. As we saw in the last chapter, the Renaissance looked to the golden age of antiquity in Greece and Rome for theatrical models. In the same way, modernists looked to Asia and the *commedia dell'arte*, which is presented in this chapter, for acting techniques. In our postmodern era of global cultural homogenization, this time of technology and unknown possibilities, we look to celebrate diversity through traditions rooted in community and ritual, forms that can tie us to each other and to our spiritual selves. The course of cultural history is marked by tradition and renewal, and the path to innovation is often through the past.

Every performance tradition has its own sets of conventions that influence acting, training, writing, design, and directing. Each also has its own history, but often there is

History IN PERSPECTIVE

PLOTTING HISTORY AND TRADITION

How do we recount history? In Chapter 3 we looked at the many ways playwrights tell their stories. History is also a kind of storytelling, and when we set out to tell a history of theatre and its development, we decide what should be told and then determine a structure to help arrange our points and express our perspective, just as playwrights do.

The events included in a history reflect what is valued by the historian or the culture. No history of any kind can be all inclusive, so subjective judgments are made as to what is of interest and worthy of study. Decisions about which histories to tell change over time. If you were to look at an American theatre history book written fifty years ago, you would find little attention paid to non-European or nontext traditions. Africa and South America might not even be mentioned, and the contributions of women and minorities would be marginalized.

The one important difference between the work of the playwright and the work of the historian is that history presumably tells a story based on facts. The very notion of a "fact" can be questioned, however, especially as we move back in time beyond living memory and written records. What some groups consider history, others might call myth and vice versa. The ancient Greek mythology we read today was history for the ancient Greeks, as were the epic tales of Homer, which we read today primarily as literature. Yet archeologists have found evidence that Homer's stories were based in fact. Some think of the events recorded in the Hebrew Bible and the New Testament as fact, searching for geological action that might account for the parting of the Red Sea in the story of Moses. Others regard such events as true miracles, while still others see them as inspired literary invention. The determination of "fact" is clearly subjective.

The models we use to express history reveal how we think about the subject at hand. One of the most common models for expressing a view of history is a time line. On a time line, events are located at specific dates or points in time. A time line resembles the Aristotelian dramatic structure, since it shows events in a singular, linear, continued progression. Important dates and events appear like the climaxes in the Aristotelian play as the result of a sequence of causally related events.

Some might argue that human development from birth to death necessarily gives us a linear view of time. This idea holds only if we regard birth as a beginning and

no clear point of origin. There are so many performance traditions around the world that it is difficult to select only a few representative models. The ones presented in this chapter are of particular interest because of their longevity, ubiquity, influence, or the strange journey they traveled.

Indian Sanskrit Theatre

The sophisticated, poetic theatrical form of Indian Sanskrit theatre flourished sometime between the first centuries before and after the common era. The specific dates and the historical background of the form are difficult to pin down, but the tradition traces a mythic origin to the god Brahma, who, at a time when the world was full of vice, took important parts of the four Hindu *Vedas*, or sacred texts, and combined them to create a fifth *Veda* called *natya* or "theatre." Unlike the other *Vedas*, this sacred performance would be available to people of every class and contain every kind of knowledge and art.

Sanskrit theatre developed elaborate codes of performance, but the plays survived divorced from a continuous performance tradition, leaving us only dramatic texts and what we know of the performance codes from a manuscript called the **Natyasastra**, which means "authoritative text on the theatre." Written sometime between 200 B.C.E. and 200 C.E., it is a veritable encyclopedia of information about theatre from the classi-

death as an end, but many cultures do not view time in this way. For the Yoruba of Nigeria, newborn babies are in a liminal state between this world and the one from which they have journeyed, and death is a process of journeying back to the other world again. Souls may make many journeys back and forth between the earthly realm and the other world, but each time they come bearing a different personality, and with each journey there is transformation.

A standard time line proves inadequate for representing many performance traditions that evolved over an extended period and had no specific moment of creation. This is especially true of traditions that reach back before written records. The word *tradition* itself evokes what has been continually handed down, rather than a moment of birth or inception. It implies something that has seemingly always existed. Even the *noh* theatre, which began in the work of Kannami and Zeami, evolved from other preexisting traditions.

When dates do exist for performance traditions, they are often approximate. In the case of the Sanskrit *Natyasastra*, dating of the text ranges over a period of four hundred years, from the second century B.C.E. to the second century C.E. Although the text proclaims itself to be written by Bharata, who inherited the tradition of Sanskrit drama directly from the god Brahma, it is obviously a compendium of what had to have already been well-established theatrical practices. Even if we knew the exact date of this text, it might not help us pinpoint the origins of the tradition it codifies.

No tradition is static. Performance forms naturally change as new performers take up the mantle and either through strong conviction or gentle refinement adapt the form to their own times and cultural interests. How do we determine when enough changes add up to something new? When does one form end and a new one begin?

Even traditions that have come and gone may continue to exert their influence on future generations in new and unpredictable ways. The *commedia dell'arte* resurfaced in silent film, vaudeville, cartoons, and today's situation comedies. In recent times the San Francisco Mime Troupe and others have created contemporary *commedias*. Traditions live on in their continued influence on new theatrical forms in new generations. Traditions may also be disseminated throughout a wide geographical region, dying out in one area even as they achieve a new vitality in another. Today's global communication has increased this phenomenon.

How can we historically map out the lives of theatrical traditions whose dates of origin are uncertain, whose vitality varies depending on time and place, whose forms evolve with each new generation, and whose longevity overshadows their significance at any single point in time? A standard time line fails to capture the reality and nuances of the lives, deaths, and rebirths of many performance traditions that have left us no tangible record of their trajectory. We are challenged to find new models to represent their historical evolution.

cal Sanskrit tradition. Although it is credited to the mythic sage Bharata, whose one hundred sons were said to be the first performers of *natya*, it is thought to be an accumulation of knowledge and performance rules based on already well-established theatre practices. This ancient text influences Indian theatre to this day.

Just as Aristotle's *Poetics* provides a lens through which to read and understand Western tragedy, the *Natyasastra*, the earliest critical writing in India, functions as a guide to understanding Sanskrit theatre and many subsequent Indian performance traditions that draw on its prescriptions. In contrast to the *Poetics*, the *Natyasastra* does not focus on the written play text, but addresses all aspects of production equally. It describes how actors should train for and perform a variety of role types, what kinds of makeup and costumes they should wear, what types of theatre spaces are appropriate for performances, and even what makes an ideal spectator. Influenced by the *Natyasastra*, discussion of theatre in India has not emphasized the centrality of the dramatic text as in Western countries. In India, as in many other Asian countries, the line between theatre and dance remains fluid, and most traditional theatre forms are performed to musical accompaniment. Indian classical dance forms such as *bharata natyam* and *odissi* have their roots in temple dances that blended the sacred and the sensual. Under British rule, these temple dances fell into disrepute. After independence, artists looked to the *Natyasastra* to help in their revival and reconstruction.

The Theory of *Rasa*

The *Natyasastra* introduces the idea of **rasa,** tastes or flavors that contrast and complement each other. Although they do not exactly correlate to Western genres, each *rasa* presents a different mood or feeling. A play should offer a mixture of *rasa*, and a good Sanskrit drama is expected to offer all eight of the *rasa* that the *Natyasastra* defines—love, mirth, sadness, wrath, vigor, the terrible, disgust, and the marvelous—although one *rasa*, or mood, should dominate. Theatre practitioners prepare a piece for their spectators as a master chef would make a sumptuous meal for a gourmet, mixing the flavors or *rasa*. They take care that the venue and atmosphere of the performance contribute to the overall effect. The theatre event is understood as an aesthetic moment that unites the theatre artists and the connoisseur. This is an aesthetic model that underlies many Indian performance traditions and highlights the important connection between performer and spectator.

According to the *Natyasastra*, the best theatrical events are those in which text, acting, music, and dance all combine to create multiple emotional experiences meant to satisfy the most discriminating theatrical palate. This view contrasts with Aristotle's clear distinction between comedy and tragedy as separate genres as well as the view of Renaissance neoclassicists that these genres should never be mixed. The final goal of a Sanskrit theatre performance is not a purging of emotions, as in Aristotle's tragic catharsis, but a sensual banquet that brings its audience a sense of peace and fulfillment. In fact, later Indian scholars described "peace" as a ninth *rasa*.

Performance Conventions

Sanskrit performances began with a number of preliminaries including a benediction to a god, for whom the play acted as an offering, and a prologue in which the head of the company not only told the audience about the play and players they were about to see (much like today's programs), but also eased the audience into the fictional world of the performance by interacting with characters from the play.

The *Natyasastra* devotes numerous chapters to the actor's art, especially to movement. It breaks down the body into parts—eyes, head, hand, limbs—and describes a number of different positions for each. These positions are combined to represent different emotional states. Both *nritta* (pure dance) and *nritya* (gestural dance) were part of performance, and songs accompanied by drums, cymbals, and flutes were used for a number of different purposes such as introducing characters or underlining the mood of the action.

Since the *Natyasastra* has no illustrations, figuring out exactly what costumes, sets, props, acting, dance, and music were like in performance still entails a good deal of guesswork and interpretation. The *Natyasastra* notes three kinds of stages—square, rectangular, and triangular—recommending the rectangular stage because of its superior sightlines. Scene location may have been designated by simple set pieces representing a house, temple, or mountain on a mostly bare stage, and an actor could indicate a new location simply by moving from one part of the stage to another. Costumes were highly ornamented, with characters dressed according to type. Makeup was used on the actor's face and body with colors, again, accorded by type.

Sanskrit Plays

The Sanskrit plays that have survived are polished dramatic works written in poetic verse. The main action of a Sanskrit play is the hero's struggle to attain an object of desire. As the ultimate objective is to leave the audience with a sense of well-being, the hero is always successful in the end, even if temporarily thwarted along the way. The plays reflect the Hindu values of their original cultural context: The hero achieves one or more of the three ends of Hindu life—*dharma* or duty, *kama* or controlled sensual pleasure, or *artha*, the wealth that allows one to provide for others.

In *The Little Clay Cart*, said to be written by King Sudraka, the hero Charudatta's poverty at the beginning of the play derives from his former generosity. His honorable nature leads a wealthy and virtuous courtesan, Vasantasena, to fall in love with him. The king's villainous brother, Sansthanaka, pursues her and, in the process, accuses Charudatta of her murder. In the end truth is revealed, the king is deposed, and the lovers are united. The cart of the title is Charudatta's son's simple toy. Vasantasena put her jewels in it, showing that even a humble vessel can carry great wealth inside. It is this spiritual wealth that Charudatta, Vasantasena, and many characters in this tale display.

The play's dominant *rasa* is that of love or the erotic, but the story's scope and its myriad characters express many other *rasas* as well. The villain creates a situation of trepidation for the lovers, and characters such as Charudatta's comic friend Maitreya bring in humor.

Like many plays of the tradition, *The Little Clay Cart* reflects the Hindu idea of *maya*—a force that misleads people to believe that the sensory world around them is permanent, when in fact it is marked by constant change, blinding us to the ultimate reality beyond. *Maya* allows one to become attached to worldly desires instead of realizing that everything is an illusion, part of God's dream. In this play Charudatta's poverty, Vasantasena's life as a courtesan, and Sansthanaka's high position all obscure their true natures to the unwary observer. Sansthanaka appears to murder Vasantasena, but she revives from her apparent death. Throughout the play we discover that, ultimately, things are not as they appear at first glance. The ending brings clarity to all issues and a happy resolution to events.

Kutiyattam and *Kathakali*

Although Sanskrit drama as a performance tradition is lost to us, *kutiyattam*, one of the oldest continuous performance traditions in India, going back before the tenth century, may be its direct descendent. Performances in temples (see page 251) by temple servants as part of a ritual sacrifice are primarily in Sanskrit and include some

Photo 5.1a
A performance of *nangiar kuttu*, a form of solo performance that is an offshoot of *kutiyattam.*
© *Dinodia/Omni-Photo Communications, Inc.*

Photo 5.1b
Kalamandalam Raman Cakzar costumed for the role of Shandilya, the traditional Vidusaka (stock comic character) in the *kutiyattam* tradition in the one-act Sanskrit farce, *The Hermit Harlot.*
© *Photograph by Phillip Zarrilli*

Kutiyattam and *nangiar kuttu* use physical gestures and facial expressions drawn form the ancient tradition of Sanskrit drama as outlined in *The Natyasastra*. Actors wear traditional makeup and costumes that define their characters. Male actors are drawn from the *Chakyar* community, whose performances are part of their duties in care of the temple. Female *kutiyattam* actors come from the *Nangyar* community, and the community's men serve as *kutiyattam* drummers. *Nangiar kuttu* is a related form done only by women of the *Nangyar* community, to the rhythms of *Nambiar* drummers. Their performances tell stories from the life of Krishna.

plays of the older tradition. Performers, in fabulous costumes and makeup, use elaborate facial and hand gestures in presentations that can extend over a period of several days.

Kathakali, a vigorous seventeenth-century form, originally performed by members of the warrior class, may have developed its own language of hand gestures and vibrant stage makeup and costuming from *kutiyattam*. Both are from the region of Kerala. In Chapter 7 we will take a closer look at *kathakali* and see how it uses the theory of *rasa* as a basis for its acting technique, giving us some idea of what Sanskrit acting may have been like. Through *kathakali* and other forms that feel the influence of the *Natyasastra* and Sanskrit drama, we may yet be able to glimpse this extinct performance tradition in action.

Mime and the Commedia dell'Arte Tradition

The Mime Tradition in Antiquity

What do circus clowns, acrobats, stand-up comics, silent film comedians, mimes, and sitcom actors have in common? They can all trace the origins of their performance style to the oldest European tradition. Although we often think of the European theatre as one that focuses on the text, we know that perhaps as long as two hundred years before the first written ancient tragedy, there existed a popular unscripted theatrical performance form—Greek **mime**. Many scholars believe that tragedy evolved from the fertility rituals honoring the god Dionysus, and that parallel secular mime performances either spoofed these rites or provided comic relief from their intensity. Mimes continued to perform as street entertainers during the Athenian theatre festivals, and unlike the government-sponsored theatre, we have evidence of women among mime performers. From Aristotle we know that these comic players were itinerant. They traveled the ancient Mediterranean world spreading their performance tradition, which entailed stock characters, short improvised comic sketches, broad physical and acrobatic humor, juggling, music, and bawdy jokes. They were often masked and wore padded phalluses to aid in lewd innuendo.

No one knows to what degree Roman mime, comedy, farce, and popular entertainment were indebted to these Greek traveling players. We do know that they all shared various similarities. The Atellan farce, named for the town of Atella in southern Italy, began in the third century B.C.E. as an improvised form resembling Greek mime, using masks and stock characters that spoofed local types; later the texts were written down. Many of the same types appear in the written comedies. Roman mime and popular entertainment extended the variety entertainment form made popular by the Greeks. Concurrently a Roman **pantomime** form developed that resembled a silent storytelling dance, and was a distinct performance genre from mime. As Christianity spread, the mimes turned their satyric eye on the Catholic Church, just as they had spoofed the rituals and gods of antiquity. This provoked criticism and censorship, and the mimes were driven underground during the Middle Ages when the church controlled much of everyday life. Some scholars believe the traveling players and troubadours of the time were the heirs of the mime tradition, wandering to stay one step ahead of church authorities.

The Birth of *Commedia dell'Arte*

During the sixteenth century, with the freedom and humanism of the Renaissance, a form resembling ancient mime and early Atellan farce with its masks, stock characters, local types, and improvised form springs to life—the **commedia dell'arte.** This is the start of a performance tradition that would dominate European theatre for the next three hundred years and whose influence can be felt to the present day. Because of the many similarities with ancient forms, some historians believe the *commedia* is a direct descendent that emerged from hiding after the Dark Ages. Others believe that it is a fresh creation of the Renaissance, and that improvisation and stock types are common to all societies and will come to life given the opportunity. The form was first called **commedia all' improviso** or improvised drama. It came to be called *commedia dell'arte* out of respect for the great "*arte*" or skill for improvisation shown by the professional actors of this tradition. The *commedia* was treated like any other fine art of the time, with masters, apprentices, and families transmitting skills from generation to generation.

The *Commedia* Form

Commedia dell'arte players used **scenarios**—general outlines of plots with short descriptions of each scene—as the basis for improvisation. These were always simple in outline—young lovers kept apart by a cruel parent must be united, or a rich man must be bilked of his money in some elaborate scheme, for example. Once on stage, there were certain standard *lazzi*—set bits of comic stage business—to which an actor

Photo 5.2

This eighteenth-century French engraving shows a scene of two *commedia dell'arte* zannies, or comic servants. On the left, Arlecchino, recognizable by his black mask and his patchwork patterned suit, performs one of the acrobatic stunts for which he is famous.

© *The Granger Collection, New York*

could turn for comic effect. These ranged from pure slapstick to acrobatic stunts, poems, and set speeches, all guaranteed to get a laugh. Actors inserted these comic turns as needed to warm up an audience, heighten humorous effect, or save a lackluster performance. Because actors played the same stock figures throughout their careers, they mastered their characters' speech patterns, movements, and reactions, which facilitated improvisations.

The *commedia* used grotesque leather half masks that revealed the mouth, enabling characters to speak; however, language was secondary to physical expression, and like all masked styles, the *commedia* demanded enlarged stylized movement. Each character, except for the women and young lovers, was represented by a particular mask that expressed specific traits. Set patterns of movement belonging to each character were learned and passed from one generation of performers to the next.

Through time a set repertory of characters developed: Pantalone—the miserly, lecherous, sometimes impotent merchant, often cast as a father figure who thwarted young love; Dottore—the pedantic, pompous intellectual scholar or medical doctor who quoted in bad Latin and dispensed idiotic advice under the guise of elevated knowledge and prose; Capitano—the braggart soldier who is really a coward; the *inamorati*—young lovers with frustrated passions; a group of female maids who scolded or aided and abetted plotters; and last, but most vital, a collection of male servants who schemed, manipulated, and challenged authority. Some were wily, some were fools, some were cruel, but all advanced the comic plot. The most famous of these servants were Arlecchino or Harlequin, Brighella, Piero, and Pulcinella, also known in English as Punch. This cast was recycled into endless comic plot permutations.

Commedia performers were the darlings of the Italian public during the sixteenth century. Their antics pleased royalty and commoners alike, and they played on street corners and in palaces. Most often, *commedia* acting companies wandered from town to town in wagons that could be transformed into stages to the delight of the local population. Many of the characters represented regional types who were easily recognizable to locals. When Catherine de Medici (1519–1589) married King Henri II of France who reigned from 1547 to 1559, she brought her love of things Italian to France, including the *commedia dell'arte*.

It was not long before the Italian players were the favorites of France, where they metamorphosed French acting and playwriting. French actors imitated the robust style, and Molière's first plays were actually written *commedia* scenarios. Unwelcome at first in Protestant England, by the late seventeenth century the *commedia* had found an audience there as well. To put their popularity in today's perspective, through much of Europe from the sixteenth through the nineteenth centuries, the *commedia dell'arte* was as popular as your favorite television situation comedy is today and offered easily accessible entertainment to all in an era before mass media.

The Evolution of *Commedia*

As with all traditions, in time the *commedia* responded to social change and metamorphosed into other forms. By 1760 there were almost no Italian-born *commedia* players in France, and the robust, earthy performance was falling victim to French refinement. *Commedia* characters and scenarios were integrated into written plays in Italy and France, but the incorporation of an actors' tradition into a written text diminished the vibrant physicality that marked the *commedia* at its high point.

If the *commedia* was unwelcome in England in the late sixteenth century, its British descendants were embraced one hundred years later. The English pantomime form, born in the early eighteenth century, traced two story lines—a traditional *commedia* scenario and a narrative balletic dancing of a mythological tale. The two came together when, after a wild, acrobatic, knockabout chase scene called a Harlequinade, Harlequin whirled a magic wand and resolved the two stories, accompanied by dazzling scenic effects. This was the most popular theatrical form in England for over a century, aided by the Licensing Act of 1737, which restricted plays, but did not apply to pantomime. The greatest performer of the English pantomime was Joseph Grimaldi (1778–1837), whose character, named Clown, usurped Harlequin's dominant position as the hero of the new urban working class. Grimaldi created original makeup for Clown—whiteface, two bright red triangles on the cheeks, heavily colored enlarged lips and eyebrows, a comic wig, a brightly patterned shirt, and baggy pants with big hidden pockets for stolen goods. This became the origin of a tradition of circus clowns known today as "Joeys," and named for Grimaldi, showing the link between character and actor in non-text-based traditions.

The French Revolution created a newly liberated class of citizens who wanted to see themselves reflected onstage. Fairs and variety shows continued the *commedia* tradition. Licensing laws limited the use of spoken words on stage, and a new form of mime captured the spirit of the *commedia* in silence, demonstrating how traditions will adapt to social conditions. This is the first time the terms *mime* and *pantomime* come to be used interchangeably. Again, a single actor transformed the *commedia* tradition. Jean-Gaspard Deburau (1796–1846), like Grimaldi, used his character Pierrot to create a hero of the working class, and he too usurped the lead position of the character Arlecchino or Harlequin. He played in simple *commedia* scenarios where he always prevailed over the upper classes. Tall and thin, he chose as his costume a billowing white chemise with wide sleeves and large buttons, loose pants, no collar, and a tight-fitting black cap against his white-face makeup. The costume we traditionally associate with Pierrot today is in fact the creation of the actor who brought the character to prominence.

In later generations, as the pantomime form waned in popularity, many performers moved to music hall and vaudeville variety entertainment, or to the circus, and later to silent films. Charlie Chaplin (1889–1977) and Buster Keaton (1895–1966) are heirs to the great *commedia* tradition. In the twentieth century in France, a modern mime form is created and Marcel Marceau's (b. 1923) Bip character is

Photo 5.3
The French actor Jean Louis Barrault portrays the famous nineteenth-century mime Jean-Gaspard Deburau in a still from the film *Les Enfants du Paradis (Children of Paradise)*, shot in occupied France during World War II.
© *SUNSET BOULEVARD/CORBIS SYGMA*

the embodiment of *commedia*'s spirit more than four hundred years after its first incarnation (see Photo 6.5). *Commedia* is now a tool for actor training, and many young performers have tried to revive the form. If we look around, we see the influence of the *commedia* everywhere—in the written drama, in television sitcom characters and plots, in the circus, and in the tradition of new vaudeville we will examine in the next chapter.

Japanese Traditions

The *Noh* Theatre

Like an apparition from another realm, an imposing figure holding a red and gold fan and wearing a small white mask, a golden headdress, and several layers of beautifully embroidered robes glides so slowly down the smooth wooden pathway leading to the stage that the movement is almost imperceptible. Though the mask displays the subtle, delicate features of a young woman, a middle-aged male actor's robust chin sticks out from underneath. Once on stage, his voice is low and guttural, and his movements are accompanied by the droning chants of a male chorus, the high-pitched sound of a flute, intermittent beats of two drums, and strange yelps from the onstage musicians. The main character of this play, *Hagoromo*, or *The Feather Mantle*, is an angel. In return for her feather cape, picked up by a fisherman while she bathed, the angel offers a dance of blessing. Her appearance marks a union of heaven and earth, and the angel serves as a personification of Buddhist wisdom.

Japan's *noh* theatre is a highly stylized ritualistic form in which a few pages of text can take hours to perform. The plays of the *noh* have been passed down from generation to generation as performance texts that include dance, movement, music, vocal patterns, mask, and costuming, reflecting both the performance style and the Buddhist and Shinto religious practices and values of the fourteenth-century Japanese court world that gave birth to them. Combined with their distinctive staging, *noh* plays create an atmosphere or mood through poetry and do not focus on action and dialogue.

Many ritual and performance forms contributed to the creation of *noh*, which evolved into a highly refined art in the court of Shogun, Ashikaga Yoshimitsu (1358–1408). There the performers Kanami Kiyotsugu (1333–1384) and his son, Zeami Motokiyo (1363–1443), considered the founders of *noh*, wrote poetic texts inspired by the literary tastes of their elite audience that remain a substantial part of the *noh* repertoire. From 1603–1867, *noh* was the exclusive privilege of the ruling samurai. The ascetic ideals of Japan's medieval warrior class are evident throughout the conventions of *noh* performance.

Buddhist and Shinto Influence on Performance Practices

Zen Buddhism, an esoteric religious practice popular at the Shogun's court, was an important influence on *noh*; indeed, all aspects of the art blend the formal simplicity and hidden mystery reflective of Buddhist ideas. In Zen, the visible world is an illusion. Enlightenment, an insight into the essence of all things, can be achieved only through meditation and by relinquishing all attachments to the physical world. In his treatises on *noh*, Zeami describes the two "pillars," or aesthetic tenets, of *noh* as *monomane*, or dramatic imitation, and *yūgen*, usually translated as "grace," "suggestive beauty," or "mystery." These two pillars constitute a balance between concrete reality and the intangible truth that transcends it. They parallel the Buddhist division between the illusory material world and its true metaphysical essence. Today the feeling of mystery or *yūgen* dominates *noh*, which has become more slow-paced and ritualistic than in Zeami's time.

Noh staging practices continue to reflect a Buddhist sensibility, exemplified in its emphasis on stillness. For Zeami, the actor's body should move only seven-tenths, while his soul moves ten-tenths. Zeami advised actors to move differently when playing an old man or a young woman, but professional *noh* actors, who are all male, make little attempt to disguise their low voices for female roles, reflecting Buddhism's view that all reality is illusory. Masks and stage properties also reject theatrical illusion. The actor's face always protrudes from beneath the mask, so the actor and the image on the mask are visible at once. Fans carried by actors can represent a variety of objects, such as a sword or a sake ladle. The stage itself is bare except for one or two set pieces that may indicate a special location associated with a spirit. These set pieces are always minimalist in construction because their evocative qualities are more important than what they literally represent. They are constructed by the actor for each performance. In *Matsukaze*, or *Pining Wind*, a hut where two sisters live is just an outline of a structure, too small for both actors to fit inside; one sister remains outside, but the audience accepts the convention that she is inside for the purpose of the play.

Many conventions of the *noh* theatre play with time and space, reinforcing a sense of inhabiting a realm of dreams. Walking around the stage or simply stating that one has traveled a long distance and arrived at a new location makes it so. The ghosts that appear in *noh* are caught between realities: the domains of the living and the dead, the present and the past. Their memories draw them back to earth and entice them to reenact events from the past. *Noh* also breaks down one's sense of individual identity. Characters talk about themselves in the third person, as distant observers, and the eight-member chorus often speaks their lines for them, freeing the actor to act and dance without having to project through the mask.

The *noh* theatre reflects Shinto's animistic belief that spirits inhabit all elements of the natural world and must be appeased to bring health, happiness, and good fortune to individuals and the community. Traditionally, Shinto priestesses, or *miko*, acted as shamans, whose handheld objects, such as fans or flowering branches, served as conduits for spirits to enter and possess them. *Noh* actors continue to use these simple objects in performance, harkening back to their ritual function. The plays present the visitation of gods, demons, or human spirits to the earthly realm, and the space itself is modeled on Shinto shrines. The *hashigakari*, or bridgeway, that leads to the stage from which actors make their entrances, is like a passage between the world of spirits and our own. (See Chapter 9).

Photo 5.4
This *noh* actor, wearing a delicate female mask and exquisite *kimono*, moves slowly along the *noh* theatre's bridgeway toward the main stage. The tension the performer creates in stillness is valued in the art as much as the beauty of the costumes and stage properties.
© *Scala/Art Resource, NY*

Noh Plays

There are five different categories of *noh* plays—god plays, warrior plays, women plays, miscellaneous plays, and demon plays—and each has a different sensibility and dynamic, ranging from the slowest and most refined (the god and women plays) to the fastest and most vigorous (the demon plays). Ideally, a day of *noh* would include a play from each category in the preceding order, reflecting a rhythmic pattern known as *jo-ha-kyu*: introduc-

Photo 5.5

A scene from the *noh* play *Tsuchigumo (Earth Spider)* in which the spirit of the earth spider causes the illness of a samurai lord and must be exorcised. Note the *shite* or main character, the Earth Spider played by Umewaka Rokuro in a demon mask, who later, in a highlight of this most dramatic of *noh* plays, unfurls strings of webbing across the stage. The *waki,* or secondary character, Lord Minamoto Raikou, played by Kakuto Naotaka, does not wear a mask. The musicians sit behind the actors in front of the painted pine tree on an otherwise bare stage. This play was the first *noh* witnessed by Westerners when it was presented to General Ulysses S. Grant in 1879, as recorded in the diaries of Umewaka Minoru (1828–1909), whose great grandson performs the role of the Earth Spider here. Legend has it that Grant's appreciation of the *noh* greatly contributed to the Japanese of the period guaranteeing preservation and support of the *noh.* Japan Society, New York.
© *Jack Vartoogian/FrontRowPhotos*

Photo 5.6

A Japanese Edo period (1603–1868) illustration of a traditional outdoor *noh* temple stage. An audience on blankets enjoys a performance of the *noh* play *Dojoji (Dojo Temple).* In this play a young maiden, turned into an angry spirit by her thwarted love for a Buddhist priest, foils the re-consecration of his temple's bell. We see the beginning of the second half of the play when the main character, having changed from a woman mask into a demon mask, comes out from under the bell. On stage are the secondary character and his assistants, who play the priests who attempt to exorcize the angry maiden's spirit, and the *noh* musicians and chorus.
© *National Noh Theatre, Toyko*

tion (*jo*), development (*ha*), and climax (*kyu*). This movement from slow to fast governs all aspects of a *noh* performance, from the structure of a play to an actor's every move.

"God," "warrior," "woman," and "demon" refer to the main character, or *shite*, literally the "doer" of the action of the play. The main characters of *noh* are drawn from history, literature, and legend. In the first half of a play they usually appear in humble form, and then in the second they reveal their true natures as spirits. A change of mask or costume actualizes this transformation.

Many *noh* plays focus on the longing and sadness of characters who cling to the ephemeral world, even in death, thus highlighting the Buddhist belief that release from earthly attachments is necessary to put the soul to rest. In *Matsukaze*, a woman play, the spirits of two young fisherwomen return to Suma Bay where in life they met and fell in love with Yukihira, a court poet. As they scoop brine into their cart, their poetic text speaks of the salt tears they shed over their lost love when Yukihira re-

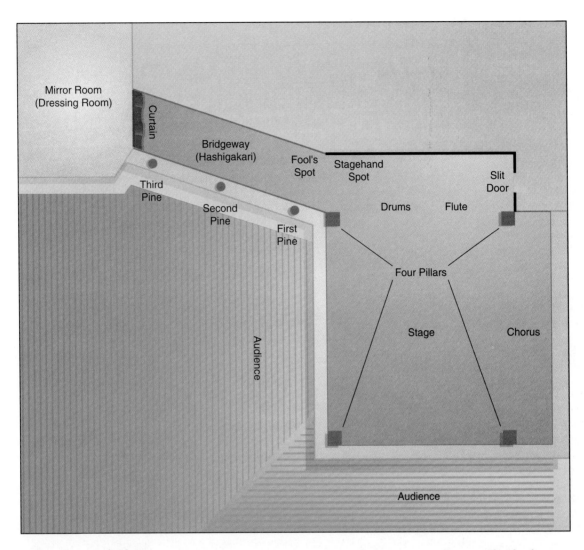

Figure 5.1 *Noh* **Theatre** Actors emerge from behind the curtained mirror room and are considered to be on stage as soon as they step onto the bridgeway. They share the stage with the chorus and musicians. With the exception of a few set pieces, the stage is basically bare and the rear wall of the stage is covered by a painting of a pine tree. This stage is used for all *noh* performances and is not altered for specific plays.

turned to court without them. In their pails they see the reflection of the moon, a symbol of Buddhist enlightenment. In the final dance sequence, Matsukaze puts on Yukihira's hat and cloak and, as she dances, declares that she loves him still. In the end, lost in a kind of mad melancholy, she clings to her earthly love. Just as Matsukaze sees only the moon's reflection and not the moon itself, so too is she blind to true Buddhist happiness. Her spirit continues to live in longing, never finding peace. The play expresses the poignancy of love, which, like all earthly desires, can never be fully or finally attained.

Imagery in *noh* is densely packed. Words with more than one meaning, image patterns, and other forms of poetic language make *noh* plays richly symbolic and difficult to translate. They are replete with allusions to famous poems that courtiers of the period would have recognized. Word play deepens the thematic content and the feelings it evokes. The name Matsukaze, for instance, combines the word *matsu*, meaning both "pine" and "to wait," with *kaze*, meaning "wind." Matsukaze waits for her lost lover and describes their love as wind in the pines; they are two beings intertwined and inseparable. The play is also saturated with images of water—for example, the women's salt tears and the brine they collect.

History IN PERSPECTIVE

KOREA'S *T'ALCH'UM* TRADITION: SUPPRESSION, RESURRECTION, AND RENEWAL

The history of the Korean *t'alch'um* performance tradition demonstrates the durability of ancient performance traditions as they adapt to political, social, and religious change. T'alch'um (*t'al* for mask and *ch'um* for dance), the ancient Korean masked dance theatre, finds its roots in shamanistic ritual, and according to some scholars, can be traced back as far as 5000 B.C.E. T'alch'um's ritual origins are evident today in the *kosa*, the ritual ceremony honoring local spirits that precedes a performance, and in the grotesque masks once used to drive away evil spirits. In some regions of Korea, the masks are still burned at the end of a performance in a shamanistic exorcism. *T'alch'um* grew increasingly secular as Korea moved from early shamanistic belief to Buddhism and later Confucianism and Neoconfucianism.

The stock characters—an old Buddhist priest, monks, noblemen, servants, a lion, a prodigal, an old couple, a concubine, and coquettes represent the types of an ancient era. They were recycled into several basic sketches that satirized the piety of monks, insulted the power of the nobles, rebelled against patriarchal rule, exposed the harsh life of the common peasant, and ridiculed marriage and the competition between wife and concubine. Music is played on traditional Korean instruments and evokes tunes and rhythms known to the audience. The outdoor performances usually begin at sunset and can last the night. The improvisational nature of the performance permitted the insertion of topical names and events that kept the satirical content current over hundreds of years. The audience is drawn into the action and encouraged to shout out *pullim*, well-known phrases that can comment on the action.

T'alch'um, the most popular form of Korean theatre, came to a crashing halt when the Japanese invaded Korea in 1910 and banned any form of performance that embodied Korean cultural identity. The Koreans were forced to adopt Japanese theatre styles including *sinp'a*, which ironically was a Japanese adaptation of European theatre. The Korean intelligentsia who studied at Japanese universities were exposed to Ibsen, Chekhov, and other plays of social realism, and brought these plays back to Korea in the hope of establishing a new drama movement that could supplant Japanese forms with modern European ones. During the 1920s, socialist theatre groups wandered the countryside performing short agit-prop pieces exposing Japanese oppression.

The ten-year period from 1935 to 1945 saw the most brutal oppression. The Korean language was banned, Koreans were forced to take Japanese surnames, youths were conscripted into the Japanese army, and many women were shipped into war zones to provide "comfort" for Japanese soldiers. All theatres were closed except those performing pro-Japanese propaganda plays. When Japan was defeated in 1945, Korean traditional theatre, forbidden since 1910, had long been forgotten. The civil strife that ended in the division of Korea saw left-wing theatre in the north and imitations of Western theatre in the south.

As the situation stabilized in South Korea, there was a call to recover Korean cultural identity, and with it

---

Challenges and Choices

Why preserve a tradition whose appeal has waned?

The Art behind the *Noh*

Noh actors and musicians devote a lifetime to honing their craft. Actors grow up in *noh* families or enter the profession through study with a master artist. Actors specialize in either primary (*shite*) or secondary (*waki*) roles. Like opera singers, *noh* actors learn a repertoire and only then come together with other actors and musicians for a performance, usually with only one group rehearsal beforehand. Performances are singular events that bring a particular cast together for only one presentation, eliciting a heightened sense of concentration from all involved and lending each presentation a unique intensity. *Noh* actors never retire, and elderly performers play some of the most challenging roles, which often call for evocations of deep emotion by means of little movement.

The artifacts of *noh* are treasures created by masters who have devoted a lifetime to learning and perfecting their craft. *Noh* masks are carved from specially treated wood

came the resurrection of *t'alch'um*. Through government preservation initiatives, university research, and a national festival, *t'alch'um* was seen again in the late 1950s for the first time in half a century. In 1964, the Korean government named *t'alch'um* an "Important Intangible Cultural Property of Korea." *T'alch'um* became a required course at the Seoul Drama School in 1964, and student clubs emerged at other universities. During the political repression of the 1970s, students used *t'alch'um* as a form of protest, updating the old peasant characters with factory workers and replacing the noblemen with new topical political figures. The hybrid form came to be known as *madang-kuk* (yard or town square plays).

Simultaneously, during the 1970s, the experimental theatre movement in Korea found ways of interweaving *t'alch'um* elements into productions of Western classical plays. New dramas were written incorporating ritual elements from *t'alch'um* reflecting the influence of Artaud's ideas. Such a production by O T'ae-sŏk, *The Order*, played at La MaMa Experimental Theatre in New York in 1974, and was the first Korean play to be performed abroad. Many contemporary Korean theatre artists continue to combine traditional *t'alch'um* elements with new plays that seek to balance Eastern and Western influences.

Today, Korean new wave theatre artists draw from various traditions. The recent production of *Cookin'* (2004) in New York via Seoul and the Edinburgh Festival has a loose story about a restaurant kitchen whose harmony is upset by the entrance of the owner's nephew. The cook-off that ensues includes a *kosa* ceremony to honor the kitchen spirits, a traditional wedding ceremony with members of the audience as bride and groom, spectacular *t'alch'um* choreography with streamers attached to hats, and the playing of traditional rhythms on traditional and not so traditional instruments. Slide projections direct the audience to participate in the performance as in days of old, and they do so with gusto. Juggling, acrobatics, and martial arts are added to the mix, and the evening ends with an explosion of indigenous Korean percussive rhythm. This fusion of forms and styles with the once outlawed *t'alch'um* demonstrates that old traditions never die; they simply evolve in the postmodern era.

The enthusiastic drumming of the cast of *Cookin'* harkens back to the rhythmic drumming of early *t'alch'um* ritual dance drama. Cast: Kang Il Kim, Won Hae Kim, Bum Chan Lee, Chu Ja Seo and Ho Yeoul Sul. Originated in Seoul, Korea and performed at the Minetta Lane Theatre, New York
© Joan Marcus

and delicately painted in such a way that the actor's subtle movements completely transform their apparent expressions. The masks' facial features follow traditional models, yet each has a life of its own. Like other such artifacts, they are cherished and passed down from one generation to another in performance families. The richly woven and embroidered kimonos of *noh* are also beautiful artistic creations treasured by performers.

Kyōgen

Noh's partner, *kyōgen*, which means "mad words" and developed from some of the same antecedents as *noh*, is a comic form that shares the *noh* stage, but has its own acting, speaking, and costuming conventions. Whereas *noh* deals with the metaphysical realm, *kyōgen* engages with the concrete world and exposes everyday foibles, conflicts, and follies.

Kyōgen are generally performed between *noh* plays and often complement them, although today they are sometimes performed on their own program. In the past a full presentation might have included a *noh* from every category, each followed by a complementary *kyōgen*. *Kyōgen* performers come from different performance families than *noh* actors and appear in *noh* plays only in the roles of commoners or to perform the *ai-kyōgen*, or interlude, between the two main sections of a *noh* play. All *kyōgen* pieces use colloquial language rather than poetry, and the *ai-kyōgen* explains the events of the *noh* play in easily understood terms. These sections were not usually written out in *noh* texts; the *kyōgen* actor was expected to improvise.

Kyōgen acting, though not nearly as subtle as that of *noh*, is surprisingly formal and stylized for physical comedy. Whereas some *kyōgen* characters require masks, masks are less prevalent in *kyōgen* than in *noh* because the actors' facial expressions are essential to the comedy. The most common masks are of animals, and most *kyōgen* actors begin their training as children playing the role of a monkey.

Kyōgen characters are rarely the extraordinary spirits of *noh*, but ordinary people, masters and their servants, husbands and wives, fathers and sons. *Kyōgen* is often compared to the *commedia dell'arte* in its reliance on stock figures, its master and servant types (see Photo 5.7), and in the fact that there were no written scripts until late in the tradition. Tarōkaja, like Arlecchino, is a clever servant who outwits his master, and many plot lines revolving around this character interestingly parallel *commedia* scenarios. In *Busu*, or *Sweet Poison*, the master tells his servants that a barrel of molasses is filled with poison so they will not eat it while he is away. Tarōkaja and his naive sidekick Jirōkaja, enticed by curiosity and the sweet smell from the barrel, eventually realize there is no poison and finish all the molasses. Tarō has Jirō rip the master's precious scroll and break a fragile bowl so that when he returns they can escape punishment by telling him that on accidentally ruining these treasured objects while wrestling, they sought death by devouring the poison. In *Boshibari*, or *Tied to a Stick*, the two servants manage to drink the master's *sake*, sing, and dance while he's away, in spite of his having tied their hands. In *kyōgen* social hierarchies are overturned, and a life spirit flourishes in spite of circumstances.

When gods do appear in *kyōgen*, they are literally and metaphorically brought down to earth and forced to endure the indignities of daily life. In *Kaminari*, the thunder god

Photo 5.7
In this *kyōgen*, the clever servant Tarōkaja has convinced his master that he can only sing when drunk and lying in his own wife's lap, so the master gets him drunk and provides him with his own confortable lap to coax a song out of him. Shigeyama Masakuni as the master pours sake for grandfather, and Living National Treasure, Shigeyama Sensaku as Tarōkaja in *Neongyoku* or *Horizontal Singing*, Japan Society, New York
© *Jack Vartoogian/FrontRowPhotos*

accidentally falls to earth through a hole in the clouds and hurts his rear end. A doctor cures him with a big needle and then asks for a fee. The god, short of cash, pays him with the promise that no floods or droughts will come for eight hundred years. The ending of this play acts as a blessing for future good health and fertility.

Noh and *kyōgen*, both treasured national arts in Japan, continue with the support of the government and devoted fans. Professional performers are still exclusively men, but amateur performers, who are not members of professional families, include many women who study *noh* and enjoy developing their skills. Although there is some resistance to experimentation within these traditions, Japanese theater artists have created *noh*-style adaptations of Shakespeare and Beckett, along with other experiments.

Kabuki

To find a theatrical form that is the complete aesthetic opposite of the *noh* theatre, you can look to *kabuki*, Japan's other major theatrical tradition. *Noh* is subtle and introverted; *kabuki*, explicit and extroverted. *Noh* is elite and refined; *kabuki*, popular and brash. *Noh* focuses on enlightenment; *kabuki*'s goal is entertainment.

Originating in the seventeenth century, the Japanese *kabuki* theatre is an actor-centered tradition whose extraordinary costumes and makeup, lavish sets and scenic devices, and moving domestic and historical plays all developed to draw in popular audiences and spotlight the talents of celebrated performers. *Kabuki* originally catered to Japan's merchant class at a time when their wealth and power were on the rise, offering them a place to spend their money and their leisure time. *Kabuki*'s lavish entertainment contrasted sharply with the ascetic ideals of the warrior elite embodied in the *noh*, and stiff competition among *kabuki* theatres led to a constant search for novelties. Passed down from generation to generation, today's *kabuki* is more about preservation than the innovation of the early years, and its current role is as a Japanese national artistic treasure and cultural export. Nonetheless, *kabuki*'s unique performance style and imaginative theatrical devices still thrill audiences and inspire artists the world over.

The origin of *kabuki* goes back to Okuni (c. 1570–c. 1610), a woman calling herself a priestess of the Grand Shrine of Izumo, who, around 1603, performed radical dances in the dry bed of the Kamo River. According to screen and scroll paintings, she dressed in men's clothes, wore a Christian rosary, and performed scenes of assignations with prostitutes. These performances were called *kabuki*, whose original meaning is "tilted" or "off-kilter." Today the word *kabuki* is written with three Japanese characters that mean music, dance, and craft or skill.

The form appealed to boisterous crowds who chafed under the Tokugawa Shogun's rigid government based on Confucian ideals. Okuni's dances were copied by female prostitutes until 1629, when the Tokugawa banned women from performing in an attempt to control this growing rebellious and disruptive form. Young male prostitutes, who had also borrowed Okuni's sensual dances to promote themselves, filled the gap until 1652, when the Tokugawa banned their performances as well. When only older men were left to perform in this style, *kabuki* evolved toward its present form, the domain of male actors, but it has retained its early emphasis on dance, its highlighting of the performer's physical beauty, and a close connection between performer and spectator.

Kabuki Acting Conventions

Kabuki acting openly expresses its theatricality, and the actor's identity is acknowledged alongside that of the character he portrays. Costumes often display the actor's family crest, and a stage assistant might bring an actor a cup of tea or a glass of water during a

Photo 5.8
Kabuki onnagata actor
Tamasaburo Bando V completely fulfills an ideal of female grace and beauty in his performance of the dance solo *Kanegamisaki (The Cape of the Temple Bell)*, a *kabuki* dance version of *Dojoji* (see Photo 5.6). The Japan Society, New York.
© *Jack Vartoogian/FrontRowPhotos*

particularly long or arduous scene, or arrange his costume to make sure he looks good. These assistants, usually dressed in black, make no attempt to hide themselves; the audience is meant to read them as invisible.

Kabuki uses several basic character or role types that are depicted through movement, makeup, costume, and vocal pattern. When women were banned from the stage, *kabuki* developed the **onnagata** or female role type: an idealized woman played by male actors in white makeup, black styled wigs, and women's kimonos (see Photo 5.8). Their high-pitched, singsong voices and constrained, graceful movements make them paradigms of feminine beauty with which, some say, no real woman could compete. Most *onnagata* actors play women's roles exclusively throughout their careers, and every woman character on the professional *kabuki* stage, whatever her age or social class, is played by a man.

Two different styles of male performance forged by prominent actors developed in Kabuki's two centers, Kyoto-Osaka and Edo (today's Tokyo), eliciting different kinds of scripts. In the Kyoto-Osaka area, the actor Sakata Tōjuro (1647–1709) created the soft or *wagoto* style of acting, used for figures in domestic dramas (*sewamono*), which usually depict middle-class merchants caught between their love of a courtesan and their duty to family and business. *Wagoto* characters are almost feminine in their movements and speak with soft, high-pitched voices. They wear simple white makeup and kimonos that are modest in color and style. They are effeminate heroes appealing in their pathos.

In Edo, actor Ichikawa Danjuro (1660–1704) developed the *aragoto* or rough style of performance used for superhuman figures from heroes to gods incarnate. Many of the more extravagant aspects of *kabuki* are associated with this style. These characters are found in history plays *(jidaimono)*, and wear the bold red and black makeup called *kumadori* and wild, colorful costumes. In *Shibaraku*, or *Wait a Minute*, one *aragoto* character's costume is so large it requires steel supports for its enormous square sleeves. (See the chapter opening photo on page 112.) *Aragoto* movements are broad, taking up space in every direction to accompany the characters' booming voices. They display their superhuman strength in *tachimawari*, or stylized fight scenes in which, with a simple push, they can send up to twenty attackers reeling in somersaults.

Kabuki began in dance, and physical movement still remains central to *kabuki* performance, allowing an actor to display his personal beauty, charisma, and talent. Mastering the physicality of the role types is of primary importance. *Kabuki* actors begin their training by learning *nihon buyo*, Japanese classical dance, and some *kabuki* solo pieces are told entirely through dance. In all *kabuki* plays the high points are captured in physical poses called **mie.** Underscored by the beats of wooden clappers (see Photo 10.7), the actors wind into poses that serve as physical exclamation points for the scene. Aficionados wait for these climactic moments.

Catering to the Audience

The close association between actor and audience gives *kabuki* its dynamism. Audience members have always supported their favorite actors, both by yelling and applauding as well as with more substantial gifts of money or goods. At performances, fans can get up close to their idols by sitting near the flower path or **hanamichi**. A descendant of the bridgeway used in *noh*, this runway cuts through the audience. The name *hanamichi* likely derives from the flowers that fans threw to their favorite actors as they came on stage. Actors use it for most exits and entrances and to make important speeches and perform famous *mie*. The spot on the *hanamichi* where the actors stop, called the "seven-three" position, is seven-tenths of the way to the stage. It is visible from anywhere in the house and allows actors to grab the audience's attention for dramatic moments before taking the stage or making a final exit.

Catering to audiences fed *kabuki*'s search for novelty and theatrical marvels. Some pieces have actors fly over the heads of the audience, and one crowd-pleasing feat, revived in the twentieth century by the actor Ichikawa Ennosuke III (b. 1939), calls for one performer to play an entire cast of characters, changing into elaborate costumes and makeup beneath the floorboards on his way to the next entrance. Without the aid of electricity the *kabuki* developed many mechanical stage devices including an elevator trap, first used in 1736,

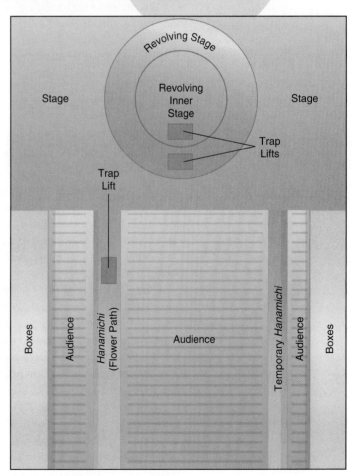

Figure 5.2 *Kabuki* Theatre Actors enter on the *hanamichi* through the audience (see the Chapter 2 opening photo.) Note the technical devices of traps, elevators, and revolving stages developed to create dramatic effects.

an elevator stage in 1753, and a revolving stage platform in 1827. Each device allowed for astonishing transformations and fed the merchant class's desire for theatrical excitement.

The *kabuki* repertoire covers a wide range of themes, but plays were first and foremost vehicles for star actors and meant to highlight their talents. Under the guidance of a head author who put the whole play together, each member of a team of writers wrote the kinds of scenes at which he excelled. Plays filled a whole day, but the most interesting scenes appeared at the time of day when most spectators were likely to attend. Today's *kabuki* performances are shorter than the original daylong offerings, and famous scenes are performed on their own, without the rest of the original play. The Shogun forbade the *kabuki* from making political commentary or speaking about current events, so theatre companies thinly disguised contemporary subject matter and altered the settings to other historical periods or legends. This was just one way the *kabuki* evaded restrictions to please its audiences and participated in the counterculture of its day.

Today's *kabuki* is more a cultivated taste than the popular form of the past, but *kabuki* continues to grow. Ichikawa Ennosuke III has repopularized the form in Japan with his energetic "super *kabuki*" that uses high-tech special effects like a real waterfall on stage, dynamic stage lighting, a faster pace achieved by cutting long, slow passages, and adding contemporary Japanese language. Nagoya Musume Kabuki, founded in 1983, is an all-woman *kabuki* company approved by the Ichikawa *kabuki* family. *Kabuki*'s larger than life emotions and artistic displays are adopted for highly stylized productions in many places outside the world of *kabuki* families. Ariane Mnouchkine borrowed from *kabuki* for the Théâtre du Soleil's 1982 *Richard II*, as did Ninagawa Yukio (b. 1935) for his 1985 production of *Macbeth*. Both Shakespearean plays echo *kabuki*'s own historical tales of intrigue. *Kabuki* continues in its traditional form and in contributions to imaginative new productions that borrow both its conventions and exuberant theatrical spirit.

Challenges and Choices

Should all-male performance traditions permit women to perform professionally today for the sake of equality, or should an age-old tradition preserve its original conventions?

Chinese Opera

Cymbals clang and gongs ring out as a battalion of acrobats in ornate red, green, blue, and gold flip across the stage in succession. A battle scene from Chinese opera is an explosion of excitement and physical virtuosity, a stylized fight that combines gymnastic feats and martial arts. It is just one piece of a theatrical form that brings together music, dance, song, acting, mime, spectacular makeup, conventionalized characters, and dramatic storytelling.

Beijing Opera, because of its association with the capital, is the most famous of the more than three hundred local opera traditions that exist in China. They all use the same basic role types and staging practices, but different regional music. Although drawing from traditions that date back to the earliest Chinese rituals and entertainments, Beijing Opera solidified as a new form around 1779 when it blended with practices that performers from Hubei and Anhui provinces brought to the capital to celebrate the Qialong emperor's seventieth birthday. *Kunqu*, born in the district of Kunshan, dates back to the sixteenth century and is the oldest, most refined, and most literary form of Chinese opera. It contributed to the birth of the many popular regional forms. Today, all Chinese opera performers train in this classical form as well as a regional style.

The plays of Chinese opera cover a range of subject matter from comic to serious to fantastic. Many are love stories such as Tang Xianzu's (1550–1616) sixteenth-century *kunqu* opera classic, *Peony Pavilion*, which follows a love that goes beyond death. In this fifty-five-scene play, a young woman, Du Liniang, grows old and dies pining for an ideal man she fell in love with in a dream (see photo on page 178). After death she wanders as a ghost until the man, Liu Mengmei, comes across her portrait and falls in love with her as well. With the blessing of the king of the underworld, Du Liniang is resurrected, and the rest of the play traces her path to love's fulfillment. Some operas tell tales of battle that capitalize on martial skills. In *Mu Gui Ying* the heroine is a legendary female general from the Song dynasty who never loses a battle and rises for combat even after giving birth on the battlefield. *Prince Lanling* is the story of a warrior who is so handsome his enemies are not frightened of him until his wife gives him a horrifying mask. He wins subsequent victories and makes the king so jealous that he poisons the warrior. In *The Legend of the White Snake*, a fantastic tale, a man marries a beautiful woman who is actually a white snake. A monk who suspects her true nature gives her a drink that reveals her as a snake to her husband. The shock kills him. Proving her love, White Snake travels to a magic mountain to retrieve a special herb to bring her husband back to life.

Chinese opera uses four basic role types: the female (*dan*), the male (*sheng*), the clown (*chou*), and the painted face (*jing*) for strong male characters such as generals and high officials. Each role has a number of different subcategories, and within a character type, performers can specialize as singers or experts in martial arts. Starting in childhood, actors train in a particular type determined by their physical features and talents and then spend a lifetime mastering a role's moves and the repertoire associated with it. Chinese women performed in various theatrical traditions up until the eighteenth century when the Emperor Qianlong banned them from the stage. From this period on, men performed all the roles. Today women take part again, and one form, Shanghai opera, is performed exclusively by women.

Makeup and Costume

The makeup and costumes of Chinese opera are arresting, and their vibrant colors help define the characters. Especially remarkable are the painted-face characters whose makeup is detailed with elaborate swirling lines and patterns. There are over a thousand different facial patterns for Chinese opera characters, but spectators familiar with the conventions know that a character in red makeup is courageous or assertive, one in white is wicked, and one in blue is cruel, and Chinese opera clowns wear a patch of white around the nose and eyes (see the illustration on page 273 and the photo on page 277, top). The costumes of Chinese opera are sumptuous with lavish embroidery and

Photo 5.10
In this group pose at the end of an acrobatic fight scene, we see actors who specialized in martial roles in the traditional makeup and highly ornamented costumes of Chinese opera. Note the elaborate makeup of the *jing,* or painted face, characters, the use of a traditional fake beard in the character on the left, and the more natural makeup of the young women down front. The Peking Opera Company of Heibei in *Havoc in Heaven*, World Music Institute, City Center, New York.
© Jack Vartoogian/FrontRowPhotos

brocades. They reflect the fashions of the Ming Dynasty (1368–1644), and the colors indicate the characters' social status: members of the imperial family wear yellow, characters of high nobility wear red, and students wear blue. Emperors have dragons embroidered on their costumes. The large padded outfits and high shoes worn by generals make these socially powerful characters physically impressive as well. The pennants on their backs symbolize the armies they lead. Long, flowing "water sleeves" made of light cloth add grace and beauty to the movements of actors playing the male and female roles. Jewels and headdresses add further adornment to stage dress.

Movement and Music

Chinese opera is primarily a performer's art. A table, a chair, and a red rug suffice as a stage set; the actors depict the rest of the setting through conventionalized gestures. Actors step over an imaginary threshold to indicate a doorway; they carry a whip if they are riding a horse and have prescribed motions for mounting, riding, and dismounting; and they bend up and down at the knees to step into an imaginary boat swaying in the water. Entrances, exits, and startling moves are underscored by beating cymbals and gongs. Actors punctuate important moments by turning their heads in a single dramatic move and fixing their eyes on the audience.

As its name implies, the soul of Chinese opera is its music. In China, all theatrical performances contained music and singing until the twentieth century when the Chinese borrowed Western models and created *huaju* or spoken drama. Each of the over three hundred different forms of Chinese opera is specific to a region and uses a set of musical pieces that match the tonal dialect of its geographic area.

Unlike Western operas, Chinese operas are not linked with particular musical compositions. Instead, each form of Chinese opera has its own collection of tunes from which musicians select songs to create the score for a production. This process can be compared to the way piano players accompanying old silent films chose their music from standard tunes each time a film was run. The process in Chinese opera is somewhat more complex, however, because a large number of conventions govern these choices. Singers try to select musical pieces best suited to their own vocal strengths. The singing and musical dialogue of Chinese opera may seem slightly shrill or jarring to Western ears unfamiliar with the form. To the trained ear, subtleties in musical delivery make the difference between a good performance and a great one.

The Twentieth Century and Beyond

In the twentieth century, Chinese opera underwent many changes. During the Cultural Revolution (1966–1976), traditional operas were outlawed because of their perceived aristocratic and bourgeois content. Chairman Mao Zedong's wife, Jiang Qing (1914–1991), sponsored the creation of new "model" operas such as *Taking Tiger Mountain by Strategy* and *Raid on the White Tiger Regiment*, which combined some old conventions with new Western influences and were meant to exalt communist heroes and the proletariat. Until the

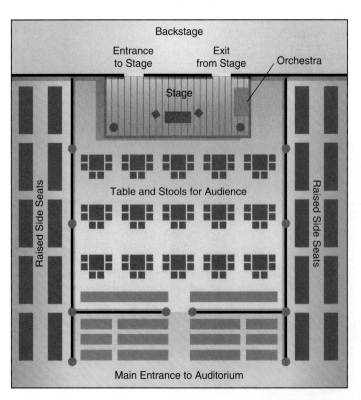

Figure 5.3   Traditional Chinese Teahouse Theatre   Traditional Chinese teahouse theatres allowed spectators to partake of tea while watching performances on a raised platform stage furnished with the basic set pieces of most Chinese opera: a table and two chairs.

Artists
IN PERSPECTIVE

INFLUENCE OF THE MASTER ARTIST:
MEI LANFANG (1894–1961)

The famous performer Mei Lanfang introduced the world to Chinese opera through his many tours from 1919 to 1956 to Japan, the United States, and the Soviet Union, where he gave demonstrations witnessed by Charlie Chaplin, Constantin Stanislavski, and Bertolt Brecht, among other theatre luminaries. Mei Lanfang's demonstration influenced Brecht's views on acting for the epic theatre. Trained from the age of 8, Mei, attained stardom while still in his teens.

Mei innovated within the form of Chinese opera. He mastered song, dance, and martial arts in the female role, developing an original style. New pieces were created as vehicles for his enormous talents. Although artists usually master only a single role type, Mei perfected both the role of the loyal wife or daughter and the woman warrior role, eventually creating a new type called *huashan,* a female who is both vivacious and seductive. He revived many classical dances and redefined costumes and acting technique, revitalizing Chinese opera.

Although Mei was a female role performer himself, he supported bringing women back into these roles at a time when they did not perform, which ironically led to the end of the male performer in female roles, the art that had brought him fame. He wore modern dress from his wife's closet to play victimized heroines in "contemporary costume plays," a short-lived form that took its subjects from current events.

The actor Mei Lanfang, famous for performances of female roles in Chinese opera, poses offstage in formal Chinese dress, 1930.
© Bettmann/CORBIS

end of the Cultural Revolution, only these operas and works based on them could be performed. Many former actors were vilified for their association with the traditional form and were sent to work camps or to prison. When traditional operas were again cultivated as an important part of the national heritage, a generation had lost the opportunity to learn the tradition from masters, and audience members were no longer knowledgeable about the form's codes of performance. A lapse of continuity can spell the end of any form that relies on direct transmission from teacher to student. Nonetheless, today Chinese opera flourishes in its homeland and in communities in the United States and elsewhere that have welcomed Chinese immigrants.

New experiments continue to challenge the form and reach out to new audiences. Two versions of *Peony Pavilion* drew international attention in 1999. One was the New York–based Chinese director Chen Shizheng's (b. 1963) nineteen-hour production with the Shanghai Kunqu Opera Company, using all fifty-five scenes of the original play. The Chinese authorities called Chen's version, done in Chinese opera style but with new interpretations, "feudal" and "pornographic" and refused to have it performed abroad. The other was American director Peter Sellars' pared-down, four-hour version, which used Chinese performers alongside Western-trained actors, video sequences, and composer Tan Dun's musical mix of traditional instruments and synthesizers. Performance tradi-

Challenges and Choices

Who should be responsible for preserving a tradition— the government, an international organization, the community of origin, or the people who perform it?

Challenges and Choices

Who, if anyone, owns a theatrical tradition or has the right to innovate within it?

tions still offer possibilities for daring innovations, perhaps even giving birth to something wholly new. Some people, however, may question a particular artists' right to experiment with an age-old form.

Carnival Tradition

Carnival's European Origins

The tradition of carnival across Latin America traces a peculiar lineage from ancient Rome through medieval Europe to the present. Its history demonstrates the indefatigable need for cultural expression through the performing arts, even in the face of brutal oppression. What began as festive revelry evolved into a complex hybrid theatrical tradition, with role-play and dress-up used to subvert authority.

Almost all societies observe periods of approved exuberant merrymaking, through which people give vent to pent-up emotions in communal celebrations where they can transcend normally acceptable behavior. New Year's Eve and Halloween often provide that release in our own culture. The ancient Romans had festivals throughout the year that served this social function. The most extravagant display came at Saturnalia, the celebration of the winter solstice at which people exchanged gifts and engaged in elaborate role-play in which the world returned to a time when all were equal under the reign of the god Saturn. Slaves exchanged roles and even clothing with their masters. They dined at the master's table and rejoiced in this brief period of freedom. With the spread of Christianity, the Church understood that it could not stop these celebrations and win converts. It chose instead to adapt them and incorporate them into Christian ritual.

Saturnalia was transformed by the Catholic Church into a celebration of wild festivity before the period of Lent, observed by abstaining from the eating of meat. Carnival literally means "farewell meat" (*carne vale*), and throughout the Middle Ages it was observed with banquets and masked costume parties. The custom spread from Italy across Catholic Europe, although the exact nature of the festivities varied from country to country as it interacted with local customs. As the Spanish, Portuguese, and French colonized the world, they brought carnival celebrations to Latin America where the European tradition encountered the cultural influences of African slaves and indentured labor from China.

African Influence in Colonial Latin America and the Caribbean

During the eighteenth century, European colonists continued their carnival masquerade celebrations in the colonies, mainly as private masked costume parties. Just as the Romans released their slaves from work for the Saturnalia, many colonial slave masters gave the carnival as a single time of rest in the year, and African slaves were permitted to celebrate carnival as long as no ritual worship occurred that would violate Christian religious belief. It was not long before slave celebrations reflecting African customs developed. The ancient African traditions of circular parading through villages at festival time immediately took hold as part of the carnival form. While the colonists celebrated at private banquets, slaves and their descendants turned carnival into a lively outdoor street theatre. As in Africa, when skits were performed, the parading crowd would encircle the performers. African dance, music, and drumming accompanied the pre-Lent celebrations as did sculptural masks and costumes made of feathers, beads, and grass, typical of African tribal festivals. Many of these elements can be seen in carnival costumes to the present day.

Carnival as Political Street Theatre

In the Caribbean, after the end of slavery in 1838, metaphorical combat was often part of carnival celebrations and was meant to challenge repressive authority structures. Stick fights, a combat sport amusement of the slave yards, were choreographed into elaborate mime routines. Calypso, with its call and response format, was used to both engage the public and create a competition among calypso singers who would vaunt their prowess in suggestive lyrics of praise and challenge. The combative mode was also used to harpoon colonial authorities and satirize public figures. Performers used masks and the anonymity they provided as protective cover for the transgressive behavior displayed in carnival skits. In the British colonies, a *commedia*-like form that was the verbal counterpart of the stick combat routines developed. The character of the English Pierrot appeared as a Dottore type who spoke in elevated language filled with lapses of logic about the rule of law. His foil was provided by the Pierrot Grenade, a lowborn comic servant figure who improvised in the local patois and depended on his wits to survive. As the dialogue performances grew and a host of local stock characters were added, a talk tent was created to house these improvised comic sketches.

By the late nineteenth century, slaves and their descendants had transformed this celebration of white European colonists into an element of black culture and a theatrical celebration of freedom from slavery. Eventually, whites stopped participating in carnival festivities. The transgressive nature of the event often created a spirit of lawlessness in the streets. In 1883 the British colonial authorities banned the use of African drums. In keeping with the improvisational nature of carnival, musicians devised instruments out of bamboo sticks, calabash shells, cookie tins, and dust pans, and finally turned to discarded oil drums as devices for percussive expression. The origin of the steel band lies in carnival's creative response to oppressive authority.

Around Latin America, carnival took slightly different forms and lasted from a single day to two weeks. Everywhere the European celebration was co-opted by slaves and those on the lowest rungs of society. The Cuban carnival, one of the oldest traditions in the region, was for some time celebrated on January 6, the day of Epiphany, also as a single day of rest. It is now celebrated in July as a festival of the revolution. In Cuba, the music mixes a Chinese trumpet-like instrument with conga drums revealing not only African roots, but the influence of the many indentured Chinese laborers brought to the Island. Chinese motifs also appear in the visual elements of Cuban carnival, notably in the large lanterns carried aloft during the procession. The carnival in Brazil is actually a later development of the mid-nineteenth century and was basically a European affair of polka and waltzes until the slaves were freed in 1888. The *samba*, a fusion of Angolan *semba* rhythms (*semba* is an erotic dance brought from Luanda by slaves) with polka, the slow Cuban *habanero*, and other Caribbean dance influences, was created in the

Photo 5.11
Carnival street performers in colorful costumes parade through the streets of Port of Spain, Trinidad, in community celebration.
© *Hideto Sasamoto/HAGA/The Image Works*

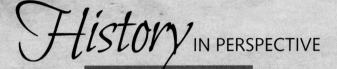

History IN PERSPECTIVE

PRESERVING ENDANGERED THEATRICAL TRADITIONS

Many performance traditions around the globe are endangered species of theatre unless we choose to cherish and preserve them. The legacy of colonial repression and the rapidity of today's economic, social, and political change have placed many forms at risk of extinction. They are losing their place in community life, their artists, and even the languages that sustained them. Attempts to save these cultural practices for future generations are underway. International organizations, national governments, universities, and local communities are experimenting with strategies for preserving endangered theatrical traditions.

In the last few years the United Nations Educational, Scientific and Cultural Organization (UNESCO) has expanded its notion of cultural heritage from tangible artworks to include intangible heritage such as language, know-how, and the performing arts, and has spearheaded the preservation and revitalization of cultural heritage worldwide. UNESCO has currently designated twenty-eight "masterpieces of oral and intangible heritage," outlining a unique plan of action for preserving each.

Among these masterpieces is *The Mystery Play of Elche* from Elche, Spain, a sacred musical drama mixing medieval and Renaissance stage practices that has been performed annually in the Basilica of Santa Marìa de Elche since the mid-fifteenth century. Sung in Latin and the Valencian language, the play uses three hundred participants to enact the assumption of the Virgin Mary for the entire community. A dearth of local performers who know the Valencian language and how to maintain the play's stage devices may lead to the extinction of the form. Restoration of the stage devices, the creation of a museum of the performance, and the training of new singers are all strategies for saving this practice.

In Benin, Nigeria, and Togo, the *Gelede*, a yearly Yoruba-nago right that includes singing; dancing; and the use of carved masks, costumes, and satyrical characters to retrace local history and myth is endangered because of a loss of skilled artists. Preservation efforts have led to the recording of the rites, the identification of master artists, and the creation of arts festivals as a place for performance and revitalization.

UNESCO's efforts have a global scope. The *kutiyattam* Sanskrit theatre from Kerala, India, the *kunqu* opera tradition in China, and the *bunraku* puppet tradition of Japan are all among the masterpieces cited by the organization, as are various carnival traditions from Oruro, Bolivia; Baranquilla, Colombia; and Binche, Belgium, and storytelling forms such as the *lakalaka* sung and choreographed speeches from Tonga, Korean *pansori* chanting, and the *Al-Sirah Al-Hilaliyyah* epic storytelling tradition of Egypt.

Many communities have long been engaged in preserving their own traditions. On the island of Bali in Indonesia, the impact of tourism on performance traditions and village life inspired the community to devise innovative means to preserve a rich heritage of dance-drama, shadow puppetry, and masked performance forms that blend Hindu and pre-Hindu practices. The Balinese cultivate two streams of performance, one for tourists and one with religious elements observed for the Balinese. They founded the Kokar Conservatory and the STSI School of Dance and Music to pass down traditional performances, create tourist presentations, and encourage the growth of new forms. The annual month-long Bali arts festival enables artists to perform traditional works to discerning audiences, maintaining a high technical standard. The revival of Thailand's *nang-yai* shadow puppet

early twentieth century in the slums of Rio. In a semantic confusion, it was called *samba* which means "praying to the spirit of the ancestors" in Bantu. Its rhythms permitted performers to dance, parade, and sing simultaneously, and it is now closely associated with Rio's carnival festivities, when community groups called samba schools challenge each other with dance performances, paralleling calypso's singing duels in the Caribbean.

Carnival Adapts and Evolves

During colonial times, attempts to ban carnival as unruly and lawless were repeated around Latin America to no avail. The form itself triumphed as an expression of freedom. Eventually carnival's jubilations became a government-sanctioned social release

tradition is indebted to monks who house the puppets and use their unique position within the community to assist local performers, mostly farmers, in maintaining the tradition.

Around the world, government-sponsored national theatres, training schools, and international festivals sustain traditional performance, and universities often harbor cultural centers for the study and promotion of indigenous art. This institutional support is key to preserving traditional forms. In Papua, New Guinea, The National Performing Arts Troupe trains performers and presents both traditional forms and new theatrical works, and the annual Hiri Moale Festival organized by local government offices provides an important opportunity for performance.

Often theatrical traditions fall victim to political events. During the brutal communist dictatorship of Pol Pot (1975–1979), 80 to 90 percent of Cambodia's artists died or were killed, endangering all of the indigenous Cambodian arts. The National Department of Arts, the School of Fine Arts in Phnom Penh, the University of Fine Arts, and royal patronage have united to revive

Cambodia's classical arts, including dance-dramas and shadow puppetry. Princess Norodom Buppha Devi herself has served as principal dancer for the royal dance troupe. The Tibetan Institute of Performing Arts (TIPA) in Dharamsala, India, keeps Tibetan cultural heritage alive for the Tibetan government and community in exile. TIPA receives support from international institutions working to preserve Tibetan culture.

These solutions, whether undertaken locally or by international groups, inevitably create their own contradictions and may transform the forms in their attempts to revitalize them. The questions of who pays for these measures as well as how traditions are elected for salvation and by whom remain hotbeds of debate. The reality that long-standing traditions can disappear within a single generation if they are not passed down to new performers galvanizes the search for workable options.

A masked dancer in a Tibetan opera at the annual Shoton Festival in Lhasa Tibet at Norbu Lingka Park, former resort of the Dalai Lama. Performances like this one, done in Tibet under Chinese rule, have different cultural and political implications from the same Tibetan operas done by Tibetans living in exile in India, who are preserving their own cultural heritage.
© Liu Liqun/ChinaStock.
All Rights Reserved.

valve for the poor. Caribbean peoples have taken their carnival heritage with them wherever they go. Large celebrations can be found in London, Brooklyn, and Toronto, and smaller festivities in many other cities continue to spring up. Months of costume preparations and rehearsals for these performances bring communities together. In keeping with old practices, festivities adapt to local surroundings, customs, and music, in an ever-evolving tradition.

Today's Caribbean artists find themselves in a position of contradiction toward carnival. With the tourist trade a staple of many Caribbean economies, carnival has become an object of touristic voyeurism performed to entertain the very people it co-opted, satirized, and demonized. Simultaneously it is the true voice of a culture and its fight for freedom and independence. Carnival has been a tremendous presence in Caribbean written drama, where the rhythms of calypso inhabit the language, and movement is an

Challenges and Choices

What is the difference between developing a form and transforming it into something new?

Photo 5.12
Participants in the annual Children's Parade and festival in Brooklyn, New York, display the spirit and style of carnival brought by West Indian immigrant groups to their new home in New York.
© *David M. Grossman/The Image Works*

inherent part of performance. The dueling songs of calypso can be felt in intense dialogue exchanges; the English Pierrot is personified in various postcolonial authority figures, as is the Pierrot Grenade, the poor fool outwitting his betters. The Nobel prize–winning Caribbean poet and playwright Derek Walcott (b. 1930) pits these two carnival figures against each other in *Dream on Monkey Mountain* through the characters of the mulatto prison guard Lestrade and Makak, his captive. Caribbean plays also reflect on the moral ambiguity embodied in the transgressive carnival, born at a time when the law and justice could be upheld by a corrupt colonial authority.

Puppet Traditions around the Globe

In the United States puppetry is often considered a form primarily for children, but around the world, from Belgium to Brazil, from Thailand to Turkey, from Mali to Myanmar, we find sophisticated puppet traditions that entertain adults and children alike. Puppets pass on myths and legends, illustrate moral teachings and philosophical questions, and present stories of emotional complexity. They are used in political activism and rituals of magic and healing. Some traditions go back hundreds of years and have served as the essential theatrical experience for a community.

An inanimate object brought to life is the captivating force of puppetry. Where once a human performer claimed center stage, puppeteers, puppets, and sometimes a narrator join to take the actor's role. Puppetry uses all the elements of theatre, but the visual takes precedence over the oral in this form. Traditions identify themselves by the kinds of puppets they use, and the special capabilities of particular objects determine the nature of the performance.

Puppets can take many forms and have various methods of manipulation: Hand puppets, string marionettes, rod puppets, and shadow puppets are the most common. The number of puppeteers required to operate a single puppet depends on its size and type. An operator can manipulate two small hand puppets at a time, whereas string marionettes, generally more complicated, might require two hands for a single figure. Some Burmese marionettes with many strings can perform amazing feats, such as the Alchemist, who does flips and other acrobatics. In many shadow traditions the puppeteer manipulates an entire world of characters by placing cutout figures, usually of leather, against a screen lit from behind by a lamp or other light source. In Thailand large shadow puppets representing a whole scene are danced across the screen by an operator holding the puppet by two handles. There are various types of rod puppets. Some, like those found in Sicily, are quite large; from four to five feet tall and dressed in full armor, these puppets can weigh up to eighty pounds each. The puppeteer works from above, holding a metal pole attached to the puppet's head and ropes attached to the arms. Other puppets, such as the West Javanese *wayang golek*, are small, and the puppeteer grasps the wooden sticks that support the bodies and hands from below.

There are as many kinds of puppets as there are ways of manipulating objects, and each is adapted to its performance context. Vietnamese water puppets—carved and painted wooden figures that have mechanical motions—perform on water stages in rice paddies and temple pools. The puppeteers stand behind a screen in water up to their waists to operate underwater poles attached to the floating figures.

Puppets and Ritual

An ancient art, puppetry's origins may lie in rituals in which objects imbued with life revealed the presence of a god or became a god incarnate and were worshiped as totemic figures. According to Indian legend, puppetry began when the god Shiva and his wife Parvati, seeing some excellently carved wooden figures, possessed them and made them dance. India boasts numerous puppet traditions whose performances all begin with prayers, and puppet figures have been found in some of the oldest archeological sites. Indian puppets are still treated reverently, and many continue to serve ritual functions.

Native peoples in the Americas used puppetry for both ritual and enjoyment long before colonists brought European puppet theatre to their land. In one Northwest Coast Indian ritual, a carved mythical snake chased a sacred dancer who appeared to eat it and then spit blood to exorcize a spirit. The snake was controlled by hidden manipulators who pulled strings from behind a hut. The Hopi Indians also used secretly manipulated snakes in a corn ritual.

According to the ancient Greek historian Herodotus, the Egyptians had a processional figure whose phallus was lifted by a string as part of a celebration of the god Osiris,

Photo 5.13

Wayang golek, pictured here, is a wooden rod puppet tradition from West Java, Indonesia, similar in many ways to the *wayang kulit* shadow puppet traditions found throughout Java and Bali. The delicate features and white paint of the puppet on the left belong to the *alus,* or refined character, while the bulbous eyes and nose and the red color of the puppet on the right show this to be a *kasar,* or unrefined character. The puppeteer or *dalang,* considered a spiritual leader, operates all of the puppets to the music of a *gamelan* orchestra, which he conducts by banging a small metal hammer held between his toes. The stories of *wayang golek* are drawn from Hindu epics or the tales of Panji and may express Muslim as well as Hindu religious and philosophical themes. Here we see puppets from Warno Wakito's puppet workshop, Yogyakarta, Java, Indonesia.
© *Michael Freeman/CORBIS*

History IN PERSPECTIVE

JOURNEY OF A THEATRICAL TRADITION: THE *ZARZUELA*

In places as far apart as Spain, the Philippines, Paraguay, the Caribbean, and New York, the term *zarzuela* means "musical theatrical entertainment." This theatrical form has journeyed through colonization and immigration and has taken root in new homelands, regenerating in unexpected ways.

Zarzuelas are romantic comedies or satires that incorporate music and dance and familiar characters. The name is derived from the shooting lodge of Philip IV of Spain, the Palacio de la Zarzuela, where many of these comic performances were done in the seventeenth century under his patronage. Some scholars contend that the form existed long before its name, as far back as the thirteenth century, descending from *sainetes* or short farces to which music and dance were added. Others believe it was born in Spain's Golden Age of theatre, the time of Lope de Vega and Calderón de la Barca, both of whom helped popularize the tradition.

The influx of Italian opera troupes to Spain caused the decline of *zarzuela* in the eighteenth century as it came to be regarded as an inferior musical form. A revival in the nineteenth century paralleled the rise of the operetta in France and Austria and resulted in two new forms: the *zarzuela grande* meant to rival Italian opera, but it was long and tedious, and it could not compete; and the *genero chico*, one-act *zarzuelas* first inserted between the acts of full-length plays and later presented on their own program. These appealed to popular audiences and were more successful.

The Spanish brought their theatre to their colonies in the sixteenth century as a means of converting the local population to Christianity. They were so successful that religious spectacles and *comedias* on religious themes, which all served missionary purposes, are still presented today across Latin America and the Philippines. Inevitably the forms blended with local influences. The *zarzuela*, a secular form, did not come to these areas until the nineteenth century when Spanish touring companies visited the colonies.

In 1878 playwright Dario Cespedes's Spanish troupe was the first *zarzuela* company to perform in Manila. In 1880 Alejandro Cubero and Elisea Raguera came from Spain and organized the first Filipino *zarzuela* troupe, training many future Filipino stars. They popu-larized Spanish-language *zarzuelas*, but a tradition of *zarzuelas* written in Filipino dialects soon emerged, spearheaded by Mariano Proceso Pabalan (1863–1904). Writers from across the islands followed suit, writing in their own tongues and introducing Filipino subjects and characters.

Tagalog language *zarzuelas* had revolutionary content, turning the colonizers' own theatrical form against them. Severino Reyes's *Walang Sugat* spoke against Spanish imperialism. Anti-American plays were written during the period of American colonization, such as Juan Abad's *Tanjikalang Ginto* (1903), which led to the author's arrest by American soldiers. The popularity of the *zarzuela* declined in the Philippines with the introduction of cinema, although the first Filipino silent film was based on a *zarzuela*, with live singers performing from behind the movie screen.

Cuba was one of the first countries in the Americas to receive *zarzuela* troupes in 1853 and provided a port of entry for *zarzuela* throughout the Americas. As early as 1868, at least two foreign companies competed for Cuban audiences. Touring companies then popularized the form throughout South America, Central America, and the Spanish-speaking Caribbean.

In each country, artists adapted *zarzuela* to local tastes and needs. In Chile it combined with the *costumbristas*, using local traditions, characters, and costumes to create a hybrid tradition. In Cuba, *zarzuelas* were both objects of scorn during the revolutionary period, and, as in the Philippines, a means of making anti-Spanish political commentary in a fight for independence. Race relations and colonialism have served as themes of Cuban *zarzuelas*.

Latin American immigrant communities in the United States brought the *zarzuela* with them as part of their cultural heritage. A Cuban American theatre in Florida performed *zarzuelas* under the Federal Theatre Project in the 1930s. Repertorio Español and Thalia Spanish Theatre continue to perform *zarzuelas* in Spanish for members of New York's Latino community seeking to reconnect with a cultural heritage they see as Cuban, Puerto Rican, or Dominican, not as a colonial tradition imported from Spain. Each nation has made *zarzuela* its own.

in what was probably a fertility rite. In ancient Rome the statue of the oracle of Jupiter-Ammon appeared to move on its own and spoke with voices that emerged from tubes in the wall. During the Middle Ages, European churches housed statues of holy figures with moving eyes and nodding heads, and some even wept or bled. Medieval marionettes also performed plays with religious themes.

Many puppet traditions still serve various ritual functions. In Awaji, Japan, puppeteers go from house to house conducting rituals of blessing for the new year. In Indonesia, puppeteers, or *dalang*, are people of power and perform with either shadow or rod puppets at weddings, births, and other ritual celebrations. They enact tales from the Hindu *Ramayana* and *Mahabharata* epics, adapted to fit the performance occasion. The final battle sequences are thought to bring forces of good and evil back into balance.

Africa has a rich heritage of masked performance, but surprisingly few ritual puppet traditions. In Mali masquerade performances combine masks and puppets, all of which are referred to as "masks." Puppet figures in the shape of mythical animals and symbolic characters pop out from the back of costumes and from the top of masks worn on the head. The performers dance about moving both their own bodies and those of the puppets accompanied by a singing chorus and drumming. Although not a sacred ritual, this community performance is a celebration of heritage and the natural world, and it acknowledges a connection between the world of spirits and that of humans.

Puppets and the Popular Voice

In Europe the tradition of popular puppetry extends back to ancient Greece and Rome. There is little evidence to reliably state what these puppets performed, but some may have done comic sketches akin to Atellan farces. Later puppet theatres incorporated *commedia dell'arte* characters and its improvisational style, relying on scenarios rather than play texts even for long and intricate stories.

The sixteenth century spawned a progeny of rabble-rousing *commedia dell'arte* puppet characters defiant of authority, including Italy's Pulcinella, England's Punch, and later Belgium's Tchantches, France's Guignol, and versions of these characters in Russia, Argentina, and elsewhere. First performed with hand puppets and small portable stages on street corners and in marketplaces, these shows provided popular entertainment and served as a voice for the common people. They relied on knockabout humor, but also took up topical issues of the day. Guignol, a nineteenth-century figure developed by a laid-off factory worker, reported on contemporary events for illiterate workers. The Turkish and Greek shadow traditions served a similar cultural role, centering on an anti-authoritarian rogue like Punch and his brethren called Karaghioz in Turkey and Karaghiozis in Greece. In both Sicily and Belgium, rod puppets perform medieval tales such as Ariosto's *Orlando Furioso* (1516) and *The Song of Roland* (eleventh century). Battle scenes draw the main focus, with comic relief provided by popular *commedia*-style characters.

In the eighteenth century string marionettes rose in popularity in Europe especially as entertainment for bourgeois audiences, and puppetry's role in catering to popular audiences declined. Joseph Haydn (1732–1809) and Wolfgang Amadeus Mozart (1756–1791), among other great composers, wrote operatic works specifically for marionettes. The Salzburg Marionette Theatre, founded in 1923, tours the world with its renowned opera, operetta, and ballet marionette performances.

A long-established tradition of Czech folk marionette theatre found its political voice in the Czech nationalist movement of the late nineteenth century against the Austro-Hungarian Empire. The puppet form, which predated the empire, kept local languages and legends alive and stood as a symbol of the indigenous Moravian and Bohemian cultures from early Czech history. Before World War I, Czech puppet plays protested

Photo 5.14
An old couple express their affection in a scene from the silent puppet play *Em Concerto (In Concert)* from Paraty Brazil's *Grupo Contadores des Estórias.* Director Marcos Caetano Ribas; puppets and props by Marcos and Rachel Ribas.
Courtesy of GRUPO CONTADORES DE ESTÓRIAS— TEATRO ESPAÇO

Austrian domination, and during the Soviet period they cleverly critiqued Communism. The Drak puppet company, founded in 1958, is still one of the Czech Republic's most important puppet theatres, mixing traditional marionettes with new ideas.

Today puppets also have a decidedly political role, with large processional puppets staples of political rallies. Peter Schuman's (b. 1934) Bread and Puppet Theatre began this trend in the 1960s when he brought his papier-mâché figures (masks and puppets of all sizes) to anti-Vietnam War protests. These silent images of women in pain and mourning made a dramatic impact and proved an effective means of conveying the antiwar message. Large puppets carried down the street by a crowd made puppeteering a communal act of protest. Schuman drew inspiration from European medieval processional figures, and his theatre promotes its grassroots politics by inviting all who so desire to participate in creation and performance (see photo on page 260). The Bread and Puppet Theatre derives its name from the belief that art is as necessary to health as bread, and the actors hand out their homemade bread to spectators when they perform. Bread and Puppet is still active, and it continues to inspire new generations of political puppeteers.

Puppets and Written Texts

In puppetry, the performing object is of more interest than a written text. As a result, many puppet traditions rely on the puppeteer's improvisations. Even when a written epic tale exists as the basis for a performance, such as the *Ramayana* and *Mahabharata* in India and Indonesia or *The Song of Roland* in Belgium, puppeteers often improvise, model a performance on an earlier puppeteer's practices, or use language passed on through an oral tradition. Nonetheless, some forms have developed great written literature for the puppet stage.

Japan's ***bunraku,*** a combination of puppet manipulation, ballad singing, and playing the three-stringed *shamisen*, has engendered both exquisite puppets and literary masterpieces. *Bunraku* puppets are three to four feet tall and operate through direct manipulation by three puppeteers who work together to create a seamless unity of action. Performers spend ten years learning to manipulate the puppet's feet and ten years learning to work the puppet's left hand; only then can they take the place of master puppeteers who manipulate the doll's head, face, and right hand. A chanter sits at the side of the stage narrating the story and performing all the voices and dialogue to musical accompaniment. Narrating for *bunraku* is a demanding art of its own, and famous chanters are the primary attraction for many aficionados. Chikamatsu Monzaemon (1653–1725), often called the Shakespeare of Japan, wrote his most famous plays for *bunraku.* They are beautiful literary works like *Love Suicides at Sonezaki* (1703) and *The Battles of Coxinga* (1715) with themes of love and honor that combine dialogue and prose description.

Other important playwrights have tried their hand at writing plays for puppets including Belgium's Maurice Maeterlinck (1862–1949) and Spain's Federico García Lorca (1899–1936). Lorca first wrote plays for hand puppets starring a Punch-like figure called

Don Cristobal in 1923. Lorca's visit to Argentina from 1932 to 1934 inspired puppet theatre presentations of European classical plays as well as Lorca's own work. Argentine puppeteers traveled through South America expanding interest in the form. Today, most Latin American puppet theatre serves a social and educational function, but young daring artists are exploring new forms that interact with other technologies.

Puppetry in the Twentieth Century and Today

In the early twentieth century the development of psychology and the explosion of technology made the puppet—an anthropomorphic figure moved by outside forces—an important symbol for artists commenting on the modern human condition. European writers such as Michel de Ghelderode (1898–1962), Jean Cocteau (1889–1963), Paul Claudel (1868–1955), Ramón de Valle-Inclán (1866–1936), and Gerhart Hauptmann (1862–1946) either wrote plays for puppets or used the puppet as a figure or metaphor in other dramatic works. The theatre designer and director Edward Gordon Craig (1872–1966) theorized that an *übermarionette*, a large puppet figure, should replace imperfect live actors to create a seamless stage world fully under the control of the director. Visual artists Wassily Kandinsky (1866–1944), Xanti Schawinsky (1904–1979), and Oscar Schlemmer (1888–1943) worked together at Germany's Bauhaus, a center for modernism based on the union of art and technology. Here they created mechanical puppets and designed costumes that transformed actors into moving objects. The Swiss artist Paul Klee (1879–1940) brought his abstract style to fifty hand puppets he made for his son Felix that were used in a Bauhaus performance.

Puppetry's ability to captivate spectators with dynamic visual images makes it a perfect theatrical answer to today's media age, and performing objects are an increasingly popular theatrical tool. Jim Henson (1936–1990), following in the footsteps of Howdy Doody; Kukla, Fran, and Ollie; and Shari Lewis's (1933–1998) Lamb Chops, introduced generations of children to puppetry through television with his Muppets, whose sophisticated humor addresses adults as well. Jim Henson's Creature Shop puts technologically innovative puppets to work on film and television, while the Henson Foundation continues to support puppeteers creating new works for the stage. *The Lion King* and

Photo 5.15
Woyzeck on the Highveld uses rod puppets and artist William Kentridge's film animations to transport Georg Buchner's nineteenth-century play *Woyzeck* to contemporary South Africa. Here Woyzeck is a migrant worker. The sense of despair and the struggle with poverty in a barren landscape are carved into the puppets' faces. In productions like this and *Ubu and the Truth Comission*, Handspring Puppets, the Johannesburg-based company, uses puppetry and animation to reflect on the realities of contemporary South Africa.
Photo by Ruphin Coudyzer FPPSA, www.ruphin.com

Photo 5.16
Performer Paul Zaloom makes comic cultural commentary using performing objects collected from America's trash heaps.
© *Jim Moore*

Avenue Q appear on Broadway with puppets, and Pulitzer Prize–winning author Paula Vogel's (b. 1951) *The Long Christmas Ride Home* (2003) uses puppets alongside live actors.

Today puppeteers experiment with an endless array of performing objects. They use found objects as puppets, they create their own figurative and nonfigurative forms with novel materials, and they blend aspects of every tradition with other visual imagery and media technology. South Africa's Handspring Puppet Company working with artist William Kentridge incorporates music and video animation in its work and has toured internationally with *Woyzek on the Highveld* and *Ubu and the Truth Commission*. Paul Zaloom (b. 1951) spent his early years with the Bread and Puppet Theater before creating his personal hybrid form combining mime, clowning, and puppetry to make political commentary. He can use ordinary objects on an overhead projector to create a modern shadow theatre, or create an entire puppet city of New York out of disposal garbage as a metaphor for our throwaway culture. Trained as a visual artist, Theodora Skipitares combines video projection with shadow puppets made from synthetic materials, stuffed figures that use the actor's hands as their own, and imaginative visual sights, such as the beautiful Helen of Greek mythology represented by a walking sheet and pillow adorned with a naked Renaissance female form. A give and take between established traditions and new experiments continues to expand the art of puppetry and its theatrical possibilities.

Traditions Evolve

Each of the performance traditions described in this chapter has had a long and colorful history and a large international sphere of influence. Many other traditions such as Korean *t'alch'um* have had less of an impact on other forms, but have held deep cultural meanings for their societies. They all reflect how varied theatrical expression can be, and how the imaginative and creative spirit can instigate change and challenge seemingly fixed forms. As we look at our own traditions, it is important to remember that they were once innovations. The true theatre artist looks to tradition and sees only possibilities.

■ KEY IDEAS

- Almost every culture has performance traditions, each with its own set of conventions that influence acting, training, writing, design, and directing.
- Performance traditions tend to present a heightened theatricality through the integration of music, dance, movement, masks, and elaborate costumes and make-up that create a total sensory experience for the audience.

- Indian Sanskrit drama is a sophisticated poetic tradition whose plays survive but whose codes of performance are lost to us, except for the description in the *Natyasastra*, a more than two-thousand-year-old authoritative text on the form that continues to influence Indian arts today.
- The mime tradition dates back to antiquity. The *commedia dell'arte* was an improvised Renaissance the-

atrical form with stock characters, whose influence can be felt in theatre, circus, vaudeville, film, and television to the present.

■ Japan has several important theatrical traditions. *Noh* is a highly stylized ritualistic form that developed in the medieval court. *Kyōgen* is its comic partner. *Kabuki* is a seventeenth-century tradition that evolved dynamic staging, costuming, and acting styles to cater to its popular merchant-class audience.

■ Singing is the heart of Chinese opera, a form that combines music, dance, song, acting, mime, spectacular makeup, conventionalized characters, martial arts, and dramatic storytelling.

■ Carnival, a theatrical form born in pagan Europe, traveled through colonization to the Caribbean and Latin America, where African slaves transformed it into an expression of freedom.

■ Almost every culture has a vibrant puppet tradition that can serve a ritual function or as popular entertainment. Puppets come in many shapes and sizes and have various modes of manipulation.

■ All traditions transform over time.

Alternative Paths to Performance

In "Sleep," one of three tales by Japanese author Murakami Haruki adapted for the stage by director Simon McBurney in *The Elephant Vanishes*, an alienated housewife tries to transform her mundane existence by staying up for seventeen nights. The multiple-eye imagery captures her forced wakefulness and speaks metaphorically about her process of self-examination. *The Elephant Vanishes* is a Complicité co-production with Setagaya Public Theatre, performed at the New York State Theater.

© Stephanie Berger

Every theatrical performance has a text that provides coherence and form for the events on stage, but that text is not always a play script, and the author is not always a playwright. A theatrical text can come in many guises—a musical score, movement notation, or visual images—and can be created in many ways. The author may be a playwright, but the author can also be an actor, a director or designer, a choreographer or composer, a clown or mime, or an ensemble of artists. A theatrical work often defies notions of authorship because its very nature is collaborative.

Other Authors, Other Texts, Other Forms

Plays give rise to a linear creative process that begins with ideas in the mind of a playwright that are expressed in a script that is turned over to directors, actors, and designers for interpretation on the stage. The creative process does not always follow this course from page to stage, however. Often the process is inverted, and rehearsals and performance shape the text. Sometimes the result of alternative paths to performance is alternative theatrical forms. The forms discussed in this chapter are both old and new; some are popular and easily accessible while others are unfamiliar, but all are created without a traditional play as the starting point. Understanding how a theatrical text created in unusual ways structures the performance can help us appreciate the variety of experiences we might encounter in the theatre today.

New forms develop when theatre practitioners believe old ones are exhausted or unable to express current concerns. Some artists try to use traditional styles in original ways. Still others seek a more personal means of expression. Whatever the impulse, they all search for new ways to create that can reinvigorate the stage. This leads to innovations that may defy accepted conventions. Artists who rebel against tradition are referred to as the **avant-garde** from the French term for the soldiers who march ahead of a military formation. Metaphorically, that is what these artists are doing, scouting out new artistic territory. Many of the forms and artists discussed in this chapter broke new ground, but now their path to performance is well trodden as others have followed in their footsteps. As you will see, when enough theatre practitioners follow new conventions for a period of time, a new theatrical tradition may be established. The avant-garde must be prepared to be challenged in a continual cycle of renewal through innovation.

Creating through Improvisation

Many theatrical forms rely on the improvisational creativity of the actor rather than on the playwright's written words for dialogue and dramatic action. In such forms actors take center stage as creators of drama, not just as performers. Such was the case of the improvised *commedia dell'arte* discussed in the last chapter, whose demise was hastened by its assimilation into written plays. Because it depended on the spontaneity of improvisation and physical humor, something inherent to its very nature—the freedom of the actor—was destroyed by the written word.

Improvisation is a central element in African culture, and the spontaneous interaction with an audience can transform a performance. Many African countries continue a tradition of improvised theatre that very much resembles the *commedia dell'arte*, with actors working off an outline prepared by the leader of the troupe. The stock characters reflect African types—the aged and crippled female crone, the cocky young stud, and the

 IN PERSPECTIVE

COMMEDIA SCENARIO

Commedia dell'arte performers improvised on a scenario, like the one pictured here from act three of *The Captain*, drawn from a collection of scenarios published in 1611 by Flaminio Scala, a *commedia* actor. Scripts like these would have hung backstage for the actors to look at before performing. On the left we see the names of the characters in the scene and on the right the description of events that will inspire improvisation.

The Captain: ACT THREE

FRANCESCHINA	Franceschina enters, grieving because she will never again see her husband, Pedrolino.
CASSANDRO	Just then, Cassandro enters, looking for the Captain. He sees Franceschina; recognizing her as the nurse, he begins to berate her, and falling to her knees, she tells him all that has happened to his daughter and where she left her.
DR. GRATIANO	At that moment, the Doctor enters, rejoicing about the wedding. He sees Cassandro, who tells him that Franceschina is the nurse and he now hopes to find his daughter. They go into the Doctor's house.
PANTALONE ORATIO	Pantalone and Oratio enter with jewels for the bride.
PEDROLINO PORTERS	Thereupon, Pedrolino enters with porters who are carrying things for the wedding, and they all go into the Doctor's house.
CAPT. SPAVENTO ISABELLA	Just then, the Captain enters with Isabella, who is dressed as a soldier. They say they want more than anything to stop the wedding, and they hide.
ARLECCHINO MUSICIANS	Arlecchino now enters with the musicians, instructing them that the banquet will be held in a garden at the Tosa Gate. The Captain and Isabella, having heard everything, leave. Arlecchino knocks.
ORATIO FLAMINIA	Oratio comes out holding Flaminia by the hand.
PEDROLINO FRANCESCHINA	Pedrolino comes out, holding Franceschina by the hand.
PANTALONE DR. GRATIANO	Pantalone comes out, holding the Doctor by the hand. The musicians start playing and they all dance off to the garden at the Tosa Gate.

From Scenarios of the Commedia dell'Arte, *Flaminio Scala's* Il Teatro delle favole rappresentative, *trans. Henry F. Salerno. (New York: New York University Press, 1967), 83. Used with permission of Michelle Korri.*

usual collection of gluttonous servants and tricksters. Most of these companies are traveling troupes, like their European counterparts.

Improvisation plays an important role in many Asian theatrical traditions as performers adapt well-known stories or prepared material to topical events. In the *bhavai* tradition of Gujarat, India, traveling players hone a repertoire of *veshas,* or sketches. These sketches are not written down, but passed on from father to son through practice and performance. When the players arrive in a town, they inquire about current events and issues of importance to the local people. This information helps them choose what *veshas* to perform, so their improvisations will be relevant and filled with topical allusions to which the audience can relate.

Photo 6.1
Members of the Second City improvisational troupe perform routines at the troupe's cabaret-style theater on Chicago's North Side. Second City has branched out into the multibillion corporate training market, using improv-based learning methods to polish the skills of business people.
© *AP/Wide World Photos*

Improvisational theatre is alive and well in the United States. Second City and Chicago City Limits are long-running improvisational theatre events in which actors improvise and often create from ideas given to them by the audience. A simple subject or title volunteered by an audience member can serve as the dramatic text and form the catalyst for comic sketches, much as they did for the *commedia dell'arte. Whose Line Is It Anyway?*, the television show based on these techniques, has been enjoying great popularity. The excitement of the form lies in the spontaneity and virtuosity of the actors as they interact in performance.

Improvisation is an inherent part of the theatrical process. Before performances are set, there is a period of rehearsal that usually begins with improvised trial and error, so what appears to be a fully scripted and blocked performance is actually created through improvisation. The discoveries made during rehearsals are often incorporated into published plays. At each performance, actors face a set of unknowns that can alter the playing of the text: an unexpected laugh, a forgotten line, or a malfunctioning prop can trigger improvisation. Even fully scripted texts are in some way scenarios for the action on stage.

The Performance Ensemble and Collaborative Creation

Although all theatre is always collaborative, sometimes traditional hierarchies of decision-making dissolve and a group of artists share the responsibility for creating the text. They may work through improvisation, discussion, and sharing of ideas. In this process, there may not necessarily be a single author. Collaborative creation is often favored by those with strong political and social beliefs in the power of the community.

1960s Experimental Collaboration

During the 1960s, when the social revolution sent the theatre into a search for new forms, some theatre artists rebelled against the established written text and the hierarchy of control within the theatrical process. The supremacy of the playwright's words was seen as a metaphor for the social and political power structure that needed to be overthrown. Following the ideas of French theorist Antonin Artaud (1896–1948), for a time even language itself was decried as the source of manipulation of the masses, and the primal expression of sound and movement was given priority. Groups such as Joseph Chaikin's (1935–2003) Open Theatre (1963–1973) and Peter Brook's International Center for Theatre Research (founded in 1970) searched for a new system of language based on sound and movement that attempted to transcend cultural boundaries. Many new theatre companies began rehearsals with an idea or concept but no written text. The actors, designers, and director began a process of collaborative creation; the performance text and the dramatic text evolved together, and the creative performance team was the author of both texts.

One of the earliest groups to work in this manner was The Living Theatre, whose political work we discussed in Chapter 2. Founder Julian Beck described their process as follows: "We find an idea that we want to express physically. Then we do what is necessary to realize it. If it requires special physical exercises, then we do them."[1] Some of their work involved audience participation, and spectator reaction influenced the dramatic text. Even when they worked with playwrights, such as Jack Gelber (1932–2003), some parts of the script were worked out in performance. In fact, their production of Gelber's *The Connection* (1959) not only used jazz improvisation as a metaphor for the actor's work, but had jazz musicians improvising on stage with the actors in performance.

Although such collaborative groups proliferated in the United States, this was an international phenomenon. Peter Brook began his work in London and then set up in Paris. Jerzy Grotowski's (1933–1999) famed Polish Laboratory Theatre used physically based acting techniques to reconstruct and construct dramatic texts, and his efforts were an inspiration to many groups around the world. (There is further discussion of Grotowski in Chapter 7.)

Contemporary Collaborative Work

Today many theatre groups continue to use collaborative improvisation and experimentation to create a performance text. Although dramatic texts may develop out of this work, they are "written" through an active working process on the stage. The idea that a play can be authored by a company of people and that even the audience can claim some part of authorship is a marked departure from the traditional concept of a playwright as the sole author of the dramatic text.

One important example of this is the collaborative docudrama *The Laramie Project* (2001), about the events surrounding the gruesome 1998 murder of Matthew Shepard, a young gay man who was severely beaten and left to die on a roadside in the harsh Wyoming winter. Members of the Tectonic Theatre Project served as researchers and interviewers, and then as dramaturgs, writers, and actors. Director Moisés Kaufman took his actors to Laramie, Wyoming, where they interviewed the murdered Shepard's friends and family, the friends and family of the men who killed him, the person who found his

---

1. Julian Beck, "Acting Exercises," in *The Twentieth Century Performance Reader* (London: Routledge, 1996), 61.

Texts IN PERSPECTIVE

THE OPEN THEATRE'S GROUP CREATION: *TERMINAL*

The work of the Open Theatre was created in collaboration with actors and writers, and pieces often developed over two years of experimentation. The script for *Terminal* is the result of a group search for an expression of cultural attitudes toward death and mortality. Performed with ritual elements of choral movement and chanting, words were evocative of deeper meanings, and images of the transitory nature of the human body were everywhere present as the living and the dying became one. The name of Susan Yankowitz, who is credited as the "playwright" for this piece, was often not mentioned in publicity or reviews, and she openly acknowledged the awkwardness of being "the author of an 'authorless' piece." She would write lines for the actors to try out. They would work with them and then accept or reject them. Sometimes the actors suggested the lines for her to write. Most often, sound and gesture expressed more meaning than the words.

The Dying Resist   *Lights. A circle of actors walk at a brisk, regular pace. When individuals break out of the circle, the others maintain its original size and shape by adjusting pace and distance. Two Team Members stand outside the circle. One gives instructions. The other drones words of approval, which eventually become empty sounds.*

TEAM MEMBER 1:
Keep moving.
Everyone is part of the
  circle.
Everyone must keep the
  circle moving.
Follow instructions.
Don't accelerate or slow
  down.
Don't stop.
You are each responsible
  for keeping the circle
  moving.
Everyone is useful.
You are each keeping the
  circle alive.

TEAM MEMBER 2:		
Very	good.	Nice.
Very	good.	Nice.
Very	good.	Nice.
Very	good.	Nice.
ery	ood.	ice.
ery	ood.	ice.
ery	ood.	ice.
ery	ood.	ice.

Individuals step out of the circle, or stop abruptly where they are.
First one. Then another. Then more.
Individually, and finally in unison, the Resisters punctuate the drone with the word "out."

RESISTERS:		TEAM MEMBER 2:		
Out			ery	ood.	ice.
out	out		ery	ood.	ice.
	out		ery	ood.	ice.
out				(*Etc.*)	
out					
out					
out					
out					

The actors continue their circle.
They ignore both the physical obstacles presented by the Resisters and the word of protest.
The circle and the protest exist simultaneously.

The Runner Who Never Gets Started   *The Runner crouches over an imaginary starting line on hands and toes. He holds the racing position for several moments, then jumps to his feet, panting. Behind him, a Second Runner runs frantically in place. The First Runner repeats his action.*

The Dying Are Drugged   *Several of the Dying sit or lie on the beds. We see them in their drugged condition—vacant, tranquilized, harmless. A high-pitched hum is heard.*

Note: *This fragment should bear a rhythmic and thematic relationship to The Dying Resist.*

The Open Theatre was known for its strong physical acting and vocal work. In the 1971 production *Terminal*, written by Susan Yankowitz and directed by Joseph Chaikin and Roberta Sklar, sound, movement, and incantation evoke images of death and dying. The work of this group was revolutionary in its time.
© Photograph by Max Waldman. All Rights Reserved.

Source: Copyright © 1969 by Susan Yankowitz and Joseph Chaikin and the Open Theatre Ensemble.

Photo 6.2
Using current events as a springboard for collaborative creation, actors of the Tectonic Theatre Project portray members of the Laramie community they interviewed to create the text for the *Laramie Project*. The production toured widely. Shown here, the southern California premiere in La Jolla, directed by Moisés Kaufman, with additional staging by associate director Leigh Fondakowski.
© *Ken Friedman*

body, the sheriff who led the investigation, other gay men in town, church leaders, teachers, and other members of the community. The actors turned these interviews into short monologues, attempting to reproduce the voices, actions, and words of the people they had interviewed as authentically as possible. They performed these vignettes for each other, arguing for and against keeping different pieces. The result was *The Laramie Project*, which painted a theatrical portrait of Laramie, Wyoming, and examined the various ways its individuals and the community as a whole dealt with issues of prejudice. The actors took a strong hand in aspects of the production that would normally be left to the playwright and the director. A written play was not the starting point of this project, but the end, and the program lists the director and all the members of the company in

Photo 6.3
Cast members Stefan Metz, Hannes Flaschberger, Aurelia Petit, Dan Fredenburgh, Kostas Philippoglou, Tim McMullan, and Susan Lynch examine the remains of a 5,000-year-old man as a means of using the past to find meaning in the present. Simon McBurney's production of *Mnemonic* devised by the company Complicité at Riverside Studios.
© *ArenaPal/Topham/The Image Works*

Photo 6.4
Sarafina, written and directed by South African Mbongeni Ngema with music by Ngema and Hugh Masekela, dramatizes the struggle of South African youth against the oppression of apartheid. The central character wrestles with the need to use violence to overcome injustice and confront the racist government's authority figures. First produced in South Africa in 1987 by Committed Artists, the play was later moved to New York, where it was nominated for five Tony Awards.
Photo by Ruphin Coudyzer FPPSA,
www.ruphin.com

addition to several writers as the authors of the final script. In the program, the director welcomed the audience to the "performance of '*our*' play."

Similarly the Complicité's collaborative production *Mnemonic* (1999) traced the intersecting stories of the search for the identity of a frozen five-thousand-year-old man with a contemporary woman's search for her origins (see Photo 6.3). Using visual images, music, movement, text, and sound, the performance was constructed from interwoven memories and associations of the various company members in what its director Simon McBurney described as a "collision" of personal stories that awaits the final collaboration of the audience. Again, the program credits the entire company with authorship.

Black South African director Mbongeni Ngema created Theatre of the Ancestors, a political people's theatre of little means and great theatricality using collaborative creation. In the community spirit of the African tradition, he brings together an ensemble of untrained actors who live together for many months, building the spirit of *ubuntu*, or brotherhood, out of which collaborative creation will grow. He provides rigorous training while the actors are building a performance about matters of immediate concern to them through improvisation and collaboration. Using the storytelling, dance, and choral song at the heart of African performance, he built his production of *Sarafina*, which tells the tale of a murdered civil rights lawyer. Through impersonation and storytelling, the actors in this group invite the spirit of the fallen ancestor to live within them. Acting becomes a vehicle that combines traditional beliefs with education, personal growth, and creative expression. Ngema used the same method in *Woza Albert!* to call up the spirit of memorable political leaders and enact them on stage.

Mime and Movement Theatre

Around the world, in many performance traditions, the actor's movement is the primary conveyor of meaning or story. The literary text is either nonexistent or given secondary dramatic value. Most performances that use masks focus on the body and emphasize movement over language. The Indian *kathakali*, Balinese masked comedies, Native American performance, African festivals, and *commedia* and clown traditions around the world use movement as a primary text. Because mime is embodied in the mutable physical being, there are few records of movement-based performance through history. We do have enough evidence, however, to know that such forms seem to have existed in all periods, in all cultures.

Modern Mime

Although movement-based theatre is a global phenomenon, the term *mime* usually evokes images of a story acted out without words as in a *pantomime*. Actors working in the manner of Marcel Marceau to conjure up the existence of unseen objects and people on stage perform what is called *illusionary mime*. Many mime performances are actually *mimodramas*—silent plays that have characters, plot, and a story; the absence of language means that they are conceived in the body, and not through dialogue. Less well known are various forms of abstract mime that do not rely on a narrative and whose expression lies in the kinetic energy of the body. This abstract corporal expression feels closer to modern dance, but it does not have the focus on the conscious aesthetics of movement we find in dance performance. If the dancer seems to work with or against the forces of gravity, mime is always earthbound and emotionally rooted. *Statuary mime*—the creation of Étienne Decroux (1898–1991)—uses

Photo 6.5
Renowned artist Marcel Marceau is the master of illusionary mime. He can make us see what is not there, as in this photo of a performance at the Geffen Playhouse in Westwood, California.
© Michel Boutefeu/Getty Images

suggestive movement bursting out of immobility to create a series of moving sculptures, each position capable of multiple interpretations just like an actual piece of statuary art. Statuary mime also liberates the actor from expressing only human forms. Decroux's famous pieces *Les Arbres* (*The Trees*) and *L'enveloppe* (*The Envelope*) use abstraction and metaphor. In *L'enveloppe*, a draped amorphous form struggles for freedom. Decroux's disciple, Jean-Louis Barrault (1910–1994), sought a "subjective" tragic mime that dealt with the metaphysical human struggle for existence in a difficult world. Jacques Lecoq (1921–1999) created a famous mime school in Paris devoted to the development of a fundamental and natural mime that preexists language and is transcultural. The Mummenschanz, a company originally formed by Lecoq students, masks not only the face, but the body as well, turning the actors into abstract shapes that express meaning much the way it is expressed in abstract art. Many of Lecoq's students have used his philosophy of mime to energize stage movement within more traditional theatrical forms.

Unlike dance, which is structured through rhythm, music, and line of movement, the mime begins with a narrative, idea, or image and then gives physical life to that concept. Mime performance is created through improvisational trial and error until a performance text is concretized into fixed patterns of movement. Most often, the author of the movement text is also the performer, creating the same organic link between the dramatic text and the performance found in all performance traditions and particularly in solo work. Some movement texts can be passed on to new generations of interpreters because they are carefully choreographed and notated.

The Variety Entertainer

Variety entertainment is as old as recorded theatre history. We know that street performers, "mimes" performed in ancient times. Aristotle alludes to them in *The Poetics*. The theatre in the late Roman Empire was largely a variety show. These performances are always high on fun and low on intellectual demands because of the lack of a sustained narrative. They have appealed to the general public through the centuries by featuring diverse entertainments not connected through a single story.

Clowns and Fools

Clowns and fools occur in most cultures, and as discussed in the section on comedy in Chapter 4, serve a variety of social functions. What they have in common is minimal written text and a dependency on tradition, improvisation, and physical action. Ceremonial clowns of Native American traditions may use texts based on ritual, and circus clowns may develop personal texts based on movement that is idiosyncratic to their individual clown characters. Sometimes daring acrobatic feats may provide the text for circus clowns, or they may depend on the knockabout humor of the English pantomime and music hall tradition that we saw extended into silent film. The talking clown used verbal humor as a nontraditional written text that has led to an entire tradition of stand-up comedy.

In certain regions of Anglophone Africa, a form of variety entertainment called **concert parties** evolved in the 1920s, and its touring companies have performed all over West Africa ever since. A hybrid combination of African culture and American and European entertainments brought by traders, it includes musical numbers, brief topical sketches, female interpreters, and comic routines with clowns and tricksters winning the day in slapstick romps with stock characters out of West African society. The concert party clown, in an intriguing bit of cultural borrowing from early American films, often appears to this very day with the heavy white painted lips of the American **minstrel show**, a nineteenth-century racist performance style in which whites both appropriated African American culture and music and simultaneously created the denigrating blackface, white-lipped racial stereotype (see Photo 6.6 and page 335). Today's concert parties continue a blending of traditions, incorporating gospel, rock, and soul music with African themes. The Yoruba Opera in Nigeria is similar in form and practice, and its development was probably influenced by concert parties.

African performances also included elements of **vaudeville**—a popular American variety show form that incorporated many different kinds of dramatic texts and relied heavily on the stand-up routines and knockabout humor that had evolved out of earlier clown traditions. Vaudeville had its heyday toward the end of the nineteenth and the

Photo 6.6
"The Akan Trio," a Ghanaian concert party, during an opening chorus in the late 1950s. Joseph Emmanuel Baidoe, playing the Lady, is flanked by Kobina Okai on the left and E. K. Nyame on the right. Note the use of the exaggerated makeup of American minstrelsy, whose negative racial stereotype traveled the globe and became a form of self-parody in West Africa.
Courtesy of J. E. Baidoe and Catherine M. Cole

early twentieth centuries, and billed itself as family entertainment. Its counterpart was the less family-oriented **burlesque** show, which had bawdier humor and usually included striptease. Both popular entertainments were eventually eclipsed by the movies. To keep audiences in the theatre by offering something for everyone, vaudeville and burlesque could include musical numbers, acrobatic bits, comedy duos, and even animal tricks. The evening usually ended with an extended theatrical scene.

Variety Entertainment and the Avant-Garde

The early twentieth century avant-garde, especially the futurists, focused on variety show performance as a means of developing a new artistic sensibility. They wanted to destroy the illusionary realistic stage world through the destruction of the convention of the *fourth wall* and foster an active interaction with the audience. The clown, the acrobat, and the juggler were the perfect performers to achieve this; they do not represent anything other than themselves and are not caught up in the illusion of narrative; and their acts rely on a logical presentation of concrete skills—feats that inspire ongoing interaction with the audience.

In the tradition of the avant-garde, these old popular entertainments have now come back in the form of *new vaudeville* and *new burlesque* and are performing in theatrical venues. They bring an aesthetic and social self-consciousness that seeks to alter audience sensibilities. These clowns, comics, acrobats, mimes, and jugglers are distinguished from their antecedents who played for pure entertainment value. Their physical humor and movement are part of a dramatic text with other messages and goals. The best known of these new clowns is Bill Irwin, who trained as a circus performer, dancer, actor, and mime, and has extended comic clown routines beyond their pure amusement value. In *The Regard Evening*, Irwin spoofs the avant-garde as well as the conventions of realism and variety theatre. Using costume elements as symbols (the baggy pants, ruffled collar, and big shoes of the clown; the top hat and cane of the vaudeville hoofer; the goofy hat of the stand-up comic; and a groucho Marx disguise), Irwin humorously explodes each tradition (see Photo 6.7). In *Largely New York*, which played in the commercial Broadway theatre, Irwin appeared as a "post-modern

Photo 6.7
In *The Regard Evening*, Bill Irwin shows the skill of an old Broadway hoofer in a new vaudeville performance directed by Bill Irwin and created in collaboration with Doug Skinner, Michael O'Connor, and Nancy Harrington. Set design by Nancy Schertler; costume design by Catherine Zuber; music by Doug Skinner; sound design by Douglas Stein; lighting design by Brett R. Jarvis; Signature Theatre Company.
© *Carol Rosegg*

FUTURIST PERFORMANCE

In futurist performance the stage was experienced concretely and not as representing some other place. Scripts emphasized the illogical and rejected a narrative based on cause and effect. In this short piece by Giacomo Balla (1871–1953), the gibberish of the lines destroys the narrative thread. The stage is empty and draws attention to itself by the division into zones of red and green light. This empty space was a novel idea at the start of the twentieth century. The actors come out and perform as variety show entertainers, not belonging to any dramatic context.

GIACOMO BALLA

To Understand Weeping / *Per Comprendere il Pianto*

MAN DRESSED IN WHITE (*summer suit*)
MAN DRESSED IN BLACK (*a woman's mourning suit*)

Background: square frame, half-red, half-green.
The two characters are talking, always very seriously.

MAN DRESSED IN BLACK: To understand weeping . . .
MAN DRESSED IN WHITE: mispicchirtitotiti
MAN DRESSED IN BLACK: 48
MAN DRESSED IN WHITE: brancapatarsa
MAN DRESSED IN BLACK: 1215 but mi . . .
MAN DRESSED IN WHITE: ullurbusssssut
MAN DRESSED IN BLACK: 1 it seems like you are laughing
MAN DRESSED IN WHITE: sgnacarsnaipir
MAN DRESSED IN BLACK: 111.111.011 I forbid you to laugh
MAN DRESSED IN WHITE: parplecurplototplaplint
MAN DRESSED IN BLACK: 888 but for G-o-d-'-s sake don't laugh!
MAN DRESSED IN WHITE: iiiiiirrrrririrriri
MAN DRESSED IN BLACK: 12344 Enough! Stop it! Stop laughing.
MAN DRESSED IN WHITE: I must laugh.

CURTAIN

Source: Futurist Performance, *by Michael Kirby, with manifestos and playscripts translated from the Italian by Victoria Nes Kirby. Copyright © 1971, 1986 by Michael Kirby. English translations of manifestos and playscripts in Appendix copyright © 1971 by Victoria Nes Kirby. Reprinted by permission of PAJ Publications, New York.*

hoofer" whose doomed attempts to learn a variety of modern dance styles end up trapping him inside a television set. All this is performed with ongoing banter with the audience. Despite his light-hearted veneer, Irwin ends up delivering pointed social and aesthetic commentary.

The Quebec-based Cirque du Soleil has found a way to use circus performance as a theatrical text playing on the inherent dramatic content in feats that defy gravity and the limits of the human body, and it has spawned imitators around the world. Performed with attention to every aesthetic detail from dramatic lighting to costumes and sound, these circus artists assume theatrical characters as they dazzle us with circus skills enhanced with the accoutrements of theatre performance. Unlike other circus performances in which the focus is on the raw energy of the skill and danger, Cirque du Soleil clothes its acts in an air of mystery, mysticism, and the exotic. The Flying Karamazov Brothers, who can juggle almost anything from meat cleavers and sickles to chunks of tofu, fish, and eggs, engage in an ongoing comic patter with the audience that titillates the mind while their feats titillate the eyes. Here circus is combined with impeccable comic timing.

The Storyteller

Storytelling has long been considered an origin of theatre. It contains all the fundamental elements of the form—a performer, an audience, characters, and narrative. In fact, gifted storytellers can transform into the characters in their tales, turning their narrative into a form of theatrical performance. Solo storytelling performance has a long and continuing history.

Telling the Community's Story

In many African cultures storytelling is a vital way of educating the young while entertaining the community. Narration, acting, drumming, and song are interwoven into a participatory art form, and audience response can create improvised moments. Often stories begin with riddles posed to the children of the community as a teaching device. Subjects tend to stress the continuity of the community and its values and may include tribal heroics, feats of strength and wit, and tales of magical powers. The legends tend to have morals and imply behavioral dictates. The African storyteller is a talented impersonator who can portray all the characters, human and animal, through alterations in voice and body. Narrative descriptions are recounted with sound effects and expressive intonations.

The stories belong to their communities and are passed on from one generation of storytellers to the next, with each adding its own embellishments. The idea of authorship for these stories can be an anathema to societies in which cultural property belongs to the community and ideas of ownership are not reflected in methods of creation. Often community members interrupt the story to act out particular passages or sing an appropriate song, and the audience can spontaneously enter the playing space to dance and sing and add to the performance. Although much storytelling consists of myth and legend, the *griots*—storytellers of West Africa—have provided an oral history of their communities through their recitation of epic heroic tales that can go on for hours. These sagas are filled

Photo 6.8
An African griot woman, Ya Jalahatuma Jabate, performing a song of praise at a gathering to celebrate the istallation of the Chief Griot of Kita. She is playing the *karinya*. In West Africa, insruments are allocated by gender. Only men can play drums and stringed instruments, while women play percussion.
Photo by Barbara G. Hoffman, 1985

with music and songs, praises for leaders and their ancestors, genealogies that connect the past to the present, and proverbs that ensure the continuity of cultural values.

Telling Personal Stories

Sometimes a storyteller may recount a personal history. Solo performance has become popular in recent years, evolving from several traditions from stand-up comedy to **performance art**, in which performance is an extension of visual art in time, with more significance accorded to the visual image than the spoken text. Today, individual actors create solo pieces to highlight their unique talents, their personal experiences, and their own deep concerns.

All of today's solo performers owe a debt to Spalding Gray (1941–2004), who pioneered with his solo performances in the 1970s and was instrumental in turning solo theatre into a respected performance form. His performances were a place for personal exploration and confession, and many younger artists cite him as their inspiration. His texts sound and read more like diary entries than traditional theatre pieces. When he performed *Swimming to Cambodia* or *Monster in a Box*, monologues that relate very personal stories from his own life, he did not just reveal his particular personality on stage; the audience also witnessed his attempt to come to grips with his own life experiences through the medium of theatre. Although written, published, and available to other interpreters, Gray's monologues are deeply connected to him and his life experiences.

Unlike our image of a playwright toiling alone at a desk, Gray's texts developed out of his performances. To create a piece, he sat at a desk on stage and improvised from an outline in front of an audience. The performance was recorded and the tapes transcribed. He then edited and expanded the performance transcripts, continuing this process of performance, taping, editing, and expanding until the written monologue was complete. Early audiences did not hear the completed dramatic text, but rather, a text in process. The dramatic text was actually created in front of the audience, and the audience's responses became a collaborative element. Interestingly, many solo performers create in this way. Because the writers and performers of these solo texts are the same person and the material is so deeply connected to their lives, the texts can be composed organically during the performance process.

The growing number of performers who have taken to this form reflects a confluence of forces. As theatre becomes increasingly expensive to produce, the single artist sitting alone on stage with little or no set or costume elements is an economical and portable way to create theatre that can be taken to different venues with little effort. On a deeper level, as the world moves toward multicultural awareness, individual voices representing groups who had been largely silent can now be heard and welcomed in the public arena. Performers from marginalized groups often take to the stage to represent the political and social agendas of their communities.

Personal Stories, Political Agendas

Challenges and Choices
When an artist wants to make a strong statement of social protest, should there be limitations in how far he or she can go in violation of social taboos?

Although early male solo artists such as Spalding Gray often focused on political or social commentary in their work, when women claimed the solo stage for feminist performance, often the personal became political. A generation ago, it could seem unsettling just to see a woman alone in command of a theatre; now women are not only solo, but have created daring pieces that often blur the line between public and private acts. Performers such as Karen Finley (b. 1956) and Holly Hughes (b. 1951) use the shock value of nudity, obscene tirades, and sexual images—including Finley's smearing her naked body in chocolate and offering the audience a lick—to raise awareness of their political concerns. Some of the disturbing effects were visual statements, reflecting solo performance's origins in performance art.

 IN PERSPECTIVE

SPALDING GRAY

Spalding Gray's texts read more like diary entries than traditional theatre pieces. Recounting actual incidents from his life, Gray made astute observations that became sharp social commentary.

FROM "NOBODY WANTED TO SIT BEHIND A DESK"

The summer was completely planned. All I had to do was get safely from Amsterdam to New York, where Renée was to meet me with a car. Then we had three solid weeks to drive to San Francisco, where I was to perform.

I had had trouble getting out of Amsterdam before. It was not so much the city itself, but the airport, the Schiphol airport, where I had a tendency to get bogged down. In 1976, when I was returning from India with an open ticket on KLM, I decided that I wanted to avoid the bicentennial and spend the summer in Amsterdam instead. Just as I was about to board, I told the stewardess at the gate, "Take the luggage off the plane. I'll stay here." She said, "I'm sorry, Mr. Gray. I'm afraid it's too late for that." Then I said, "Very well, send the luggage on to New York. I'll stay on without it." She said, "We can't do that, Mr. Gray. It's a rule, you have to accompany your luggage on the flight." So I flew all the way back to New York to accompany my luggage.

In his usual posture at his desk, Spalding Gray is seen here performing *Terrors of Pleasure* at the Lincoln Center "Serious Fun" festival.
© *Paula Court*

Source: Sex and Death to the Age 14 by Spalding Gray, copyright © 1986 by Spalding Gray. Used by permission of Vintage Books, a division of Random House, Inc.

Feminist performance gave way to explorations of class, race, ethnicity, and sexuality. Daring, provocative, and often naked, Tim Miller challenges audiences to see past his homosexuality to his humanity (see Photo 6.9). In pieces such as *Glory Box* (1999), *Body Blows* (2002), and *US* (2003), he thrust himself into the American cultural war over gay marriage and immigration rights for gay and lesbian binational couples. Similarly, London-based Muslim performer Shazia Mirza (b. 1976) uses comedy to pierce our ethnic and religious stereotypes and fears with jokes about terrorists and the "veil." Solo artists use their art to probe the nature of identity and social definitions of difference, self, and other, while bringing visibility to the concerns of disenfranchised groups. Their work challenges us to think about how we define ourselves and those we do not really know.

Photo 6.9
Tim Miller performs his autobiographical solo act *Shirts and Skin*, in which he traces significant moments in his life by stripping naked and trying on different shirts that aid in his reminiscence.
© *Paula Court*

Although some solo artists perform themselves, sometimes as diarists of their own lives, other solo performers create character sketches by imitating or performing people they know—family members or others they have met or interviewed. John Leguizamo (b. 1965) in *Mambo Mouth* and *Freak*, singlehandedly populates a stage with as many as thirty-nine different characters from the Latino community. Korean American Margaret Cho (b. 1968) not only explores Asian American identity, but crosses racial lines to play characters she knows of other races and ethnicities, forcing us to examine our own social typecasting. Sarah Jones in her acclaimed show *Bridge and Tunnel* (2004) examines assimilation and identity as she portrays a dozen or more New York characters of different races, religions, and ethnicities who reveal their deepest longings at a community poetry contest.

As the solo form of stand-up comedy turns increasingly "in your face" and agenda driven, it often becomes difficult to draw a clear line between stand-up and other forms of solo performance. Many festivals of solo performance include entertainers who bill themselves as comedians and those who consider themselves performance artists. If the comic is always looking for laughter as a release, performance artists often provide no outlet for our shock or outrage. What all of these artists have in common is the authorship of texts that require their personal presence on stage. The actor's intimate relationship to the individuals and experiences presented is integral, and unlike a play written as a monologue, these personal performance pieces can't be reproduced by another actor.

The Journalist and Social Historian: Documentary Theatre

Historical sources have long been mined to create theatrical fare. Some believe the events depicted in Greek tragedy are based in fact; Shakespeare wrote history plays; Arthur Miller went to Salem, Massachusetts, to study the court records of the witch trials before writing *The Crucible*. These documentary records served as the inspiration for fictional drama. Today we see a new kind of **docudrama**, or **documentary theatre**, in which actual primary sources become the text for a performance. Unlike reality television and its frivolous invented drama, documentary theatre tends to have political and social messages and tries to address pressing issues with theatrical immediacy.

Solo Social Documentarians

Although solo performance is a personal form, it does not have to use personal material. Several solo artists have used the medium to explore social and political issues through the transformation of material collected from various primary sources into performance vehicles. The work of solo artists like Eve Ensler and Anna Deavere Smith (b. 1950) are in the category of docudrama.

Anna Deavere Smith's performances are all part of a larger project she calls *On the Road* that explores the way individuals negotiate their ethnic, religious, racial, and American identities. Her characters are all people she has met in real life, and Smith lets them speak for themselves—the dialogue she uses is taken directly from transcripts of interviews she has done. Performing their words, Smith recreates the speech patterns and mannerisms of her interviewees with great precision and changes before our eyes like a chameleon. Race relations have been a central focus in her work: *Fires in the Mirror* (1992) is an investigation of the racial and religious attitudes that triggered the riots and murder that took place in Crown Heights, Brooklyn, in 1991 after a car driven by an orthodox Jew hit a black child. *Twilight: Los Angeles, 1992* (1993) deals with the urban unrest following the beating of a black man, Rodney King, by Los Angeles police in 1992. The racial conflicts that followed showed the fragility of our social coexistence as whites, African Americans, and Koreans were pitted against each other. In these pieces, Anna Deavere Smith, a light-skinned African American woman, performs men and women of every ethnic and racial background. She moves so seamlessly from one role to another that the characters' ethnicity, race, and gender seemingly obliterate her own. Her magical transformations through only body and voice allow the audience to maintain a degree of detachment and objectivity as they encounter

Photo 6.10
Anna Deavere Smith transforming into a male character in *House Arrest* at the New York Public Theater.
© *Michal Daniel, 2000*

volatile issues through emotionally involved characters. Watching Smith, we think about how gender and race are portrayed in our culture and on stage. Smith's performance of her characters is an essential and untransferable part of her pieces.

Eve Ensler's *Vagina Monologues* (1996), discussed in Chapter 1, contained many documentary pieces about sexual violence against women during the war in Kosovo, where Bosnian women were systematically raped as part of a program of ethnic cleansing. Her piece has opened doors for other artists to continue to explore world events through a woman's eyes.

More recently, in 2004, Heather Raffo, an American of Iraqi descent, assembled ten years of collected interviews with Iraqi women into *Nine Parts of Desire*, a collage of personal perspectives on conditions in Iraq before and after Saddam Hussein (see Photo 6.11). Here the authentic voices of women whose families have been literally and figuratively torn apart by a brutal dictatorship followed by a brutal war can be heard as a sharp contrast to the distanced portrayal of events in the mass media. The piece serves as a sharp reminder of the very personal and individual consequences of government policy.

Docudramas

As we have seen from *The Laramie Project*, docudrama need not be a solo art. The moral questions surrounding capital punishment are explored in *The Exonerated*, a piece constructed primarily from court transcripts and interviews with six exonerated

Challenges and Choices

Can theatre that uses documentary material or interviews be objective, or does a performance always express a point of view, no matter what the intention?

inmates released from death row after serving prison terms of two to twenty years. The performance applies no theatrical razzle-dazzle. Actors sit on chairs and face the audience giving testimony to the horrors of a judicial system that could haphazardly kill in error. The piece has been performed in New York with a rotating cast of stars. The authentic words speak for themselves, and interestingly, heighten the emotional response in the audience.

Documentary work can also take a comic turn. The group Culture Clash, featuring three performers with roots in El Salvador and Mexico, combines the methods of Anna Deavere Smith with wild comic sensibility. Creating portraits of communities through interviews with diverse populations, they fashion stinging social satire by connecting the documentary sources with original humorous material. Their performance of *Chavez Ravine* described the uprooting of a Chicano community to make way for the new Dodgers' stadium in the 1950s. *Radio Mambo* explores the urban problems of Miami through interviews with people representing the racial and ethnic mix of the area. Although each show raises the specific issues of particular locations as seen through the eyes of those who live there, each piece is also representative of the general concerns of our urban multicultural society.

Docudrama is not a new form of text. As discussed in Chapter 2, during the 1930s, the Federal Theatre Project, created by the Roosevelt administration to provide work for unemployed theatre artists, performed "living newspapers" with texts drawn from newspaper articles, speeches, and government documents interwoven with dialogue to dramatize the pressing social problems of the day.

Even medical writings and therapy sessions can be turned into dramatic texts. Peter Brook turned Oliver Sachs' book on neurological disorders into *The Man Who*, an exploration of the boundaries of normalcy. Storytelling workshops with Alzheimer's patients use the disjointed memories of ordinary people to form a performance called *Time Slips*, which depicts the internal confusion of people with dementia.

In each of these examples, the dramatic text is not a traditional play, but an assemblage of primary source materials recast in theatrical form. There is no "playwright" creating characters and dialogue; rather, a writer or group of writers, who may also have functioned as interviewers, historical researchers, or archivists, structure the material into an effective piece of theatre.

Reenactments or Living Histories

Historical reenactments have made a new theatrical use of documentary materials and are found at historic sites around the United States. At Plimoth Plantation, a reconstructed seventeenth-century village, actors study the history of the period and then are assigned to take on the identity of one of the original colonial inhabitants (see Photo 6.12). Costumed in period clothes and

Photo 6.11
Heather Raffo in *Nine Parts of Desire*, which she wrote as her Master's thesis at the University of San Diego out of concern for her family still living in war-torn Iraq.
© *Joan Marcus*

speaking in the appropriate accent during their workday, these actors replicate the social and cultural life of a historic community. Actors interact with visitors as their historical characters. They improvise banter and explain the colonial way of life. No matter what is asked of them, they never break with their characters or the historic time and place. A tourist's request to take a picture will be met with, "If you bring it back." The dramatic text uses historical documents as a scenario for improvisation to create a new kind of docudrama—a "living history."

Music and Dance Theatre

Wherever we go in the world, music and dance are used as theatrical texts. Blended with other elements, music and dance enhance dramatic effect by permitting sustained heightened emotion and the externalization of profound passion or spiritual yearning. Music and dance texts can reveal character, set pace and rhythm, create a mood, enliven, and entertain. Most important, music and dance permit us to transcend ourselves and the ordinary boundaries of our emotional lives. There is an African expression: "If you can walk, you can dance. If you can talk, you can sing." Dancing and singing are activities basic to the human spirit through which we directly express our emotions and deepest longings.

Photo 6.12
Pilgrim Barbara Standish, portrayed by Tara Brooke Watkins, talks to visitors to Plimoth Plantation, a living history museum.
© *Brian Snyder/Reuters/Landov*

Opera was a major form of musical theatre in Europe, but it did not hold a monopoly. By the mid-nineteenth century, bourgeois audiences in Paris were demanding new entertainment, and Jacques Offenbach (1819–1880) obliged with the **operetta** form, which borrows many features from opera and incorporates dance, farce, and clowning to tell a simple story that always culminates in romance fulfilled. Often satiric in nature, it was a readily accessible popular entertainment form whose primary goal was to amuse its audience. Later it was popularized in German-speaking countries by Johann Strauss (1825–1899), and in England by W. S. Gilbert (1836–1911) and Sir Arthur Sullivan (1842–1900). The nineteenth-century *zarzuela* in Spain shares many elements. Operetta was in many ways the forerunner of today's musical theatre.

The lines that divide opera, operetta, and musical theatre are not clear, and it is hard to generalize about the distinctions. Opera has always been written in the tradition of great European art music; operetta and musical theatre have no such pretensions, yet much great music has been written for these forms. In general, opera has less spoken dialogue than the operetta and the musical, but contrary to common belief, many operas have spoken text. Operetta always deals with lighthearted subjects, but there are many comic operas. Comic opera's sentimentality is replaced in the operetta with a witty and satiric tone whose goal is to amuse and not to move, so most operettas lack opera's overt appeal to the emotions, yet here again there are exceptions, especially among the Viennese repertory. Although we often think of opera as

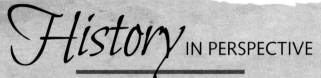

History IN PERSPECTIVE

OPERA IN THE WEST

The fusion of music and drama transcends cultural boundaries. Many traditional Asian forms of performance have maintained a mixture of music, dance, and spoken drama, all working together to enhance the audience's enjoyment. The earliest Western dramatic forms, tragedy and comedy in ancient Greece, were very similar in this regard. Over the centuries, Western concepts of realism led to the gradual elimination of musical and dancing components from drama. Of course singing and dancing were as popular as ever in the West, but traditional dramatic forms began to strictly separate nonrealistic dance and song from tragedy and comedy.

In the late Renaissance period several Italian performers and theorists, eager to recapture the effect of ancient Greek tragedy as it was originally presented, experimented with performances reintegrating drama with continuous music. By the end of the 1500s, opera was born and soon spread throughout the Western world. The new form of music drama mixed comedy and tragedy in such unpredictable ways that the early Italian practitioners, used to pigeonholing art into convenient classifications, wound up calling their new invention "opera," which is simply the Italian word for "work." The name has stuck.

Why should so elaborate and ostentatiously unrealistic an art form have caught on in an artistic climate so concerned with verisimilitude—the appearance of truth? Why is opera more wildly popular today than ever? Opera is one of the few performance styles in the West that allows its audience something of the expanded theatrical effect of traditional Asian forms like *kabuki* or Chinese opera. Emotionally charged stories become larger than life when performed with continuous, powerful musical accompaniment. Everyone can tell the impact an effective soundtrack gives to a movie or television program. Good soundtrack music guides the audience's emotional response to the unfolding dramatic events.

Such "scoring" is of course allowed fuller rein in opera. There the orchestra joins the characters' singing voices to support their self-presentation and to add emphasis where the composer desires.

Opera's power derives from the fusion of different elements. Poetic dialogue written by a librettist portraying dramatic situations is united with a composer's music, which heightens the emotional content and "interprets" the dramatic events and psychological states of the characters for the audience. When Mimi in Puccini's *La Bohème* is in a serious crisis and has evocative words to sing to a compelling melody and that melody is enriched by a large orchestra playing along with her, the audience is free to enjoy an overwhelming emotional experience that conventional spoken drama, or nondramatic music, cannot provide. Often ironic tension is created between what the characters are singing and what the orchestra is suggesting by the music it is playing. Mozart in his *Don Giovanni* has his orchestra "contradict" his singing characters in this way and even make fun of them using wry instrumental commentary.

Opera derives much of its expressive vocabulary from the contrast between lyrical, or melodic, music such as arias and choruses and a style of music called recitative. Recitative is a kind of "musical speech." It is a nontuneful declamatory kind of singing that serves to move the dramatic action forward. Many popular songs and numbers from musicals to this day begin with recitative to introduce the song's subject before the song "really" begins with its principal lyrical tune. Recitative and lyrical music may be seen as the prose and poetry of opera. Lyrical, tuneful music is used in arias to accent the character's strongest emotional states.

Dramatic action usually stands still for arias to allow an audience to savor the emotional high point. This explains why arias or lyrical music are the most popular features of operatic performance and why an audience may

highbrow entertainment for the elite, in many places, opera is a people's theatre. One significant difference between musical theatre and operas and operettas as they are performed today is that operas and operettas are performed by singers who act, whereas musical theatre is performed by actors who sing, indicating a shift of some of the emotional burden from music onto the text. Operettas, although still performed, are not written today, and their audience has been claimed by the musical theatre, which borrowed much of its form and added elements from other popular entertainments. Musical comedy, with its light-hearted stories, has given way to today's musical theatre, which can treat topics across the spectrum.

well burst into applause when they are over. In these passages, the drama has been translated into music that talented opera singers are able to bring to life through the beauty and range of their voices, their handling of melodic phrases, and their sensitivity to the meaning of the words they are singing as well as the dramatic situation. Operatic arias act like the freeze frame on a video tape or DVD player. In some respects this freeze frame quality is analogous to the posing effect in *kabuki* performance. Opera is one of the only living Western theatrical forms that allows for a similar manipulation of time and encourages a similar kind of aesthetic savoring.

The German Romantic opera composer Richard Wagner (1813–1883) famously described opera as a *gesamtkunstwerk* or "total art work." Wagner meant that opera should unite the skills of librettists; composers; dancers; singer-actors; and set, costume, and lighting designers in an artistic unity that will thrill, elevate, and move modern audiences the way Greek tragedy did in ancient times. The growing complexity of operas in the 1800s, especially Wagner's, was a contributing factor to the development of the modern director. Wagner's operas with their ambitious staging requirements were responsible for important innovations in

lighting, set, and auditorium design that affect much of Western operatic and spoken theater to this very day.

Operas are always helped by coherent and interesting librettos. Nevertheless many successful operas have been created by great composers working with texts that would be considered silly without music to clothe them. No successful operas offer fine texts but ineffective music. The composer is the ultimate dramatist in the opera house. The composer's choices govern the audience's perception of what they are hearing and seeing.

The important opera composers of history may be regarded as great composers as well as among the finest theater artists of their time. Major opera composers include Claudio Monteverdi (1567–1643), George Frederick Handel (1685–1759), Wolfgang Amadeus Mozart (1756–1791), Giuseppe Verdi (1813–1901), Georges Bizet (1838–1875), Modest Musorgsky (1839–1881), Wagner, Giacomo Puccini (1858–1924), and Benjamin Britten (1913–1976). Operas by contemporary composers such as Philip Glass (b.1937), John Adams (b.1947), and John Corigliano (b.1938) ensure that the operatic repertory continues to grow.

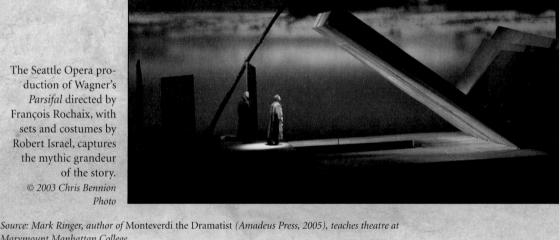

The Seattle Opera production of Wagner's *Parsifal* directed by François Rochaix, with sets and costumes by Robert Israel, captures the mythic grandeur of the story.
© *2003 Chris Bennion Photo*

Source: Mark Ringer, author of Monteverdi the Dramatist *(Amadeus Press, 2005), teaches theatre at Marymount Manhattan College.*

The American Musical

When we think of contemporary musical theatre, we think of the form that grew up in the United States and is today embraced by countries around the world. Many of the alternative forms we have looked at may seem unfamiliar, but musical theatre is one with which we are all acquainted. Its creation combines the talents of many artists. The American musical has always combined textual materials and involved the collaboration of several authors.

Composers, Lyricists, and Choreographers as Authors

Music, lyrics (usually in rhymed verse), choreography for a danced text, and spoken dialogue that fleshes out the story line and comprises the **book** or written text of the musical are combined to create the musical form. These are created by a composer, a lyricist, a choreographer, and a book writer, although often the roles may be combined, as in the case of Stephen Sondheim (b. 1930), who writes both words and music for most of his work. Although each of these texts can be read separately for meaning (we can listen to a recording of the songs or read the book), the way the various texts interrelate and reinforce each other in performance defines the musical form. What was once a simple story told through song and dance interspersed with spoken dialogue has become the subject of new experiments that play with the relationship among these various textual elements. The history of the musical is itself one of change and transformation.

Musical theatre has always been a composite form. In its origins, it combined elements of American melodrama, dance, popular song, and variety show entertainments such as vaudeville, burlesque, and minstrel shows, in combination with the European operetta. As the importance of story line grew, plots became more complex resulting in the development of the **book musical**, a story told through spoken text and song. Recent decades have seen a return to the **revue** or nonstory musical form as a parallel development to increasingly serious subject matter in the traditional book musical. The British musical, such as *Phantom of the Opera* (1989) and *Cats* (1981), emulates the high art of opera and reduces the element of spoken text. Productions of operas that emphasize theatrical elements over the musical text such as Baz Luhrman's *La Bohème* (2003) are staged in commercial theatre houses. Simultaneously, opera companies are staging American musicals in opera houses not only in an attempt to appeal to a broader audience base, but also as a recognition that what was once popular culture has reached the status of high art.

Multiculturalism and the American Musical

Musical theatre was one of the first forms to explore multicultural textual elements and themes, as if dance and music provided a distancing that permitted contributions from marginalized groups. As early as the 1920s, African American musicals appeared on Broadway, starting with Eubie Blake (1883–1983) and Noble Sissle's (1889–1975) *Shuffle*

Along in 1921, although three more decades would pass before serious drama by an African American could receive a Broadway production with a black director and cast. Ragtime and jazz were musical texts appropriated by white composers, and black dance forms were incorporated into the standard dance repertory. George Gershwin's (1898–1937) *Porgy and Bess* (1935) openly uses the sounds and rhythms of African American culture as text.

Musicals also daringly explored racial themes before society as a whole was ready to confront such issues. In 1927, *Showboat* by Jerome Kern (1885–1945) and Oscar Hammerstein (1895–1960) explored the impact of antimiscegenation laws on race relations and provided one of the earliest examples of a musical with a complex, tightly woven plot whose drama is heightened by the musical text. Richard Rodgers (1902–1979) and Hammerstein used *South Pacific* (1949) to explore the roots of personal prejudice, and *The King and I* (1951) to examine cultural barriers to understanding. In 1957, Leonard Bernstein (1918–1990) and Stephen Sondheim exposed cultural clashes in America through *West Side Story* (see Photo 6.13). More recently, the 1998 *Parade* by Jason Robert Brown used a historic court case to expose religious intolerance and antisemitism in the American South. In each of these productions the musical and dance texts reflected particular cultural idioms or an outsider's concept of music and dance texts of other cultures, reinforcing the thematic material presented in the written book. The history of the American musical reflects the multiculturalism of our society and its use of music and dance as a tool for assimilation and understanding of difference.

Dance in Musical Theatre

Recently, more and more musical theatre is using dance as the central dramatic element in the text. While dance has always been part of the musical form, it moved from an entertainment vehicle for showgirls to a vital part of the dramatic text. Starting in the 1930s, dance came to be used much the way songs were to further the plot or reveal a character's state of mind or emotions. George Balanchine's choreography for Rodgers' and Lorenz Hart's (1898–1943) *On Your Toes* in 1936 brought new stature to the role of dance and may have been the first time the word *choreographer* was applied to a popular entertainment form. The 1940 Rodgers and Hart *Pal Joey* featured Gene Kelly, who used

Photo 6.14
Movin' Out captures the coming of age of a group of friends in the late 1960s and 1970s through music and lyrics by Billy Joel and extraordinary dancing choreographed by director Twyla Tharp. Note how the production combines dance and acting to tell a tale. Scenic design by Santo Loquasto; costume design by Suzy Benzinger; lighting design by Donald Holder; sound design by Brian Ruggles and Peter J. Fitzgerald; hair design by Paul Huntley.
© *Joan Marcus*

dance as an expression of character. In 1943, Rodgers and Hammerstein's *Oklahoma*, choreographed by Agnes de Mille (1905–1995), drew on her classical training and gave dance a significant role in helping to tell the story with added psychological dimension. De Mille's dances went beyond the simple narrative in sequences such as Laurey's dream to express the character's inner life and unconscious longing. Jerome Robbins (1918–1998) made dance an integral part of the dramatic text and the choreographer the central figure in shaping a musical production with his work on *West Side Story*. He was at the advent of a line of director choreographers—among them Bob Fosse, Tommy Tune, Susan Stroman, and now Twyla Tharp—who have placed dance as the central text in musical performance. Imagine *Chicago* without Fosse's choreography. Musicals such as *Bring in da Noise, Bring in da Funk* now find their drama entirely in the dancing.

Musical theatre texts sometimes have no dialogue, or almost none; dance stands in for the word or goes beyond the word to express pure sensation and emotion. In Matthew Bourne's production of *Swan Lake* (1999) on Broadway and in London, the music served as the inspiration for a danced dramatic text about sexual obsession and repression, although not one word was spoken; the music and choreography combined with an idea to form the text. Several other danced theatre pieces without dialogue such as *Contact* (1999), which its choreographer Susan Stroman referred to as a "**dance play**," and Twyla Tharp's *Movin' Out* (2002), based on songs by Billy Joel, have come to Broadway in recent years (see Photo 6.14). These are categorized as theatre, not dance performances, because characterization, narrative, and dramatic conflict are the departure point for the choreographer's conceptualization of movement and serve as the primary consideration in the dancer's rehearsal process. Usually the focus of dance performance is on the quality and line of the movement. In these "dance plays," the dancers may also be working with or against the lyrics of the music as the verbal text that regulates the dance, internalizing the musical score and lyrics the way actors internalize dialogue. Innovative avant-garde directors such as Pina Bausch and Martha Clarke (discussed in Chapter 8) have also created dance theatre pieces that push the limits of both arts.

The American Musical Abroad

Today, the American musical is ubiquitous. Broadway musicals are performed the world over, and other cultures have created their own versions of the form. American musical

Photo 6.15
B. D. Wong, front, and Sab Shimono in the Roundabout Theater's revival of *Pacific Overtures,* a musical that explores the clash of cultures when Commodore Matthew Perry and the American fleet arrive in 1853 to "open" Japan to the West. Director Miyamoto Amon is the first Japanese citizen ever to direct a Broadway production.
Sara Krulwich/The New York Times

Texts IN PERSPECTIVE

DANCE NOTATION

Expressive dance movement is generally passed on directly by teachers or choreographers who model physical work for their protégés to follow. Because this leaves no tangible record of a dance, the difficulties transmitting and preserving choreography for new artists has led to attempts to create notation systems that record physical movements the way musical notation records sound.

The Frenchman Thoinot Arbeau's (1520–1595) *Orchesographie*, published in 1588, set out a system for European court dance that remained in use for two hundred years. As there was one basic posture for all court dances, the system was simple. In the early eighteenth century, Raoul-Auger Feuillet and Pierre Beauchamp created a system that accommodated the more complex footwork of court ballet, a developing form at the time. Women ballet dancers of the period wore long dresses covering most of their bodies, so the system only had to communicate floor patterns and the dancer's feet.

In the nineteenth century ballet costumes became shorter, and in the wake of Romanticism, ballet itself became freer with more expressive upper body movements rendering the old recording system inadequate. Both the Frenchman Arthur Saint-Leon and the German Friedrich Zorn tried systems using stick figures, but these could only show static positions, neglecting the flow of movement.

Today, the most common notation systems are Labanotation and Benesh Movement Notation. Labanotation was developed in the 1920s by Rudolf Laban. It uses principles of space, anatomy, and dynamics to record all kinds of movement, not just dance. Benesh Movement Notation, developed in the 1940s by Joan and Rudolf Benesh, also aims at a general use and has been employed for physical therapy as well as dance. Because of the complexity of human movement in three-dimensional space, these systems are complicated, and recording a piece of choreography can be a time-consuming process. Most choreographers still create and pass on their dances in the studio and find videotape sufficient for recording and preserving their work. Written notation systems still have their advantages, and libraries such as the Dance Notation Bureau in New York commission and preserve choreographic notations for future study and restaging of artistic works.

The figure at left shows one page of Labanotation from Bob Fosse's choreography for "There's Gotta Be Something Better Than This" from the musical *Sweet Charity* (1965). Bob Fosse was also a director whose signature dance style in Broadway shows such as *Pippin* (1972), *Chicago* (1975), and *Dancin'* (1978) made dance the central element in his productions. This page shows the dance movements of three performers for about ten measures of music. The whole number takes up thirty-four pages of dance notation.

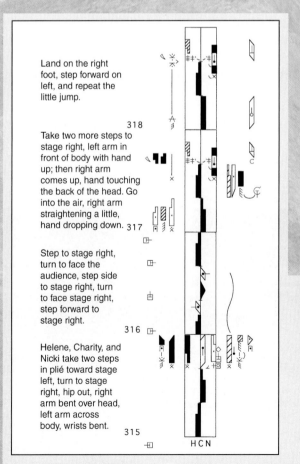

Land on the right foot, step forward on left, and repeat the little jump.

318

Take two more steps to stage right, left arm in front of body with hand up; then right arm comes up, hand touching the back of the head. Go into the air, right arm straightening a little, hand dropping down. 317

Step to stage right, turn to face the audience, step side to stage right, turn to face stage right, step forward to stage right.

316

Helene, Charity, and Nicki take two steps in plié toward stage left, turn to stage right, hip out, right arm bent over head, left arm across body, wrists bent.

315

H C N

Figure 6.1 Dance Notation This labanotation was drafted by Billie Mahoney in 1977 for Elaine Cancilla's reconstruction of Bob Fosse's choreography of "There's Gotta Be Something Better" from *Sweet Charity* done for the American Dance Machine at the American Theatre Lab, New York City, May 5 and 6, 1977. Staging and rehearsal direction by Bick Goss. Directed by Lee Becker Theodore. This notation should not be considered final, as Fosse could have reworked it. The description alongside, provided by Ilene Fox of the Dance Notation Bureau, explains the notation.

Reprinted with permission from Nicole Fosse. Art courtesy of the Dance Notation Bureau.

texts are combined with foreign books and lyrics. In Singapore, the Western musical is the most widely embraced theatrical form, and the homegrown musical *Nagraland* by Dick Lee used Asian themes and written text to create a hybrid cultural piece that then toured successfully in Japan. *Mother Teresa, the Musical,* was presented in Rome to celebrate her beatification, mixing this most secular of forms with holy text. Sondheim's *Pacific Overtures* was staged by Japanese director Amon Miyamoto (b. 1958) using *noh, kabuki, bunraku,* and *rokyoko* techniques to present the Japanese perspective on Commodore Perry, using the American musical form as a distorting mirror (see Photo 6.15). The Japanese version of the musical then toured the United States. *Riverdance,* the Irish Broadway musical, recently performed in the seven-thousand-seat Great Hall of the People in Beijing, where the legislature normally meets. The play immediately sold fifty thousand tickets as proof that music and dance texts can transcend culture.

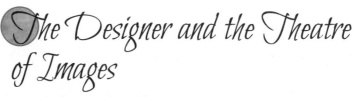

The Designer and the Theatre of Images

During the first decades of the twentieth century, European avant-garde visual artists became interested in performance as a way of repudiating the establishment's merchandising of art. These modern artists experimented with ways of expressing the modern aesthetic in living visual forms that incorporated the ideas of time and action. They mixed media, forms, and incongruous images to create performance collages that defied traditional categories. This early work provided the inspiration for American and Asian performance art of the 1970s and 1980s, and new theatrical forms continue to evolve from these roots to the present. Performance art has gone in several directions, including the exploration of solo performance. One of the lingering results of this movement is the idea of a nonliterary visual dramatic text conceived as a series of visual images often incorporating mixed media and grand spectacle. Here, stage pictures, video, film, slides, and even lights are part of the dramatic text and are privileged over the written word, narrative plot, and developed character.

One of the best known artists working in this image-dominated form is Robert Wilson (b. 1941), who begins his work with a visual idea as the structuring element. What little language is used does not necessarily tell a coherent story, and the dramatic action moves from image to image. Actors are manipulated as visual elements on the stage. The

Photo 6.16
Robert Wilson's image text shown in Figure 6.2 is realized in this performance of *The Golden Windows* at the Kammerspiele Theater, Munich. The moment corresponds to sketch X in the figure on page 175.
Copyright by Mara Eggert, Franfurt/Main

IN PERSPECTIVE

IMAGE TEXT: ROBERT WILSON'S *THE GOLDEN WINDOWS*

Following is the visual text for *The Golden Windows*, a performance piece created by Robert Wilson with music by Tania Léon, Gavin Bryars, and Johann Pepusch, which premiered at the Münchner Kammerspiele in Munich in 1982 and later played in Vienna, Montreal, and New York. For Robert Wilson, trained as a visual artist, visual images are the primary text that structure the performance. These storyboard sketches show how Wilson envisioned the progression of the piece.

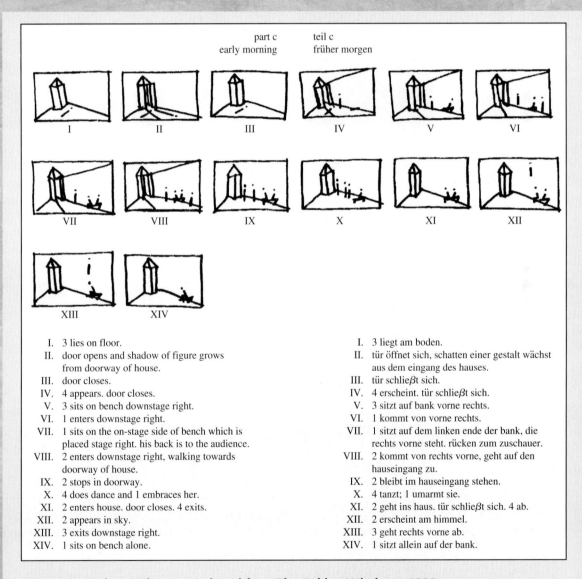

I.	3 lies on floor.	I. 3 liegt am boden.
II.	door opens and shadow of figure grows from doorway of house.	II. tür öffnet sich, schatten einer gestalt wächst aus dem eingang des hauses.
III.	door closes.	III. tür schließt sich.
IV.	4 appears. door closes.	IV. 4 erscheint. tür schließt sich.
V.	3 sits on bench downstage right.	V. 3 sitzt auf bank vorne rechts.
VI.	1 enters downstage right.	VI. 1 kommt von vorne rechts.
VII.	1 sits on the on-stage side of bench which is placed stage right. his back is to the audience.	VII. 1 sitzt auf dem linken ende der bank, die rechts vorne steht. rücken zum zuschauer.
VIII.	2 enters downstage right, walking towards doorway of house.	VIII. 2 kommt von rechts vorne, geht auf den hauseingang zu.
IX.	2 stops in doorway.	IX. 2 bleibt im hauseingang stehen.
X.	4 does dance and 1 embraces her.	X. 4 tanzt; 1 umarmt sie.
XI.	2 enters house. door closes. 4 exits.	XI. 2 geht ins haus. tür schließt sich. 4 ab.
XII.	2 appears in sky.	XII. 2 erscheint am himmel.
XIII.	3 exits downstage right.	XIII. 3 geht rechts vorne ab.
XIV.	1 sits on bench alone.	XIV. 1 sitzt allein auf der bank.

Figure 6.2   Robert Wilson's storyboard from *The Golden Windows*, 1985.

Reprinted with permission

Photo 6.17
Hashirigaki, from Theatre Vidy Lausanne, directed by Heiner Goebbles, is a fusion of diverse elements. Beach Boys' tunes are juxtaposed against Japanese folk music and a text by Gertrude Stein. A talented international cast and dazzling visual and sound effects enable this unlikely combination of styles to achieve impressive theatricality.
© ArenaPal/Topham/The Image Works

images are supported by sound and music, often by his longtime collaborator Philip Glass (b. 1937), whose minimalist style is a perfect complement for Wilson's nonnarrative pieces. Attending a Robert Wilson performance is like sitting before a giant living, moving painting with sound effects and words and music. You assimilate the total effect as you might looking out at a panoramic vista while listening to the birds and reading poetry. You simply respond to all the sensory input. We will discuss Wilson's work in more detail in the next chapter.

Sound and Image Theatre

Some theatrical creators think of music as a structuring device for the visual world. Postmodern composer and director Heiner Goebbels explores the relationship between images and sound. Dazzling stage pictures are juxtaposed against a global array of music and poetry. In his production of *Hashirigaki* for the Théâtre Vidy in Lausanne, Switzerland (2003), the title was translated from the Japanese to mean "the act of walking, thinking, and talking at the same time." These very acts are explored by three performers—Japanese, Swedish, and Canadian—against a background of Gertrude Stein poetry, Brian Wilson's Beach Boys music, and Japanese and original compositions on a cross-cultural collection of instruments, while fantasy set pieces and fabulous lights create dazzling visual effects. The actors, of opposing physical types and different accents, mutate the sound and action much as the repeating language of Stein's poems mutates words. If Robert Wilson's work resembles that of a landscape artist, Goebbels is a creator of soundscapes. The audience is asked to have a sensory experience without connecting narrative line.

The Diversity of Theatrical Forms

As we have seen, the many methods of theatrical creation have led to a diversity of theatrical texts and forms that defy easy labels. Much of the work we have examined in this chapter is deeply tied to the artists who created and performed them and is not easily transmitted to new generations of interpreters. Some are so rooted in the actual physical body of the actor who created them that they cannot be given to others. Unlike plays, these kinds of texts lack transmissibility, are temporal, and underscore the ephemeral quality of the theatre. The acceptance of alternative texts and methods of creation has led to the era of the director-auteur, a creator who has envisioned both the written and the performance text, who will be discussed in Chapter 8.

Drama, comedy, and musical are no longer adequate for categorizing the performance forms we see today. To some degree, however, exceptions to the rules have always existed. Renaissance theorists divided genres into comedy, tragedy, and pastoral, omitting the *commedia dell'arte*—the most vital theatre of their time, perhaps because it had no play text. In other eras, secondary forms were also given short shrift (consider the two sentences Aristotle devotes to Greek mime in the *Poetics*). The difficulties involved in categorization are pointed out each year at award time when awards are defined by category. The Pulitzer Prize committee took back its nomination for "best drama" from Anna Deavere Smith because her work was seen as documentary, and not a play. In the last decade, the Tony Awards given to outstanding Broadway productions have been the subject of running disputes about how to categorize the new forms that have evolved. Is an opera musical theatre? Is a stand-up comedy routine a comedy? Is a musical with dance and no book or singing a musical? Is a solo performance a play? To accommodate the problem, a unique category was created called "Special Theatrical Event," and everything that didn't fit neatly into a traditional niche has been placed there ever since.

These controversies reflect the changing concept of theatrical text that has reached even the commercial theatre. Accepted categories of texts have always been determined by the groups that dominate a particular society. These are the people who award prizes, sponsor festivals, write criticism, or subsidize the arts. As artists push creative boundaries, they force us all to reassess the limits of established theatrical models. Today alternative forms are given a place alongside traditional works, reflecting the more inclusive social power structure and the increasing acceptance of diversity and innovation in our culture.

KEY IDEAS

- A dramatic text can come in many guises—a musical score, movement notation, or visual images—and can be created in many ways and have many different authors.
- Sometimes new forms and methods of creation develop when avant-garde artists rebel against tradition.
- Improvisation is a form of theatre that relies on the actor's skill to create a performance without a fully written text.
- Mime and movement-based theatre, created by the performer, exists around the world and rarely has a written text.
- Often a group of artists will create a piece together, beginning with an idea or concept but no written text. A written text may evolve from their collaborative work.
- Traditions of variety entertainment have used improvisation, clowning, music, and circus skills.
- In some societies storytellers are part of an oral tradition, passing on the heritage of a community.

- Solo performance has become increasingly popular. It allows individual voices of particular groups to be heard and has been used to express political content.
- Docudrama uses primary source material as the basis for a performance and usually has a social message. Historical reenactments use historical research to create living history.
- Music and dance are used as dramatic texts throughout the world.
- The American musical combines the work of a lyricist, composer, and choreographer. It was one of the first American forms to explore multicultural and racial themes. Today the dance musical uses dance as the central dramatic text.
- Theatre can be created like an abstract painting using the impact of sound or images without an elaborate text.
- Today's increasingly diverse forms of theatrical expression defy traditional categories.

PART THREE

Peter Brook explores the elements of theatricality in *Qui est là?*, a meditation on the art of theatre drawn from Shakespearean text and the writings of the most important theatre theorists of the twentieth century. In this rehearsal moment, the basic elements of creation—the actor, director, and space—become the subject of the photo.

Shaping the Performance

Every theatrical performance creates an imaginary world and transports the audience in time and space. This world of illusion, like the real world, has shape, dimension, rules, and inhabitants. We have already looked at how the playwright and tradition can contribute to the definition of this artistic territory. In performance, a new set of players establishes the imaginary realm. Theatrical space defines the physical parameters of performance interactions. Directors decide what rules, or theatrical conventions, will operate within that space. The actor embodies both and makes them a tangible presence for the audience to behold.

The Actor
Theatre's Living Presence

7

Actress Qian Yi as Du Liniang, the young romantic female lead, uses her entire body to express her longing for the man she fell in love with in a dream. The delicate, stylized gestures of her fingers are typical of acting in Chinese opera, as is the graceful lifting of the long water sleeve. Both convey feeling and add beauty to the performance. Director Chen Shizheng's controversial production of Tang Xianzu's sixteenth-century *kunqu* opera *Peony Pavilion* was performed at the Lincoln Center Festival, New York and is discussed in Chapter 5 on pages 135–136.

© Stephanie Berger

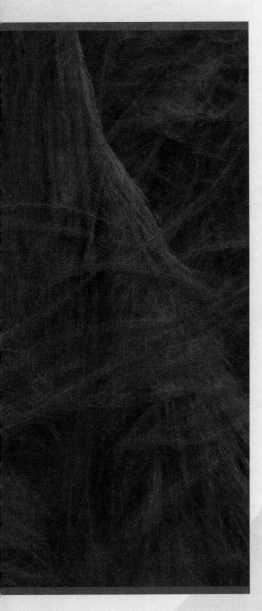

Imagine a theatre: houselights dim, stage lights illuminate the empty stage, and we, in the audience, wait expectantly. What are we waiting for? We are awaiting the entrance of the actor, without whom there can be no theatre, for the theatre depends on the presence of the live human being. The actor's body, voice, heart, and mind become the embodiment of the human narrative portrayed in the theatre.

The Thrill of Simulation

In Roman times, a famous actor named Parmenon was renowned for his imitation of a pig. Audiences would journey far to see Parmenon perform his famous sow. One day, a jealous fellow actor leaped onto the stage with a live pig and said to the audience, "You who so idolize Parmenon, what do you think of his acting next to this real pig?" The audience replied, "It's a good sow, but it's still not as good as Parmenon's sow." What does this ancient parable tell us about acting? Acting is more than just imitating the behavior of everyday life. Acting adds artistic interpretation; it produces metaphor and meaning; it captures the essence of a being. Acting is not simply reproduction and imitation.

In fact, it is the very artifice of the performance that thrills us. Things that we would find disturbing, upsetting, or even frightening in real life excite us and give pleasure when we see them acted in the theatre. We would not choose to be at someone's deathbed, or to witness a violent duel or acts of war, but in the theatre, through acting, we are permitted the aesthetic distance with which to examine human conduct. No matter how close to life it seems, no matter how real the emotions feel, we are aware that we are watching a simulation, and this fills us with awe. Actors have the power to appear to be living a part, and yet we, the audience, know it is not so.

To Act Is Human

Acting is a fundamental human activity. It is part of our very nature. You can see this when you watch children at play. Whether it's playing house, or doctor, or soldier, there is a basic need to express ourselves through impersonation and fantasy. Aristotle wrote about this in the fourth century B.C.E., and it is an observation unchanged through the centuries. He tells us that imitation is a necessary and pleasurable human activity and a source of knowledge about the world and ourselves. Anthropologists have observed the need for play-acting in every society. Sometimes it is channeled into storytelling, sometimes into ritual drama, festivals, pageants, or parades. While this predisposition takes many forms around the globe, it appears to be present everywhere.

Social psychologists believe we "perform" aspects of ourselves in various situations in everyday life. This daily role-play, however, is quite different from the imaginative, vital transformation required to act in the theatre. Imagine for a moment that you were placed on the stage in any of your various daily roles—student, boyfriend, girlfriend, child, parent, employee, brother, sister. Would the audience find you interesting or compelling? You most likely would not even be audible beyond the first row. The audience would not have the sense of a consciously created and shaped artistic performance. Although you may be playing a role, you are not *acting*. Your behavior would not possess the essential universal qualities required of an actor. Although actors use their own physical and emotional beings, they are not necessarily portraying themselves.

The Universal Qualities of Acting in the Theatre

All acting is a special form of behavior that transcends the everyday and consists of universal principles applicable in any theatre anywhere: energy, control, purpose, focus, enlargement, dynamics, and transformation. Although actors learn various methods and work in ways that accommodate different theatrical styles and traditions, these special qualities are shared by all performers all over the world.

■ **Energy.** All theatrical performance requires the harnessed use of physical, emotional, and mental energy. This gives intensity and vitality to an actor's work and holds the audience's attention. Directed energy creates the quality we have come to call stage presence. In life, our energy is the result of our personality, mood, physical state, and our environment. On stage, actors must shed their everyday concerns as they work to create a vigorous and radiant stage presence. The release of this inner energy source requires removing physical and emotional blocks, and actors study for years the techniques that permit them to access and free the channel for energy flow.

■ **Control.** The actor must feel in control of a performance. Even in highly emotional moments or states of ecstatic movement, some aspect of consciousness oversees what happens. From the interpretation of a role to the voice and movement of a character, actors study techniques to remain in control of their instrument. They do physical exercises to increase strength and flexibility, and vocal exercises to free the voice

Photo 7.1a
Jude Law as Faustus in Christopher Marlowe's *Doctor Faustus*, directed by David Ian at the Young Vic Theatre, London.
© *Donald Cooper/Photostage*

Photo 7.1b
Kabuki actor Nakamura Kankuro of the Heisei Nakamura-za company in *Natsumatsuri Naniwa Kagami*, directed by Kushida Kazuyoshi, at Lincoln Center, New York.
© *Stephanie Berger*

Jude Law and Nakamura Kankuro are trained in different traditions, but they both embody the universal qualities of acting: energy, control, purpose, focus, enlargement, and dynamics. Note the dynamisms of their stage presence and the rootedness of their physical postures. Each actor draws us to him with the special magnetism of great acting.

Photo 7.2
Actors use their minds and bodies and the aid of makeup and costume to step outside themselves to transform into characters. In deep concentration as he puts on his makeup, Georges Bigot of the Théâtre du Soleil prepares to perform the title role in Shakespeare's *Richard II,* directed by Ariane Mnouchkine at the Cartoucherie de Vincennes.

© *Martine Franck/Magnum Photos*

and make maximum use of various resonators. They study diction. They may study fencing and circus skills to develop coordination and timing, or dance for grace and flexibility. If they are learning a set performance text, as in many Asian forms, they will need to study every gestural and vocal detail. If they are interpreting a character in a play, they will carefully analyze the text so their understanding of the role is complete and can guide their interpretation. Mastery of all the components of expression enables the actor to achieve a controlled performance.

■ **Focus.** Acting requires a heightened awareness and level of concentration. The body is on the alert in the theatrical environment, and attention cannot wander. We spoke of the imminent danger for the actor on stage in Chapter 1, and it is this peril that puts the senses to the test. Actors are even careful to guard against thoughts from everyday life intruding on their creative process. They are aware of the audience and adjust to the audience response, but they must keep their primary focus on the onstage action. They are constantly selecting and adjusting focus. Actors on stage react as we all do when we are in a situation that might threaten us— they proceed in a state of heightened sensory awareness and discipline.

■ **Purpose.** All action on stage is purposeful and meaningful. Aimless action can defuse the energy of a performance and confuse the audience. Even the smallest gesture is read by the audience as having significance, and so actors develop an awareness that every sound and movement they make has meaning. The famous acting teacher Eugenio Barba (b. 1936) refers to this as "decided" action—determined and directed.

■ **Dynamics.** A performance is constructed much like a piece of music. It has dynamics, rhythm, and tempo. It strikes various notes and keys, with moments of rising and falling intensity. Actors shape a performance to have texture and interest and to reflect the cadence and rhythm of the text and their character.

■ **Enlargement.** Acting requires the expression of common emotions in an uncommon way. Actors must fill large theatres with feeling and project vocally so as to be heard in the last row of the theatre. Actors must be able to enlarge their movement, voices, and energy field without losing a sense of authenticity of emotion and character. In particular styles, they may need to project heightened imagistic texts or unusual physical expression. This is an enormous task that is carried out through a mastery of technique.

■ **Transformation.** The mask is a symbol for the theatre because it expresses the stepping outside the self that transforms the actor on the stage. Put on a mask and you can become anyone. In theatre traditions that use masks, the transformation is palpable. In our own theatre, where actors rarely use masks, the actor uses the self—the body, mind, and feelings—to transform the self. Technical manipulation of the body, voice, mind, and feelings creates another persona. Sometimes the audience is unaware of the transformation; they wonder whether the actor is actually just like the role. But no performance is ever an exact replica of who the actor is in real life. Even actors who play themselves, as often occurs in solo performance pieces, are playing the role of themselves. They are heightened, theatricalized, and transformed by the conscious use of energy, control, purpose, focus, enlargement, and dynamics.

These fundamental qualities form the basis of all acting for the theatre, however diverse the theatrical style. All actors try to find a pathway to these universal principles.

What Does an Actor Do?

If you are American and have only limited theatre-going experience, this may seem like a simple question. You might respond, "An actor plays and interprets a character in a play." But in fact, the answer to this question is complex. Actors in different theatrical traditions actually do different things, and their training is a function of how and what they will be expected to perform.

A great deal of American and European theatre is constructed around a *play-text*. The actor is seen as an interpreter of the dramatic text, and the training for such a theatre involves text interpretation and character analysis and learning the ways to best transmit the playwright's ideas and portray the character. In contrast, *performance* traditions pass on all aspects of a performance that can be read for meaning including all that an actor does. Specific gestures, movement, and vocal elements, musical accompaniment, mask, makeup and costume elements, and precise staging have already been determined and fixed. The actor's role is to learn a performance and to preserve a tradition. The training passes that tradition on through teaching rules of prescribed behavior—codified acting. Improvisational theatre demands yet another kind of acting based on spontaneity and freedom, and training for this kind of performance involves removing blocks to self-expression and freeing the imagination. In traditional African theatre, the actor must sing, dance, tell tales, and manipulate the audience into participatory response. In such traditions, there may be no formal training at all; performers absorb oral and movement traditions, and an entire community can participate. Different traditions and styles pose different technical demands, so technique is a function of what kind of acting is expected.

Presentational versus Representational Acting

The earliest recorded musings on the art of acting in ancient Greece and Rome identified two approaches to performance. Some actors seemed to truly feel their characters' emotions as if transported or possessed by another being, whereas others presented their characters' feelings with virtuoso technique that thrilled the audience through their overt artifice. The living of the emotions came to be called **representational** acting and is seen in more realistic styles, and the openly artificial reproduction of emotion was labeled **presentational** and appears where there is a heightened theatrical style. Almost all ancient performance traditions embrace a presentational style. The modern era has advocates of both approaches.

Through the centuries, the question remains, can the actor really feel the emotions portrayed, or is the actor always, through technique, dissembling and presenting the external signs of emotion? From the time of Plato in the fifth century B.C.E. to today, these two approaches to acting have been presented as polarities—between the rational and the irrational, between art and craft, between mind and body. In eras and cultures in which the rational mind was celebrated, acting that was contrived and virtuosic was acclaimed. In periods that celebrate nature and the natural, a more emotionally driven acting style has been hailed. Today, through neuroscience, we have come to understand that we cannot so easily compartmentalize the mind, the body, and the feelings. All good acting actually combines both techniques because all our thoughts are recorded in our bodies, just as all our movement has an effect on our feelings and how we think.

The Actor's Dual Consciousness

The question of how an actor can appear carried away by emotion and yet still deliver a controlled performance continues to intrigue. What keeps the actor from going mad? The actor's sanity is ensured through the ability to stand simultaneously inside and outside oneself.

Denis Diderot (1713–1784) in his famous essay *The Paradox of the Actor*, framed the discussion of dual consciousness for future generations. He believed that the actor presented the "ideal model" of the truth as created by the actor's imagination, and that a part of the actor's consciousness was always outside of the role, shaping and guiding the presentation of the ideal. Diderot's essay raised questions that haunt discussions of acting to this day: How is it possible, if the actor really feels the part, to maintain control of a performance? Is the actor working internally for real emotional connection or externally like a sculptor for a desired effect? Is there a creative process we can outline as a method, or is acting intuitive and instinctual? Can we create controlled illusions of emotional authenticity? What is the "ideal model," and how does it reflect the culture and theatrical conventions of a given time and place? Is the actor's imagination culture bound?

The idea of dual consciousness was present even in ancient times. In ancient Greece, the original word for actor was *hypocrite*. This literally meant "to judge from underneath." It implied that the actor under the mask was defining the character. This standing outside the self enables the actor to shape and mold a performance as though it were a piece of sculpture. By the third century B.C.E., as the art of acting became the province of professional actors, the word *hypocrite* had taken on the meaning it has today to characterize a deceiver or dissembler. The other word the Greeks used for actor was *thespis* (the name of the first known actor), whose root is in the word *theos*, which means God, and can be found in our word *thespian*. The actor was someone filled with the words of God, reminding us that Greek theatre had its origin in Dionysian ritual and ecstatic dance. Depending on the cultural viewpoint, actors may be speakers of divine truths or divinely inspired deceivers.

We have all experienced this sense of double consciousness whenever we tell a lie. What makes lying closer to acting than other behaviors is the constant self-awareness that we have when we lie. We know the truth, and yet we are fabricating another reality. We choose how to create this alternative reality, what story to tell, and how to deliver it. We are ourselves, and yet we are outside of ourselves.

Acting Reflects Culture

The Holy or Profane Actor

Acting has always been seen as "special" behavior outside of everyday life, so actors are always viewed as set apart from the norm. In some cultures they are revered, in others they are scorned or reviled, but always they provoke some exceptional response. To see the actor outside of the role gives us a glimpse into the magical process of transformation. Today's celebrity worship of actors combines a sacred sentiment with secular activity.

As we see from the derivation of the Greek word for *actor*, in many cultures acting is a holy act. Whole theatrical traditions have sprung from religious inspiration, and often the spiritual process of the actor is a primary part of a technique that uses trance, meditation, and ecstatic dance to extol the gods. Actors express their devotion to the gods by delivering themselves as offerings. In India the tradition of the holy actor goes back to the *Natyasastra* and its account of theatre as a creation of the god Brahma that was first performed by sages and meant as a ritual sacrifice. Many Indian traditions continue to manifest this sacred view of performance and the actor. The *Rāmlilā* is a cycle play that reenacts the life of Rama and Krishna; it is performed throughout the north of India during the Hindu festival of Dashahara. Community actors are believed to actually be the gods and goddesses they portray, and spectators worship them by touching their feet, praising them, and participating in postperformance rituals. The *Rāslilā*, a devotional dance-drama on the life of the god Krishna, takes place yearly at temples in Uttar-Pradesh, a region associated with Krishna's life that is also the destination of many devotees and pilgrims. It uses music and poetry to bring the spectator to an ecstatic vision of the god Krishna and his consort Rādhā. Throughout the performance spectators worship, make offerings, and bow before the performers. The *bhāgavata mela* from Tamil Nadu is performed once a year in honor of one incarnation of the god Vishnu, a half man, half lion called Narasimha. It is enacted in front of the deity at the temple where the props and masks are stored. The mask of Narasimha is worshiped as a holy object all year long. The actor who performs Narasimha fasts all day before donning the mask, is then transported into a trance, and becomes possessed by the god.

Photo 7.3
Here we see a member of the Nambe Pueblo taking in the spirit of the buffalo he has hunted and depended on for survival in a celebration of thanksgiving as part of the Nambe Waterfall Ceremonials, New Mexico. Performing the Buffalo Dance is a great honor, and this is an event with deep spiritual meaning.
© Craig Aurness/CORBIS

Many cultures see the actor's ability to impersonate the creatures of the natural world as a special power, so often the actor is viewed as a kind of shaman traveling between the world of the spirits and the world of the here and now to bring back knowledge. Many Native American performances use mime and dance with actors portraying revered animals to ensure the continued survival of the tribe in its natural environment. Similar mimetic-dance performances occur the world over from the Bushmen of the Kalahari to the Navajo and Lakotas of the American Plains.

Although the European theatre derived from ritual acts, it was not long before professional actors were seen as unholy purveyors of entertainment. In many eras actors were considered of low moral repute, and actresses were even labeled as prostitutes and courtesans offering their bodies for secular, not religious, consumption. The Roman Empire found slaves and prostitutes performing in the theatre. It is said the Emperor Justinian first spotted his future empress, Theodora, performing her striptease act. In China one of the early words for actor also meant harlot. The Elizabethan theatre banned women from the English stage, and from 1642 to 1660 during the era of Puritan rule, the theatre was seen as morally offensive and public performances were forbidden. When the Restoration period returned, the female actor to the stage, she was often of dubious reputation. The famous actress Nell Gwynn

(1650–1687) was the daughter of a brothel owner and the mistress of King Charles II. It was not unusual for prostitutes to work the audience, and wealthy noblemen often sought their pleasure backstage. The legacy of the profane actor can be found in today's fascination with the lurid details of actors' personal lives.

In the modern era, Jerzy Grotowski (1933–1999), the famed Polish director and acting teacher, tried to unite the sacred and the profane with the concept of the "holy" actor, offering himself in an act of humility as a sacrifice to his art. Stripped bare of all personal psychological and physical blocks, the actor is freed to release a deep spirituality through art. (See the photo on page 191.) To lead the actor to this state, Grotowski incorporated many of the techniques of ritual performance—trance, meditation, physical endurance, and ecstatic dance. The state of "secular holiness" that Grotowski sought reflects the interest in Asian philosophy and religion in Europe and the United States in the 1960s.

Convention and Believable Acting

Audiences come to the theatre with expectations that actors will perform on stage in a manner that reflects their society's values and its view of beauty, emotion, psychology, and behavior. This in turn affects the way actors will use the human body to portray feelings on stage. What is viewed as authentic or believable acting is culturally determined and can vary widely. Japanese culture values beauty as an integrated part of existence revealed through subtlety and simplicity, a hidden part of the way things are performed. Unlike the Western concept of time passing, the Japanese, influenced by Zen, believe that we pass, but time is still. Understanding how the Japanese view the world is crucial to understanding the nuanced slow movements of the *noh* actor. Understanding the American focus on individualism and psychological motivation can help someone outside our culture comprehend the authentic emotion sought in most American acting. Around the world today, the wide variety of acting styles reflects these differences. In other periods, actors behaved in very different ways and used techniques unlike those practiced today.

Acting Conventions in the European Tradition

Because the play text has been so central to the European tradition, most acting has been about the interpretation of a role. Actors begin with the question, "How can I enter my character's world to understand and portray my character's situation and emotions?" While the question has remained the same through the centuries, the answer has been different in various eras, and individual actors have sought personal solutions that reflected the conventions of their times.

American and European acting until the early twentieth century bore no resemblance to what we think of as good acting today. Actors of the past would appear artificial and melodramatic to us. You have only to look at an early silent film to get a sense of how different acting was just a short time ago within our own tradition. The few films we have of the great star of her day, Sarah Bernhardt (1844–1923), appear almost as parodies to our sensibilities. Early recordings from the late nineteenth and early twentieth centuries of actors performing Shakespeare indicate that vocal technique was as exaggerated as the physical work we see in films of the time. Actors intoned their lines and gave what we would call unnatural readings. All this was to change as the theatre increasingly turned to realism and an interest in the new science of psychology during the twentieth century.

For centuries, it was believed that there were universal forms of emotional expression, that everybody expressed a particular emotion in the exact same way. Emotions were seen to fall into only a few categories. Aristotle in the fourth century B.C.E., writes of fifteen major emotions in his *Rhetoric*. Descartes speaks of six primitive passions in 1666; and Aaron Hill (1685–1750), in his *Essay on the Art of Acting* in 1746, speaks of ten dramatic passions. Such categorization of the emotions continued well into the twentieth century. If each emotion had a set form of physical expression, and there were only ten or twenty emotions, then actors needed only to learn the standard body positions and facial expressions of each emotion to communicate feeling from the stage. The few manuals of rhetoric we have from earlier periods catalog the portrayal of emotions by positions of the body and facial expressions. These manuals are a strong indication of how actors were expected to behave, and many of the paintings we have of actors from earlier centuries show them in the poses depicted in these books.

Not only were emotions generalized, but character types were generalized as well. Actors were hired to play a particular **line of business**—a particular type—from young lover to old miser. Actors made their reputations in these types and brought the same qualities to every role, much the way Hollywood in the 1930s through the 1950s typed actors as leading men, gangsters, femmes fatales, heroes, and ingenues. To some extent, the practice continues today.

Audiences accepted the convention that character and emotions would be portrayed in these external and generalized ways, a style well suited to the heightened poetic language that was the written convention of their time. The vocal skills of the actor were most significant. What we call *declamatory* acting emphasized phrasing, diction, and a mellifluous voice. All were vital for the successful performer, who struck appropriate poses while delivering speeches. Today, it is hard for us to imagine that there was no attempt to make dialogue sound like natural speech, or stage movement seem like everyday life. Although some actors talked of developing a more "natural" style starting in the eighteenth century, we would not find their emotionalized acting realistic today. *Presentational* acting reigned, and there was no disguise of theatrical artifice. Actors were openly acting.

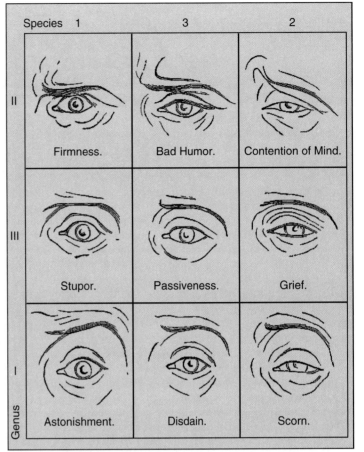

Figure 7.1   Delsarte's Expressions of the Eye   Each nuanced position of the eye and flexing of the facial muscles around the eye and brow was meant to depict a particular emotion. Delsarte developed corresponding charts for the positioning of other body parts such as the hands, feet, head, and mouth. He trained actors and orators to take these positions to express specific emotions through outward physical gesture.
Adapted from Delsarte System of Oratory, 4th ed. New York: Edgar S. Werner and Co., 1893.

The Development of Actor Training

Schools of acting, as such, did not exist, before the twentieth century. Acting, like most other crafts, was learned by apprenticeship, and often skills were passed down through families. Young actors joined companies and learned by watching those more accom-

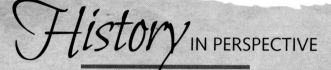

History IN PERSPECTIVE

A UNIVERSAL LANGUAGE OF EMOTIONAL EXPRESSION

Actors have long searched for a universal language of emotions; however, the last decades of the twentieth century, fueled by globalization and interculturalism, saw an accelerated interest in, and even a quest for, expressive forms that could transcend cultural frontiers. The question of whether there exists or can exist a universal language of emotions, a fundamentally human form of expression that can be understood by all people everywhere, stands at an interdisciplinary crossroad of art, anthropology, psychology, and biology.

The impulses behind this search have come from opposing forces. Rejecting language as the tool of power and the camouflage of feeling, actor-director Antonin Artaud and his followers called for a primal preliterate universal language of screams, sounds, and movement to take over the theatre and break down the barriers between actors and audience. From rational science came the understanding of emotion as a biological response to the environment shared among all members of our species and even with animals, prompting the view of the physical expression of feeling as a universal biological form that actors can be taught to release. Theatrical experiments motivated by either rational science or romantic primitivism have produced interesting results.

In 1970 British director Peter Brook assembled a troupe of international actors at his Centre International de Recherche Théâtrales (CIRT) in Paris to explore the possibility of intercultural theatrical communication. Through exercises and improvisations inspired by Artaud, Brook stripped his performers of the cultural specifics of their individual training to find a shared theatrical expression. Exercises in voice and movement drawn from *t'ai chi*, Zoroastrian sources, and other traditions gave the company a shared physical and vocal technique. Using only a series of rhythmic syllables chosen by the company (ba-sh-ta-hon-do) as a vocal language for exercises, the actors searched for a more primal and emotionally direct nonverbal communication system.

Brook's most ambitious experiment in finding a universal language of expression was *Orghast*, a production commissioned by the Shiraz Festival in Iran and performed at Persepolis with Brook's company and a group of Persian actors. The twelve-hour performance drawn from many myths and legends, but generally based on the primordial story of Prometheus stealing fire from the gods, was performed outside overnight in the natural environment of mountains surrounding the tombs of Per-

sian kings. The text of *Orghast* was written by the poet Ted Hughes in a mixture of Avesta, a now dead language from the time of Alexander the Great, ancient Greek and Latin, and mostly Orghast, a language Hughes invented based partially on English, but using the most evocative sounds possible for each word and idea. The cast played with the sounds of this new language over a long rehearsal period, using its music, expressive possibilities, and the movement it evoked to discover a more organic emotional eloquence. In performance there was no shared language between cast members and audience, only a vital theatrical encounter attempting a universal, primal human communication.

Polish director Jerzy Grotowski's exploration of the possibility of organic human exchange began in the early 1960s in his Laboratory Theatre, where rigorous physical training for actors was meant to tear down social barriers to free expression. In productions like *Acropolis*, Grotowski emphasized the direct, vital interchange between the actor and the spectator. Starting in 1970 his investigations took him beyond theatre to "active culture" and "paratheatrical experiences." He had already stripped his theatre of luxuries in costume, makeup, set, and lighting that might overshadow the actor–audience encounter. He looked to tear away the cultural trappings of daily life that stood in the way of direct human connections. In a series of special projects he took small groups to remote locations where, without the use of language, they could rediscover human communication and the natural rhythms of life. Freed from ordinary social rules, habits, and activities, participants tapped into previously unexplored emotions and ways of interacting. Grotowski reintroduced songs and ritualized movements in his final work, with the aim of discovering an essential communion between human beings that was not overshadowed by false cultural expressions.

Italian-born director Eugenio Barba (b.1936), who worked with Grotowski in Poland for three years and subsequently started his Odin Teatret in Norway, brought Grotowski's research in universals back to the field of theatre proper. In 1979 he founded ISTA, the International School of Theatre Anthropology, to investigate the shared qualities of physical presence in performers across cultures. For Barba, the performer has three levels of expression. The first is based in the actor's unique persona and gifts, and the second is based in the cultural tradition in which the performer has trained. The third level of "pre-expressivity" is the universal vibrant presence of the physical actor on stage before any culturally specific technique is expressed. This shared theatrical energy has been the subject of Barba's investigations. In *A Dictionary of Theatre Anthropology: The Secret Art of the Performer,* written with Nicola Savarese, Barba lays out the fruits of ISTA research and defines the pre-expressive state of performers from different theatrical traditions as an altered and often precarious physical balance, a dilation of the body, opposition of directions within the body, a direct gaze from the eyes, and a codified intentional use of hand gestures, all of which make actors seem supremely alive on stage.

Psychologist Paul Ekman offers a more scientific point of view on a universal language of emotions. Fascinated by individuals who are particularly good at reading facial expressions to perceive emotions, Ekman investigated whether these talented face readers were seeing something concrete that the rest of us miss. Working with Wallace Friesen, he codified almost all the possible movements of the human face in a Facial Action Coding System (FACS) and correlated different expressions to different emotions. Looking carefully at films of politicians, criminals, and mental patients who were caught lying on camera, he discovered that there are involuntary, transitory facial expressions that spontaneously reveal emotions. These "microexpressions" are generated by a different physiological system than the one that governs our intentional facial expressions, revealing emotions we consciously try to hide. Because they are involuntary, like breathing, they are universal. Ekman also discovered that intentionally making a facial expression, unmotivated by the emotion it displays, creates physiological changes in heart rate and body temperature associated with having the real emotion. Making an angry face can elevate the heart rate. Pixar, creators of *Toy Story*, and Dreamworks, creators of *Shrek*, have both used FACS in their computer animation.

Chilean neurophysiologist Susana Bloch was developing similar ideas as she produced experiments to record responses to emotional situations. She noticed universal physical patterns of response that she called "effector patterns." Dr. Bloch discovered that repeating the posture, breath, and facial expression of these patterns could induce an emotional response akin to a real emotion. During the 1980s, Dr. Bloch worked to establish a set vocabulary of effector patterns, documenting the breathing, facial expression, and physical position that could best elicit each of six primary emotions. She called the system **Alba Emoting.** The application to acting technique was obvious, and Dr. Bloch began working with actors in Chile and France to teach them to use her system to create emotions for a role. During the 1990s, she began holding workshops all over the world. Although there are many zealous advocates of the system in the United States, there is also a great deal of resistence to a technique that works externally to create emotion. Currently no effective application of its principles has been developed for use during a performance.

Ekman's and Bloch's scientific studies echo the prescribed codified positions of early European acting, the Desarte system, and the *rasa*-based acting technique of *kathakali*. Science has now documented the interrelationship between external expression and internal feeling that these traditions advocated.

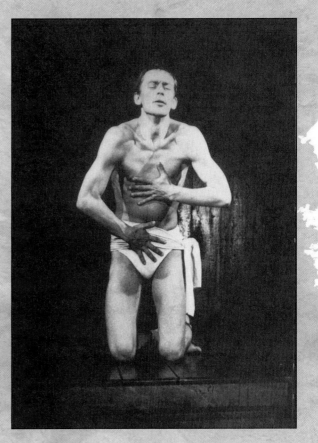

The actor Ryszard Cieslak trained with Jerzy Grotowski and exemplifies Grotowski's intense physical acting style. The fundamental human emotions expressed in this performance can be read across cultures. Here Cieslak performs in Calderón de la Barca's *The Constant Prince.* Teatr Laboratorium, director Jerzy Grotowski.
Zygmunt Samosiuk, Teatr Laboratorium. Courtesy of the Archive of The Grotowski Center, Wroclaw, Poland.

Challenges and Choices

From your observations of people speaking languages you don't understand, what part of an actor's performance can transcend linguistic barriers?

plished at the art. The first attempt to create a training method came from a Frenchman, Francois Delsarte (1811–1871), whose system of oratory provided a pseudo-scientific, mystical approach to the subject. Although Delsarte's system was created for public speaking, European actors, whose art was still based on declamation, found his ideas useful.

Delsarte's system was a revival of the old manuals of set positions for each emotion, only this time, broken down into the smallest body parts and positions, and coordinated with speech patterns and inflections, all carefully illustrated on charts (see Figure 7.1 on page 189). This gestural and vocal code for emotional presentation was learned by rote. Although Delsarte seemed to understand that an organic connection existed between gesture and feeling, his method was totally external and in no way provided links to text or character. The only American known to have studied with Delsarte was Steele MacKaye (1842–1894), who founded what was to become the American Academy of Dramatic Art in 1884 to teach the Delsarte method in the United States. This was actually the beginning of formal actor training in the United States. The Delsarte system became the most popular system of actor training in America through MacKaye's work during the first part of the twentieth century.

Constantin Stanislavski and the Science of Psychology

It is hard for us to realize today that the idea of individual psychology was born in the late nineteenth century and is only a little over one hundred years old. The psychological approach to acting that we identify with the American theatre is even more recent than that. It is rooted in the work of the Russian actor and director Constantin Stanislavski (1863–1938), who created the first systematic approach to acting that included script analysis and role interpretation. His ideas are now taught the world over.

Stanislavski believed that the methodology of science could be applied to acting technique and that the actor's laboratory was the studio, not the performance hall. With a group of talented actors in his laboratory at the Moscow Art Theatre, Stanislavski searched for a technique that would enable actors to inhabit the new naturalist plays of his time that presented situations close to everyday life and used natural language and a realistic portrayal of character and emotion. The ensemble style demanded by these plays required an approach to acting different from the bombastic, melodramatic acting of the period. Stanislavski worked to develop a training methodology that could address psychological realism.

Using some of the new theories of post-Darwinian psychology, Stanislavski sought the triggers for emotion and natural behavior within the imaginary world of the play. This was truly pioneering work entirely different from any other approach to acting before it. Stanislavski observed that we adapt our behavior to the conditions in which we find ourselves. Every play sets out a series of such conditions for its characters. Stanislavski called these the **given circumstances**. Actors must ask themselves many questions as they read a play. What has just happened? What is happening now? Where am I? What country, location, building, or room am I in? When is it? What period, time of day, and season? Who am I? Why am I here? These questions are asked in the first person so the response to each question is personalized and has an immediate effect on the actor's behavior. If it were a cold winter night in medieval Denmark, and I were on night watch on the ramparts of a castle where yesterday a ghost had appeared, as in *Hamlet*, my walk and bearing, the feeling in my body would all be different than if I were in a small tenement apartment in twentieth century New Orleans on a sweltering summer day, as in *A Streetcar Named Desire*. Stanislavski also emphasized the importance of detail and specificity in describing a character's circumstances. For example, if I said I was in a restaurant, this would not be specific enough. It might be a McDonald's or a four-star restaurant in Paris. I certainly would not behave the same way in both of those places. How I eat, my table manners, how I sit, talk and hold myself would completely change. Specificity of detail is important for determining specificity of behavior.

The most important question is, "Who am I?" It serves as the basis for all physical and psychological work on character. Stanislavski emphasized the importance of combing a play for buried information to create a complete picture of the character. The emphasis is on the detail that prevents the actor from playing a cliché instead of a distinct and unique individual. The facts of the plot, the social situation, the psychological relationships, all must be examined to form the basis for characterization. This contrasts sharply with the method of playing generalized emotions and types before Stanislavski.

Once the *given circumstances* are outlined, the actor must ask, How would I behave *if* I were this character in these circumstances? We have come to call this the **magic *if*** because it stimulates the imagination. The circumstances cause the character to desire a certain outcome—the **objective**—the goal that drives a character every moment she is on stage. Characters have larger **superobjectives** that carry them through the play, and they have more immediate scene objectives that they live each moment on stage. Stanislavski made the significant observation that we want something every moment we are alive. We are never completely passive. This observation became a key to his technique. Because the character always wants something, the actor is launched into *action* to achieve that objective. This action becomes the source of interesting and compelling stage behavior. As the character moves through the play pursuing objectives, circumstances are altered by the character's actions. The actor must make internal *adjustments* or adaptations to these changing circumstances, each of which marks a unit or **beat** of the drama. This results in shifting objectives and actions, and it is this pattern of stimulus and response that energizes an actor's inner life and movement through the play.

Truthful acting for Stanislavski meant behaving in a way that was consistent with the imaginary circumstances of the play. Until the twentieth century, it was an accepted European convention that actors faced the audience directly when they spoke, even when their lines were directed toward other characters. We even have anecdotal reports of actors on stage during a performance discussing at what tavern to drink after the show and other matters outside the sphere of the play when they were not speaking lines. To combat this convention, Stanislavski developed the idea of **concentration of attention**, insisting that actors keep a circle of attention with their eyes that did not encompass the audience and focused instead on objects and characters within the stage reality. Stanislavski also imposed an inner concentration of attention on the imaginary reality of the character. He emphasized the importance of actors truly talking to each other on stage instead of focusing on the audience. He called this *communion*, deliberately choosing a term with spiritual connotations to reflect the deep emotional connection that actors must make when relating to each other on stage. This becomes the basis of ensemble performance.

One part of Stanislavski's early technique remains the subject of controversy to this day—**emotional** or **affective memory**, sometimes called emotional recall. The technique requires focusing on the sensory stimuli surrounding an event in the actor's personal life that was similar to the situation in the character's life in order to evoke an emotional response. Acting teachers have disagreed about the effectiveness of the use of an actor's personal mem-

Photo 7.4
Actors must give us a strong sense of the circumstances in which their characters find themselves. Here we sense the characters' desperate plight. *The Trojan Women,* adapted and directed by Alfred Preisser, Classical Theater of Harlem. *Courtesy of The Classical Theatre of Harlem, Inc.; photo by Christopher McElroen*

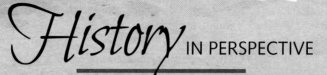

History IN PERSPECTIVE

THE STANISLAVSKI SYSTEM BECOMES AMERICAN METHOD ACTING

Method acting, that distinctly American brand of theatrical performance marked by force of personality and raw emotion, and personified by figures such as Marlon Brando, James Dean, and Paul Newman, evolved from the Stanislavski system. The system came to American consciousness during the 1923 tour of the Moscow Art Theatre. Two actors who had studied with Stanislavski, Maria Ouspenskaya (1881–1949) and Richard Boleslavsky (1889–1937), remained in the United States and taught his technique to a group of American actors at the American Laboratory Theatre in New York. Here, during the 1920s, the young Lee Strasberg (1902–1982), Stella Adler (1902–1992), and Harold Clurman (1901–1980) would come to learn their craft. All began their theatrical lives inspired by the Yiddish theatre that then thrived on the lower east side of Manhattan, and each followed a different path to fame on the American stage as teachers, actors, and directors. Together with Cheryl Crawford (1902–1986), they later formed the core of the Group Theatre (1931–1941), where they were joined by Robert Lewis (1909–1997), Sanford Meisner, (1905–1997), and Elia Kazan (1909–2003), among others. This passionate ensemble of young actors and directors would transform the American theatre and turn the Stanislavski system into something distinctly American.

Using the Moscow Art Theatre as a model, they set out to reform the commercial theatre through their socially conscious plays, their ensemble style, and the emotional authenticity of their acting, which was startling and fresh. In time, however, artistic and personal differences brought friction to the Group. Notably, Stella Adler and Lee Strasberg clashed over his focus on emotional or affective memory. Adler felt the technique was tearing her up emotionally and traveled to France in 1934 to meet with the ailing Stanislavski to hear the truth of the system from the horse's mouth.

In fact, Stanislavski had long since abandoned his focus on emotional memory. Even at the time of the 1923 tour, he was already working on a psychophysical approach to acting that emphasized physical action and took the actor's attention off the personal emotional life. Ouspenskaya and Boleslavsky, who had trained during the earlier stages of Stanislavski's work, had passed on an incomplete system to their New York students. By the time he met Adler, Stanislavski was concerned for his legacy in America. He taught her his new technical approach, focusing on the *given circumstances* and *action*, with emotion as a by-product, not a goal. When she returned, Adler shared the method of physical actions with the Group and challenged Strasberg's authority as lead acting teacher for the ensemble. Although Strasberg and Adler have different recollections of their encounter, this was the start of a rift. Strasberg believed Stanislavski was contradicting himself and that he, Strasberg, had now developed his own method that was as valid as the evolved Stanislavski system.

In 1947, six years after the Group disbanded, several of its alumni—Harold Clurman, Elia Kazan, and Robert Lewis—met to discuss continuing its work. Out of this meeting came the idea to start The Actors Studio, the

Challenges and Choices

If actors need to be free and have open channels of expression, is there any limit to what an acting teacher can ask actors to experience during training (e.g., nudity, intimacy, smoking, drinking, pushing actors to physical and emotional limits)? If you refuse to take a risk, are you denying a range of expression?

ories to portray the emotions of the character. Not only is the technique often unsuccessful, but it takes the actor out of the imaginary world of the play and onto personal issues that may be painful and unequal to the circumstances of the drama. It also prevents the actor from standing fully outside the self to shape a role. Stanislavski himself abandoned this technique during the 1920s when he came to believe that emotions could not be directly called up but needed to be stimulated indirectly through physical action, reversing his earlier theories.

Stanislavski was under the influence of the theories of French psychologist Théodule Ribot (1839–1916) and Russian physiologists Ivan Pavlov (1849–1936) and Ivan Sechenov (1829–1905), who were studying conditioned reflex. Stanislavski came to believe that emotional reactions arise as a result of our physical interactions with the environment and that feelings are evoked by our physical responses. If the actor created the proper physical stimulus, the emotions would be evoked. Stanislavski substituted his theory of **psychophysical action** for emotional recall as the center of his technique, now believing that physical behavior that reveals the character and the objective can provoke the emotional response more directly than internal work can. Disputes over how much

name recalling Stanislavski's first studio where his search for a new technique began. Its initial class included many who would become luminaries of American theatre and film—Marlon Brando, Montgomery Clift, Julie Harris, Karl Malden, famed choreographer Jerome Robbins, and film director Sidney Lumet among them. In short order, Lewis and Kazan had conflicts. Kazan's landmark production of *A Streetcar Named Desire*, with Brando in his definitive performance, had led to a busy directing schedule. They needed someone who had ample time to devote to the school. Strasberg, at first kept out because of his difficult temperament, was having little success in his career and was called in for the task. In 1948, Strasberg joined the Studio. By 1951 he had become its artistic director, a position he held until his death in 1982, and the rest is American theatre history. Method acting, Lee Strasberg, and The Actors Studio would become synonymous.

Authenticity of emotion became the focus of Strasberg's work, and actors turned inward to mine their psyches for the experiences and feelings that could translate to the stage. He developed emotional memory exercises and the famous "private moment" that put actors' personal issues into public view as they enacted private behavior that they would normally only do behind closed doors. Although alerted to be tasteful in the choice of activities, many actors crossed social boundaries with daring nudity and intimate behavior. Much rumor still circulates around this exercise, although most work was quite tame. In the Studio's early years, little emphasis was placed on the vocal and movement work of British and European conservatories. Without that training, studio actors rarely developed the skills for character roles and the

classics, and one criticism of the method was that it prepared actors only for realism and roles in which they could play themselves in heightened theatrical terms.

Strasberg was at once a dominating force, a bully, and a father figure to his students. He traumatized many young talents with his harsh criticism and nurtured others. Some felt that the atmosphere created in his classes was emotionally perilous; others thrived. Many who studied with him became the great actors of the American theatre, ensuring his reputation as a guru. Strasberg also spawned a cult of acting teachers who used his method to push young actors to their emotional breaking point, misunderstanding the method as a license to practice psychoanalysis.

Although Strasberg was well aware that Stanislavski was influenced by behavioral psychology and not versed in Freud, Strasberg's techniques meshed well with the American obsession with psychoanalysis during the 1950s and 1960s. As more and more of the public were examining their inner demons, watching actors wrestle with theirs was a public projection of the American psyche. The personal and emotional approach of Actors Studio performers became the hallmark of a new American acting style that would captivate the world.

Marlon Brando, who died in 2004, exemplified the intensely emotional style represented by American method acting. He burst onto the theatrical scene in 1947 with his portrayal of Stanley Kowalski in Tennessee Williams's *A Streetcar Named Desire*, directed by Elia Kazan at the Ethel Barrymore Theatre in New York. Pictured with him is Jessica Tandy as Blanche Dubois.
Photofest

an actor's personal psychology must enter into actor training continue today, along with the continuing debates over the necessity of "feeling" or "living" the role versus technically "presenting" the role. This is another manifestation of conventions of acting reflecting the cultural viewpoint of a particular society.

Today, almost a century after Stanislavski began his innovative work, the system he pioneered remains at the center of actor training programs on every continent. Various interpreters have expanded or modified the core techniques, and new exercises have been created, but the fundamental concept of purposeful behavior on stage within the imaginary circumstances has proven a key to acting in various theatrical styles. Recent discoveries about the physical basis of emotions in modern neuroscience seem to confirm much of Stanislavski's thinking.

Explorations in Physical Training

Stanislavski's ideas spread through the tours of the Moscow Art Theatre, whose ensemble performances were hailed for their realistic acting. Although he had talked

History IN PERSPECTIVE

CURRICULUM FROM THE PROFESSIONAL SCHOOL OF THE VIEUX COLOMBIER, 1922–1923

The Professional School of the Vieux Colombier was one of the earliest actor training programs to fully integrate complete physical training for the actor, including dance, acrobatics, mask, mime, flexibility and strength training with elocution, declamation, text analysis, theatre history, and design.

COURSES AND WORKSHOPS FOR THE APPRENTICE GROUP

1. Theory of Theatre—Prof. Jacques Copeau

   Religious origins and social significance. Birth and development of dramatic feeling, of tragic form, of the theatrical instrument. The architecture and materials of the theatre. The performance. The playing of actors and scenic arrangements. The works.

2. Dramatic Education—Profs. Jacques Copeau and Suzanne Bing

   Cultivation of spontaneity and invention in the adolescent. Stories, games of wit, improvisation, impromptu dialogue, mimicry, mask, etc. Staging of the diverse means acquired by the student in the course of his general instruction.

3. Schools, Communities and Civilization—Prof. Georges-Chennevière

   The country. The race. The spirit. Overview of history and civilization. Great men and great collectives. Philosophical schools. Philosophical and religious communities. Literary and artistic schools. Corporations. Daily life of individuals, groups, and cities. How it expresses itself in poetry, music, theatre.

4. Course in French Language—Prof. Mme Line Noro

   Exercises in grammar, vocabulary. Explication of texts.

4b. Memory Exercises—Prof. Mme Line Noro

   Rational cultivation of the memory. Recitation of texts.

5. Elocution, Diction, Declamation—Prof. Suzanne Bing

   Mechanism of elocution. Syntax. Study of genres and styles. Ensembles.

6. Music—Under the Direction of Daniel Lazarus

   a) Musical Culture—Study of ancient music and that of the Middle Ages. Lecture commentaries on the works of the great classical, romantic and modern masters.

   b) Singing—Prof. Louis Brochard—Study of a cappella and accompanied choruses of the 16th, 17th, and 18th centuries.

   c) Dance—Prof. Mlle Lamballe—Technical study of the steps and figures of classical dance. Dramatic applications.

7. Physical Culture—Monitor M. Moyne

   Hygiene and physical training. Outdoor exercises. Flexibility. Breathing. Endurance. Stability.

about the need for muscular relaxation and physical training for the actor, Stanislavski left behind no set methodology for achieving these goals. Other figures, often with very different views of the theatre, pioneered the work in this area. The early decades of the twentieth century, inspired by the new behavioral sciences and new theatrical forms, were marked by a search for the techniques that could train the modern actor.

8. Acrobatics, Games of Strength and Skill—Profs. Paul and François Fratellini

Work at the Cirque Médrano.

9. Craft Workshops

a) Drawing. Sketching. Modeling. Moulding. Life Drawing. Prof. Emile Marque.
b) Costume—Prof. M. Ruppert
c) Design. Study of materials—Prof. Mlle Mathilde de Coster.
Shop Leader: Mlle Marie-Hélène Copeau.

The craft shop work leaves place to the initiative and spontaneous taste of the student. Classes will alternate according to opportunity, with lectures, games, outings (visits to museums, monuments, gardens, etc.).

II. Courses Reserved for the Company of the Vieux-Colombier

1. Study of Poetic Styles (Preparation for Poetry Matinees)—Prof. Jules Romains

Exceptionally, some amateurs will be admitted—upon their request and after a preliminary examination—to participate in these classes and in choral recitations.

2. Principles of Production (staging)— Prof. Jacques Copeau

3. Singing Course (individual and choral)—Prof. Louis Brochard

4. Dance Course—Prof. Mlle Lamballe

5. Perfecting Diction and Stage Practice—Prof. S. Bing (Course for student-actors of the Company).

III. Courses Reserved for Outside Professionals
Diction—Principles of Production— Prof. Georges Vitray. Under the direction Jacques Copeau.
Conditions of admission: 500 francs per year.

Jacques Copeau used masks to help actors find a more dynamic and physically expressive form of acting that could replace the declamatory style of most French theatre of the early twentieth century. Copeau actors (left to right) Monique Schlumberger, Yvonne Galli, Eve Lievens, Madeleine Gautier, and Charles Goldblatt wear masks made for the chorus of demons in André Gide's *Saül*.
Courtesy of Mime Journal

Source: Vieux Colombier *curriculum from Barbara Kusler Leigh, "Jacques Copeau's School for Actors,"* Mime Journal #9 and #10. With permission of Barbara Leigh, Ph.D.

In Russia, Stanislavski's student Vsevolod Meyerhold (1874–1942) created **biomechanics**, a physical training system for efficient and expressive movement. Departing from his mentor's emphasis on emotional truth, Meyerhold believed that the key to actor training lay in the actor's physical being. Biomechanics offered a developed system of exercises, based in organic patterns of movement, that taught the actor complete control over the body and developed the capacity for quick response to stimuli, so necessary for the actor on stage. The training reflected Russian developments in neurophysiology pioneered by Pavlov and others. The system is still studied today.

In France, in the 1920s, Jacques Copeau (1878–1949), upset with the tired ham acting of the commercial theatre and the static oratorical style of performing classical texts, founded the École du Vieux Colombier to resuscitate the theatre. The school integrated circus, mask, mime, Asian movement, and *commedia dell'arte* training into the acting curriculum in the hope of revitalizing the actor's art (see pages 196–197). Modern French mime found its origins in this school. Copeau's nephew, Michel Saint-Denis (1897–1971), created the first English acting school—the Old Vic Theatre School in 1946, followed by the National Theatre School of Canada in 1959, and in 1968 the Julliard School in New York, all based on Copeau's ideas of physical training for the actor. Not until the 1970s were similar regimens of physical training incorporated into the curricula of many American acting schools, and it took almost a decade before such work was widespread in the United States. Today, it is impossible to imagine a professional actor training program that does not provide extensive courses to develop an expressive and articulate body.

Freeing the Actor's Energy

The 1960s and early 1970s, like the early decades of the century, were marked by a search for new forms of theatre. The revolutionary political atmosphere had a profound impact on the theatre and in turn on acting. As social structures were seen as obstacles to certain freedoms of expression, they were also seen as obstacles to free expression in the theatre. New forms of theatre broke down the barriers between audience and performer, and a new form of actor training focused on releasing the blocks to expression. Learned social inhibitions were seen as obstructing the flow of energy and feeling and blocking the actor from reaching a primal emotional source.

To achieve this free energy flow, ideas and techniques drawn from Asian philosophy and religion that emphasized the impossibility of separating the physical from the psychological human functions were applied. From Zen came an understanding of the importance of proper relaxation and breathing techniques as a support for all voice and movement work. Focus on the breath creates a greater awareness of the whole body, and through awareness comes the control so necessary to acting. The influence of Asian religion and philosophy is evidenced in the idea of a *body center*, or a point in the body where breath, movement, feeling, and thought are integrated through focused relaxation. The process through which an actor reaches this integrated state is called **centering**. It permits the harnessed and economical use of the body's physical, emotional, and intellectual energy resulting in a dynamic performance. To achieve this centered state, contemporary actor training focuses on removing muscular tension that blocks the free flow of the body's expressive potential. Various approaches to movement training such as Alexander and Feldenkrais tech-

Photo 7.5
The impact of the 1960s emphasis on phsycial training can be seen in contemporary groups like the Minneapolis-based Theatre de la Jeune Lune, who use acrobatics along with other acting techniques to create theatrical events. Pictured is *The Circus of Tales,* a collaboratively created production directed by Robert Rosen.
© *Michal Daniel, 2002*

Photo 7.6
Actors train in the Suzuki method with New York's SITI Company. Through stomping and other exercises that focus on the lower half of the body, Suzuki actors develop a connection with the ground that gives them physical strength as well as breath and vocal control.
Photo courtesy of John Nation/SITI Company

niques have focused on proper alignment and good body imaging and use to free physical movement from muscular tension. Simultaneously, vocal techniques have been developed in the past forty years to facilitate a free, natural, and fully projected voice. Vocal coaches Kristin Linklater, Cecily Berry, Arthur Lessac, and Patsy Rodenberg have all been at the forefront of this type of voice training, which replaced the old emphasis on elocution with the free release of feeling on sound.

During this period, the European and American avant-garde moved away from traditional plays or used texts as a basis for improvised action which placed new demands on actors. Notable European directors of the 1960s created productions that relied on exquisitely trained actors capable of physical and vocal virtuosity. Jerzy Grotowski, with his Polish Laboratory Theatre, not only created productions that required his actors to offer their bodies as sacrifices to their art, but also developed a set of difficult exercises called **plastiques** that could only be performed by physically trained actors. Jean-Louis Barrault (1911–1994) trained as a mime and incorporated elaborate group pantomime sequences into his work. The 1970 production of *A Midsummer's Night's Dream*, directed by Peter Brook, serves as an example of the demands of the new theatre. Scenes were played on trapezes, and actors juggled while reciting their lines in perfect Shakespearean rhythm. The performers were required to have all the traditional skills of accomplished Shakespearean actors and be able to do circus tricks as well. Theatre groups in the United States such as the Open Theatre, The Performance Group, and The Manhattan Project worked improvisationally to create performances with the actors as both creators and performers. These pieces, created out of sound and movement, required actors to have complete mastery of their bodies and voices and to be excellent improvisors.

It is now almost one hundred years since the importance of physical training for the actor was just an experimental idea in Europe. Today new systems of training continue to develop around the world. The Japanese director and teacher Suzuki Tadashi (b. 1939) developed a technique based on the physical rootedness of ancient Japanese acting traditions, placing special emphasis on the feet and a feeling of connectedness to the earth (see Photo 7.6). Through stomping, the actor coordinates the movement of the upper torso and the feet, creating an awareness of the energy at the center between the upward and the downward forces. American director Anne Bogart (b. 1951) cofounded with

Challenges and Choices

Since the actor uses her own body, heart, mind, and emotions, do we see the real person when the actor performs a role?

IN PERSPECTIVE

In Their Own Words

CHRISTINE TOY JOHNSON

Christine Toy Johnson is an actor, writer, producer, and advocate for inclusion in the arts. Her extensive acting career spans Broadway, Off-Broadway, national tours, regional theatres, episodic and daytime television, and feature films. Christine's short film All American Eyes *played the festival circuit, and she is in development with a feature-length screenplay. She has been active in the Nontraditional Casting Project, which promotes employment opportunities for minority and disabled actors.*

■ **Can you explain your work with nontraditional casting and its goals?**

I became involved in advocacy for nontraditional casting and inclusion in the arts about fourteen years ago. At the time the discussions of nontraditional casting were ripe because of the hiring of the non-Asian Jonathan Pryce to play the Asian (later justified as "Eurasian") "Engineer" in the Broadway premiere of *Miss Saigon*. The issues that surfaced have continued to fuel both the Asian American community and those in the theatrical community who have a commitment to fighting discrimination in the arts.

I remember thinking that if Cameron McIntosh could argue that actors (such as Jonathan Pryce) should be able to play other races, then the door had to swing both ways. At the time we were still fighting to get the opportunity to play our own ethnicity. I lost many *King and I* jobs to Caucasian women with brown, or in one instance even blonde, hair, so it seemed only fair that in plays where race was not germane to the plot, Asian American actors should also be allowed to play non-Asian roles.

■ **Is authenticity important in portraying Asians on the stage?**

Given the lack of opportunities that Asian actors have had, I stand firm on fighting for our right to portray Asians on the stage. Unfortunately, Asian roles have often not been portrayed with the dignity, respect, and lack of stereotypical characteristics that most Asian American actors would bring to the same roles. It was vital for us to start portraying our multicultural society through the characters we played on stage. After all, the theatre has always been an educator and a mirror to our society.

Authenticity in portraying any role is the quest of every actor worth his or her salt, and I believe that certain culturally specific roles must be portrayed by culturally specific actors when that specificity is germane to plot or character development. I have had to explain the abhorrent concept of "yellow face" being the equivalent of "black face" in the eyes of the Asian American community. One would never cast an African American role with an actor who is not African American, yet it is still common to find non-Asian actors in "yellow face" portraying Asian roles on stage. When an actor is cast nontraditionally in a role that has been routinely played by a Caucasian actor, he or she does not don "white face" in order to assume the character.

■ **Why is nontraditional casting important?**

The arts and the media have a unique opportunity to influence the way we look at each other. Nontraditional casting has always been about enriching the quality of storytelling, expanding boundaries, portraying the universality of the human spirit. We can send the message that our important plays reach beyond race, ethnicity, and disability. The opportunity to help heal society by highlighting the beauty of both our similarities and our differences is an incredible gift, and this is the power of theatre.

In 1991, I was called with an appointment to audition for "Julie" in a production of *Carousel*. I was stunned that I was even being given the opportunity to audition. I felt sure the other actresses were wondering what I was doing there. I got the job. And this changed my life and my perception of what I could do in the theatre. I realized that I connected to the character of "Julie" so much more than any Asian character in the musical theatre and learned that getting the essence of the character right was more vital to the storytelling than the color of the actor's skin, unless it's a story specifically about ethnicity and race.

■ **What special efforts, if any, do you make when preparing for a role that is outside your personal racial background?**

I prepare all roles in the same way, no matter what their racial or cultural background might be. Trained to examine the text and to mine the details that are there in order to illuminate the life of the character, I aim to understand what makes a character tick, and why they do what they do. In getting to the root of a character, the basic questions I ask are the same: What does she want? What will she do to get it? What's standing in her way? What does she think will happen if she doesn't get what she wants? Why is she motivated to do the things she does? The fascinating part of the process for me is to figure out how the pieces of the puzzle fit together. I also do extensive research on a person's cultural, societal, and professional background, developing the backstory of a character as much as possible in order to understand the richness of their life history.

■ **Considering the history of *Flower Drum Song* and its Orientalist perception of Asians, did you have any hesitation about accepting the role?**

The Broadway tour of *Flower Drum Song* was actually a new, retooled version by Asian American playwright, David Henry Hwang. I knew he had made the roles more three-dimensional than in the original version, and that he emphasized the clash in the cultures between being Chinese from China and being Chinese American from America. I was excited by the prospect of playing a person who, like me and millions of others, is of Asian heritage but was born and bred in the United States. There has been no other Broadway musical with Asian American characters in it! I also knew that audiences had not had much opportunity to see this particular Asian American story—a love story as well as one about the complexity of assimilation, being accepted as American, fitting into a society that is more comfortable choosing who is "All American" based on a European prototype. This show did more to bash the "Orientalist perception" of us than any other show I can think of.

■ **Can you discuss your personal experiences and the ease or difficulty of finding work?**

I have been making a living as an actor for over twenty years, and the unlikelihood of this fact does not escape me. First, our industry is impossible at best, but I have to believe that talent, perseverance, and complete and utter faith that you're doing what you were born to be doing, all contribute to longevity in the business. Add to that an unwillingness to view obstacles as obstacles. I have definitely run into discriminatory barriers. I have experienced people blatantly not hiring me because of my ethnicity, in one case saying they needed a "regular girl" instead. I know, after all these years, when I am not being taken seriously at an audition before I even open my mouth.

That said, as a character in Stephen Sondheim's *Follies* says, "I'm still here!" I've also had wonderful opportunities to play fabulous roles on Broadway, Off-Broadway, and all over the country. I am grateful that I've been able to build a reputation for myself and hope that by being prepared and constantly honing my craft, I will always continue to work in this business. And I'm intent on creating new roles for myself and other Asian American actors in the screenplays I am writing and producing. This is where our future lies, I'm certain.

■ **What advice would you give to young actors starting out today?**

I talk to young actors all the time and always tell them to keep studying, keep enjoying life, keep growing as a human being, and never, never give up! Stay aware, keep your antennas alert, observe all you can, and use it later! Learn to stay generous, listen and respond with passion—and know that being a storyteller is a great and glorious task, one that the world has always relied on for inspiration, education, and thought.

An example of non-traditional casting is Asian-American actor Christine Toy Johnson as Ethel Toffelmier in the Broadway production of *The Music Man*, directed by Susan Stroman at the Neil Simon Theatre in New York.
© *Michael Duran*

Source: Used with permission of Christine Toy Johnson.

Challenges and Choices

Should all roles be open to casting with any actor, regardless of ethnic or racial identity? With so few roles available in the commercial theatre for minority actors, should those roles be reserved for them?

Suzuki the Saratoga International Theatre Institute. She uses **Viewpoints**, a physical training system developed by Mary Overlie which fosters awareness of the basic components of movement—line, rhythm, tempo, and duration, as a basis for group creation. Workshops in these recently developed methods are given around the world, evidence of the globalization of actor training.

Once acting schools would teach only diction, script analysis, and scene study. Today's professional actor training programs stress voice and movement as the key to effective use of the actor in scene work. It is now common for acting schools to offer classes in circus to develop coordination and strength, mime and mask work to create an articulate and expressive body, *t'ai chi* for balance and form, yoga for breath control and focus, Suzuki for centering, African dance for centered control and rhythm, Alexander technique for alignment and "good use," fencing for focus and coordination, Viewpoints for spatial awareness, vocal production for a free voice, diction for clarity of speech, and singing. All of these techniques are now seen as vital and reflect borrowings from many different cultures. Today's fully trained Western actor would have extensive physical and vocal training in addition to work on script analysis.

The Acting Profession Today

The glamour of the acting profession draws many people to the theatre, but, in fact, the actor's life is a mixed blessing filled with hard work, endless training, and many disappointments. For minority actors, the road to success may be even more difficult. Actors will tell you that nothing compares to the thrill of performing, of feeling all your physical, mental, and emotional energy flowing and focused. It is an exhilarating sensation that keeps people in the profession despite its attendant difficulties.

A great misconception is that actors are somewhat unstable and that they can work out their personal problems through acting. In fact, actors need to be emotionally and physically healthy to deal with the technical challenges of training and to have the ability to analyze characters objectively. The knocks of the profession and the constant risk and rejection, along with prolonged periods of unemployment, require a strong ego and sense of self.

Challenges and Choices

When so many highly trained actors are unemployed, is it right to bring in a nonactor with celebrity appeal to play a coveted role? Is it justified if it lures new audiences to the theatre?

Once, actors joined companies where they performed with a group of people for many years. Actors sometimes even became shareholders in the profits. Shakespeare and Molière, both actors, wrote for their own acting companies and had specific actors in mind for the roles they wrote. Today we have few ongoing theatre companies or repertory troupes in which actors stay together for years. Instead, actors are hired for a single role for the run of the play and frequently find themselves unemployed for long periods between engagements. The advantages of ongoing companies are many. Actors have a sense of family and ensemble that does not have to be created afresh after every production. Work can be developed that fits with the talents of particular actors, and of course, there is the advantage of not being perpetually unemployed.

Repeatedly, perhaps many times a year, actors seek work through an **audition**, where they perform either prepared material or read from the play being cast for the director. A small number of actors are asked to return for a second audition called a **callback**. They may or may not be cast, even after repeated efforts. If cast, there will be a rehearsal period during which actors explore their roles, analyze the text, and develop physical characterizations—a walk, a voice, and mannerisms for their characters. During rehearsals actors explore actions and objectives with the guidance of the director. They must find a way to have their interpretations and choices mesh with the choices of other actors to create a seamless imaginary world. They adjust to costumes, sets, and lights and ready the production for performance.

Sometimes actors do not begin with a written play, but with a concept, and are expected to create the text. Rehearsals here become a series of improvisations and explorations, until a performance text is fully created. We discussed some of the groups that work in this way in Chapter 6.

Before every rehearsal and performance, all trained actors perform a **warm-up** to relieve tension that could block emotional flow, to loosen and limber, and to get centered and focused. There is no single way to warm up. Actors construct warm-ups that suit the roles they are playing or particular vocal or movement problems they may have. Some theatre companies warm up together as a way of getting the energy flowing among the actors before they are on stage. The acting warm-up is not unlike the warm-up for athletic events. Actors, like athletes, must ready the body to give its all.

Over a period of weeks, an actor's performance develops. The intellectual analysis gives way to physical embodiment, and the actual performance becomes second nature. At this point, actors no longer think about the meaning of the piece, the voice or movement or feeling. It all becomes an organic part of the actor's being, an integrated whole. All the training of the body, voice, and mind frees actors to transform themselves into imaginary beings with beating hearts.

Stage and Film Acting

The technical demands of the stage are much greater than those of film, although some of the basic principles of acting for these two very different media remain the same. Actors analyze the script, the character, and the circumstances for a film the same way they would for the theatre. They choose physical characterizations, voices, and gestures. However, stage actors must have mastery of vocal technique if they are to be heard in a large theatre without vocal strain; they must radiate physical energy and choose actions that read across space, and they must learn to play off a live audience. On the other hand, film actors are supported by microphones, close-ups, and camera angles. They rehearse for very short periods, in small bits, and often out of sequence so they do not have to create a sustained and developed performance. Ultimately, actors in film have less control over the shape of their final performances than actors in the theatre do because the film director and editor can cut, determine camera angles, and shape what the viewer sees. Many actors who work in both film and theatre say that when they work in film they miss the contact with the live audience and the sense of immediacy and control of the arc of performance they have on the stage. As a result, many, like Kevin Spacey, Kevin Kline, Kathleen Turner, and Nathan Lane, return to the theatre for challenge and renewal. On stage, there is no safety net, no chance for a retake.

Acting in Performance Traditions

In most performance traditions, the exuberance and the theatricality of the spectacle takes precedence over the quest for emotional authenticity. Traditions that involve music, dance, song, masks, and exaggerated makeup demand a very different kind of acting than realism with its attempt to portray real life on the stage. The style of acting among various traditions varies widely, and the training can be formal or informal. In Africa and among the indigenous peoples of the Americas and Australia, many traditions are passed on through initiation, imitation, and apprenticeship, and the burden is on the student to observe, absorb, and practice techniques. In Asia many codified systems are rigorously taught.

Photo 7.7

A teacher at the College of Dramatic Arts in Bangkok helps a student perfect the stance of a vigorous character from *khon,* a Thai classical masked-dance tradition. *Khon* students are matched to role types such as a young man, a young woman, a demon, or an athletic character, usually used for the monkey Hanuman in the *Ramayana* epic. Students train to perform the single role type that best matches their physical potential. Precise physical positioning is an important part of the art, and students learn and repeat their characters' traditional postures and dance sequences before using masks. The college is the major school for training in classical Thai dance and is the descendant of the old palace department of performing arts.

© *Claudia Orenstein*

Traditional Asian Acting Styles and Training

Asian theatre traditions revel in the artificiality and artistry of a presentational style. Plays in these traditions generally tell tales of gods or legendary heroes, and an amplified style of performance usually integrates dramatic presentation with mime, dance, music and sometimes acrobatics, supporting the mythic dimensions of these larger-than-life characters. Asian theatre forms use colorful costumes, vibrant makeup or masks, and exaggerated styles of movement. On the Asian stage, to move is to dance and to speak is to sing. Actors do not concentrate on the development of psychologically realistic portraits, but instead practice embodying archetypal figures.

Asian actors master codes of performance that previous artists have developed and perfected, sometimes over hundreds of years. These codes usually delineate physical postures and gestures as well as vocal styles for a defined number of role types. They may also determine patterns of stage movement as well as costume and makeup. The emphasis in these traditions is on the accomplished execution of a completely envisioned role, rather than on developing an entirely new or unique interpretation.

Traditional Asian forms were passed down through families, from one generation to the next. From their infancy, future actors were exposed to the art they would later take up as they watched their parents rehearse and perform and listened to the music and stories of the theatrical repertoire. Because changing economic and social realities throughout Asia have endangered these family traditions, special schools, now provide training to students who are not from artistic families.

In many Asian traditions, training in the early stages involves the master's manipulation of the student's body. The student's process is marked by intense observation and imitation of the master's movement patterns, and then endless repetition until formal perfection is attained. Eventually the mastery is complete and it is up to the actor to fill the forms with life. If you have ever studied a martial art, you may have experienced some similarities in approach.

Formal training usually starts at a young age, when the body is flexible. Asian theatre forms demand extraordinary physical expression in which every part of the body, including fingers, toes, and even the eyes and mouth, are fully articulated. Much early training involves preparing the actor's body for performance. The closest parallel in the West is the training of classical ballet dancers, who must start at an early age to develop the strength and flexibility required to master a set repertory of positions and movements.

It is common for students to be chosen to study particular kinds of roles based on how well their faces and bodies conform to preconceived ideals. Traditions usually offer a range of types from characters who are poised, calm, and refined, with graceful, subtle movements, to those who are vigorous and passionate with larger, more energetic gesticulations. Actors may learn complete dances or roles in gradations of growing complexity, rather than isolated, individual units, or positions, that are then put together. A full day of training will usually include work on physical characterization, dancing, and acrobatics as well as music and vocal instruction and study of texts from the theatrical repertoire.

Kathakali: A Case Study of Asian Training

Kathakali theatre from the state of Kerala in India offers a good example of the arduous demands placed on the traditional Asian actor. *Kathakali*, which means "story-play," dates back to the late sixteenth and early seventeenth centuries. In *kathakali*, all-male companies of actor-dancers enact tales from the Indian epics, the *Mahabharata* and the *Ramayana*, as well as stories from popular Hindu lore. They are accompanied by percussion music and vocalists who sing both narration and dialogue. *Kathakali*'s derivation from the Kerala martial arts tradition accounts in part for the demanding physicality inherent in the form. The actors must also be fit to carry the voluminous skirts and large headdresses that are traditional costuming. In fact, it takes two to three hours for the actor to don traditional makeup and costume in preparation for performance (see Photo 10.3). They then act, dance, and leap through shows that can last from 6:30 in the evening until 6:30 the next morning.

Kathakali actors traditionally begin their training by the age of seven or eight, although today some may start as late as sixteen. Class can fill an eight- to thirteen-hour day that includes both philosophical and text study, as well as rigorous physical training. Instruction concentrates on preparing the actor's body for the physical demands of performance and includes building general strength and flexibility and learning jumping, body control, and footwork patterns. Actors remodel their bodies to the basic posture that is the basis for all *kathakali* movement—head straight with chin tucked in, heels together with knees turned out forming the shape of a flat rhombus with the legs. The outer edges of the feet are never placed flat on the ground and yet perfect balance is maintained. The spine is held in a concave curve with the rear end pointing up, arms out to the side, elbows slightly bent, and hands limp so that from the side the performer looks flat. Starting from this position, the actor must be able to execute all the prescribed dance patterns as well as occasional feats of physical virtuosity. To attain this stance, actors undergo deep, painful massages. As the young actors lie on the floor with their knees turned out, their teachers step on their backs, molding their bodies into the ideal shape.

Photo 7.8
At a training school in Kerala, India, a young student develops the flexibility required for the physically demanding art of *kathakali*. Traditionally artists begin training when they are young and their bodies are supple.
© *Henri Cartier-Bresson/Magnum Photos*

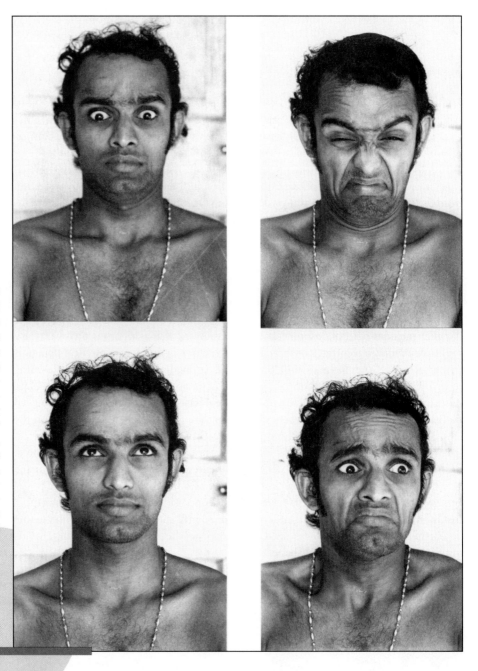

Photo 7.9
Basic *Kathakali* Facial Expressions
Kathakali actors convey the basic *bhavas* or emotions through facial expressions that require total control of all facial muscles. The audience savors the corresponding *rasa*, or flavor of feeling, produced by each expression. Pictured here, clockwise from top left, are the emotions of fury, disgust, fear, and peace. Interestingly, Delsarte, working in nineteenth-century France, developed a system that echoes this late sixteenth-, early seventeenth-century Indian performance tradition, which draws from more ancient roots. Compare these expressions with those in Figure 7.1.
Photograph by Phillip Zarrilli

Kathakali actors neither speak nor sing on stage. Some Asian actors, such as those in Chinese opera, do both, and *kabuki* actors don't sing but do use expressive, stylized vocal patterns. Both narration and dialogue in *kathakali* are presented by a vocalist who stands with the musicians. Actors communicate the Sanskrit texts to the audience not in speech but in a language of hand gestures known as **mudras** that can be used to represent the entire syntactical range of the Sanskrit language. Actors use a basic set of *mudras* whose meanings change in relation to various body postures and facial expressions. As part of their training, *kathakali* actors learn five hundred *mudras* and the texts from as many as eighteen plays.

The *kathakali* actor is not just an athlete, dancer, and gestural storyteller, but, like all actors, he embodies characters and presents their emotional states and experiences to the audience. In the *kathakali* theatre a variety of role types are defined by their traditional

Photo 7.10
Kathakali dancers Amaljeet and Rewati Aiyyer as Lord Krishna and Draupadi in a scene taken from the *Mahabharata* at a cultural festival in Patna, India. Note the traditional makeup and costuming of *kathakali* and the use of expressive facial and hand gestures to convey emotions.
© *EPA/Landov*

makeup and costuming. Unlike some Asian forms in which actors specialize in one role type their whole lives, *kathakali* actors learn all the roles and how to perform each within the entire dramatic repertoire.

Kathakali acting identifies nine basic emotional states or *bhavas*: erotic, comic, pathos, fury, heroic, fearful, repulsive, wondrous, and peace, plus a tenth state, shyness, used only for female characters. Actors express these states by executing prescribed facial expressions with specific positioning for the eyes, eyebrows, and mouth. They practice these articulations independent of particular plays or characters. They also do exercises to render their faces flexible and expressive. In one such exercise, actors sit facing a wall as they listen to their teacher tell a story. They must enact everything the character of the story sees and feels using only their eyes. When performing, actors place small seeds in their eyes to redden them and make them more remarkable.

Like many Asian performers, *kathakali* actors play on a mostly bare stage and create the imaginary world around them through physical gesture. An actor's movements will tell the audience that he is mounting, riding, or dismounting a horse.

Mastering *kathakali* performance takes a lifetime of practice. Actors do not truly reach their prime until their forties, when their technique becomes second nature and can serve as a vehicle for artistic expression. The following often-quoted statement reveals the philosophy embedded in the *kathakali* approach to actor training (The term *bhava* means the actor's expression of the character's emotional state, and the term *rasa* means the audience's aesthetic savoring of the theatrical experience):

Where the hand [is], there [is] the eye;

where the eye [is], there [is] the mind;

where the mind [is], there [is] the *bhava*;

where the *bhava* [is], there is the *rasa*.[1]

---

1. Phillip B. Zarrilli, *Kathakali Dance Drama: Where Gods and Demons Come to Play* (London: Routledge, 2000), 91.

The Puppeteer as Actor

To be a puppeteer is to be a kind of actor. Using a marionette, glove, shadow, or rod puppet, whether of Asian or Western origin, the puppeteer needs to master the ability to create and project character, just as actors do. The difference is that puppeteers project their performances through the medium of a performing object rather than through their own bodies. In Asia, the close relationship between human and puppet performance provides some insight into the stylized acting found in Asia, and may even explain some of the training methodology. The marionette theatre in Myanmar (Burma) is said to predate live-actor performance forms there. Dance postures of human actors mimic the movements of puppets. One frequently performed novelty act pits a prince marionette in a dancing contest against a human performer also playing a prince. The puppet and the actor dance the same movements together. In Indonesia the **wayang kulit**, or shadow puppet tradition, one of many different types of puppetry there, predates *wayang orang*, a masked-dance form with human actors with which it shares many similarities. Puppets and human actors can provide mutual inspiration.

Puppeteers have traditionally trained informally in families or with performing troupes, and this is still the case for many traditional forms. Today institutions throughout the world offer workshops and courses of study for aspiring puppeteers. They teach the art of manipulating a variety of performing objects. It is relatively easy to learn to manipulate some puppets, such as shadow puppets, whereas others, such as marionettes or *bunraku*-style puppets, take a good deal of patience, coordination, and dexterity. Most programs teach movement and mime to help puppeteers understand their own physical actions and centering, so they can impart physical expression to a performing object. Voice training is also important because vocal characterization helps define a speaking puppet (imagine Sesame Street's Kermit the Frog with a low, husky voice and the character would be transformed). Also, puppeteers may do the voices of several characters in a single show. Because puppeteers often create their own shows from scratch, many programs teach puppet construction. Some also provide classes in playwriting for the puppet theatre to help puppeteers develop scripts for performance.

Freedom within Constraint; Constraint within Freedom

Western actors often believe that the strictly defined codes of traditional Asian performance hinder the actor's freedom and creativity. Asian performers, by contrast, feel that the constraints of tradition that guide their performances actually liberate them artistically. Freed from having to make new choices in terms of action, characterization, physicality, and vocal placement, they are fully available on stage to execute a role for which a lifetime of practice has prepared them.

Most Asian theatre codes of performance are not as strict as they might seem at first glance, and the actor's creativity may be called on in ways that would seem surprising to Western performers. In Chinese opera, for instance, actors master a single role type, such as the vivacious young female or *hua dan*, which they play their entire lives. However, they choose which gestures from the character's physical vocabulary they will use to reflect feelings at particular moments, often varying choices from one night to the next. Chinese opera audiences are sensitive to these changes and judge the

Artists

IN PERSPECTIVE

In Their Own Words

MATSUI AKIRA

Matsui Akira is a master actor-teacher of the Kita School of Japanese classical noh *theater. He began studying* noh *at the age of five and at age thirteen became a "live-in apprentice" to Kita Minoru, the fifteenth generation of* noh *masters of the Kita School. Since age twenty he has been performing and teaching throughout Japan and has been active in disseminating* noh *abroad by training student actors around the world, acting in productions of plays by Shakespeare, W. B. Yeats, and Beckett; cocreating new "English* noh;" *and choreographing* noh-*style dances to jazz ballads and poetry. In 1998 he was designated an Important Intangible Cultural Asset by the Japanese government. He is an Affiliated Artist with Theatre Nohgaku, whose mission is to share the beauty and power of* noh *with English-speaking audiences and performers through English language productions, training workshops, lectures, and professional residencies.*

■ **Could you describe your own training in *noh*? How did you become a *noh* performer?**

I'm not from a traditional *noh* family. When I was five years old and growing up in Wakayama City, I was quite small and my doctor suggested I do *utai* (*noh* chant) to make me stronger. In fact, he was a teacher of chant, and so I started taking lessons from him. My parents had the doctor introduce me to his teacher, a Kita School performer named Wajima Tomitaro. I began to take lessons with Wajima sensei, and he had me occasionally perform *kokata* (child) roles in plays in Wakayama and Osaka. When I was thirteen years old, I was very fortunate to have Wajima sensei arrange for me to go to Tokyo to live with the *iemoto* (headmaster) of the Kita School, Kita Minoru. I was one of seven *uchideshi* (live-in disciples) of the *iemoto* and the youngest. We would wake up early in the morning and practice chant and dance for a couple of hours before going off to regular school. After school we would come back and have lessons in the *hayashi*—the four instruments of *noh*. A different *hayashi* teacher would come every day. Then we would rehearse more chant and dance. Some days we would have performances where we began to learn how to help backstage.

Of course, what we were doing as *uchideshi* was not just learning how to perform *noh*. We were doing what we call *shugyô*, which includes much more than just learning how to perform. It is learning how to live. We had to clean the house, we had to open and close all the house shutters, we had to do the things our seniors told us to do. And of course the most important is learning proper greetings and etiquette in the house and then backstage. Even if you think your senior isn't a particularly good performer, you must learn to respect him. We don't have exams to determine who has the highest score, and we are not like sumo or other sports where you have a winner or loser. It is difficult to determine who is a better performer, but even if one thinks one is better, someone else might eventually be a better teacher. So we always have to show respect for our elders.

What we come to understand in the process is that etiquette is the basis of one's *noh* training. And it becomes important in passing along the art to our own sons. If I died young, who would teach my own son? It really is necessary that my association with other performers is good so they can help in the training of my son no matter what the future.

Noh is a group performance. One can't perform it by oneself. If you don't have a good relationship with other performers, you won't be asked to perform and you won't be able to ask others to perform with you. You might be more talented than someone else, but what good will that do if no one is willing to perform with you? So it is not just a question of technique. A major part of one's training is learning how to work with others. If you don't learn this while you are young, you will suffer for it later. Actually, even if you aren't such a good performer, if you have a good association with other performers, you will get work. We have a saying that "a great talent matures late." One might be a very good performer as a youth but later not be so good. Or you might not be so skilled as a youth but then become better with age.

■ **To many Western actors, the idea of learning a codified performance form can seem constraining. Can you explain how it frees you to create within the form, or how you see your own creativity emerge within the form?**

In the West, dance and theatre have become separate things. In both *noh* and *kabuki*, dance and theatre are melded together. When you do dance, you of course

(continues)

Artists

IN PERSPECTIVE (CONTINUED)

have to learn the forms of dance which we call *kata*. But then as you begin to add more levels of theatre you need to add inner elements of expression. Even with those inner elements, the basis for movement still is dance in terms of how you move or even walk. Classical ballet still uses balletic movements as its base even though a theatrical story is being presented. So *noh* isn't theatre in the sense that Shakespeare is theatre. *Noh* has dance that follows rules, which makes it different from Shakespeare. And it also has music, which means that movement has to fit along with the rules of music, and that of course is what dance is.

Kata, the set movement patterns of *noh*, are thus born of dance. How one expresses those *kata* then becomes the source of creativity for the actor. Do you express those *kata* in a large fashion or a small fashion? Do you make them simple or complex? Each *kata* might have its parameters of expression, but there is a lot of freedom within those parameters. *Kata* might have set rules, but the actor

has freedom to vary those boundaries. *Noh* actors use *suriashi* "sliding feet" movements to walk, but there is a great variety in how you execute that walk.

If you can execute the *kata*, you can perform. In turn, that might make it difficult to stand out as a performer because you might think that everyone is doing the same thing. But not all actors look the same doing the same *kata*. Some might be very precise, others not so. For the audience members who know *kata*, that difference is interesting. It is up to the actor to take the expression of those *kata* to a higher level to create something that deepens a sense of understanding of the story. And that is what creates the difference between performers and performances.

■ **What do you believe are the most important qualities or skills for a *noh* actor?**

For the head of a school, more important than performing itself is passing on the tradition and the per-

Matsui Akira in the *shite*, or main role, of the play *Nomori (The Watchman of the Plains)*. In this play a traveler looks into a magic mirror, which displays an image that can only be tolerated by someone with divine power. He calls on the deity of the "unmoving" and, in this mask, becomes one with the deity, enabling him to look into the mirror.

Noh actor Matsui Akira in *shimai* pose, on a *noh* stage.

Photos by Ikegami Yoshiharu; reproduced with the permission of Matsui Akira

formance standards of the tradition. But for other performers in the school, the question is how can one learn the tradition but make it feel new, relevant, and vital to the present. And that is really the most difficult thing for a performer to do. If one just takes the patterns and performs them without giving them new life, they are just antiques and the actor just becomes a museum of ancient performance.

In the last fifteen years, the world of *noh* has suddenly opened up and many performers are involved in new creations. There is a fine distinction where what you are doing is an extension of the tradition and at the same time feels fresh and new. So in the end, the performer must learn absolutely the basics of the tradition so even if he goes off to explore things outside the tradition, he can always find his way back to the tradition.

■ **What differences have you found in working with Japanese actors and the many Western performers whom you have trained?**

If you are talking about Japanese actors who are not *noh* actors, there really is very little difference between Japanese and Western performers. But if you are talking about *noh* actors, then of course there is a big difference. *Noh* actors only know *noh* and so it is very easy to work with them. We always follow the fundamentals of putting together a performance—the fundamentals that are a part of the *noh* world but not of any other performing world even in Japan. In the *noh* world, we all work on the part we are to perform and then we come together, have basically one rehearsal, and then do the performance. If you work with actors outside of the tradition, you usually need to get together for a number of rehearsals. If you are teaching them *noh*, then you have to teach them, then rehearse them, and then finally perform with them. It is a long process.

If I am going to perform with a Beijing opera performer or with a ballet dancer, I have to learn about Beijing opera or ballet. I've had the experience of taking workshops in both just to get some insight into those traditions so it is possible to perform with them. Even if what I personally do as a performer is based in *noh*, we all have to work together to understand characteristics of each other's art so we can somehow find a point of meeting. That meeting point is always the same with other *noh* actors, but with non-*noh* actors, that point is inevitably different.

■ **You have also worked with new plays created for the *noh* repertoire, like Samuel Beckett's *Rockabye*. What is your view of these new plays, and how do you approach a completely new text?**

When one does something new like this, there is always a director. In *noh*, we don't have a director. But in any new piece I have done, such as *Rockabye* or *Siddhartha*, there has always been a director. The question then is what the director wants me to do. Does he want me to do something in *noh* style, or does he want a *noh* actor to do something in some other style? Clearly, if the director just wants an actor to act realistically, he should get an actor who normally does that kind of thing. They will certainly be better at it than I am. But they have probably asked me to perform because they want something that a *noh* actor can give them—maybe not *noh* itself, but a certain something. So treading the fine line between the two styles is what is difficult. It's like walking on a wall. If you fall off to one side, you will be doing *noh*. If you fall off to the other side, you will be doing realistic theatre. So by somehow walking on the wall itself you are able to do something that is neither but is something special in itself—something that not just any actor can do.

To deal with a new text, I often first try to figure out how it would be done in a *noh* style. Then when I come to something that I can't figure out, I think about how it might be portrayed in realistic theatre. Then I usually try to create new *kata* by basically making dance out of realistic gestures. You have to discover the essence of what you want to express and work from there. An apple drawn by Cézanne has to be something unique but at the same time must be something everyone will recognize as an apple. What makes his apple special is the perspective that is his alone. Yes, everyone sees immediately that it is an apple, but the essence is clear and something special is created. In the end, when I do something new, the essence of *noh* has to be there. Even if you think what I created with *Rockabye* is different from *noh*, the essence of *noh* is still there.

Source: The interview with Matsui Akira was conducted in Japanese and translated and transcribed into English by Richard Emmert, the founder and artistic director of Theatre Nohgaku.

actor in part by these creative decisions. Chinese opera singers also help select the music that accompanies a performance. During Chinese opera rehearsals, actors indicate to the musicians what kind of music they feel would be appropriate for a particular moment on stage, and the musicians select a musical piece from a repertoire of known melodies.

In the Japanese *noh* theatre, actors make interpretive statements about their characters through choices in costuming. The appropriate style of kimono for a role might be prescribed, but a performer will decide on a particular design or pattern for the garment, perhaps one with cranes or fall-colored leaves, to reveal his view of the play. In Western theatre this type of choice is made by costume designers and directors rather than performers.

Whatever performance codes exist, however, living traditions are always in flux as they react to the needs of new actors, changing times, and contemporary audiences. No current performance can be a complete replica of any done in the past. In Asia today new social, political, and economic realities are continually altering time-honored traditions. *Kathakali* plays once done outdoors in the round by firelight for local audiences are now presented indoors on proscenium-style stages with electric lighting for audiences from all over the world. Such changes inevitably influence performance style and technique.

Just as traditional Asian forms are relaxing some of their strict performance codes, American and European stage acting is becoming an increasingly refined and disciplined art. Once actors took to the stage by whim or passion, today's American stage actor is a highly trained professional who has usually studied the craft intensively for an extended time. Most have been trained in conservatories or MFA programs that often require a minimum of three years of study. Physical rigor and control is demanded and often taught through Asian training systems. A standard book often handed to first-year acting students in the United States is *Zen and the Art of Archery*, whose focus on breathing, relaxation, focus, and effortless release of energy as a path to emotional freedom and performance (in Zen the emphasis is more spiritual) now serves to prepare American actors for the rigors ahead. The extreme discipline of modern mime and mask work is often integrated into the training, and many of the theatre's most significant young talents have emerged from Jacques Lecoq's mime school in Paris.

Freedom within constraint and constraint within freedom have been the hallmarks of contemporary acting around the world. This has been achieved by looking toward tradition for innovation.

KEY IDEAS

- Acting is not simply reproduction and imitation. The excitement of live acting comes from watching the process of simulation.
- All actors transcend everyday behavior through energy, control, focus, purpose, dynamics, enlargement, and transformation.
- Actors in different theatrical traditions do different things on stage, and their training is a function of how and what they are expected to perform.

- Representational acting is seen in realistic theatrical styles in which actors live the emotions. Presentational acting appears where there is a heightened theatrical style and an openly artificial reproduction of emotion.
- Actors' dual consciousness allows them to stand simultaneously inside and outside the role they are playing.
- Acting generally reflects a society's views of beauty, emotion, psychology, and behavior.

- In the European tradition most acting centers on interpreting a written role. Before the twentieth century, actors in the European tradition generalized emotions and character types.
- Beginning in the twentieth century, formal training systems and schools for actors were developed that worked on the psychological and physical development of a role. Stanislavski's system of actor training took a scientific approach based on psychology and dominated American actor training during the twentieth century.

- Actor training in performance traditions can be very rigorous, including many years of physical work, vocal work, and practice of the repertoire that may begin in childhood.
- Puppeteers project character through a performing object and may train informally or in schools that include physical and vocal work for the actor as well as practice in various methods of object manipulation.
- All actors balance the constraints of technique with the freedom of artistic expression, although the balance is different in different theatrical traditions.

The Director
The Invisible Presence

Director Robert Wilson's unique vision marks this production of Georg Büchner's *Woyzeck*. The title character's alienation from the world around him is represented through the isolation of light and color and the distortion of the windows as much as through acting. Such metaphorical visual elements and the use of actors and their costumes as part of a visual landscape are all typical of Wilson's style. Jens Jørn Spottag (right) as Woyzeck with Marianne Mortensen and Morten Eisner as the Doctors in the Robert Wilson/Tom Waits production of *Woyzeck*, Brooklyn Academy of Music, Harvey Theater, New York.
© *Jack Vartoogian/FrontRowPhotos*

Actors embody the characters who engage us; playwrights pen the words we hear; designers create the sets, costumes, and lighting we see before us. These are all palpable aspects of the theatrical experience, and it is obvious to us who is responsible for the artistry behind each one. So where is the director? Everything we experience in the theatre is infused with the director's unique style and personal perspective. The director molds each dramatic interaction and movement on stage, shapes the reading of every line, and selects each detail of design. Though absent from the scene during the moment of performance, the director's presence is everywhere.

Directors provide a unified artistic vision of what the world of the production will be, and sometimes it is literally a vision as they imagine the stage in concrete visual theatrical images. Sometimes their vision may be about the process of creation. Sometimes it redefines the very nature of a particular text or theatrical style, but there is always a guiding vision, and the director leads the creative process toward its realization.

Directors Mold the Theatrical Experience

Directors decide how to manipulate theatrical elements to create meaning on stage. Aware that audience members consciously and unconsciously read significance into all aspects of a theatrical performance from the color of an actor's shirt to a momentary silence, directors carefully frame and shape the audience's theatrical experience. They select each tangible detail of acting, staging, movement, design, sound, and special effects, as well as intangibles that can be felt but not seen such as mood, rhythm, and tempo. Often directors can determine where the audience sits or how and when they enter the theatrical space. A director might put notes in the program or set up a lobby display to help contextualize a piece for the audience. The director's art lies in making decisions about how to use all the means available to create a compelling theatrical encounter.

Establishing and Manipulating Stage Convention

Every director possesses a vocabulary of theatrical conventions from which creative choices are made. While some directors stay within the traditional stage conventions for particular works and styles, many directors achieve acclaim precisely because they challenge the prevailing notion of how to realize a play or what kind of text to use. Setting a Shakespearean play in Nazi Germany or the American Wild West, having video projections interact with live actors, making the audience change location and seats, or turning an unsuspecting group of people into an audience in a public space are just a few of the ways directors have chosen to defy convention. Today, we put a premium on such originality, and it often feels as though directors resist the traditional to create bold new concepts.

Even the most shocking confrontations with convention can in time become the norm. So many 1960s avant-garde directors such as Julian Beck and Richard Schechner involved the spectator in the performance that eventually it became an accepted theatre practice, and audience participation in the action became a new convention. The same is true of nudity on the stage. Director Tom O'Horgan (b. 1926) in *Hair* created an uproar in 1968 with female nudity; fleeting male nudity followed. In 2003, you could watch an entire baseball team shower naked in director Joe Mantello's (b. 1962) *Take Me Out*. Consider how shocking such a thing would have been in 1965, and you will realize how fast theatrical innovations can evolve into new conventions when directors consistently push the limits.

Photo 8.1
The naked body, once a taboo in serious drama, is now an accepted stage convention. Nudity is an important narrative and imagistic element in *Vienna: Lusthaus (Revisited)*, a dance-theatre piece reflecting the deep anxieties of *fin de siècle* Vienna through a sequence of dream and nightmare images. New York Theatre Workshop; text by Charles L. Mee; music by Richard Peaslee; conceived and directed by Martha Clarke.
© *Joan Marcus*

Directors Play a Double Role

Directors work as artists engaged in creation, but they must also step back from the process and look at it from a distance. They act as the audience's eyes and ears, reading what they themselves have helped lay out on stage, just as a spectator would walking in off the street. To do this successfully, directors must possess a heightened visual sense and a keen ear for language and phrasing. They continually shift back and forth between these two roles of creator and spectator as they make decisions about which elements of the production to keep and which to change.

Rehearsal is the director's time. During this period the director, having conceptualized the piece, molds the theatrical work, exploring the text with the actors and designers to construct meaning through every theatrical moment on stage. On opening night, the director's work is done; the stage manager takes over the show and acts as the caretaker of the director's vision. It is then up to the performers and the crew to enact the production that the director envisioned and created with them. At this point the director's omnipotent role is diminished. The director becomes powerless, having bequeathed artistic trust to the members of the company. The arrival of the audience completes the director's process.

Directing, a Recent Art

Considering the enormous task of the director, it is difficult to believe that the art of directing is a relatively recent phenomenon in the history of the theatre. In fact, the idea of the director, as the role is defined today, begins to take shape in the late eighteenth and early nineteenth centuries in Europe, and is not established in its current form until the early twentieth century.

Before Directors, Who Ran the Show?

Of course, the theatre has always needed someone to run the show and organize the performance. In different eras, this role was performed by either the playwright, an actor, or a manager, but these were organizational roles, not visionary or interpretive ones. In ancient Greece, the playwright acted in his plays and trained the chorus; in ancient Rome **actor-managers** also often functioned as playwrights. In the Middle Ages, towns and guilds provided organization and named **pageant masters** to organize theatrical events. The sixteenth through the nineteenth centuries saw the rise of actor-managers, who provided coordination for performances. In Europe, for the most part, actors worked on their roles alone and wore costumes they owned. There was little concern for a conceptually unified production. It is hard for us to believe, but most actors never read the entire play they were performing; they received only "**sides**," actors' individual lines and cues, copied by a stage manager. Rehearsals did not take place, so no one was needed to run them or serve as an acting coach. Performances took place on bare stages or in front of reusable backdrops or flats, not specific to any particular play, so no one was needed to coordinate the designers' efforts with a specific concept. Actors stood in set patterns on the stage, usually a semicircle, stepping forward to speak their lines, so no one was needed to stage a play.

Theatrical traditions outside of Europe simply did not need a director because they had preestablished codes that dictated exactly how a performance should be done. The master performer, who knows every piece of the repertoire by heart, as well as its staging, teaches every detail to others, fulfilling the function of director. What we might consider directorial choices—selection of costume, makeup, and movement—are left to the actor. For example, the performances of great *kabuki* actors were passed down *en toto* to their successors with each move, gesture, facial expression, and vocal inflection scrupulously imitated. Even today, *kabuki* actors learn to perform famous roles exactly as their predecessors performed them.

Rise of the Modern Director

During the late eighteenth century in Europe, an increasing interest in scientific precision and "natural" behavior resulted in a growing dissatisfaction with the lack of coherent approach and artificial acting style. Rehearsals were begun in some theatre companies, and theatre practitioners began to search for a more organized and natural approach to staging. Several figures made important initial contributions to defining the role of the modern director.

Johann Wolfgang von Goethe, the great German playwright, poet, essayist, and novelist, experimented with new methods of theatre production during his twenty-six years as director of the Court Theatre in Weimar from 1791 to 1817. The plays Goethe and Friedrich Schiller wrote in the small dukedom of Weimar presented an elegant poetic style called "Weimar Classicism" and required acting skills beyond those of the Weimar actors, who were more at home with clownish farces. Goethe established rules for actors' comportment on stage so the company could form well-composed stage pictures that he modeled on great paintings and sculpture. Goethe had his actors read the text together in rehearsal, rather than just memorizing their own lines from "sides." Using a stick, he beat out the rhythm of each line so the actors would present the verse musically on stage and in a unified style. To control visual composition, he drew grid lines on the stage floor to permit precise instructions about how and where to move. Taking control of all the artistic elements on stage, Goethe became a prototype for the future director.

Georg II, The Duke of Saxe-Meiningen (1826–1914), working out of his own small German court theatre, brought the idea of detailed visual unity in production to new heights. He spared no expense to achieve his goals of historical accuracy in costume and setting and, using the visual arts as his guide, arranged actors in interestingly composed stage pictures. His company was renowned for its crowd scenes in which each actor displayed an individual character, yet worked in unison with the others. Between 1870 and 1890, the Meiningen Players made frequent performance tours throughout Europe, disseminating their impressive new staging practices.

The idea of a thematically unified stage work, or ***gesamtkunstwerk***, came from Richard Wagner (1813–1883), who asserted a directorial vision for the operas he composed. For Wagner, the musical score unified the theatrical work and set the tone and the mood for each character, each scene, and all the visual elements of the staging. Using music as the unifying force, Wagner offered a prototype for a unified production style that related form to content.

With the publication of Charles Darwin's (1809–1882) *Origin of Species*, in 1849, interest in the environmental and hereditary factors that shape human behavior preoccupied the world and the theatre. These ideas gave birth to the social sciences of sociology and psychology, removing the study of human nature from the province of religion and philosophy and putting it squarely in the scientific domain. Playwrights such as Emile Zola (1840–1902), Henrik Ibsen, August Strindberg (1849–1912), and Anton Chekhov wrote plays with psychologically complex characters who grew out of particular social milieus. Naturalist plays that examined social and biological forces that determine human interactions required sets and costumes that reflected the reality of characters' lives specifically and truthfully in order to scientifically expose the truth of social ills. The generic settings of the past were now insufficient for understanding characters within their own dramatic worlds.

Theatre practitioners now saw the need to create specific environments for particular plays, and the need for an artistic eye—a director to unify the stage elements with the play text. At the Théâtre Libre, André Antoine (1858–1943) went to every length to recreate his characters' environment on stage. In his production of *The Butchers* (1888), he bought the contents of a butcher shop and hung real rotting beef carcasses on stage, leaving nothing to the imagination. He arranged rooms as you would find them in real life and during rehearsals decided which side to remove as the audience's "fourth wall." Antoine feared that professional actors of his day, known for heightened emotional ham acting, would ruin the stage illusion, so he engaged amateurs who he believed would behave more naturally, in an attempt to make the stage represent a *slice of life*.

Constantin Stanislavski (1863–1938) came up with a better and more influential solution to the problem of melodramatic acting, with the creation of his famous system, discussed in Chapter 7, that focused on psychologically motivated behavior and ensemble work. He integrated the acting with the play, set, costumes, light, and sound to create the seamless illusion of reality on the stage. The modern director as visionary, unifier, and guide to actors was born in Stanislavski's early work.

Photo 8.2
Andre Antoine's 1902 production of *La Terre (The Earth)* in France. Note Antoine's emphasis on naturalistic detail in this farm scene with real hay and live chickens. The actors' mundane activities also stress the "slice of life" naturalism of the scene, as does the natural light of the candles. The set gives the impression that a real barn is presented with the fourth wall removed.
© Bibliothèque Nationale de France

Because the director evolved from the need of realistic plays for a coherent, unified presentation of the world of the drama on stage, the role of the director is originally conceived as an interpreter of the dramatic text. The first modern directors were found in Europe or in cultures that had inherited that theatrical tradition's emphasis on the written play. As we saw in Chapter 6, today, directors may begin their creative process in many different ways.

The rebellion against realism in the early twentieth century fostered the emergence of influential directors drawn to nonrealistic aesthetics. Before long, it was clear that the unified vision the director gave to realism could be applicable to any theatrical style, and directors carved out expanded roles. They became more than just realizers of plays and turned themselves into wizards of stagecraft and manipulators of conventions. Directors were able to move between the written tradition and performance traditions, and in some cases they became the creators of their own performance traditions, usurping both the role of the actor as the guardian of stage technique and the role of the playwright as the author of the text. Many of the alternative forms we examined in Chapter 6 illustrate how the director can take on multiple roles.

Today the director can be found the world over, working with and without traditional play texts. The primary role of the director in the American theatre remains the interpretation and realization of plays. Increasingly, in the avant-garde, we find the role of the director transformed into that of conceptualizer and author of every aspect of a production. In the sections ahead, we will examine some of the ways directors create theatre.

The Director's Process: A Multiplicity of Approaches

There is no single description of the working process of the director. Although all directors present a guiding vision and make the final decisions about what will be seen and heard on stage, directors work in different ways, toward different goals, and under diverse circumstances. Their approach to the collaborative effort is personal. The work of some directors reenvisions the process of directing and the very idea of what a director and a theatrical event are supposed to be. Some have carefully planned all aspects of a production and expect the team to fulfill a set concept, while others offer actors and designers the freedom to contribute to the director's vision. Some directors see themselves as interpreters of a dramatic text; others see themselves as creators of the text. Some believe they lead and dictate to the creative team; others see themselves as collaborators and organizers of a group effort. No matter what the process, directors are ultimately in charge of every aspect of a production. For this reason, they must understand the possibilities and pragmatics of design, technology, stage effects, sound, and acting to get optimum results from the efforts of others.

The Director as Interpreter of a Dramatic Text

The director, as the interpreter of a play, guides its journey from the written word to the performed action. Under this model, the director's work begins long before the first rehearsal. Selecting, researching, analyzing, and interpreting the text, and determining a concept and stylistic approach, all must be done before the hands-on work begins. Sometimes, in the commercial theatre, producers or artistic directors may choose the text and then hire a director suited to the project based on the director's experience with similar material or because of other talents the director might bring to the project.

Choosing the Text

In the interpretive model of directing, a production begins with a play. The first job of directors is to choose the text, a vehicle through which they can speak to a subject in a personal voice. They read many scripts looking for the play that can trigger their theatrical imaginations while meeting their pragmatic concerns. A play may address an important issue or present themes the director wants to explore, or it may provide an intriguing image or character. Even when theatres hire directors after choosing a season of plays (a very common practice), directors need to uncover inspirational elements of a play before they begin their work.

Many considerations go into play choice. Practical constraints such as budget and working conditions, or the availability of performance rights may be influential. A director may want a script that accommodates a particular actor or theatrical space. The intended audience also plays a key role. Directors may think about the needs of their particular community, considering what might provide enjoyment or illuminate issues of concern. At a university theatre, staging a classic play such as *Oedipus the King* or *Waiting for Godot* may be beneficial for training student actors or because students are reading these plays in their classes. Sometimes a director chooses something daring to challenge prevalent tastes and lead the community toward new visions of the theatre and its possibilities.

Directors also have to know themselves, their particular talents and abilities. Some directors are particularly good with musicals, others with classical language, still others at staging productions that rely on mime and movement. Although many directors want to stretch their talents, in the commercial theatre, a director is expected to assess what he or she can deliver before committing to the job. In the end, the play must be exciting to the director, who will communicate that enthusiasm to others involved in the project to sustain their work through the rehearsal process.

Challenges and Choices

Should directors choose plays that appeal to the intended audience's taste, or should they seek to expand audience taste?

Establishing the Directorial Vision

The process of interpretating the play text begins with the first reading. The director's immediate visceral response often serves as an anchor for all the other discoveries that follow. From the start, a director will begin to imagine the physical world the play will inhabit. What are simply words on the page to others are relationships, movement patterns, line readings, stage business, and theatrical moments to a director who will read the play over and over again to become familiar with all of its nuances, to know the characters intimately, to feel its imagery and structure. A director will search the play for a central idea that can unite all the elements of a production and that sums up the meaning of the piece—a thematic statement, a demonstrated lesson, an eternal truth.

Directors may do research to broaden their understanding of a piece. Learning about the time period in which the play is set or when it was written illuminates its historical context. Information about the playwright can also help probe a play's hidden meanings. Research on a subject the play deals with, such as AIDS or environmental hazards, makes the director more knowledgeable. Directors may also read critical interpretations of the text written by scholars to broaden their perspective on the play. Reviews and photos of past productions can show them how other directors dealt with the problems the play poses. Some directors, however, scrupulously avoid looking at such material to leave themselves open to a spontaneous response. Some directors work with

IN PERSPECTIVE

In Their Own Words

LLOYD RICHARDS

Tony Award–winning director Lloyd Richards (b. 1923) made history with his 1959 production of Lorraine Hansberry's A Raisin in the Sun. *Not only was an African American woman playwright's voice heard on Broadway for the first time, but Richards became the first black man to direct a serious drama on the Great White Way. He has returned to Broadway many times since his groundbreaking efforts and is known most recently for his direction of the works of August Wilson, whose career he launched as artistic director of the National Playwrights Conference at the Eugene O'Neill Memorial Theater Center. His theatre credits are too numerous to list, but he can boast six Tony Award nominations and a Tony. He also directed segments of* Roots *for television. Throughout his life he has nurtured young talent, serving as head of the actor training program at New York University's School of the Arts and professor of theatre at Hunter College before becoming dean of the prestigious Yale University School of Drama and artistic director of the Yale Repertory Theatre in 1979.*

■ **In your career you made significant changes for African Americans in the theatre, and you didn't do it by being a radical but by working in established theatres and institutions. What does it take to make radical changes in our culture?**

This depends on how you define radical. Radical to me is doing, or attempting to do, something which is different than that which is easily accepted by the powers that be in society.

Take nontraditional casting. It is now a subject of great interest. I questioned myself about that fifty years ago. It is an issue that would come up regularly every ten years, then it would disappear and reemerge. But I dealt with it every day. I don't know what radical is, but I know that this was not an acceptable way of thinking or trying to do things when I began, and it is now. To be involved in nontraditional casting was not easy, but it was how I wanted to live my life.

All art belongs to me. All of it! Not any one piece of it. Any artist who creates a thought puts it out into the world, and that thought then belongs to me where I can accept it as something to consider and say whether it is mine or it is not. When somebody says to me, "Why are you doing Chekhov?" I answer, "Because I like him. He speaks to me. I understand him.

He has things to say that I want to hear and pass on." His art is my art because I accept it. Art may stem from a particular individual in a particular culture in a particular time, but it speaks to the centuries, to all times, and it is there for me.

■ **How then do you react to August Wilson saying his plays should only be directed by black directors with black actors and his ensuing debate with Robert Brustein who sees theatre as unifying and cross-cultural?**

I don't agree with Wilson. I don't challenge him. That is what he believes. He came up at a particular time in our history, in a particular place, in a particular theatre. I have been concerned by the debate between him and Brustein. Here are two liberals from two different eras who are stuck with the liberalism from the particular time in which they matured. I cannot look at this as a serious battle, and there is no niche for me in this debate. People are dying in the world. We have plenty of enemies. We have essentially too much in common to be debating this.

■ **Doesn't nontraditional casting today now work in only one direction? Would you cast a white actor in a black role?**

Yesterday, in an acting class that I was teaching, an excellent mature white actor and a beautiful mature black woman played a scene from *Cry, the Beloved Country* in which the white man played the black minister. It was a beautiful scene beautifully done, and the concern that those two characters had as to whether or not their son would come home was not an African subject, it was a human subject. What that playwright was writing about came through. If I were to ask him why as a white man he would choose to play that role, how silly I would sound. This was a man trying to understand the human dilemma by putting himself into a particular culture at a particular time. And the black woman also had to inject herself into that time and that place, and they shared the problem of probing the humanity of the characters' struggle. And that is what the playwright was trying to provoke. I would not ask this actor if the character belonged to him. It belonged to him because he is concerned with him, because it struck him, because he wanted to know more.

■ **When you look for a play to direct, do you look for anything in particular?**

I don't look for anything in particular. I read it, I'm interested. What I look for is a play that says to me YOU must do this. YOU. Not because it is a good play, or a black play, but I want to do something that expresses ME and my concerns.

■ **Do you think Broadway has changed from the 1950s to the 1990s?**

There are so many things that I would not have been considered for fifty years ago at all; thirty or forty years ago I would have been considered and rejected. Everyone was living in the world and had pressures that they had to respond to as they must. When I came to New York, I was an experienced radio actor, and I made the rounds and I got rejection after rejection.

■ **Did you feel angry?**

No. I was facing this all the time. You can't waste all your energy just being angry. Yes, I was displeased and unhappy that this was the circumstance. But there were people who were able to take a chance. It was an issue in the business.

■ **Did you know that *Raisin in the Sun* would be an historic production at the time?**

No. People come to me and say, "You are the first black in history to direct on Broadway." That had nothing to do with why I did this. It had to do with how the play affected me. And the playwright concerned me. Those were the things that talked to me. You have historic consciousness to the extent that somebody might mention it, but I did it because of the provocation of the material itself, not because I'll be the first black director on Broadway. It gives me nothing to create from in terms of the work itself.

■ **What do you think is the primary role of theatre?**

To make people think and feel. During an out-of-town tryout of an August Wilson play, one night an elderly white couple stopped and said to me, "We want to thank you and Mr. Wilson for permitting us to be in the kitchen of a black household." They meant the nitty gritty aspects of life.

"Thank you for letting us know your thinking as a black person." Today Jewish audiences go to plays about Jewish families and Irish audiences go to Irish plays, and I long for the time when we will be part of each other's audience.

■ **You have worked on many new plays. How does a director best help a playwright in rehearsal?**

I am not a playwright. I don't write plays or tell playwrights how to write. One day I told August Wilson to fix the scene that was not working in his play, but I didn't tell him which scene, and he fixed it, because he understood that I wanted him to reexamine his work and think about it again. Working with a playwright is like a marriage. You find a way of communicating and working things out. If you can't, you get divorced.

■ **What do you look for in an actor?**

I want the actor to show me who he or she is, not what they think I want them to be. When I audition, I look for the point at which the actor as a human being overlaps with my concept of the character. The audition happens between the wings and the center of the stage. The actor that comes from the wings and comes alive in the center of the stage is the one who can live there.

■ **Are there any themes the theatre needs to engage with today?**

Yes. What is the meaning of our democracy? The people running our country today wouldn't know how to begin to write our constitution.

Lloyd Richards's direction of the historic 1959 Broadway production of Lorraine Hansberry's *A Raisin in the Sun*, with Claudia McNeil as Lena Younger and Sidney Poitier as Walter Lee Younger, brought the yearnings and conflicts of a black family to the attention of the general culture.
Photofest

Source: Used with permission of Lloyd Richards.

dramaturgs (see Chapter 15), who provide additional research and interpretive ideas that will help shape the director's perspective on the script.

When directing a new play, directors work closely with the playwright, who is often in attendance at rehearsals. They usually come to an agreement about the interpretation of the text. The director may request rewrites, identifying staging problems in the script that need to be solved, character elements that are lacking, speeches that need to be cut, even scenes that might be juggled. This of course is a delicate process with competing egos, but ultimately it works because of the shared goal of a successful production.

Conceiving the Play for the Stage

Directors are now ready to imagine the theatrical world the play must inhabit on the stage and to develop a clear concept of how they will communicate the central meaning to the audience. The concept will lead to a stylistic approach to the material that will guide all the collaborators involved. Style, the manner in which life will be portrayed on stage, can mean realistic staging that approximates real life, or an abstract, symbolic, or emotionally heightened stage world. The director's chosen style must capture something essential in the play and permit it to realize it's full dramatic potential and meaning.

Some directors find a central metaphor that can provide a clear image for the directing and design. Perhaps *A Doll's House* is about a caged bird trying to fly free; communicating this metaphor would inform the acting and design choices. Nora may flit around the stage, or speak in a high lyric voice. The set designer might try to find ways to enclose her in her space. Some directors follow Stanislavski's principles and formulate a **spine**, or superobjective for a play, to establish a central line of dramatic action that can guide actors in their choices. Using a strong active verb, they try to describe the central action in a single phrase that will propel actors through the play. A superobjective for *Romeo and Juliet* might be "To reach for love over all barriers," an image that demands physical urgency. Bertolt Brecht (1891–1956) used the term *fable* to describe the often complex heart or lesson of the theatrical story a director needs to grasp. Other directors avoid these metaphors and spines and prefer using a personal vocabulary to talk at length with designers and actors about their vision and interpretation. Different directors will find different meanings, fables, metaphors, and spines for the same play, depending on their point of view.

High-Concept Directing

Often, directors believe they can reveal more of a play's themes to a contemporary audience if they challenge conventional staging. They may choose to move a play's time period; change its location; invert the genders of the actors; or add music, masks, or puppets. Lee Breuer's (b. 1937) *Dollhouse* (2003) presented a version of the Ibsen play with female roles played by tall women and male roles played by four-foot men; the miniature set was sized to the male characters (see Photo 8.3). This inverted the metaphor of the play; in this production, women dominated the psyches of men, toying with them as puppets. These kinds of alterations are called **high-concept productions**, and they can often provide illuminating new readings of well-known works.

Contemporary directors often break with traditional staging and interpretations of well-known plays. **Deconstruction**, the movement in literary criticism that questions the idea of fixed meanings, truths, or assumptions about texts, is the hallmark of the postmodern aesthetic and has given license to directors to search for new meanings and forms in plays once thought to be confined to particular interpretations and styles.

In the 1960s, following the publication of Polish critic Jan Kott's *Shakespeare, Our Contemporary*, it became fashionable to recontextualize productions of Shakespeare, a practice that continues to the present with many daring reconceptions. The practice has

Photo 8.3
In *Dollhouse,* Lee Breuer's high-concept production of Henrik Ibsen's play, Nora (Maude Mitchell) towers over her husband Torvald (Mark Povinelli) and Dr. Rank (Ricardo Gil). Her house, and the miniature furniture inside, are suited only to the men. Nora's cute gestures and frilly dress add to Breuer's interpretation of her as a grown woman playing at being a child. Mabou Mines, St. Ann's Warehouse, New York; set, Narelle Sissons, costumes, Meganne George.
© *Richard Termine*

now extended to other works in both the classical and modern repertory. Peter Brook, famous for his reimagined Shakespearean worlds, opened the doors for others to push the boundaries of original and classical texts, often to the point where they are free of any formal constraints. The European theatre has a long tradition of such adaptation of classic texts by directors. Bertolt Brecht had his version of Shakespeare's *Coriolanus* and Sophocles' *Antigone,* long before the 1960s. From Ariane Mnouchkine in France, to Peter Stein in Germany, to Miyamoto Amon in Japan, prominent directors have felt empowered to use plays for their own ends.

Such appropriations of well-known plays have been used to stamp a personal imprint on the material and to open up interpretive possibilities. The Dutch director Ivo Van Hove has taken classical American works by Eugene O'Neill and Tennessee Williams and reinvented them. His *A Streetcar Named Desire* featured a bare stage with little more than a water-filled bathtub and chairs; characters plunged naked into the tub at moments of heightened dramatic tension. Of Swiss origin, Heidi Abderhalden of the Mapa Teatro in Bogotá is representative of South American directors who use traditional plays to reflect on the political realities of the current world. Her recent adaptation of *Richard III* used seven actors to play all the parts in a pared-down text. The stage was strewn with piles of skulls, symbolic of the death and corruption that has plagued Colombia as well as Elizabethan England (see Photo 8.4).

Elizabeth LeCompte (b. 1944) and the Wooster Group are known for their conceptual staging of well-known plays that are deconstructed to reveal hidden meanings. These productions often incorporate technological effects to startling results. Their adaptation of Racine's *Phèdre* (*To You, the Birdie*) depicted a constipated Phaedra receiving enimas from her servants, while male characters engaged in an ongoing badminton game and bodies were severed on video screens.

Productions that turn expectations on end can be the subject of controversy. Samuel Beckett objected to director JoAnn Akalaitis' reimagined *Endgame,* when he felt her concept violated his original intentions, just as Arthur Miller was distressed by LeCompte using portions of *The Crucible.* Both raised questions of authors' rights versus directors' rights of free interpretation. Despite the dispute, appropriations of plays by directors have become standard in the international avant-garde; they are safer, of

Challenges and Choices

Is there something in the play text—form, convention, style, language—that must be respected, or should the director be free to interpret a play without constraint?

Photo 8.4
Shakespeare's plays have inspired many high-concept productions. *Ricardo III (Richard III),* from Mapa teatro in Bogotá, used an all-male cast of seven to play more than 35 roles. Imagistic and suggestive staging brought the play's chilling moments into sharp focus. Hoisting two toddlers' outfits up on a pulley represented the taking of the child-princes to the tower for later slaughter. Women's roles were effected through costumes, including the donning of a naked plastic torso, pictured upstage. Dramaturgy and direction by Heidi Abderhalden Cortés, with Julian Diaz, Walter Luengas, Pedro Miguel Rozo, Mauricio Navas, José Ignacio Rincón, Rodolfo Silva. Set design and props by Christian Probst; costume design by Elisabeth Abderhalden; music by Santiago Zuluaga; lighting by Marcela Flores; Mapa Teatro, Colombia.
Courtesy of Festival de théâtre des Amériques, Montreal; photo by Mauricio Esguerra

---

Challenges and Choices

Does a playwright's insistence on a particular interpretation of a work risk making it moribund and a cliché?

---

course, when the playwright is dead and cannot challenge the director's concept. Traditionalists believe that such liberties violate the sanctity of the playwright's work, and that the intentions of the author should be respected. Others argue that it is never possible to know the playwright's true intentions, that a dramatic text is a pre-text for the action on stage and should be used as a jumping-off point for the creative leaps of the director.

Interculturalism has inspired many directors to freely incorporate elements from diverse cultures into their production concepts. Together, deconstruction and interculturalism have opened up the expressive potential of many well-known plays. Mnouchkine's famed production of *Les Atrides* (*The Orestia*) used acting styles, costumes, makeup, and musical instruments and rhythms inspired by Asian traditions. Her European actors use Asian acting techniques to learn to work at a psychological distance from their characters for heightened theatrical effect. Intercultural borrowings have gone in all directions. Japanese directors have taken European texts and used Japanese acting styles to stage them. Suzuki Tadashi's interpretation of *The Bacchae* used the slow movements and sculptural poses of the *noh* theatre to startling dramatic effect, and Ninagawa Yukio, has done stunning *kabuki*-esque versions of ancient Greek tragedies and Shakespeare.

Shaping the Visual World

In the commercial theatre, producers, who run the business side of the production, or artistic directors may be responsible for putting together the team of designers, technicians, and stage managers who will realize the director's vision. In noncommercial ventures, this job may fall to the director. Even when producers select the designers, they usually seek the director's input in assembling the creative team whose collaboration will fall under the director's watchful eye.

Directors seek designers who "can speak their language"—that is, designers who can translate their conceptual language into tangible costumes, sets, and lights on stage. Partnerships often develop, and successful director–designer collaborating teams are often rehired for many productions. Usually, long before actors are cast, the director meets

Artists

IN PERSPECTIVE

ARIANE MNOUCHKINE

The French theatre company Le Théâtre du Soleil, founded in 1964 as a collective, is today identified primarily with Ariane Mnouchkine, its director and main artistic force. Mnouchkine looks to Asian theatrical forms and other stylized traditions using masks, colorful makeup, and extraordinary movement to help distance her actors from psychologically based acting techniques and create a theatre of symbols and archetypes rather than realistic representation. In *L'Age D'Or* (*The Golden Age*) (1976), Soleil actors drew from both European and Asian stock characters to create modern characterizations of immigrant workers and Parisian citizens.

Between 1981 and 1984, the company's sumptuous Shakespeare productions contributed to "interculturalism" becoming an active theatrical idea and subject of debate. *Richard II* echoed the imagery and techniques of Japanese *kabuki* and *noh*; *A Midsummer Night's Dream* took influences from Indian *kathakali*; and *Henry IV* combined motifs from all of these forms. For *Les Atrides* (1990–1994), a cycle of four ancient Greek plays that included Aeschylus's *Oresteia* trilogy preceded by Euripides' *Iphigenia in Aulis*, the company created a gestural language resonant of the *mudras* of Indian *kathakali* and hand movements of Armenian dance. Jean-Jacques Lemêtre's musical accompaniment fused motifs from musical traditions the world over. Mnouchkine doesn't attempt to replicate performance traditions, but uses them as a springboard for developing a unique theatrical idiom.

Mnouchkine's rehearsal process is unusual. Actors rehearse in costume from the beginning and may help develop the characters' costume by adding, changing, and eliminating elements. Final casting of roles may not be settled until very late in the process. Several actors may try out the same role, collectively creating a character that one of them will eventually embody in performance. Mnouchkine works on general actor training during the rehearsal process, especially now that most of the original company members have left and been replaced by a new generation of performers. Once or twice a year she offers a public acting workshop from which new company members are drawn.

A Théâtre du Soleil production is a total theatrical experience that begins with a trip to the outskirts of Paris and a special bus ride through the woods of Vincennes to the Cartoucherie, the troupe's home in a converted ammunition factory. In the theatre's large entrance hall spectators read books related to the theme of the production and purchase homemade food from the actors, who also serve audience members during intermission. Mnouchkine is always present before and after the show and at intermission, helping out and talking with spectators. She takes personal care of the theatre and trains her actors to do the same. On entering the vast theatrical space, before taking a seat in the informal auditorium of bleachers, spectators watch the ensemble put on their makeup and costumes as they prepare for the performance. A mostly bare stage puts the focus on the actors and their accomplished, dynamic performances. The highly ornamented costumes and other carefully crafted design elements enhance this experience.

Director Ariane Mnouchkine of the Théâtre du Soleil working closely with her actors during a rehearsal of Shakespeare's *Richard II* at the Cartoucherie de Vincennes.
© *Martine Franck/Magnum Photos*

with the set, costume, lighting, and sound designers who will be working on the show. At this first meeting, directors will share their interpretation of the play and their vision or concept for the production. This first encounter begins a dialogue between director and designers that continues until opening night. Through a process of discussion and negotiation, the director guides designers in creating sets and costumes that are appropriate for the production.

Occasionally a director will have a very specific costume or set piece in mind, or be planning a particular bit of staging that will require specific set or costume demands. The designers, drawing on their own artistic training, research, and imagination, invent specific designs that express their artistic realization of the director's interpretation. It is the director's role, however, to make sure that the various design elements come together to project a unified artistic vision on stage.

Although all the designers attend production conferences together, occasionally the set, costume, and lighting designers create conflicting elements—perhaps colors that jar or costumes or set pieces from different eras. It is up to the director to catch such contradictions and to facilitate a dialogue among designers to determine what will be cut and what will be kept or changed. Designers also share needs with each other; for example, the set designer may want a piece lit in a particular way for the proper effect, or a lighting designer may request a placement that aids a lighting effect. These are all negotiated for the director's approval.

Working with Actors

Auditions and Casting

Directors generally hold auditions to cast actors for a show. They come to auditions with basic ideas about what qualities they seek for each role. Physical type is often a secondary concern because most directors focus on the predominant personality and presence an actor projects as well as particular talents and technical know-how. If a director knows a role will be physically demanding, it will be more important to find an actor who is agile and expressive than one who is tall. A play may need an actor with good comic timing, or an ability to speak poetic language or to sing within a certain musical range. Traits like a character's age or gender may also be fairly restrictive. Final casting choices are always based on the way the ensemble comes together. A particularly strong audition by an actor who was not the original physical type the director envisioned may lead the director to rethink other casting choices.

Auditions give directors a chance to test an actor's range and abilities, and to see if the actor is someone compatible with their working style. Directors may ask auditioners to perform prepared monologues or to read from the play they are casting. They might have actors try a part in different ways to see how flexible they are or how well they take direction. Amazingly, the director learns to use a five-minute audition to identify exactly the qualities required. In the commercial theatre, the producer may have already cast a star in the lead, so the cast will need to be assembled around that central presence. Occasionally none of the actors who audition will match the director's vision of a character, and the director may need to reinterpret the role to suit the casting pool. At other times an actor's inspired reading may give the director fresh insight into a part. Often a very talented actor is not suitable for any of the roles but might be remembered by a director for future projects. Like all parts of the creative process, casting requires negotiating between ideals and realities.

Leading Rehearsals and Determining Staging

At the first rehearsal, you can feel the anticipation in the air as the ensemble's creative journey begins. This is the opportunity for the director to set the tone for the project and to explain his or her personal working process. Usually, everyone present sits around a table and takes notes. The director will talk at length about an overall interpretation for the play and the way each role fits into the larger picture. The excitement begins when the actors read through the script, many encountering and relating to their fellow cast members for the first time. If the director has done his or her job well, there is a simmering energy and a palpable sense of potential.

At the next set of rehearsals, the director looks at smaller units of the play as scenes are rehearsed with groups of actors. The director frames each scene within the interpretation of the play and defines the relationships and goals of the characters. Actors are filled with questions about their parts, and early rehearsals are often spent in discussion. Although directors may come into these sessions with fairly strong ideas of what they want, rehearsal is a time of exploration and experimentation. Actors explore the meaning of their lines and the best readings while searching for physical actions that embody meaning, are interesting to watch, and move the play forward. For much of the early rehearsals, the director may serve as an acting coach, often creating improvisations to help actors discover relationships and physical action, or to facilitate their ensemble work. The best directors encourage actors to take creative leaps and to try out new ideas. They offer suggestions to the actors and are open to their ideas. Rehearsals are hard work, but they are also exciting times of discovery and uncovering layers of meaning in the script. Eventually the experimentation comes to an end as the director sets the **blocking** (the pattern of how the actors will move on stage at particular moments) and selects the best ideas for action and line readings. The scenes are strung together until the actors are ready to do a **run-through** of the play from beginning to end without stopping.

Integrating the Elements of Production

The first opportunity the director has to see how all the conceptual pieces fit together on stage is during **technical rehearsals**. Although many directors have **paper techs**, a time when they walk through the technical aspects of the production with the designers and staff, until this point, the total vision of the performance has remained in the director's imagination. The technical rehearsal is the moment for the director's vision to come alive.

Work with the actors now takes a backseat to integrating other elements of production including lighting, sound, and set changes, and choosing how the technical aspects of the play will run during the show. Much of this time is spent with the director deciding on the exact timing for certain cues. When will a sound effect be heard? How many seconds should it take for the lights to dim, or should there be a rapid blackout? The director, the designer, and the stage manager confer about these kinds of choices, and the director makes the final decision as to what will best support the text, the acting, and the world the director has created on stage. Once all the pieces are in place, and the timing has been decided *to the second*, the actors and the crew are ready to run through the play while the director watches and takes notes about parts of the production that need to be adjusted in some way.

Run-throughs offer directors the opportunity to make sure that all the elements of the production are running smoothly together and to test the pace and rhythm of the piece. There may be notes to the designers, to particular actors, or to the stage manager and running crew, as tiny adjustments are made. A **technical dress rehearsal** gives the opportunity to see the costumes under the lights and to make any final changes to actors' wardrobes before **dress rehearsal**, the last step in bringing all the elements of production together for a trial run.

In the commercial theatre, **previews** give the director an opportunity to try the production out in front of a live audience. In most cases, previews provide the director with a final opportunity to make changes. Because theatre is essentially about actor–audience interaction, it is only at this point that the theatrical piece can be appreciated fully. The director listens and watches the audience. Their responses can alert the director to parts of the production that need to be altered. The pace of a scene may be too slow, making the audience restless. The audience may not get a joke, so the director will try to clarify it or remove it. Language that is particularly difficult may need to be slowed down so the audience can follow it more easily.

Because of the enormous financial investment at stake in large-scale Broadway productions, these shows usually have several months of out-of-town tryouts before they open in New York. During this period, directors may oversee drastic changes, such as rewrites of the script. Often work continues until **opening night**, when finally, the director's work is done. The director has guided the company in making choices about every element of production. Although the director will not appear on stage, every aspect of the piece reflects the director's artistic hand. Every night the actors and the crew will recreate the performance as the director has staged it with them.

The Director as Acting Guru

Sometimes the director's vision is so specific that a particular acting style is required to fulfill it, and directors have trained their actors in a particular methodology to carry out their concept. In the crudest way, that is what Goethe did when he set out his rules for actors. Later directors developed sophisticated training systems to create their ideal actor. Many of the approaches to actor training we discussed in the acting chapter were created by directors. Perhaps the first director to work in this way was the great Stanislavski. Confronted with the direction of the plays of Anton Chekhov, he recognized that actors of his time were ill equipped to create the psychological realism he wanted in these works. In his "laboratories," Stanislavski trained the Moscow Art Theatre company of actors in his famous system, and the naturalistic acting in his productions was the hallmark of his directorial work.

One of Stanislavski's own students and star actors had an alternative view of the theatre. Influenced by antirealist movements in art, Vsevolod Meyerhold envisioned a highly stylized directorial art that used sets inspired by Russian constructivist art. The biomechanics training system he developed, which turned the actor into an efficient worker for the stage making optimum use of body movement and rhythm, was meant to facilitate the actor's integration into his production concepts. His directorial work featured acting with vibrant physicality.

Jerzy Grotowski's *Poor Theatre* focused on the primacy of the actor in space. Grotowski developed a physical training system that pushed the actor's limits through excruciatingly difficult exercises called *plastiques*. Training with Grotowski was a test of body and spirit, but necessary if you were to be able to act in his productions, which placed extraordinary demands on the actors.

Suzuki Tadashi developed a technique of feet stomping to give proper physical and vocal support to actors in order to meet the challenges of his highly stylized directing. Today Anne Bogart is working with actors on Viewpoints, a training methodology used to orient the actor and direct energy in space.

These are but a few examples of directors who developed serious training systems for actors. Each of the methods mentioned here has had a significant impact on actor training, but they were all inspired by directors in search of a cohesive company of actors who could fully realize their directorial vision.

Artists
IN PERSPECTIVE

SUZUKI TADASHI

Japanese director Suzuki Tadashi has gained international fame for forceful productions of Western classics such as Sophocles' *Oedipus Rex* and Euripides' *Trojan Women*. Even in stillness actors from the Suzuki Company of Toga (SCOT), originally the Waseda Little Theatre, realize a riveting intensity on stage. Suzuki's theatre is driven by the organic "animal energy" of the actor, which he celebrates in opposition to the machine energy that runs modern society and much modern theatre as well.

Suzuki's system of actor training was developed as an alternative to the realistic *shingeki* style that dominated Japanese theatre when he entered the profession. The system is physically arduous and aimed at drawing out this human, animal energy. Through a series of exercises that involve vigorous stomping and various ways of walking, actors become conscious of how their feet connect to the ground. They discover an inner physical sensibility and create a strong base to support the kind of breathing and dramatic expression necessary for acting classical texts. Although many critics see a particularly Japanese style of expression reminiscent of *noh* and *kabuki* in Suzuki's work, Suzuki feels his training distills the virtues of these traditional forms to create a universal theatre that restores the body's wholeness, and his system is now practiced by followers throughout the world.

Suzuki thinks of his theatre company as a family, and he has adopted some aspects of the traditional Japanese *iemoto* family system of teacher and disciple relationships. He takes the role of *sensei*, or master teacher, acting as both a taskmaster and spiritual guide. The demands of his training make him an autocratic force in training sessions, in which all company members participate to cement a sense of community and the group's performance aesthetic. Actors participate in every part of running the company, from cleaning rehearsal halls to administration, and technicians connect with the actors' work by participating in the physical training sessions.

The company spends several months a year living and working together in the remote village of Toga when they are not touring abroad. It is difficult for some ac-

tors to give complete physical, emotional, and personal dedication to a theatre company in the way Suzuki requires, but many of Suzuki's actors have devoted years of their lives to his work. The actress Shiraishi Kayoko's performances as Clytemnestra and Agave most exemplify Suzuki's theatrical vision. Her extraordinary physical and vocal control and stage presence are the rewards of her dedication.

Suzuki has collaborated closely with the architect Isozaki Arata to create outdoor theatre spaces that combine spatial values from traditional Japanese theatres with those of ancient Greece and Elizabethan England. These new sacred spaces revitalize the audience's connection to the performance. In building such theatres throughout Japan, Suzuki and Isozaki have assisted in decentralizing Japan's Tokyo-based theatre world.

Suzuki has helped foster interculturalism in the theatre through the worldwide popularization of his actor training system, his own exchanges with international theatre artists, and his creation of the Toga Festival, the first international theatre festival in Japan. His productions, which bring a Japanese sensibility to bear on Western classics, have toured the world. Suzuki's 1981 version of Euripides' *The Bacchae* brought Western and Japanese performers together. American actor Tom Hewitt, speaking in English, played Pentheus, the rational ruler of

Thebes, while Shiraishi Kayoko, speaking in Japanese, played both the feminine, mystical god Dionysus, who comes from the East and falls into conflict with Pentheus, and Pentheus' mother Agave. The recognition scene in which she realizes that she has killed her own son is played in a dramatic moment of stillness drawn from Japanese classical traditions. This unique casting gave contemporary resonance to the ancient clash of East and West embodied in Euripides' play.

Playing the title role in Suzuki Tadashi's production of Euripides' *Electra*, actress Saito Yukiko embodies Suzuki's physical acting training, which energizes the entire body through a stance rooted through the feet to the floor. Suzuki Company of Tokyo at the Japan Society, New York.
© *Jack Vartoogian/FrontRowPhotos*

The Director as Auteur

When the origin of the idea for a performance comes from the director, not the playwright, we call that director an **auteur**. Significantly, in French, the term means not only author, but also the originator of a concept. The term *auteur* was first applied to film directors who created and controlled every aspect of a work from inception to realization, creating the screenplay and the film. Stage directors can envision a total project in much the same way. The original idea can come from their own imaginations, not from a playwright, and they can set about creating the production as a reflection of their personal viewpoint.

The development of the director-auteur followed a natural progression. The acceptance of high-concept productions liberated directors from basing their work on prevailing assumptions about either the form or content of the dramatic text or expected stage conventions. As directors felt free to adapt a play for their own ends, it was a short step to the director as the creator of the text. Director-auteurs exercise much more control and authority over all aspects of the production, and performance is the realization of a complete and personal vision. In recent times, the director-auteur has become a phenomenon of the international avant-garde. Today, at any major international theatre festival, the majority of the productions present the director as author or adapter of the dramatic text.

The director-auteur creates a different kind of play text called a **performance text** that records all that will happen on stage. It is born as part of the directorial conception that cannot easily be handed to others because the text and the staging are conceived as a unified whole expressing a distinct and personal point of view. Richard Foreman is representative of this kind of director-*auteur*-playwright. He writes his own works for his Ontological-Hysteric Theatre, where his quirky texts and performances represent a unique and personal vision. Lee Breuer, when he is not reinventing traditional plays such as his *Lear* with reversed gender roles set in the American South, or his *Oedipus at Colonus*, staged as a gospel musical, does much the same kind of personal exploration in the texts he has written for Mabou Mines, a theatre collaborative. Because this kind of work is so personal, it is not unusual for these directors to have their own theatre companies where they can exercise complete control over their artistic vision.

Although much of this kind of work is intellectually difficult for mass audiences, Mary Zimmerman has shown that the director-auteur can create works that appeal to a more general public. Her adaptation of Ovid's *Metamorphosis*, with a text based on Greek myths, was created collaboratively with the actors. It played on Broadway for two years and won her the Tony Award for direction.

The work of director-auteurs should not be confused with that of traditional playwrights who elect to direct their own work. Today playwrights Douglas Turner Ward, David Mamet

Photo 8.5
The bizarre costumes and odd juxtaposition of scenic elements in *King Cowboy Rufus Rules the Universe,* written, directed, and designed by Richard Foreman for his Ontological-Hysteric Theatre in New York, reflects Foreman's idiosyncratic style of authorship and direction. He writes randomly every day, and when he has accumulated several months' material, he searches through his writings for bits of dialogue on similar themes. He shuffles the material into a collage on a theme and then assigns the lines to characters.
© Paula Court

(b. 1947), Irene Fornes (b. 1930), George C. Wolfe, and Sam Shepard are among the preeminent American playwrights who have acted as directors for their own plays. Unlike director-auteurs, these playwrights create works that are not uniquely tied to a particular and personal directorial concept and can be passed on to other realizers for their directorial vision. For *auteurs*, the concept is part of the text and so performance texts cannot easily be passed on to others for reconceptualization.

Alternative Beginnings

When directors find inspiration for theatrical projects in sources other than plays, they may begin their creative journey in a variety of ways. Directors may assemble texts not originally written for the stage—poetry, novels, diary entries, historical documents—and create a collage of the material for dramatic effect. They may write an original text or create one with a group, or they may envision the text in nonliterary terms, as discussed in Chapter 6, creating an alternative form of performance text.

Directors may also create out of nontextual elements of performance, turning that into their text instead of a play. Their visions emerge from images, sounds, movement, dance, music, stage technology, or other theatrical elements. Some of this work does not resemble traditional theatre experiences and may appear as hybrid forms—theatre crossed with dance, rock concerts, music video, opera, mime, and the visual arts. Alternative forms always require new ways of conceiving a performance, and Chapter 6 traced the work of many directors who begin their process without a play.

Many directors come to the theatre from other artistic disciplines, and those biases are reflected in the way they create. Choreographer-directors Martha Clarke (b. 1944) and Pina Bausch (b. 1940) have created dance-theatre pieces that mix dance, dialogue, and striking visual design with theatrical and nontheatrical texts and music. In Clarke's *Garden of Earthly Delights* (1984), she used a painting by Hieronymous Bosch (1450–1516) as the central text she brought to life through mime and danced enactment of stories she imagined from the canvas. Using a dance vocabulary and theatrical elements, the piece defies simple categorization. Because theatre encompasses so many art forms—writing, design, painting, sculpture, acting, mime, dance, music, and media—each can provide a starting point for the performance text. Whatever the point of origin, as adapter, writer, designer, or collaborator, these projects sometimes follow alternative creative processes for the director.

Photo 8.6
The paintings of Hieronymus Bosch served as inspiration for this dance-theatre piece, *Garden of Earthly Delights*, conceived and directed by Martha Clarke. Story and image are presented through the dancers' physical postures and gestures. Minetta Lane Theatre, New York.
© *Carol Rosegg*

Director as Designer

Some directors come to the theatre with a strong visual aesthetic of their own that can govern their creative process and the way they work with a design team toward the final production. In the last chapter we looked at the image text of Robert Wilson, who is

Artists
IN PERSPECTIVE

ROBERT WILSON

Trained as a visual artist, Robert Wilson brings these talents to bear in all his work for the theatre. Although he has brought his signature style to traditional plays and operas, he is best known for the conceptual work he has created as a director-auteur. He functions as writer, designer, and director, controlling every detail of his staging, and structures his directorial concept with a strong visual picture that is extended through a series of thematically linked images and associated meanings. A sample of the storyboards he creates as texts for his work constructing the progression of the theatrical event through images is shown in Chapter 6.

Wilson's stage pictures may include human figures and set pieces that may or may not have realistic dimensions. When working with actors, Wilson gives very precise instructions about where they need to be on stage and how slowly or quickly they need to move to create the visual moments he envisions. Wilson manipulates actors as pictorial elements, and he does not play the traditional directorial role of acting coach. Language, far from providing a cohesive narrative, functions as background music for the visual images.

The experience of time and space in the theatre is a focus of Wilson's work, and time is deeply felt in his slow-moving images. He made his initial mark with pieces of great length. His seven-day-long piece *KA MOUNTain and GUARDenia Terrace* performed in Shiraz, Iran, in 1972, ran day and night for a week, erasing the sense of firm boundaries between art and life. Fame came to him in 1976 with *Einstein on the Beach*, a five-hour uninterrupted opera with minimalist music by Philip Glass for which he did a series of drawings that Glass set to music. Wilson described their process: "We put together the opera the way an architect would build a building. The structure of the music was completely interwoven with the stage action and with the lighting. Everything was all of a piece."[1]

Einstein on the Beach established Wilson as the preeminent American artist in this genre, but his epic productions and spectacular stage pictures necessitate opera-house scale, and he has often more easily found funding for his work in European government-supported venues. When Wilson turns his hand to more conventional plays, such as his *Woyzeck* (2002) with music by Tom Waits (see photo on page 214), they are always unconventionally staged, mixing unexpected elements and music, and always giving preeminence to the visual realization. They may mix live actors with puppets and speech with recorded sound; they play with rhythms and scale, challenging our perceptions. The Wilson style has reached wide audiences in the United States and Europe and inspired many followers. Wilson spends summers at the Watermill Center in New York developing new works with international artists in a spirit of collaboration.

1. *http://www.glasspages.org/eins93.html*

The blending of powerful visual images is a hallmark of Robert Wilson's Work. *Einstein on the Beach* was, among other things, a meditation on time and the effect of Einstein's theories on twentieth-century consciousness. The giant clock, Einstein's presence on stage, the mathematical quality of Philip Glass's music, and the slow pace of the lengthy performance all reinforce these ideas.
© *Jack Vartoogian/ FrontRowPhotos*

profiled on page 234. Wilson has paved the way for other artists. Director Ping Chong (b. 1946) also comes to the theatre from the visual arts, so he thinks about space and light as primary elements in his creations. Puppets and dance are featured in his work because of their sculptural qualities.

Julie Taymor, the first woman to win a Tony Award for directing in 1998, works with traditional texts in nontraditional ways. She is a director-designer, puppet and mask-maker, mime, and choreographer who uses her design skills to tell a story. Because she controls all aspects of the production, her work provides an integrated artistic vision with emphasis on visual storytelling. Taymor studied mime in Paris and traveled extensively through Asia to study various puppet and masked theatres. Her work often provides a synthesis of intercultural theatrical traditions. Her production *Juan Darién* used different kinds of puppets interacting with live actors to create a carnival-like spectacle with dialogue, narration, mime, mask, and shadow puppet visual play (see Photo 8.7). This strong visual text was used again in Taymor's famous production of the popular *Lion King*, in which Taymor served as mask and puppet designer as well as director. Although Taymor mixes puppets with live actors, unlike Robert Wilson, she relies on the talents of actors to support the fantastic masks she creates. She does not view the actor simply as another visual element to manipulate. The atmosphere of the performance and her directorial concepts are embodied in her designs for a show, although she does not predetermine every theatrical image. She also collaborates with lighting, set, and costume designers, who work with her to create a seamless visual world on stage.

Photo 8.7

Masks, puppets, and butterflies on wires are just a small part of the visual world director Julie Taymor creates on stage. In *Juan Darién: A Carnival Mass,* a South American tale about a jaguar cub who becomes a boy, magical transformations are effected through the combination of masks, popular puppet traditions from around the globe, and live actors. Co-conceived and written by Julie Taymor and Elliot Goldenthal, based on a tale by Horacio Quirogà. Directed by Julie Taymor and designed by Julie Taymor and G.W. Mercier. Vivian Beaumont Theater, Lincoln Center, New York.
© Joan Marcus

Designers were directors in earlier generations as well. Gordon Craig (1872–1966), the pioneering director and theorist who developed abstract sets and understood early on the importance of light, color, and sculptural elements, directed actors in ways that would complement his visual designs. He envisioned a perfect actor, free of psychological realism, highly trained and capable of symbolic gesture. Until such an actor appeared, he put forth the idea of a marionette that could substitute for the fallible human actor on stage. The Polish artist and designer Tadeusz Kantor (1915–1990) worked as a set designer and then moved into performance art and happenings. His later work was a theatre of living images with actors manipulated like mannequins. His art was influenced by the atrocities of World War II, which demonstrated that human beings are not always on a higher plane than objects (see Photo 8.8).

Director and Actors as Collaborators

Some directors feel uncomfortable with the hierarchy of the traditional structure, with the powerful director controlling the creative process, and prefer a collaborative approach to creation. For this to succeed, the creative ensemble must share goals and expectations about the process and the end product. Communication among the ensemble

Artists
IN PERSPECTIVE

SIMON MCBURNEY

Simon McBurney (b. 1957), the brilliant and idiosyncratic British director, brings his incisive intelligence and a style marked by strong visual images and virtuoso physical acting to all his creations with the English theatre company Complicité. Formerly known as the Théâtre de Complicité, the group was founded in 1983 by four actors trained in physical theatre with the mimes Jacques Lecoq and Philippe Gaulier in Paris. They brought the collaborative method they had practiced in France to their new company in England, which has today grown to international fame under McBurney's direction. Complicité now claims a large number of actors, directors, and designers from around the world as company collaborators. As the company's work continues to evolve, the key element of a Complicité production remains the collaboration of an ensemble building on a shared physical and artistic language.

A Complicité production can begin with either a thematic idea or a text. *The Street of Crocodiles* (1992) was inspired by the stories and the life of Polish writer Bruno Schultz (1892–1942). *Mnemonic* (1999) grew from shared memories of the cast inspired by a tale of the discovery of the body of a five-thousand-year-old man in the Alps (see Photo 6.3). *The Noise of Time* (2000) used sounds and images to explore the life and work of composer Dmitri Shostakovich, and *The Elephant Vanishes* (2004) was based on three short stories by contemporary Japanese writer Murakami Haruki.

No single method is used in the evolution of a Complicité performance. The approach is marked by a general openness to the material, which allows the group to play with ideas and follow where they lead through research, improvisation, discussion, and artistic exchange. The group sometimes fills the rehearsal space with videos, images, clothes, and objects that inspire them and that later may be incorporated into their improvisations and performance along with lights, movement, silences, and

sounds. McBurney describes this process as a series of collisions between actors and with the elements of performance—music, text, images, and action. The long rehearsal process can lead to many dead ends, but at other times it culminates in serendipitous and compelling theatrical images and actions that could only emerge from collaborative experimentation.

As a director in a collaborative process, McBurney's role includes choosing the point of departure for creation, moving the work along so that it continues to yield new insights, and the excruciating task of making final decisions about how to shape the performance. In *Mnemonic*, McBurney also played a main role in the performance. For the collaboration to move smoothly, McBurney must mold each group into a working ensemble, help them discover a common artistic language, and keep the feeling of childish play that allows the imagination to flow alive in the rehearsal hall. He must inspire the company with the confidence that this sometimes haphazard form of theatrical exploration will yield an engaging piece of theatre. Like all directors, he acts as the eyes and ears of the audience, deciding whether the actors' inspiration and invention are yielding something theatrically viable and pushing the performers toward dynamic discoveries.

McBurney's theatrical productions are testament to the strength of his collaborative artistic vision, and he combines different elements for each new project. In *The Street of Crocodiles* and *The Three Lives of Lucie Cabrol* (1994) McBurney focused on the actor's physical expression and inventiveness, whereas in *The Noise of Time* and *The Elephant Vanishes* he integrated the human performer within a world of video, projected images, and recorded soundscapes. In a McBurney production there are many images that leave a lasting visual impression on the spectator. In the opening scene of *The Street of Crocodiles,* the cast emerges from the most unlikely places, one actor walking perpendicularly down the wall, another popping up from inside a bucket. In *Mnemonic*

Challenges and Choices

In the theatre of images, where language is less important than the visual elements, do we lose something vital, discover something new, or both?

must be facilitated through a common artistic vocabulary and methodology. Although the image of coequals working together to create a performance is an appealing one, more often than not, there comes a time in the collaboration when someone steps forward as the leader, or director, to make the choices necessary to finalize a performance. It is almost impossible to arrive at a polished production in a leaderless vacuum, although many groups have tried to find ways of equalizing the roles of the co-creators. Some directors, such as Simon McBurney, may act in their productions; others give the actors free rein during a prolonged rehearsal process.

the preserved remains of the five-thousand-year-old ice man are brought to life by actors manipulating an old leather chair so that it stands erect and appears to walk along the mountain range. These images are born of bursts of imagination brought forth through collaboration and shaped by directorial acumen.

McBurney has demonstrated his ability to work with more traditional texts as well. His 1998 production of Ionesco's *The Chairs* was an extraordinary realization of a difficult play, in which the tragicomic poignancy of the writing was revealed through the physicality of the acting. His production of Shakespeare's *Measure for Measure* (2004) brought his ability to use technology to highlight contemporary themes to the fore. Each of McBurney's works dazzles in unexpected ways, and theatre connoisseurs look forward to the next flight of his imagination.

In "Sleep," one of three tales by Japanese author Murakami Haruki, adapted for the stage by director Simon McBurney, an alienated housewife tries to transform her mundane existence by staying up for seventeen nights straight reading *Anna Karenina*. In her insomniac state, the words on the page subsume her just as they spread across the visual space of the stage. Her surreal condition is expressed by several actresses embodying the character at once. Projections, scenic imagery, and acting are integrated under McBurney's direction. *The Elephant Vanishes*, coproduced by Complicité and Setagaya Public Theatre, Tokyo. © *Robbie Jack/CORBIS*

The Théâtre de la Jeune Lune, based in Minneapolis, a company known for its energetic physical explorations of the classics, has solved the problem by creating a company in which the duties of the artistic director are shared among the group, and all the performers also write, design, and direct. Because of the revolving roles, no one is given absolute authority. Significantly, all of the company members are graduates of Jacques Lecoq's famous school of mime in Paris, so they share a common creative method and technique. The members of McBurney's Complicité Company also share the Lecoq training as a technical base. Many of the actors in the collaborative groups of the 1960s

Photo 8.8
Director Tadeusz Kantor's artistic vision is evident in all aspects of his productions. In *Wielopole Wielopole,* a powerful portrayal of Poland's traumatic wartime experiences, Kantor explores memory, loss, and survival, as rigid human effigies and lines of empty chairs speak of mass murders and human tragedy. Long musical sequences often support the stage imagery of Kantor's shows.
© *Bogdan Korczowski*

were committed to a particular physical approach to acting as well, and often the director served as an acting teacher for the company. In collaborative groups, adaptations of plays or original performance texts are created through the rehearsal process; as the members of the company explore the theatrical values embedded in a particular play or improvise on a theme. In all of these collaborative ensembles, although the rehearsal process is more open and egalitarian, eventually, a director steps forward to determine the final text, fix the staging, select the design elements, and set sound and lighting cues.

Indonesian director Putu Wijaya of Teater Mandiri draws on the Balinese view of *desa, kala, patra*—that every presentation naturally changes in relation to the time, place, and mood of the moment. Putu sets only some aspects of a piece and concentrates instead on training his actors to respond to each other. In his highly abstract presentations, which use shadow play and loud music, there is always room for new ideas and improvisations and even for unrehearsed performers to jump in and take part. Sound and lighting operators are given license to adjust their artistic elements depending on how the actors are performing on any given night. Putu himself will also take part in production, adjusting elements during the show to challenge the actors to connect spontaneously.

The Director's Personal Qualities

With so many different directorial processes, the director's temperament can range from the maniacal control freak to the open egalitarian. Directors have been described as coaches, trainers, mother hens, psychoanalysts, midwives, and confessors, as well as tyrants, despots, and mad geniuses. Despite this gamut of possibilities, some general qualities are required of all directors. Leadership and organizational skills are necessary to guide and coordinate an artistic staff of actors, crew members, and designers in realizing an artistic vision on stage. Directors need to have the same qualities any good leader does, including self-confidence, interpersonal skills, and good problem-solving capabilities. Because the theatre relies on collaboration and engages its artists' intellectual, emotional, and physical faculties, each individual's contributions must be valued to hold an ensemble together and elicit the best work possible from everyone involved in the production process.

While some mavericks still see themselves in a godlike role, most directors working today approach their jobs in a more collaborative spirit. The image of the dictatorial director is mainly a relic of past eras. Some directors are authority figures, but most strive not to be authoritarian and to encourage others to have creative impulses. So much of the rehearsal process is spent in exploration that a director must be a good listener, be open to questions, and know how to ask just the right questions of others to open new pathways to expression. Because so much of artistic creation requires risk, the director must inspire trust. All artists must feel that their efforts will be respected and that the director has created a safe environment for experimentation. Simultaneously, directors must build confidence in their creative process and its results, so that all participants are fully committed. When a strong artistic and intellectual vision is combined with the personal attributes that enable others to reach their full creative potential, a director becomes inspirational.

KEY IDEAS

- The director molds every moment of performance and provides a unified vision of the production.
- Directors manipulate theatrical elements and stage conventions to create meaning on stage.
- Directors shift between the roles of creator and spectator, acting as the audience's eyes and ears during rehearsals.
- The role of the modern director as we define it today is only about one hundred years old. In the past, playwrights, lead actors, or company managers helped organize the performance, but did not determine the vision of the production.
- The role of the director emerged with the rise of stage realism, which elicited the need for an outside eye to bring all the elements of production together to create a complete, unified environment on stage.
- Some directors interpret a play, taking it from the page to the stage through a process that begins with choosing and analyzing a play and developing a production concept.
- Directors guide designers and actors through the rehearsal process and, in the final stages of rehearsal, integrate all the design and technical elements into the production.
- Director-auteurs begin a production with a personal vision rather than with the work of a playwright. They may assemble texts not originally written for the stage, write an original text, create one with a group, or envision the theatrical text in nonliterary terms, sometimes creating hybrid theatrical forms. Some begin with visual ideas, and others develop special training systems for their actors.
- Whether dictatorial or collaborative, all directors must possess leadership skills and present a strong artistic vision.

Theatre Spaces and Environments
The Silent Character

9

Carved out of the mountainside, the open air Theatre of Delphi, Greece, provided ancient audiences a breathtaking panorama as part of the scene before them—a potent reminder of the power of the gods portrayed in Greek tragedy. The entire community could attend the performance with seating for ten to fifteen thousand.

© Kevin Schafer/CORBIS

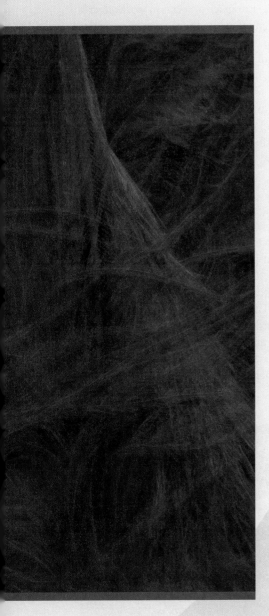

All theatrical encounters occur in time and space. Space determines the nature of the relationship between the performers and the audience and among audience members. It affects the nature of the performance and its reception. It may be planned or determined spontaneously, but space is always a silent character in the series of interactions that characterize performance.

Space Creates Meaning

Often, we are not conscious of the way the entire theatre space or location works to create meaning and context for a theatrical event. When we attend the theatre in an ornate opera house with opulent lobbies and bars serving champagne, we develop certain expectations for a lavish production, meticulous detail, and performances by stars. When we venture into a fringe theatre behind a storefront, in a warehouse, or in a church basement, we expect experimentation, provocation, and minimal visual or technical elements. In an African village where the entire community is assembled in a circle with drummers and musicians, we expect celebration and participation. We measure what we see against what we expect, and make sense of a performance accordingly. The next time you go to the theatre, take note of how the location and space affect your expectations and interpretation of what you see.

Space and Theatrical Convention

The theatrical space encompasses the world of the actors and the world of the spectators. Every spatial arrangement is a negotiation between protecting the magic of the actor's domain and meeting the audience's need to connect to each other and the world of the performance. Theatre spaces develop within a cultural framework that establishes the rules of the encounter between these two worlds. The tacit understanding among participants of how these worlds relate is one of the basic conventions of theatre. Consider how rarely an uninvited spectator willfully violates the actor's space, even when it would be easy to do so. When performers invite us to enter their world, we know that stepping into the playing space changes us from observer to performer and brings with it burdens,

Photo 9.1
Division 13 performs Samuel Beckett's *Play* in the store window of Right-On-Futon in Chicago. This unconventional theatrical venue, at a busy three-way intersection, brought a new public to Beckett's esoteric work. The isolation of the characters, each confined up to the neck in an urn, is augmented by their encasement behind the store window and the eerie reflection of their images on the glass. Actors Anne DeAcetis, Megan Rodgers, and Katie Taber had microphones in their urns, their voices brought to the street through speakers. Directed by Joanna Settle; scenic design by Mark Bello. *Photo by Joe Ziolkowski*

responsibilities, and power. A nontraditional use of space can surprise the audience and alter the dynamics of a performance. Space contributes to the regulation of the actor–audience relationship.

Space and Performance Evolve Together

Theatre spaces evolve organically to serve the needs of performers, audience members, and the larger community. Gathering in a circle to watch an event is the way human beings naturally congregate when a public presentation occurs. In city parks, on college campuses, and in small villages—wherever performers set up—spectators form a circle around them. No one orchestrates this audience formation; it is the natural result of a desire to see up close and to feel the energy of the performance. Encircling the performance provides optimum proximity and **sight lines**—clear vision for the greatest number of people. Whether we are in Tibet or Ghana, Greece or Mexico, theatrical spaces find their origins in the spontaneous circular surrounding of performers by the audience.

As the needs of actors and audience grow in complexity, more elaborate spatial arrangements develop. Spaces of concealment for the actors behind doors or curtains are created to provide protection for the actors' magical transformation and to house props, prompters, and costumes. When the circle is abandoned, we find raised platforms forming elevated stages, moving stages, or **raked seating** on an incline providing solutions to sight line problems for growing audiences. A reciprocal relationship exists between theatrical spaces and the theatrical forms they house. Performance forms can define their spaces, just as spaces can delineate performance forms and possibilities.

Photo 9.2
Spectators naturally form a circle around street performer Whistler eating fire at this beautiful outdoor performance site in British Columbia, Canada.
© *Leanna Rathkelly/Getty Images*

The Boundaries of Theatre Spaces

The exact entry point into the theatrical space is not easily defined. Many of us think we enter the theatre space when we come into the auditorium where the performance will take place, but if we actually analyze our experience, we will see that we have entered the theatrical environment long before taking our seats. The moment we break with our everyday lives and are enveloped by the aura of the theatrical event, we have entered the realm of the theatre. If we have read or seen anything about the performance, we may have formed a mental picture of the space before we arrive, and this image will be an orientation point for us within the actual physical space. As we approach the theatre, we start to feel a sense of anticipation and excitement that prepares us for the event.

If the theatre is in an unusual setting, just getting there can become part of the performance. Journeying to a residential area in Brooklyn where you enter through the basement of a private house can turn the trip itself into the first entry into the environment of the drama. *I'm Gonna Kill the President! A Federal Offense* uses the trip to the theatre to set up the subversive themes of the performance. Audience members are not told the theatre location when they reserve tickets and must show up on a street corner in the East Village section of Manhattan. There a contact sends them to meet up with another contact around the corner where they are subject to a security check before being

Performance

IN PERSPECTIVE

THE LAST SUPPER: HOME THEATRE

To reserve seats for *The Last Supper*, you telephoned the playwright-actor Ed Schmidt at home and left a message on his personal answering machine. You were told that dinner would be served and then given only the numerical address of a brownstone on a quiet residential street in Brooklyn. The building appeared no different from the other houses on the block and had no external signs of theatrical activity. Once on the stoop, you discovered a small marker sending you to the basement entry. You entered a low-ceilinged unfinished cellar, then traversed and exited into the backyard. Although there were no signs, the only place you could go in the enclosed yard was up a back stairway that led to a door opening into a comfortable family kitchen, unusual only because of the church pews seating approximately sixteen people placed where you would expect to find a dining table. The programs on the wooden bench were the only sign that a performance was about to take place.

Mr. Schmidt appeared and began to prepare dinner, interrupted by his six-year-old son who was hushed and sent upstairs to bed. You were treated to the actor's opening monologue until he discovered that he had not defrosted the fish. You were then sent to the living room to chitchat with other audience members and eat cheese and crackers while the host made other dinner arrangements. By the end of the performance, the line between fact and fiction was successfully blurred; the reality of Mr. Schmidt's home, child, and food underscored his theme that truth is an illusion. The unusual journey and theatrical venue prepared you for an unusual evening in the theatre, and the audience was not disappointed.

The intimacy of Ed Schmidt's kitchen as a performance space set the audience up for an unusual and often mind-bending performance of *The Last Supper*.
Courtesy of The Last Supper *and Ed Schmidt; photo by Greg Choate*

led to the theatre several blocks away. The program continues the stealth, as none of the actors' names are mentioned lest they be associated with a federal offense.

Outdoor summer theatres often have an atmosphere of festivity around them that transports us into the theatrical environment and its excitement (see Photo 16.5). In more traditional venues, if there is a crowd milling outside the theatre, we may join the group before actually going into the building, or we may congregate in the theatre lobby, united with others by our status as audience members. Broadway theatres have huge marquees under which audience members gather before a performance; being part of this group immediately draws us into the world of the theatre. We look around to see who else is in attendance and what kind of people have chosen this show. We may listen to conversations about what people are expecting or share our own expectations with companions. These interactions are already shaping our audience response. Today, theatre architects spend a great deal of time thinking about how the public will arrive at the theatre, and they conceive of the atmosphere in lobbies and ticket areas as a part of the theatrical environment.

Photo 9.3
The lobby of the Elsinore Theatre in Salem, Oregon, was built in 1925-1926 to resemble the historic castle of Elsinore in Denmark, where Shakespeare's tragedy *Hamlet* is set. This theatrical entry space inevitably creates a mood for audience members coming to see a performance and is an architectural draw in its own right. STAGE, the theatre's current owners, maintain and renovate the space and have brought it up to today's building codes.
© Ron Cooper

Cultural Meanings of Theatre Spaces

The location of performance spaces within the larger community says something about the nature of the performance and the way it is valued by its society. The tribal celebration in West Africa is organically rooted in the community's daily life and is performed in the center of the village or inside the chief's home. Plays written with artful awareness of European models are often performed in specially designed culture centers or theatres in large cities. The ancient Athenians placed their theatre next to the temple of Dionysus, underscoring theatre's ritual origins. It was built on public land into the slope of a hill just below the acropolis—the seat of government and power in ancient Greece, emphasizing the civic role theatre played in Athenian life. The public theatres of Elizabethan England were constructed in the rough neighborhoods on the outskirts of the city, reflecting the general moral disapproval of theatrical activity. Under Louis XIV in France, state-sanctioned theatres were built close to the king's palaces, elevating the status of theatre-going within the society at large. Compare the *kabuki* and *noh* theatres of Japan. *Kabuki* developed in the "pleasure quarters" of cities where brothels and courtesans operated, reflecting the outcast position of actors at that time in Japanese culture. In contrast, the earlier *noh* theatre took shape within the samurai courts. It was performed in palaces and temples and was considered to be a poetic, refined tradition.

Theatre Spaces and the Social Order

Theatres have always reflected the social hierarchy. Where you sit and how you enter and exit confer status. In highly stratified cultures, a protected space, from tents in Tibet to the royal box in London, is often created for the ruling classes, reflecting the social structure outside the theatre. For centuries, the nobility used one set of entrances and the rabble, another. Opera houses and theatres were constructed with private boxes that "insulated" the elite from the general public and provided a private domain within the public performance space. Kings were often placed where they could be seen by the audience, performing their royal roles as the actors performed on stage (see Photo 9.4).

History IN PERSPECTIVE

TIMES SQUARE: THE TRANSFORMATION OF A THEATRE DISTRICT

New York's Times Square at Forty-Second Street and Broadway has been synonymous with theatre since 1895 when developer Oscar Hammerstein, grandfather of the composer and lyricist Oscar Hammerstein II, opened the Olympia, a huge entertainment complex housing three theatres on what was then Longacre Square. The Olympia's success led Hammerstein to build several more theatres in the same locale, which in turn attracted other theatre developers. Soon a theatre district was born.

A theatre district sets a tone for its offerings, and success or failure of the whole community outweighs the fortunes of any single production. During World War I, Times Square experienced its first real boom time, producing 113 shows in a single season despite the war. The Great Depression then hit the theatre district, forcing many owners to transform their establishments into movie houses, an inexpensive form of entertainment. In the 1960s and 1970s, Times Square's legitimate theatres competed for space and attention with the X-rated movie theatres and nude shows that had crowded the district, bringing with them other illicit activities. Theatre-goers who lingered to dine or drink after a show were greeted by the area's alternative nightlife; prostitutes looking for clients and drug dealers pushing their wares. The area had one of the highest crime rates in the city.

Since the 1990s, Times Square has undergone a guided transformation. Spearheaded by the Walt Disney Company's refurbishing of the New Amsterdam Theatre and supported by the City and State of New York, the Forty-Second Street Development Project has worked to make the Times Square area an inviting place for out-of-town tourists. Most of the X-rated shows in the area have been closed down, replaced by wholesome enter-

tainments, including several Disney productions, as well as large commercial enterprises, an enormous Toys "R" Us housing a full-size Ferris wheel, and a Disney Store. Times Square's streets now bustle all night long with crowds of tourists going to shows, watching the blaze of neon lights and huge video screens while spending their money.

What has been called the "Disneyfication" of the area pleases some and leaves a good number of New Yorkers and theatre aficionados unsettled. While the old Times Square may have had a high crime rate, its legitimate theatres still catered to the taste of seasoned and discerning theatre-goers. Today's theatrical fare is noticeably less challenging. The area supported a large number of local businesses that have been pushed out by national chain stores, and much of the area resembles an urban version of the suburban mall.

Times Square is losing its unique cachet and becoming a carbon copy of other commercial developments. Because of Disney's strong presence, many fear the area is being turned into a theme park. If the culture of Times Square becomes as carefully crafted and monitored as that of Disney's other fantasy worlds, Times Square may rid itself of "adult" entertainment and replace it with children's fare and family entertainment. Under "Disneyfication," what will happen to local culture and the ability of Broadway theatres to address important and controversial issues? Will there be a place for challenging productions in New York's theatre district?

The Disney Store and Disney's stage version of *The Lion King* dominate this view of the revived theatre district around Times Square, New York, where once peep shows and porno films dominated the urban landscape. Neon lights and bustling crowds are part of the thrill of the Broadway theatre experience.
© *Andy Caulfield/Getty Images*

Photo 9.4
At Garnier Hall, home of the Monte Carlo Opera in Monaco, the late Prince Rainier III and his entourage create their own spectacle as they enter to watch the show from the theatre's lavish royal box. Positioned to give the monarch the best view of the performance, it also gave his subjects the best view of him.
© *SETBOUN/CORBIS*

When the industrial revolution brought people to cities, large theatres replaced smaller houses to seat the growing theatre-going public. With the democratic revolutions of the eighteenth and nineteenth centuries, more egalitarian seating arrangements developed, yet even today, audience members may enter through the same doors, but they are segregated by the economics of ticket prices for various places in the theatre.

It is interesting to look at the space allotted to actors in various theatres. Often dressing rooms are small and cramped and meant to be shared. Actors' comfort has clearly not been taken into account in much theatre architecture, which reflects the social status accorded the profession. Today, the union Actors' Equity sets minimal standards of accommodation for the actor's needs, forcing this to be a consideration. The theatre's social order is customarily reflected in dressing room assignments. Around the world, star performers are traditionally given quarters closest to the stage. In Japan, among the lowest ranking actors are the *sangai* meaning "third floor," referring to the faraway location of their dressing rooms.

The tradition of the **green room**—a space where actors could socialize and audience members could greet them after a performance—developed during the late seventeenth century in England, indicating the increased fraternization between performers and their public. We have some evidence that these spaces were originally green, but today the term refers to rooms of any color that serve this social function. European theatres developed similar spaces usually called artists' salons or conversation rooms.

Theatre Space Reflects Technological Change

As theatre artists incorporate technological advances into their artistic process, theatre spaces need to accommodate change. The development of perspective painting in the Renaissance led to several changes in theatre architecture and the creation of a picture frame stage through which the illusion of a perspective painting could be achieved. When a system for changing painted wings was invented, the stage area needed to expand to hold a series of painted panels or **flats** on the side of the stage, and stage depth increased to heighten the illusion (see Figure 14.3).

Challenges and Choices

Is a cleaned-up neighborhood worth the price of a loss of local culture and challenging theatre?

IN PERSPECTIVE

AKWASIDAI FESTIVAL'S SYMBOLIC SPACE

This ritual celebration of the Akan tribe of the Ashanti clan in Ghana takes place every forty days, nine times a year, in a never-ending cycle, reflecting the Ashanti view of time. The enactment honors dead ancestors and procures their blessing on the community. It is a ceremony of purification and thanksgiving. Art, ritual, and politics merge as the entire rite serves as a prelude to a town meeting. The space, the seating arrangement of the participants, and all the props have symbolic value and reflect the central values of the culture expressed through performance.

Drumming starts the night before the festivities while the chief remains in prayer to the tribal ancestors in his ancestral home—the chief's "palace," the largest building in the town with a central interior area that can accommodate the entire population. The next morning, all the townspeople and invited guests assemble in the courtyard of the palace. This space is the source of spiritual, ancestral, and political power for the community.

The drumming intensifies and all the villagers dance, stopping abruptly upon the chief's entry. The chief, adorned in all his gold regalia, comes out to receive the homage of his people surrounded by dancers, praise-singers, and horn-blowers. He takes his seat upon the Akan-Ashanti golden stool, the symbol of Ashanti nationhood, the embodiment of ancestral spirits and of the chief's authority over his tribe. An umbrella with a tribal symbol at its point is held overhead as protection. The chief is surrounded by elders in two rows to his left and right, linguists who speak the chief's words, and court criers. Next to the elders are placed the town's children, symbolizing the

During the Akwaisidai festival, the Ashanti king sits in state surrounded by tribal elders and criers and wears a robe of kente cloth reserved for chiefs. Symbols of Ashanti belief are everywhere, from the painted stool to the elaborate gold medallions. The townspeople celebrate this tribal festival with officials in Kumasi, Ghana.
© *John Isaac/Peter Arnold, Inc.*

Electricity made it necessary for theatres to adapt to the needs of lighting instruments and overhead hanging grids. Developments in sound and lighting created the need for a control booth from which to operate equipment. Some older theatres have lights and sound operated from an open place behind the orchestra seats. Newer theatres consider current technology in their architectural design and create spaces to house technical equipment and the staff needed to run the show.

Theatre Architecture as Symbolic Design

Ritual acts sanctify the places where they are performed and delineate a symbolic space where gods and humans can participate in an exchange between two worlds. Theatre forms that evolved from religious practice occurred in spaces that contained spiritual meaning. Today, traditional African theatre, so closely linked to its ritual origins, occurs

Ashanti belief in connections between the living and the dead, the old and the young, through endless cycles of ritual and renewal. Outsiders are offered a bowl of palm wine, and the residue is thrown at the visitors' feet. If the wine flows in a straight line, the visitor is considered an honest person and may stay and participate. Those whose presence is accepted can now greet the chief and the elders. All dance in communal celebration.

The elders now engage in narrative dance, two by two or solo, and the chief accepts the dedication of these dances by touching the dancer's head with the golden sword that symbolizes ancestral authority. Many of these dances are about the chase of woman by man and are meant to ensure the continuation of the community and fertility. The chief now dances with the sword raised toward him, followed by the subchief. They resume their seats in state as the villagers rejoice in song and dance. The drumming subsides and one drum softly beats the rhythm of the town meeting while the town criers bring the villagers to order. The chief speaks to his people through the linguists, who enact his words. They bring his message for renewal and his prayer that the ancestors make all be one.

A telescoping of time and space occurs as the world of the ancestors and the world of the present are brought together through song and dance in the ancestral palace. The chief's seat in state is also a symbol of secular and spiritual power and mystery. The danced offerings are meant to please the ancestors through the approval of the chief, and the space and all the elements of performance—the costumes and the chief's robe of coveted kente cloth—and the props—the stool, sword, staffs, sculpted umbrella, and wine bowls—have symbolic value.

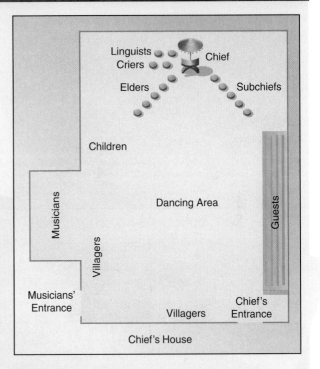

Ground Plan for Akwasidai Celebration This ground plan of the chief's home in the center of the village shows the communal space used for participation in celebratory dance. Before taking his seat on the Ashanti throne, the chief walks through the area where his people sit.

in a circle that permits the physical and psychological interpenetration of the actors and celebrants as they commune with the divine.

The architectural space of early theatres was itself an expression of the dominant values of the culture. Because the architecture provided a universal backdrop for the dramatic action, specific scenic environments and designs for every drama were unnecessary. In fifth-century B.C.E. Athens, the performance space provided a metaphor for the Greek worldview expressed in the plays. It was adjacent to the temple and even contained an altar to the god Dionysus. The **orchestra**, the circular playing space on the lowest level, was the province of the chorus, who often represented the voice of the people. The architectural wall of the **skene**, the retiring house, contained doors that symbolized royal places of power. The province of the gods was on the upper level from which a *deus ex machina*, a god figure descending from above, could appear (see Figures 9.1 and 14.1). (Take a virtual tour of the

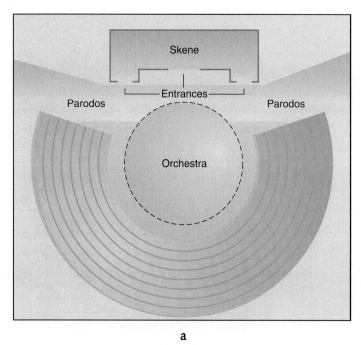

a

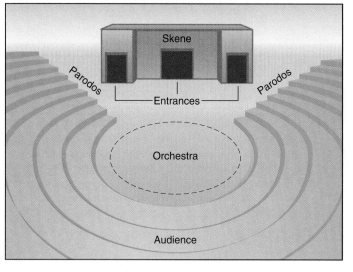

b

Figure 9.1 The Ancient Greek Theatre These figures show two views of the ancient Greek theatre. The chorus entered the orchestra, the area where they would sing and dance, through the *parodos,* or large aisle. The *skene,* or scene house, served as both a backdrop and a place from which actors entered. Gods were often placed atop. No one knows exactly what the *skene* looked like during the fifth century B.C.E. Rendered here is one possible configuration. The doors at the center could represent the entrance to a palace and were wide enough to allow the *ekkyklema* (discussed in Chapter 14), a platform on wheels with a scene displayed on it, to be pushed through. The stage behind the orchestra was probably at or close to ground level, although the stage was elevated several feet off the ground in later periods. The audience is configured around the orchestra area in steeply rising rows of seats set into the hillside.

Theatre of Dionysus at www.theatron.co.uk/ athens.htm.) The audience, seated on levels carved out of a hillside, often looked out on spectacular natural vistas behind the action, as exemplified by the theatre at Delphi, setting the scene for a drama ruled by divine power (see the opening photo for this chapter on page 240). The ancient Greek theatre space reflected both its ritual origins and dramatic themes, while serving the structure of the plays.

The Elizabethan theatre had the cosmos painted on the roof of the stage to symbolize the universe against which the actions of human beings played. The theatre's circular shape rendered, in the words of Shakespeare, all the world a stage—and the stage, a simulation of the world (see photo on page 257).

The Japanese *noh* stage is modeled on the porches of Shinto shrines where sacred performances are held, and where the *noh* was performed in its early days (see Photo 9.5). The pine tree, a favorite place for spirits to alight, is painted on the back wall of every *noh* theatre, and real pines representing heaven, earth, and man are placed at the bridgeway or *hashigakari,* which leads to the stage. The Japanese word for pine has a dual meaning and implies faithfulness and long life, giving the trees' presence symbolic meaning. The trees are also a reminder of the original outdoor performances at shrines surrounded by pines. The *hashigakari* can be interpreted as a bridge that connects the world of the spirits to the human realm, and the actor's slow entrance across this bridge is a journey from the beyond to our world.

Analogously, early Indian dramas took place in temples, and early European passion plays grew out of Christian ritual in churches, where the symbolic architecture of these religious structures provided emblematic background for the theatre. With these symbolic elements part of the permanent theatre architecture, the theatrical space itself was filled with multilevel meanings that expressed the values and beliefs of the culture. The drama could be staged against an unchanging backdrop representing a seemingly universal worldview.

Once the idea of a single world order and an entrenched cultural value system gives way to individualism, subjectivity, and social fragmentation, spaces and environments are needed that can express varying perspectives and values. As that happens, the theatrical environment moves from the symbolic to the representational.

Performance
IN PERSPECTIVE

THE SPIRITUAL SPACE OF *KUTIYATTAM*

India's sacred *kutiyattam* performances take place in open-air rectangular wooden structures found in the compounds of Kerala's Hindu temples. Sacred temple grounds are open only to practicing Hindus, so they are the only spectators for *kutiyattam* in sacred space. Spectators must purify themselves by bathing before entering the temple to witness performances. The performances take place from late in the evening until sunrise, by the light of a single oil lamp. The performers are drawn from a special cast of temple servants charged with specific rites, among them, acting *kutiyattam*. Unlike most performances in India, *kutiyattam* takes place in relative quiet, as the vendors and stalls that usually spring up for outdoor performances are not allowed within temple compounds.

The nine *kutiyattam* stages found in the region of Kerala are the only surviving examples of permanent theatre structures from ancient India, and they conform more or less to the descriptions of ideal performance spaces set out in the *Natyasastra*. Only three of these sites remain in use. The largest, the stage at the Siva Temple of Trichur, can seat around five hundred spectators and is used on only one highly auspicious day a year.

The slightly raised, square *kutiyattam* stage is set facing the temple deity since performances are considered a form of visual offering. Actors play toward the deity so mortal spectators, who can sit on three sides of the stage, find the best seats in front. A roof supported by pillars covers the stage. Its underside is usually highly decorated with paintings and carvings that are not visible to the audience, presumably serving ritual purposes of their own. Before setting foot on stage, actors here, like those throughout India, put their right hand to the floor of the stage and then to their eye and head to acknowledge the sanctity of the space and the performance and to entreat blessings for the event.

View of a *kutiyattam* temple theatre in Kerala, India. The space is bare, audience members sit on three sides. The interior of the roof is highly ornate.
© *Rakesh H. Solomon*

Theatre Spaces and Environments

Some spaces have been specifically constructed to be theatres; others have been converted or co-opted for theatrical use. In some performance spaces the relationship of the audience and the performers reflects prevailing theatrical conventions and is predetermined by architectural design. In others, this relationship is flexible and can be reconfigured to meet the needs of particular performances. In every case, the way the artists perform their work is affected by the nature of the space and its impact on the theatrical aesthetic.

Traditional Theatre Spaces

Despite the myriad of possibilities, several arrangements, each altering relationships within the performance dynamic, have become traditional in architect-designed theatres.

Proscenium Stage

Most of the theatre you have seen has probably taken place on a **proscenium**, or **picture frame stage**. In this arrangement, the audience sits facing a raised stage. During the Italian Renaissance, a **proscenium arch**, sometimes in the shape of a rectangle, was constructed over the front of the stage, separating the audience from the performance space and forming a frame for the newly developed painted perspective stage scenery. Spectators had the impression that they were looking into a framed living picture, and the perspective painting could give the impression of great distance behind the actors. The **stage curtain** is usually contained just inside the frame and can be raised and lowered to conceal set changes and to reveal the stage action. In some eras before electrical lighting, a large **apron** (a raised extension of the stage) protruded past the proscenium arch and was often used as the major playing space for the actors, who were lit with **footlights** at the front of the stage while the arch framed the scenery behind them. Today, the apron is usually small, and actors perform behind the proscenium arch. We sometimes find an **orchestra pit** below the apron of the stage to house musicians. Sometimes the orchestra pit can be elevated to form an extended apron when an orchestra is not required.

To the left and right of the playing area are **wings**, empty spaces that can be masked to hide actors, technicians, props, and scenery that can move laterally onto or across the stage. Scenery that once moved mechanically can now be moved electrically and can be run by computers. Some proscenium theatres have very high ceilings behind the arch called **fly spaces** or **lofts** that can house painted scenery that is literally "flown" up and down on a system of pulleys to change the sets. These lofts must be at least twice as tall as the proscenium opening so scenery can be completely concealed. Proscenium theatres provide the possibility of rapid set changes through both horizontal and vertical movement of scenery creating illusory magic to thrill audiences. Even today in our technologically advanced world, audiences often "ooh" and "aah" at such scenic wonder and often even applaud the new set. The descent of the helicopter in *Miss Saigon* provided such an effect.

Directly facing the stage is the large raked audience seating area we call the orchestra, named for the space in the ancient Greek theatre. **Balconies** in proscenium houses usually overhang a third to a half of the orchestra when they are facing the stage, or they may form horseshoe-shaped tiers around the periphery of the auditorium. The horseshoe shape was the dominant form in European theatres and opera houses during the seventeenth and eighteenth centuries because it permitted private **boxes** that could separate the nobility from the rest of the theatre-going public. As democratic revolutions overturned the rigid class structure, the architec-

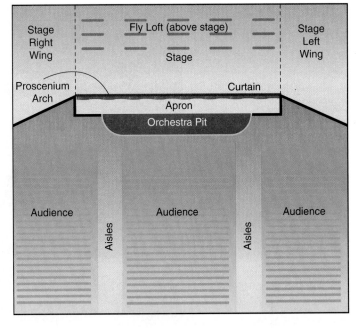

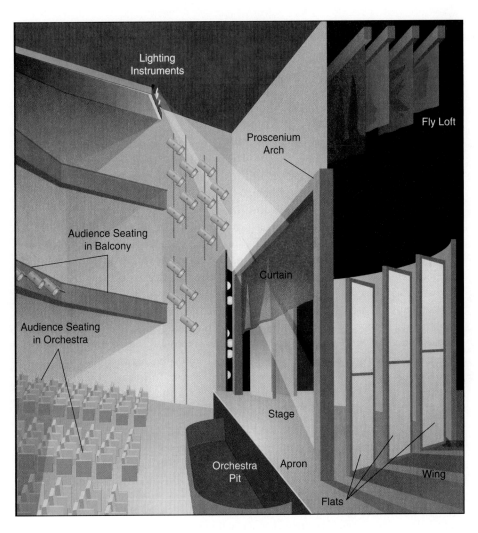

Figure 9.2 Ground Plan and Cross-Section Views of a Proscenium Stage

Photo 9.6
In this lovely proscenium theatre in Sarasota, Florida, the audience waits for a performance to begin. The action will be framed by the proscenium arch, and spectators will look into the picture of the stage world.
© *Wayne Eastep/Getty Images*

ture of the theatre accommodated newfound egalitarianism by creating open balconies facing the stage.

Proscenium theatres create a clear boundary between the world of the audience and the world of the actors, and the audience is farthest from the stage action in this arrangement. Spectators are positioned as voyeurs peeking into another world. For this reason, the side of the stage closest to the audience and framed by the arch is referred to as the *fourth wall*. Watching a proscenium performance, you feel as if the fourth wall of a room has been removed to allow you to see what is happening. Because the audience views the action from only one side, actors learn to play frontally toward the audience and to **cheat out**—that is, to avoid turning their backs completely toward the audience by remaining on an angle even when talking to someone slightly behind them. When standing center stage facing the audience, the area of the stage to the actor's right is called **stage right**, and the area to the actor's left, **stage left**. The area of the stage closest to the audience is referred to as **downstage**. The area of the stage farthest from the audience is **upstage**, a reminder of the seventeenth and eighteenth centuries when the stage was raked upward. During a performance, one actor may walk upstage of another, forcing the downstage actor to turn away from the audience to address lines. The first actor thus claims the full attention of the audience. When this happens, we say the downstage actor is **upstaged**. To upstage now also means to steal the spotlight.

Realistic sets work especially well behind a proscenium frame. The separation of the stage world from the auditorium increases the illusion while focusing the audience forward toward the stage. Performances requiring elaborate special effects and scenic changes are also a natural for proscenium houses, so musicals that require an orchestra and multiple sets usually are staged in this kind of theatre.

Theatre-in-the-Round or the Arena Stage

Encircling a performance is the natural way to gather. Many scholars believe that Greek tragedy and the European tradition originated in rituals enacted in a circle. Once theatres moved indoors and became a formal tradition, arena staging all but disappeared until the twentieth century, when it was reborn as a reaction to the proscenium's separation of au-

Photo 9.7
Performance space of Arena Stage, Washington, D.C., where audience members surround the action on four sides. Note the lower level *voms* by which actors enter the stage.
Courtesy of Arena Stage

dience and performer. In this configuration, the audience sits on all four sides of a round or rectangular performance space. Actors can enter through four or more **voms**, aisles named for the *vomitoria* or entryways of the ancient Roman amphitheaters that often ran through the audience. Because there are fewer rows, this arrangement brings more spectators closer to the stage action and permits a sense of intimate involvement with the actors. Simultaneously, audience members can see each other across the playing space and are aware of being part of the event. This creates a sense of heightened theatricality and awareness of the fragility of the theatrical illusion.

Arena staging places demands on directors, actors, designers, and the audience. Large pieces of scenery cannot be used because they would block sight lines from some part of the audience. Set designers must develop clever, small set pieces that serve the needs of the play and suggest location without any backdrop or flats that would obscure vision. Lighting designers have the difficult task of directing the light to keep the playing area separate from the audience without any existing architectural boundaries. Directors' staging must keep the physical action moving so that no actor has a back to a particular side of the audience for too long. Actors must invent justifications for movement and turns to play to all four sides of the house. Unlike the single point focus of the proscenium stage, arena staging does not direct the spectators' attention in any particular direction, and audience members must select focus. Despite all of these difficulties, many artists enjoy working within these constraints and believe the arena pushes the imagination to find inventive solutions for many practical necessities, while the forced movement enlivens a production. Actors often love the intimacy with the audience. Audience members enjoy this too, as well as the sense of community in a space where they are aware of each other's reactions.

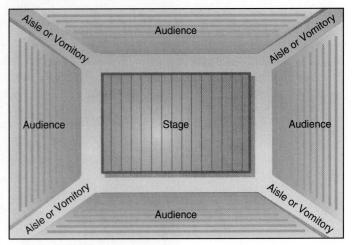

Figure 9.3 Arena Theatre Ground Plan

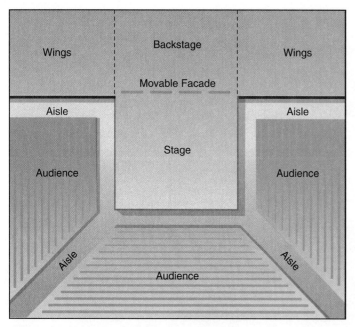

Figure 9.4   Thrust Theatre Ground Plan

Of course, many plays would be extremely difficult to stage effectively in the round. Bedroom farces, in which the timing of slamming doors and entrances and exits hold the play together, require great skill to stage in arena, as do plays that require enormous realistic detail. Imaginative theatre artists often find original ways to overcome the obstacles, and many directors even elect to do plays that would more naturally lend themselves to other spacial arrangements in order to conceive the play in fresh new ways.

Thrust Stage

The thrust stage provides some of the intimacy and theatricality of the arena and some of the practical solutions offered by the proscenium. In this configuration, the audience sits on three sides of a performance area that projects into the audience, while the fourth side provides a backdrop for the action and an area for concealment and scene and costume changes. Actors can enter from the backstage area or through aisles or voms.

The thrust stage was one of the first arrangements to be used architecturally in formally designed theatre spaces. The ancient Greek and Roman theatres are, in fact, thrust stages. Through the centuries, wherever itinerant actors set up stages on their wagons, audiences would gather on three sides to view the action, creating an impromptu thrust stage. During the Middle Ages, when theatre moved outside the church, **platform stages** with a **scene house** or curtained area at the back for concealment and costume changes, were set up for outdoor performances. Often the platform was on wheels and formed a **wagon** or **booth stage** that moved throughout the town performing in different locations, creating a mobile thrust stage.

Challenges and Choices

In a historically accurate reconstruction, how much of the original theatrical experience can be recaptured? What elements would be missing?

Photo 9.8
The Maclab Theatre at the Citadel Theatre in Edmonton, Canada, accommodating 686 spectators on three sides of a thrust stage is reminiscent of the ancient Greek theatre. Compare it to the theatre at Delphi and to Figures 9.1a and b.
Courtesy of The Citadel Theatre, citadeltheatre.com

History IN PERSPECTIVE

THE RECONSTRUCTION OF THE GLOBE THEATRE

William Shakespeare was one of six original shareholders in the first Globe Theatre built in 1599 to house the performances of the Lord Chamberlain's Men, the acting company responsible for the premiers of the great writer's most significant works. Here it was that Hamlet, Macbeth, Lear, and Othello first strutted across the stage in a disreputable district just outside the then city limits of London.

Burned down in 1613 when an ember from a stage cannon set the thatched roof on fire, the Globe Theatre was rebuilt a year later only to be torn down by the Puritans in the 1640s because they condemned the immorality of theatrical activity. For centuries the Globe existed as a theatre of legend, living only in panoramic London drawings, maps, building contracts, and written accounts of Elizabethan theatre-goers.

All this was to change when American actor and film director Sam Wanamaker came to London in search of the Globe, only to discover that there was no lasting theatre monument to the theatre's greatest writer. In 1970 he created the Shakespeare Globe Trust to raise money for a reconstruction of the original theatre based on the existing records, drawings, and accounts, as well as archeological excavations and extant structures from the period. From 1987 to 1997, construction proceeded on a site two hundred yards from the original building. Using materials such as oak timbers, handmade bricks, thatched roof, bright paints, and lime-washed walls, the builders of the new theatre approximated as closely as possible the first Globe. The painting of the heavens is recreated on the roof of the stage. Unfortunately, Wanamaker died in 1993 and never saw the completion of his dream.

Since 1997, summer performances at the Globe of period plays have been produced with attention to historical accuracy in costume, props, set pieces, music, and sound. Musicians are placed on the stage itself or on the stage balcony. No recorded sound is ever used. An all-male cast performs the plays as in Shakespeare's time, and **groundlings**, lower class spectators who could not afford seats, still stand for the duration of the performance, rain or shine, in the open pit area in front of the stage. There are still many unknowns about the acting and pronunciation of the period as we have no tangible evidence to reproduce.

The limited backstage dressing room and storage areas pose challenges to the actors and theatre personnel, but the only concession to today's needs has been in issues of safety. There are twice the number of entrances, illuminated exit signs, and a sprinkler system, lest the fire of 1613 be repeated. The contemporary audience need only cast off their modern attitudes and expectations to experience history.

The New Globe Theatre in London tries to reproduce the feeling of Shakespeare's original Globe with audience members sitting in three tiers of galleries and standing in the pit up to the very edge of the stage itself. The roofed playing area, supported by pillars, follows scholarly assumptions about what Shakespeare's original playing space was like. This photo captures the circular theatre interior, the three galleries of seating around the perimeter, and the general atmosphere in the pit.

© Andrea Pistolesi/Getty Images

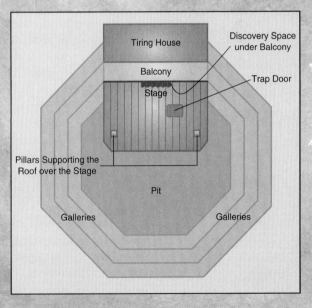

The Elizabethan Globe Theatre The ground plan of Shakespeare's Globe theatre. Audience members stood in the pit or sat in three tiers of galleries, surrounding the action on three sides. Actors made their entrances from the tiring house. The discovery space and trap door on the stage allowed for special effects and revelations.

Challenges and Choices

Should old spaces be adapted to modern expectations of comfort, or should historical accuracy be preserved?

The theatre buildings of renaissance Spain and England grew out of the idea of the medieval platform stage. The Elizabethan theatre was basically a circular structure open to the sky, with a roofed, raised platform stage on one side and three floors of gallery seating built into the outer walls of the theatre (see photo and figure on page 257). Around the three sides of the thrust stage was an area called the **pit** in which spectators could stand to watch the performance. On the level of the stage, two doors on either side at the back were used for entrances and exits. It is believed that a small balcony at the back of the stage provided the roof for a curtained **discovery space** where events or items could be concealed or revealed. The balcony provided a second-story playing space that could represent high places such as turrets, windows, or balconies. Interest in the Elizabethan theatre provoked a resurgence of the use of thrust stages in the twentieth century.

The thrust stage has been adapted the world over. Many Asian theatre traditions used some version of the thrust configuration. The *noh* stage of Japan, established in the seventeenth century, is a modified thrust (see Photo 9.5). It has a roofed platform stage resembling the shrines where the *noh* was originally performed, with audience seating on two sides. The *kabuki* first used the basic *noh* stage until its growing use of elaborate scenery and effects required a curtain and other aspects of the proscenium stage.

Actors on the thrust stage must keep moving to ensure that the entire audience gets maximum frontal visibility. Unlike actors in arena theatres who must play to all four sides, actors on thrust stages need only play to three sides. This eases the director's staging problems and offers designers many options.

Flexible and Found Spaces

Challenges and Choices

Should the audience's comfort be a consideration when selecting found spaces, or is discomfort part of the novelty of the experience?

Sometimes traditional theatre spaces are not desirable to theatre artists for aesthetic or economic reasons. This often means finding and adapting spaces not originally conceived as places of performance. Anywhere actors and audience can be accommodated—lofts, churches, basements, warehouses, or factories—can serve as theatre spaces. This often leads to improvised spatial configurations dependent on the parameters of the found space. Practitioners needing spaces hospitable to new theatrical forms now seek flexibility within designed theatre spaces as well.

Today, cyberspace has opened up new possibilities for found space. Once it was thought that theatrical space, whatever its size, shape, or nature, had to encompass the performers and the actors, but technology now permits us to transcend this limitation. We will discuss the implications of these advances in Chapter 14.

Street Theatre

The ultimate noncommercial space is the co-opting of public space for performance. Often used by theatres with political or social agendas, **street theatre** brings the performance to the people. Because the spectators are often coerced into becoming audience members, they may resist their role, obliging street theatre artists to use compelling theatrical devices—music, spectacle, masks, costumes, dancing, drumming, or direct audience confrontation—to engage with the public. Such theatre is limited in its use of text and is mostly comprised of simple short scenes. Political action theatre in the street is often called **guerrilla theatre** because it sneaks up on the audience where they least expect it and aggressively exhorts them to engage politically. Street theatre often concerns itself with the interests of a particular community, and performers hope the public will focus on their work because its subject is of immediate concern.

IN PERSPECTIVE

ROBERT LEPAGE: *TRILOGIE DES DRAGONS:* LOCATION AND SPACE AS THEATRICAL EXPERIENCE

For the production of Robert Lepage's *Trilogie des Dragons* for the Festival des Ameriques, the audience journeyed far from public transportation through rail yards on the outskirts of Montreal to a huge abandoned railway maintenance building on the waterfront. No attempt was made to permanently convert the space into a theatre, and evidence of its original use refitting railcars was everywhere—from old pipes on the walls to obsolete equipment notable only for its decrepitude and filth. The cavernous space had a large central rectangular playing area sixty-four feet long by twenty-eight feet wide. Two sets of steep bleachers were constructed facing each other on the opposite long sides of the ground-level stage. These were furnished with flimsy folding chairs that provided seating for the six-hour performance.

No acceptable accommodation was made for the spectators' needs. Approximately a dozen portable toilets were set outside in the yard for the large audience, who often needed to wait

in the rain for a turn. Two water coolers were provided. Refreshments were sold at intermission.

All the performances were sold out, and Lepage's imaginative staging of this collaboratively developed piece made it worth the inconvenience. The large space permitted special effects and dramatic lighting not achievable in tighter locations. Characters rode in on mopeds, video projection screens were set up on the short sides of the rectangular playing area, and a wheelchair was set ablaze. The scale of the space was a perfect backdrop for the thematic sweep of the production tracing the Asian immigrant experience from China to Canadian cities, via the world of fantasy, dreams, and hopes over six decades. In some sense, the out-of-the-way place, the strange space without any cosmetic enhancement, even the endurance of uncomfortable seating and lack of facilities made the audience feel part of a special event for those "in-the-know" who would take the journey.

Far from public transportation, spectators walk through rail yards to get to this remote performance site. The interior of the railway car repair space was left unrenovated and without any public accommodations, yet sellout crowds came to see Lepage's work.

Both photos courtesy of Festival de théâtre des Amériques, Montreal

Multifocus Staging

At every moment in life, many things are going on around us, and we choose where to direct our attention—to the television, a phone call, noise on the street, or the ongoing conversation in a room. In a reaction against single-focus realism, some theatre artists felt that **multifocus theatre**, in which several playing areas are set up simultaneously, would give the audience the same choice they exercise in daily life. The demands on the actor are high in this kind of presentation because they are actually competing with their fellow performers for the audience's attention. Sometimes multifocus staging requires that the

IN PERSPECTIVE

THE BREAD AND PUPPET THEATRE: CLAIMED SPACE

Bread and Puppet Theatre's large-scale political puppets demand theatrical arenas befitting their stature, leading the company to perform in city streets, open fields, or unusual large indoor spaces. At political rallies and marches the group's enormous puppets, designed by Peter Schuman, built by a community of volunteers, and carried by contingents of ten or more, are visible for blocks. These processional figures disrupt our usual sense of scale and proportion, holding their own against the tall buildings that dwarf their human companions. Their rough papier-mâché features bring a humanizing presence to industrialized urban environments as the puppets claim public space for communal art and political commentary. The company's slow-moving, silent procession of giants can transform their surroundings, halting the hustle and bustle of traffic and demanding the attention of passers-by unwittingly transformed into spectators.

Bread and Puppet performed its *Domestic Resurrection Circus* every summer from 1975 to 1998 at the company's home in Glover, Vermont. At Cate Farm, grassy fields, pine

trees, majestic mountains, and open sky provided a natural backdrop. The great outdoors gave the puppets a vast landscape for performance and brought Mother Nature into the company's political dramas as a silent observer and implied character. The first part of the annual puppet circus consisted of "side-shows"—small-scale puppet works that took place on little stages scattered throughout the fields, open to the sun or tucked in the shade of the pines. The second part, a multiact political circus, took place in a seminatural amphitheatre created when gravel was removed from a hillside to build the nearby interstate. The final part of the performance, a grand-scale pageant, stretched across the fields, a panorama integrating theatre and nature. In the dimming light of the setting sun, huge figures emerged over the sloping hillside. At the annual bonfire, which brought the performance into the realm of primal ritual, the year's ills were burned in effigy to make way for Mother Earth. This symbolic puppet of resurrection reconnected participants to the cycle of life, death, and rebirth.

In Bread and Puppet's final *Domestic Resurrection Circus* at Cate Farm in Glover, Vermont, Mother Earth, an enormous processional puppet operated by a crew of volunteers, arrives over the hillside with arms outstretched, ready to embrace the naked, destitute figures in brown cardboard below. The figures stand in contrast to the real humans in suits. The scene takes place at sunset and uses the natural change in the light to dramatic effect.
© *Ronald T. Simon (www.fineprintphoto.com)*

audience move from place to place to follow the action. It may also use moving instead of stationary stages, and the audience can choose to follow a particular moving stage or wait for the next wagon stage to appear as part of a **processional stage**, with new elements of the performance appearing on each subsequent rolling platform. African festivals in which characters are carried through the crowd on hoisted litters use this form, and many medieval performances used the moving wagon stage. During the 1960s and 1970s the processional stage was resurrected by experimental artists. Companies such as Bread and Puppet Theatre staged large outdoor and indoor multifocus events.

Environmental Staging

In the 1960s the avant-garde theatre movement viewed the proscenium as promoting a passive audience that could sit back and relax at a comfortable distance from the action. The politically active experimental theatre of the period sought a new and vital kind of performance that would engage the audience more completely. Influenced by the writings of theorist Antonin Artaud, work that involved audience participation eventually led to the idea of removing all the spatial boundaries between performers and spectators to allow them to share space.

Jerzy Grotowski in Poland and Richard Schechner in New York experimented with configurations that permitted various kinds of performer–audience interactions. Schechner's famous production of *Dionysus in 69* was an adaptation of *The Bacchae* staged in a garage with large open areas on the floor and scattered scaffolding (see Photo 9.9). The audience could choose to sit anywhere in the space, and each night the actors adjusted their performance to the way the audience had arranged themselves. Certain scenes were performed practically in the laps of some spectators, and lines were whispered in audience members' ears as the actors moved through the space. This created a multifocus environment where the audience could choose not only where to sit, but also where to look and listen. No two audience members had the same experience of the performance, as where you chose to sit exposed you to particular scenes and lines. During the performance, the entire audience was invited to join in a bacchanalian dance with the actors, erasing all boundaries.

Revolutionary at the time, environmental staging freed more traditional theatres to experiment with audience involvement in performance by seating the audience on the stage or close to the action. Although the audience may seem to be in the same space with the actors, in a sense there is never a complete sharing. The actors bring with them a halo of energy, an invisible space that surrounds them and empowers them in their interactions with the audience.

Site-Specific Staging

Often theatrical environments are specifically connected to the content of a performance. Staging a play about prison life inside an actual prison, or Reverend Billy's Church of Stop Shopping performed in an actual church are ways of creating a hyper-reality within the performance space. Many historical reenactments take place on original historic sites. Director Joanna Settle set two short Beckett plays in site-specific locations in Chicago (see Photo 9.1). *Rockaby*, which reveals the internal thoughts of a woman in a rocking chair, was staged in the bay window of an apartment for audiences of fifteen to twenty people, and *Play* was staged in a store window at a busy Chicago intersection. Deborah Warner's *Angel Project* actually provided audi-

Photo 9.9
In this environmental staging of Richard Schechner's *Dionysus in 69* at the Performing Garage, the audience could choose to sit anywhere in the space—from the floor to the multi-level scaffolding, just as actors could choose to perform anywhere and engage anyone. The performance therefore takes place amidst the audience. Here one actor at the top of the scaffolding connects with another actor, on bent knees on the floor, interacting with audience members as they take their positions. The audience was invited to participate in communal dance and in smaller moments.
© *Fred Eberstadt*

Performance
IN PERSPECTIVE

THE ANGEL PROJECT: SITE-SPECIFIC STAGING

Deborah Warner's *Angel Project* took spectators on a tour of New York into spaces that framed the city spaces in unusual ways, some populated by actor-angels, others with unusual props. Warner considers the urban architecture she revealed as the text for the production, providing a new kind of visual space where the familiar is made strange through the heightened awareness created by solitary exploration. A quotation from *Paradise Lost* in the program and bits of Christian imagery scattered throughout the sites, such as religious books and objects in an abandoned porn theatre, feathers floating to the ground, and a nun reading the Bible in Times Square indicate that the work had intended the-

matic unity. Spectators picked up a guidebook at the first site and were guided on their way through the city. The timing of each tour was staggered so that each ticket holder traveled alone, turning the usual theatrical dynamic on end with its lone audience of one wandering through open public space.

When you look at the world through the eyes of an audience member walking the streets, everyone appears to be performing. For much of the time, the spectator is deciding where to focus, what image to seize, and what meaning to construct. Each audience member, in a sense, becomes the author, director, designer, and actor of the theatrical space as he or she decides which site-specific spaces to frame in his or her field of vision.

A moment in *The Angel Project*, conceived and directed by Deborah Warner. A country landscape of flowers pushing through the snow at an indoor venue, where windows provide a new perspective on the urban cityscape outside. Audience members navigated solo journeys throughout New York to experience known sites through fresh eyes. Lincoln Center Festival.
© *Stephanie Berger*

ence members with guides to various sites around New York, where often just being in the site itself was the performance (see photo above).

Black Box Theatres

As you have seen, each of the various stages presents advantages and disadvantages, options and restrictions. Theatre artists in the twentieth century desired flexibility to choose the staging arrangement that would best suit a particular project. The idea of a flexible space theatre was pioneered by Walter Gropius (1883–1969) in 1926 with his

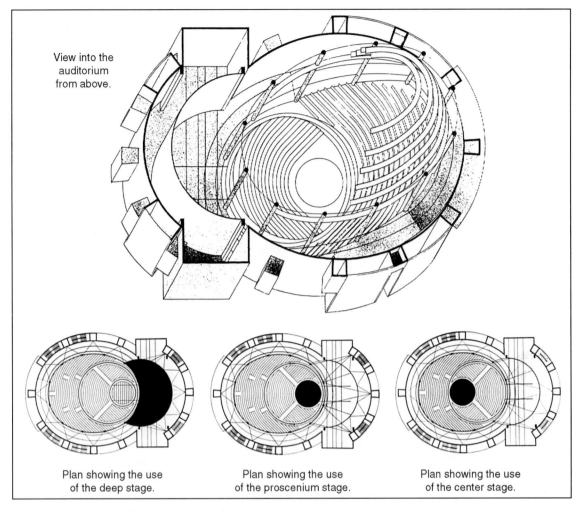

View into the
auditorium
from above.

Plan showing the use
of the deep stage.

Plan showing the use
of the proscenium stage.

Plan showing the use
of the center stage.

Figure 9.5   Walter Gropius's Flexible Bauhaus Theatre

Walter Gropius and Arthur S. Wensinger, "Plans and Model of the Synthetic Total Theatre, 1926," The Theater of the Bauhaus. (Wesleyan University Press, 1961). © 1961 by Walter Gropius and Arthur S. Wensinger and reprinted by permission of Wesleyan University Press.

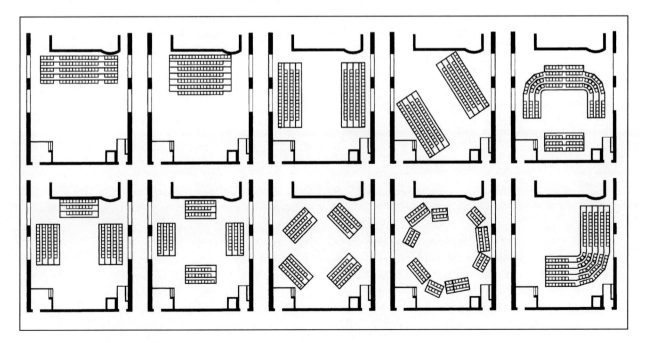

Figure 9.6   Ground Plans for Configurations of a Black Box Theatre   Louisa Thomspon's renderings of possible arrangements for the Frederick Loewe Theatre at Hunter College

Reprinted with permission from Louisa Thompson.

Challenges and Choices

If you were to imagine the ideal theatre from the audience's point of view, what elements would it contain?

plans for a synthetic "total theater"—a circular space with revolving platforms that could move the stage from arena to thrust or proscenium, or encircle the audience with scenic projections on surrounding screens.

Gropius believed the theatrical space itself should feed the imagination. Although the construction of this ingenious space was halted when Hitler took power in Germany, the plans sowed the seeds for later flexible configurations. Today, **black box theatres** that permit the rearrangement of seating and playing areas for every production are an accepted convention and are found everywhere. They require only a large room painted black, of course, and permit not only the traditional proscenium, arena, and thrust arrangements, but corner stages, L-shaped stage or seating areas, and audience-surround performances as well as environmental and multifocus performances (see Figure 9.6). Once used only in found spaces adapted for theatrical use, today many new theatres are architect-designed flexible black boxes.

The Actor in Space

The theatrical environment can be created in many ways, in many places. There is no need for an architecturally designed theatre building. What is required is a space that facilitates the interaction between the performer and the audience and serves the content of the event. Each of the environments discussed in this chapter imposes expectations on the audience and constraints and freedoms on theatre practitioners. The impact of the theatrical environment, however, is felt most directly by actors, who must fill the theatrical space each and every performance with their physical energy. Although aided by designers and directors, the actor must ultimately build the invisible channel through the theatrical environment to the audience. Some arrangements like the arena are more actor centered. The proscenium best showcases the designer's work. But ultimately, theatricality is created by the presence of the actor in space. The Greek philosopher Protagoras claimed "man is the measure of all things." In the theatre, the actor is the measure of all things. In the theatrical space, scale, visibility, audibility, and the transmission of energy allow the actor to touch the audience.

KEY IDEAS

- Space determines the nature of the relationship between the performers and the audience and among audience members.
- Location and space influence the audience's expectations and interpretations of a performance.
- Theatre spaces evolve to serve the needs of performers, audience members, and the larger community.
- The boundaries of the theatrical space go beyond the walls of the playhouse to its geographical location and even to the journey audience members take to the site.
- The geographic location of theatres reflects how a culture values its theatre.
- Theatre spaces reflect social hierarchies.
- Theatre structures and stages can embody symbolic ideas through their spatial configurations, design elements, and unique architectural features.
- The proscenium stage, with the audience sitting on one side of a picture frame stage; the arena stage, with the

audience encircling a central playing space; and the thrust stage, with the audience sitting on three sides of the stage are all common theatrical arrangements that can be architecturally predetermined.

■ Found spaces, multifocus staging, environmental staging, site-specific staging, and black box theatres can provide more flexible and unusual arrangements between the audience and the performers.

■ The size, shape, and arrangement of the theatre space must always permit the actor to reach the audience.

PART FOUR

Video projections on the upper level work in conjunction with more traditional design elements and live actors below in *Alladeen*, a collaboration between The Builder's Association and the London-based company Motiroti. The live production can be combined with interactive video and web presentations. The high-tech design reflects the show's exploration of the impact of media and technology on global culture, as well as on the lives of individuals whose longings can travel as far as their telephone voices. Directed by Marianne Weems, and co-conceived and designed by Keith Khan and Ali Zaidi, with performers drawn from both companies. Lighting, Jennifer Tipton; sound, Dan Dobson; video design, Christopher Kondek and Peter Norman; dramaturgy, Norman Frisch.

Courtesy of The Builders Association; photo by Simone Lynn

Art and Technology
Design for the Theatre

The sensory world of the theatre speaks to us directly, and we interpret it more quickly and more viscerally than we do the spoken text. When the lights come up and the curtain music begins, we feel the mood of the scene before any action occurs. When we see the set and costumes, we wonder about the time and place and who these people will turn out to be. In the contemporary theatre, designers create the elements of set, costumes, light, and sound that enfold us in a performance.

Although the live actor and audience are the basic theatrical elements, it is almost impossible to see theatre unadorned by design. All aspects of theatrical design, from simple props, lights, sets, sound, makeup, and costumes to elaborate special effects, depend on some level of technology, and the history of the visual elements of theatre reflects a reciprocal relationship between technological developments and design concepts. Artists will naturally exploit all the means at their disposal for creative purposes just as we find uses for new inventions in our daily lives. Theatrical artistry is in a constant interaction with scientific advances and technological inventions.

In the chapters ahead, we will look at theatrical design and its role in performance and text traditions. Some theatrical designs have come down to us through long and venerable traditions that continue to inspire the contemporary world. Others are recent and depend on new technology. Because design develops in a constant partnership with technology, innovation in design is often tied to technical advances.

Approaches to Design

10

In this intercultural performance, Greek tragedy and Japanese *kabuki* styles merge. While Samuel Barber's *Adagio for Strings* swells around them, Medea's painful rejection by her husband is expressed by the chorus of Corinthians who slowly pull long red ribbons from their mouths, a move adapted from *kabuki*. Medea's large headdress and her wide, colorful costume, with its protruding, breasted torso, visually convey the character's mythic dimensions. Euripides' *Medea*, Delacorte Theater, New York. Director Ninagawa Yukio; set, Asakura Setsu and Takahashi Mutsuo; costumes, Tsujimura Jusaburo; lighting, Yoshi Sumio; sound, Honma Akira.

Drumbeats, music, and cymbals. A shaft of golden light. A blood-splattered glass wall. A grotesque painted face. The theatre is a world of sights and sounds, textures, tones, and atmospheres that permeate our being. Around the globe, whatever the culture, theatre captivates the audience through the elements of sound and spectacle.

Performance traditions inherit design conventions that are relatively fixed, while designers in the interpretive tradition imagine the world of the stage afresh for each new production. In either context, design can be subtle or dazzling. Today's artists have adapted the interpretive model to suit alternative forms as well, and sometimes, as we have seen, the design itself may serve as the text.

Photo 10.1

Arlecchino or Harlequin holding his slapstick, and wearing his traditional mask. The diamond-patterned suit has become the emblem of this character and is reminiscent of the servant character's original patchwork garment of rags.
© *The Art Archive/Casa Goldoni Museum Venice/Dagli Orti (A)*

Design in Performance Traditions

Performance traditions often highlight the sensory provocation of the theatrical event and are associated with particular visual and aural elements that are essential to understanding their dramatic world. When we see a *noh*, Chinese opera, or *commedia dell'arte* performance, we can identify the tradition immediately by its stage setting, costumes, sounds, and the masks or makeup worn by the performers. Although these design features may have originally emerged from individual invention or novelty, they are now emblematic of the forms themselves.

Performance traditions have some of the most sumptuous, artistic, and tasteful stage designs in the theatrical world. Set, costume, lighting, and sound complement each other to create a singular theatrical environment. Chinese opera is a realm of rich colors and elaborate details seen in its brocade costumes and painted face characters. *Noh*, by contrast, is minimalist even in its silk kimonos that, despite their beautiful woven patterns, are relaxing to the eye. *Noh* theatre reveals its essence in its sublime wooden masks with slender painted lips and eyes. *Commedia* displays its earthy spirit in rough leather half-masks with grotesque features. Balinese performances are dynamic, and masks can have bulging eyes, enormous fangs, bold lines, and vibrant colors. Performers wear large headdresses and wide ornate collars over long robes, and they support these visual accoutrements with animated physical movements as they perform barefoot on the hard ground in or in front of open outdoor Hindu temples. The design elements in these traditions have evolved over time so that today we may read each form as having a distinctive aesthetic with its own dramatic impact.

Costume, Makeup, and Masks

In actor-centered traditions, the performers are the primary visual elements on stage, and colorful dress, masks, and makeup enlarge their presence and convey important information about the character's age, temperament, social status, and personal

affiliation. These elements are more than mere dress or adornment; they form a visual, symbolic language that describes the characters and their roles in the drama.

Costume

Traditional costumes differentiate young from old, peasants from nobility, and good from bad through conventions of color and style. In Iranian *ta'ziyeh* discussed in Chapter 1, characters who support Hoseyn dress in green, whereas those who are against him wear red. The lighthearted patterns of *kyōgen* costumes, bearing images of peaches, radishes, turnips, dogs, and monkeys, reflect the comic servants' earthy qualities and contrast with the somber costumes of their masters and the rich, dignified robes of *noh*. *Commedia*'s Arlecchino (Harlequin) is immediately recognizable by the diamond-shaped pattern of his suit (see Photo 10.1), which evolved from a patch-covered outfit reflecting his poverty.

In *kabuki* a change of costume can indicate a change in a character's temperament or a moment of magical transformation. In *Narukami*, the title character, an ascetic, has ensnared the rain dragon and caused a drought. A seductive princess distracts him and frees the rain dragon, ending the drought and leading to Narukami's transformation into the Thunder God. Already partially altered in newly emboldened white makeup with heavy black lines and a wild-haired black wig, Narukami's costume is transformed by stage hands who deftly pull out threads from the top of his pristine white kimono so that it falls forward to reveal a design of red flames (see Photo 10.2). This trick, called *bukkaeri*, or

Photo 10.2
Kabuki actor Ebizo (who now carries the name Danjuro XII) in the title role of *Narukami*. On the left, we see him before his transformation into the Thunder God and, on the right, afterwards. Notice the metamorphosis of the hair, from tame to wild, the makeup, emboldened in the second picture, the costume, from plain white to flame-patterned, and the actor's gestures, from constrained to expansive. The costume change is effected in front of the audience by a trick known as *bukkaeri* or "sudden change." The Grand Kabuki of Japan, Metropolitan Opera House, New York.
Both photos © Jack Vartoogian/FrontRowPhotos

"sudden change," is used in many *kabuki* plays to accomplish startling transformations in order to display a new dimension of the character before the audience's eyes. *Hikinuki,* or pulling of the threads, is a similar technique to effect onstage costume change.

Makeup

Makeup has been with us since antiquity and is seen on ancient artifacts in many cultures. Its first use seems to have been linked to religious ritual, and many theatrical forms that evolved from ritual use elaborate formal makeup patterns. Facial designs in performance traditions are often spectacular and draw the audience's focus to the actor's face, reinforcing the overt theatricality of the performance style. Conventions of color and pattern allow the audience to read the most abstract or ornamental designs. *Kathakali*'s imaginative, detailed makeup follows strict protocol, with the most refined, "green" characters—gods, kings, and heroes—identifiable by their green makeup base (see Photo 10.3). *Katti,* or knife characters, are of a noble class but have an arrogant or evil nature indicated by an upturned red mustache. There are also white-, red-, and black-bearded characters, whose colored beards communicate their status and dispositions. In Szechuan opera, painted face designs, already startling, create an even more dazzling effect when actors change from one to another in the time it takes them to do a flip or turn, sometimes making several changes in a row.

Masks

Masks can refashion the face to the very limits of the imagination and make possible the portrayal of an entire cosmos of beings: people, animals, ghosts, gods, and devils. **Half-masks**, like those of the *commedia dell'arte,* leave the mouth uncovered, allowing the actor to speak clearly. Some masks cover the whole head or the entire body, blurring the line between mask and costume. Traditional masks can be made of wood, papier-mâché, grass, or leather. The texture of the mask determines how an actor performs and how much it blends in with the human figure. Leather molds itself to the actor's face, while wood maintains its shape, putting more constraints on the actor's movement.

Photo 10.3
A *kathakali* performer in Kerala, India, has makeup applied to his face as he prepares for the role of a lion-god. This makeup type falls in the category of *tēppu* or "special," designs used only for unique characters or animals. Like *kathakali* beards, the lion's white ruff was traditionally made of rice paste and today is cut from paper.
© *Charles & Josette Lenars/CORBIS*

History IN PERSPECTIVE

CHINESE OPERA: FROM MASK TO PAINTED FACE

The elaborate facial makeup of Chinese opera finds its roots in primitive religious rites in which participants donned animal skins and feathers to drive away spirits and disease. Such practices are thought to have contributed to the use of animal masks of jackals, bears, and dragons in dances during the warring states period (475–221 B.C.E.). These entertainments developed into theatrical performances, and during the Tang dynasty (618–907), actors wore masks to play ordinary people as well as gods, demons, and animals. During this period some performers began using makeup instead of masks to adorn their faces. Sometime between 960 and 1130, face painting overtook the use of masks in comic plays. A large array of facial images had already developed through the use of masks: one set of wooden masks given as a gift to the emperor contained eight hundred masks, each with a unique design.

These early facial designs fell into two basic categories: simple makeup for basic male and female roles and more dynamic "parti-colored" painting for strong male roles such as generals and clowns. During the Yuan dynasty (1206–1368), the art of using makeup to highlight character traits developed, and the Ming dynasty made facial patterns more complicated. As folk operas flowered throughout China during the nineteenth century, the dazzling and intricate facial designs of "painted face" characters fell into the more specific classifications used today.

Face painting in Chinese opera reveals character traits through patterns that divide the face along various lines and principal and subsidiary colors. In "principal color" patterns, used for positive characters, the face has one main color (red, black, or white) with minor touches added to the eyes, eyebrows, nose, and lips. Other basic face patterns include the "vertical-cross-front" pattern, in which a bold black cross organizes other design elements; the "three-tile pattern," which brings attention to the forehead and the cheeks; and the "saddle-shape" pattern or "half-face," usually used for low-class characters, which divides the face in two by focusing design around the eyes and eyebrows. "Parti-colored" pattern is the most complex, mixing elements from "three-tile" and "vertical-cross-front." It expresses vileness or ferocity. "Clown pattern" uses only black and white and features a white patch between the eyes. Clowns with martial skills use one kind of pattern, "date-pit," while others use "bean-curd." "Abnormal-face" patterns distort the facial features and are used for odd or repulsive characters. "Animal-image" patterns depict the qualities associated with the animal, such as a rat image on a character who is, in fact, a low-life thief.

The colors in Chinese opera face painting reflect moral qualities and derive from traditional color associations. Red indicates loyalty and bravery; blue, valiance; purple, honesty; green, righteousness; black, uprightness; yellow, cruelty or sinisterness; and white, wickedness and deceit. Pink is used for elderly characters, and gold and silver are used for gods, demons, spirits, and monsters. These characters have some of the most fantastical designs, expressing their supernatural qualities.

Facial designs developed for particular roles and often display the unique features of a specific character. Yang Yansi, a powerful black tiger god, has the Chinese character for "tiger" on his forehead. Cao Cao, a sinister figure, has a sword on his nose showing his murderous intentions.

The hundreds of face painting patterns in Chinese opera are used in the over three hundred forms of opera throughout China. These beautiful images are an art unto themselves, and molds of opera face patterns adorn the walls of Chinese homes and businesses.

Dragon-Tiger Marshal   Aged Clown

God of Thunder   Big Ghost

Makeup Patterns from the Chinese Opera Four traditional makeup patterns from the Chinese opera. The Aged Clown is a *chou* role, while the other three designs all fall under the category of *jing* or painted-face characters.

In Bali, only people considered ritually strong are chosen to wear the mask of the witch Rangda. These performers are blessed with holy water to protect them from Rangda's power, and the masks themselves are also subject to religious rituals to empower them. In the past, at the end of Korean *pyolsandae* (masked dance performances), the players burned the masks, perhaps originally as a way of exorcizing their spirits. Today the masks may be sold to tourists.

Throughout Africa powerful masks are used in ritual performance and have found their way into more secular theatrical activity. In West Africa, to achieve social unity, masks are often used satirically to depict members of outside tribal groups, and animals and spirits are often portrayed by masked actors, sometimes to comic effect.

Clowns

Clowns, iconic figures in cultures throughout the world, wear traditional costumes, masks, or face paint that herald their foolishness and irreverence. The very unconventionality of their dress is itself a convention codified by tradition. Particular clowns are immediately recognizable within their own societies. In America the word *clown* brings to mind the white face, red nose, big shoes, and baggy pants of the circus clown. The image is so well known that the red nose alone can be enough to transform an actor into a clown. Many Native American tribes recognize a clown mask by its crooked nose. Members of the Iroquois False Face Society wear masks made of basswood with a crooked nose and a twisted half-smile to perform exorcisms of demon diseases, while the Pueblo Indian clown is identified by black and white stripes painted across his entire body. In Medieval Europe, court jesters wore ass ears with bells and multicolored outfits. The *chou* clowns of the Chinese opera wear makeup with a white patch around the nose and eyes and a few black marks. Great performers leave their marks on clown types. Groucho Marx's bushy eyebrows, enlarged nose, painted mustache, and thick-rimmed glasses became the *commedia* Dottore mask for our time. The outrageous nature of their masks, makeup, and costumes allows clowns to comment on social norms by placing them outside normal behavioral expectations.

Photo 10.4
Dogon men wear traditional Dogon masks to perform a dance in Sanga, Mali.
© *Wolfgang Kaehler/CORBIS*

IN PERSPECTIVE

ONE TABLE, TWO CHAIRS: INNOVATING WITH TRADITION

Zuni Icosahedron, a cultural collective in Hong Kong developing alternative theatre and multimedia performance, created the One Table, Two Chairs project. They invited directors to make new performances using the simple one table and two chairs setup of traditional Chinese opera. Each director extracted a different theme from these basic elements. Hugh Lee, director of the Taiwan Pin-fong Acting Troupe, suspended the chairs and table from the ceiling where they rotated and evoked the instability of a continually shifting political situation. Movie director Stanley Kwan used these furnishings to tell the story of his relationship with his dead

father. One chair was placed behind a white screen and the other in front of the screen where rolls of film fell on it from above. A voice-over evoked the image of the father and son in the empty chairs. Hobin Park of JoBac Dance company saw "one table, two chairs" as embodying the smallest social unit. This theatrical experiment demonstrated how the basic unit of a venerated tradition can be transformed through innovative directorial concepts.

A scene from director Hugh Lee's In the Name of Li Denghui . . . Dust to Dust, Ashes to Ashes from Zuni Icosahedron's One Table, Two Chairs project, curated by Danny Young. The minimalist set pieces of Chinese opera are removed from their traditional context, hung from the ceiling and amplified with projections in this contemporary production.
Courtesy of Zuni Icosahedron

Set

Set elements tend to be sparse in actor-centered performance traditions, but every form has a particular kind of frugality and is governed by its own set of conventions. The two chairs, one table, and rug that are the sole set features of Chinese opera don't represent a particular setting, but the way actors use them can define almost any location from a room, to a mountain, to a temple. The rug can serve as padding for the benefit of acrobats or help delimit the acting area. These simple portable pieces, which transform into any Chinese opera set at a moment's notice, suit the needs of this once itinerant tradition. *Commedia dell'arte* solved transportability issues and accommodated its outdoor venues with modest, elevated wooden platforms and a few painted backdrops. The stage of the *noh* theatre reflects the architecture of Shinto shrines with beautiful polished wood floors and an elegant roof. The few set pieces the *noh* does require—a tomb, a hut, or a cart—are made of natural materials and shaped into simple structures, preserving the open, airy feeling of the stage. In each of these performance traditions, a few simple stage elements or props, in harmony with the overall design, serve a variety of purposes.

The *kabuki* theatre, by contrast, has flamboyant sets, an exception within performance traditions. Its vast stage boasts vivid painted backdrops, constructed

Clowns

The clown or fool has existed in almost every society as far back as recorded history. These figures exist across time and cultures because they respond to universal human needs. We all long to be free of the constraints of social rules regulating our behavior, and clowns always stand outside of mainstream society. From that position, they can comment on or transgress society's rules. We laugh at these transgressions, and this laughter provides us with a psychotherapeutic release valve for pent-up emotional energy. Often clowns are part of rituals that cement a society's value system. They can teach by bad example.

Their very ability to break the rules also affirms the rules and values that govern normative behavior.

The clown is free to express our profound longings and deepest anxieties—our need for love and companionship, and our fear of death. Clowns can provide an ironic commentary on our lives, and the greatest wisdom often comes from the mouths of fools. Many Shakespearean fools can see when wise men are blind. They provide the wisdom that is beyond reason, and the knowledge that is only obtained through instinct, intuition, and proximity to the forces of nature.

Many Native American tribes had ceremonial clowns who performed comic exorcisms. They might dance, whistle, sing, shake rattles, or throw cinders or water to chase away evil spirits and cure disease. Pictured here is an Iroquois Native American wearing a false face fright mask, as he kneels in the snow outside a reconstructed traditional Iroquois longhouse. These masks are carved from living trees and are thought to be inhabited by the spirits of the forest with the power to frighten away demons in order to cure illness.
© Nathan Benn/CORBIS

Groucho Marx was the twentieth-century equivalent of the *commedia* Dottore. His clever wordplay made a show of false erudition while his anarchic spirit turned society's order on end. He took his clown character from vaudeville to Broadway, Hollywood, and television. The wisecracking antics that defied the boundaries of permissible social behavior brought laughter to every venue.
© Ralph Crane/Time Life Pictures/Getty Images

A *chou* or clown role performer from the Jiangsu Provincial Opera performing for locals in Qufu, in Shandong Province, China. The patch of white on his nose identifies him as a clown character, as does his comic expression. Clowns in Chinese opera speak more directly and colloquially to the audience than other characters, and many are trained in martial arts and have a repertoire of martial and acrobatic stunts. Clowns can be traced back to some of the earliest Chinese performance traditions.
© *Dennis Cox/ChinaStock, All Rights Reserved.*

At the International Clown Theatre Festival in Philadelphia, a clown from the Russian mime group Litsedi in Saint Petersburg wears the traditional red clown nose and makeup. Openly expressing his deepest yearning, this clown wears his heart on his sleeve.
© *Jim Moore*

Photo 10.5
Shadow puppeteers in Southeast Asia create dynamic shadow effects by moving flat leather puppets in relation to the light, traditionally an oil lamp with a flickering open flame. The colors of these beautifully painted puppets are somewhat visible on the shadows they project. Some Indonesian audience members prefer to sit behind the screen and watch the performer at work rather than watch the shadow effects from the other side.
© Reuters/CORBIS

interiors, and even rotating platforms. Yet *kabuki* set design, however extravagant, is also based on established conventions. Specific designs are customary for particular plays or types of plays, and all design conventions highlight the performer. The actor's three-dimensional figure stands out against backdrops that are intentionally painted with two-dimensional images that provide a background, but don't upstage the actors. When a large number of characters enter at once, stagehands may remove the sliding doors behind the actors to reveal an expansive landscape. The visual transformation makes the stage appear less crowded. Small set pieces, such as trees and rocks, appear only if actors interact with them, never just to decorate the space or indicate location. The *kabuki* stage, with its flower path jutting out into the audience, stretches beyond its scenery. It does not represent a realistic place, but presents a theatrical space appointed for the actor's use.

Light

Since performance traditions date back before the advent of electricity, they have used natural light, candles, lamps, and torches for visibility and to create special effects. Only recently has electric stage lighting replaced some traditional practices, affording new options, but often at the expense of a form's inherent dramatic impact. From its inception in the seventeenth century, Indian *kathakali* drama took place outdoors at night by the light of only a single oil lamp. The flickering of the flame in the dark cast eerie shadows and illuminated the actors' colorful makeup in magical ways that helped establish *kathakali's* mythic world of gods and heroes. Today, when *kathakali* performances take place in modern indoor auditoriums with electric lighting, that other-worldly quality can be lost. Traditional shadow theatres, such as those found in India and Indonesia, also take place at night with only a single light source to project shadows on the screen. The surrounding darkness, the solitary flame or light source, and the fluctuation of the shadows themselves lend these performances a sense of the supernatural. Some of this feeling has been lost today with a crisper electrical light.

In Indian *bhavai*, male actors playing female roles create provocative highlights and shadows on their faces by moving candles inserted in a paper cup and attached to the ends of the index and middle fingers back and forth as part of their seductive

Challenges and Choices

Do traditional forms need to adapt to new technologies to appeal to contemporary audiences and meet modern safety standards?

Artists

IN PERSPECTIVE

In Their Own Words

STANLEY ALLAN SHERMAN, MASK MAKER

Stanley Allan Sherman is a master craftsman mask maker specializing in leather masks for theatre, opera, dance, and wrestling. His masks were shown in a long-running exhibition at Lincoln Center Library of the Performing Arts in New York. A graduate of Ecole Jacques Lecoq, he has had a career as a clown, mime, and Off-Broadway and television actor. He teaches in the Roving Classical Commedia University (totally unaccredited).

■ **How did you become a mask maker?**

I am self-taught. When I trained in mime at Ecole Jacques Lecoq in Paris, one of the assignments was to make a mask. After I graduated, I needed masks for my own shows and made them. Then people started coming to me and asking me to make them masks.

A friend, Vasek Simek, asked me to make him a leather *commedia dell'arte* mask. I said, "The only one who knows that skill is in Italy and he's dead." Vasek said, "Stanley, think you can do it." He guaranteed me payment, but I did not have to guarantee him a mask. I asked everyone I knew for advice. After a month, at the moment I gave up, I discovered the first secret to getting leather to move and stay in place. After that it was discovering and developing. Carlo Mazzone-Clementi gave me many insights, and at two international leather conferences with leather craftsmen and artists from around the world, we all traded techniques, tips, and secrets of working with leather.

■ **What kinds of masks do you make?**

I make leather theatrical masks and am known for my *commedia dell'arte* masks as well as pro wrestling masks. I make masks for live performers and performances, opera singers, dancers, clowns, and films. That is very different from making decorative masks that exclusively hang on a wall. My masks come alive when a person puts them on. They are designed that way. So a somewhat unimpressive mask on a wall will become very powerful and amazing when a performer puts it on.

■ **In what ways do you consider the tradition of mask-making craftsmanship that preceded your work as you craft a mask?**

There is much leather crafting information that has been lost over the last five hundred years, and the tradition of mask making only came back in full force in the last fifteen to forty years in large part because of the Ecole Jacque Lecoq. I discovered and developed my technique on my own, then over years picked up tricks and techniques from master leather craftspeople around the world.

One tradition is not to steal someone else's mask design, even if that design is from the 1500s, but to develop your own mask for a particular actor based on the character and its emotions. My masks are generally very natural; they do not rely on the use of modern chemicals to help hold the mask in place, but a traditional wet molding process. I use animal hair rather than synthetics and never use human hair. I am developing different finishes for my masks that I feel may have been used back in the 1500s. I watch and meet the performer who will wear the mask. I also use a Balinese mask-making technique of putting a soul into the mask.

■ **When you are working on a traditional *commedia* mask, in what ways do you consider yourself to be making an artistic contribution to the mask's creation?**

One cannot create a mask without making a total artistic contribution. With *commedia dell'arte* masks one is not copying masks from an artistic sketch from the sixteenth century, but creating a mask for a performer or a group of performers for today. The only true choice is creating as a mask artist, and knowing the character is how you know the mask is right. One must remember that there were many *commedia dell'arte* troupes that we know nothing about. Look at all the different Arlecchinos that developed, and each Arlecchino had his own mask. As the mask maker, I must make the artistic and creative decisions that flow through me in the process.

■ **Can you describe the steps in your process?**

I write a list of character elements, the emotions and colors I want the mask to express. Then I sketch the mask on paper. I then create a clay sculpture from which I make a mold that will shape the leather. Once the basic shape is given to the leather, there is drying, cutting, gluing, coloring, adding hair, and elastic. The most important step in the process is selecting the right piece of leather to take the shape of the mold. It must be supple, yet stiff, and not too thin for it to be durable.

■ **How much innovation is permissible before you have violated a tradition?**

When making *commedia dell'arte* masks, I am sculpting in a certain style. To be in the tradition, you must know the characters and have an idea of how they are

(continues)

Artists

IN PERSPECTIVE (CONTINUED)

performed. I base my mask making on the character and its range of emotion.

My biggest transformations or innovations have been in my pro wrestling masks, inspired by my opera masks. I developed what I call a free-floating-moveable-jaw so the characters can do anything they want and the mask stays on. When I developed the Mankind Mask for the then WWF, I saw from watching the performer that the performance was at least 65 percent talk, so some of the same concerns that go into opera masks are addressed in pro wrestling masks. Sight, air flow, comfort, wrestling safety, and the mask staying on when wrestling are all issues. But I also drew upon *commedia dell'arte*. Only a handful of people know this, but the Mankind Mask I made is basically a form of a modern Arlecchino. That came through in the performances of the man who played the character.

Living in NYC during 9/11, I made a set of masks inspired by the event. With one of these I call the Longest Moment Mask, I developed a surfacing on one side that is rough powder, using sand or stone as well as leather. A dear friend of mine said they are my best designs.

■ **Since you are also a performer, do you physically become the character as you work?**

Being a performer is a major advantage to a mask maker. I know how the mask works; I

know what needs to be added and not added to the design. I know what to avoid. But the only way to make a great mask is to become the character. I must move around, jump, talk, sing, walk, and whatever else this creation that I am giving life to will do. I am the first person to be any of the mask characters, and I perform it before that mask has ever taken a shape. I become the mask and live as the mask in whatever world that mask is going to be as I am creating.

Mask-maker Stanley Allan Sherman
at work on a leather mask.
© *Jim Moore*

Source: Used with permission of Stanley Allan Sherman.

dances; in effect they act as their own lighting designers and operators while they perform. With sari material covering their heads, their challenge includes not catching on fire while they dance. Other lighting sources for these performances included torches, now often replaced by halogen lights attached to poles or rooftops that weaken the effect.

Sound

The sounds of performance traditions are as iconic as their visual manifestations. They alert spectators to the beginning of a show, establish the mood of a scene, provide musical accompaniment for singing and dancing, and create aural effects that reinforce stage action. In France, the *trois coups* (three knocks of a stick against the stage floor) have alerted the audience to the start of a performance for centuries. Spectators can anticipate the opening of a *kabuki* performance by the clap of wooden sticks, which becomes increasingly frequent until it explodes in a crescendo of beats as stagehands, grabbing the curtain, run it across the platform to reveal the stage. These wooden clappers also punctuate the actors' movements at climactic moments, just as the clang of cymbals and other percussion instruments underscore the physical actions of Chinese opera performers. In *commedia*, Arlecchino's flat wooden sword helped him provide his own sound effects for the beatings he habitually receives and gives. Drumbeats set the tone for all traditional African festival performances.

Specialized vocal techniques in performance traditions help actors establish and differentiate characters while aiding projection. Each tradition has a distinctive sound. *Noh* performers chant in a low guttural hum, while Chinese opera singers use a high-pitched nasal sound when singing and speaking. A range of pitches and tones within each unique oral style allows for differentiation, so the strong male characters of *kabuki* have deep, booming voices, and the female characters have high falsettos.

Master Artisans

In performance traditions, set, costume, and mask designs have generally developed over time, so there are no designers creating new costumes and sets for a particular production based on their own unique interpretation.

Photo 10.6
Noh actors in Kamakura, Japan, perform a *takigi noh* outside at night, by the light of bonfires. This haunting lighting is well suited to *noh*, in which the main characters are generally spirits, gods, or demons.
© Katsumi Tanaka/HAGA/The Image Works

Photo 10.7
Kabuki performances are punctuated throughout by the sound of *tsuke* or wooden clappers struck onto boards. Increasing beats alert spectators that the show is about to begin, and a *battari* sound accompanies the actors' *mies* or dynamic poses.
© Linda Vartoogian/FrontRowPhotos

Instead we find craftsmen who build the sets, props, masks, and costumes for performance, bringing the visual elements of living traditions to the stage. In some forms, master artisans bring a lifetime of study and artistry to their work. In Bali, talented mask makers gain a reputation on the island, and performers seek them out and commission their masks. The masks sold to tourists do not generally have the same artistry or sturdiness as those made for performance, which entail ritual practices as part of their construction to give them power. Because Balinese masked performance depends on improvisation, new masks can find a way into performance, such as the recent addition of a mask of a Western tourist. These new characters invite mask makers to develop their own visions, but they must first master traditional forms. Within the world of *kabuki*, every job is highly specialized, and many years of training are required for those making *kabuki* sets, props, costumes, and wigs. Both the masks and kimonos of *noh* are made by master craftspeople proficient in the art who pass down their skills and artistic reputation. *Commedia* mask makers also study special techniques for crafting leather masks on a carved wooden mold, and would-be mask makers learn as apprentices. Masterful execution of established designs is of greater value than originality in all of these forms.

In performance traditions there are also personnel who take care of the material objects of the performance. Some are in charge of setting up the stage, replacing items that have been damaged, or cleaning and caring for items between productions. Amateurs, trained professionals, or the actors themselves may take on these tasks. By preserving the stage artifacts, they preserve their traditions.

Western Design before the Interpretive Model

In Europe, before the late nineteenth and early twentieth centuries, designers as interpreters of particular plays did not exist. Rather, established conventions governed set and costume choices. These conventions have not been passed on to us as performance codes, but they were part of the expectations of the audiences of other times.

In ancient Roman comedy, for example, actors wore everyday Greek dress for plays set in Greece and daily Roman dress for those set in Rome. Their masks, wigs, and costumes depicted a few typical characters who were immediately recognizable. Slaves wore red wigs, old men wore grey wigs, young men wore black ones, and courtesans wore yellow—perhaps the origin of the blonde bombshell. The plays were set outside, and architectural portals on the theatre's back wall stood in for the doors of the houses used in the action. It is believed that entering from stage right indicated that a character had come from the town, and entering from stage left indicated that the character had come from the harbor.

In the Middle Ages, costume and set elements for religious dramas were based on iconic imagery drawn from the conventions of painting and sculpture. The Virgin Mary always wore a blue robe; devils had horns, tails, and other beastlike features; the shepherds of Bethlehem dressed like their counterparts in the European countryside; and God wore the regal robes of an emperor. The sets for these productions, placed inside the church for liturgical dramas or on outdoor pageant wagons for religious cycle plays, used stage elements that quickly evoked the familiar Biblical stories—an apple tree for the Garden of Eden or a cross for the crucifixion, rather than detailed locations.

During the Renaissance, when theatre moved indoors, Italian stage design adopted new artistic experiments in perspective drawing for theatrical sets. Professional artists painted detailed wings, drops, and stage floors to create the illusion of a three-dimensional world receding toward a central vanishing point beyond the limits of the actual stage. These sets were visually impressive and functioned as a backdrop for the actors. If performers stepped too far upstage, they could easily disrupt the illusion and scale. These designs and accompanying experiments with stage machinery discussed in Chapter 14 were not text specific: the front of a palace suited any tragedy; a city street, any comedy. Lighting was of course limited by the technology of the times to candles and oil lamps and for the most part was used only for general illumination of the stage and the performers. Actors in comedy and tragedy wore the fashions of the times on stage and usually supplied their own costumes. Togas or tunics and helmets evoked the classical world, and exotic costumes represented Asia and the Americas. European court masques, Italian intermezzos, and the entertainments that grew out of them were more fanciful, reflecting courtly opulence and expressing the ruler's prestige in allegorical terms. Sets might represent the heavens, and courtiers or kings often participated, dressed as Greek and Roman gods and goddesses or allegorical figures such as Power or Sovereignty. Some had special effects that were accompanied by music and sound.

These basic conventions of stage design with generic sets for particular genres continued to be the norm in Europe through the eighteenth century. Experiments in multiple vanishing points, mood painting, and greater historical accuracy did begin a movement toward more specificity in visual elements, but for the most part, calls for the truthful portrayal of everyday life by people such as Diderot were ignored. Some acting companies developed stocks of costumes to supplement actors' individual wardrobes. On the whole, costume and set were only loosely connected to a play's time and place or to particular characters and themes.

Interest in greater realistic and historical detail grew during the nineteenth century. Painted wings and backdrops gave way to a three-walled box set with three-dimensional set pieces that could actually be used by actors. Midcentury, theatre managers often engaged designers to create sets, costumes, and wigs for particular plays. Improvements in lighting, first gas and then electricity, allowed actors to recede into the stage environment instead of playing in front of it. Ultimately, naturalistic plays and the rise of the director demanded increasing specificity in the stage world. By the twentieth century, European and American stage designers were creating specific designs that interpreted a director's vision of a text and unified all of the production elements. Today, set, costume, lighting, and sound designers are collaborative artists who help realize a complete production concept.

Realistic Design

When all that we see and hear on stage closely resembles the natural world, we are in the presence of realistic stage design. Set, costume, light, and sound are used to depict a specific location, time, and social milieu that explains the behavior of the characters. Solid three-dimensional elements such as furniture, trees, and boulders are part of a habitable environment in which characters can conduct themselves seemingly as they would in life. The concrete reality of a play's universe is expressed in every sensory element on stage, and the psychology, temperament, habits, and tastes of characters are further conveyed in the costumes actors wear and how they carry them. All is seen under stage lights that attempt to reproduce naturally occurring light sources. The dramatic action is accompanied by the sounds of the real world. Despite the imitation of observable reality, realism is actually a created environment composed of carefully selected elements that communicate meaning.

Challenges and Choices

If you lift all the elements of a set from real life, is it designed? Is the simple act of selection an act of design?

Photo Essay

Illusions of Reality

Girl of the Golden West with Blanche Bates and Robert Hell, written and directed by David Belasco in 1905, Belasco Theatre, New York.
© *Bettmann/CORBIS*

These two photos show a transition in design from naturalism to selective realism. In the famous card game from *Girl of the Golden West*, a woman saloon owner plays poker to save the man she loves. The environment so completely represents the location and time that we could mistake it for a room in the real world. The fully delineated walls, floor, furniture, clothing, fur pelts, and bric-a-brac paint a detailed picture of the environment. The set is evocative of the replication of reality in early films, and the growth of film partially explains the shift away from detailed naturalism in the theatre. *Joe Turner's Come and Gone* is set in 1911 Pittsburgh.

In this 2004 staging, we find realistic details in the wooden table, the floor treatment, but the bric-a-brac in the room only suggests some of what we might find in such a home. The frame of the house is visible; the floor is not fully covered; and the walls are merely skeletal structures that allow us to see beyond them to the adjacent room, and beyond the house to the outside world, where Pittsburgh's industrial smokestacks can be seen in the background as a symbol of the social change that dominates the characters' lives. Realistic design in theatre today selects the key elements that telegraph information about the world of the play.

August Wilson's *Joe Turner's Come and Gone* at the Saint Louis Black Repertory Company, directed by Andrea Frye in 2004.
Courtesy of St. Louis Black Repertory Company; photo by Stewart Goldstein

During the late nineteenth and early twentieth centuries, a detailed and heightened realism called *naturalism* was used to create vivid replicas of the real world on stage to scientifically expose the truth about social ills. Often actual rooms were moved from stores, restaurants, and houses to create precise environments for particular plays. Eventually naturalism was replaced with a realism that used representative elements of the natural world. We now identify this style as *representational*, in contrast to *presentational* stage worlds that make no attempt to disguise their theatricality.

Abstract Design

As a reaction to naturalism and its detailed literal depiction of reality, artists in many fields believed that there was a higher truth that could not be found in the objects of real life. Direct sensory provocation could lead to meanings and associations not found in the concrete, much the way the juxtaposition of words and images in poetry can lead to a more profound sense of the world. Designers began to think of the stage as a symbolic realm of evocative meanings, and symbolism became the first theatrical movement to embody these ideas, using color, texture, and light to express the essence of a play. Sometimes symbolist designers presented scenes through veiled gauze, which gave the impression of entering a realm of reverie and dreams to connect the audience to unconscious feelings and ideas.

Adolphe Appia and Edward Gordon Craig developed the work of the symbolists in their expressive use of light and shadow on stage. Expressionism further captured emotional force through its dramatic use of angles, lines, and distortions to paint the world as perceived by the inner character. As modernism developed, there was faith that feelings could be communicated without all the trappings of reality, that color, texture, and pure form could express the intangible truths and hieroglyphs of the unconscious mind. Set designs that suggested meaning through nonrepresentational forms emerged. Eventually even human beings were reduced to abstract forms, and many early modernist movements, futurism and Bauhaus in particular, experimented with costume design that turned performers into geometric objects moving through space. Constructivists, inspired by industrial structures, created functional sets using scaffolding, wooden platforms, and piping, turning the stage into an abstract machine in which actors worked like cogs in a wheel.

The high point of modernism in theatrical design occurred when Pablo Picasso created the set and costumes for the Ballets Russes production of *Parade*. The surrealist Jean Cocteau wrote the scenario, and the impressionist Erik Satie composed the music. This inspired many other great modern painters—Henri Matisse, Georges Braque, and Juan Gris, among others—to apply concepts from artistic movements such as cubism, Fauvism, futurism, and surrealism to theatrical design. The influence of this work can be felt today in the sets of many contemporary designers who continue to use color, line, form, and movement beyond the confines of realism. Director-designer Robert Wilson has even extended this impulse to include the actor as an element of design.

During the 1920s, the impact of these European modernist movements was expressed in the United States in what came to be known as the **new stagecraft**. Robert Edmund Jones (1887–1954), Lee Simonson (1888–1967), and Norman Bel Geddes (1893–1958) were the most influential American designers calling for a renewed theatricality in the visual world. The naturalism that had dominated the American stage gave way to more modernist approaches. Eventually, realistic and abstract design borrowed from each other's vocabulary. Many American theatrical designers followed a theatrical realism, while others continued to design in more abstract forms.

Challenges and Choices

When borrowing design elements from traditional forms, must one acknowledge the cultural significance they carry, or can they simply be recontextualized within new forms?

Photo Essay

Modernism in Design

Painted pictorial realism dominated theatrical design from the Renaissance through most of the nineteenth century. Illusions of perspective were rendered on flat surfaces. Actors did not interact with their stage world but performed, for the most part, in front of a painted set. As stage lighting improved, first through gas and later through electricity, actors were able to move away from the front of the stage.

Adolphe Appia (1862–1928), the Swiss designer, sought a way to unite the three-dimensional actor with the two-dimensional scenic design. He started by envisioning the stage space in three dimensions and considering its volume and mass as he designed. To achieve his goals, he employed steps, ramps, and platforms that were usable by the actor. There was minimal painted detail. The resulting sculptural set could then harmonize with the sculpted body of the actor. He underscored the importance of lighting as the art that could unite the actor with the space. Today we take for granted the idea of three dimensional sculptural sets, but it was revolutionary in the 1890s.

During the early decades of the twentieth century, many great visual artists were actively involved in designing for the theatre. Pablo Picasso (1881–1973), Henri Matisse (1869–1954), Georges Braque (1882–1963), and Juan Gris (1887–1927) are just a few of the many painters whose work graced both the stage and art galleries. This group of avant-garde artists brought the new aesthetic of modernism to the theatre, replacing pictorial realism with pictorial abstraction. These early abstract works were still based on objects in the real world. Cubism tried to capture multiple perspectives on the same object simultaneously by breaking the subject down into the basic geometric shapes of which it was composed.

Eventually modern art moved away from abstractions of objects found in the real world to pure abstraction. Russian suprematism and constructivism combined cubism's fragmentation of objects with futurism's attempt to capture the dynamism of the modern world into an art of pure form. Geometric shapes and colors and architectural forms replaced any attempt to render reality. Sculptors began to use a variety of hitherto unusual materials—wood, glass, tin, cardboard, nylon, plaster—juxtaposing materials and textures as well as shapes and

Design by Adolphe Appia for the descent into the underworld from Gluck's *Orpheus and Eurydice* in Hellerau in 1912. Note the absence of any realistic detail and the three dimensional use of space that allows the actor to work within the elements of the set.

colors. The great Russian director, Vsevolod Meyerhold, who developed an intense physical training system to make the actor an efficient worker in the theatre, saw these sculptural pieces as the ideal set for his stage direction. Lyubov Popova (1889–1924), a leading female artist of the Russian avant-garde, designed her now famous constructivist set for Meyerhold's production of *The Magnanimous Cuckhold* (1922) with wheels, steps, catwalks, ramps, and windmills, to capture the dynamism of the new age and its new actor. As you will see in Chapter 11, the ideas of these early pioneers in modernism are still present in scenic design today.

A reconstruction by the Joffrey Ballet of Leonide Massine's ballet *Parade*, originally produced by the Ballets Russes in 1917. The libretto by Jean Cocteau and music by Erik Satie complemented the cubist set and costumes by Pablo Picasso. The costume in the photo was over ten feet tall. The production captured the "new spirit" of modernism.
© *Jack Vartoogian/FrontRowPhotos*

Lyubov Popova's design for Meyerhold's production of *The Magnanimous Cuckhold* in Moscow in 1922 was an abstract sculptural composition with moving elements that could act as a functional machine for actors.
© *St. Petersburg State Museum of Theatre and Music*

IN PERSPECTIVE

THE LION KING: INTEGRATING TRADITION AND INVENTION

Julie Taymor's visual conceptualization of *The Lion King* is an example of stage design borrowing elements from different traditions and cultures to create something unique, dazzling, and fresh. In this production, the design inspires the movement and the acting, and the entire event becomes a visual feast in which costume, set, lighting, and performance become an integrated form.

The Lion King appropriates design elements from African and Asian traditions that seem to fertilize Taymor's imagination. The lion masks mix African mask features with Taymor's own sculptural style. African geometric motifs decorate the bodies of jungle animals. Textures such as fiber, wood, grass, and cloth lift the characters out of their cartoon world and integrate them into the natural environment. The yellows of the savannah setting, the greens of the jungle world, and the greys of the elephant graveyard are the colors of the African landscape. The scene at times comes to life with an explosion of colors and forms drawn from African festival designs. Other aspects of Taymor's design like the shadow puppets, the *bunraku*-style puppets, and the streamers pulled from the eyes of masks to represent tears and grief are influenced by Asian theatrical forms.

Taymor's emphasis on the human dimension of the story of *The Lion King* creates a stage world in which actors play both flora and fauna, and in which the human presence is visible in every costume, mask, and puppet. Dancers in striped leotards blend into the zebra figures they carry, their own legs serving as the animals' front legs. Performers portraying giraffes walk on stilts, supporting headdresses that are the animals' long necks and tiny heads. Singers wearing palettes of grass on their heads rise out of the stage floor, bringing

the savannah to life; their headdresses provide a grassy field for puppet characters to romp through. Timon, a comic meerkat, is a life-size puppet operated by a performer in a green outfit and green makeup. His costume gives the character an ever-present foliage backdrop. Dancers adorned with leaves lie on the floor or hang like vines from above to create the jungle setting.

Highly mechanized effects, operated by sophisticated computer consoles, play alongside less elaborate, but equally theatrical displays. Pride Rock, the lion king's throne, is a large ramp that rotates in a spiral as it rises from the stage. The elephant graveyard echoes this image with two ramps whose counterrotations evoke chaos as opposed to nobility. Daybreak is depicted by a large unfolding cloth sun that rises from the stage floor to loom over the savannah. Its blue mirror image on the floor is a watering hole; drought is indicated by pulling it down through the stage floor from its center.

Rich saturated lighting, designed by Donald Holder, transforms the sets with deep oranges and yellows for the heat of a savannah sunrise, and purples for a cool jungle evening. At a crucial moment in the story, lighting, props, and dance all come together to produce the image of the dead lion king's face emerging from the starry sky. Taymor also uses music to capture the spirit of the African environment depicted visually in the film. The production combines Elton John and Tim Rice's pop tunes with the South African vocal music of Lebo M. In the end, it is the performers who bring all the various artistic elements together as they move with and through the rotating sets, dance with their masks, and sing in a variety of musical styles and languages. Time-honored theatrical tradition, new popular forms, the latest technology, and creative invention merge in *The Lion King*.

Innovation and tradition merge in the set, costume, makeup, and lighting design for *The Lion King*. In this scene, Tsidii Le Loka as Rafiki is surrounded by the chorus as living earth. Directed by Julie Taymor; scenic design by Richard Hudson; costume design by Julie Taymor; lighting design by Donald Holder; mask design by Julie Taymor and Michael Curry; puppet design by Julie Taymor and Michael Curry; sound design by Tony Meola; hair design by Michael Ward; projection design by Geoff Puckett; New Amsterdam Theatre, New York.
© *Joan Marcus*

Photo 10.8
East meets West in Heisei Nakamura-za's production of the traditional *kabuki* play *Natsumatsuri Naniwa Kagami (The Summer Festival: A Mirror of Osaka)*. Here, in a twist on the play's traditional ending, actors dressed as New York City policemen arrest Danshichi Kurobei (Nakamura Kankuro, right) for the murder of his father-in-law, and Issun Tokubei (Nakamura Hashinosuke) for helping his friend escape. This innovative plot turn connected the performance with the contemporary world of the New York audience, reviving the popular spirit of the early *kabuki* tradition.
© Jack Vartoogian/FrontRowPhotos

Contemporary Design: Collaboration and Evolution

Today designers are free to borrow, combine, and juxtapose elements from various conceptual movements, traditions, and cultures. Stylistic eclecticism is the hallmark of postmodernism and defines a shift in sensibility from earlier periods. With access to images from every culture past and present and the benefit of global cultural exchanges, designers have a varied palette of visual vocabularies and stage techniques from which to draw. These can merge and cross-fertilize or remain distinct. Designers are called on to realize a written play text as well as alternative forms of performance. The result is productions with their own visual styles, unique unto themselves and the designer's imagination.

KEY IDEAS

- Theatre captivates the audience through sound and spectacle. Performance traditions inherit design conventions, while designers in the interpretive tradition imagine the world of the stage afresh for each new production.
- Each performance tradition is associated with particular visual and aural elements that have become emblematic of the form.
- In actor-centered traditions, colorful dress, masks, and makeup convey important information about character through a visual, symbolic language. Set elements tend to be sparse.
- In performance traditions master craftspeople build the sets, masks, and costumes. The skillful execution of established designs is often of greater value than originality.

- In Europe, in the late nineteenth and early twentieth centuries, naturalistic plays and the emergence of the director gave rise to the interpretive design tradition.
- In realistic stage design, all that we see and hear on stage closely resembles the natural world.
- Symbolism, expressionism, futurism, and constructivism were reactions against realism's search for truth in everyday reality. The impact of these European movements was expressed in the United States in the *new stagecraft*.
- Today designers borrow, combine, and juxtapose elements from various conceptual movements, traditions, and cultures. They work in a collaborative process to create the world the characters will inhabit.

With lighting changes and the addition of a few set pieces, this basically bare set accommodates the many locations of Shakespeare's *Pericles*. In a turn borrowed from Chinese opera, billowing blue cloths transform the stage into a sea for a small boat. The circular opening, stage center, creates a visual focal point and provides a second frame for stage action within the larger frame of the stage itself. By stepping through the circular opening, actors create a division between inside and outside, or enact other physical or metaphorical transitions. Ron Menzel as Pericles and Shawn Hamilton as Gower. Director, Joel Sass; scenic design, John Clark Donahue; costumes, Amelia Busse Cheever; lighting, Marcus Dilliard; Guthrie Lab, Minneapolis.

© Michal Daniel, 2005

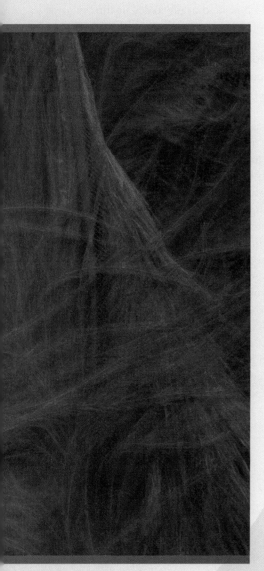

The idea that production design should be unique and specific for each theatrical event emerged from the Western theatrical tradition. Today, the set designer as the visual interpreter of a particular play or performance text is common around the globe. A good set design is not just aesthetically interesting or pleasing for its own sake, but functional and evocative, and deeply connected with a total production concept. It is a kinetic element through which actors move and the audience's eye travels. The set itself may move and establish performance rhythm, and it always both surrounds and inspires the actors' physical actions.

In life we enter rooms and hear sounds without responding to each detail. Place your bedroom on stage and it suddenly becomes a space of hidden meanings. What book is on the night table? Is the bed unmade? Are clothes left around neatly folded or thrown on the floor? Are there bottles of pills on the dresser? Are the blinds or shades up or down? All that we take for granted, when placed on stage, fills with import. We start asking ourselves questions about the characters who inhabit the stage space. Who is the person who lives in the messy room with shuttered windows and empty junk food packages? Suddenly we hear the screech of car brakes and a usual sound of urban life becomes a signal—a portent of dramatic action to come.

Although most of the time the world around us is assembled haphazardly, at particular moments we decide to take control of the messages our world communicates about us. You may have chosen a piece of music to play when a date arrived to create a particular impression or mood. Perhaps you left an interesting book open, rearranged furniture, or cleaned the room so that you would be perceived as a certain type of person. You may have turned down the lights or lit candles to create a romantic atmosphere. Surely we have all chosen items of clothing to express aspects of our personality or to indicate how sexually appealing we are. Just as you tried to set a mood and create a portrait of you and your world through the deliberate selection of visual and sound elements, designers create a portrait of an imaginary world inhabited by characters through the careful selection of visual and aural signals of meaning. These signals serve as clues that the audience will read as they interpret the action on stage.

Designers work in a collaborative process with each other and with other members of the creative production team. Together they decide how best to create the world the characters will inhabit. Every step of the way, they remember that the audience will read every visual and sound element for significance, so each choice they make will contribute to the totality of the theatrical experience.

Goals of Set Design

■ **Facilitating the Dramatic Action.** The most basic requirement of a set is to *serve the text and the performance.* All sets should provide a playable space that allows actors to move about and make their entrances and exits freely. Since the set will either limit or open possibilities for physical action, set designers consider a text carefully to make note of all special needs such as the number of entrances and exits, changes in location, and important set elements that take part in the action. In Georges Feydeau's (1862–1921) farce *A Flea in Her Ear* (1907), the fast-paced action of over two hundred comings and goings of characters trying to catch each other in *flagrante delicto* while escaping discovery by spouses and lovers requires a number of doors and corridors. Molière's *Tartuffe* has a character hiding in an armoire to eavesdrop, so the position of this set piece is crucial to the action. In Eugène Ionesco's *Frenzy for Two or More*, explosions tear apart the walls of an apartment where two lovers quarrel, so the set designer needs to create a set

Photo Essay

Designing the Character's World

Eugene O'Neill's *Moon for the Misbegotten* at the Long Wharf Theatre, New Haven, directed by Gordon Edelstein. Scenic design by Ming Cho Lee; costumes by Jennifer Von Mayrhauser; lighting by Jennifer Tipton.
© *T. Charles Erickson*

These two sets each tell us much about the character's lives and set the time and place for the action, yet their approaches are quite different. How a set expresses the world in which the characters will live is the result of a collaborative process in which the designer and director determine what visual style will work best with the directorial concept for the text. Ming Cho Lee's set (above) uses a single scenic location and includes a weathered wooden house, an old water pump, rocks, and even dirt to tell us where we are and to reflect the dismal lives of the characters. *Man from Nebraska* tells of a man in a mid-life crisis of faith and his search for meaning. Todd Rosenthal's set (below), with its twenty different locations simultaneously visible, gives a sense of the journey the lead character will take toward self-discovery. Each box on this grid is fully dimensional, except for a few printed backgrounds, such as the road, that were printed onto backlit vinyl.

Tracy Lett's *Man from Nebraska* at the Steppenwolf Theatre Company, Chicago, directed by Anna Shapiro; scenic design by Todd Rosenthal; costumes by Mara Blumenfeld; lighting design by Ann Wrightson.
© *Michael Brosilow*

Photo 11.1
A bright orange flip hairdo frames the proscenium to provide a visual metaphor for the theme of *Hairspray*. The comic, quirky style of the production is reinforced by the addition of the barrette to the frame of this stage musical adaptation of a John Waters film, in which exaggerated hairstyles play a major role. Note the bright, bold colors in the set and costumes that set a joyful mood. Director, Jack O'Brien; scenic design, David Rockwell; costumes, William Ivey Long; lighting, Kenneth Posner; at the Neil Simon Theatre, New York.
© *David Joseph and Rockwell Group*

that can be completely destroyed each night and yet be easily reconstructed for the next performance. The requirements of the action need to become part of the set designer's vision, and often are the source of inspiration.

■ **Establishing Time and Place.** The set can place the action in time and tell us *when* the action is unfolding—the era, the time of year, as well as the time of day. A medieval castle, a high-tech office, or a flourishing garden all tell us something about time. Sometimes set designers strive to remove the play from any particular time period and deliberately avoid any defining elements. *Waiting for Godot* is often placed in a no-man's-land outside of traditional time periods to express the continuity of the human condition.

The set can also tell us *where* the action is happening—what part of the world and what kind of environment we are in, indoors or outdoors, in a natural environment or an urban setting. Design can tell us what type of building, home, or room we are in. In *The Lion King* the African settings include the open savannah with its jutting Pride Rock, an elephant's graveyard infested with vicious hyenas, and a lush jungle for carefree characters. The cramped urban apartment of *A Streetcar Named Desire* sets the scene for the events in that play.

■ **Creating Mood.** Design elements can capture the emotional tone of a production. We often know in an instant whether we are at a comedy or a tragedy by the feeling of the stage environment. Somber, heavy architectural elements create a different feeling from light, airy, open space. Edward Gorey's somber neogothic sets for *Dracula* were filled with motifs of skulls and bats and set the tone for the horror tale.

■ **Providing an Environment that Embodies the Characters' Lives.** Set designers enter the characters' world and express in visual terms the religious, political, economic, or social rules that govern it. Whether the stage environment is historically accurate, invented by the playwright, or redefined by the director, it will determine how the characters act and whether they are constrained or free. Federico García Lorca's *House of*

Bernarda Alba (1945) depicts a world imprisoned by Spanish Catholic doctrine. Bernarda Alba holds her five daughters at home under lock and key for an eight-year period of strict mourning. Forbidden social activities and intimate relationships, the daughters watch their youth recede from inside the house that has become a jail cell. A set that can express this feeling of oppression will help the actors live the reality of their situation and give the audience a sensory experience of the characters' longings.

The set immediately relays information about the people who live within it. Class, taste, education, personality, and occupation are all revealed by the physical environment. The characters' emotional state can be captured by the placement of walls and objects. Realistic sets try to capture the specific details of the environment that can enable us to understand the characters' actions and desires (see photos on page 293).

- **Telling the Story.** The set can chart the characters' physical or emotional journey. In Chekhov's *The Cherry Orchard*, an aristocratic family facing financial pressures and changing times is forced to sell its estate to a former servant. Returning from a trip abroad at the start of the play, they pull the dust cloths off the elegant furnishings that fill their home. In the final scene, they have lost their estate, and the set, reflecting their loss, is almost bare. The set provides the visual expression of the characters' changing circumstances.

- **Presenting a Visual Metaphor for the Director's Concept.** The set captures in concrete form the abstract ideas present in a work that govern the director's choices. David Rockwell's set design for *Hairspray* frames the set with a metaphorical curtain (see Photo 11.1). In the set for *Thoroughly Modern Millie*, David Gallo provides a backdrop of the city that shapes the characters' dreams (see Photo 11.6).

- **Defining Style.** The set designer manipulates stage conventions to create a visual style for the set. This "look" will reflect the director's concept and the approach to acting and movement. The set designer can choose to use the conventions of realism by creating the appearance of real rooms and places for actors behaving in seemingly natural ways, or the stage can be a place of abstraction using ramps, platforms, and geometrical or symbolic objects where actors can behave in an artificial, exaggerated, or aestheticized manner. Sometimes directors request a particular stylistic approach to the visual design

Photo 11.2
This spiral structure, designed by Stefan Mayer, which descends to the center of the playing area in Part II of Peter Stein's production of Goethe's *Faust*, is one part of a set that establishes the spiritual journey of the central character and a style for the production. Here Faust's impending heavenly redemption is made visual as he is led up the ramp by angels dressed in white. Costumes, Moidele Bickel.
© Ruth Walz

and direct the actors in a style that contrasts with the design to heighten certain meanings in the text. The very familiar bourgeois living room of *The Bald Soprano* is set off by the anomalous behavior of the characters to reveal the deeper truths of our daily lives (see Photo 3.5).

■ **Determining the Relationship between the Audience and the Dramatic Action.** Creating a set that regulates the relationship between performers and spectators is an integral part of the set designer's work with the director. The set designer can move everything to a distance by framing the action behind a proscenium arch, or draw the audience into the action by using the front apron of a proscenium stage, entrances through the audience, and places for interaction. In a black box theatre, in which the seating is flexible, the director and set designer determine the spatial configuration that will work best for the director's concept. These choices will affect every aspect of the production—staging, lighting, and acting, as well as the interplay with the public.

■ **Expressing the Director's Point of View.** The ultimate goal of set design is to express the director's point of view. At each step in the process, the director must approve of the choices the set designer makes. The final design should therefore be a visual statement of the director's concept for a production.

Challenges and Choices

When a set is nothing more than an arrangement of the space—seating and playing areas—in what way can we consider this a complete design?

The Set Designer's Process: Collaboration, Discussion, Evolution

With the exception of director-designers such as Robert Wilson or Julie Taymor, or those working in collective environments, set designers are usually engaged after a production project has been selected. They begin their creative process with several careful readings of the text, or if they are designing for a work evolving through collaboration, they attend rehearsals. Set designers might ask themselves: What kinds of images does the work

Photo 11.3
The Renaissance-style painting on the backdrop of the set demonstrates how researched images can make their way onto the stage to provide an atmosphere for a production. Shakespeare's *The Winter's Tale.* Pictured are Keith David and Aunjanue Ellis; director, Brian Kulick; set, Riccardo Hernández; costumes, Anita Yavich; lighting, Kenneth Posner. The Public Theatre/New York Shakespeare Festival, Central Park.
© *Michal Daniel, 2000*

Photo 11.4
Todd Rosenthal's model for *Man from Nebraska* demonstrates the amount of detail a designer may put into a model to give the director, cast, and technical director a clear idea of how the set should look when completed. Compare the model to the actual completed set shown in the Photo Essay on page 293 to get a sense of how ideas develop in the design process as elements are added.
© *Todd Rosenthal*

bring to mind? What feelings are evoked? What elements are necessary to the dramatic action? What visual ideas stand out or seem most important?

Although set designers may have many immediate responses to the piece, they do not start designing until they have had lengthy discussions with the director. Here they learn the concept that will guide the production, significant needs the interpretation may require, and special moments the director wishes to highlight. Scenic designers often see potential problems adapting the text to particular theatre spaces as well as specific needs for the dramatic action. Because set designers are always thinking with the visual elements foremost in their minds, they often foresee difficulties and needs the director may have missed. A good designer also finds unexplored opportunities for the design to create interesting moments and serve the text. During this first meeting there is an exciting exchange about the text, the concept, and how particular problems will be solved. Designers can stimulate this conversation and help the director clarify ideas by asking questions about the concept that clarify the director's vision.

A set designer may do visual research to find images—photos and drawings—that reflect the time, place, or directorial interpretation of the production. These may provide inspiration and are often presented to the director to see whether they capture the concept the director has in mind. This research takes place on three levels: the objective world of the play—its historic moment, sociology, and period style; the subjective level—the history and sociology and style of the director's concept; and the inspirational level—images that are not necessarily specifically related to the play but can spur the designer's imagination.

For example, if the director were setting a seventeenth-century French play in post–World War II Paris, the set designer would need to research both periods. The seventeenth-century photos would give a feel of the original period and help the designer translate that feeling into late 1940s terms. Researched images offer a tool for clarifying ideas in discussion and are vital to formulating a shared vision of the visual world. Old magazines, art books, or historical photographs are all good sources. Most set designers keep files of images to sift through when they begin work on a new production.

Challenges and Choices

Does reassembling researched images constitute an act of design?

Artists
IN PERSPECTIVE

In Their Own Words

LOUISA THOMPSON

Louisa Thompson won the Obie and Hewes awards for the set of the critically acclaimed Off-Broadway production of [sic]. Her work has been seen around the country at such theatres as the La Jolla Playhouse, The Children's Theatre Company of Minneapolis, Philadelphia Theatre Company, Actor's Express, Geva Theatre, Triad Stage, The Empty Space Theatre, and the Yale Repertory Theatre. Among her many New York credits are Suitcase, Molly's Dream, and The Year of the Baby for Soho Repertory Theatre; Fat Pig and The Distance from Here (MCC Theatre); 21 Dog Years at Amazon.Com (Play All Day Productions); The Roaring Girle (The Foundry Theatre Company); The Cherry Orchard (SALT Theatre); Tulpa (Target Margin Theater); First in Flight, and Just So Stories (Theatreworks/USA); and People Are Wrong, 131 (P.S. 122). She holds an MFA from the Yale School of Drama and is currently on the faculty of Hunter College in New York.

■ **How much do you think about the entire theatrical space—both that of the audience and that of the performer—when you design?**

When I work in any type of theatre—proscenium, thrust, or black box, I am always thinking about the entire space; this includes both where the performance is happening and where the audience is sitting. For me, the relationship between these two spaces is always echoed in the architecture, so the architecture of the space must be included in the design. There are times when the architecture is so powerful, or present, or has so much opportunity inherent in it that you can actually use it to frame a production or to create moments within the production.

So I can use the architecture to help the production or use it in an unexpected way to change the relationship between the actor and the audience. In both cases, the audience grasps when they enter the theatre that their relationship to the performance is specific in terms of the way the architecture is either highlighted or reconfigured, and this makes the relationship of the spectator to the event feel more immediate.

You can take a proscenium and put the audience on the stage and place a ramp over the seating area for the performance. The second you bring the audience within the frame of the proscenium, the frame tends to go away. You can also make a transition between the

proscenium frame by creating aprons, stairs, ramps, to break the proscenium, even within realistic plays, because the theatre is always a heightened reality, so even realism makes its own rules.

■ **What if an audience member has never been in a particular space?**

All people have an inherent understanding of architecture. You sense naturally where a door should be and how you should move and be placed in a particular space, even if you haven't been in it before. Audience members have expectations, so if the space is turned around, or the seating reconfigured, you sense it as an active choice, and you automatically start asking questions about your relationship to what is about to happen. When I designed *Molly's Dream* by Irene Fornes at Soho Rep in New York, I turned the room around so that the audience sat facing the longest wall in the room. To watch the play you had to move your head from left to right to encompass the long set.

I am always interested in placing the audience in an unusual position within the space because it awakens the audience's relationship to the performance and the performer and heightens the awareness of the self as an audience member. Sometimes this can be uncomfortable; potentially it is challenging; ideally it is done in a way that serves a specific project. Take the production of Suzan Lori Parks' *Venus* at Hunter College where the audience was on swivel chairs surrounded by the performance; the audience was also on stage performing as they negotiated the performance and each other and which way to look. This reinforced the episodic nature of the play, and an unexpected and exciting demand was placed on the audience.

■ **When you read a play, does it call out for a particular space?**

Yes, some speak to me as flat and presentational, and I feel that the actors are on display. This evokes a proscenium and is difficult in a thrust or arena space, where the actors can be seen front, back, and side—sculpturally, but not pictorially. You can't make flat pictures when the audience is on more than one side.

■ **Can you talk about the relationship between space and set pieces?**

The world of the play is always my starting point, and as soon as I begin to imagine that world, I see it within a specific space, and when I do that, I am dealing with architecture. Architecture is a framing device that helps us focus and block out the distractions of our lives. Sometimes you want to use it; at other times you want to acknowledge it and let it drift away. Sometimes set pieces help to do this. Set pieces can define the performance and the audience space; sometimes they do more than the architecture, when you construct the space within which the pieces fit. A **box set,** where flats form the back and side walls, and sometimes even the ceiling of a room, does not acknowledge the space around it and tends to make you want to forget the architecture and focus on the space within it. Some box sets can make you do both, focus within and without. As a designer, I am interested in making the relationship between set and architecture as active as possible.

In arena staging, your walls are essentially defined by the audience surrounding the playing area, and you are much more aware of the floor and ceiling. So these horizontal planes in space are more active, and props and smaller set pieces are seen in relation to the ground. In arena I think about designing the floor as the field or frame against which you are envisioning the composition. Thrust is a mix that allows some picture frame as well as a sculptural space, and my job is to find a way to connect those two ideas.

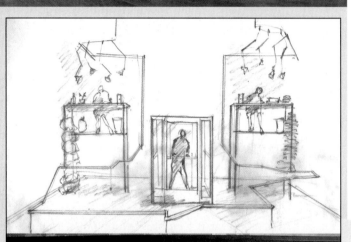

These three images show the progression of Louisa Thompson's set design for Melissa James Gibson's *Suitcase, or Those That Resemble Flies from a Distance* from working drawing to presentation model to finished design in performance. The actual process included many more sketches and rough models. Note the use of human figures in the sketch to show how the set and scale figures in the model can be used to give an accurate sense of proportion. The two scaffolds represent separate apartments, and the isolation of their inhabitants, buried in scholarly research, is represented by the tower of books on the right. Directed by Daniel Aukin at the Soho Rep, New York.

© Louisa Thompson

Challenges and Choices

How much autonomy should a set designer have? At what point should artists subsume their creativity to the collaborative experience?

Once they have an understanding of the vision of the production as a whole, set designers will start to imagine the set in more concrete terms. They may ask: What does the audience need to see? What is essential to the visual expression of the text? Synthesizing the director's ideas with their own and taking into account practical considerations about the theatre space, budget, and building time, designers translate their ideas into concrete visual images. Sketches serve as the basis for further discussion. Several sketches may be presented for the director's response, and they may be modified for the final design. A designer may even do a **storyboard**, a series of sketches showing how the set changes to tell the story through time. This technique is often used to solve practical problems. Out of this process, a **ground plan** emerges that gives a view of the dimensions of the stage and the placement of set pieces.

Most set designers build a scale **model** of the set. This three-dimensional model gives the production team more specific information about how the design will actually look and work in the space, as well as a sense of the viewers' angle on the action. Some set designers prefer to develop their ideas through multiple models. Directors often use models in rehearsal to give themselves and the actors a better sense of the environment and to help adjust movement patterns. A scaled human figure is always placed in the model to help everyone visualize the actor in space. Models can reveal places where ideas that looked good on paper may not work in reality, precipitating changes before the set is built. Models of rooms often have movable pieces of furniture and scenery, and directors and designers toy with placement for best effect. The other designers (costume, lighting, sound) usually come to see the model because it can help guide their choices.

Discussions between set designers and directors take place throughout the production process in production meetings and during informal exchanges. Costume, lighting, and sound designers will also be part of these exchanges because the design elements need to complement each other and work together: A lamp that needs to turn on in performance raises problems for both the set and lighting designers; a stereo that plays music involves the set and sound designer. In *The Lion King*, costume elements form the set, requiring coordination between costume and set design. Open channels of communication are vital to coordinate practical and aesthetic needs.

For most commercial productions, the basic designs will be completed before the first rehearsal and then refined through part of the rehearsal process to accommodate the discoveries of actors, directors, and designers. For this reason, set designers must be flexible. They attend rehearsals to get a better sense of how the stage is being used in the action. The set design must be finalized and signed off long before the first performance to allow time for construction.

The set designer drafts construction drawings to send to the shop. These are first shown to the lighting designer for a check of any lighting difficulties the plans might present. Today, more and more of these drawings are being done on computers because most shop technicians prefer receiving computer drafted plans. Computer-drafted designs can also be used to program computerized machinery in the scene shop. Set designers may visit the shop to see how things are going, but they are not around to supervise. Therefore, their drawings need to be extremely accurate and contain as much information as possible about the shape, size, function, and look of every set piece. Paint elevations show the application of color to all stage surfaces and are also provided with sample colors for the scenic artists. Set designers need good drafting skills to execute these documents. They rely on the technician's knowledge of materials, carpentry, or engineering to find solutions to design problems, and often make changes based on the technical director's suggestions. They work closely with technical staff to make the set design a reality that fulfills the artistic promise originally set out in discussion and sketches.

Artists
IN PERSPECTIVE

In Their Own Words

PAMELA HOWARD

An internationally recognized scenographer and teacher, Pamela Howard has moved from just design to directing and design and creating original perform-ances. She is equally adept at interpreting texts and the possibilities of space. While continuing an extraor-dinary professional career, Howard has maintained a parallel career in education. Many designers working in international theatre, opera, and film have studied with her. She was founder and artistic director of the European Scenography Centres, an international masters course in scenography based at Central Saint Martins College of Art and Design in London, with centers in Utrecht, Prague, Helsinki, and Seville. She was artistic director of SCENOFEST, a groundbreaking international annual festival held in a different city each year, and which is now integrated into the Prague Quadriennal. She is professor emeritus of Central Saint Martins and a visiting professor at Royal Holloway College, the University of London, and Tel Aviv University and a consultant to the University of the Arts in Belgrade. Her book What Is Scenography? *is now translated into many languages. Her most recent work includes* The Greek Passion *for the Opera of Thessaloniki in 2005, for which she was both direc-tor and designer, and* The New Jerusalem, *an original work she created for the Oxmarket Centre of Arts in August 2005.*

■ **How do you define the role of a contemporary set designer?**

When considering the role of the contemporary set de-signer, I have to ask myself if there really *is* a role any more. When I started off in 1954, all a set designer was required to do was to provide a reasonably practi-cal and decorative background for the actors to per-form in front of. Now, fifty years later the former "set designer" fulfills a more creative and virtually directorial role as a major instigator of the work. So, a contempo-rary theatre designer (I cannot subscribe to the U.S. habit of separating set and costume—these two inter-linked disciplines) has to be above all an artist of vision, but one who is able to initiate ideas—even the subject of the work, and know how to carry out the commission so that the artistic integrity is universally maintained.

■ **How has your work as a designer led you to directing, and what impact has directing had on your creative process as a designer?**

My work as a designer was for many years fulfilling, and I achieved a high level of recognition and success. However, I was increasingly frustrated. Sometimes this was by the inability of the directors I was working with to see how to best use the spaces I provided. More fundamental was the realization that there were so many plays I really wanted to do, but the actual work depended on someone else asking me to do what they wanted to do. I am very very concerned with human-ity, tolerance, politics, peace—all those current conflicts that inform our everyday lives. Theatre is a marvelous medium for exploring and addressing these issues, and they are well reflected in the dramatic repertoire since ancient times. However, choices of plays are usually made for very different reasons—marketing, availability of a "star," balance of an established pro-gram. Although I do not intend giving up designing, the only way I can do work that really means some-thing to me is to do it myself. Martinu's opera *The Greek Passion* from the book *Christ Recrucified* by Nikos Kazantzakis is one such example, since it deals with how we react when faced with asylum seekers and refugees. Though written in 1957, it has never been more appropriate than now; yet, the likelihood of a director asking me to design it is so remote. I pro-posed it to the Opera of Thessaloniki myself. I am also writing a lot of performance work, where the text and the vision are so unified that there would be no point in anyone else putting in another layer by directing it.

Most of the work I am currently creating also uses and exploits spaces that may or may not be conventional theatres. As soon as one moves out of the "hierarchical space" into a fluid space, it ceases to matter so much who does what, so even the word *directing* seems inap-propriate. I call myself a "creator." However, my long ex-perience as a designer has definitely given me a personal aesthetic that informs all the choices I make either as a director or a designer—and the art is definitely in making the right decisions time after time. When I have directed productions, for example my own version of Fernando de Rojas's *La Celestina* at the Hopkins Center in Hanover, New Hampshire, in 2002, it has been pure pleasure just to feel in control of my own creativity. It feels like I have taken a bite out of the golden apple, and there is no going back now! However, when I set up a creative team, I look for people who are interdisciplinary and are able to move from one area to the other. In this way, an

(continues)

Artists

IN PERSPECTIVE (CONTINUED)

object-maker may also perform; a performer may make a costume; and a nonhierarchical group of performative artists can come together to realize a piece of work with a shared aesthetic.

■ **Can you talk about the relationship between the architectural space and the set design? How do site-specific works change your creative process?**

The most significant factor in contemporary design is the use of architectural space. This does not have to be a "site-specific" space—a warehouse, a derelict customs shed, for example. But like *Concierto Barroco*, created with Edwin Erminy, which took place in the basement paint shop of the Teresa Carreno Theatre in Caracas, theatre can rejuvenate unloved and forgotten spaces in the theatre itself. Very often I go into a theatre and look at the space and try to imagine the performance there. Sometimes I can see how a perfectly normal space could be better used for the particular project in mind. The fact is that when one is able to work creatively in a space with performers in costume and light and sound, "set design" just becomes irrelevant—and on the whole, I now really think it is. It just seems mad that we all recycle newspapers and bottles like mad, and then throw away expensive scenery that has a short life, can't be stored, and no one wants to use again. Increasingly set design hardly features in my work at all. In the drawings for *The Greek Passion* (see photo) you will see the characters against a rough and rocky background that represents the site itself. The only added elements are simple pieces of constructed furniture. The whole work has a very limited color scheme that looks as though it is all black, but in fact there is no black at all. There is greenblack, redblack, purpleblack, etc. It all deceives the eye, but is not at all naturalistic—it is totally invented.

Working in a new or revised architectural space demands per se a revision of working attitudes, since immediately boundaries are blurred. In *The Greek Passion* the acoustician is suddenly "the boss"!! I had not expected that. I am challenged by how to use the space. I look at the possibilities of surprise—where can I bring people in from, and what can be happening in one place, while in another something else is getting prepared.

■ **How do you find a fresh vision for classical works?**

Unfortunately classic plays often become national monuments, and when that happens, it becomes a vehicle for bravura acting, and the real meaning is obfuscated. By placing classic plays in different architectural spaces, the piece is often released from its monumentality and the story just flows. I did a very interesting production

of Ibsen's *Hedda Gabler* with the director Stephen Unwin in 2000 in the Donmar Warehouse in Covent Garden, and just forcing this "big" play into a tiny place, where the spectators seemed to be in the room of the play, made an enormous impact. However, the truth is that so many directors are timid and full of fear and really only want the comfort of lots of scenery so that their own work is less exposed. I love to use classical work to "paint pictures with people." The whole point of my work is how it is received by the spectator, and when I hear people saying, "Oh so that is what that play is about" and arguing about the issues, I feel I have been reasonably successful.

■ **Is there a design project that you've done that you thought was particularly memorable, and why?**

The most memorable design project I have ever done was with the late John McGrath in 1990 at the Tramway Theatre Glasgow as part of Glasgow City of Culture. It was *Border Warfare*, written and directed by John, but really jointly created. The story was six hundred years of wars between the Scots and the English told by twelve actors, a pop group, and not much money in a promenade type performance that lasted nearly four hours! I was just inspired by the story, and by chance saw a football cup final between England and Scotland on TV, which gave me the idea to convert the Tramway into a football field by laying down grass on the floor and painting a white line across the middle. Scotland was one end of the space and England was the opposite end. The six hundred spectators followed the fast-moving action moving around and through the spaces, guided by huge wooden horses pushed by stage management. It was really wild, but tickets were like gold!

■ **Can you talk about the role of research in your process?**

Research is my motivation. I read, write, study all the time. I search and research. I visit museums in all the countries I find myself, listen to people's stories, and keep sketchbooks and copious notes that line the walls of my studio, which I did think once had plenty of room. Through research, I am able to find connections through history and use this information eclectically in my work. As I try so often to tell students, research is not just about collecting photocopies from books. One has to develop techniques for recording research so that it is useful, and drawing is a very good way of memorizing colors, textures, the shape of people, the small ephemera of everyday life that have not changed much throughout the ages. In a production of Shakespeare's *Henry IV* Parts

1 and 2 for English Touring Theatre, with the director Stephen Unwin I used the dying king's speech "There is a history in all men's lives" (Part 2) to create costumes that spoke of a history in all men's clothes. For this I researched how people lived through different centuries according to their occupations.

■ What is the impact of your professional work on your teaching?

I have always followed the dictum that I teach what I practice and practice what I teach, and all my life these two things have gone hand in hand. I am very happy when I see the huge number of students who were my students doing really well all over the world, and even more happy to be part of an international community of scenographers that we started in 1994 at the European Scenography Centres, who are making work together. As an educator, I have tried to show that working in the theatre is a privilege, not just a job. This subject encompasses more than just knowing how scenery is constructed. Through the visual medium of theatre, we can touch humanity, as only art can—mysterious and indefinable, but concretely felt by the spectator and the creator. We have the privilege through our art to clarify those issues and find a form of expression that enhances understanding. What could be more important than educating younger colleagues to do that while striving to practice it at the same time? I also have felt that the commitment to the student is not just for the fleeting moment the student is working with you, but rather a cradle to grave commitment. This way education is continuing and shared.

Pamela Howard's design for Nikolios, The Shepherd Boy, for Bohuslav Martinu's opera *The Greek Passion*, which she both directed and designed. The costume integrates the character with the ancient architecture of the setting within "The Old Prison Courtyard" at the Heptapyrgion (Old Byzantine Citadel), as well as with the site's natural outdoor landscape. Performed by Opera of Thessaloniki (The National Theatre of Northern Greece), Thessaloniki.
© Pamela Howard, 2004–2005

■ What advice would you give to young prospective designers?

I receive many letters every week from desperate young prospective designers, and I am often shocked at how dismissive schools are once their people have graduated. My best advice is to be hungry and starving for work, and to really go out and seek it. That means going to see work whenever you can, and then contacting the creators of that work to discuss it.

I travel all over the world, and go and see productions wherever I am, and try to meet the people who make the work. Generally creators really want to talk about their work to colleagues. I tell people, "Don't ask—offer." Don't ask for a job (the answer is likely to be no)—but offer to be involved in a project that interests you, or engage in a critical debate. Eventually it does work out. Be well prepared and create a logical portfolio so that someone looking at it can share your journey of development. Above all, dream and have passions. As I said, it's more than a job. Oh yes, and the best bit of advice is not to forget that no one ever wants to employ someone who is a misery. A smile and a sense of humor is a great passport!

Early in the rehearsal process, the set designer will work with the director and stage manager to create a prop list of the objects necessary for the stage action. Items may be added or deleted from this initial list as the actors' blocking is developed and fixed. Some props are set out on stage; others are hand props carried on stage by actors. Often personal props carried by actors, such as a briefcase or umbrella, are part of costume design. Set designers select items for use on stage that conform to the style of the set. There is always discussion with the director about how each object should look and how it will be used. A bowl of fruit can use artificial fruit unless actors eat it as part of the action, so it is important for the director to describe how every prop will function. Set designers may transform everyday objects with paint, varnish, finishes, and ornamentation, perhaps antiquing an aluminum bowl, distressing a wood box, or bejeweling the handle of a cane. Some props may be built from scratch. Sometimes antique replicas or other original objects are purchased or drawn from stock. All props used on stage are chosen by the set designer and approved by the director. Set designers may attend rehearsals to see exactly how a particular prop is used by actors to help in their selection process.

When all the pieces are built, the set is *loaded in*. With the set in place in the theatre with actors working on it, the set designer can now see how the set looks and functions. Except in the case of very well-funded productions, it is too late to make major changes. Designers can make minor adjustments for visual quality, functionality, and safety. They may oversee or do scenic painting to create textures and finishes, and they may **dress the set** with final touches: upholstery, small objects for tables and shelves, pillows, and curtains.

Set designers supervise the creation of the set from conception to implementation. Their ideas may be modified along the way so the final stage image fits the director's concept, the space, and the stage action. The set's ultimate realization, however, only takes place when the performers bring it to life.

Principles of Composition

Spectators rely on stage composition to orient them within the visual world of the stage. Composition directs their gaze and guides their interpretation of the visual elements. How we look is actually informed by how we read, whether we go from left to right or up to down. The composition of the stage elements (how they sit in relationship to each other) plays on our visual habits to create meaning.

Focus

All elements of design can be used to direct the audience's vision toward parts of the stage that have theatrical, practical, or metaphorical value. The arrangement of objects on stage orients the audience within the space. The lines of a set draw their eyes in particular directions, as do certain colors, textures, and relative masses. Set designers have many ways to bring focus to a particular point on the stage. To rivet our eyes to the palace doors where Queen Clytemnestra lures King Agamemnon to his death, designers might put them center stage, paint them bright red in an otherwise dull-colored set, make them appear of massive sculptured bronze, place them on an otherwise bare stage, or have all the lines of the set point toward them wherever they are placed. Perhaps they will create several smaller frames within the frame of the stage itself, with a window or some other kind of border. Set designers can even take our eyes on a journey through the set, with circular lines that move our vision from one side of the stage to the other. Designers are responsible for controlling the audience's line of sight and may sometimes need to work with existing obstructions.

Balance

If you draw a line down the middle of the stage and the two sides mirror each other, there is symmetry. If more set elements are gathered on one side than another, there is asymmetry. We tend to associate balance with stability, excessive symmetry with rigidity or artificiality, and imbalance with disorientation. Manipulating balance is a set designer's tool that can reflect a point of view on the world the characters inhabit.

Proportion

Proportion refers to the scale of the set elements in relation to each other and to the actors. Large set pieces can dominate the space and tower above the human figures, while unusually small ones may seem like toys, as in the example from Lee Breuer's *Dollhouse* (see Photo 8.3). The relative scale of objects may reflect reality or distort the world for stylistic or metaphorical purposes. The imposing machine that dominated the 1923 set of Elmer Rice's expressionist play *The Adding Machine* served to underscore the dehumanization of people in the modern industrial era. Scale also tells audiences where to look as their eyes are drawn to large objects on stage (see Photo 11.5 and the photo on page 169).

Rhythm

The visual world of the stage has a rhythm. Visual statements can repeat in a regular manner or shift abruptly and disjunctively. They can impart a sense of calm or frenzy. In his famous 1926 production of Gogol's *Inspector General*, Meyerhold put fifteen doors in a line across the stage. Officials emerged from each one to bribe the inspector. The visual repetition of the doors and the repetitive action on stage reinforced the thematic exposition of the machinelike workings of government bureaucracy. Robert Wilson's set for *Einstein on the Beach* used a scaffolding to create a three-dimensional grid of square spaces. A performer in each frame reinforced the sense of visual repetition but with variations since each one had a different physical stance.

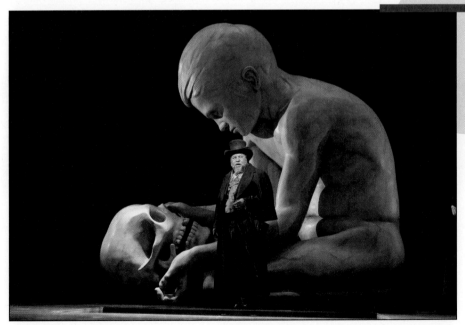

Photo 11.5
The exaggerated proportions of an enormous statue of a youth cradling a skull lends a sense of unease to this graveyard scene in *Dracula, The Musical,* directed by Des McAnuff. Scenic design, Heidi Ettinger; costumes, Catherine Zuber, lighting, Howell Binkley; at the Belasco Theatre, New York.
© *Joan Marcus*

Unity

The words *harmony, unity,* or *integrity* describe a set in which all the elements are in agreement with each other. Often dissonant notes are deliberately struck to drive home a point about the world in which the characters live. A play set in an undeveloped land might present a hut with a satellite dish to demonstrate the reach of globalization. Discordant elements always assume meaning and are carefully selected. However disproportionate or asymmetrical individual set pieces may seem, in a unified design, the composition is justified and meaningful. The characters see their world as whole, and the set should reflect this world with its own integrity.

The Visual Elements of Set Design

All objects have some form of *line, mass, texture,* and *color,* properties that convey meaning through their artistic use. Designers manipulate these elements to accomplish all the goals of set design while composing the space. Our ability to read a set is informed by the general visual culture, the associations we have with certain colors or shapes and how these make us feel.

Line

The visual world is constructed of lines—straight, curved, and zigzag—set horizontally, vertically, or diagonally. These lines give definition to walls, furnishings, and every object on stage and impart a particular feeling to the viewer. Straight horizontal lines can give a sense of rigidity or confinement, reminiscent of a jail cell, or they may convey stability and security, like the columns on a stately building. Vertical lines can give a sense of soaring and power. Curved lines give a feeling of freedom and openness or of instability, like waves on the ocean. Zigzag lines can create a topsy-turvy world. Expressionist sets of the early twentieth century often used steeply angled lines to express an emotionally charged world seen through the eyes of the central character of the drama.

Photo 11.6
The repetition of straight, vertical lines in the backdrop of skyscrapers is echoed in the dancers limbs, also stretched long and upward. The set speaks of modernism, industrialization, and striving skyward to reach new heights. *Thoroughly Modern Millie,* director, Michael Mayer; choreographer, Rob Ashford; scenic design, David Gallo; costumes, Martin Pakledinaz; lighting, Donald Holder; Marquis Theatre, New York.
© *Joan Marcus*

Photo 11.7
For Charles L. Mee's *Big Love*, the padded floor covered in pink vinyl served as a trampoline on which actor's could throw themselves in paroxysm of passion and rage in the play's dramatization of the battle between the sexes. Director, Les Walters; set, Annie Smart; costumes, James Schuette; lighting, Robert Wierzel; Brooklyn Academy of Music, Harvey Theatre, New York.
© Richard Termine

Mass

Mass refers to the shape of objects on stage, their size and weight and the way they occupy space. The balance of mass in the stage environment set against the figure of the actor imparts a sense of our human value and power in the stage world (see Photo 11.5). Heavy objects can create a dense, oppressive space and even give a sense of mental weight or claustrophobia. Light ones can create an airy, open space, unleashing a feeling of freedom.

Ornamentation is a related idea that refers to the quantity of objects and detail on a set. Every inch of the set can be filled with patterned textiles, small objects, and set pieces, or the stage may be relatively bare and open. Each creates a different stage world and places different demands on the actors inhabiting the space.

Texture

We don't usually get to touch the objects on stage, but the textures of the design speak to us nonetheless through the play of light on surfaces. Sets often have fake textures—wooden pillars painted to resemble marble; styrofoam carved to look like brick. Whether real or false, these textures give a particular feel to the environment. Marble can be cold and stately on a government building. Wood can be rustic and homey like a log cabin. Steel is cold and harsh; velvet, soft, luxurious, and inviting. In Les Waters's 2001 staging of Charles Mee's *Big Love*, the stage floor was a springy trampoline. Actors repeatedly threw themselves on the floor at emotional moments and bounced back while speaking about the vagaries of love. The springy floor reflected how relationships can literally send you reeling.

Color

Color affects us powerfully. Simply changing the back wall of a theatre from black to white or yellow will completely alter our sense of the space and the associations it draws from us. Set designers think of the play of colors in relation to the actors' skin tones. There are warm colors—those in the red and yellow families including pinks and oranges—and cold colors—those in the blue, green, and white families. Warm

colors tend to create empathy for the characters, while cold colors distance us. A bright, garish red can be disturbing, just as a deep, lush gold can be welcoming. Edward Gorey's 1977 design for *Dracula* conjured up the count's castle using only black etched lines on a white surface and the occasional splash of red. In Chen Shizheng's *The Orphan of Zhao* performed at the Lincoln Center Summer Festival in 2003, the main playing area was a white square surrounded by a moat of red paint. The actors, barefoot, walked through the pool of red and painted the white stage floor with their red footprints. The final red-splattered canvas was an appropriate visual metaphor for this tale of bloody revenge.

The Set Designer's Materials
The Architectural or Natural Space

The theatrical space itself is always a component of the set designer's process. It defines possibilities and dimensions, and a set designer always works within some limitations. A theatre with a low ceiling has no fly space and cannot have flying backdrops. A theatre without any wing space cannot house set pieces for multiple scene changes. A black box can allow the set designer to play with spatial configurations by manipulating seating and shaping the playing area; a proscenium fixes the relationship of the set to the audience. An arena stage limits the use of walls and massive objects that would obscure sight lines. Sometimes set designers know a production will go on tour, so they design scenic elements to travel easily and be adaptable to different theatre spaces.

The architectural features of a space can become the unadorned design. French director Jacques Copeau was the first person in the modern era to look back to the iconic stage spaces of ancient Greece and Elizabethan England and revive the idea of a bare stage to showcase the actor and reconnect the theatre to the performer's vocal and physical power. In the open space the body's expressive power takes center stage.

A theatrical space may also have architectural or decorative elements that can enhance a set and become incorporated into the design. Peter Brook first staged his version of the Indian epic *The Mahabharata* outdoors in a stone quarry. When he moved it indoors, the bare, distressed back walls of the Bouffes du Nord theatre in Paris worked as an expressive backdrop. Transferred to New York, the distressed walls of the Harvey Theatre at the Brooklyn Academy of Music matched those of the Paris space and remain one of that theatre's identifying features (see the photo on page 19). When churches are transformed into theatres, the architectural gothic arches are often incorporated into set designs.

Many of the New York Shakespeare Festival productions at the open-air Delacorte Theatre in Central Park incorporate the lake and the surrounding greenery of the park as a backdrop for their designs as a perfect depiction of the world of many Shakespearean plays. Some set designers search for pre-existing settings in which to place a production. Several companies have made use of the New York urban environment as a stage set.

Photo 11.9

Walt Spangler's set for this production of Shakespeare's *Twelfth Night,* staged at the outdoor Delacorte Theatre in Central Park, uses the park's natural setting as part of its backdrop. The huge hull of the shipwreck that sets the action in motion looms in the background. An oriental carpet and pillows suffice to suggest the interior of Count Orsino's (Jimmy Smits) court. His velvet robe expresses his romantic nature. In contrast, Viola (Julia Stiles), disguised as a boy, wears an almost military uniform that hides her passion. Director, Brian Kulick; costumes, Miguel Angel Huidor; lighting, Michael Chybowski; the Public Theatre/ New York Shakespeare Festival, Central Park.
© *Michal Daniel, 2002*

Photo 11.10
Ralph Koltai's design for Shakespeare's *Twelfth Night* swathes the stage in rich colors that set a romantic mood. The square frame center stage, seemingly superimposed on the background and designed with an all too perfect tree and hillside, along with the staircase that appears improbably on the left, impart a sense of fantasy for this production's land of Illyria and its tale of love. Directed by Sorn Iversen at The Royal Theatre, Copenhagen. Compare this design concept with Photo 11.9.
© *Ralph Koltai*

Challenges and Choices

In various eras, audiences were drawn to the theatre primarily because of its visual spectacle. In today's visual culture, can set design exist alone as an art form?

Flats, Platforms, Drapes, Drops, and Scrims

Set elements do not need to meet the building codes of real objects for everyday use, but they must meet many fire and safety codes as well as union regulations. They only need to be as fully constructed or as sturdy as production use requires. The theatre offers a variety of special scenic elements habitually used as modular components of scenic design. Set designers can completely transform the theatrical space using flats, platforms, drapes, **drops**, and **scrims** that mask the architectural elements of the theatre itself as they configure a new environment.

Flats have traditionally been the building blocks of stage construction. These single units of canvas or other material stretched over a wooden frame can be connected to each other to create walls that outline an entire room or building. They can be painted any color and to resemble any number of textures and materials. With flats, set designers create structures that are light enough to move into the space, but strong enough to last for the run of a show. **Platforms** give dimension to the acting area by providing different levels and isolating locations. A platform brought into an empty space can itself serve as a stage.

Drapes can be used as decorative elements on stage. Hung across the upstage wall, they can turn the theatre into a neutral space. Drapes can also be used to outline the playing area. Black drapes can mask lighting or scenic elements and conceal actors before they make their entrances.

Drops (large pieces of painted canvas hung at the back of the stage) are used to set particular locales. The Cheek-by-Jowl Company's production of *Duchess of Malfi* used a bare stage with narrow fabric panels to delineate various scenes and locations.

A *scrim* is a special kind of cloth or gauze that allows light to pass through it. When light shines on it from the front, the cloth appears opaque. When light shines on it from the back, it becomes transparent and can magically reveal scenic elements it once obscured. This provides a clever means of creating magical transformations. A painted scrim can reveal different settings and scenes with a simple lighting change.

Furniture and Properties

Furniture and *properties* (or "props") make spaces specific and relate the scale of the actor to the set. A set depicting a realistic apartment or a store may require extensive furnishings and props and a great deal of dressing to make it reflect the lives of the characters who live and work in the space. Furniture can also be used in a symbolic manner. A throne can evoke an entire palace, a cot can indicate a jail cell or an army barracks, and a giant flower can suggest a garden. Set pieces may be specially constructed for the show, or bought new or secondhand. They may be rented or come from the company's stock of furniture and be repainted or restyled for a particular production design.

IN PERSPECTIVE

DOGUGAESHI: SET TRANSFORMATION AS PERFORMANCE

Through his own artistic pursuit of nonlinear, abstract puppet performance, American puppeteer Basil Twist encountered a Japanese theatrical tradition in which watching sets change is the main attraction. Twist is best known for his award-winning piece *Symphonie Fantastique*, in which hidden puppeteers create visually compelling images to the music of Hector Berlioz by moving scarves and other objects in a huge tank of water. After seeing a performance of *dogugaeshi* at a puppet exhibit in Paris in 1997, where a black and white monitor played a brief film of Japanese screens opening and closing, Twist traveled to Japan to visit those who still perform this endangered art and then created his own performance, which pays homage to the tradition as it creatively reimagines it.

Dogugaeshi literally means "changing stage sets" in Japanese. It is a form of theatre developed on the island of Awaji and in nearby Tokushima prefecture as part of a broader regional folk tradition of puppet performance. Large puppet figures play in front of beautifully painted sliding screen backdrops, which move along tracks set into the stage at various levels of depth to reveal new scenic backgrounds. At intermission, the movement of sliding screens and revealed sets is offered as its own entertainment, accompanied by candlelight, the music of the three-stringed *shamisen*, and the pounding of wooden clappers.

In *dogugaeshi* up to eighty-eight screens move in and out of a small puppet stage, in various configurations, opening on to new images, receding upstage or advancing downstage. One of the most startling effects is produced by a series of screens that act as wings and backdrop to create a perspective view of a large *tatami* room. The number of heavy and intricately painted mulberry paper screens used in a performance expresses the theatre troupe's prosperity and reflects the overall sense of illusion created by the puppet theatre. In the half-light of evening, *dogugaeshi* brings the spectator to a dreamlike state of demi-consciousness, much as Japan's *noh* theatre does, by providing a plane of associative images—plums, cherry trees, dragons, and phoenixes drawn from Japanese myth and

poetry.[1] The Inukai Theatre, declared an important tangible asset in Japan in 1998, holds the largest collection of painted screens for puppet shows or *fusuma-e*, with 132 pieces, some reportedly one hundred years old.

Twist's *Dogugaeshi*, which premiered in November 2004 at the Japan Society of New York, reenacts the form's near demise during World War II, when puppeteers sold off sacred puppets and performance equipment to stay alive, or burned them to keep warm. It also documents the tradition's recent rejuvenation. Setting a monitor within the frame of the puppet stage, Twist begins with the actual black and white film of the tradition as it was originally performed that he first saw in France. After this brief introduction, the live action begins with a shadow puppet representation of performers hauling their equipment up a hillside and building an outdoor stage, recalling old performance practices. A parade of sliding screens ensues, followed by a recreation of the traditional perspective-set *tatami* room in all its glory. The show is accompanied by various types of recorded music and the live music of *shamisen* composer and performer Tanaka Yumiko.

Soon the perspective set begins to tremble. Screens go flying, and sheets of screen paper fall from the top of the stage. Flaps turn over to transform the picture-perfect room into an image of destruction and decay. A large hand puppet of a seemingly magical white fox, introduced earlier, moves in and out of the distressed screens like a spirit in search of a home.

The scene then changes to modern-day Japan, mixing live and recorded action with a landscape of cutout, shadow puppet skyscrapers superimposed with video images and a soundtrack of television babble. A video projection of local women from the region where *dogugaeshi* is performed follows. Dressed in the rural outfits of this seaside area, they all talk at once, pouring out memories of the *dogugaeshi* shows they saw in their youths—the phoenixes, the views of Mt. Fuji, the candles.

The scene then returns to live action without projection, with the demolished *tatami* room partially

1. *Jane Marie Law,* Puppets of Nostalgia: The Life, Death, and Rebirth of the Awaji Ningyo Tradition *(Princeton, NJ: Princeton University Press, 1997), 199–200.*

restored. A row of candles slides in and, starting from within the frame of the *tatami* room, then moving to encompass the entire set, a full *dogugaeshi* is performed, with screens moving in and out, revealing ever more marvelous colorful patterns and images—new doors continually opening onto new vistas. In one memorable moment, a screen of a bright green bamboo forest breaks up into individual panels. Half of them turn sideways to reveal an orange tiger peering through its bamboo cover. The performance ends with a continuous flow of colorful screens receding upstage. Within the smaller frames at the back,

Twist recreates a live version of the film that began the show with screens the size of the television monitor painted in black and white. White gauze curtains that parted to open the show are each consecutively drawn to a close. Through the visual beauty and movement of panels and screens, the audience has been taken on a journey through the recent history of *dogugaeshi* and into a realm of dream, imagination, and memory. The addition of video footage gives a contemporary turn to this tradition of visual imagery as theatrical spectacle.

Screens opening one after another show a continually receding perspective in Basil Twist's *Dogugaeshi*, Japan Society New York.
© *William Irwin—IrwinPhoto.com*

Photo 11.13
In *Metamorphosis* a large pool of water serves as the main playing area in the set designed by Daniel Ostling. Actors work with the movement, feel, and experience of real water. This natural element brings a vitality to the action and is the perfect setting for the primal, emotional relationships captured in the play's tales from ancient Greek mythology. Seen here are Anjali Bhimani and Chris Kipiniak. Written and directed by Mary Zimmerman; costumes, Mara Blumenthal; lighting, T. J. Gerckens.
© *Joan Marcus*

Technology

As we will see in Chapter 14, the newest technologies have always found a place in theatre design, and today high-tech equipment is becoming an ever more integral part of set design, from the conceptualization and visualization of design ideas to the construction of set pieces and the regulation of their stage movement. From turntables and treadmills to screen projections and interactive computer imagery, the set designer's ability to use technical tools for scenic effects continues to grow.

Other Materials

Set designers adopt many materials for the stage, drawing on their evocative qualities. Natural elements, such as water, earth, and fire reconnect us with our organic nature. They are manipulable, but don't necessarily conform to the dictates of a director. Their very reality captivates us with its potential for surprise and subversion of the theatrical frame. Mary Zimmerman used a pool of water as the central image and playing area of her *Metamorphosis*, based on tales from Ovid. Actors could dive into its depth, wade across it, and float over it on plastic floats. The pool represented transformation, rebirth, and the power of the gods to create chaos and offer redemption as expressed in the ancient myths. Peter Brook's *Carmen* created a metaphorical bullring and filled the stage with sand. Constructivist designers in the 1920s used steel and wire to create sets that spoke of technology and industry. For Ralph Lemon's dance piece *Geography*, set designer Nari Ward used wooden palettes within a structure of plastic for a backdrop that reflected the idea of commerce and transport. In each of these cases, the material of the design was a source of meaning and significance within the production concept.

Set designers create a world where the director's vision can be realized. Never before have they had such a broad palette from which to draw. Today, their images may be transcultural. Their materials are both natural and synthetic, and their styles may be traditional, eclectic, or innovative. Their collaborative role has grown. Whatever the result, however, the set always awaits the live actor to breathe life into the design.

KEY IDEAS

- The set designer is the visual interpreter of a performance text. A good set design is deeply connected with the total production concept.
- A theatrical set facilitates the action of the play, establishes time and place, creates mood, provides an environment that embodies the character's lives, helps tell the story, presents a visual metaphor for the director's concept, defines style, determines the relationship between the audience and the dramatic action, and expresses the director's point of view on the text.

- Set designers collaborate with the director and other designers in developing a theatrical design. The process begins with a careful reading of the text, discussion, and research.
- Set designers imagine the set in concrete terms, creating sketches, storyboards, ground plans, and a scale model.
- Set designers work closely with technical staff to make the design a reality on stage.
- The stage composition directs the audience's gaze and guides their interpretation of the visual elements.
- Set designers manipulate line, mass, texture, and color to convey meaning and compose the stage space.
- Set designers create sets using the architectural features of a theatre, flats, platforms, drapes, drops, scrims, furniture, properties, and new technologies.

Dressing the Character

Designer Constance Hoffman's head-to-toe costumes and makeup help Annalee Jeffries and David Patrick Kelly make the fantastic transformation into reptiles in Edward Albee's *Seascape* at the Hartford Stage Company, directed by Mark Lamos. Note the texture of the costumes.

© T. Charles Erickson

What we wear tells others who we are: our tastes, habits, social class, profession, gender, and sexuality. Clothing changes the way we inhabit our bodies and consequently alters the way others perceive us. When we dress for work or a night out on the town, we are making choices, often unconsciously, about how we want to present ourselves and what we hope our clothes will say about us. In the theatre costume designers make such decisions for imaginary characters. Each choice they make defines the character for the audience while contributing to a unified production style.

Costuming and the Actor

The seemingly magical power of costume to shape our identity is a major part of role-play in the theatre. We've all had the experience of putting on a piece of clothing and feeling transformed. Slipping into a sexy dress inspires us to walk in a sultry manner; a suit and tie make us more aware of posture and bearing; a certain pair of shoes can make us feel athletic or restrained. Actors use important costume pieces—a suit jacket, a long skirt, or a tight corset—to feel the character in their bodies. In some situations they rehearse in costume elements or makeup, so that their performances grow out of a psychophysical understanding of character.

For designs to be both expressive and functional, costumers need to consider not only the director's concept, but also what physical actions the actor will be performing on stage, the psychological nature of the character, as well as the limitations and potential of the actor. The living, moving actor is ultimately the canvas on which costume designs are realized. Actors' body shapes, size, and skin color, as well as their physical mannerisms and feelings, affect how a costume will appear and be worn. Costumers therefore work more closely with performers than do other members of the design team. Sometimes costume reveals or supports the actor's own physique, and sometimes it attempts to transform it. In either case, the actor's body is always at issue; it is the material substance that must work in concert with costume design.

Actors, of course, are not just brute material, but psychological beings with deep feelings about their own bodies. They have strongly expressed preferences about what makes them look good or feel comfortable, and what clothing inhibits or frees their movement. When creating characters, they formulate strong opinions about what those individuals would wear. Costume designers assist in bringing the director's vision and the actors' personal sentiments together so performers can act with ease and confidence, while being faithful to the production's artistic goals.

Costumes help actors express character through gesture. Actors play with their clothes and accessories, integrating them into stage business and body language. Specific details such as a scarf, a tie, or the placement of buttons can offer actors the character-defining choices of tossing a scarf flamboyantly over a shoulder, loosening a tie, or undoing a constricting or revealing button.

Goals of Costume Design

■ **Establishing Time and Place.** Clothes can immediately suggest the period in which a scene takes place and with it the feeling of a cultural moment. A long skirt with a tight corset points to the sexual repression of the Victorian period, while a miniskirt reflects the more permissive 1960s. When a director chooses to set a play in an era other than the one indicated by the author, clothing helps situate the production. Gestapo uniforms and formal evening dress placed Sir Ian McKellen's *Richard III* in the era just before World War II, although the language remained Elizabethan.

History IN PERSPECTIVE

CROSS-DRESSING

What does it mean when a man appears on the stage dressed in women's clothes or a woman in men's clothes? This simple question opens what has become in recent years a library's worth of criticism about how different cultures in different times and places have understood and represented gender. Because theatre is a place where we engage in role-play, how we play at being male or female on stage reflects how we define and understand gender roles in society at large. The theatre can replicate commonly held social ideas about males and females or put them into question. **Cross-dressing**, by its very nature, implies crossing the boundaries of what is accepted as appropriate for one gender or another. Today's costumers need to confront these social expectations as they select and design clothes that portray gender on stage.

Throughout the world cultural views about how men and women should behave are portrayed in the clothing they wear. Sometimes cross-dressing on stage presents a complete disguise in which an actor completely assumes a role type. This is the case for male *onnagata* performers in *kabuki* who present idealized female characters. (See Photo 5.9) The image they create through makeup, costuming, and studied movements are so complete that it is impossible to discern the male actor inside the kimono. Tradition asserts that women characters in *kabuki* are presented so perfectly that no real woman actor could do justice to the roles. The female form portrayed by men on stage, although astonishingly unlike the male actors themselves, is also unlike any real woman.

The tables are turned on *kabuki* in Takarazuka, a twentieth-century Japanese theatrical company, popular for its musicals, in which women play all the roles. Female Takarazuka performers play such idealized, romantic male leads that the male role performers are the true box-office draws for Takarazuka's devoted fans, who are primarily women.

Instead of allowing an actor's gender to dissolve inside the role, cross-dressing can also juxtapose the gender of the costume and that of the performer. This is the case for the tradition of the "drag queen," whose presentation of "female" is so exaggerated it is denaturalized. Audience members are continually aware of the tension be-

tween the costume and the actor, the role and the player. On stage it is not always the case that "the clothes make the man," or woman.

At different periods in history, cross-dressing on stage has channeled different kinds of sexual desire. In Elizabethan England, the belief that it was immodest and immoral for women to display themselves publicly led to young boys playing all the female roles. Recent scholars have examined the homoerotic tension that existed in these performances. This tension was further complicated when boys played women who disguise themselves as men, such as Viola in *Twelfth Night* or Rosalind in *As You Like It*, allowing a male homoerotic relationship to be played out openly on stage.

During the English Restoration, women appeared for the first time on the public stages of England. Beautiful young actresses were often called on to play **breeches roles**, in which they played young men dressed in short pants or "breeches." These male accoutrements allowed male audience members to ogle the actresses' alluring ankles, a taboo sight in society outside the theatre.

Although several contemporary theatre companies and directors such as Edward Hall and Declan Donnellan have experimented with all-male casts in Shakespearean productions, we cannot recreate the experience of Elizabethan cross-dressing in the modern era. Today when women are permitted on stage the sight of men in women's costumes brings with it different associations and values. On stage dressing male or female comments on the existing social hierarchies and power structure associated with gender and has implications in the realm of sexual desire. Today's costumers need to be aware of the notions of gender, power, and desire inherent in every garment they choose.

Modern audiences grow accustomed to cross-dressing as the all-male cast in Edward Hall's production of Shakespeare's *A Midsummer Night's Dream* convincingly portray both male and female roles. As the performance goes on, it becomes easy to understand how the Elizabethan public accepted this stage convention. Designed by Michael Pavelka at the Brooklyn Academy of Music, Harvey Theater, New York.
© *Richard Termine*

Although designers research historical costume detail, they are rarely completely faithful to period style. Stage fashion always seeks a compromise between accuracy and contemporary audience tastes and knowledge. Particular aspects of a costume may be exaggerated to depict class and social role in an unfamiliar world. Compromises are also made for the actor's comfort and to facilitate the stage action. Stage dress also indicates the time of day and the time of year, reflecting social and seasonal conventions. Tuxedos and long gowns suggest evening; business clothes and briefcase evoke the workday. Sweaters, scarves, and gloves tell us it is winter; bathing suits, shorts, and sandals bring thoughts of summer or the tropics.

Costumes can tell us if we are in Mexico or China, in a hospital or a hotel. When sets are minimal, costuming often fills in information and implies settings in the spectator's imagination. Bowling shirts and shoes set the scene in a bowling alley, even if there are no lanes or pins. A silk kimono can place a scene in Japan, even if the stage is bare.

■ **Revealing the Essence of Character.** Clothes are very personal and can become a second skin. They are worn close to the body and are transformed through movements and habits. Costumes become a part of who characters are. Costumes define a character's identity for the audience. Consider the dress of Stella and Blanche, the sisters in *A Streetcar Named Desire*. Stella's acceptance of her working-class life and Blanche's flamboyance and desperate need to be perceived as wealthy and desirable would be reflected in every article of their clothing and accessories.

Costumers express what is distinctive about each character through the smallest details. A simple business suit is transformed by the cut, color, lapel size, vent, number of buttons, and cuffs. The addition of accessories such as ties, shirts, ascots, and jewelry can make a statement about each character's personal psychology.

■ **Setting the Social and Cultural Milieu.** Costumes are always read within a social context. Presentations of social and economic class, of sophistication and innocence are particular to time, place, and situation. Designers don't conceive of a costume in isolation but attempt to describe an entire world and what it considers normal, outrageous, delightful, or suspicious. A character in an old T-shirt and torn jeans is unremarkable at a

Challenges and Choices

When dressing someone in traditional dress, must costume designers abide by all the codes of dress, all the costume elements? Is it disrespectful to take only the elements one needs from another culture?

Photo 12.1
Large feathered hats, shawls, corseted tops, and long skirts with trim set the 1912 era for the musical *The Music Man*. Note the variety in patterns, styles, and hat adornments that give each character an individual look within the period style. Directed by Susan Stroman; scenic design by Thomas Lynch; costumes by William Ivey Long; lighting by Peter Kaczorowski; at the Neil Simon Theatre, New York.
© *Joan Marcus*

baseball game, but conspicuous at a corporate board meeting, and the audience could read much into such an appearance. The way a character's costume relates to the social milieu says volumes about that individual's position and emotional state. In productions of *Hamlet*, the king, queen, and courtiers are often costumed in splendid regalia, whereas Hamlet is in simple black mourning clothes, setting him emotionally apart from other members of the court. William Wycherly's (1633–1688) Restoration comedy, *The Country Wife* (1675) puts Pinchwife, a Puritan from the countryside, in the midst of fashionable, libertine London society. His conservative dress separates the spoil-sport Pinchwife from the fun-loving social world.

- **Telling the Story.** Sherlock Holmes could look at an ink-stained glove or a pair of mud-spattered boots and trace a person's path on a particular day. Clothing and accessories all tell a tale: A character's threadbare coat in the first act and elegant dress in the second depicts a change in fortune. A tear in a shirt may be the outcome of a barroom brawl. A lipstick stain on a collar is the trace of an illicit affair. Garments and the state they are in tell us where characters have been, what they have been up to, and how they have fared. Costumes chart changes in the character's circumstances.

- **Demonstrating Relationships among Characters.** Costumes articulate social hierarchies, family connections, political antagonisms, emotional relationships, and other distinctions (see the photo on page 325). Just as members of a club or gang might wear the same jacket, costumes can imply union, separation, or shared status. Complementary colors or patterns can emotionally unite two young lovers in the spectator's eyes before the script ever brings them together. Military uniforms with medals and stripes imply rank status and relationship. Clashing colors can distinguish warring armies.

- **Specifying Characters' Social and Professional Roles.** Costumes can define profession or occupation. We identify doctors by their lab coats, policemen by their blue uniforms, and chefs by their puffy white toques. Such dress can be realistic or iconic—representing a category of people.

- **Defining Style.** Costumes can create a representational or presentational stage world. They may be realistic or creations of fantasy or exaggeration. They can stimulate associations with historical periods or help to create a mood and point of view. Because actors comport themselves differently in realistic dress than in elaborate theatrical clothes, costumes will affect their acting and help them contribute to a production's unified style.

- **Meeting the Practical Needs of the Production.** A text may call for a particular costume piece to take part in the action: a locket to display a picture, a pocket to conceal a letter, a hood to act as a disguise. Designers accommodate these needs so that clothes

Photo 12.2
Costume designer Fabio Toblini sets a production style and brings a sense of comic whimsy to the Courtesan (Christina Baldwin Fletcher) by enhancing the stylized clothes with the absurd additions of a bee hive bustle, complete with bees, and a butterfly hair adornment. Shakespeare's *Comedy of Errors* directed by Dominique Serrand; lighting design by Marcus Dilliard; sound design by Scott W. Edwards; at the Guthrie Theater, Minneapolis.
© Michal Daniel, 2002

can play their parts. In Eugene Labiche's *The Italian Straw Hat*, the madcap action revolves around a hat; when a horse eats one, it places a young wife's fidelity in question; when a replacement hat appears, it puts her jealous husband's mind to rest. In *Twelfth Night*, Malvolio reads a forged letter expressing Viola's desire to see him in yellow stockings worn "cross-gartered." His costume must fit the description in the text to serve the comic action.

The physical demands of a production are a primary consideration in costume design, and all choices must facilitate the actors' blocking. Costumes need to move with the actors, allowing them to bend or stretch, do dance or acrobatics, or any other movement required by the staging. Costumes are three-dimensional objects that travel with the actors across the stage and must offer the audience views from all angles. Some stage costumes need to accommodate quick changes or comic stage business and are designed to facilitate split-second timing.

The Costume Designer's Process

Costume designers come to an understanding of the characters and their world through a close analysis of the text, discussions with the director and the rest of the production's creative team, and research. Costume designers and directors share ideas about how story, concept, and characterization can be realized through costume. They may offer each other specific images through photos and paintings that suggest the feeling they want to capture on stage.

Before the first meeting, costume designers read the text with a particular eye on character analysis. They try to figure out what makes the characters tick and how they function in the text. They also note any practical requirements for clothing or personal props and any information that reveals location, period, time of day, and season. Costumers note the number of costume changes required for each character as well as any potential difficulties.

A costume designer's visual research serves as a springboard for discussion and the inspiration for ideas that develop over time. They consult books on period style, artworks, magazines, and other visual resources to learn the fashion of different times and places. Research can reveal specific period details, the range of a style, and images that stimulate new ways of thinking about the production's look or visual motifs. Visual research is an important part of exploring and exchanging ideas with a director.

Sketches help designers communicate ideas to the director. Simple *thumbnail sketches* of each character help find a direction for the evolving costumes. *Final sketches* show each costume in detail and present all the clothes and accessories the designer envisions. *Fabric swatches* attached to the sketches for the director's approval communicate as nearly as possible the precise color, pattern, and texture of the fabric the designer intends to use (see Photo 12.3). Costume designers also consider other visual elements when making choices. They think about how a particular color or texture of fabric will look under certain lights and how their choices will mesh with the set and directorial style. Sketches can give a clear idea of how the actors will look together on stage and how costume will define their relationships.

Costume designers usually ask to attend a rehearsal as soon as the cast is set because they must adjust designs to the performers' body types. Costume designers work closely with the actors throughout the process. They take performers' measurements and see them in fittings. Actors are apt to share their views on their costumes and express the need for changes or additional items. If actors are particularly uncomfortable with an item of clothing, costume designers will usually try to accommodate their needs. Some-

Photo 12.3
Maggie Morgan's sketch and final costume for Claudia Shear's *Dirty Blonde* directed by Barbara Bosch at the Sacramento Theatre Company, California. This Mae West outfit is worn by two characters in the play. The researched images attached to the sketch show Mae West's actual garb and serve to inspire the design. The attached fabric swatch gives a precise sense of the color, texture, and ornamentation of the fabric intended for the dress. The designer's sketch includes accessories—hats and jewelry—as part of the overall visual image of the character.
Sketch reprinted with permission from Maggie Morgan.
Photo © Steve Kolb

times dealing with demanding actors can be a costumer's challenge. Costumers attend rehearsals to see how actors move on stage; a designer may rethink a tight short skirt or billowing coat if an actress has to climb a ladder or engage in a physical fight.

Once designers and directors finalize designs, the costume designer begins to assemble the costumes, working closely with costume shop personnel, who carry out the designs. Costumes can be *built* from scratch in a costume shop, *bought* from a store, *pulled* from the company's stock, or *rented* from a rental house. Building new costumes for all the actors in a production can be costly and time-consuming. For many productions, costumers build one or two special items and create others from existing pieces, adapting them by tailoring, dyeing, distressing, or removing or adding ornamentation to reflect the original design concept. A **costume plot** helps designers keep track of all the items each character wears in every scene. The costume designer is responsible for managing the time, labor, and cost involved in costume construction and for overseeing the purchase of materials and the progress of work in the costume shop. The amount of assistance the designer has in this process depends on the financial constraints of a particular production.

After a series of fittings, the costumes are finished. A **dress parade** can offer the director and designer an opportunity to see all the actors together in costume under stage lights. Costume designers make sure the clothes fit, move well, and look good together. Dress rehearsals put the costumes into action, often revealing where practical problems might arise so costume designers take notes on final adjustments they must make before opening night. Actors are usually anxious to complete their character portrayal through costume, and this is an important moment for pulling the production together. The costume designer's work is finished once the show opens, but a wardrobe staff

IN PERSPECTIVE

In Their Own Words

LINDA CHO

Since graduating from the Yale School of Drama, Canadian designer Linda Cho has been working around the United States and in Asia at such venues as the New York Public Theatre, the Arena Stage in Washington, D.C., the old Globe Theatre in San Diego, the Dallas Theater Center, and the National Theatre in Taipei, Taiwan. Her work has been nominated for several important awards.

■ **Can you talk about the role of research in your process?**

Research is the backbone of any design. Over the years I have collected a basic library of costume books, and generally I begin there to get a visual and historical overview of the period. In addition to the look of any period, I try to understand the basic political, social, and economic landscape of the time. I find this is helpful in putting the characters in context and in better understanding their relationships. Other resources I find useful are paintings to find popular colors of an era, or cultural interests like the interest in Orientalism at the turn of the century. Sculpture provides insight into line and texture, and crafts like quilts or stained glass give you a feel for materials. Photographs of actual people help to understand how the garments were worn and how people moved in them, which is sometimes even more interesting than the actual garments themselves. Armed with images and information, I can take the next step in the design and tailor the costume to the characters. Sometimes the research is a point of departure and the design is abstracted from the original. Even if the intent is a fantastic made-up world, I try to ground the design in concrete research.

■ **How do you deal with racial and ethnic stereotypes when they provide a visual shorthand for the audience?**

In our twenty-first-century global village and particularly in North America's multicultural society, I think the average audience member has been exposed to many different cultures and is able to identify the differences between different racial groups. Having said that, I think that there is no need to portray characters as broad stereotypes unless of course the play calls for some sort of parody. I think it is very important when dealing with ethnic characters in

a production to research the nuances of that culture and to get it right. Authenticity just makes the design more interesting and may even serve to educate the audience.

■ **How do you negotiate your ideal costume design with the reality of the actor's body type?**

I consider the costume sketch a first step, not the final step in a design process. The sketch is a general framework, and it is open to change depending on the situation. Whenever possible, I try to get a general idea of the actor's body type before I render the final designs. When I do not get that information, if I can manipulate the body with padding, corseting, and such, and if it is appropriate and the actor and director want to go in that direction, we essentially change the appearance of the actor from the inside out. In some instances I will work from the outside in by tweaking the design, perhaps changing hem lengths, necklines, or adding sleeves to best suit the actor. Sometimes body type is not the motivating factor in changing a design. If the actor who has been cast is different from how I had imagined the character and brings something new and different to the table, I will speak to the director and actor and adjust accordingly. On occasion, I have completely redesigned a costume to work with how the actor is playing a particular role. Ultimately, this is a collaborative medium and if I cannot get the actor to a place of comfort and confidence either through conversations or adjustments, I feel I am not doing my job.

■ **Is there a design project that you've done that you thought was particularly memorable, and why?**

For me, one of the most memorable shows was *Pericles* at the Old Globe Theatre in San Diego. The show was abstracted from the ancient Greco-Roman era; also we looked at the images of Gustave Dore's biblical etchings as our point of departure. *Pericles* can be a very confusing story, and we took pains to make each of the six kingdoms as distinctive as possible through the use of color and silhouette. I really enjoyed the challenge of executing such a wide range of costumes, from the daughter of Antiochus in a decadent snake-like gown whose train served as both cape and tail, to the whores of Mytilene dressed in the colors of rotting citrus fruit with their sagging, misshapen bodies. The goddess Diana was wearing a white gown with a twenty-foot train, which was gracefully lifted into the air by a dozen actors like a giant sail. It was a breathtaking image thanks to a successful collaboration with director Darko Tresnjak, who really takes the time to work with costumes to use them to their best effect.

■ **Do you feel a designer brings their personal psychology including race, ethnicity, and gender to the design process? If so, how?**

I don't think you can help but bring who you are into a design. I think the influences are endless. In terms of race, I was born in Korea and was brought up in Canada in a multicultural environment, and certainly that had an influence on my tastes. I have a keen interest in Asian culture. I have borrowed ideas from sources such as Japanese *kabuki*, Korean *ponsori*, and Chinese opera on numerous occasions, even for non-Asian productions. For example, in a production of *Orpheus and Eurydice* at the Virginia Opera, set in Europe circa 1910s, I used the *kabuki* technique of *hikinuki* (which is a way of transforming a kimono instantly on stage by removing basting threads along the sleeves) for Eurydice's gown when she comes back to life.

Often my personal psychology manifests itself subconsciously; choices I make in line, color, and textures probably have something to do with my upbringing. I know I have been asked to design certain shows because I am Asian. Initially, I found this disturbing; I didn't want people to think that was the limit of my range of abilities as a designer. But the more I thought about it, I realized that my personal history gives me firsthand knowledge about certain things, and that is what makes me unique as a designer.

■ **You have also designed for film. What is the difference between designing costumes for film versus costumes for theatrical production?**

I found the biggest difference between designing costumes for film and theatre is time. In theatre you can design several shows at the same time. The average regional

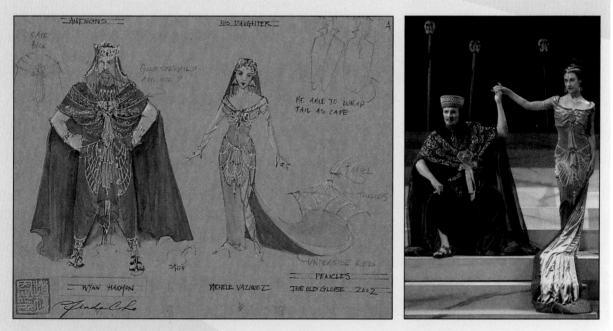

Sketch and final costumes of Antiochus and his daughter designed by Linda Cho for Shakespeare's *Pericles*, directed by Darko Tresnjak at the Old Globe Theatre, San Diego, California. Note how the costumes define the characters as a pair through the inversion of the red and gold color scheme and through the parallel details and ornamentation. The daughter's long train is made even more regal when draped along the steps of the stage, a connection between costume and set that helps express character. The sketch includes notations about how the tail of the costume can be used as a cape and other notes on color and construction to help the designer communicate her ideas fully to the director and costume shop personnel.
Sketch reprinted with permission from Linda Cho. Photo © Craig Schwartz

(continues)

Artists

IN PERSPECTIVE (CONTINUED)

show takes about one month for design and one month for production, so you can be in the design phase for one show while in the production stage for another. In film the schedule is intense and requires months of uninterrupted attention; shooting days can begin as early as 5 A.M. and end at midnight to take advantage of sunlight and to get to multiple locations.

Another difference is the amount of time you get with actors. In theatre you often get three fittings. In film, sometimes extras are cast only days before their shoot date and the only fitting you get is that same day; design decisions have to be made quickly on the spot because there is a constant pressure of time.

■ Is there a play you long to design, and why?

I would love to design the opera *Madame Butterfly*. I remember seeing it for the very first time at the Canadian Opera Company when I was about ten years old. My parents got season tickets and I started going regularly from a young age. I loved going to the opera; I loved getting dressed up, the big sparkly chandelier in the lobby, the little binoculars, eating a Toblerone chocolate at intermission. As far as I was concerned, the actual opera only played a small part in the event. In the earlier days, the COC didn't have surtitles, and I had trouble following the story and even more trouble staying awake. But all that changed when I saw *Madame Butter-*

fly. When Butterfly killed herself, you would have thought she had stabbed me by the way I cried and cried. I loved that production, I still remember it, and I would love to design it myself one day.

■ What advice would you give to young prospective designers?

I think it is important to remember to treat all your collaborators with the utmost respect—not just your director and fellow designers, which goes without saying, but also your drapers, wig masters, craftspeople, and actors, who are experts at what they do. If you can listen to suggestions and welcome input, it can only make your designs better. The sketch, as I mentioned earlier, is a starting place; there are many steps and people involved in getting a costume to the stage.

We are lucky to be theater artists. We chose to be costume designers because we love what we do, and very few can truly say as much. However, this is a world that will probably not pay extravagantly and will require sacrifice and hard work, so try to truly enjoy what you do, for at the end of the day the privilege of doing our art is the ultimate payoff. I remember in graduate school, someone in our class cried (which we all did at least once) over a brutal critique. Ming Cho Lee, our professor, patted her on the back and said, "Don't cry; it is only theatre." Words to live by.

Source: Used with permission from Linda Cho.

Challenges and Concerns

Do costumes need to reflect the designer's and the audience's social stereotypes in order to communicate?

remains on deck during the run of the show to help launder and repair the clothes for each performance.

Principles of Composition

The principles of composition discussed in set design—focus, balance, proportion, rhythm, and unity—are applicable to costume design as well. Styles and fashions of different periods suggest particular compositions that may circumscribe the costume designer's work. Principles of composition guide the creation of both a single character's dress and an ensemble of costumes.

Costume composition directs the audience's attention to particular parts of the body. A ruff at the neck draws attention to the head. Trim on the sleeves sets off the hands. A low-cut neckline pulls our eyes to cleavage. Composition also tells us whom to look at on stage, perhaps bringing our focus to central characters over secondary roles with the use of color or adornment.

Costumes can change our impression of the body's natural proportions and play with the body's natural symmetry. In the sixteenth century men wore puffy sleeves that gave bulk to their torsos and stockings that emphasized the trimness of their legs. Women who wore wide sleeves matched by a wide skirt had a more symmetrical look. Empire dresses are slender with high waistlines that divide the body in two unequal portions just under the breasts rather than at the natural waist. Bustles created the impression of an arched spine and a protruding derrière.

When creating a world of costumes, designers consider the relative proportions of different costumes within an overall scheme. A costume or set of costumes can show repetition or variation in motifs to create a rhythm. Touches of lace at the neck, the sleeves, the waist, and the hem can unite the various actors on stage. An absence of complementary elements can create a tense stage world.

Costume designers articulate compositions through their use of line, texture, and color displayed on the body in motion. These elements draw on the audience's personal and cultural associations and sensory reactions.

Line

Line refers to the **silhouette** or overall shape of a costume. We associate silhouettes with specific historical periods, but inherent in particular silhouettes are associated social ideas. In the 1950s, American women wore long flair skirts, layers of petticoats, pointed bras, and high heels that impeded freedom and movement. The line emphasized almost to the point of caricature the hourglass shape, depicting a false idea of femininity that imprisoned women in traditional roles during a sexually repressed decade. Compare that profile with the short flapper dresses of the liberated 1920s that marked women's newly acquired right to vote and with the miniskirts of the late 1960s and early 1970s women's liberation movement. Women's silhouettes can express social restraint through corsets, high necklines, long skirts, and bustles. Costume line can also draw our eyes in a particular direction. Elizabethan men's garments draw the eyes to the codpiece, and the fashion of seventeenth-century Europe enhanced women's cleavage.

Texture

The feel of the surface of a costume affects how it catches the stage light and can accentuate the form and style of a garment, especially if folds are an important design feature. Thick textures such as velvet absorb light, while smooth ones such as satin reflect it. Texture also influences how garments move on stage, whether they are flowing like silk or stiff like felt or burlap. In turn this affects the actors' physical actions. Textures help define the character's social, emotional, and physical state. The actor's skin is set against the feel of the fabric, so the audience reads the two textures together, eliciting cultural and sensory responses. Satin and velvet seem opulent and give a sense of wealth. Wool can feel cozy and warm and may remind us of sitting by a fire on a snowy evening. Burlap is rough and scratchy and may bring with it an association of poverty, earthiness, or discomfort. Polyester can seem kitschy.

History IN PERSPECTIVE

MODERN DESIGN AND THE BALLETS RUSSES

The innovative dance company, the Ballets Russes, was founded in Saint Petersburg in 1898 by Sergei Diaghilev (1872–1929). Breaking from the story-telling tradition of classical ballet, the troupe presented a dance form capable of evoking pure emotion through form and movement within a total artwork in which set, costumes, movement, music, and dance worked together to induce specific emotional states. Their work provided an inspirational source for today's modern dance. What Wagner had envisioned as a unified production bound through music and opera, the Ballets Russes actually achieved through dance. To compliment these abstract ballets, designs moved away from the conventional pictorial realism of painted perspective wings, drops, and flats into the realm of abstract art. Many of the greatest modern painters of the day—Pablo Picasso, Henri Matisse, Juan Miró, Georges Braque—among a host of other luminaries of the art world participated, as well as the great Russian designer Léon Bakst (1866–1924).

Using such dazzling new talents to create sets and costumes, Diaghilev hoped to move away from the staid tradition of nineteenth-century European stage design. The stage technology for the Ballets Russes' scenic work was, with the exception of a few sculptural sets, not revolutionary. Old-fashioned wings and drops were the standard, but what was painted on them was revolutionary. These great artists who were revolutionizing the art world provided painted backdrops using vibrant color, stylized composition, abstraction, geometric forms, and either forced or flattened perspective that made these drops unique works of art. As dazzling as the sets were, the company's designers were most revolutionary in the realm of costume. These costumes not only clothed the human form, they transformed it into sculptural elements of abstract art. Never before had costumes been so specifically rendered to unite with the other elements on stage in the creation of mood, form, and feeling.

Bakst's designs for a series of ballets based on ancient Greek themes used images from ancient Greek vase paintings that also served as the inspiration for the choreography, which emphasized the primitive passions of the Greek myths. The famous *Afternoon of a Faun* (1912)

Leon Bakst's set design (watercolor on paper) for Gabriele d'Annunzio's *La Pisanelle, Ou La Mort Parfumée*, performed at the théâtre du Chatelet, Saisons des Ballets Russes in 1913, shows Orientalist influence in the lush, colorful, patterned designs on the walls and floors as well as the vivid colors of the fauve movement in modern art.
Private Collection, Archives Charmet/www.bridgeman.co.uk

Color

Color is one of the costume designer's most powerful tools. Because color is energy transmitted through light, it provokes a direct physical response in the audience. We interpret color through sensory experience and cultural conventions: Red signals danger and passion in our culture, yet to the Chinese, it represents happiness and celebration. White stands for innocence and purity, but in Japan it is a sign of death and mourning. Psychological studies indicate that red, yellow, and orange are sensory stimulants, while blues and greens can have a calming effect. The impact of color is modified by its intensity. The deeper the hue, the more it attracts the eye. While light blue may calm, royal

featured the electrifying dancer Vaslav Nijinsky (1890–1950), who was instructed on the angular poses and two-dimensional rigid stances of ancient Greek painted images by the designer, Bakst. The ballet, in many ways, looked like an animated ancient Greek urn painting. Bakst's costumes were modern vibrant renditions of these earlier images whose colors harmonized with the set. In a similar unified manner, designer Natalia Gontcharova created sets and costumes for *Le Coq d'Or* (1914) using motifs from Russian crafts and folk art in a neoprimitivism that was marked by primary colors, distorted perspective, and stylized floral patterns that reflected the dynamism of the Fauvist movement in modern art.

The Ballet Russes, with their international tours, provided wide exposure for painters and a new venue in which to experiment. In search of a unified visual world, Picasso created sets and costumes for the ballet *Parade* (1917) (see top photo on page 287) and Henri Matisse for *The Song of the Nightingale* (1920), set in China, in which the visual world became a European fantasy of the exotic Orient. Matisse saw the costumes as an opportunity to turn the dancers' bodies into architectural blocks, which he viewed as mobile modern sculpture. Matisse commented that painters have always been "choreographers," creating compositional groupings of the human form. Often, these dynamic and experimental costumes that masked the curves of the body to create a generic building block of shape inspired the choreography. In all cases, the visual and performing elements of every production were united by a common aesthetic and by the mutual inspiration they provided.

The early decades of the twentieth century were marked by an Orientalism that romanticized the Far East. Following the Paris Exposition Universelle in 1900 and tours of theatre performers and dancers from Siam, Cambodia, India, China, and Japan, Europe was intoxicated with Asian arts. A period of intercultural borrowing began, although few Europeans truly understood the cultural context of the forms they were appropriating. Art, fashion, fragrance, and every form of design reflected this fascination. The impact of the Russian tour of the royal Siamese ballet troupe on the Ballets Russes was marked. Siamese gesture and technique were incorporated into performances and training and was reflected in the visual motifs Bakst created for sets and costumes. Nijinsky tried to master Siamese hand movements and the use of the upper torso. Bakst created a series of costumes that borrowed heavily from Siamese forms using short skirts and headdresses with geometric designs. These early intercultural efforts saw culture as fashion and expressed a superficial exoticism. Nonetheless, they provided us with some of the most striking costume designs of the period, if not the century, and elevated costume design to the highest of art forms.

Nijinsky in the Blue God costume designed by Leon Bakst for the Ballets Russes. Nijinsky's gestures and his costume show an Orientalist influence, reminiscent of Southeast Asian performance traditions. Note the stylized positions of the hands and feet. They do not quote any single tradition and remain a fanciful interpretation.
© Snark/Art Resource, NY

blue may arouse. Costumers manipulate our responses to characters by playing with our cultural associations and sensory responses to color.

The way colors are combined or set against different backgrounds affects the way they are read, so costumers must consider the set design and the way various characters will appear in relation to each other as they select costume elements. Through color, costume designers can make immediately apparent relationships among characters and help tell the story: In *Romeo and Juliet*, the Capulets might wear gold while the Montagues wear silver, or one family might appear in hues of burgundy and the other in hues of

Artists
IN PERSPECTIVE

In Their Own Words

JUDITH DOLAN

Designer-director Judith Dolan is best known for her work with director Harold Prince, including the Broadway productions of Alfred Uhry's Parade *and* Candide, *for which she received a 1997 Tony award for best costume design.* Candide *was revived at the New York City Opera in 2005. The musical* The Petrified Prince *at the Public Theater in New York City earned her the Lucille Lortelle Award for Excellence in Costume Design and a 1995 Drama Desk nomination. Her credits include costumes for Andrei Serban's production of* The Miser *for the American Repertory Theatre and the original Broadway production of* Joseph and the Amazing Technicolor Dreamcoat. *Among several Off-Broadway credits is John Houseman's revival of Marc Blitzstein's* The Cradle Will Rock.*

After an extensive design career beginning at the Abbey Theatre in Ireland, she earned a Ph.D. from Stanford University in directing and design. As a director-designer she has mounted productions of the work of Bertolt Brecht, Tennessee Williams, and August Strindberg. At the Directors' Company in New York City, she has developed new plays and musicals. Judith Dolan's work has also been seen in such venues as the Old Vic in London, the Kennedy Center, the Brooklyn Academy of Music, the Mark Taper Forum, and the Alley Theater in Houston. She is currently professor of design in the Department of Theater and Dance at the University of California at San Diego.

■ **What is the key to developing your total concept for a production?**

In the art of poetry, two forces that seem to be in opposition, word and image, are united in a powerful dynamic. As a designer-director, I approach my work as an exercise in poetry where word and image work together cooperatively. As such, the images that the play suggests to me are as vital as the words of the text. My method is to discover those images and begin to interpret them through physical experiences.

■ **What specific design techniques do you apply as a director?**

The chart of character/scene breakdown is the first step through which a costume designer brings the words on the page into a physical reality. It suggests entrances and exits, costume changes, what characters are on stage together, and begins to lift the flat experience of the page onto the dimensional stage. Making the organizational

decisions for the chart begins the commitment to the play that reflects my own directorial focus. From the early reading erupt images, questions, prejudices as well as physical needs, which become a structural springboard to the textures of the world of the play. Ultimately, the chart becomes for me a time/space document—a visual orchestration of the rhythms and music of the play.

To this I add storyboarding, image research, and collage, other means of visually interpreting the text as a designer-director. The storyboard drawings (the figures are often stick figures) keep the work focused on how the narrative relates to the spatial demands of the production. The storyboard is intentionally "not pretty" so that visual choices are not prematurely made, but in a graphic way, it provides me with the first concrete step into designing the set. The shape and structure of the play is then directly linked to the space of performance.

If the play is a period piece, I research the period from dramaturgical and historical viewpoints, and acquaint myself with the architecture, artifacts, and art of that period. I leave myself open to all sorts of possibilities from contemporary sources to capture the textural qualities of the play for contemporary audiences. This may include music exploration, which serves to connect me to unspoken visceral and emotional responses. Through this process evolves the visual relationships that will transform into scenic, costume, lighting, and sound designs.

The research period allows me to wander in many potential artistic directions, in order to choose the images that are most vital to the collage that will be the world of the production. The collage includes not only two-dimensional images, but also three-dimensional textures. It should reflect the dynamics of the play—whether brutal or lyrical, lighthearted or heavy. This struggle with editing images and then assembling them with other newly introduced textures is an anchor to the preproduction design process, as I become increasingly involved in directing during the rehearsal process.

■ **How does your experience as a costume designer affect your work with actors as a director?**

Casting decisions affect the visual nature of the world being created on stage. The actor's singular presence, his/her style—face, body, movement, voice, and internal rhythm—suggest the boundaries of the world. Casting choices related to age, race, size, gender, and nationality contribute to the human texture in performance. My design work has been significantly centered on costume design, and the actor, for me, has always been an important collaborator. My experience as a costume designer has allowed me to operate as a bridge between the world of the design and that of directing. It gives me

Judith Dolan's sketch and final costumes for *Parade*. The three mill girls on the right of the photo are treated as a group by the director and designed as a group in the sketch. Dolan's sketch is full of detailed notes about costume and hair. The costumes capture period, class, and occupation. *Parade,* book by Alfred Uhry; music and lyrics by Jason Robert Brown and co-conceived by Harold Prince; director, Harold Prince; Vivian Beaumont Theater, Lincoln Center, New York.
Sketch by Judith Dolan. Photo © Joan Marcus.

as a director an opportunity to unite the details of the costume with the interpretation of the character as the performance evolves in rehearsal. It also collapses the boundary between actor, director, and designer and can enrich the work of all three collaborators.

■ **Is something lost when there is a single voice conceiving more than one element of a show?**

The art of the theater is based on collaboration. If there is a danger in the role of designer-director, it lies in the narrowing of the pool of collaborators, thus tapping into the nineteenth-century concept of the director as the visionary of theater production. I never design more than sets and costumes for any play that I direct. In losing some of the rough and tumble of the artistic exchange between various designers and the director, my compensation is that as a director, I engage in a more intimate collaboration with the performers. It is up to the designer-director to resist the potential tyranny of that role, and to include as many other collaborators as possible in the process of artistic discovery.

Source: Used with permission from Judith Dolan.

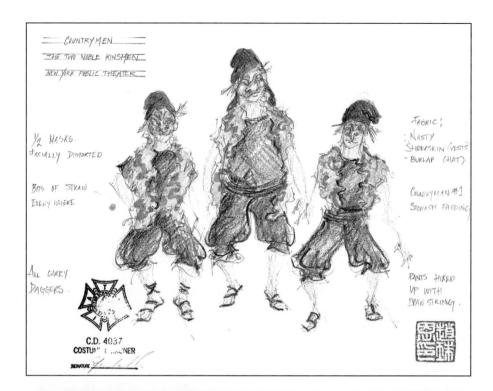

Photo 12.4
Linda Cho's sketch and final costumes of the three countrymen for *The Three Noble Kinsmen,* directed by Darko Tresnjak at the Joseph Papp Public Theatre, New York. Notice the importance of texture in conveying a rustic feel. The costumer specifies the "nasty sheepskin" of the jackets, the burlap of the hats, and the "distorted" masks. Cho's detailed comments on the sketch for "bits of straw everywhere" and "pants held up with drawstring" add to the definition of these characters as unrefined peasants.
Sketch reprinted with permission from Linda Cho. Photo © Craig Schwartz

green (see photo on page 325). Personality is evoked through color, so choices reflect an interpretation of character. Would Juliet wear red? Would Hamlet wear yellow? The colors of an individual costume need to work with the actor's skin tones so that the actor's face stands out. Designers specify a palette of costume colors for a show within a scale of color values that coordinates with the colors chosen for the sets and lights that provide the environment for costumes.

The Costume Designer's Materials

Fabric

The costumer's most basic tool is fabric. Its color, elasticity, movement, and texture all influence how actors move and feel on stage and how the audience understands the characters and the world of the play. Costumers also use other materials, such as metal or plastic, along with fabric to shape, disguise, and reveal the human form.

Ornament

Ornaments are the elements costumers add to clothes to give them extra detail and style, such as lace, buttons, tassels, embroidery, and sequins. Each of these decorations can evoke a period, style, social class, or personality. Aunty Mame might wear sequins, large buttons, and jeweled collars, while Juliet might have some tasteful lace or embroidered trim (see Photo 12.2).

Accessories

Just as we might "accessorize" to bring finishing touches to our own wardrobes, costumers fill out the details of a character's costume with hats, scarves, shoes, jewelry, canes, and handbags. Some accessories help actors create character mannerisms: bracelets to jangle, a cane to point, a scarf to twist. Some participate in the action, such as the bowler hats the tramps exchange in *Waiting for Godot*.

Hairstyles and Wigs

Hairstyle completes the actor's visual image and falls under the costume designer's purview. Designers use wigs and hairpieces to reflect a historical period, to reveal a character's personal habits or taste, or to reinforce the overall style of the production. They often alter the actor's own hair through dyeing, cutting, shaving, and styling, or they might ask an actor to grow a beard. In the Broadway musical *Hairspray*, large bouffant wigs sum up the campy style of the piece and comment on attitudes toward female beauty in the 1950s.

Makeup

Almost all actors wear some kind of makeup. Actors transformed through makeup feel their character develop within when they look in the mirror. Stanislavski wrote much about makeup as a tool for literally getting into the character's skin. Makeup can be divided into three categories: straight makeup, character makeup, and special effects.

Straight makeup can enhance facial features, especially the eyebrows, eyes, cheeks, and mouth to keep them from washing out under stage lights, allowing the actor's expressions to be read at a distance. Makeup can define a character, create old

Photo 12.5
An absurd little hat on top of an enormous wig looks like an inappropriate afterthought. Costume designer Michael Krass combines two elements of period style—the hat and the wig—in an unexpected way to express comic character in Nicholas Martin's production of Richard Brinsley Sheridan's *The Rivals*. Huntington Theatre Company, Boston.
© *T. Charles Erickson*

History IN PERSPECTIVE

BLACKFACE

In the 1820s, an American performer named Thomas Dartmouth Rice put burnt cork on his face, dressed himself in rags, and did a shuffle dance while singing "Jump Jim Crow," claiming he had copied the routine from a black slave he saw down South. This marked the beginning of **blackface** minstrelsy, a popular entertainment that dominated the American stage throughout the nineteenth century. The iconic makeup of the minstrel clown, a blackened face with white circles around the eyes and mouth, topped off by a wild fright wig, has today become emblematic not only of the theatrical form that gave it birth, but also of African American oppression in the United States. The minstrel show's legacy of songs, dances, and comic routines brings with it a derogatory, comic black stereotype that continues to haunt American culture.

The first minstrel performers were white men who put burnt cork makeup on their faces to blacken them and claimed to be imitating the dances and songs of Southern slaves. Such individuals eventually pooled their talents, performing in groups and calling themselves "minstrels." Black makeup gave these performers license to perform someone racially different from themselves and, in the process, to construct that identity for white Americans.

White Americans in the North, who had little direct contact with black slaves, believed that what they saw in minstrel shows was an authentic rendition of Southern black culture, no matter how ridiculous the characters seemed. Showing blacks as foolish and naive, minstrel shows presented blacks as happy with their status as slaves while perpetuating a nostalgic view of plantation life. This helped many whites accept slavery, even as the abolitionist movement was on the rise.

During the Civil War, blacks began performing in their own minstrel troupes, thinking they could cash in on this theatrical form by providing a more authentic look at black culture than white performers could. Ironically, the minstrel stereotype was so strong that black performers also had to cork up and put on wigs to conform to audience expectations. Burnt cork makeup had come to represent blackness on stage more than real skin color.

We could compare minstrel makeup to clown makeup and masks found in many cultures, but because blackface makeup points to a racially specific group, it is different from other types of clown makeup. Audience members of the period transposed the ridiculous image built up on stage to real human beings outside the theatre. Oddly, although presenting blacks in a demeaning role, it provided an innocuous facade that permitted black performers the freedom to speak forthrightly on topics such as politics and religion that would otherwise have been taboo.

The great vaudeville and musical theatre entertainer Bert Williams (1876–1922) discovered both freedom and constraint in blackface performance. Born in the West Indies, he was unfamiliar with the minstrel stereotype when he first entered show business. He soon found that he had to cork up, and he developed a character called "Mr. Nobody," who, conforming to the stereotype, was humble and shiftless. The blackface makeup, he claimed, freed him to find himself as a performer and develop his comic style. Although he rose to great fame, offstage he continued to experience the oppression that accompanied a real black face in America. The popularity of minstrelsy gave black performers in the United States an avenue to display their talents and make a living, but it also enlisted them in the perpetuation of the very stereotype that oppressed them. That stereotype imprinted itself on the culture through the image of blackface makeup.

By the mid-twentieth century, the black clown character developed in minstrelsy appeared on television and film without the exaggerated makeup but preserving its demeaning character traits. The grotesque vision of the blackface clown continued to lurk behind the real black faces that appeared in mainstream entertainment and continued to constrain these performers from finding roles outside the stereotype.

In the late 1950s, the civil rights movement took pointed aim at the minstrel clown, replacing the demeaning image it promoted with expressions of "black power" and "black pride." Theatre artists appropriated the minstrel mask for political purposes, using it to challenge racial oppression. The San Francisco Mime Troupe's 1965 production *A Minstrel Show, or Civil Rights in a Cracker Barrel* used a cast of three black and three white men, all wearing blackface. Using a traditional minstrel show format, it forced its audiences to examine their racial prejudices. Try as they might, audiences could not distinguish the black and white performers on stage. In a scene called "Black History Month," the minstrels, performing famous blacks in history, became increasingly militant as the figures became more contemporary. The Interlocutor, a traditional character from the minstrel show who was always white, forced these minstrels to reassume their tame, subservient roles. In Ntozake Shange's 1979 theatrical choreopoem, *Spell #7*, a large minstrel face hangs as an imposing image over the set and the lives of the characters, who strive to free themselves from received stereotypes. In Amiri Baraka's *Slave Ship*, blacks who conform to the minstrel stereotype are transformed into revolutionaries. More recently, George Wolfe's *Colored Museum* used the image of blackface minstrelsy to comment on popular African American entertainment. A video image of performers in minstrel makeup appears, reminding the audience of the legacy of performing "black" for white audiences. In Spike Lee's 2001 film *Bamboozled*, the extraordinary success of a minstrel-style sitcom comments on the position of blacks in media entertainment.

The use of "whiteface," in which African Americans wear white makeup or play "white" to comment on white culture, has become a dramatic device. Douglas Turner Ward's 1965 one-act comedy *Day of Absence* is a reverse minstrel show in which a black cast dons whiteface to portray a Southern community that wakes up to find that all the blacks in their town have mysteriously disappeared, sending their lives into chaos. In Suzan-Lori Parks's 2001 play *Topdog/Underdog*, one of her two black characters has a job at a carnival wearing white makeup as he portrays Abraham Lincoln, and patrons are invited to shoot at him. In the Wayans brothers' 2004 film *White Chicks*, the black comic duo make up as rich blond women using latex masks, blond wigs, and blue contact lenses to poke fun at white values.

The presence of blackface, whiteface, and Asian makeup continues to make us question how much racial identity is something we perform according to socially imposed stereotypes. It reminds us that performing racial identity on stage, whether our own race or another's, determines how we as a culture think about race.

Left: Actor Bert Williams wearing the traditional blackface minstrel makeup that was expected in the performance of black roles by both white and black actors in the late nineteenth and early twentieth century. The "minstrel mask" helped Williams find acceptance on the stage but confined his talents within a debasing stereotype.
© CORBIS

Right: The civil rights movement fostered a Black theatre movement that sought to reclaim racial identity. Actors Tracy Johnson and Trisha Jeffrey wear "whiteface," a turnabout on "blackface," to parody whites in this production of Douglas Turner Ward's 1965 play *Day of Absence,* directed by Alfred Preisser, at the Classical Theatre of Harlem, New York.
Courtesy of The Classical Theatre of Harlem, Inc.; photo by Jake Nixon

age, accentuate character traits, or reshape the face completely. Elements attached to the face such as beards, mustaches, bushy eyebrows, and fake noses permit actors to make amazing transformations. Certain kinds of characters wear traditional makeup such as the Restoration fop's rouged cheeks and beauty mark. Special effects makeup can create bruises, scars, and other infirmities. Teeth can be stained or blackened to create a toothless look. In highly stylized performances, a wide palette of makeup colors and designs can totally transform and even camouflage human features. *Cats* used makeup to transform an entire cast into animals.

Masks

Masks immediately set a presentational style for both the visual elements and the acting and demand a heightened theatricality in all the accompanying stage elements. Masks provide the opportunity for even greater alteration of persona and imaginative flights of fancy than makeup. They can turn a group into a chorus with similar faces, reveal a fully defined unique character, or create figures of fantasy. Because masks cover the face, performers compensate by enlarging movement and corporeal expression. Robert Wilson's 2004 production of *The Fables of la Fontaine*, staged at the Comédie Française, used fantastic masks to bring these animal allegories to life. Actors who normally worked in the declamatory style of French classical theatre were free to leap, hop, and prance, croak and roar. Because of the demands masks place on actors, rehearsals began with movement exercises as the key to the embodiment of the masked characters. The pairing of animal masks with human clothing supported the thematic symbolism of the allegorical material.

Costume designers turn the director's vision of the world on stage and the relationship among the imaginary people who inhabit it into a tangible reality. They translate psychological traits into visual language that telegraphs the essence of character to an audience. Ultimately, they are the actor's silent partner in the creation of a vibrant physical character portrait.

Photo 12.6
Director-designer Robert Wilson uses a combination of animal masks and elegant evening wear to create the anthropomorphic characters of La Fontaine's moral fables in *The Fables of la Fontaine* at the Comédie Française, Paris. Unlike the lizards in *Seascape* (see photo on page 316), animal masks alone transform the characters and underscore the thematic relevance of the animal fables to human life. The scene pictured here is from the fable "The Ears of the Hare" with, left to right, Florence Viala as The Grasshopper, Céline Samie as The Raven, Charles Chemin as The Stag, Julie Sicard as The Hare, and Bakary Sangaré as The Lion.
© *Martine Franck/Magnum Photos*

KEY IDEAS

- The power of costume to shape identity is a major part of role-play in the theatre.
- Costumers consider the director's concept, what physical actions will be performed on stage, the psychological nature of a character, and the actor's physique.
- Costumes help tell the story. They establish time and place and the social and cultural milieu. They reveal the essence of character and express relationships among characters while defining the production style and meeting its practical needs.
- The costume designer's process begins with a careful reading of the text, discussion with the director, and research.
- Sketches help costume designers communicate ideas to the director and other designers. Costume designers consider the other visual elements when making choices and think about how all the costumes will look together.
- Costume designers work closely with the actors and with costume shop personnel to make the design a reality.
- In costume design, principles of composition take place on the human form.
- Costume designers draw on the audience's personal and cultural associations and sensory reactions as they display line, texture, and color on the body in motion.
- The costume designer's materials include fabric, ornamentation, hairstyles and wigs, makeup, and masks.

Lighting and
Sound Design

13

Low, rich red stage lighting along with the flickering flames of the candelabra held by Aphrodite (Felicity Jones), the goddess of love, set a romantic mood in this scene from Mary Zimmerman's *Metamorphosis*. Note how the actor's face and shoulder are selectively and seductively illuminated. Directed by Mary Zimmerman; scenic design by Daniel Ostling; costumes by Mara Blumenfeld; lighting by T. J. Gerkens. New York.
© Joan Marcus

Although lighting and sound have always been taken into account in theatrical performance, they are the newest arts to be fully integrated into the theatre. As technology has advanced, their roles in theatre production have expanded, demonstrating how artists take advantage of invention to find new modes of expression. Nowhere is the partnership between art and technology more in evidence in today's theatre than in lighting and sound design.

Stage Lighting

Many of the good feelings we associate with springtime—warmth, the promise of renewal, the approach of the end of the semester—are brought home to us subliminally by changes in the illumination of our visible surroundings. The dwindling light of autumn, by contrast, may bring on feelings of melancholy or the desire to huddle inside and hibernate. Natural light and the way it changes with the time of day, the weather, and the passing of the seasons affects people both physically and emotionally. Since the discovery of electricity, we have become more conscious of the power of artificial light. We may be drawn to the warm lighting of a cozy, romantic restaurant, or we may want to quickly leave the harsh neon and fluorescent lights of a fast-food joint.

Although lighting design is a vital aspect of every theatre production today, it is rarely the first thing we think about when we watch a performance. We do not think of light as something we see, but rather *what we see by*. Light illuminates the theatrical world, and it is in and through light that things are revealed to us.

Lighting designers master the art of controlling light. They think consciously about how natural and artificial light connect us to the world, and they specialize in translating that understanding into lighting effects for the stage. Some lighting designers use light conspicuously, allowing it to become a character within the drama itself.

Light often affects us unconsciously. We attribute our emotional reaction to a theatrical moment to the acting or dialogue and often ignore the supporting role of a lighting effect. However, lighting creates the emotional atmosphere for a theatrical event and plays a crucial role in unifying the visual elements on stage.

Technological Advances and Design Innovations

The development of lighting design as an art has been closely tied to technological advances in lighting itself. Theatre in ancient Greece and Rome and the religious pageants of the Middle Ages all took place outdoors, with sunlight illuminating both performers and spectators, uniting them in a shared physical environment and social atmosphere. A passing cloud or a dynamic sunset might provide a natural special effect, and torches added illumination as the daylight faded, but generally the control of light was minimal. Indoor court performances during the Renaissance made visibility a greater concern and led artists to experiment with lighting effects in creating theatrical illusions. Chandeliers set with candles or oil lamps illuminated both the stage and the auditorium. Footlights strengthened the light on stage, and mica or tinsel basins placed behind the lamps as reflectors increased their intensity. Stagehands brightened and darkened the scene by lowering or raising cylinders over the lamps or turning lamps on rotating poles to or away from the spectators. Containers filled with colored liquid or colored glass placed in front of the lights gave a colored tint to a scene, and a crystal orb filled with colored liquid made a glowing moon.

In the nineteenth century, gas lighting allowed directors and producers to control both the intensity and distribution of light across the stage. With a *gas table*, the precursor of the lighting board, a technician could manipulate all the lights from a single spot, making light changes more efficient. Philadelphia's Chestnut Street Theatre was the first to use gas in 1816. Gas lighting was found in many urban theatres by the 1840s. Other lighting options included the arc light, an early experiment in electric lighting, which produced an extremely harsh and bright light, and *limelight*, in which gas, hydrogen, and oxygen heated a column of lime, rendering it incandescent. Limelight, which remained popular until World War I, created an effect of sunlight or moonlight, and was most often used as a spotlight. Today, we use the expression "in the limelight" metaphorically to mean that someone is the focus of attention.

Lighting design became an essential theatrical art in the twentieth century with the development of safe, efficient electricity. Edison's invention of the incandescent lamp in 1879, the first lighting source without an open flame, saved theatres from the plague of fire and also permitted control of intensity. New lighting instruments designed specifically for stage use permitted lighting design to develop as an art.

Artists quickly learned how to exploit each new invention. In England Henry Irving (1838–1905), known for extravagant theatrical spectacles with massive moving sets and many actors, was one of the first to contrive innovative lighting effects as part of his productions. He darkened the audience to give full focus to the stage, he used lacquered glass for coloring gaslights, and he put up black masking to prevent light from spilling into unwanted areas. His productions regularly involved fantastic lighting effects that often upstaged the actors. In 1902, David Belasco (1853–1931), another innovative producer, built a light laboratory in the dome of the Republic Theatre in New York where he and Louis Hartman, his electrician, experimented with new lighting techniques and invented devices such as the "top hat" to control the spill of light. The famous sunset scene Belasco created for his production of *Madame Butterfly* (1900) produced a nuanced naturalistic effect extended over fourteen minutes of gradual change. In 1911, Munroe Pevear contributed to lighting design with advances in lighting color theory.

Drawing on Wagner's conception of theatre as a "total work of art" (*gesamtkunstwerk*), Adolphe Appia (1862–1928) theorized that light, as a visual counterpart to music, could unify the three-dimensional actor, the stage set, and the floor of the playing area. His interest in light's ability to respond to shifting moods and emotions was shared by director-designer Edward Gordon Craig, who experimented with these ideas in production.

Challenges and Choices

Is our theatre richer today because of our ability to control lighting, or have some aspects of the theatre such as language and acting been diminished by the use of sophisticated lighting design?

Photo 13.1
This haunting lighting links the Canadian immigrants' present to images of their family's distant past in China, a homeland now surrounded in myth and mystery, and sets the mood for Robert Lepage's *Trilogie des Dragons*. Original set design by Jean-François Couture and Gilles Dubé; lighting design by Sonoyo Nishikawa; original lighting design by Louis-Marie Lavoie and Lucie Bazzo. Quebec, Canada.
© *Erick Labbe*

The futurists, as part of their celebration of new technologies, made light a central actor in short dramas. In Francis Canguillo's *Lights!* (1919), actors planted in the audience instigated spectators sitting in the dark to cry out more and more vigorously for light until all the lights came on full blast. Augusto Mauro's *Death and Transfiguration* is a four-part symphonic poem performance that tells the story of a confrontation with death acted out entirely through different colored lights. Light shows in the 1960s and 1970s made light the central attraction for more abstract, psychedelic events.

Goals of Stage Lighting

■ **Creating Mood.** Creating an atmosphere that provides a logical surround for the characters' behavior is a key to good lighting design. Since light strongly affects feelings, it can help define and justify the character's psychological state and actions. It also conveys the mood of a scene to the audience in subtle ways. Lights coming at odd angles can lend an eerie feeling to the stage, while low rose lights can establish a romantic atmosphere. Serious dramas are often performed in stark or dim lighting; comedies, in brightness and color.

■ **Providing Selective Visibility and Focus.** Lighting illuminates the stage, revealing colors and forms. There must be enough light on stage and enough coverage of the stage that any area that needs to be seen *can* be seen. Lighting can emphasize one part of the stage over another, open the entire stage area up at once, or break the stage up into different sections of brightness and shadow. Light marks the limits of the theatrical environment and establishes the visual composition of the stage. Because lighting tells the audience where to look, it focuses their attention.

■ **Defining Style.** Lighting can impart a sense of reality or of the unreal and echo the stylistic approach of the other visual elements on stage. A realistic play may work well with effects that reproduce light the way we experience it from natural sources, whereas an expressionist piece may benefit from saturated colors at harsh angles to produce a nightmarish quality. A poetic piece can be enhanced through dramatic changes in color that support the images in the text and its inherent theatricality.

■ **Establishing Time and Place.** Creating an environment that expresses the location and time of the dramatic action is an important role of lighting. The color and angle of light can convey the time of day, whether it is early morning, late evening, or mid-afternoon; it can also indicate if it is summer or winter, and whether the characters are indoors or out. Lighting can also evoke specific interiors, from the low lights of a tavern to the brightness of a department store at Christmastime.

■ **Telling the Story.** Lights follow and express the dramatic action. The dimming of the house-

Photo 13.2
Spotlights have been used for nearly a century to provide selective visibility and focus on stage. Follow spots move with an actor, maintaining a constant pool of light. The expression "being in the spotlight" has become synonymous with being a star. In this scene from *Gypsy*, the spotlight is used for both its practical and metaphorical value to capture Mama Rose (Bernadette Peters) dreaming of fame. Note the circular lights on the stage floor that repeat the visual theme established with the spotlight. Directed by Sam Mendes; scenic and costume design by Anthony Ward; lighting design by Jules Fischer and Peggy Eisenhauer. Shubert Theatre, New York.
© *ArenaPal/Topham/The Image Works*

Photo 13.3
Focused areas of deeply saturated blue, green, and red light color the floor as well as the actor and help establish the brash, dynamic, and celebratory style of this historical review of the music and dance of Harlem. Lighting also sets the chorus apart from the main performer, David St. Louis. *Harlem Song*, written and directed by George C. Wolfe; music by Daryl Waters and Zane Mark; scenic design by Ricardo Hernandez; costume design by Paul Tazewell; lighting design by Jules Fischer and Peggy Eisenhauer; Apollo Theater, New York.
© Michal Daniel, 2002

lights in the auditorium and the raising of the stage lights on the set open a performance. Lights create a transition from scene to scene as they change in brightness or color, perhaps **cross-fading**—slowly diminishing one lighting cue while adding another to gradually transition from one scene to the next. They punctuate the end of an event, usually with a **fade**—a gradual dimming—or a quick **blackout**. They move our interest from one location on the stage to another and from one character to another, telling us where to look to follow the story. These changes can express an emotional movement as alterations in colors and intensity indicate changes in the circumstances of the characters. Light coming up, whenever it occurs, inevitably gives a sense of discovery and a new beginning, whereas lights going down suggest closure.

Photo 13.4
Swirling lights on the stage floor and the minimal set pieces capture the rhythm and movement of the location of this scene on a New York City subway train in Amiri Baraka's (LeRoi Jones) *Dutchman*. The dizzying lights reinforce the whirlpool of emotions that erupt between the main characters in this drama of racial conflict directed by Jonathan Wilson. Scenic design by Scott Bradley; costume design by Susan Hilferty; lighting design by Rui Rita. Hartford Stage, Connecticut.
© Jennifer Lester

Photo 13.5

Playwright Samuel Beckett's precise directions for lighting *Come and Go* are nearly the same length as this short play itself, emphasizing the importance of light in his conceptualization of the text. Following Beckett's directions, light isolates the actresses' hats and dresses, leaving their faces dark, and reinforces the play's thematic concerns of human isolation and the interchangeability of identity. Dublin's Gate Theater production of *Come and Go,* directed by Bairbre Ni Chaoinh; lighting design by Alan Burrett; scenic and costume design by Simon Vincenzi. Lincoln Center Festival, New York.
© *Stephanie Berger*

- **Reinforcing the Central Image or Theme of the Play.** Lighting can embody the very idea of a theatrical work. In *Metamorphosis*, the constantly changing dramatic colors and patterns of light captured the image of the pool of water in which the action took place, extending the feel of the watery surface to the walls of the set and reinforcing the theme of transformation. Samuel Beckett's *Not I* features a spotlight focused on the mouth of an actress. The isolated beam of light echoes the stream-of-consciousness monologue expressing the isolation and dislocation of the central character. The alienation and loss of self in Beckett's plays is often achieved through lighting effects. The order in which things are revealed as the lights go up can fix a central idea in spectators' minds and give the components of the set relative levels of importance. The shell of a house might be illuminated before the furniture to make a statement about the emptiness of the family living within.

- **Establishing Rhythm.** The speed and frequency of light changes sets the pace of a show. Lights going on and off with a bump can startle, enliven, or underscore dramatic impact, whereas gradual fades may extend an emotional moment. Short scenes paired with light changes can create a sense of movement through time.

The Lighting Designer's Process

Lighting designers begin by reading the text and thinking about what kinds of design elements the production requires as they develop a concept for the performance. They look for specific indications of time and place and any important references to light and its influence on the characters and the mood of the play. They hunt for **motivated light** cues specifically indicated in the text, such as a lamp being turned on, and make lists of the basic requirements. They meet with the director and discuss the director's vision for the production, desired special effects, and the way the lighting will function. Lighting designers make suggestions as to how light might serve the production, enhance a moment, or solve a problem. These collaborative discussions lead to decisions about *unmotivated light cues* not specifically required by the text but that serve the director's concept.

Unlike other members of the design team, lighting designers do not usually bring sketches of their ideas to the first meetings. Since the lighting designers' goal is to unify all the elements of the production, they must wait to see the set and costume designs to know what they will be lighting. Their presence at early meetings is essential because they can spot potential problems in set design such as tall structures that might block an angle of lighting, an area of action on a part of the stage that may be difficult to light, or the choice of a reflective surface that might cause the light to blind the audience. These issues are more easily resolved while designs are still on paper than after they have been built.

Artists

IN PERSPECTIVE

In Their Own Words

JENNIFER TIPTON

Jennifer Tipton has brought her talent in lighting design to dance, opera, and theatre and has earned prestigious awards for her work in the United States and abroad. Her versatility and ability to adapt to the demands of each art make her a unique talent. Although in demand by notables in the dance and theatre worlds, she still finds time to teach at the Yale School of Drama.

■ **What inspired you to change paths from dancing to lighting?**

I began lighting theatre after lighting Jerome Robbins's *Celebration, the Art of the Pas De Deux* at the Spoleto Festival in Italy 1972. Several theater directors asked me to work with them after seeing that production. Santo Loquasto saw the work and asked me to light Shakespeare at the Mitzi Newhouse Theater for the New York Shakespeare Festival, which began a long relationship.

■ **Do you believe having been a dancer yourself has given you a distinct consciousness or sensibility toward the human form in space that influences your lighting?**

I am sure that I light space because of the people moving in it rather than because of any text or music.

■ **How does your approach to lighting dance, opera, and theatre differ? Is the source of the inspiration different when working with a spoken text, or pure movement, or the music and singing of opera?**

My approach to anything that I do is more or less the same. I try to make the story clear and to respond to the dynamics of the space and the timing. I feel that each production is specific, and I try to find the lighting language or vocabulary that best expresses that production. Of course my approach is often determined by the scenery, by the time given for lighting, and by the circumstances of the production (it may be in a repertory plot).

■ **Is there something that you feel distinguishes your lighting from others who work in the field?**

I have often been asked about my "style" by people who write about lighting. I point out that there is no way for me to know. I simply do what I do. I must leave characterizing what I do to other people.

■ **How does your lighting for the Wooster Group have to negotiate with the many other technological elements the company uses onstage?**

In my first production with the Wooster Group, *BRACE UP!*, I was very aware of "competing" with the sound and video technology (see photo on page 381). At the time I realized that there was no way. Sound and video are show pieces and very much in evidence in Elizabeth LeCompte's aesthetic. Light takes a quieter place—totally important but following my rules of making the story clear and the rhythm dynamic.

The sailor Chito, played by Mikhail Baryshnikov, waves goodbye to his love, Tsisana (Pilar Witherspoon) as he sails off to sea and as she receives a new proposal from Ermonia (Luiz Perez). Jennifer Tipton's lighting brings the scene together in a wash of blue that captures the sea and sets the mood of departure. Light distinguishes between the events taking place in the background and the foreground. Logs were turned by hand to create the effect of waves for the puppet boat. *Forbidden Christmas* or *The Doctor and the Patient*, text, direction, and scenic design by Rezo Gabriedze; lighting design by Jennifer Tipton. The Guthrie Theater, Minneapolis.
© *Michal Daniel, 2004*

(continues)

Artists

IN PERSPECTIVE (CONTINUED)

■ **What are the pleasures or difficulties of working with someone like Robert Wilson, who has such a clear visual idea of what he wants to see onstage?**

I learned a huge amount working with Robert Wilson. I will never forget how long it took me to come to the realization that he was talking about lighting the space with lights on the floor so that he could separate the actors from the space. When I began lighting with Bob, I had been working mostly in dance where there is no time. From him I learned what could be accomplished by taking time to do everything the "right" way. But he always lights a production in the same way, and as I have said, I feel very strongly that each production should be lit in its own particular way. Once I learned that, it was only right that we should go our separate ways.

■ **You trained in an apprenticeship. How do you feel about the apprenticeship training model versus MFA training?**

I learned to light on the road with the Paul Taylor Dance Company. I still feel that is a very good way to learn, but companies today want more experienced people than I was when I began. The main reason to get an MFA is for the contacts that you make while you are at school, the directors and other designers. It is certainly not the only way to learn the craft—but it is a good way.

■ **What advice would you give to aspiring designers today?**

My best advice for aspiring designers is to respond to your passion. Theatre is a very difficult profession, and you have to be sure that you are madly in love with it. There are dozens of ways to make a better living. If you don't absolutely adore lighting, do something else.

Source: Used with permission from Jennifer Tipton.

Lighting designers keep apprised of the development of costumes and sets. Set placement determines where they hang the lights and what parts of the stage they must illuminate. The colors and textures of the set and costumes absorb or reflect light and are of vital concern to the lighting designer in the angle and placement of lights. White costumes and sets will reflect when lit, as will sequined costumes, mirrors, or shiny surfaces. Lighting designers will watch a run-through of the show toward the end of the rehearsal period to get a good sense of the placement and movement of the actors on stage so they know how the lights should follow the action. With all of this information and their understanding of the play, they create a design for the show on paper before hanging and focusing the lights in the theatre.

Lighting designers also research the historical period of the play. They study architectural features and lighting fixtures of the time. They gather information about the visual images the director is seeking. They look at photos, read about previous productions, and research the text.

A **light plot** is a blueprint of the stage and auditorium with the **lighting grid** (the metal pipe structure from which the lights are hung) and the location of each light to be used for a production specifically marked. On this plan, lighting designers give each light an identifying number and chart the different instruments they intend to use and their locations. An **instrument schedule** is a chart that lists each instrument by its number and specifies its location, its purpose, the wattage of the lamp inside, the color of the gel, and other important information about its use. The light plot and instrument schedule are given to the **master electrician** to oversee the crew's installation and electrical connections. During the technical rehearsal, the lighting designer can refer to this chart to know which light to adjust.

After lighting designers focus the lights in the theatre, a significant part of their task comes during technical rehearsals when the blocking is fixed and sets and costumes are finished. The lighting designer and the director now observe all the production elements

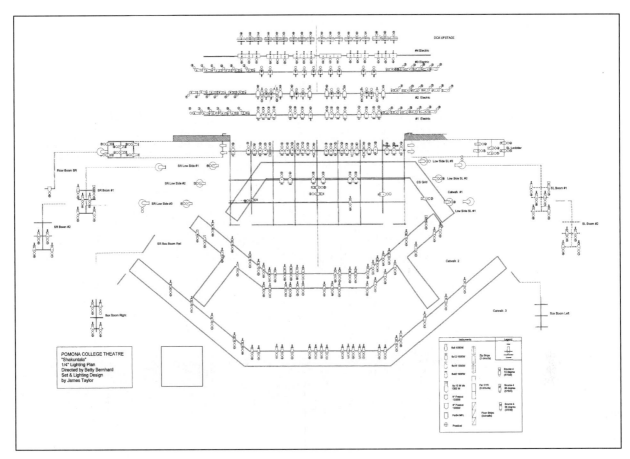

#	"Shakuntala"	#	Fall 2003	#	Design	#	
1	Front Warm A/D/E	48	Back Warm T	95	Spot SL	142	SR Tree
2	B	49	Back Cool A/D/E	96	Spot Sr	143	Bench
3	C/G/H	50	B	97	Cyc Bottom Lt. Blue	144	Throne
4	F	51	C/G/H/	98	Dark Blue	145	Heavenly Ashram
5	I	52	F	99	Red	146	
6	J	53	I	100	Cyc Top Lt. Blue	147	"Magic" Tree SL
7	K	54	J	101	Dark Blue	148	SR
8	L	55	K	102	Amber	149	Vedic Light
9	M	56	L	103	Kanva Warm Front	150	Vedic Light
10	N	57	M	104	Back	151	River Front
11	O	58	N	105	Side SL	152	River Sides
12	P	59	O	106	Side Sr	153	River Back
13	Q	60	P	107	Kanva Cool Front	154	Clouds
14	R	61	Q	108	Back	155	Menaka
15	S	62	R	109	Side SL	156	
16	T	63	S	110	Side SR	157	Mountains
17	Front Cool A/D/E	64	T	111	Cool Leaves DS SL	158	War Dance A
18	B	65	Side Warm SLIn1	112	SR	159	War Dance B
19	C/G/H	66	In 2	113	Cool Leaves Mid SL	160	Signer
20	F	67	In 3	114	SR		
21		68			Cool Leaves US		

Figure 13.1 Lighting designer James P. Taylor's light plot (top) and instrument schedule (bottom) for Kalidasa's *Sakuntala* at Pomona College Theatre, California. The plot shows the placement of lighting instruments on the light grid and throughout the theatre. The key on the lower left identifies the different kinds of lighting instruments on the grid. Notice how lights are placed over the audience, on the stage, and offstage in the wings to allow the designer to control light from a variety of angles. The schedule identifies each lighting instrument by a number and gives various details—such as its purpose, color, and position—to identify the light and its function.

Reprinted with permission from James P. Taylor.

Photo 13.6
The Demon Dance performed by the noted Kathakali artist Sasidharan Nair in Kalidasa's *Sakuntala*, as the action moves to a hermitage in the sky. Lighting designer James Taylor chose colors to correspond to the wild demonic quality of the dance and music. Directed by Betty Bernhard and Kailash Pandya; choreography by Sasidharan Nair; set and lighting design by James Taylor; costume design by Sherry Linnell. Pomona College Theatre, California. Figure 13.1 is the light plot and instrument schedule for this performance.
© Donna Ruzika

under the lights. This is a time for setting final lighting levels, making adjustments to focus to make sure all the action is clearly illuminated, and changing gel colors if needed. The most complex part of the process is setting the actual timing of light cues—changes in light settings—with the director and the actors. Often this is a time of experimentation. The director may want a slow fade at the end of an act; the lighting designer may suggest that a blackout would be more effective. The scene is run both ways, and the best result becomes the final cue. Each lighting change is examined in this careful manner until all the cues are set. A simple show may have twenty cues; complex events can have hundreds of lighting cues that all need to be carefully timed. The lighting designer coordinates with the stage manager to make sure each cue is properly noted in the **prompt book** (see pages 422–423), which serves as a guide to changes in light and sound during the performance. The work of the lighting designer, like that of the other designers, ends on opening night.

The Visual Elements of Light

Look at any panorama over several days at different times. Use the view from a window in your home, or even better, some natural vista. If you are truly observant, you will see that things look different at different times of day and under various weather conditions. The objects you are looking at have not changed; what has changed is the pattern of light, the highlights and shadows that play across these objects and alter your perceptions and, in turn, change your emotional response to what you see. How are these many effects achieved with something as elusive as light? Light has four basic qualities that affect perception and that designers manipulate for various effects: *intensity, distribution, color,* and *movement*. These qualities can be manipulated to create line, mass, color, and texture through light.

Intensity

Intensity is the degree of brightness of a light. The most fundamental and controllable level of a light is whether it is on or off. Dimmers control power and allow the designer to adjust intensity gradually just as you do with the dimmer on a lamp or light switch at home. Because our eyes continually adapt to lighting conditions, simple changes in the relative brightness of two different light cues can produce a new effect.

Distribution

Distribution refers to where light falls on stage and from what direction, the angle of the light, and the texture or edge of the light. Light can fall in a single stark beam or be diffused in space. Lighting designers control the angle and coverage of a beam of light in the way they hang and adjust lighting instruments. Theatre lights come equipped with either shutters or flaps called *barn doors*, which close over a beam of light to give a narrow or wide focus. *Spill* refers to light that flows beyond the area of desired focus. A spill of light indicates a need to refocus, although spill can sometimes be used intentionally for artistic effect.

Color

The lighting designer uses the color of light as a fundamental expressive element. Thin colored films called **gels** inserted in slots in front of the lighting instrument color stage lights. Some gels are lightly tinted and help create the slightly orange or pinkish white lights to which we are accustomed; others are more saturated and turn the stage a deep blue or red. Lighting designers mix colored gels to create a broad palette of tones. Focusing two lights with different colored gels on the same stage area produces a textured effect of color. Mixing colored light is a different process from mixing paint. Mixing the three primary colors of paint (red, blue, and yellow) yields something close to black, whereas mixing the primary colors of light (red, blue, and green) yields white. White light contains the entire spectrum of colors that we see. Looking carefully at the white lights we encounter on a daily basis will reveal that some are more orange, yellow, pink, or blue than others, and these different light colorings elicit different associations and feelings. Color is essential in creating mood on stage.

Photo 13.7
The precise, triangular distribution of a shaft of golden light outlines the cramped garret in *La Bohème* and heightens the dramatic impact. Directed by So-young Kim; scenic design by Hee-jae; lighting design by Woo-hyung Lee. The Hanjeon Art Center, Korea.
© *Hae-Jin Hwang*

Photo 13.8
The use of richly saturated colors and backlighting for silhouettes produces a dazzling visual scene for the Broadway stage production of *Aida*. Music by Elton John; lyrics by Tim Rice; book by Linda Woolverton, Robert Falls, and David Henry Hwang; directed by Robert Falls; choreographed by Wayne Cilento; scenic and costume design by Bob Crowley; lighting design by Natasha Katz.
© Joan Marcus

Movement

The placement and duration of light on stage are essential elements in lighting design because the audience's eyes will follow the light. Lighting designers create movement by having lights come on, go off, and shift from one side of the stage to another. These may follow developing action, character movement, or changes in scenes or locations.

Composing with Light

Although light is intangible, it is a central organizer and unifier of the visual elements on the stage. The stage is a black void until light composes the stage picture as it reveals objects in relation to each other and the actor. The visual elements of design—line, mass, texture, color, and scale—are revealed through light.

Lighting designers achieve these compositional goals through the use of several techniques that permit flexible effects. A **special** is a light with a unique and singular function. Specials are useful for bumping up the light on a particular area on stage that receives extra focus or attention. A special light might illuminate and isolate an actor during a monologue or draw attention to a particular actor in a crowd scene. A **practical** is an onstage light such as a lamp or a fire in a fireplace that needs to appear to be controlled from the stage. Usually the light produced by a practical is supplemented by a special overhead to heighten its effect. Extra lights create special effects, such as an eerie light accompanying the appearance of a ghost. Light coming from below is useful for such effects. This is why a flashlight under your chin at Halloween works so well as a cheap, portable special effect. **Backlighting**, light coming from behind the actor, creates silhouettes. **Sidelighting**, light coming from the side of the stage, can provide accents and highlights and is used often in dance and musical theatre to highlight the dancers' legs.

Photo 13.9
These six photographs demonstrate how the direction and angle of light molds the actor's face. *Top row:* left—high side light from left; center—front light hitting the actor straight on; right—high side light from right. *Bottom row:* left—front light filled out with lights from other angles to give a more three-dimensional view; center—high diagonal light; right—uplight coming from below creates an eerie effect. Model, Alex Will; lighting technician, Vanessa Rundle; lighting consultant, James Taylor.
© *Angel Herrera*

Conceiving a Design: Control and Flexibility

There are many ways of conceiving the lighting design for a specific production. Because it is impractical to think about lights and cues individually, lighting designers think comprehensively about the variety of effects they want to create, how they want to sculpt the actors in space, and what areas of the stage will be used. They then accommodate a range of lighting options within an overall design. Getting the most potential lighting effects with the fewest instruments has traditionally been a lighting designer's challenge, but today's equipment makes complicated effects created with a large number of instruments easier to handle than ever before.

In the 1920s, Stanley McCandless, a professor at Yale University, developed the first comprehensive method of lighting the stage. His system is no longer the only one designers use, but it continues to provide a basic approach. The first step is to divide the stage into areas eight to ten feet in diameter. Two lights coming from each side of the stage at 45 degree angles light each area, one with a warm amber- or pink-colored gel and one with a cold or blue-colored gel. This *area lighting* assures that each part of the stage is covered and has the option of a range of color variations from warm to cold. The areas overlap so the actors don't end up in dark spots as they move across the stage. *Double hangs* or *triple hangs*, with more than one light on each side for each area, offer an even greater variety of color options and coverage. Backlight and sidelight are then added to this plan for greater three-dimensionality. The designer then fills out this general lighting with other instruments used for more specific purposes. A *color wash* that bathes the entire stage can then be layered in.

Other systems of lighting include dividing the stage in horizontal zones rather than areas to create a layered effect with a lot of sidelighting. This method separates the front of the stage from the background and is useful for dance performances and in productions in which scenery flies on and off. Jewel lighting is common in Broadway productions. It emphasizes paths of strong light and adds other lights to fill in the stage along with specials. Each of these systems provides general illumination of the stage, some areas of emphasis, and the ability to create special lights for more particular purposes. However, lighting designers often create new approaches to solve the problems posed by specific productions.

The Lighting Designer's Tools

The two main types of lighting instruments used in the theatre are the **fresnel** or **spherical reflector spotlight**, which gives a soft edge to beams of light, and the **ellipsoidal reflector spotlight**, which projects a sharper, more clearly defined edge. **Follow spots** have clearly defined beams and can follow an actor in movement across the stage. **PAR lamps (parabolic aluminated reflectors)** are smaller, cheaper, more portable alternatives that can generate different types of light beams. Remote-controlled moving lights are increasingly becoming part of a lighting designer's arsenal of instruments.

Gobos are small metal plates with stencil-like shapes cut out of them that slide into a slot on the front of an ellipsoidal reflector spot, allowing light through in selected areas to create a specific shape or pattern on stage. Gobos come in many shapes and can create the dappled effect of light shining through the leaves of trees, or the bars of a prison indicated by vertical lines of shadow and light. Designers can also create specific gobos for specific effects.

Lightboard operators execute lighting cues on **dimmer** and **control boards**. The dimmer board actually controls the intensity of the light, and the control board tells the dimmer board the timing and level. Today the majority of theatres use *computer control boards* to control the lights. Every light cue—which lights are to go on and off, to what levels, and at what speed—is programmed into the board. In the past, lightboard operators set up each lighting cue on the dimmer board individually and performed cue changes by manually moving dimmer switches on careful counts for rising and falling intensity. This required split-second timing because a minute slip of the hand could change the cue. The number of lighting cues and the speed at which they could change was limited by the number of boards and operators; most preset boards only stored two cues at a time. Computerized boards have made possible the elaborate and dynamic lighting effects we see today at rock concerts and big Broadway spectaculars. The rapidity of technical advances has expanded the lighting designer's possibilities.

Sound Design

The theatre is as alive with sound as the rest of the world around us and has always appealed to the ear through the resonance of the actors' voices, live music, and sound effects both on stage and off. In Elizabethan England people would say they were going to "hear" a play, rather than "see" one. Only recently, however, has sound design emerged as a theatrical art in its own right with sound designers offered admission into the designer's union, United Scenic Artists.

Advances in digital technology now afford a greater ability to create, control, and amplify every kind of sound. What was once the art of creating realistic sound effects to support the dramatic action has evolved into an art of composition that supports the performance emotionally, thematically, and practically. Theatrical sound now creates an aural world that reflects the visual world of the stage, drawing many composers to the profession. Theatre has joined other forms of entertainment, such as film, television, radio, and rock concerts, in which designers and technicians thoroughly craft sound to enhance the totality of an experience.

Sound Practices in the Past

Theatre has always been attentive to sound, with audibility always a central concern. The science of acoustics dates back to ancient times. Greek open-air theatres built into the hillsides had exceptional acoustics. At the Theatre of Epidaurus, originally built in the fourth century B.C.E. and still used for performances today, you can sit at the top of the fifty-five-row auditorium that seats fourteen thousand and hear someone speak from the stage. Ancient Greek and Roman actors projected their voices from wide mouthpieces in their masks, which functioned as megaphones. They intoned their speeches, often to the accompaniment of musical instruments, which allowed their voices to carry. The Romans built a shallow roof over the stage that also helped in vocal projection. They placed large shallow basins around the playing area for amplification.

Sound effects have long played a role on the stage. The Romans created the sound of thunder by pouring stones into copper jars; the Elizabethans and their successors achieved a similar effect by shaking sheets of metal or rolling heavy balls down a machine with wooden channels. In modern times stagehands have dropped crash boxes filled with broken glass to produce the sound of an accident or collision or clapped together two pieces of wood to imitate the sound of a gunshot.

In the early twentieth century, Stanislavski's productions of the plays of Anton Chekhov used everyday sounds—barking dogs, croaking frogs, and clattering dishes—into the theatre as a vehicle of stage realism. Some thought this naturalistic use of sound was excessive, and even Chekhov doubted their effect. Ever since, the recreation of the sounds of everyday life has been part of many realistic productions.

In the past live music would often accomplish the goals of sound design by entertaining the audience before the show and between acts, setting the mood, pacing the action, and accompanying the singers. Today's theatrical soundscapes include the traditional and nontraditional use of actors' voices, live music, recorded music, synthetic sound and stage effects, and a specifically composed sound score that clarifies the story and heightens the emotional impact. Much of theatrical sound is created, played, and adjusted by digital and computerized sound systems.

Goals of Sound Design

■ **Audibility.** One of a sound designer's tasks is simply to ensure that the audience can hear the actors, the musicians, and both on- and offstage sound effects. Sound designers use microphones, amplifiers, and speakers for amplification. Contemporary theatre design and changes in artistic expectations have made today's performers increasingly dependent on technology for amplification, relying less on their natural ability to project. Sometimes sound designers create effects to camouflage unwanted noise such as the thud of set pieces falling into place.

■ **Establishing the Environment.** At the 1952 debut of *4′33″*, avant-garde composer John Cage had his pianist present four minutes and thirty-three seconds of silence. He wanted the audience to focus their attention on the naturally occurring sounds of their environment, to which they usually pay little heed. In this case, the audience became aware of the patter of raindrops, the wind through the trees, and the murmur of puzzled spectators. Cage wanted to demonstrate that silence does not exist in the natural world; it is the result of inattention. Every environment is alive with its own acoustic symphony: crickets chirping, car engines revving, footsteps falling and echoing. Such sounds evoke particular settings and can even indicate a specific time of day. Many of our associations with sounds may be unconscious; like Cage's audience, we often simply block out ambient noise. The sound designer, by contrast, studies and reproduces the aural specificity of times and places to help create a world on stage. Just as set and costume designers use a specific palette of colors to create a visual identity for the play, the sound designer chooses from a specific sonic palette to create an aural identity for the play.

■ **Telling the Story.** Tires screech. A crash. Silence, then sirens from a distance. Hearing these sound effects, we have already constructed a narrative in our imagination. Theatrical texts often require sounds to set the scene, give exposition, or help define the action. Events taking place off stage can be given life: The clop-clop of hooves announces an unexpected visitor; a steam whistle signals an imminent departure. **Motivated sounds** like these have an identifiable source and immediately give concrete information to the audience and work the same way as motivated lighting.

Sound can affect the way the audience experiences the story, and often this is achieved with abstract rather than realistic effects. Sound designers often consider the emotional arc of the plot and create its aural embodiment. Rhythmic pulsing increasing in tempo can underscore the tension in a scene. The wail of a violin can signal an emotional change. A crescendo can alert us to an explosive moment to come. Whether concrete or evocative, sounds tell stories and tell us how to relate to the narrative.

■ **Defining Mood and Style.** Sounds can establish the mood of a scene: The ticktock of a clock underlines the lateness of the hour and produces a feeling of suspense. Distorted eerie sounds of chanting can unsettle the audience and prepare them for a strange experience to come. The hustle and bustle of a fairground, carnival music, the hum of the crowd, laughter, and shouting barkers intimate excitement and a carefree mood. If the music becomes too slow and the laughter too loud, the feeling can change to one of discomfort or apprehension. Exaggerations and distortions can shift the style from realism to heightened theatricality.

Sounds heard by the audience that are outside of the characters' world can also establish an atmosphere. Musical scores, like those in films, draw on our emotional responses to indicate the moods dominating various scenes. This practice, reminiscent of nineteenth-century melodrama, has long been part of the theatre. Today recorded rather than live music often achieves the effect. Preshow music, played as audience members arrive and take their seats, sets a tone before the show even begins, and plays with audience expectations. Exit music, played as the audience leaves, reinforces a feeling for the audience to remember.

■ **Aiding the Flow of the Action and Providing Rhythm.** Sound designers can punctuate dramatic action aurally with sounds or music that herald the beginning or the end of a scene. Sound can cover a stage transition, either carrying the audience along in an even flow or emphasizing a break between scenes. The timing of these sound cues, when they begin and how long they last, sets a pace for the production as a whole. In David Ives's *All in the Timing*, multiple scenes replay attempts at a pickup in a café. Every time one of the characters says the wrong thing, a buzzer goes off. The frequency of the sound accelerates the more the characters fumble, adding to the rising comic action.

Today, as more and more playwrights write plays with short scenes or plays that are collections of unrelated short sketches, sound becomes even more important for its ability to provide a unifying element and a means of making repeated transitions. More and more playwrights are aware of how sound can help their work and write suggestions for

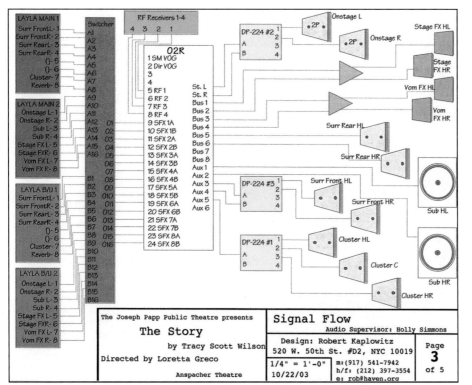

Figures 13.2a–c illustrate aspects of the sound designer's work on a production.

Figure 13.2a Sound designer Robert Kaplowitz's signal flow chart for Tracy Scott Williams's *The Story* at the Joseph Papp Public Theatre, director Loretta Greco. The chart shows what sound devices are being used for the show, where they are placed, what switches operate them, and the flow of sound from microphones and players to speakers.

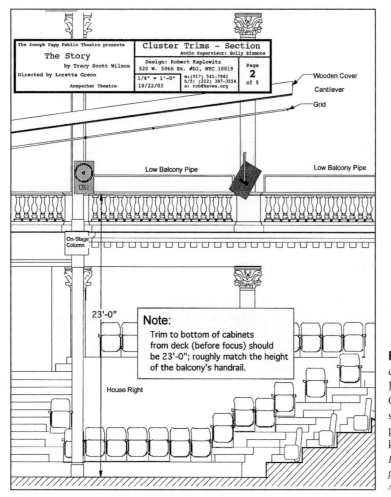

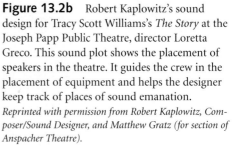

Figure 13.2b Robert Kaplowitz's sound design for Tracy Scott Williams's *The Story* at the Joseph Papp Public Theatre, director Loretta Greco. This sound plot shows the placement of speakers in the theatre. It guides the crew in the placement of equipment and helps the designer keep track of places of sound emanation.

Reprinted with permission from Robert Kaplowitz, Composer/Sound Designer, and Matthew Gratz (for section of Anspacher Theatre).

directed by Loretta Greco Sound Q Synopsis - "The Story" by Tracy Scott Wilson design: R Kaplowitz				
Cue	Cue Name	Placement	Description	
167	Fade out	p 096 Transition complete	Fade out	
SFX	VO? ☐ Y ☒ N			O2R Scene 03
168	Theme	p 098 J: You're lying. I know you are.	marimba from theme	
SFX	VO? ☐ Y ☒ N			O2R Scene 03
169	Fade out theme	p 099 Yvonne in place	Fade out	
RF	VO? ☐ Y ☒ N			O2R Scene 03
172	Radio Transition	p 103 P: You're under the arrest for the obstruction of justice.	News radio hit (redman) into voice over text plus low traffic rumble and hi traffic add	
SFX/RF	VO? ☒ Y ☐ N			O2R Scene 03
173	Pulldown to Radio	p 104 With butts in seats	Pull down level to "Radio Like"	
SFX	VO? ☐ Y ☒ N			O2R Scene 03
174	Fade Traffic	p 104 With reporter text complete in VO "48 hours to reveal her sources"	Traffic add out plus hit of garbage truck	
SFX	VO? ☐ Y ☒ N			O2R Scene 03
175	Traffic Out	p 105 Y: Went into an apartment	Pull main traffic out of surrounds to subs only	
SFX	VO? ☐ Y ☒ N			O2R Scene 03
178	Cop and Girl, RF 1&3	p 107 J: Two days, Yvonne. Two days.	Tension rhythm (hip hop) plus RF 1, 3 Up O2R SCENE 45	
SFX	VO? ☒ Y ☐ N			O2R Scene 45
178.5	Music Fade	p 107 A As girls exit/Yvonne moves to chair	Music fade	
RF	VO? ☒ Y ☐ N			O2R Scene 45
179	RF OUT	p 107 A Girl: I ain't do nothin'	RF 1, 3 out - O2R Scene 3	
SFX	VO? ☐ Y ☒ N			O2R Scene 03
180	Trans to 12C	p 111 P: And one for people who think she'll get caught.	Single bass note, distant.	
SFX	VO? ☐ Y ☒ N			O2R Scene 03
180.5	Trans to 13 - Prayer	p 112 A P: ... you're not taking Outlook with you.	Walking Bass version of theme	
SFX	VO? ☐ Y ☒ N			O2R Scene 03
181	Fade Music	p 112 B Yvonne in place Up Center	Fade out with Yvonne in place	
SFX	VO? ☐ Y ☒ N			O2R Scene 03
182	RF 4 UP	p 112 B Y: What am I going to...	RF 4 UP - O2R SCENE 58 RF into surrounds, ambiant reverb.	
RF	VO? ☐ Y ☒ N			O2R Scene 58
184	RF Out	p 112 D Latisha Exits	RF 4 Out -O2R SCENE 3 UP.	
RF	VO? ☐ Y ☒ N			O2R Scene 03

Figure 13.2c Sound designer Robert Kaplowitz's Sound Cue Synopsis for Tracy Scott Williams's *The Story* at the Joseph Papp Public Theatre, director Loretta Greco. Each sound cue has a number and a name, and the chart records a description of the sound and the line of the play that cues the sound.
Reprinted with permission from Robert Kaplowitz, Composer/Sound Designer.

sound into the script. Producers have discovered that changing scenes through sounds can be easier and less costly than doing it with sets.

■ **Reinforcing the Central Image or Theme of the Text.** Sometimes sound can sum up the action of the drama in a way that gives the audience a visceral, intuitive understanding of its meaning. At the end of Chekhov's *The Cherry Orchard*, the script indicates that the audience hears the sound of a breaking string dying away followed by the thud of an ax hitting a tree. The sound of the ax reveals that the destruction of the cherry orchard has begun, but together these sounds poignantly convey the end of an era and the dissolution of the world of the aristocracy, the central theme of the play.

Challenges and Choices

How should a designer balance audience comfort against the need to use light or sound for a shocking effect?

The Sound Designer's Process

Because comprehensive sound design is a relatively recent development, the work of sound designers varies from production to production and differs according to their specific skills. Some may work on amplification only, whereas others will create an overall

Photo 13.10
Small, unobtrusive body microphones, like these worn around the ear, are now commonly used to amplify the actors' voices on stage, especially in musical theatre. Kia Glover, NaTasha Yvette Williams, and Dwayne Grayman wear mikes that are barely visible from the audience in *Ain't Misbehavin'*, the Fats Waller musical conceived and originally directed by Richard Maltby, Jr. Directed and choreographed by Kent Gash; music director, Darryl G. Ivey; costume design, Austin K. Sanderson; set design, Emily Beck; lighting design, William H. Grant III; sound design, Peter Sasha Hurowitz; at the Trinity Repertory Company, Providence, RI.
© *T. Charles Erickson*

sound score. Some use original music and effects, whereas others draw from existing material to meet the needs of a production.

The sound designer's work usually begins with reading and analyzing a text for sound requirements and meeting with the director to discuss how sound can help realize the director's vision. Before this meeting some sound designers ask themselves what the rhythm, impulse, or energy of the play is to locate a feeling for the sound. Sound designers conceive of their work as an art in time. Because audiences experience sound through change, sound designers consider the structure of the story and how rhythm and tempo can support that dramatic structure. They think about a field of possibilities without making specific choices. The director usually has some very specific ideas in mind that further limit the range of effects. The director will discuss the style and setting of the play and how its time and place, concept and mood can be evoked by sound. When a director already has very specific ideas, the sound designer becomes a researcher to hone the director's choices. Some directors describe a feeling they want and set the sound designer free to create that feeling in an individual way.

Sound designers work with the other members of the design team to determine the placement of sound equipment and microphones on stage (see Figure 13.2b). They may even need to hide a microphone in a costume. Attending rehearsals can give a clear idea of the required timing and duration for sound cues and may provide new ideas about how sound might support the production.

Many sound designers own libraries of recorded sound. Today many effects can be downloaded from the Internet. Preexisting recordings can be purchased. Sound designers, like others on the creative team, do research to find material appropriate to particular settings and times: A setting in the Middle East may require a call to prayer and chanted passages from holy texts; Latin America might require particular music and rhythms. Discoveries and creations are shared with the director as part of the evolution of the design. When sound choices are finalized, the designer edits the sound samples onto separate discs or tapes (depending on theatre equipment) or onto one disk or tape in the order in which the cues are to be played during the course of the show. Multiple

IN PERSPECTIVE

In Their Own Words

ROBERT KAPLOWITZ

Robert Kaplowitz has been a part of the development of hundreds of new plays as designer, composer, and sometimes dramaturg. He spent five years as the resident sound designer at the Eugene O'Neill Playwrights Conference, where he worked with writers from Lee Blessing to August Wilson. Selected New York premieres include An Almost Holy Picture; The Story *(Lortel Nomination);* Light; Raise the Roof; Fat Pig; The Distance from Here; Bexley, OH!; Urban Zulu Mambo; True Love; Meshugah; Hurricane; White Chocolate; *and* Touch. *His musical designs include the tours of* Promises, Promises *and* Leader of the Pack. *He is also the producing artistic director of the Relentless Theatre Company.*

■ What drew you to this profession?

I studied jazz saxophone as a child and was enamored of the notion of composition through improvisation. In high school, while I was never interested in being a performer, I did think all those actresses were cute, and so I became a stagehand. That, coupled with an amazing electronic music lab where I studied tape loops, analogue synthesis, and basic recording techniques, led me to explore the idea of creating soundscapes and music for plays.

I attended NYU's undergraduate design program, which did not teach sound design; however, the conceptual training I received—learning to understand my visceral response to a text and translate it into a concrete landscape—was invaluable to my growth as a designer. I continued writing music, picking up new instruments, and watching plays throughout college.

My first year in New York, I saw Mark Bennet's sound design for Caryl Churchill's *Mad Forest*. The play featured an amazing score, and in the middle of it was a two- or three-minute scene that took place without any words—just a deep silence accentuated by a very subtle set of environmental sounds and actor movement. In that instant, I became fully committed to my choice to become a sound designer.

■ Can you outline the steps in your creative process?

I begin, always, with the text. I read a play all the way through in a single go to grasp the flow, the rhythms, the linguistic evolution of the world. I do this without a pencil or any music in the background. I then read it again and write down anything at all that comes to my mind—words, phrases that stand out, responses

to moments, scenes that excite me, questions. I never censor myself. I am also looking for the moments when the text must stand on its own, without any other sounds. The third reading is for what is essential, sonically, to the text—I make a list of everything from "doorbell, p. 15, rich house" to "playwright says to score sc. 4, think about how." The fourth reading prepares me for my first conversations with my director. I make a list of every possible cue I might throw in, including the above "essentials" list. I take that list, plus all of my other thoughts, into conversation with the director, and this leads us to a complete list of possibilities, which eventually gets honed down into the actual cue synopsis.

The other major leaping off point for my work is time in the theatre. I try to arrange for ten or fifteen minutes alone in the space, just to listen. Not for any advanced acoustical research; I just like to hear the room and get a sense of the environment in which the play is going to happen. The theatre is my palette, and I like to get to know it before I begin. I also double-check all of the technical drawings—measuring out the room, adding information about the house. My main concern is the propagation of sound into the ears of the audience, and I need to have accurate spatial information about the room. How does the stage relate, physically, to the house? How far is the closest point between actors and audience? How far is the farthest? How deep is the balcony overhang? What's the distance between potential speaker positions and various audience locations? Are the walls parallel, or slightly angled or broken up with architecture? Where can I put surround speakers and subwoofers? A million more questions like these must be answered before I can design the physical sound system.

The next step is my favorite—I get to sit in the rehearsal room and play with my collaborators. The symbiosis between performers and the music or sound around them is probably the single most thrilling part of sound design for me. Modern technology enables me to sit in the room with a laptop and alter whatever work I've done in the studio. I've actually written entire scores while in rehearsals, gleaning an understanding of rhythm, pace, counterpoint, support, and dynamics as the actors and director are making similar discoveries for themselves.

■ Do you consider yourself a composer?

Yes, but I would be whether or not I was a sound designer. However, I do not in any way want to imply that one must be a composer, in the traditional sense of the word, to become a sound designer. I have heard soundscapes created entirely out of preexisting music and effects that certainly feel like compositions to me, from designers who never refer to themselves as composers.

■ What skills must a sound designer possess?

The ability to make writers and directors comfortable and confident. To be able to read for dramaturgical analysis. To be able to talk with everyone on the team, accepting their notions and offering your own. Sometimes, you need a lot of restraint—tongue-biting is a good skill to have. Every collaborator is an artist, and it's sometimes important to let the others make choices without throwing your own two cents in.

You really need to know how to listen—to what the characters are saying, to what the room is doing, to the real world around you, and to every piece and style of music that comes your way. To understand that in theatre, everything is heightened. If you were to stop reading, right now, and sit totally still for sixty seconds, listening, you would notice a whole lot more than we do ordinarily. Try it. When an audience steps into a theatre, all perceptions are heightened. So you need to understand how the ordinary becomes extraordinary in theatre, and to stay specific with every choice you make.

What we do is a marriage of the artistic to the technical, so there are also a slew of technical skills to be developed. You must learn an array of sound system details—terms like *phase coupling, feedback loops, precedence effect, equalization, delay,* and *microphone field patterns.* We have to understand how the sound moves through the room, the best way to get it there, and how the room itself is going to behave in the process. How I deliver a sound cue is as important as its content. And how I deliver an actor's voice is probably even more important.

■ How do you see the profession evolving in the future?

Writers and directors have become aware of what we can do, as artists, and are becoming interested in working with designers as we find new ways to add meaning, emotion, excitement, and environment to the plays themselves. More and more, I come across scripts that ask the designer to become a co-creator, which thrills me to no end. Much of this is a result of recent advances in technology—the flexibility brought to me by computing allows me to make changes in the theatre as rapidly as a lighting designer.

Technology has also advanced reinforcement to unprecedented levels of subtlety. Microphones are becoming more invisible, both acoustically and physically. Technology allows for new ways of mixing a show as well as increased flexibility in configuring a sound system. And innovations in speaker technology have allowed designers to deliver precise reproductions of actors' voices. So I imagine growing more flexible, more artistically free, and more involved with the ideas of theatre, rather than with the nuts-and-bolts of how things work.

■ Are you concerned about amplification removing the immediacy of the human voice?

Of course—it's actually what we try to avoid. Well-designed sound systems provide that immediacy of voice. Every designer's goal is to create a transparent sound system, where the reinforcement seems to disappear and it feels like the audience is hearing just the performers. Listeners have become more sophisticated as the field has grown. Our goal is to stay a step ahead of the audience's ears at all times.

There is also a constant conflict—producers and audiences are often asking the sound team to "turn it up" because people today listen to music very loudly, in intensely personalized environments. If you've spent the past month listening to the *Chicago* soundtrack in your SUV, with its six-speaker surround sound focused on you alone, and then you go and see the show, you're going to have a very different experience. Scott Leher's terrific sound design for that show has preserved the immediacy of the human voice, its real nature, its sense of human origin. Your SUV's sound system has placed you in the middle of a recording session.

I am astounded when supposedly qualified critics ask why musical theatre performers need any reinforcement at all, when opera singers can fill the Met with no assistance. Stop and think about this for a moment—opera singers perform two or three times per week, at a maximum. They're usually performing in some of the most brilliantly designed acoustics on the globe. And they're singing music written to be performed before the advent of modern reinforcement. Musical theatre performers are going on stage eight times each week, often singing scores that have evolved from blues and rock—styles that are dependent on amplification for their very sound. They are often singing in theatres designed by "modern" architects, who, in the dismissal of all things "classical," somehow managed to lose track of the acoustical advantages of sculptural decoration and the horseshoe-shaped auditorium. We designers must continue to strive for better means of supporting and delivering those voices in a way that feels direct, real, and like it is coming from the performers.

(continues)

IN PERSPECTIVE (CONTINUED)

■ Do you feel you are helping to define this new profession, and how?

Not alone—I am standing on the shoulders, and in the company, of many giants. The first sound design credits on Broadway went to Abe Jacobs and Otts Munderloh in the 1970s. They're still out there in the trenches designing for musicals. In the 80s and 90s, soundscapes began to really play a part in the theatre, as directors and writers began to appreciate the artistry of what designers can add with the increased subtlety modern systems allow us. Music has always been a part of theatre, since early shamanistic ritual and Greek chant. But now, we have the ability to transmit this music with such flexibility that all theatre artists are reconsidering our roles.

I try to push sound further forward by creating soundscapes, scores, and systems that alter the audience's relationship to the events of the play. By helping writers to hear what they've written into their plays; by creating another layer in the world of the play that can talk to the audience through a set of senses they use less often, and less consciously; and by encouraging emerging sound designers to "risk, fail, and risk again," I am helping the profession.

■ Do you have any advice for aspiring sound designers?

Aspiring designers should pursue all knowledge—read, listen to music, go to museums and galleries, follow politics, learn about genetics, study a language . . . the more influences a designer has, the more open he or she can be to the world that we, as a profession, comment on. Avoid bogging down in any sort of "personal aesthetic"—a designer, at his or her core, is meant to be responding to the world of the play, rather than letting personal taste steer the soundscape. The key, for me, is to become a blank slate. I have a lot of information rattling around in my brain, but I never have any answers until I've spent time with the words, and with my collaborators. Only then can I create a sound design that is an accurate reflection of the play.

Source: Used with permission from Robert Kaplowitz.

sound sources can be layered and mixed by the sound operator with a *mixer,* a device that merges the sound sources into one or more streams of sound.

Sound designers may use sound systems already in place in the theatre, or they may be responsible for acquiring and setting up the necessary sound equipment. A **sound plot** shows all the equipment the show will use and how the different pieces (microphones, amplifiers, etc.) connect to one another (see Figures 13.2a and b). Before technical rehearsals, the sound designer makes sure all the equipment is working properly. During technical rehearsals, the sound designer, in consultation with the director, helps set sound levels and timing for sound cues, often coordinating sound effects with lights, set changes, and the actors' physical actions (see Figure 13.2c). Designers adjust equipment and balance the sounds coming from the loudspeakers so they reach all areas of the auditorium evenly. They also adjust the sound so that amplified and recorded sounds reach the audience at the same time as live sound from the stage. The sound designer's job, like that of other designers, ends when the show opens. Technicians continue to test, run, and maintain the equipment during the run of the production.

The Sound Designer's Tools

Stage microphones detect the sounds on stage and amplify them through loudspeakers. *Area mikes* pick up sounds in a wide area, whereas *shotgun mikes* focus on a specific direction. Today many actors wear wireless *body mikes,* attached either to their clothes or to their heads.

New technologies for creating and playing sound cues in the theatre continue to give designers greater control of sound quality. Although some theatres still use reel-to-reel tapes, digital sound technology is becoming the norm, with sound designs stored on compact disks, minidiscs, stand-alone digital workstations, or a computer's hard drive.

Both lighting and sound design have evolved in the last one hundred years through advances in technology unthinkable in past eras. The number of possible cues and the complexity of effects, the accuracy and timing of the execution of designs, and the range of artistic vocabulary far surpasses those of even a generation ago. Technical progress will surely continue to offer new innovations, and light and set design will be limited only by the power of the imagination.

Challenges and Choices

Are sound and light shows theatre?

KEY IDEAS

- Lighting designers translate their understanding of how natural and artificial light connect us to the world into lighting effects for the stage.
- Light is not what we see, but rather what we see by, and it often affects us unconsciously.
- Lighting creates the emotional atmosphere for a theatrical event and plays a crucial role in unifying the visual elements on stage.
- The development of lighting design is closely tied to technological advances such as safe, efficient electricity and new lighting instruments.
- The goals of stage lighting include creating mood, providing visibility, defining style, establishing time and place, focusing attention on stage, telling the story, reinforcing a central image or theme, and establishing rhythm.
- Lighting designers develop a design through careful reading of a text, discussion with the director and creative team, and research. A significant part of their work is accomplished during technical rehearsals.
- Lighting designers manipulate the four basic qualities

of light—intensity, distribution, color, and movement.
- The visual elements of design—line, mass, texture, color, and scale—are revealed through the composition of light.
- Lighting designers accommodate a range of lighting options within an overall design.
- Sound design has only recently emerged as a theatrical art. Advances in digital technology now afford a greater ability to create, control, and amplify every kind of sound.
- Today's theatrical soundscapes include the traditional and nontraditional use of actors' voices, live music, recorded music, synthetic sound and stage effects, and specifically composed sound scores.
- The goals of sound design include audibility, establishing the environment, telling the story, defining mood and style, aiding the flow of the action and providing rhythm, and reinforcing a central image or theme.
- Some sound designers use original music and effects, whereas others draw from existing material to meet the needs of a production.

Clown Bill Irwin provides comic commentary on our fascination with technology as he finds his identity fragmented between his physical and technological selves, in *Largely New York*. Written and directed by Bill Irwin, St. James Theatre, New York.

© Joan Marcus

The human exchange between an actor and an audience is so central to the theatrical experience that we often think of the world of science and machines as antagonistic to live performance. Yet in every period of recorded theatre history, the world of the stage made use of available technology to heighten its expressive power. Every costume, mask, prop, set, and theatre structure requires technical skill and tools to create. Technology is a force in our lives, and theatrical forms use, reflect, and comment on its power.

The curtain rising, sets changing, and lights illuminating the stage were once novel inventions that we now take for granted. The front curtain goes back to ancient Rome; rapid set changes date from the Renaissance; the spotlight was introduced only in the nineteenth century. Electric stage lighting, now an essential design element complementing sets and costumes, was not in wide use until the twentieth century. Innovative artists and engineers brought these new technologies to the stage, inspired by their novelty or their aesthetic potential.

Theatre artists have always made use of available technologies to create stage effects, and often they prompt engineers, technicians, and craftspeople to develop new devices

Artists IN PERSPECTIVE

JOSEF SVOBODA (1920–2002): VISIONARY ARTIST, TECHNOLOGICAL INNOVATOR

Czech designer Josef Svoboda redefined stage design in the twentieth century. In a career boasting over seven hundred productions at major theatres across the globe, Svoboda brought kinetic sets; expressive lighting; and slide, film, and video projections into an overall aesthetic in which new technologies supported dramatic action. He preferred the title "scenographer" to "designer," feeling that it better expressed his role as a vital participant in creating a comprehensive, active space for performance. For Svoboda "design" suggested beautiful stage pictures conceived in two-dimensional sketches or superficial decoration, whereas "scenography" applied to a conceptualization of space in three dimensions. Filling a stage with vapor or cutting it with strong beams of light was scenography.

Svoboda first gained international recognition in 1958 at the Brussels World's Fair, where he and director Alfred Radok presented two multimedia works, *Polyekran* and *Laterna Magika*. These performances combined multiple projections with sound design and live actors performing ballet and pantomime. The precise coordination of live and recorded elements and Svoboda's new multiscreen projection system made *Laterna Magika* the most popular exhibit at the fair and won it first prize. *Laterna Magika* later lent its name to the Laterna Magika theatre in Prague, which has continued to experiment in this mixed-media format. Svoboda became the principal designer for Laterna Magika in 1973, but the bulk of his innovative design work was accomplished at the National Theatre in Prague, where he served as principal designer

and technical director from 1948 to 1992, and where he would bring his new techniques to theatre and opera production.

Svoboda's training in architecture led him to see space as a primary organizing principle in life and on stage. Moving set pieces that could reconfigure the space during the course of a production were a central motif in his work. For Wagner's *Ring Cycle* at Covent Garden (1974–1976), the main set unit was a large central platform supported by telescopic columns that could tilt in numerous directions. The surface of the platform would transform into stairs at an angle proportional to the tilt whenever the platform tilted more than 15 degrees. The underside of the platform was covered with a mirrored surface, so Rhinemaidens in the trap area under the stage appeared to the audience as a mirrored reflection.

Sometimes Svoboda effected a change of space with projections, a trademark of his work, or with light, an element he crafted with precision. In his design for Chekhov's *The Three Sisters* at the National Theatre in London in 1967, stretched cords hung at the back of the stage were used as screens. With frontal projections, they became a wallpapered interior; with rear projections, a forest with beams of sunlight peeking through.

Svoboda found traditional design sketches and renderings inadequate for conveying his ideas and used kinetic, lit models instead. These models and the exhibits he created for world expositions were a source of the technical innovation he would bring to the stage. His background as a master carpenter and architect gave Svoboda the practical knowledge to turn his powerful artistic visions into theatrical reality. When the available technological instruments fell short of his needs, he invented his own, including the Svoboda light curtain, the Svoboda light ramp, and the Svoboda footlight, instruments he intro-

or techniques. At other times new tools themselves inspire theatrical innovations and lead artists in imaginative new directions. Technology helps stage all aspects of the human experience, from everyday domestic exchanges, to confrontations with natural disasters, fantastic journeys of the imagination, and spiritual encounters with the divine.

We have come to take technology for granted as today's advances are rapidly incorporated into our daily existence and change the way we live. Just think of how the home computer and the Internet have altered so much of our lives. In the theatre, just as in life, each advance opens a realm of expressive potential and spurs innovations that can alter theatrical forms. Today theatre has unprecedented technical means at its disposal.

Media such as film, television, video, and the Internet surround us; they entertain us, educate us, and move us emotionally, as at one time only theatre could do. Now these new media compete with the theatre, find their way into productions, and create the cultural background that frames our theatrical experiences. To understand theatre's relation to contemporary technology, we must appreciate the role technology has always played in both enhancing and transforming theatrical traditions.

duced to theatres around the world. His inventions enabled projections and controlled lighting to become functional elements of stage design. To eliminate light reflecting off the stage floor when projections were used, he tilted the floor backwards and covered it with a non-reflective surface. A specially designed screen gave clarity when projections were used alongside other theatrical lighting. His 1967 design for *Tristan and Isolde* at the Hesse State Theatre in Wiesbaden became famous for its pillar of light created with illuminations of a special aerosol mixture of water vapor and fog droplets holding an electrostatic charge. The light image disappeared when droplets with an opposite charge were released. In reorganizing and modernizing the technical procedures at the Czech National Theatre, Svoboda gave the company

the latest equipment and a fully trained staff of over three hundred personnel, support that helped him realize his artistic goals.

Svoboda used the most modern materials and techniques, but saw them only as tools. Without a meaningful theatrical text, these sophisticated techniques to him were merely gadgets. He once claimed that he would design a set with cheese if it was appropriate for the play. Svoboda was also aware that his designs needed to speak to the cultural climate outside the theatre as well as to the play on stage. In a career that extended over some of his homeland's most turbulent sociopolitical times, his visionary theatrical spaces reflected change and the hope for the future his audiences needed in their own lives.

For the 1962 production of Milan Kundera's *Owners of the Keys,* a domestic drama that focuses on a young man's inner struggle with his duties under Nazi occupation, Josef Svoboda used lighting and kinetic sets to accommodate the play's fluid, back-and-forth movement between two realistic rooms and a series of visions that revealed the main character's inner world. The realistic locations, set on wagon stages, evaporated as the wagons were pulled behind a black curtain. The visions, like the one pictured here, were enacted in a space of physical and emotional emptiness, defined by a pyramid of light reflected from a mirror at the top. Directed by Otomar Kreja, Tyl Theatre, Prague.
© Dr. Jaromir Svoboda

What Is Technology?

The word *technology* comes from the Greek *techne*, meaning "skill," "art," or "craft." While *technology* suggests sophisticated, scientific means, it refers more broadly to any technique we use to shape our physical environment and facilitate our cultural practices. Technology sets human beings apart from other animals because it takes us beyond mere biological instinct. Carving stone tools, making fire, weaving cloth, and forging metals are some of the earliest technologies of humankind. Writing is a technology that not only helps us keep track of objects and ideas, but also makes possible new modes of expression. The production of artifacts through technological means is so bound up with our cultural practices that it is impossible to imagine or describe human beings without it. It is equally impossible to describe the world of theatre in the absence of technology. A theatre without technology would consist of a naked actor performing outside without props, sets, or musical instruments, in front of a group of naked spectators seated on the ground.

Even so, some technical devices stand out because they are novelties, create amazing special effects, or require specially trained technicians. They may even threaten to displace the actor as the center of the theatrical event, especially when they incorporate cutting-edge scientific achievements that impress us in their own right, beyond what they contribute to the art.

We can draw a distinction between *low-tech* and *high-tech* devices. These fall along a continuum, and the high-tech devices of one generation may end up being the low-tech devices of the next. The difference between them generally reflects the degree to which they replace human power with nonhuman power. The more high-tech a technology is, the less physical human effort it requires to make it work. Sometimes these devices replace or supplant the human presence on stage, and because theatre essentially features humanity at its center, the introduction of new high-tech elements inevitably raises questions about their influence on theatre as we know it.

The Impact of Technology

When new technologies enter the theatre, we are not always clear how best to exploit their theatrical potential. Artists and technicians may play with them in rehearsal and performance, discover their possibilities, and develop ways to make them work on stage, often through trial and error. Over time, as they prove their worth, the theatre adopts them as general practice. Once the technology is mastered, new personnel train in the field and continue to discover novel ways of bringing out the technology's full theatrical potential.

Audiences also adapt to new technologies. A quick set change captivated Renaissance audiences, but has less impact today. Color washes over the stage permitted by the introduction of electricity to stage lighting astounded early-twentieth-century spectators, but today we expect this effect. New technologies can disrupt the audience's focus on acting and text, but as familiarity grows, they can heighten the effect of both.

Whereas some uses of technology *enhance* production, others *transform* the theatrical form. Technology enhances a production when it works in conjunction with other artistic elements to illuminate meaning. When technology supplants the acting and text, it may transform the theatrical event into something different.

Deciding whether a particular technological element is enhancing or transforming is a subjective matter. It can depend on our general attitude toward technology, our ex-

Challenges and Choices

Can theatre as an art form absorb any kind of technology over time? Do some technologies overwhelm or transform the essential actor–audience relationship?

pectations concerning the theatrical event, and ultimately how we understand the nature of theatre itself. Some theatre practitioners are resistant to new technology because of its potential to eclipse the live performer, while others embrace new possibilities to enhance their productions. In either case, it is impossible simply to ignore the technological changes that continue to reshape our daily lives and their potential influence on how we experience the theatre.

Technology and Culture

Technological devices shape our interaction with the world around us, but they also reveal how we see ourselves within that world. Some theatrical traditions use very few devices and rely on the actor or dramatic language to carry meaning. Others exploit a variety of means to create a theatre of spectacle and illusion. In every historical period, the use of artificial devices on stage has exhibited not just technical accomplishments, but cultural values.

Ancient Greece

The ancient Greeks did not make extensive use of technical devices in their theatrical productions, but the few they did use clearly reflected their cultural attitudes and their aesthetic sensibility. The **mēchanē** was a large hand-powered crane that hoisted actors

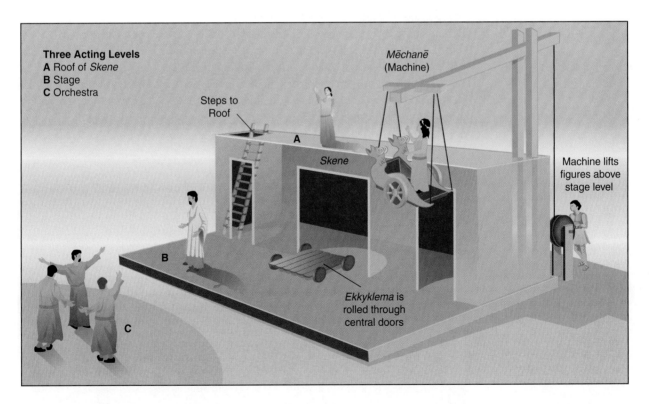

Figure 14.1 Stage Devices of the Ancient Greek Theatre. The *mēchanē* on the right was a crane used to lift actors playing gods above the *skene*. The *ekkyklema*, a platform on wheels, could be rolled out of the central doors to display a tableau, a visual scene depicting the aftermath of an off-stage event.

above the *skene*, or back wall, of the performance area. The flying actor usually portrayed a god, so the *mēchanē* suggested the gulf between human and divine power (see Photo 3.2). It captured the philosophical issues at the heart of Greek tragedy in a visual theatrical metaphor.

The ancient Greeks also made use of an **ekkyklema**, a platform on wheels that rolled on stage displaying actors prearranged in a tableau—a staged picture. The Greeks did not like to depict violence on stage, but the *ekkyklema* allowed them to show the aftermath of violent action without showing the graphic brutality that caused it. Aeschylus probably used the *ekkyklema* in *Agamemnon* to reveal the dead bodies of King Agamemnon and Cassandra after they had been caught in a net and stabbed to death by Queen Clytemnestra, although the murders took place off stage. The *ekkyklema* allowed the Greeks to contemplate tragedy as an idea, rather than just a sensational, often bloody, spectacle.

It is impossible to know whether the Greeks first brought these devices into the theatre to accommodate plays already written as we know them, or whether playwrights introduced ascending gods and offstage action in their works because they knew the *mēchanē* and *ekkyklema* were available. What we do know is that both devices were part of Greek theatrical convention and today inform our understanding of that tradition.

Ancient Rome

More so than the Greeks, the ancient Romans were brilliant engineers and tended to be more interested in concrete practical realities than abstract philosophical reflection. Consequently, theatre in Rome was never a forum for social debate, as it was in Greece. During the period of the Roman Empire (27 B.C.E.–476 C.E.), when Rome had an extremely large, diverse population and performances catered to the tastes of the masses, Romans used their engineering skills to create spectacular events. They flooded arenas for theatrical naval displays called **naumachiae** (see Photo 14.1), in which sea vessels did battle on water before spectators, often resulting in real casualties. The Romans also invented the front curtain, back curtain, and sliding scenery. They even developed new ways to accommodate the audience such as retractable awnings at outdoor amphitheaters that protected spectators from rain and sun. The Romans made technology a focus in a theatre of spectacle.

Photo 14.1

This eighteenth-century engraving of a *naumachia* offers one visual interpretation of these ancient Roman spectacles in which flooded arenas were the site of nautical battles. Engraving by Johann Bernhard Fischer von Erlach, part of *Entwurf einer Historischen Architektur*, circa 1721.
© *Historical Picture Archive/ CORBIS*

The Middle Ages

During the Middle Ages, when liturgical dramas took place inside churches and cathedrals, young celebrants costumed as angels adorned with wings and halos were hoisted on ropes and pulleys to the highest rafters to portray God's heaven on Earth. Occasional accidents only reaffirmed the importance of faith in the afterlife. When religious dramas moved outdoors, local guilds constructed pageant wagons that traveled through the town to carry the settings for cycle plays that depicted Christian history from Creation to Judgment Day. Each guild designed and constructed the set for one biblical story, so these productions gave artisans a chance to display their skills to the community. In England the shipwrights' guild staged the story of Noah with a swaying ark. Other effects included fountains springing from the ground, trees withering, and miraculous transformations such as Moses' staff turning into a snake. The Hellmouth, the mouth of a beast representing the entryway to hell, spat out real fire. These Christian religious plays used machinery and special effects to bring God's miracles to life for their audiences.

The Renaissance

The Italian Renaissance prompted new explorations in science and art, and both found their way onto the stage in the form of elaborate, illusionistic perspective sets. Later, between 1641 and 1645, Giacomo Torelli (1608–1678) perfected a system for transforming all the elements of a stage set at once. The **chariot-and-pole system** consisted of a series of ropes and pulleys attached to a succession of painted flat wings set in grooved tracks on the stage and then hitched to a pulley system located beneath the stage. When the gears moved, it pulled the ropes, moving all the flats simultaneously to reveal a new scene instantaneously. This device startled and amazed audiences at the time, both for the magical transformation it effected on stage and for the ingenuity that accomplished it. Torelli's fame led to a royal summons to the court of France, where he introduced his scenic practices.

Figure 14.2 A device to create a Paradise effect for the Feast of the Annunciation, developed by Filippo Brunelleschi (1377–1446) in Florence, c. 1426. A wood structure holding three rings of lanterns representing stars and twelve choir boys dressed as angels, held by iron belts, was hoisted through a pulley system high up into the rafters of cathedrals, and suspended from the church roof. Below this device, eight more angels and the angel of the Annunciation hung from the pictured copper *mandorla*, or almond-shaped structure, also studded with star lanterns, which could be lowered toward the actor playing the Virgin in the church when the annunciation arrives.

The chariot-and-pole system was a perfect addition to lavish court productions that already had glorious sets and costumes created by professional artists and featured music and dance rather than dramatic text. It put new developments in art and science to use for the theatre and seemed to confirm the divine right of the princes who commissioned these entertainments by manifesting heavenly magic in the form of grand theatrical illusion.

Figure 14.3   The Operation of Giacomo Torelli's Pole-and-Chariot System for Simultaneous Scene Changes.   The scene is actually created by a series of flats along the side of the stage painted to create a receding perspective. The scenic flats are placed in grooves on the stage and can be moved into the wings along these tracks by a system of interconnected ropes and pulleys below the stage. When the mechanism for running the pulleys is turned, one set of flats slides out and another set with a different scenic design rolls in simultaneously, creating rapid scenic changes that dazzled seventeenth-century audiences. Photo 14.2 below shows a Torelli set created through a series of painted flats manipulated in this manner.

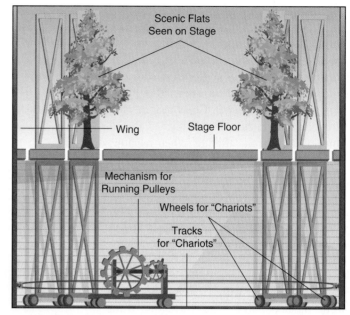

Torelli's position in France was later usurped by Gaspare Vigarani (1586–1663), who created the Salle des Machines. This hall of machines was the largest theatre in Europe, and its curious dimensions led to both its success and failure. Only 52 feet wide by 232 feet long with a stage depth of 140 feet, spectacular effects of perspective were possible through the 32-foot-wide proscenium arch. Unfortunately, technological feats were put before practical needs, resulting in the acoustics being so poor that the theatre was seldom used.

The Nineteenth Century

The nineteenth century saw an increased interest in the application of science to all aspects of life, including the arts. Even popular journals such as the *Scientific American* ran articles on the application of new technologies to the theatre, and one of its editors,

Photo 14.2
Engraving by Pierre Aveline of the forest landscape designed by Giacomo Torelli for the third act of the opera *Venere Gelosa* (Jealous Venus), first performed in Venice in 1643.
Photo from Sveriges Teatermuseum

Albert A. Hopkins, wrote "Magic: Stage Illusions and Scientific Diversions" (1897) to describe scientific applications in performance.

Nineteenth-century American melodrama, with its emphasis on sensationalism as mass entertainment, was quick to draw on the new technologies. Producers kept devising ever more startling stage effects to compete for audiences. *The Mansaniello; or, The Dumb Girl of Portici* advertised its explosion of Mount Vesuvius with burning lava and fireworks as a featured attraction, and *Timour the Tartar* had the hero rescue an unfortunate from the surges of a simulated waterfall.

During the early part of the century, technology itself was often the theatrical event. Audiences would come to see panoramas that encircled them in round buildings. Later, continuous scenes painted on lengths of cloth were wound on spools and unfurled as moving scenes rolling across the stage behind stationary objects such as ships or carriages that appeared to be changing location. This technique can be seen in many films. Louis-Jacques Daguerre (1751–1851) pioneered the use of painted transparent cloth bathed in changing light manipulated through overhead shuttered windows to give the impression of movement through time and space. His famous double effect dioramas were painted on both sides. Through the regulation of light, one or the other side, or both, could be made visible. His diorama, "Midnight Mass at St. Étienne-du-Mont" showed an empty church gradually filling with people for midnight Mass and then emptying again. Daguerre's work with light led him to make pioneering discoveries in the field of photography.

Rejecting Technology

The absence or willful omission of elaborate technological stage effects can also make a theatrical statement. As we have already seen, in Asian traditions such as Chinese opera, *noh*, and *kathakali*, forms more concerned with the art of acting than with stage realism, the actor defines the environment and creates theatrical effects through subtle gestures and suggestive movements; stage elements are few and preserve the actor-centered aesthetic. In Chinese opera a billowing blue cloth held at either end by a stagehand is sufficient to indicate ocean swells.

During the Vietnam War, Western theatre artists created actor-centered productions that deliberately avoided high-tech stage effects and devices. This movement was

> **Challenges and Choices**
>
> If the central element of theatre is the actor, is theatre that relies on technology to make an impact inferior theatre?

Photo 14.3
Nineteenth-century audiences enjoyed events in which technological innovation was the primary spectacle. Here, moving scenes of a Daguerre diorama provide entertainment. The scene is of interest itself, but the main attraction was watching it transform into another, effected by the turning of the scrolled canvas behind the screen.
© Bettmann/CORBIS

IN PERSPECTIVE

FROM PUPPETS TO PERFORMING OBJECTS

Puppetry, one of the earliest forms of performance, is becoming a central player in today's world of media entertainment. The term *performing object* is replacing the term *puppet* to describe a wide range of inanimate objects found in theatrical performance and on film, all manipulated either directly by a performer or through a variety of technological means.

Puppeteer Stephen Kaplin[1] describes how performing objects range along a continuum that begins with the actor in costume and moves to the most technologically sophisticated computerized creatures. When actors put on wigs and costumes, they are using inanimate materials to help them project character. When they wear masks, the separation of the performer and the performing object is more distinct. Actors manipulate masks by moving their heads and, in so doing, bring the mask, and the character, to life. A puppet is an object fully removed from the actor. The farther the object is from the performer, the more technology the performer requires to manipulate it.

Sometimes the technology is simple—a wooden stick for a rod puppet or a set of strings for a marionette. At a greater distance the technology can become more complex, such as radio signals or computers to control animatronic or mechanized puppets. Even computer-animated

1. *Stephen Kaplin, "A Puppet Tree: A Model for the Field of Puppet Theatre,"* The Drama Review 43, 3 *(Fall 1999): 28–35.*

figures can be considered performing objects. They are manipulated by someone projecting character through advanced computer technology. In the first *Star Wars* film in which the character Yoda appeared, he was primarily operated from underneath, like a hand puppet, by Henson puppeteer Frank Oz. The size of the figure was partially determined by the length of Oz's arm. In his second movie appearance, Yoda was primarily an animatronic or mechanically operated puppet, controlled by a puppeteer working the controls from off the set. In his final appearance, the animatronic Yoda was assisted for two scenes by a computer-animated counterpart, whose every move was crafted in cyberspace.

The transformation of puppets into performing objects links puppetry with computer animation, one of the most innovative and popular forms of entertainment of our times. It draws connections between the ancient skills of puppeteers and the new skills required for technological media. It also reflects the aesthetic approach of many contemporary stage artists who combine a range of performance techniques on stage.

Director-designer Julie Taymor freely mixes masks with *bunraku*-style puppets, shadow puppets, and other manipulated objects of her own invention in a single production. To call her work "puppetry" underestimates the variety of stage images she employs. Performing artists Janie Geiser and Kazuko Hohki combine performing objects with film and video, a match that often works more fluidly than live performers working in concert with video and film.

The performing object is a meeting point for theatre and technology. Any performing object can threaten to

to some extent a theatrical response to the military-industrial complex that supported the war. Its aesthetic affirmed the ability of ordinary people to take control of society, politics, and culture through human strength, ingenuity, and grassroots initiatives. Some groups, such as the San Francisco Mime Troupe and Bread and Puppet Theatre, delighted in a low-tech aesthetic, using basic portable stages, masks, and papier-mâché puppets. These simple techniques empowered participants to take control of the theatrical means of production. Other groups, such as the Living Theatre, the Open Theatre, and the Performance Group, did away with even these low-tech elements and focused on the physical and emotional transformations of unadorned actors on a mostly bare stage.

Challenges and Choices

Is a theatre that rejects technological effects necessarily more humanistic?

During the 1960s, many avant-garde groups around the world focused on the emotional power of the actor. Most notable was Jerzy Grotowski's Polish Laboratory Theatre. Believing that the essence of theatre was the actor and the audience, Grotowski rejected technology and replaced it with a "poor theatre" that relied on the actor's phys-

displace the actor's central position on stage, especially when it is operated electronically. However, some of the most technologically advanced performing objects have a performer, or several, behind them who give life to what is otherwise inanimate matter. In the case of computer animation, in which a tangible object doesn't even exist, the actor who performs the voice of a character may be its primary life source. Actors are recorded first, and the animation must complement their vocal renditions. Ani-mated figures are even made to look like the actors doing their voices. The Henson Digital Performance Studio allows a puppeteer to operate a computer-animated figure in real time, bringing it closer to live puppetry.

In the past puppeteers were often masked or hidden on stage. Today they are often visible, drawing focus to their skills in performance. By featuring object manipulators in this way, the theatre continues to emphasize the central role of live performers. Are new technologies such as computer animation replacing live performance, or are they allowing us to better appreciate live puppetry as a valued contemporary art form?

Audrey II, a plant that needs human blood to grow, is the true star of the Broadway revival of *Little Shop of Horrors*. Pictured here, with Hunter Foster as Seymour, Audrey's mix of low- and high-tech components includes foam, universal joints, and a lighting system that allows her veins to glow. Throughout the show, as Audrey II grows bigger and more ominous, the series of Audrey II puppets designed by The Jim Henson Company and Martin P. Robinson increase in size and complexity. The final Audrey II is twenty-three feet high and can stretch into the audience to look for tasty morsels. Michael Leon-Wooley gives Audrey II her voice while several different puppeteers, led by *Sesame Street* veteran Martin P. Robinson, manipulate the puppets. Directed by Jerry Zaks. Virginia Theatre, New York.
© *Paul Kolnik*

ical presence. Using little scenery, no recorded sound, simple costumes, and interesting spatial arrangements, he led a group of exquisitely trained actors toward a potent theatricality.

Competition with Other Media

Since the invention of film in the early twentieth century, new media technologies have given theatre stiff competition and usurped its central position in the world of entertainment. Early film and television often imitated theatre, defining themselves as a recorded form of theatrical performance before developing their own specific techniques. Vaudeville houses showed short films along with their live acts. Live performance drew in crowds, and movies were used as "chasers" to chase the audience out of the theatre at the

Challenges and Choices

At what point does an object cease to be a puppet embodying human qualities and become merely a machine? What are the essential qualities a machine must have to be considered a puppet or a performing object?

end of the show. But film quickly expanded into an art form of its own, taking audiences away from live theatre with cheap ticket prices and easy access. Television dealt an even greater blow to the theatre than film did, largely because of its convenience. Early television producers actively competed with the theatre by broadcasting television dramas based on stage plays or written by known playwrights and advertising television as "theatre in your living room," without the hassle of going out for the evening.

Today additional media such as video and the Internet provide an endless assortment of mass-marketed entertainments at the average person's disposal any time of the day or night. They are ubiquitous, easy to access, and have saturated our cultural environment with characters, storytelling techniques, and thrilling special effects, elements that had long been the sole possession of live theatre. Theatre practitioners have to compete with these new technologies and often do so by asking, "What can the theatre do that these other media entertainments can't?" Answers usually address the live human presence in theatre and its ability to incorporate audience interaction in the artistic moment itself.

Today our vast exposure to other forms of media entertainment shapes the way we approach and understand theatre itself. Large corporations that sponsor and control the aesthetic and expressive dimensions of television and film now shape theatre, too. We might worry that rather than providing its own unique forms of expression, theatre will come to look more and more like the entertainments we see elsewhere. The Disney corporation is responsible for the renovation of the Times Square theatre district in New York, where it now produces its own shows based on Disney movies. Disney's stage version of *Beauty and the Beast*, for example, is an attempt to replicate the popular animated film. While in the past a good play might serve as the basis for a movie, today movies are being turned into Broadway shows such as *The Lion King, Hairspray!, Enchanted April, Forty Second Street, The Producers*, and *The Graduate*. The types of stories and scenarios produced in other media now guide the creation and appreciation of much theatrical fare.

New Technologies in the Theatre Today

Today's new technologies are entering every aspect of theatrical production, from how artists think and plan a show, to the very nature of the theatrical event audiences see and experience. Each new invention offers new ways to conceive and carry out theatrical work and forces us once again to ask the question, "What is theatre?"

Technology Behind the Scenes

Audiences are usually unaware of the many ways sophisticated technology contributes to the theatrical event. From conception to execution, theatre professionals now make use of the latest technical resources to produce a play. Designers rely on computers to plan and execute designs; directors use computers to envision the space; scene shops use computers to interpret those designs during construction; and the backstage staff relies on computers for the efficient running of a show.

Computers in Design

Computers offer artists new ways to visualize their work in three dimensions before setting foot in an actual theatre. Set and costume designers use **CAD**, or computer-assisted drafting, programs such as Autocad or Vectorworks to help them draft precise and uniform drawings. Computer sketches allow them to visualize and modify colors, textures, and forms as they contemplate different design options. Use of a scanner or design programs such as Photoshop and Illustrator can be helpful tools in creating backdrop images, designs for props, wallpaper, and signs on stage. Lighting designers use these programs to test lighting effects on virtual sets and costumes. Computer models are used to solve technical problems and make aesthetic choices before carpenters and costumers begin building actual sets and costumes.

Designers and directors also explore virtual reality equipment to experience a stage space in three dimensions before it is built. Using systems developed by NASA to simulate environments for astronaut training, theatre artists can create an imaginary fully equipped performance space and tour it to see how staging ideas will work and how set designs feel from the inside.

Some artists are now experimenting with creating scenery by projecting virtual computer models on stage. In the work of San Francisco director George Coates, actors move through projected environments that continually change around them, transforming their world at a moment's notice. In his 1996 piece *Wings*, head-mounted displays allowed audience members to watch actors and 3-D virtual stereoscopic scenery at the same time.

Computers help artists communicate at a distance. Theatres send designers blueprints of the theatre space by e-mail, and designers send computerized images of their ideas for sets and costumes to directors for review, and then to the shops for construction. It is now possible for designers to work at theatres all over the country without being on site.

Computer-generated designs can also be converted into software that programs the power tools used in the construction of scenery. Computerized routers can cut wood and metal to the exact specifications of a design blueprint without the human labor of interpreting and measuring; this ensures accuracy and saves time and money.

Many designers, however, refuse to design with the aid of a computer. Some older designers were simply not trained in this way, and others claim that the computer hampers their creativity and removes them from the physical connection they have to the materials of their craft and the artistic work of designing. Although computers can be efficient for many tasks, some feel that they jeopardize the artistic integrity of theatrical design.

Running the Show

Today computers help the back-stage staff run the show. They facilitate the execution of traditional theatre tasks through automation. Computerized light and sound boards are now standard equipment, even in small community theatres and school playhouses. They can store and run a large number of complicated light and sound cues. Large theatres use computerized motion-controlled systems to effect and regulate set changes. Producers like using computers because they are more predictable than equipment that requires manual labor and thus more cost-efficient for large productions. They are also able to produce more sensational and cinematic effects. Computers give directors greater control of their work by bringing reliability and precision to lighting cues and set placement, but they may take away some of the spontaneity and excitement of live theatre.

When a show relies heavily on technological elements for its success, a breakdown in performance can lead to disaster. Early versions of Disney's *Aida* experimented with a robotic pyramid that changed shape for different scenes. Frequent problems caused the device to be cut from the show before it moved to Broadway. A rare computer failure at *The Producers* in the summer of 2003 prevented curtains from rising and scenery from moving, temporarily stopping the show. Breakdowns during performances are rare, but they can create havoc. On the other hand, they may also create opportunities for actors

Photo 14.4
Hudson Scenic Studios, a full service production and scenic fabrication company located in Yonkers, New York, regularly sends an entire bank of hi-tech equipment such as computers, monitors, and operating boards to theatres to operate and monitor the technological design elements constructed in their shops. This entire group at the loading dock is waiting to be shipped to a Broadway theatre to operate a single production.

and crew to save the day by improvising on the spot, returning the theatre to its fundamental nature as a live and ephemeral art.

Technology Center Stage

Some of the more interesting uses of new technology appear center stage, alongside actors, as an integral part of the production concept. Since the early twentieth century, directors have used projections to create scenery and provide visual and factual support or counterpoint to stage action. Erwin Piscator first used projections and film sequences in his political theatre in the 1920s to draw connections between recent historical events and the dramatic action, and to distance the audience emotionally from the play. Creating a workable interplay between live action and recorded action is a challenge, because film and video images often upstage actors. A slick media projection inevitably grabs the audience's attention. In 2003, *Ubung*, a production from the Netherlands, contrasted videos showing adults involved in decadent behavior—drinking, smoking, wife-swapping—with the same actions played live on stage by children. In this case, the live action commented on the video, giving each equal focus. The audience's attention was first drawn to the projected film because of its scale; it took a while for the audience to adjust its focus to include both the projected and live action and to grasp the thematic interplay between the two.

In contrast to film and video, recent computer technologies have the advantage of being interactive. They can play along with the live, changeable, spontaneous nature of the theatre and live within the show like the performers themselves. At the University of Kansas, Mark Reany has created interactive virtual scenery for a number of productions in which stage images change in response to the actors' movements. Dancer Bill T. Jones has performed with a computer-generated virtual dance partner (see photo 14.5), and Claudio Pinhanez used computer characters in his 1997 piece, *It/I*, developed at MIT. In David Saltz's production of *The Tempest* at the University of Georgia, the sprite Ariel was a 3-D computer animation performed by an actor in real time, using motion-capture technology. Backstage, wearing a suit wired to a computer, the actor manipulated Ariel's computer image with her own movements.

The intent of these experiments has not been to replace live actors, but to allow performers to engage with computerized characters in real time, offering novel performative and visual stage elements. Because of the expensive equipment and new research involved, many of these experiments are done in collaborations among artists, universities, and computer companies. New York's Brooklyn Academy of Music and Lucent Technologies are initiating a joint project to explore artistic possibilities and support the creation of new media performance projects that bring artists and Bell Lab scientists together. In these shared ventures, artists challenge their creativity, while media companies cultivate new applications for their equipment.

Although some new technologies live and interact on stage, others take the breath of life from the stage, replacing or mediating the live performance. Sometimes this intervention occurs without audience awareness. Most actors today in large theatres use stage microphones, small devices attached to their clothes or worn around the ear that are almost invisible to the audience (see Photo 13.10). What spectators hear is a digitized voice reproduced by a speaker rather than the actual human voice of the performer they see live on stage. These voices can seem eerily disembodied. Musical productions in particular rely on microphones, even in small houses, because their clear digitized sound reproduces vocal qualities we have become accustomed to from CDs and music videos.

The unmediated human voice often has trouble competing for our attention next to amplified sounds, but it can express a direct connection to the heart, mind, soul, and spirit that may be lost when digitized. Legend tells of the ancient Greek poet Sophocles giving up performing his own works because of his weak voice. The ability to project has separated stage acting from film acting. In film, microphones capture every vocal inflection, and voices are redubbed if they are unclear. Using microphones on stage helps film actors who may not have the same voice projection skills as stage actors. In the future, even stage actors may no longer train as they did in the past, giving special attention to vocal projection as a way of reaching out to the audience.

As artists rely increasingly on the microphone, the audience is forgetting how to listen to the text of a play and the subtle interplay between melody and words in musical theatre. In 2004, as a reminder of the emotional intimacy lost through the miking of the human voice, the show *Broadway Unplugged* featured twenty star performers singing show tunes without the aid of electronic amplification. The performance demonstrated that the emotional immediacy of direct contact may be the price of technological progress.

In 2003, a musician's strike on Broadway closed shows for several days and brought to the fore new concerns about sound technology replacing live music on stage. Theatre producers wanted to reduce the minimum number of live musicians required by the union's contract for Broadway musicals. They claimed that fewer musicians would help reduce Broadway ticket prices and allow artists

Photo 14.5
Dancer-choreographer Bill T. Jones dances with a computer-generated virtual dance partner to the music of Bach in a piece that reflects on solo performance. *Chaconne,* video work by Paul Kaiser and Shelley Eshkar, Wolfsburg, Germany.
Courtesy of the Bill T. Jones/Arnie Zane Dance Company; photo by Thomas Ammespohl

IN PERSPECTIVE

In Their Own Words

CLAUDIO PINHANEZ

Claudio Pinhanez is a computer scientist and media artist. Since 1999, he has been a research scientist at IBM T. J. Watson, where he designs and develops interactive spaces and investigates physical interfaces to information. Pinhanez got his Ph.D. from the MIT Media Laboratory in 1999, working on the design and construction of physically interactive environments and in computer theatre. Pinhanez has also been a visiting researcher at ATR-MIC laboratory (Kyoto, Japan) and Sony Computer Science Laboratory (Tokyo), where he designed, produced, and performed interactive artworks.

■ **Why do you chose to create theatre using computers as characters?**

I think the use of computers in theatre has been too limited to backdrops and stage effects. If we look into today's movie-making, we see an impressive number of computer graphics characters with striking levels of expression, from the animated creatures born at Pixar studios to the intricacies of Gollum's acting in the Lord of the Rings trilogy. So there is an enormous wealth of techniques that can be used to populate the stage with admirable new characters and worlds. So, the first answer to this question is one of opportunity. At the same time, I think computer characters simply follow the traditions of puppetry. I have always admired the cleanliness of puppet acting, where the limitations on articulation and expression force the puppeteers to deeply explore body movements to convey emotions and ideas. When I was working with computer characters in theatre, I always had in mind the *bunraku* puppet plays I watched in

Japan, which always fascinated me more than their non-puppetry equivalent versions in *noh* and *kabuki* plays.

■ **What do computers offer the art that human actors don't?**

Like puppets, computer characters can have nonhuman bodies and physical abilities. In particular, I am interested in computer characters having "bodies" encompassing multiple media, including computer graphics, video, sound, and lighting. For example, the computer character in the play *It/I* that I wrote and directed in 1997 has a "body" composed of multiple computer graphics objects that appear on stage screens; It "talks" through video segments and expresses rage through stage lighting. The mix of these elements creates a very special character on the stage that would be impossible to recreate in a human form and body. At the same time, It has a very minimal body, like a puppet, allowing an exploration of its expressiveness in depth.

■ **Do you consider yourself a theatre artist or a media artist?**

I consider theatre as my means of expression. Although I love contemporary performance and installation art, I found myself much more comfortable creating for a theatrical audience than in an art gallery or a performance space. My work does not seek to break the stage–audience connection characteristic of theatre, but instead, looks for expanding the range of stage possibilities much the way computer graphics is enabling new kinds of characters and dramatic situations in movies.

■ **Is it really possible for a computer to be spontaneous and "in the moment" the way an actor can if it is drawing from a limited range of preprogrammed responses?**

I do not think today's technology enables us to create an improvisational computer actor on stage. But for the

Challenges and Choices

When technology replaces human skills, such as when computers are used to draft sets or microphones are used to project the voice, do we risk losing these skills forever? Is that important?

more creative freedom in determining the musical accompaniment of a show. Of course, such a move also guarantees a loss of jobs for musicians and the replacement of much of the theatre's live music with electronically produced sound. Music is an interactive element that must live and breathe with the performers. Musical directors adjust the orchestra's timing to the rhythms of the actor's nightly performance and to audience response. They also cover up for missed cues and other unexpected occurrences. Recorded music is frozen; its tempo, unchangeable. Faced with the specter of performing to canned music, actors joined the musicians' picket lines, and Broadway musicals were shut down for the duration of the strike. The union eventually accepted a

more traditional theatre, based on action–reaction dynamics within the context of a "preprogrammed" story line, it is possible to build computer actors quite able to occupy the stage. However, I believe to keep computer characters alive on stage, they have to be responsive to the actions of the human actors. A computer character should never be constructed to trigger reactions based on elapsed time. Human actors are trained to be responsive and have a hard time adjusting themselves to fixed time reactions. In other words, it is essential to keep the stage action as a "dialogue" of actions and reactions from the characters. Providing the computer character with some variability of reactions, even if randomly chosen, helps keep the human actors on stage "listening" to the character and reacting/acting according to what actually happened.

In *It/I*, actor Joshua Pritchard, playing the character "I," shares the stage with an autonomous computer-actor system playing the character "It." The computer-actor controls the imagery on the screens, the stage lights, and sound effects responding to the human actor's actions detected by a computer vision system. The performance was written and directed by Claudio Pinhanez with art direction of Raquel Coelho, performed at Massachusetts Institute of Technology.
Copyright Claudio Pinhanez, 1997

Source: Used with permission from Claudio Pinhanez.

■ **How do you envision this kind of work evolving in the future? What is the next step? Does the answer depend on the creation of new technologies?**

We have to continue to explore and understand the possibilities of computer characters in theatre. The real problem may be getting theatre people and audiences acquainted and comfortable with this new means of theatrical expression. While in dance there is already a community working with technology for quite a long time, in theatre we are still restricted to a few companies, even in active experimentation areas such as New York.

compromise that diminished orchestra size, though not as drastically as first proposed. The eventual eradication of live music in the theatre was never before such an imminent threat.

Performing in Cyberspace

In the early 1990s, avant-garde artists began exploring the possibilities of cyberspace performance bringing together actors and audience members at different locations through the use of high-speed Internet. So called *telematic* performance has expanded

IN PERSPECTIVE

In Their Own Words

ELIZABETH LECOMPTE

Elizabeth LeCompte is best known for her work with the New York–based experimental theatre company, the Wooster Group, of which she is a founding member and director. For thirty years, the Group, under LeCompte's direction, has played a pivotal role in bringing evocative and technologically sophisticated uses of sound, lights, and video to the stage. Since 1975, LeCompte has constructed (choreographed, designed, and directed) numerous dance, film, and video pieces as well as seventeen multimedia theatre pieces with the Group.

■ **Why is technology such an important part of your directorial concept? Are you more drawn to its stage effect or to the commentary it makes on human existence in the twenty-first century?**

I don't know. I just like having all kinds of technology in the room when I work. For fun. It's fun to play with and it stimulates a more free-wheeling work environment. I like to put the real thing next to its copy and have them play off each other. It gives the actors power by amplifying and doubling them, and I can imagine worlds that couldn't be in the theater thirty years ago, and ideas that inform old texts in new ways.

■ **How does your use of technology in a production evolve during rehearsals?**

It's different for every piece, and it depends on what people are bringing into the space new, and what we worked with in the last piece. We discover how to use the technology over time and in relation to the text. It happens naturally, so that in the end there is no separation between form and content.

■ **Do your actors require any particular skills in order to perform with the technological elements you use in production?**

No. Only that they like the ideas we are working with. If they come with an opinion already formed that technology is bad, then it inhibits their ability to play.

■ **What is the effect on actors when they are competing with technology for attention on stage?**

They aren't competing with the technology. It's a tool for them to be creative.

■ **Does the fragmentation of the human form that you often achieve undercut the actor as the central element of the theater?**

No. No more than the fragmentation of time and space in the theater undercuts a performance. For me, the performers are the reason for the theater. The "text" (which includes the words and the technology) is there for them. No one would write a play if there were no performers to perform it.

■ **Does the fragmentation of the text undercut the playwright, and can you discuss some of the reactions of playwrights to your work?**

Texts for the theater have always been edited and shaped for the company and/or for the time. I think that's what I do too. It's a tradition from Shakespeare. To say we "fragment" the text is more radical than what we actually do. Sometimes we only do a piece of a play (a play within a

---

Challenges and Choices

Does theatre require that all the actors and all the audience be present in the same space? Does cyberspace take everyone into the same virtual world?

ever since, inspiring much original work and theoretical writing about its implications for the theatre.

In 2001, Rensselaer Polytechnic Institute and New York University teamed up for the forty-minute opera, *The Technophobe and the Madman*. Audience members at both locations, 160 miles apart, watched half the cast performing live and the other half on the Internet via large screens. Two musicians on each end accompanied the singers, and computers assisted in blending the music. In 2003, the Gertrude Stein Repertory experimented with "distance puppetry" in a production based on Stein's novel, *The Making of Americans* (1925), using simultaneous performance venues in Iowa and New York con-

play). The text isn't fragmented, we just use a fragment of the text. This use bothered Arthur Miller—who said he was afraid people wouldn't know that there was more of it. Playwrights I have spoken to are inspired by our work (Tony Kushner, Paul Auster, Romulus Linney).

■ **Could you ever see yourself returning to a "poor theatre"?**

I couldn't return to something that I never did. Technology is integral on every level—spiritual, social, aesthetic—of my way of making work. It would be the singer without the song.

■ **Of all your productions, where did technology serve your concept best, and why?**

Each one, like children, is different and unique. I wouldn't think that way about my work. I don't have a concept to begin with. I have a text, performers, and my space. The concept is the final piece, and the final piece *is* the concept.

Irina (Beatrice Roth) expresses frustration about her life in the Russian provinces to sister Olga (Peyton Smith) and Dr. Chebutykin (Roy Faudree), who appear on video monitors, in The Wooster Group's production of *Brace Up!*, translated by Paul Schmidt from Chekhov's *Three Sisters*. Directed by Elizabeth LeCompte; video work, Christopher Kondek; scenic design, Jim Clayburgh; lighting, Jennifer Tipton. The Performing Garage, New York.
© Paula Court

Source: Used with permission of Elizabeth LeCompte, Director, The Wooster Group, Creating with Technology.

nected by videoconferencing. The company projected the faces and bodies of actors at one location as masks and costumes on actors at the other venue, so the characters became a amalgamation of physical form and virtual image. By creating new characters in this way, the production hoped to mimic Stein's method of dissection and collage in creating literary characters. In other instances actors, each in a different location, performed for viewers watching from their own computers at home. In each of these examples the traditional notion of a theatrical event as a gathering of performers and spectators is being challenged and transformed. The Internet allows people at great distances to come together, disrupting the traditional connection between actors and audiences.

Techno-Theatre Aesthetic

Some theatre companies and independent artists envision their work through the active integration of film, video, computers, high-tech sound, and other digital media with theatre's live action, creating a new mixed-media techno-theatrical aesthetic. Film, video, and digital sound can barrage the audience's senses to create a montage effect. These media allow for greater and quicker shifts in location and can change a production's pace and sense of movement. In counterpoint to live action, they can break up linear stage narratives and provide spectators with links to outside or distant events as well as glimpses into a character's inner life. Daily, technology helps us move at a fast pace around our cities and the world via telephone and the Internet, facilitating and interrupting the flow of our lives. A techno-theatrical aesthetic reflects the way technology has already infiltrated our everyday existence, transforming how we think about time and space and how we connect to each other.

New York's Wooster Group works as an ensemble under the direction of Elizabeth LeCompte. Their theatrical work juxtaposes film, video, and multitrack scoring with dance, movement, and dialogue to reinterpret both new and classic works. In *Brace Up!*, based on Chekhov's *The Three Sisters*, live performers off stage appear on stage on video monitors alongside live stage action (see photo on page 381). Actors alternately speak on stage or from microphones visibly located behind the main playing area. The interaction between television and live action turns the plight of the three sisters into a staged reality TV show. Additional video clips break up and comment on the story line. Video segments included the grandmother of an actor trying out the lines of the play's elderly nanny, silverware being dropped again and again, film clips from Kenneth Branagh's *Henry V*, and an image of Godzilla accompanied by a loud sound appearing each time the character Solyony is about to speak. Actors were meant to use their video images both as masks and mirrors. *Poor Theatre* (2004) used technology to comment on Grotowski's theatre of minimal technology. Similar integration of technology is seen in much of the Wooster Group's work. The effect is that of a fragmented reality, a collage of real and electronically amplified images and sounds.

Robert Lepage brings a combination of film and theatrical sensibilities to stageworks such as the *Seven Streams of the River Ota* created in 1996 with his theatre company, Ex Machina. This seven-hour piece combines film, music, dialogue, and puppetry to show a global view of twentieth-century world tragedies from the atomic bomb to the Holocaust to AIDS, told through interconnected individual lives. The production used rear film projections and live video links to tell this epic tale. In *Elsinore* (1996), a retelling of *Hamlet*, Lepage plays all the roles, talking to his own real-time video images and distorting his voice through pitch-shifters to create an array of characters. The production disorients the viewer with a set of three moveable panels that rotate to reveal new scenes and videos depicting overhead or rear projections that shift the spectator's point of view. Infrared and thermal cameras and sonar slides allow spectators to peek behind castle walls. The final duel is projected from a video camera atop the poisoned sword.

The Builders Association makes technology's infiltration and transformation of everyday life the theme of their techno-theatrical pieces. *Alladeen*, their 2003 stage production directed by Marianne Weems, was linked to a web project and music video directed by Ali Zaidi (see photo on page 266). It explored the philosophical concerns emerging from today's global technology. The piece presents Indian men and women as they train to become phone operators at an international call center in Bangalore serving American companies and their clients. They learn American pronunciation and culture so they can pretend to be based in the United States. Video projections create a counterpoint to the stage images. The workers watch episodes of *Friends* as part of

Photo 14.6
Video projections of the Studebaker cars produced at the abandoned Studebaker factory where the production takes place serve as backdrop for this multimedia production about the social, economic, and personal disruption caused by the plant's closing. *Avanti: A Postindustrial Ghost Story,* written by Jessica Chalmers; directed by Marianne Weems; sound design by Dan Dobson; video design by Peter Flaherty, in collaboration with the University of Notre Dame's Department of Film, Television, and Theatre.
© *Matt Cashore*

their training, and their faces morph into those of the American *Friends* characters through video projections. Video fantasy sequences based on Bollywood-style films describe the workers' hopes for the future. The Builders Association collaborated with playwright Jessica Chalmers at the University of Notre Dame for a multimedia performance, *Avanti: A Postindustrial Ghost Story*. Staged in an abandoned Studebaker factory in South Bend, Indiana, this site-specific piece projected images and videos onto moving screens that functioned like Renaissance flats to tell the apocryphal story of job loss and industrial failure when Studebaker went under (see Photo 14.6). Groups like the Builders Association are experimenting, not just with technology, but with artistic perspectives that combine traditional theatrical elements and contemporary technologies to make theatre that comments on technology itself and speaks to our current experiences and concerns.

Concerns about Theatre and Technology

Along with these exciting experiments come concerns about the introduction of technology in production and how it may be changing the very nature of theatre. New media with more interactive capabilities can upstage actors or even replace them altogether. Contact through a computer projection, however interactive, can never fully replace the energy shared between people in the same space. In the last hundred years we have been both fascinated with and frightened by new innovations and technological forces. Their promise of improving our lives is enticing. Yet, as we have witnessed, these transformations are not always for the better, nor are they entirely within our control. Fear and skepticism about new technologies of all kinds, and the worry that they undermine our basic humanity, remain part of our general cultural dialogue as we continue to debate the value of every scientific incursion in our lives, from cellphones to genetic engineering.

History IN PERSPECTIVE

PLAYS ON SCIENCE

Theatre's preoccupation with science and technology can be seen in the many plays that take these subjects as their theme or even use scientific ideas as a structural model. Karel Capek's *R.U.R.* (1920) projected a world in which human life was replaced by robots (in fact, some trace the first use of the word *robot* to this play) who later declare war on the human race. Spurred by the horror of World War I, Capek sought to warn the world of the possibility of society becoming a technology-driven war machine.

Bertolt Brecht's *Galileo* (1939) is one of many plays exploring the relationship of the scientist to the political power structure and how knowledge can be compromised for self-interest. World War II and the destruction caused by the atom bomb inspired a host of plays exploring the social and political responsibility of the scientist in a morally ambiguous world. Heinar Kipphardt's documentary drama *In the Matter of J. Robert Oppenheimer* (1964) used documents from the proceedings of the United States Nuclear Energy Commission to demonstrate the results of passing awesome atomic knowledge to the military for its pursuits. The play poses many important questions: Who owns scientific knowledge, the scientist who discovers it, or the government that supports the research? Should a

In this famous production of Bertolt Brecht's Galileo, *which explores the relationship of the scientist to the political power structure, actor Charles Laughton in the title role works on an invention. Directed by Joseph Losey at the Coronet Theatre, 1947.*
Photo by Keystone/Hulton Archive/ Getty Images

scientist decide how knowledge should be used? In *The Physicists* (1962), Swiss playwright Friedrich Durrenmatt presents a nuclear physicist who pretends to be insane in order to be shut away from officials who would use his discoveries for destructive political ends. In the end, all of his attempts to prevent his discoveries from falling into the wrong hands fail, and the play ends in nuclear cataclysm. All of these plays deal with the moral burden that comes with scientific knowledge.

Some plays don't just take science as a theme, but reflect scientific principles in their structure, such as Tom Stoppard's *Hapgood* (1988), in which the plot mimics particle motion. In Michael Frayn's *Copenhagen* (1998), the play's scenes mirror the uncertainty principle in physics, showing alternative and incompatible versions of a famous meeting between theoretical physicists Niels Bohr and Werner Heisenberg.

The EST/Sloan Science and Technology Project sponsors plays that deal with science and technology. In 2003, a project called Technology Plays challenged playwrights to write a seven-minute play on the subject of man and technology, performed for one spectator at a time using only machines. The six plays included *Greetings from the Home Office* by Richard Dresser, in which the spectator, sitting in a cubicle, is cast as a new company employee and barraged by messages from a phone, intercom, and computer that give contradictory information about the boss, a colleague, and a secretary, leaving the spectator uncertain what to believe. Plays about science and technology and plays that use technology can push the boundaries of theatrical forms.

The introduction of new technological methods in the theatre can't help but stimulate a similar critical debate, even as it forces us to redefine the limits of the art form. We have always referred to theatre as "live" performance, but what does that mean at a time when we can perform live on television or the Internet, and when recorded media can be incorporated into "live" theatre. As we expand our ability to use technology, we must also question how we define the unique experience of live theatre.

KEY IDEAS

- Theatre has always used available technologies to heighten its expressive power.
- Sometimes theatre artists develop new technologies to achieve certain effects; at other times new tools inspire innovative theatrical ideas.
- Today's new media compete with the theatre, find their way into productions, and create the cultural background that frames our theatrical experiences.
- Technology refers broadly to any skill, art, or craft we use to shape our physical environment and facilitate our cultural practices. High-tech devices use less physical human effort than low-tech devices.
- Theatre practitioners and audiences adapt to new technologies as they become integrated into theatrical practice over time. What was once technical innovation can become standard practice.
- Technology enhances a production when it works in conjunction with other artistic elements to illuminate meaning. When technology supplants the acting and text, it may transform the theatrical event.

- Some theatrical traditions revel in spectacle; others reject technology and highlight the human presence.
- Film, television, and other new media compete with theatre and have usurped its central position in the world of entertainment, shaping the way we understand theatre.
- New technologies are entering every aspect of theatrical production, from how artists think and plan a show to the very nature of the theatrical event. Computers aid designers and stagehands; microphones amplify actors' voices; and film, projections, video, and virtual characters are part of a director's palette of possibilities. Some theatre practitioners make integrating new technology an integral part of their overall aesthetic.
- New technologies may be changing the nature of theatre by disconnecting audiences from actors and mediating live performance.
- Technology is forcing us to question what we mean by "live" performance.

PART FIVE

A set under construction is the backdrop for a rehearsal of Chekhov's *The Three Sisters* at the Gesher Theatre. Actors make notes in their scripts while a stagehand arranges props on a table. The hard work and dedication of the many offstage personnel who contribute to a performance is often unheralded, but no performance can come to life without them. The Russian Gesher Theater of Tel Aviv, Israel, is one of the only theatres in the world performing in both Russian and Hebrew with the same cast. Artistic director, Arye Yevgeny.

© Patrick Zackmann/Magnum Photos

Understanding Today's Theatre

Every theatrical production, whether it be the smallest community show, an ancient traditional performance, the Broadway mega-production, or the college show, begins with a daring leap of faith that an empty space can be transformed into a place of magic and illusion in the enactment of an artistic vision. Although the first step is an act of spirit, the process of realization is a tangible one. It sets in motion a system of collaboration requiring the contributions of many people. It will require hard work, commitment, sacrifice, and, however lofty the goals, money and publicity.

Like every act of faith, theatre has its risks, because every performance is subject to critical reaction from the general audience and from the critics who help shape the public's perception of a theatrical production. In fact, theatre artists toil in anticipation of the critical reception, knowing full well that theatre comes alive in the moment it provokes a response. Theatre is a public event and subject to public reaction. Without this vital response, it would cease to have a reason for being.

How we make theatre and how we learn to respond to it is the subject of our final chapters. The hope is that you will become knowledgeable theatregoers and perhaps even be inspired to become theatre makers. Theatre is an art form that draws upon many different kinds of talent, and there is a place for everyone who wants to join the creative community.

The Critical Response

In *The Real Inspector Hound*, playwright Tom Stoppard makes mock of critical distance by creating two characters who are critics—Birdboot (Kris Joseph) and Moon (Simon Bradshaw). Placing them in the audience at the start of the play, he allows the audience members to hear their running commentary and critical jargon. They eventually become entangled in the murder mystery they are there to review and lose themselves in the play within a play, raising questions about reality, authenticity, and identity. Directed by Charles McFarland, Third Wall Theatre Company, Ottawa, Canada.

Courtesy of Third Wall Theatre Company; photo by Jesse Henderson

Theatre is created to provoke a response. Whether they are trying to give pleasure, to entertain, to touch, to anger, or to move to action, theatre practitioners are always attempting to engage the audience. It is almost impossible to imagine a member of the audience leaving the theatre without something to say about the experience, either positive or negative. Although most of us are satisfied with expressing our emotional reactions, those of us who are knowledgeable about the theatre may want time to step back from our emotional experience and analyze it more objectively. We will ask ourselves questions about the event and the relative success of the text, acting, directing, and design elements. We will filter our thoughts through our experience and knowledge to come up with a critical response. One of the goals of this book is to provide the basis for such an informed critical evaluation to enhance the pleasure and meaning you will take from theatre-going.

Many have argued that criticism is unnecessary, that a creative work speaks to its audience on its own terms without the need for further reflection or discussion. This is true up to a point. The theatre does take place between actor and audience in the moment of performance, but it lives on in the memory, and how we shape our memory is part of the event's life. Our reception of the performance—what impact it has on us, how we understand it, what we think about it, and how we talk about it after it is over—keeps the theatre experience alive. When we connect a performance to the world around us and share our ideas with others, it becomes more meaningful. As a public act, the theatre has always invited and received critical response, so wherever we find vibrant theatrical traditions, we also find critical engagement.

 Criticism and Culture

How we analyze a production and what perspective we take in our scrutiny says a lot about what our culture finds interesting or valuable. Perhaps you have already experienced this watching an old movie. The values and mores expressed in the film might seem comical today. You will notice how acting styles have changed. What might have received critical praise in one era can be the subject of derision in the next. Only fifty years ago, on film and in the theatre, we would not have been shocked to see all the African Americans in servant roles. Today this would feel reactionary, if not racist, and would affect our critical response. Because theatre has a much longer history than film, these changes in critical perspective over time are even greater. Freud read Greek tragedies and found the subject matter of repressed desires, but Sophocles in the fifth century B.C.E. would not have understood such an interpretation of his plays. The Greeks paid little attention to the inner life and judged human beings by their actions. Freud applied a cultural frame of reference unknown to the ancient Greeks, but meaningful to the twentieth century. When a play can be mined repeatedly over centuries for contemporary relevance, we know it has spoken profoundly about the human condition.

Can we impose new cultural assumptions on a work of art? Shouldn't we try to approach a Greek tragedy as if we were ancient Greeks to truly understand it? No matter how hard we try, we cannot completely reconstruct the ancient Greek worldview, or become a member of a 2,500-year-old society, or imagine we are at the theatre in Athens in the fifth century B.C.E. If you are a woman, you might not have even been permitted to attend. If you are not Greek, you might have been a slave. Once we confront the insurmountable cultural gap between our era and those of the past, we are left with the realization that the best we can do is to find the interpretations that are valid for our own times, constructing meaning through contemporary values and tastes and using the methods of analysis we esteem. We use our knowledge of history to help formulate a contemporary interpretation.

Professional Criticism and Cultural Theory

Every society develops its own theatrical theories that become the tools of criticism. These theories reflect the biases and interests of its culture. For centuries, Aristotle's ideas framed most European and American theatrical analysis; he minimized the importance of certain genres, such as comedy, and reflected the antifeminist bias of his time. Today, in our pluralistic society, we find a multitude of critical lenses through which to analyze a performance. Marxist theory, feminist theory, psychoanalytic theory, gender theory, race theory, structuralism, poststructuralist, and semiotic theory are just a few of the many methods applied to critical analysis in the past fifty years. Some are falling out of favor, while others are hitting their stride, reflecting our society's changing values. Today, the lens through which the critic chooses to view the theatre represents one among many possibilities and offers us a gauge of the critic's interests and viewpoint as well as a means of understanding a work of art. It follows that critics are never completely objective. They hold their biases like other members of the audience.

The Critic as Cultural Insider

Theatre that emerges from a particular ethnic or social community often benefits from critical discussion that grows out of the community itself. In the United States theatre coming from minority groups has been the subject of critics who share the artists' experiences of marginalization. Such critics can both introduce this work to outsiders and broaden critical perspectives within the community itself. These writers are not outside observers; they form critiques from a position of alliance and understanding and are partners in formulating new theatrical models that respond directly to their community's unique social and artistic needs. Gay and lesbian critics such as David Savran and Jill Dolan have provided us with techniques for understanding the presentation of gender and sexuality on stage. Jorge Huerta has explained the myths and values embedded in Latino drama, and Errol G. Hill and James V. Hatch have placed African American theatre in historical context. Today, more and more critics are emerging from the cultures that are the subject of their examination.

The Many Faces of the Critic

Like light flooding into a dark room, good criticism defines and clarifies the theatre experience. Although some critics explain new and innovative theatre work and help the audience appreciate it, not all criticism comes after the creative act. Some artists are themselves critics, and others find artistic inspiration in critical writing. Criticism has even been presented in artistic form, and some theatre pieces could themselves be considered acts of criticism. While some criticism is descriptive, some is prescriptive, or even visionary, pointing the way toward new theatrical invention.

Partnerships in which critics and artists enrich each other's work are common. If a Broadway-bound play has an "out of town" run, the local critics may even influence the rewriting process. Boston theatre critic Elliott Norton (1903–2003) was known for writing reviews that gave playwrights new ideas. Neil Simon rewrote the ending to *The Odd Couple* based on a Norton suggestion. Scholarly criticism has influenced the theatrical interpretations of many directors. Criticism need not be just a final judgment; it can also bring thoughtful engagement with an artistic work throughout the creative process.

The Critic as Interpreter

Critics serve as interpreters of theatrical events by providing a framework for comprehension. This may simply consist of explaining the historical context of a play, or it may include introducing audiences to the theatrical conventions and values of another culture. For an experimental or particularly difficult piece of theatre, a critic may need to discover what new point of view or style is being expressed and explain how that translates into artistic choices onstage.

Martin Esslin (1918–2002) presents a good example of this kind of criticism. During the 1950s, Samuel Beckett, Jean Genet (1910–1986), Eugène Ionesco, and Arthur Adamov (1908–1971) wrote plays that were unlike anything people had come to expect in the theatre. They lacked clear story lines, recognizable plots, or psychologically rich characters, and dialogue often broke down into nonsense. Audiences were confused and even angry at these plays. On the opening night of Beckett's *Waiting for Godot*, in which there is little action as two tramps await the arrival of a mysterious figure named Godot, one critic walked out stating loudly, "I will not wait for Godot!" Esslin understood that these plays reflected the sense of alienation and meaninglessness of a generation that had lived through the horrific events of World War II, and coined the term "**theatre of the absurd**" in his book by that name. His analysis of these new plays made them comprehensible to a large audience, and today, plays of the theatre of the absurd are classics in the theatrical repertoire. We still use Esslin's term to describe them. Esslin, the critic, clarified a new world of theatrical experience for generations to come.

The Critic as Artistic Muse

Criticism is often the inspiration for artistic creation and directly influences new theatrical styles or the rediscovery of old texts or dramatic forms. The critic Jan Kott

Photo 15.1
Motorized scooters, leather jackets, and a set of metal scaffolding add a contemporary, urban sensibility to this production of Shakespeare's *Romeo and Juliet*. Directed by Ethan McSweeny; set and costume design by Mark Wendland. Guthrie Theater, Minneapolis.
© *Michal Daniel, 2004*

Artists
IN PERSPECTIVE

In Their Own Words

ALISA SOLOMON

Alisa Solomon has combined careers in journalism, criticism, and scholarship. For more than twenty years, she has written dramatic criticism for New York's Village Voice, *where she has also published pieces on city politics, feminism, sports, the gay rights movement, the Middle East, and education. Her book* Re-Dressing the Canon: Essays on Theater and Gender *won the George Jean Nathan Award for Dramatic Criticism. Her latest book, coedited with Tony Kushner, is* Wrestling with Zion: Progressive Jewish-American Responses to the Israeli-Palestinian Conflict. *Professor Solomon also teaches at Baruch College of the City University of New York.*

■ **What do you think is the primary role of a theatre critic who writes for a newspaper?**

Newspaper critics serve several simultaneous functions. Certainly there are some readers who look at reviews merely as consumer reports. They want to know: What's this play like? Would it interest me? How long is it? Is it worth my $25 (or $125)? Meanwhile, reviews often come to constitute the historical record of a production—the materials scholars pore over even only a few years after the fact to piece together a theatrical experience and its public reception. A newspaper review ought to provide a vivid description of the experience (not just of the plot) and provide information and interpretation that allow readers to decide whether the work sounds worth their while and their cash. However, to my mind, a review that seeks to address only such questions is not only incomplete, but destructive (even when it is favorable toward the work in question), for it encourages a simple-minded, thumbs-up/thumbs-down way of engaging the theatre, and, by extension, the world.

A critic has a larger responsibility: to contribute to and cultivate intelligent analytical discourse about theatre specifically, and, more generally, about our culture and our world. This sounds high-falutin'—and it is not easy to bear such a huge obligation in mind, much less try to fulfill it, when writing, say, no more than 450 words on an overnight deadline about a play not chosen by oneself, but assigned by an editor. Still, I believe a primary role of critics is to take part in fostering the critical attitude. As an unreconstructed Brechtian, I believe the theatre is a place where the public practices and sharpens their critical attitude; reviews ought to participate in that process. Critics can go a long way toward doing so not by setting out to pronounce whether a work is any good, but by seeking to discuss what a work means, how it means what it means, where and when it is conveying that meaning (its context), and why.

■ **Does the theater need critics, and why?**

The theatre needs critics because the world needs critics. Reviews (good ones, anyway) participate in and foster public discussion that values analysis, context, nuance, and reasoned argument. Public discourse on every level needs these qualities. There are more mundane reasons for theatre criticism, too: From a newspaper perspective, openings of plays are, quite simply, news, and should be reported on. The most useful format for such coverage is an interpretive analysis by an informed writer. Producers will say that critics are essential components of the theatre's economic ecology: favorable reviews sell tickets. (Of course, producers are ready to rid the world of critics when reviews are unfavorable.) A critic's moral compass loses its true north if s/he makes filling (or emptying) the seats for a particular production her/his purpose in a review—yet also loses its true north if s/he forgets that her/his work plays a part in an often venal commercial nexus.

■ **Is a reviewer of theatrical performance a journalist or a scholar, and do you see these roles as complementary or opposing?**

I don't find the distinction between journalists and scholars useful when it comes to theater criticism. The dichotomy is too often invoked by those with a stake in one of these identities to denounce or belittle the other. Scholars sneer at "mere" journalism; reviewers scoff at "arcane academic writing." Bad journalism yields bad theater criticism just as consistently as bad academic practices yield bad scholarship. Whether the shrinking amount of space allotted to newspaper reviews on the one hand, that pushes critics into simplified consumer reporting, or the intensified pressure to publish on the other, that leads to a proliferation of increasingly specialized journals and jargons in which scholars speak half-coherently to an ever-smaller and narrow readership, both realms suffer under commercial or competitive constraints that produce deficient results. Rather than saying that theater pages need reviewers and theater departments needs scholars, I prefer to say that both need critics: people who know the field well; can bring historical, political, theoretical, and analytical perspectives to bear on a given work or body of work; and who can argue cogently in graceful prose.

(continues)

Artists

IN PERSPECTIVE (CONTINUED)

■ **Your scholarly work addresses feminist concerns. What is the effect of that interest on your work as a theatre critic for the *Village Voice*, and how do you feel it affects your readers?**

I can't help but see the world as a feminist. Luckily, once consciousness is raised, it is not easy to stuff it back under repressive layers of sexist mores and crass popular culture. That doesn't mean that it's useful or interesting simply to affix the label "misogynist" to one work or another. Rather, feminism is itself a critical attitude that enables one to see how meanings are constructed and to what ends: this is a useful practice for a theatre critic. Obviously there is no such thing as objective criticism, though mainstream dailies tend to insist it's what they practice. What that really means is that they don't reveal their biases or perspectives, but allow them to guide their responses unselfconsciously. I can't say how my readers in the *Voice* respond in general as I have not surveyed them, but I expect that by declaring my subjectivity and letting them know they are reading something written from a particular point of view, I am creating space where they can assess and productively grapple with my writing more honestly and directly than with criticism by someone laboring under the pretense of objectivity.

■ **For generations theatrical criticism has been dominated by men. As a feminist, do you believe there is a special responsibility or role for a woman critic? If so, what is that role?**

I participated in a public panel discussion among critics a few years ago, and a young male colleague told an anecdote about how surprised he was to find himself liking the play *Wit* because, based on the description he'd read before going to see it, he expected "another one of those whiny victim plays." He was relieved and delighted when it turned out to be "not about a woman, but about a person." That such attitudes persist, even among young crit-

ics, suggests that feminists are as crucial as ever among the diverse perspectives that ought to make up the field.

Think of the unspoken assumptions underlying that young man's assertion: that "a person" and "a woman" are somehow mutually exclusive categories; that a woman's gender has to be discounted if she is to be regarded as in some way universal; that men are universal figures and have no gender; that being universal is important and gives a play value, even if the main character is female. (As for his invocation of a genre of "whiny victim plays" what could he have had in mind? *Uncle Vanya*? *King Lear*?)

Women aren't the only ones who can bring a corrective view into the conversation—and not all women would do so. I'm more comfortable saying that *feminists*, rather than *women*, have a special responsibility to unpack the tacit assumptions about gender that are expressed in plays (and in criticism) as part of their overall meaning. At the same time, I think we need to be careful not to fall into the trap of simply becoming cheerleaders for playwrights or directors who are women. While we might start from a more sympathetic stance than some of our nonfeminist colleagues when we encounter such work, we still must be honest. I agree with Shaw, who said that loyalty in a critic is corruption.

■ **What do you think aspiring theatre critics should study?**

History, political science, sociology, philosophy, literature, music, art: in sum, the liberal arts. In addition, they should know their theatre history and dramatic literature and the wider social and political contexts in which work was (and is) performed. They should read the newspaper every day and good weekly or monthly analyses of current events. They should go to lots of plays and also to films, art exhibits, concerts, and other arts events. They must learn to write well: with clarity, fluidity, and passion.

Source: Used with permission from Alisa Solomon.

(1914–2001) had this effect on some of the most innovative directors of his time. His 1961 book, *Shakespeare Our Contemporary*, demonstrated how Shakespeare's plays can be reinterpreted to speak to modern sensibilities. Having lived through both the Nazi and Stalinist occupations of his native Poland, Kott discovered in Shakespeare's dark Elizabethan world direct parallels to his own experiences that illuminated hidden meaning in the play texts. Peter Brook's staging of King Lear as the modern alienated man, more a character out of a Beckett play than an archetypal Elizabethan, was directly inspired by Kott's essay "King Lear or Endgame," which linked Beckett's play to a way of thinking about Shakespeare. Brook's magical staging of *A Midsummer Night's Dream* gave Kott's ideas full life on stage. Many of the thousands of reimagined Shakespeare productions since the 1960s can be traced back to Kott's inspirational book.

The Critic as Visionary

Some critics can be as passionate about transforming the theatrical world and propelling it in new, unexplored directions as those who make theatre. Antonin Artaud's (1896–1948) collection of essays *The Theatre and Its Double* became the theatre bible for the avant-garde twenty years after his death. He outlined a new kind of theatre, which, like a plague or a similar moment of crisis, pushed people to an extreme confrontation with their own existence. Artaud called for a "**theatre of cruelty**," a dynamic and poetic world of images, sounds, and movement that could cruelly assault the senses of the audience, opening up new levels of awareness. He advocated abandoning literary masterpieces in which visceral emotions could hide behind words, favoring instead a direct and immediate experience for actors and spectators alike in a shared performance and audience space. He sought a universal language of sound and movement linking the primal presocietal needs of all human beings. Artaud made a few attempts to put his ideas into practice, but his greatest legacy was the inspiration he gave to many great artists of the 1960s. Jean-Louis Barrault in France, Jerzy Grotowski in Poland, Peter Brook in England, and a host of American theatre companies, such as the Living Theatre, the Open Theatre, and the Performance Group created impressive performances drawing on his critical writings.

The Artist as Critic

Artists sometimes take on the role of critic as they try to explain their artistic intentions or gain a following. In the early twentieth century, practitioners in the movements of realism, symbolism, expressionism, and futurism wrote manifestos describing their hopes for new directions in the theatre while their productions tried to realize the goals they set in their writings. Bertolt Brecht—prolific playwright, poet, and director—also wrote volumes of criticism and theory about his epic theatre, which he contrasted to Aristotle's model of tragedy. While many people believe that Brecht's critical writings do not accurately portray what he achieved in his remarkable productions, his essays connect his novel methods of playwriting, directing, acting, and design to the political philosophy behind them and provide us with insight into his artistic process. Playwright Arthur Miller wrote essays about the theatre and defended his concept of the "common man" as the subject of tragedy. In fact, many playwrights have attempted to frame their work through critical writing.

Actors and directors have also ventured into the domain of criticism, especially when their work is innovative and needs explication. French director Antoine explained his theory of the fourth wall, Stanislavski wrote three volumes on his theories of acting, and American director Harold Clurman's (1901–1980) collected critical essays run well over one thousand pages. *Actors on Acting* and *Directors on Directing*[1] are anthologies of critical writing by artists.

The practice of artists writing criticism can be found in other periods and cultures as well. Zeami Motokiyo wrote treatises on the Japanese *noh* theatre to pass on the secrets of performance to future generations. He spoke from the point of view of both an actor and a playwright and captured the importance of crafting characters through the text.

Challenges and Choices

Is it important for creative artists to understand their own work within the larger cultural and historical context that critical and scholarly writing can give? Do theatre artists need to read criticism?

---

1. See *Actors on Acting*, edited by Toby Cole and Helen Chinoy, Crown, 1970, and *Directors on Directing*, edited by Toby Cole and Helen Chinoy, Macmillan, 1963.

Photo 15.2

The Regard Evening offered Bill Irwin a chance to poke fun at theatrical conventions and postmodernism as a clown critic on stage. Directed by Bill Irwin and created in collaboration with Doug Skinner, Michael O'Connor, and Nancy Harrington. Set design by Douglas Stein; lighting design by Nancy Schertler; costume design by Catherine Zuber; music by Doug Skinner; sound design by Brett R. Jarvis; Signature Theatre Company, New York.

© Carol Rosegg

Criticism from the Stage

Playwrights have often used the stage to speak critically about the theatre of their times. Seventeenth-century French playwright Molière used his short play *The Critique of the School for Wives* to answer the critics of his earlier work, *The School For Wives*, and then wrote *The Versailles Impromptu* to stage a mock rehearsal with commentary on acting by the character Molière. Italian playwright Carlo Goldoni (1707–1793) wrote *The Comic Theatre* to outline the reforms he was attempting to make to the *commedia dell'arte* tradition. Many have pointed to Hamlet's speech to the players telling them how to act as Shakespeare's criticism of the flamboyant acting style of his day. Ionesco took on his critics with his 1956 play *The Shepherd's Chameleon*, which spoofed the art of criticism while providing its own critical commentary. In 1966 German Playwright Peter Handke wrote *Offending the Audience*, which makes a mockery of the conventions of audience behavior. Bill Irwin's *The Regard of Flight* poked fun at the postmodern aesthetic through vaudeville and clown sketches. These and many other theatrical works reveal the power of the artist using the performance medium for critical commentary. It can be argued that many revolutionary stagings by avant-garde directors are implicit criticism of the old styles they are rejecting. These works show us that criticism can be a matter of content and perspective rather than form.

The Dramaturg

Intelligent theatre criticism is so important to the creative process that some theatre companies employ a dramaturg to serve as an in-house critic. Rather than giving their opinions after a show, dramaturgs work with playwrights, directors, designers, and actors during the course of creation—from script choice to final run—to give intellectual clarity to the work at hand. Dramaturgs have been called intellectual attachés to the theatre. They use their skills in critical analysis and knowledge about stage practice to help theatres create thoughtful and meaningful productions.

Dramaturgs have long been an established part of the theatre in Germany and other European countries, but have risen to prominence in the American theatre only in recent years. The German playwright Gotthold Ephraim Lessing (1729–1781) inaugurated the role of the dramaturg in his work with the National Theatre of Hamburg from 1767 to 1769. This theatre company strove to give Germany a national drama on par with the neoclassical plays of France and the Shakespearean drama of England at a time when no such German tradition existed. Lessing helped the company choose dramatic texts for performance, translated French and English plays into German, and wrote criticism, which he published in a theatre journal called *Hamburg Dramaturgy*. His essays educated the German audience about the company's work. The National Theatre of Hamburg was

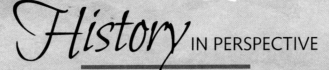

History IN PERSPECTIVE

THE AUTHORSHIP CONTROVERSY OVER *RENT*

The dramaturg's role in helping playwrights develop new work has led to questions and sometimes controversies about authorship, as demonstrated by dramaturg Lynn Thomson's legal actions against the heirs of the estate of Jonathan Larson, author of the hit Broadway musical *Rent*. *Rent* began its life at the New York Theatre Workshop, where Thomson, in the role of dramaturg, was paid $2,000 to work with Larson on his new musical and help him clarify the story line. The result of Thomson and Larson's intense collaboration during the summer and fall of 1995 was a dramatic transformation of the piece, which premiered at the New York Theatre Workshop and later found artistic and financial success on Broadway. Larson tragically died of an aortic aneurysm the night before the first New York Theatre Workshop preview of *Rent* and was never able to enjoy the success of his work.

Thomson's suit claimed she had contributed substantially to the final script's theme, structure, plot elements, and even specific language. Accordingly, she held that she deserved to be listed as a coauthor and to receive substantially more for her work than her original fee. Important members of the theatre community, including authors Tony Kushner and Craig Lucas, as well as many professional dramaturgs, supported Thomson's claims. Some testified to the important contributions Thomson's work made to the final

product. In the end the case rested not on an assessment of Thomson's contributions, which the judge acknowledged, but on a legal definition of coauthorship, a relationship that parties engaged in the work must recognize. The judge found that there was no reason to believe that the late Jonathan Larson thought of Thomson's role as anything other than that of a dramaturg and that he had not intended her to be a coauthor. The estate eventually made a confidential settlement with Thomson.

Some have called Thomson a "Rosa Parks," a pioneer for a certain kind of theatrical equal rights, because she demanded real credit for the kind of work that often goes unacknowledged. Her case has made the theatrical community at large more aware of the important role dramaturgs can play in the development of new works and has made all parties more conscious of the need to clearly articulate artistic and financial relationships in collaborative work.

The Broadway cast of Jonathan Larson's *Rent*. Controversy erupted over the extent of dramaturg Lynn Thomson's role in authoring the hit musical. Directed by Michael Greif. Nederlander Theatre, New York.
© *ArenaPal/Topham/The Image Works*

short-lived, but Lessing's model continues to be an essential one for German theatre companies, who regularly employ dramaturgs to help express each theatre's unique intellectual and artistic perspective.

Dramaturgs in the United States today take on many tasks, and their work differs from one institution to another and from one production to another. "Production dramaturgy" is done before and during the rehearsal process of a particular show. A dramaturg might help prepare a text for performance by updating a classical play, translating a text, or assisting a playwright who is developing a new script. To help the

IN PERSPECTIVE

In Their Own Words

STANLEY KAUFFMANN
Criticism: An Art about Art

*Stanley Kauffmann's critical writings have earned him in-
ternational recognition. During the 1960s, he was a theatre critic for Public Broadcasting in New York, and in
1966, theater critic for the* New York Times. *From 1969
to 1979, Kauffman was both the theatre and film critic
for the* New Republic *and later the theatre critic for the*
Saturday Review *from 1979 to 1985. He has also published two volumes of dramatic criticism and many
books of film criticism. He has taught at the Yale School
of Drama and most recently at Hunter College of the
City University of New York.*

■ **Does the theatre need critics?**

Yes, but the theatre doesn't want them—not serious critics, anyway. Theatre people usually think of criticism as a
gauntlet that a new production must run, and of course
they dislike any response that threatens the various sorts
of investment that a production entails. But to a critic,
the theatre needs perceptive and empathic comment for
its own sake, as well as an audience service. I have heard
theatre people complain, in New York and in cities with
resident companies, that the lack of respectable criticism
makes them feel that they are working in the middle of
the Sahara. T. S. Eliot said that the purpose of criticism is

the elucidation of works of art and the improvement of
taste. The number of artworks in our theatre is somewhat limited, and though taste certainly changes, it
doesn't necessarily improve. Still, Eliot's definition is
worth keeping in one's head. In any case, the theatre
needs good criticism in ways that every art needs it: as
informed response, as esthetic-intellectual ambience,
and, in the long run, as history.

■ **Does friendship with theatre artists create bias or
insight?**

Both. Obviously a critic can learn from people who are
doing theatre work, but the price the critic pays is personal linkage. I have never consciously tempered a review with a bias one way or another because I knew the
people involved, but when I knew participants, I was always aware that I was walking a fine line. One advantage in writing film criticism, as against theatre criticism,
is that the film performance is done, finished, by the time
one writes about it. With a theatre review, one is always
aware that the actor may read it before he goes on again
that night. This discomfort is intensified if one knows the
actor. I have never sought out active theatre people socially, although a few have been close friends. On the
other hand, I have found that theatre people in general
don't particularly like the company of critics.

■ **How have the position and power of the theatre critic
changed since you began?**

The critic's position and power have diminished—in New
York, at any rate—because the position and power of the

Challenges and Choices

Directors, actors, and dramaturgs often contribute to
the final play text through
their creative efforts. Do
they deserve to share credit
with the playwright as
coauthors?

director and the actors understand the world of the play, a dramaturg often does research
on the playwright; the setting of the story; and terms, ideas, or conventions of the text
that are not readily understood. If a director is altering the time and place, the dramaturg
can help recontextualize the story in its new setting. Directors draw on a dramaturg's understanding of a play to develop and articulate a vision for a production.

During rehearsals, when directors become occupied with innumerable details, dramaturgs can maintain their critical distance. They watch to see that the overall vision of
the production and the line of the story are clearly expressed. With a new play, the dramaturg often acts as a liaison between the playwright and the director, helping both to
bring the work to fruition through mutual understanding.

Just as Lessing did, dramaturgs today are often called on to bring the audience to an
appreciation of the production. They may write notes or essays for the program, for a
lobby display, or for the show's publicity. They might moderate talk-back sessions after
the show between the actors and the director and the audience or create study guides for
schoolchildren. This kind of work is usually called *audience outreach.*

Many dramaturgs in the United States hold positions as **literary managers**. Literary managers often do the tasks listed earlier, but they are also responsible for reading

theatre have diminished. In the past, what happened on Broadway and off Broadway seemed important to a large number of New Yorkers. The increased appeal of film and television and pop music has in some degree obscured the theatre, which now seems to many people a mall for tourists. Consequently, critical opinions about the theatre have less interest, let alone influence.

■ **You have been a critic for the *New York Times*, the *New Republic*, and the *Saturday Review*. How does each context change your work?**

The context affected me, as far as I was aware, only on the *Times*, not because my opinions were interfered with—this never happened—but because of something almost ridiculously physical. Column inches. I write a sentence for a magazine review, and it is just a sentence, lying there, almost awaiting the next sentence. For a newspaper I was conscious that any sentence would eat up a fat inch or more of a column, almost crowding the next sentence. Magazine ease becomes column-inch unease. This sense of space pressure affected possibilities of reference and exploration.

■ **What do you feel is your most important contribution to the theatre in your career as a critic?**

Practically, I think my only contribution was the pioneering I did against the silly pattern of opening-night re-views—rushing from the theatre, banging out a review one paragraph at a time, and handing one sheet at a time to a copy boy for dispatch to the composing room. Nowadays, in the computer world, that process is gone, but there would still be the time pressure if the pattern had not changed. I'm told that producers, who objected very strenuously to critics at a preview, now prefer them to come to previews. I hope I contributed something to the change.

Thematically, my chief contribution, I'd say, was in the matter of homosexual playwrights. In 1966 I wrote two Sunday articles in the *Times* attacking social pressures that at that time prevented gay playwrights from writing frankly about homosexuality. Proscriptions then were still so stiff in this matter that I couldn't even mention the names of the three playwrights who had prompted the piece—Williams, Albee, and Inge. The two articles caused an uproar. (Echoes of it still persist.) Conservatives were shocked, and homosexuals themselves were upset. I think they were upset, first, because, in those now unimaginably stodgy days, they didn't want such matters openly discussed. Second, they took my plea that they be allowed to write openly about homosexuality as a dictum enjoining them to write only about homosexuality. Within five years or so, the atmosphere around this subject changed drastically, on the way to present-day liberalism, and I take some pride in believing that I contributed a bit to the change.

Source: Copyright 2006 by Stanley Kauffmann.

and evaluating plays submitted to the theatre, recommending plays to the artistic director, and helping in other forms of play development such as hosting workshops or play readings.

Theatre in the United States has been slow to recognize the contributions of the dramaturg. The functions dramaturgs perform are essential and are usually done by someone at some point—the director, artistic director, or assistant director, to name a few. Having a dramaturg on staff to take on these various tasks gives a theatre someone with critical expertise and a unique set of skills to enrich the theatre's overall intellectual environment.

The Reviewer

Most of us are familiar with the **review**—the brief immediate response to a theatrical event that appears in print in a newspaper or magazine, or in a television or radio segment. This is different from the criticism that is published in scholarly journals or books, which may take a more sophisticated or intellectual approach. Some distinguish between the two types of authors, calling one a *reviewer* and the second a *critic*, but others use the terms interchangeably. A reviewer guides public opinion and shapes the market for a production; a critic hopes to shape the dialogue about a work of art. The essential differences between these two types of criticism are the amount of time the authors have to digest what they've seen, how much depth of analysis they apply, how much space they have to express themselves, and the intended audience for their ideas.

Because reviewers serve as guides to the theatre marketplace, they can influence the financial success of a production. Readers look to reviews for recommendations about whether a performance is worth the ticket price. Reviewers who write for influential newspapers such as the *New York Times* can make or break a show—a single bad review can seriously damage ticket sales, whereas a good one can bring crowds in from across the country. The reviewer can give valuable publicity that keeps a show going for years, or can destroy the months of efforts of a creative team with a few strokes of the pen. This results in an inevitable tension between critics and artists. Reviewers have become such an intrinsic part of the marketing of the theatre that they now even write in quotable sound bites for ads and commercials. Because the number of important newspapers has so greatly diminished, a few well-placed reviewers can determine the public's theatre-going practices and choices and inhibit a new or unusual production from finding its own audience.

Reviews reflect the reviewer's subjective experience and knowledge. Often, different reviews of the same play will express very different perspectives on the work, so frequent theatre-goers learn which reviewers have similar tastes to their own, and whose opinions they can trust. Even when reviewers agree about a piece, a production may have an unexpected effect on its audience. The Broadway musical hit *Cats!* was roundly panned by most reviewers but ran for years playing to audiences all over the world, who loved it. Although reviews address the general public and suggest recommendations for theatre-going, reading a review can never replace seeing a production and judging it for yourself.

Reviewers should be very astute and attentive audience members. They need to be extremely observant of all the details of a performance. Professional critics get press packets when they come to a show. These often include previous reviews of the show, background information on the artists, notes from the director or dramaturg, and other relevant material to inform their judgments. Almost all professional reviewers come to the theatre with pen and paper and make notes about the elements of production during the course of the show. Theatre reviewers need to be educated about the theatre to write with accuracy and understanding. Not only do they need a thorough knowledge of theatre history, dramatic literature, and theatre criticism, but they must also know about acting, directing, and design elements in order to discuss their contributions intelligently. Reviewers should also be informed about other arts such as literature, music, dance, and the visual arts because these all play important roles within the world of the stage. Finally, a theatre reviewer needs good writing skills to write about the theatre in a clear and engaging way. Unfortunately, many reviewers have little theatre training or knowledge, and even prominent newspapers hire theatre reviewers who are untrained in the field.

One of the great advantages of the professional reviewer is the ability to see many theatrical events. Newspaper reviewers generally get free tickets and may go to the theatre three or four times a week, sometimes more, especially if they attend a theatre festival where they might see several shows in a single day. Professional critics might see over two hundred productions a year. This familiarity with the theatrical world allows them to make informed judgments and comparisons between different productions. By knowing what the theatre can do, they are more conscious of where it may have failed to hit its mark.

Challenges and Choices

Does theatre need criticism?

Experiencing Theatre as a Critic

When you get up from your seat at the end of a performance, you will usually have some immediate emotional response to what you saw and experienced. You might share it with a friend by simply saying "I liked it" or "I didn't like it." Whether you like a theatre piece or not, another pleasure can be afforded by going beyond your first response to discover what a piece, even a bad one, was hoping to express, and how and why it succeeded or failed. Translating an emotional response into language can be difficult, but the attempt can help you clarify both your feelings and your thoughts.

You will probably be asked at some point in this class to take on the role of the theatre critic—to go to the theatre and write about your experience. Knowing that you will have to be very precise in your description of the show will probably force you to watch it with greater attention than usual. This assignment can heighten your awareness of the many disparate elements that come together to create a theatrical piece, and give you insight into how they work together successfully or unsuccessfully. You will have the opportunity to apply your newfound knowledge and take a more personal look at the job of the theatre critic.

Selecting an Event

If you live in a large urban area that is a hub of theatre activity, choosing a production to attend on your own for the first time may feel daunting. Perhaps you are confused about how to find a play or uncertain about what production will be worth your time. This is not unusual or entirely surprising. Becoming familiar with your theatrical environment, what venues exist and what type of work each produces, is knowledge that you cultivate over time. You need to develop a sense of which sorts of performances most accord with your own tastes and where you can see them. Over time you might find that you are intrigued by particular directors or actors, or you may develop a love for a certain author or types of plays. Avid theatre-goers might attend a wide range of productions to learn about innovative theatrical events or to keep abreast of whatever is happening in town. Determinations about where to go and what to see are based on knowledge and expectations acquired over time in a variety of ways—going to the theatre, reading reviews, and knowing about theatre history and literature.

Not every production you see will live up to your hopes. Performances that have received good reviews, and that your best friend loved, can disappoint you. It pays to make an agreement with yourself to be open to whatever experience is offered and judge it afterwards. Even a bad piece of theatre isn't necessarily a waste of time if it leads you to understand more about what constitutes good theatre. Because each production requires the integration of so many elements and the work of so many people, it is always a kind of miracle when everything comes together. For this reason it is important to respect good efforts. Keep in mind that any single production will give you only a minuscule taste of the variety of theatrical expression and artistry that exists. If you don't like this piece, next time try something different. You will be building a base of knowledge that will help you make more informed theatre-going choices in the future.

Reading Listings and Reviews

The best way to learn about the theatre in your area is to pick up a local newspaper or magazine and look at the theatre listings. Listings generally don't give in-depth information, but they provide a good overview of what theatre possibilities are available in your area at any particular moment. If you are in a college town, your campus newspaper or theatre department will probably have information about on-campus and off-campus productions.

Theatres also advertise through posters and on websites. Posters are designed to entice you to see a play by providing a visual summary of what makes a particular production exciting or of interest. They can sometimes be misleading. Websites can sometimes give you more information. They might include reviews of the production or a statement by the director or dramaturg about the approach to a work. Remember, though, that a website put up by the producer will give you the production team's view of what they want you to expect from their show.

Reading reviews is a useful way of finding out more about a show and learning about what theatrical events are taking place. Although a review will be one person's subjective account, you can still learn a lot about what a production is like, even if you do not agree with the reviewer's final assessment once you see the show. Making a habit of reading reviews, even when you are not looking to go out to a particular show, keeps you informed about the theatre and helps you learn about the tastes and opinions of your local critics.

Talking with others who know more about the theatre than you do, or who go more often—a theatre major, a theatre fan, a teacher—and asking for their suggestions is another good way to learn about what's worthwhile. Word of mouth from a trusted friend is sometimes the best guide. As a last resort, pick a piece at random. Challenge yourself to a new experience and see what you get out of it. It may be surprisingly good or bad. In either case it will be an event you can talk about and judge others against. This is the first step in what will hopefully become lifelong theatre-going that will enrich your life.

Getting Tickets

Tickets are usually available in person at a theatre **box office** or by phone or online and can be purchased in advance to guarantee good seats for particular dates. Some theatres will have different price ranges for tickets depending on where the seats are located, and you may even be able to pick out the exact location of the seat you want by looking at a seating chart. At some theatres you can buy a subscription for an entire season of plays. A subscription usually gives you a cheaper ticket price per play for a series of plays and a guaranteed seat. Theatres like to sell subscriptions because it ensures an audience for a whole year of productions in advance, regardless of the reviews for any particular show. If you find a theatre you like, a subscription helps support their work and commits you to seeing theatre all year long.

Cheap Tickets

There are a lot of ways for students to get cheap tickets to the theatre. Some theatres have special student prices. Others will sell discounted student rush tickets an hour or so before the show on the day of the performance. Some theatres will let you see a show for free if you usher. Most theatres offer cheaper tickets for groups of ten or more. Organize a theatre party for your class so you can all take advantage. If you are looking for discounts, ask the theatre about what options are available. If you are lucky enough to be planning a future trip to Europe, look into getting a student ID card from Student Travel. This card will allow you to get discounts at theatres and museums throughout Europe. If you can get to New York, check out the TKTS booth in Times Square, sponsored by the New York Theatre Development Fund (TDF). There you can buy tickets the day of the performance for up to 50 percent off. TDF also makes two-for-one coupons for Broadway shows available at restaurants and bookstores all over New York. Following the New York model, many major cities around the world now have discount ticket booths. There may be small theatres, cafés, or independent spaces in your area hoping to attract students that have shows for as cheap as $5 or $10. Theatre doesn't need to be expensive to be interesting.

Preparing for the Theatre

A good piece of theatre should generally not require any extra study. Nevertheless, in some cases, knowledge of the play or the production can put you in a better position to understand or appreciate what you are seeing.

If you have the opportunity to read a play before seeing it, this will influence your experience. Reading creates an image of the play's world in your imagination, and you will inevitably compare what you see to what you expected to discover. For many, the comparison is an exciting part of the theatre experience. Knowing what will happen next can lessen or heighten your involvement. Productions of new plays rarely offer the opportunity to read in advance, so the performance must be a time of discovery. If a work is particularly difficult, sometimes reading it in advance enables you to follow the language and action more easily in performance. One caution, however: Sometimes a play that seems incomprehensible on the page comes to dazzling life on the stage where it feels emotionally immediate and accessible. Reading it, you might have decided not to attend and closed yourself off to an exciting demonstration of how theatre lives in performance. There is clearly no hard-and-fast rule about whether to read a play before seeing it.

Reading reviews sets up expectations against which you will judge your own responses. For a new, foreign, or particularly difficult piece, a review can sometimes give the background you need to understand what you will see. The risk is that the reviewer's opinions may prejudice your own and shape your experience in the theatre. It is important to be aware of how the review has influenced you and to try to formulate an independent viewpoint. The choice to read reviews or not is based on the type of production you will see and your own inclinations, rather than on any strict rule.

Photo 15.3
Crowds flock to the TKTS booth in the center of New York's Times Square to buy discounted tickets to New York theatre performances. Surrounded by the excitement of the Broadway theatre district, for some this New York ritual is itself a cherished part of the theatre-going experience.
© Jeff Greenberg/The Image Works

Sometimes a theatre company will want to inform the perspective you bring to their work. They might provide notes in the program or set up a lobby display with pictures and other materials. If a production was particularly well reviewed, they may place a giant blow-up of the article in the theatre lobby to put you in a positive frame of mind. Often these are best read on the way out of the theatre so you can compare your responses to the reviewer's.

Attending the theatre can be an opportunity to expand your knowledge. You can go beyond reading the play and the reviews and look at other relevant materials. You may want to read a book or article on an actor or director, or in the case of a well-known play you may want to read a biography of the playwright, more lengthy critical writings on the piece, or other plays by the same author. Writings on the social, economic, political, or historical context of a play can also be informative. You don't need all this background to attend a production, but sometimes the experience is enriched by some intellectual exploration before or after the event.

Attending the Show

Your theatre experience begins even before the performance starts. Where is the theatre, and how does that influence your expectations? Is it a traditional theatre space or an unconventional one? What is the atmosphere in the crowd? Take a look at the people around you. Their general age, ethnicity, gender, demeanor, or manner of dress can also frame your expectation of a show. What does the nature of the crowd tell you about the play? How do you fit into this audience? How are you being received and introduced to the show? What do your surroundings lead you to expect?

You will usually find your seat with the help of an usher, who will hand you a program. A program can be a simple list of cast and crew members. Some programs give you more information such as brief professional biographies of the artists, notes from the director, indications about whether the piece has an intermission and how long it will be, and even articles about the theatre. The program of a Broadway production is contained in an issue of *Playbill* magazine, which features an array of items about the Broadway theatre. In Germany, theatre programs are put together by dramaturgs and may include lengthy scholarly essays about the play or related issues. Some American theatres have now taken up this practice as well. You should read through the information in the program before the show, because some of it is aimed at framing your experience. Pay special attention if there is a "Director's Note"; this usually explains the approach to the production and the director's concept or intentions. If you have been assigned to write a review, the program will provide valuable information for your assignment, so be sure to take it home with you.

Once you take your seat, you may find yourself in a theatre with a curtain masking the stage before the performance begins. The proverbial rising of the curtain will be your first introduction to the world of the play. Use of a curtain builds a sense of anticipation. Today many theatres don't use curtains, and the set for the play is already visible. This setup gives you another opportunity to formulate and contemplate your expectations of the production. What is the space indicating to you? How is it already speaking about the world of the play before any characters have come on stage?

During the performance, you will need to be attentive to all the details of the production—acting, setting, costuming, music, lighting, dialogue—as well as your reactions to them. It is important to think about each element of the production individually and then to reflect on how they work together to create the total effect.

Taking Notes

Like a professional reviewer, you may want to bring notebook and pen to the show so you can make notes during the performance, at intermission, or after leaving the theatre. It is helpful to make a sketch of the set so that you can remember the details when you sit down to write about it. You might also want to note moments that were significant to you because they were particularly engaging, dull, or disturbing. Write down your first impressions so that they stay with you. Your notes do not need to be elaborate, as long as they serve as reminders of what you saw and experienced. You can then go back to your notes to refresh your memory and analyze your immediate response.

Writing a Review

When you sit down to think about what you have to say, the first question you will probably ask yourself is, "Did I like it?" Although this gut reaction begins your evaluation, you want to be sure to move on to an analysis of your reactions. What captivated you, and what didn't? Did the piece leave you feeling confused, unsatisfied, joyful? Why did you feel the way you did? Think about each aspect of the production separately and note what kind of contribution it made to the overall effect. The following questions can serve as guidelines.

Acting: Did the actors embody the characters physically, vocally, and emotionally? Were the performances energized and compelling? Were there any memorable acting moments?

Directing: Did the production possess a unified vision? Was there an interesting concept? How well did the show move in terms of pace and rhythm? Were there interesting patterns of movement? Were there any significant directorial moments?

Writing: If you saw a play, were the plot and characters well developed? Was the content interesting? If you saw another kind of text, how was it structured? What made it interesting?

Design: How did the design elements contribute to the overall effect? Did they create a unified whole? How did the choices for color and line support the text, the environment, and the characters? Did the set serve the action well? Were the characters well depicted by their costumes? Did the lighting create a mood? What was the function of sound?

Finally, ask yourself, What did the piece say to me, and how did all the aspects of production express this?

Having a Point of View

When you write, it is important to have a point of view. You will express this as your "thesis," or main idea. You should be able to summarize your overall perspective in a single clear sentence. The rest of your essay elaborates, explains, and provides support for your thesis. Your point of view on the production should be reflected in the title of your essay and also stated clearly somewhere in your paper, usually in the introduction. You can think of your thesis as the light that guides you through your writing. Try reading reviews

Challenges and Choices

Is an uninformed critical evaluation by a novice theatre-goer of value?

in the newspaper and see if you can summarize the reviewer's thesis or impression of the show in one sentence. Can you point to a line in the article that states the main idea clearly?

Backing Up Your Ideas

In the course of writing a review, you will want to give your reader good reasons to understand and perhaps agree with your point of view on the performance. In a research paper the evidence you use to support your statements may be quotations from scholarly texts. In a literary essay it may be citations from a novel or poem. In an essay about a theatre production, your evidence usually resides in detailed descriptions of the performance. If you liked the acting of a particular role, you might recount a theatrical moment that highlights the actor's talents. If you didn't like the set, you should describe its color, materials, structure, and elements and explain which factors seemed inappropriate or what ways it did not serve the action well. You may need to refer to your notes to be precise.

Engage with the emotional and intellectual intentions of the production to have some sense of the standards by which to judge it. Remember that theatrical elements are introduced to reveal something about a text, characters, and ideas. They are not meant to be simply pleasing in and of themselves. A talented actor can play a character who is despicable. A dreary set may be exactly right for delineating the bleak world of a play. A tragedy might bring you down emotionally, but that is the intention.

Good Writing

An essay about the theatre should be written in clear and engaging prose, like any piece of good writing. Good ideas can only be appreciated when they are expressed articulately. Try to paint a portrait of the performance with words, using as much detailed description as possible. Sometimes writing will clarify your understanding of a performance. If you are unsure about your writing skills, use a writer's manual or seek out assistance from a teacher or writing tutor.

A few conventions are used when writing about the theatre. The title of a full-length play should always be underlined or written in italics. This practice is not only correct, but also helps in distinguishing the play *Hamlet* from the character Hamlet. It is standard practice that the first time you mention the name of an author, actor, designer, or director in your paper you give the full name; later references require only the last name.

You now have the tools to become a perceptive theatre reviewer. All you need is the practice and experience to train your critical eye and voice.

KEY IDEAS

- All theatre provokes both emotional and critical responses.
- Theatre criticism reflects its time and culture.
- Critics are not objective, but reflect their own biases and interests.

- Today criticism offers a multitude of critical lenses through which to analyze performance.
- Good criticism defines and clarifies the theatre experience.

- Critics can help interpret a theatrical event by providing a framework for comprehension, or they can inspire artistic creation and influence new theatrical styles.
- Artists may take on the role of critic as they explain their artistic intentions, and theatrical works can themselves critique the theatre.
- Dramaturgs are inhouse critics who work with theatre artists during the creative process.
- Critics and reviewers generally differ in the amount of time they have to digest what they've seen, the depth of their analyses, the space they have for expression, and their intended audience.
- All of us have the potential to develop our critical skills as we learn about the components of theatre.

Making Theatre Happen

16

Theatre can sometimes be a dangerous business, and committed actors often need to fight for their right to perform and for financial support. After the end of the Taliban rule, which forbade theatrical performance, actors in the ruins of the Kabul theatre in Afghanistan stage a play about Afghanistan's destruction in an effort to encourage the new government to sponsor future productions. The actress dressed as a bride symbolizes peace.

© Rob Elliott/AFP/Getty Images

Around the world, despite obstacles and difficulties, people are committed to making theatre. Whether in Sarajevo or Bagdad, Cape Town, or at Ground Zero in New York, artists use the theatre to express their strivings, hopes, and fears. Some overcome political barriers, some leap financial hurdles, some combat social and religious custom, and some even risk their lives to express their human yearnings through the theatrical form. Fortunate theatre artists are celebrated for their activities by the state, their communities, or an adoring public. While some find fame and fortune, most create at great personal sacrifice. In this panorama of conditions, there is no single model for creating the theatrical event. In each case artistic vision, talent, and passion confront a set of social, political, and economic realities.

How one enters a life in the theatre can vary from society to society. Some are driven by personal talent and ambition, some by cultural heritage and community values. In some places national traditions and institutions provide a conduit for artists. In China elementary school children are auditioned for theatre training and at this young age begin years of rigorous training at government-funded conservatories to receive positions in government-funded theatres; those not evidencing precocious talent are excluded from entering the national schools. *Kabuki* theatre passes roles within the family from generation to generation, so in Japan, you can be born into the profession. In Australia, the Americas, and Europe, theatre is usually the place for individual expression and self-realization, reflecting the premium placed on individual freedom in these cultures. Actors and directors peddle their talents, and even in the noncommercial world, creating theatre may require inspiring a collaborative team to assemble around you.

In some repressive cultures, such individual freedom is feared, and all theatre artists are labeled as political dissidents. Theatrical activity can land you in prison like Czech president Vaclav Havel and Nigerian Wole Soyinka, or even get you killed like Indian director Safdar Hashmi. Nevertheless, the need to make a statement in theatrical form about political conditions inspires some performers to risk all, performing in clandestine underground venues with minimal technical equipment. How and where a theatrical performance is created is inextricably tied to who is doing it and why.

Challenges and Choices

What advantages does theatre offer as a forum for controversial political issues?

Where Theatre Happens

State-Subsidized Theatres

Many countries around the world have state-subsidized professional theatres. In Europe, the tradition of state funding goes back to the royal theatres chartered by the ruling monarchs of the Renaissance. In the era before electronic media, theatre was the only way to reach mass public audiences, and state licensing was often used as a means of censorship. The central authority funded only those theatres with approved messages, a tradition that continued in many modern dictatorships. In contrast, today's subsidized European theatres are frequently places of artistic exploration and experimentation. Municipalities and provincial governments fund local theatres and cultural centers that often provide convenient schedules and child care to facilitate theatre-going.

In Africa and Asia, colonial powers used the subsidized theatre to stamp their cultural imprint on colonized populations. With the growth of democracy in many developing nations, subsidized national theatres now belong to the people and celebrate popular indigenous culture. Across Africa and Asia, countries such as Nigeria, the Democratic Republic of the Congo, Cambodia, and Thailand all provide government subsidies for national theatres to preserve excellence or local traditions. For example, the Thai and Nigerian national theatres are dedicated to the preservation of indigenous arts. The Japanese National Theatre and the French Comédie Française preserve classical theatrical forms.

Challenges and Choices

Should governments provide funding for theatre institutions or artists?

History IN PERSPECTIVE

SAFDAR HASHMI (1954–1989):
THE PRICE OF POLITICAL PERFORMANCE

On January 1, 1989, before a group of striking industrial workers in Jhadpur village on the outskirts of Delhi, Indian theatre activist, playwright, and actor Safdar Hashmi and his theatre company, Jan Natya Manch (People's Theatre Front), performed their street theatre play *Halla Bol* (Raise Hell!!), a satire on political corruption. The performance was in support of the strikers and the Center of Indian Trade Unions' (CITU) candidate running for office in local elections.

The rival candidate, backed by the Congress Party, arrived on the scene with supporters armed with lathi—sticks bound with iron—and guns. They attacked the performers, who scattered along with the audience. They grabbed an activist, Ram Badhar, beat him, then shot him to death. They pushed their way into the CITU office, where Safdar Hashmi and others had hidden for protection, and beat Hashmi so severely that he died the next day of a brain hemorrhage. On January 4, under the direction of Molyashree Hashmi, Hashmi's widow, the troupe performed the play again to thousands at the place where Hashmi had been killed—a performance of mourning that spoke in defiance of political intimidation.

Beginning in 1973, using the streets as their stage, Hashmi and his troupe brought plays addressing issues of concern to India's workers and peasants to urban and rural populations. Their short skit *Kursi, Kursi, Kursi* (Chair, Chair, Chair), about a king who cannot remove his throne from his backside no matter how hard he tries even when his successor is elected, was performed on the occasion of Prime Minister Indira Gandhi's refusal to resign despite accusations of fixing the elections. Other plays dealt with women's oppression, the problems of migrant workers, and various forms of political corruption.

Hashmi's murder revealed that political corruption in India reached even grassroots-level politics and showed the risks inherent in speaking out politically from the stage. Hashmi's murderers were finally convicted in 2003 after a trial that stretched out over fourteen years. Two of the nine perpetrators died during the interval.

Spectators of all ages gather at every vantage point to watch Safdar Hashmi's company, Jana Natya Manch, perform on a makeshift stage constructed from camel carts in the early 1980s. Hashmi's company brought not only entertainment but also an important political voice to poor Indian communities such as this one. Hashmi stands with his back to the camera.
© *Jana Natya Manch, Delhi; photo by Surendra Rajan*

The United States is actually an exception among most prosperous nations in having no national theatre funded by the government. Even many struggling countries consider government support essential for the theatre and its artists. Plans to privatize the National Arts Theatre of Nigeria led to massive protests that forced the government to restore funding. Sadly, national and local support for the arts in the United States is limited to competitive grants and subject to budget cuts and political pressure. In 1990, the National Endowment for the Arts (NEA) withdrew its support to individual artists who had been recommended by a peer review panel, claiming that their work was too sexually explicit. This engendered a protracted court battle over freedom of speech and First

Challenges and Choices

Should the government fund individual artists whose work offends certain communities but is deemed excellent by a peer committee?

Amendment protection for applicants for government grants, in a suit brought by artists Karen Finley, Tim Miller, John Fleck, and Holly Hughes, now referred to as the NEA Four. The legal battle centered on the amendment to the 1990 congressional reauthorization of the NEA that required consideration of standards of decency in awarding grants.

During the Great Depression of the 1930s, the U.S. government briefly flirted with state-supported theatres in the form of the Federal Theatre Project, founded to provide a buffer against massive unemployment in the arts. Wonderful artists emerged from that era, including Orson Welles and John Houseman. The foundations for the Black Theatre movement, the innovative work done under government auspices, and the thousands of theatre artists provided with a decent wage demonstrate that government subsidy can produce significant theatre in the United States.

In countries with state-subsidized theatres, the luxury of strong public support is evidenced in the stable working lives it provides to actors, designers, and directors. State funding allows companies to develop ensembles, to have long rehearsal periods that permit difficult projects, and to enjoy the freedom of creating without concern for ticket sales and profit margins.

Government subsidy is not without its drawbacks and controversy, however. There is always the threat of censorship as was evidenced in Eastern Europe during the Soviet era. Groups in Canada and England have argued that the government gives too much support to large national theatres and not enough to smaller local troupes, choosing to support tourism, not culture. Some theatre practitioners fear that subsidized artists will grow complacent. State-supported theatre can get embroiled in culture wars, such as when the South African government withdrew its support for theatres that produced European and American forms, preferring to allocate resources to indigenous culture. This decision put actors out of work and forced artists to abandon the theatre of their choice, or to work at great personal cost. Despite these assorted problems, most American theatre artists would relish the idea of working with dependable economic support for their efforts like their counterparts around the globe.

International Theatre Festivals

International theatre festivals have been growing in numbers since the 1960s. Begun as havens for experimental work, they now are organized around many different themes. Holding a festival can earn a particular city or country cultural recognition. Receiving an invitation to perform at a prestigious festival can give a theatre company the artistic legitimacy that facilitates grants and other funding.

One of the best ways to get a sampling of theatre from around the world is to attend one of the many international theatre festivals held each year. They offer a chance to see the broad spectrum of theatrical activity going on today, and in a week's time, you may be able to see a dozen productions. Both emerging trends and cultural difference are clearly in evidence at some of the better festivals. Almost every country in Europe sponsors at least one theatre festival, as do many cities around the United States, Canada, New Zealand, and Australia. African companies, once limited to the European festivals, have now organized several pan-African festivals (in Benin, Burkina Faso, Côte d'Ivoire, Ghana, Cameroon, and in the Democratic Republic of the Congo, to name a few,) that assert African artistic freedom from the European tradition and encourage talented African actors to work locally. New York, of course, has several events during the year.

Some festivals celebrate local theatre companies, and most festivals have an international reach. Many are open to all kinds of theatre; others have a specific focus. Some are devoted to the avant-garde and others to more traditional forms. Some are juried, and others are open to all who wish to perform. The director of the Festival des Ameriques, held every two years in Montréal, travels the globe looking for interesting performances

Artists

IN PERSPECTIVE

In Their Own Words

JANE ALEXANDER

Jane Alexander's life demonstrates the marriage of artistic excellence and distinguished public service. An acting career that includes a Tony, an Obie, and a Drama Desk Award for The Great White Hope, *she has returned to the Broadway stage many times. Numerous regional theatre performances and countless film and television roles have led to four Oscar nominations and an Emmy. In 2004, she performed in* What of the Night *in Germany, which arrived in New York the following year. In 1993, President Clinton nominated her to serve as chairperson of the National Endowment for the Arts, and her tenure in that position from 1993 until 1997, was a stormy period during which she defended the arts in a charged political climate.*

■ **Can art that really expresses diverse and particular points of view avoid offending someone?**

Art has the ability to excite and stimulate people who think differently and also to outrage them. I think that comes with the territory. The way you enhance the experience for everybody is through education. If you are doing a difficult piece of work or one where you might anticipate a negative reaction, it is important to prepare the audience through articles and news coverage, and through the schools.

■ **What if a work intends to provoke?**

We live in a free society and some people will choose to provoke, and those people should be free to do that—to provoke interest, excitement, stimulation. There is in my mind a difference between propaganda and provocative art. Propaganda is always provocative, and not all art should be. I would estimate that only about 10 percent of art is provocative, and that 90 percent is created for beauty or comfort. It comforts by reinforcing feelings and beliefs. These are roles that artists play and that audiences expect.

■ **Can you think of a specific example in which theatre was used to heal?**

After the Oklahoma City bombings, we used a lot of theatre to heal through storytelling. That was a cathartic use of theatre. Healing also happens a lot with preventative theatre that takes an issue or subject such as teen pregnancy and deals with it in the schools or in prescribed community situations.

■ **Should the NEA use government money to fund arts that might offend particular communities?**

I think it is the business of the government to honor and fund works of art that are deemed excellent by a peer panel, which is what the NEA tries to do. And I think those peer panels are first-rate. They are a diverse body pulled together from different states, backgrounds, races, and ethnicities, so as a whole they represent a community standard of excellence. Some of their choices will be provocative, and some will offend certain groups.

■ **Do you think there is an attempt to purge art by the government?**

There is definitely a chill factor with regard to the NEA, mainly because the decency clause is still in existence. Artists will not apply with their most outrageous work because they think it is going to be subject to a review of decency and then kicked out right away.

■ **How do you react to the NEA giving all its support to institutions at the expense of individual funding?**

Congress has put an end to individual funding except for literature fellowships, and honorifics for jazz, folk, and traditional artists. One-person shows like those of the NEA Four could not be funded any more through the NEA. I think that it is very important for the government to support and nurture the individual artist. I love that Mexico gives a stipend to the artists they consider national treasures. We don't have anything like that. Of course there is private giving, but I do think the federal government should be in the business of honoring our individual artists, both those that are coming up in the world and those that are at the end of their lives.

■ **What is the most salient lesson you took from your experience as head of the NEA?**

That our rights as a people in the United States are inviolable. That First Amendment rights with regard to the artist and free expression should be inviolable, and that this is a battle one has to fight again and again because there are legislators who seek to reinterpret the Constitution in a manner that treads on the sacred ground of basic human rights. And that was what was beginning to happen at the NEA when I was there.

(continues)

IN PERSPECTIVE (CONTINUED)

■ **If you could create an ideal NEA, what would it do?**

I think it would support individual artists, nurture new and promising talents, and recognize older talents. It would promote arts education. It would shore up our institutions nationally. Right now we pay about thirty-four cents per person for the NEA. If we could only increase that tax contribution to three dollars per individual, you could really award new companies and institutions their basic running expenses, especially organizations that interact with their communities.

■ **Do you believe the NEA shapes the arts in America today?**

No. For the most part, the amount of money that is given doesn't matter a whit. In the future, if there were more taxpayer dollars given to the endowment, then it would make a difference.

■ **When you look at how Europe funds its theatres, how do you compare the situation for theatre artists there to the United States?**

I thought for a long time that European state-subsidized theatre was the most wonderful thing. But after working in Germany in 2004, I saw that there was little hunger, figurative hunger, to create something wonderful. Many people have grown complacent. The state-subsidized system creates glorious design ele-

ments, but not necessarily inspired art. And it often blocks getting things done. The state-subsidized system is not a panacea. You can't buy and sell creativity.

I love the spirit here in the United States where there is no complacency. There is something to be said for struggling with a creative idea and trying to bring in others to make it viable. I do, however, wish there were more money for people to draw on.

■ **Should the government be involved in the arts?**

It is the business of the federal government to fund art in our society because the government is of the people and should be interested in developing inquiring minds, creative thought, imagination, and critical thinking, and the arts are the area of human endeavor that most readily promotes that for society. We must be secure in that opinion.

As Chairperson of the National Endowment for the Arts, actress Jane Alexander speaks at the White House. President and Mrs. Clinton watch in the background.
© Wally McNamee/CORBIS

Source: Used with permission from Jane Alexander.

and a wide range of theatrical activity that is carefully selected for presentation. The Next Wave at BAM in New York is devoted to the more established avant-garde, whereas the Edinburgh Festival Fringe in Scotland is open to almost all who wish to appear and accommodates even minor companies and solo artists. The newly developed New York Fringe Festival has followed the Edinburgh lead. Avignon, in France, is focused on the recent avant-garde. UNIMA (Union Nationale de la Marionette) unites puppeteers from around the world and sponsors international puppet theatre festivals every four years in different venues around the world. The Asia-Pacific Festival of Children's Theatre in Toyama, Japan, focuses on theatre for young audiences. The international Festival of the Francophone World held in Limoges offers the opportunity for French and postcolonial

French theatre to appear side by side. As you can see, the assortment of festivals and interest groups is wide and varied. The Internet offers guides to festivals, performances, and ticket information.

The growing number of international festivals is subject to positive and negative effects, like so much in our global world. Although these festivals are a source of cross-fertilization, as artists from various cultures exchange ideas, some fear it can lead to homogeneity and cultural appropriation, or worse, domination of indigenous traditions by the Western theatre establishment.

Colleges and Universities

Universities around the world have traditionally been hubs for theatrical activity. In Africa in particular, many universities have resident theatre companies and groups promoting classical and indigenous art forms on campus that transform the university into a cultural center for the general population. In some developing nations, universities also provide training in both European and traditional forms. In the United States, colleges and Universities have become the center for professional theatre training and have forged new partnerships with the professional theatre. As part of their training, students participate in productions that serve not only the campus, but the larger community as well. Free from financial concerns, educational theatre can do interesting and innovative work. Most college repertories range from musical theatre to the European avant-garde and multicultural presentations. Because faculty often have significant professional theatre credentials, the quality of educational theatre can be quite high. Many universities have resident professional theatres in which students are given the opportunity to perform or work backstage alongside professionals in the field. In less well-known programs, the college production is still an important opportunity for students to be exposed to live performance and to learn how theatre is made.

Summer Theatres and Shakespeare Festivals

Summer theatres and Shakespeare festivals in the United States do more than provide entertainment for vacationers. They offer the opportunity for student interns and young

Photo 16.1
Since 1947, the Avignon Theatre Festival has attracted summer crowds. Today its events play to audiences of 100,000, who come to see first showings of contemporary theatre and dance from around the world in this magnificent old city. Featured here is an outdoor performance near the Papal Palace.
© *Gail Mooney/CORBIS*

Photo 16.2
Around the United States, summer Shakespeare theatres attract crowds of theatre-goers, who enjoy these performances in an informal environment. The Utah Shakespeare festival, honored with a Tony Award for "Outstanding Regional Theatre," offers free Elizabethan music and dance on its park-like grounds, as well as seminars, classes, and Shakespearean and contemporary productions.
Copyright Utah Shakespearean Festival; photo by Karl Hugh

professionals to try out their craft under the guidance of professional directors. The quality of these theatres varies widely. Some, such as the Williamstown or Berkshire Theatre Festivals, use well-known actors and directors and also train students. They may do tried-and-true plays and experimental work in the same season. Shakespeare festivals often draw their directors and staff from the professionals teaching at local universities, who bring students along for a summer of learning in a professional setting, building yet another bridge between the educational and professional theatre communities. Others recruit actors and directors from regional theatres or New York professionals. Often these festivals are at outdoor theatres where the festive atmosphere makes theatre-going a jubilant event. The New York Shakespeare Festival founded by Joseph Papp (1921–1991) takes the festival to its populist limits, offering free Shakespeare in Central Park with high-quality star actors such as Meryl Streep and Kevin Kline performing for a general audience.

Community Theatres

Many small towns around the world that cannot attract professional resident companies rely on community theatres, although many large cities have community groups as well. Some are run on a totally volunteer basis; others pay for basic staffs and sometimes for a professional director to lead a troupe of dedicated volunteer actors. They may work in well-equipped small theatres or commandeer the town hall, a church, or the village square. Some produce high-quality work, whereas others are distinctly amateur in quality. Community theatres contribute to the cultural life of a locality and provide a place for shared experiences that reinforce the social fabric. People give of themselves to an art they love. Many young people would have no exposure to the live theatre were it not for such groups.

As we look around the world and back through time, we see the important role that community theatre has played and continues to play in many cultures. Native American storytelling and dance performances, African festivals, Mexican Corpus Christi plays, and medieval cycle plays are examples of community theatres that were part of the social glue that reinforced shared values. *The Oberammergau Passion Play* is an event that involves an entire city and has been performed every ten years as a civic event since 1634.

Citizens consider it an honor to take part, and twenty years of town residency is required to participate. Even the ancient Athenian theatre began as a state-subsidized community theatre.

Today, many community theatres have carved out an important role reinforcing identity and providing cultural education. The Sen'Klip Native Theatre Company in Canada and the Red Eagle Soaring and Thunderbird Theatres in the United States are examples of groups that provide a sense of community identity and purpose to Native

History IN PERSPECTIVE

THE OBERAMMERGAU PASSION PLAY: TRADITION IN CHANGED TIMES

To ward off the bubonic plague in 1633, the residents of Oberammergau, Germany, vowed to perform a play depicting the life and death of Jesus every ten years. The Oberammergau passion play has been the ultimate demonstration of community theatre ever since. This seven-hour extravaganza is a living link to medieval religious drama and comprises spoken text, choral and musical components, and *tableaux vivants* in which actors pose in frozen biblical scenes accompanied by narration and music. Once performed to knit the fabric of the community around core beliefs, the play now attracts tourists from around the globe.

The production performed in public spaces involves approximately half the townspeople in a cast of 2,200 performers, all of whom must be twenty-year residents of the town. The play holds such a place in the psyche of the town's inhabitants that people are referred to in the intervening years between performances by the characters they play. The death rate even drops in the year before the production as people cling to life for one more chance to participate.[1] Families often hold on to coveted roles.

Performers were limited to Catholics in good standing until 2000, when non-Christians were allowed to play pagan roles. Despite its fame, longevity, and popularity, charges of anti-Semitism have been leveled at the play, which paints the Jewish community as the killers of Christ. European passion plays were often the source of anti-Semitic senti-

1. *James Shapiro,* Oberammergau *(New York: Pantheon Books, 2000), 4.*

ment that gave rise to violence against Jews and have long been cited as part of the cultural backdrop for the Holocaust. Indeed, Adolph Hitler attended and praised the 1934 Oberammergau production for its anti-Semitic message, and passages were rewritten that year to reaffirm the Nazi agenda.

In recent times, protests from organizations around the world have led to changes in the centuries-old text. Jesus is now referred to as Rabbi and speaks a Hebrew prayer. The Roman role in the crucifixion has been acknowledged, and lines that incite revenge against Jews have been expurgated from the text along with other elements that demonized the Jews. Many believe that the historic text should not be altered to meet the demands of outside groups while acknowledging that there was no protest when the text was doctored to meet the needs of Nazi propaganda. Although the event fills the coffers of the small Bavarian town and is a source of local pride, both Christian and Jewish organizations have questioned continuing performances in a post-Holocaust world.

This *tableau vivant* from the 2000 performance of the Oberammergau passion play enacts a scene from the passion of Christ.
© *Michael Dalder/REUTERS/CORBIS*

Americans. Small towns in Africa often receive funding for their community theatres to preserve traditional cultural forms of entertainment. In Zimbabwe, local cultural centers in townships are charged with the preservation of folklore theatre. Across Africa, local groups, aware of the possible loss of traditional forms, use community theatre to provide cultural memory.

Another form of community theatre, sometimes called community-based theatre, draws on the concerns and experiences of marginalized groups to create theatre that promotes social change. Community-based theatre has been done with prisoners, youth at risk, and minority and economically disenfranchised groups. In the United States, Living Stage, an outreach of Washington, D.C.'s, Arena Theatre, has helped spread this work that is now practiced by many organizations and individuals. PETA, the Philippines Educational Theatre Association, has conducted workshops throughout Asia. Community-based theatres also exist around the globe in Costa Rica, the Middle East, Bosnia, Australia, and Kenya. Facilitators help community members dramatize their own stories, histories, or social concerns. Performances done for the community can take a variety of forms including agit-prop, comedy, musical, and melodrama and may use masks, puppets, dance, and music. In Kenya, the Kawuonda Women's Collective, which also runs a bakery and a child-care center, uses storytelling and performance to depict women's changing roles in a changing society. Theatre work is integrated with the women's daily chores, as they often work together raising crops and making meals to meet personal needs while creating public performance. Community-based theatre empowers local groups by giving them a voice through theatre.

Commercial and Not-for-Profit Theatre in the United States

In the United States, productions may be amateur (done out of love) or professional (done for money) and may fall into either the **commercial theatre** or the **not-for-profit theatre** category. Although all amateur productions are not-for-profit, not all not-for-profit theatre is amateur. In the commercial theatre, investors back a single production and take a capital return if a show is a success; a production will run as long as it is making money. In not-for-profit theatre, the profit is channeled back into the producing organization to defray costs for the institution and to fund new projects.

Commercial Theatre

When we think of the commercial theatre, we think of **Broadway** and the great concentration of commercial houses around Times Square in New York and London's **West End**, but there are commercial theatres all around the country and around the world in almost every major cosmopolitan city. Because the financial risks are high, commercial theatre is rarely the place for experimentation or performances with limited appeal. Many bemoan the dearth of serious and interesting drama on Broadway compared to the days when costs were low and investors could take greater chances with material. Nevertheless, the Broadway theatre maintains its caché and remains a symbol of "making it" in the professional theatre. Despite the burgeoning theatre activity in cities such as Seattle and Chicago, New York remains the theatrical center of the United States, with at least thirty commercial productions and well over a hundred other professional and semiprofessional performances available on any given night of the week. Touring companies will take a successful Broadway show on the road and set up in touring houses for limited runs in cities around the country and Canada. Tours can generate millions of dollars for Broadway investors. In New York, some smaller theatres in and out of the theatre district are designated **Off-Broadway** because they have fewer than five hundred seats. Often, a well-received Off-Broadway production will be moved to a larger theatre on Broadway if investors are convinced they can turn a profit and fill the house.

Professional Not-for-Profit Companies

Many important theatres in New York and **resident theatres** around the country are professional not-for-profit companies. Originally conceived as **regional theatres** to combat the centralization of theatre activity in New York, resident theatres have grown over the last forty years and now provide a permanent theatre presence in almost every major city in America including New York. Presenting a season of plays for set runs, some focus on particular kinds of performance—the classics, new plays, or multicultural performances. Others offer an eclectic repertory. They have expanded theatrical activity around the country, provided a source of employment for both local and New York theatre professionals, and enlarged theatre audiences.

To qualify for tax-exempt nonprofit status, theatres must develop goals and mission statements and file for such status with the Internal Revenue Service. Not-for-profit theatres have a board of directors responsible for fund-raising and finance and the hiring and firing of the managing and artistic directors. These theatres depend on subscriptions, grants, private donations, and foundation and corporate support for their survival, and negotiate salary waivers with theatrical unions.

In recent years many resident theatres noticed that the majority of their subscribers were over the age of fifty. This disturbing situation meant that young people in their areas were not getting into the habit of going to the theatre and that the theatres were not building their future audiences. To keep their older subscribers coming back, they had to put on traditional and less experimental pieces. They were caught in the bind of trying to hold onto their audience base while simultaneously attracting a new population to the theatre with innovative work. Theatres also found that the majority of their audience members were white. However, when they did a play by an African American or Asian American playwright, they brought in new audiences. Although these companies tried to do a varied season, audiences rarely crossed over to see plays that they didn't feel were intended for them. Resident theatres are searching for ways to bring their various audiences together around new work through special events, lectures, and talks with the artists.

Common Interest Theatres

Common interest theatres are created when groups of artists come together with particular goals or visions—be they political, artistic, or educational. Such theatres may be created by professionals or amateurs. The **Off-Off-Broadway** theatre was founded by both amateurs and professionals who sought an alternative to the artistic constraints imposed in the commercial theatre. They wanted to be free to make radical political statements, to experiment artistically with less financial risk, and to showcase their talents. Such theatres are often driven by a dominant artistic vision such as Mabou Mines, Théâtre de la Jeune Lune, or the Wooster Group, or by a community of interest, such as the Puerto Rican Traveling Theatre, the Pan-Asian Repertory Company, the Negro Ensemble Company, or Split Britches. Sometimes groups are formed around political issues and share a combined political and artistic point of view such as the Tectonic Theatre, or Teatro Campesino.

Producing Theatre

Although the scale and finances of the theatrical endeavor may vary, the process always begins with an idea that someone believes in and for which support is recruited. Who that person is and how the support will be raised depends on the nature of the venture. The originator of the idea can be a director, a playwright, an actor, a composer, an artistic director, a government agency, or a producer who must sell a group of collaborators on the validity of the project.

At some point, early in the process, every production requires a **producer** who, through a clear perception of the project, can bring together a creative team with the necessary resources to get the work done before the right audience, in the right place. We associate producers with the commercial theatre, but someone always serves that role even without the title. In university theatres, the department chairperson may set the budget, assign the space, and determine the designers and directors. In regional theatres, it may be the managing and artistic directors. In small experimental companies, it may be the director. But no production will ever be realized unless someone is doing the job of producing the event.

The producer is the artistic, financial, and administrative coordinator of a theatrical production, and the list of responsibilities is dizzying. The producer's first job is to find a worthwhile project and to secure the performance rights, which means negotiating with publishers, agents, playwrights, directors, or actors, whoever holds the rights to the piece. Once the right to perform is guaranteed, the producer must assemble a creative team, starting with the director. Then, with the director's collaboration, the producer must engage actors, designers, stage managers, and crews. This may require negotiating with agents and unions. Crews need to be assembled to carry out the work of the designers. If a scenic production studio is hired to build the set, the producer hires the technical liaison with the studio. A rehearsal and performance space must be procured that suits the nature of the project in size, layout, and location, and a rental agreement needs to be negotiated. Running crews to staff the theatre will be required for every performance. The producer must supervise the management of the theatre, making sure that box office staff, ushers, and house managers are doing their jobs properly. The producer is also responsible for advertising and programs. When things are not going well, the producer may have to fire the director or an actor. Making sure the entire endeavor is on time and within budget is an important responsibility of the producer.

The Commercial Producer

Challenges and Choices

Does producing works with broad audience appeal limit creativity and innovation?

The goal of commercial producers is to make money. That means they must have an unerring sense of what the public will pay to see. They search for a *property*—a play, a story, or an idea for which they can purchase the rights for a professional production. They find their properties by developing relationships with playwrights and directors who bring them their new work and ideas. Sometimes producers commission new work. High-end producers may employ *play readers* to read through hundreds of submitted plays in search of a vehicle for success. They may send out scouts to look at new plays in the not-for-profit theatres that may hold commercial promise. Today, very few new works begin their lives on Broadway because the costs and financial risks are too high. Instead, commercial producers often work with regional theatres, which serve as out-of-town tryouts for new plays. (Many playwrights also prefer having the first airing of new work outside of New York where the effects of negative reviews are less damaging.) Commercial producers also need to raise money to fund production costs. They find backers who invest in productions in the hope of realizing a financial return. Some commercial producers own several theatres, which enables them to control rental expenses.

Even before a play reaches an out-of-town tryout, it often goes through a process of readings. Producers use this occasion to judge its commercial viability. It is not unusual to have several readings while a play is in development. For the first reading, actors sit in chairs with scripts in hand. There are no props, and the stage manager reads the stage directions. There is an invited audience, and the actors often volunteer their time or work for a small stipend to help the playwright in the hope of being cast in the final production. This is the opportunity for the playwright to hear the characters' voices and gauge audience response, so the audience too is a collaborator in the process of developing a play. The writer then rewrites the script to address problems that became clear in the reading.

Sometimes a play goes through a transitional step called a **staged reading**. Actors are on their feet, scripts in hand, and there are minimal set pieces. This is a chance to discover practical staging problems and other needs of the script. In the commercial theatre, working on a play in this manner saves time and money and leads to a greater likelihood of success. This model is often followed for not-for-profit theatre as well.

The Not-for-Profit Producer

Many not-for-profit companies have both managing and artistic directors who share the responsibilities of producing with a board of directors. The board is responsible for overseeing fund-raising and planning. The artistic director may decide what plays to produce and whom to hire for the artistic staff, and may also work as a director. The managing director is responsible for budgets and staff hiring for specific productions, publicity, and all other aspects of administration and theatre management. If a company owns a theatre, the managing director is also responsible for maintaining the facilities.

The Alternative Theatre Producer

Both commercial and not-for-profit producers function in relative luxury when compared with producers in many small theatres around the world who have no staff, no facilities, and no money. Often directors with specific projects play the role of producer, procuring funds, renting theatres, sometimes even building the sets, buying props, and costuming out of their own closets. Often the responsibilities for production are shared

Photo 16.3
After limited rehearsal, actors sit in chairs for the first public reading of a new play. Although the physical action is limited, good actors can bring much life and interest to the spoken text. To help make the written text vivid for the audience, an actor or stage manager is engaged to read stage directions.

with the actors and designers, who give time to work on other aspects of the production. Such community-spirited theatrical endeavors provide an alternative model.

Behind the Scenes: The Unsung Heroes of the Theatre

When we attend the theatre, we are aware of the actors, we may think about the work of the designers and dramatist, but we forget the many highly skilled professionals on whose efforts every successful production relies. Readying a theatrical event requires the work of technicians, managers, and crews. Each performance depends on the teamwork of diverse personnel to run the show. In fact, a large commercial production may have as many as one hundred salaried employees working on any given performance.

The following sections introduce the set of characters who create a theatrical production. It is important to keep in mind that someone must do these jobs on every production. Sometimes money is available to hire individual personnel for each position. If a theatre cannot hire separate individuals for every function, people will take on two or three jobs to get the show up and running, no matter how tiring and difficult that may be. Theatre professionals are a dedicated group who will do whatever it takes to "go on with the show."

The Stage Manager

The figure who holds a show together emotionally, practically, and technically is the stage manager. This is the person with whom the director works most closely in preparing the production, and on whom the director depends to take care of all pragmatic concerns by functioning as a liaison between the director and all other members of the theatrical team, including the actors. All information about the developing production flows through the stage manager, and complicated shows may require the work of several assistants. Stage managers must be able to multitask and function effectively under stress. They must be organized to a fault and have strong interpersonal skills to balance all of the artistic temperaments involved in production. They must stay calm under fire and be able to think on their feet and problem-solve quickly when things go wrong in performance. They must also have enough ego to be strong leaders and enough selflessness to be the facilitators for everyone else's artistic needs.

Coordinating a Production

Stage managers must be present at all rehearsals in a managerial role, organizing and maintaining discipline. They call rehearsals to order and are responsible for keeping a precise and orderly prompt book, a copy of the performance text in which all rehearsal work—blocking, lighting and sound cues, and changes to the script—is noted. Actors rely on the stage manager's accurate recording of movement, cuts, and additions as jogs to their own memories, and stage managers may prompt actors during rehearsals.

A good stage manager will immediately recognize when an artistic discovery in rehearsal will necessitate a change in props, set, lights, or costumes, sometimes even before the director. Once the change is approved by the director, the stage manager is in charge of communicating the information to actors, designers, or technical and house staff—everyone the change affects—through written memos called *rehearsal reports*. Stage managers facilitate the rehearsal process by readying the space, taping the ground plan

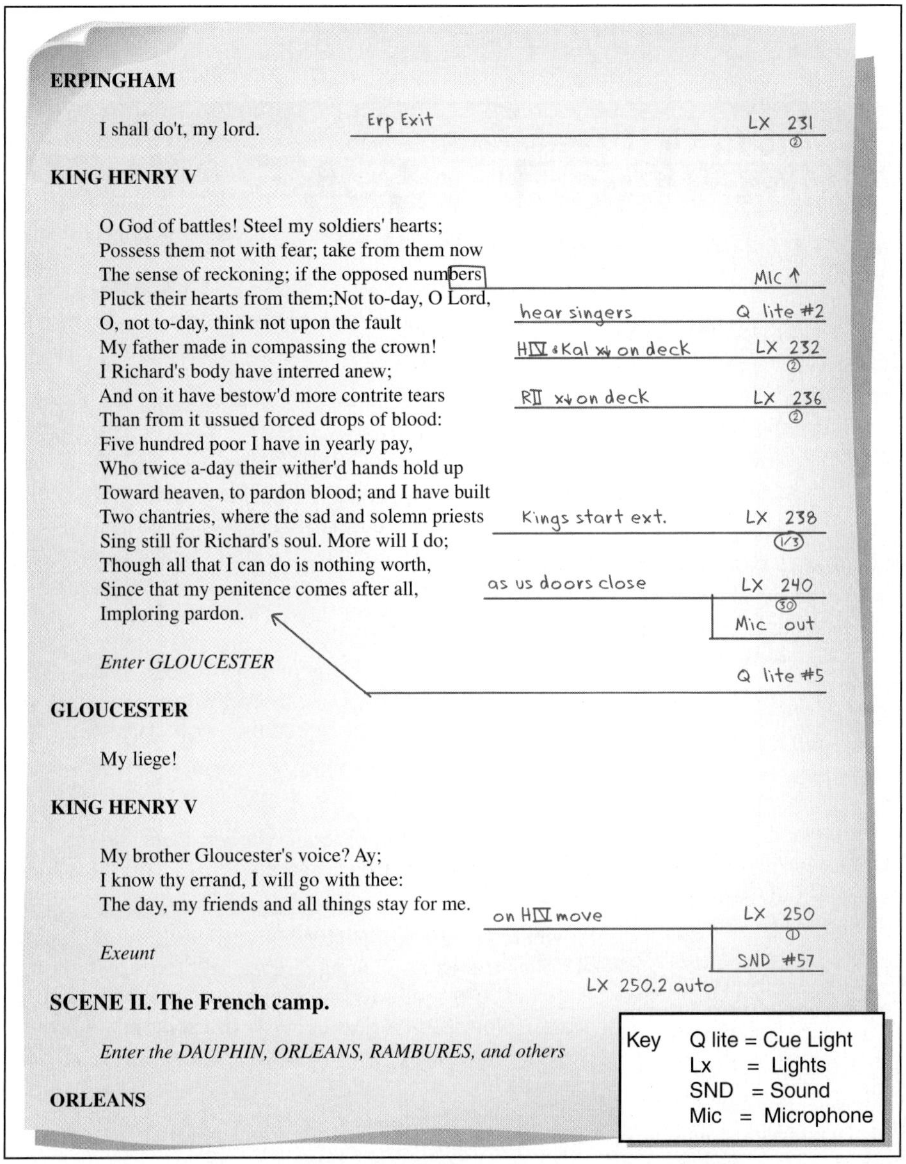

ERPINGHAM

I shall do't, my lord.
         Erp Exit   LX 231 ②

KING HENRY V

O God of battles! Steel my soldiers' hearts;
Possess them not with fear; take from them now
The sense of reckoning; if the opposed numbers   MIC ↑
Pluck their hearts from them;Not to-day, O Lord,
O, not to-day, think not upon the fault   hear singers   Q lite #2
My father made in compassing the crown!   HⅣ & Kal x↓ on deck   LX 232 ②
I Richard's body have interred anew;
And on it have bestow'd more contrite tears   RⅡ x↓ on deck   LX 236 ②
Than from it ussued forced drops of blood:
Five hundred poor I have in yearly pay,
Who twice a-day their wither'd hands hold up
Toward heaven, to pardon blood; and I have built
Two chantries, where the sad and solemn priests   Kings start ext.   LX 238 ①/③
Sing still for Richard's soul. More will I do;
Though all that I can do is nothing worth,
Since that my penitence comes after all,   as us doors close   LX 240 ⑤⑤
Imploring pardon.   Mic out

     Enter GLOUCESTER   Q lite #5

GLOUCESTER

My liege!

KING HENRY V

My brother Gloucester's voice? Ay;
I know thy errand, I will go with thee:
The day, my friends and all things stay for me.   on HⅣ move   LX 250 ①

     Exeunt   SND #57
                            LX 250.2 auto

SCENE II. The French camp.

     Enter the DAUPHIN, ORLEANS, RAMBURES, and others

ORLEANS

Key   Q lite = Cue Light
       Lx   = Lights
       SND   = Sound
       Mic   = Microphone

Figure 16.1 A sample stage manager's prompt book includes notes on the actors' blocking and cues for calling light and sound effects during a performance. The key on the lower right gives you a guide for reading the stage manager's notes.

on the floor to outline where set pieces will be, setting up rehearsal furniture, or getting props or costume pieces for the actors.

Stage managers attend production meetings to keep abreast of any new developments and make sure everyone has all of the necessary information and changes. Stage managers provide the information bridge between those who are present at production meetings and those who are present at rehearsals. They ensure that the efforts of all the people involved in the show are coordinated so work will be harmonious and efficient.

Managing the Actors

Stage managers relay information from the director to the actors. They call actors to rehearsal, let them know of changes in the schedule, and deal with actors who show up late or are absent. In union productions, stage managers must report infractions of the rules. They may help with a personal problem or be a go-between when personality conflicts arise. Stage managers look out for the actors. They alert the director when the actors need a break and make sure the theatre space is clean and safe for rehearsal and performance.

Artists

IN PERSPECTIVE

In Their Own Words

RUTH STERNBERG

Ruth Sternberg is Director of Production and Facility Management at the New York Public Theatre. She completed ten seasons heading Trinity Rep's production department and has served as production manager for the Newport Music Festival and the McCarter Theatre, as well as several international tours for Philip Glass (including La Belle et La Bête*) and Diamanda Galas. She was also the production stage manager for Philip Glass and Robert Wilson's 1992 world tour of* Einstein on the Beach. *In addition to ESPN's 1996 X Games, she has stage managed for directors Ann Bogart, Emily Mann, Amanda Dehnert, David Rabe, David Wheeler, Scott Ellis, Richard Foreman, Mark Lamos, and Ken Bryant at theaters such as Hartford Stage Company, Dallas Theatre Center, American Repertory Theatre, McCarter Theatre, as well as at the Trinity Repertory Company. Sternberg is dedicated to training future stage managers and has served as a stage management instructor at Rhode Island College.*

■ **What drew you to stage management, and what personal qualities do you think are essential for someone in that position?**

I was drawn to stage management because I love theatre and I wasn't a very good actor. I believe that the essential personal qualities are patience, lack of ego, communication, and organizational skills. You must be comfortable with the idea that your role is to facilitate others doing their art (which is in itself an art). A good stage manager can create a safe atmosphere where the artistic work comes first and therefore stays first in the minds of all those in the room.

■ **How has new technology affected the job of the stage manager in the last two decades?**

I think that the technological advancement of the last two decades has made some things easier and some things harder. The biggest plus has been voicemail systems and cellphones. You can always leave a message for someone and know that they'll get it. That wasn't necessarily true twenty years ago. Personal computers have made it easier to organize and distribute information.

The advancement in sound technology has made it much easier to run shows. More theatres employ sound operators (as opposed to expecting stage managers to run sound), and the technology is more user friendly. The equipment that theatres can afford is of a higher quality because it has become relatively less expensive. On the other hand, the advancement of computer lighting systems has made it easier for lighting designers to write more complicated cues. There are robotic lights that can be programmed to do a multitude of things. These advancements have made cues much easier to run during a performance, but it generally takes more time to program in a technical rehearsal. It is very important for a stage manager to understand what the cues are in order to maintain the show and to know what needs to happen to be able make adjustments as a show evolves.

Other technological advancements, such as DVD, video projectors, computer-generated images, automation, and others haven't really made the job any more difficult, they have just increased the vocabulary that a stage manager needs to know. It also means that there is more that could go wrong.

■ **You have worked in different venues. Does the job change with the setting, and how?**

The job of a stage manager is basically the same no matter where you are working. What changes is the protocol of different theatres. During a rehearsal process it is the stage manager's job to make sure that all pertinent rehearsal information is distributed to the appropriate people. The stage manager needs to understand how the organization works in order to facilitate that distribution. Different theatres have different crew members with different jobs; some have union requirements that can vary by venue. The key for a stage manager is to establish a basic understanding of how the organization works, and to be flexible enough to adapt to the surroundings.

■ **How does the job call on your creativity?**

A stage manager's creativity is called upon often. It starts with how to set up a room for rehearsal that will be the most efficient and that will make people feel the most comfortable in their new working environment. The stage manager is the center of the information gathering and information distribution. This makes you the logical point to solve all things logistical for everyone involved. You need to know whose conflicts and problems take priority without ever letting anyone feel that their request is not very important. The larger the production and theatre, the greater the number of conflicts that may arise. It is up to you to schedule and coordinate the needs of the various departments. This can mean setting up meetings with the director for the designers, making sure that people see new articles as they are brought into the room, scheduling costume fittings, recording sessions, video tapings, photo calls, fight rehearsals, dialect sessions, wig fittings. A good stage manager will see that all of it happens as efficiently as possible.

Calling a show can be a performance, and should be, to a point. A stage manager needs to understand what every cue does and how it should look on the stage, but also how the actors interact with what that cue is. Every part of a performance is interdependent.

It is the responsibility of the stage manager to maintain the artistic intention of the director. A director will usually leave after opening night. It is then up to the stage manager to maintain the show. The stage manager gives the actors notes on their performances, rehearses understudies and replacements, and gives notes to maintain and repair the physical elements of the production.

■ **Why did you move to production management, and can you talk about the related skills?**

I moved into production management primarily because it is a steadier job, at least in a regional theatre. A lot of the skills are the same. I think that people come to production management via different paths. Because my path was stage management, that is the approach that I take to my job. The biggest difference between production management and stage management is that a production manager is simultaneously working on several productions at any given time, and a stage manager is generally working on one at a time. The people management skills are very similar in both jobs. As a production manager you come into direct contact with more people. You are responsible for all of the hiring of personnel for a production, making sure that the designers and shops understand the limits of their budgets and stay within them. There is a lot of coordinating of the physical plant. A stage manager is responsible for setting up the rehearsal hall; the production manager is responsible for making sure there IS a rehearsal hall.

■ **What is the biggest challenge of a production manager, and are there particular challenges working with creative artists?**

I think that the biggest challenge of a production manager is to realize that your resources, both money and workforce, will ebb and flow with the economy and the political climate. The challenges with creative artists are usually much more interesting. The biggest challenge is to make sure that all involved in a conversation are using the same vocabulary. When trying to solve a problem, we are identifying what we are trying to solve, what options we have that would solve the problem, what other options would require further resources. And then, what is the solution of choice, and why? Getting an artist to explain what a specific solution represents to them within the piece makes it easier to understand what a workable second option might be, and that is only possible when you share a common language.

■ **Can you describe a particularly difficult production and how you solved the problems it created?**

Every production has its own difficulties; they just vary in size and frequency. The amount of time dedicated to planning is directly inverse to the problems that you will have on a given production. However, even with lots of planning, problems will arise. The key is to understand what the real problem is and to know what resources you have available to solve it. If a director says "I hate the color of the wall," you know that something has to change, but to understand what will solve the problem you need to understand why the director hates it. Does the director hate the color when an actor walks in front of it wearing a particular costume? Is it the contrast that he/she hates? Is it when the wall is seen under specific lighting? Does the light color need to change? Quite often people will offer a solution to a problem without specifying what the problem is. This can lead to making a change that ultimately doesn't solve the problem.

Knowing what resources are available to you at any given time is a huge help. When at Trinity rep, there were other theaters in the New England area that I made it a point to help out when possible. Help came in the form of renting props or costumes or lighting (sometimes very cheaply), or encouraging our staff to go work at that theatre when they were behind on a project. This allowed for reciprocity when a project I was working on was in trouble. The most common problem for all of us is a lack of time and you have to catch up. Unlike construction projects that just don't get finished on time, in our business the tickets are sold and there will be a show.

■ **Do you have any advice for aspiring stage managers?**

Make sure that you keep your focus on the work.

Source: Used with permission from Ruth Sternberg.

They maintain a first aid kit and always have aspirin or antacids on hand for those stressful moments.

Running the Show

During technical rehearsals, stage managers make sure that all of the director's cues are properly entered in the prompt book and executed. Once the show opens, the stage manager is in charge of keeping the rhythm and pace of the show by *calling cues*, which means telling the lighting and sound operators and the stage crew the precise moment of all changes in light, sound, and set. Communicating with other members of the crew on headsets, they alert them that a lighting, sound, or set change is coming up and then give them the go-ahead to make the change. Stage managers keep time for the entire production by making sure the actors know when to arrive at the theatre and by giving time warnings until the show begins. They communicate with house managers about the state of readiness backstage and alert them to any problems requiring a delay of the **curtain**, or starting time. When everything is set, they call "places" to get the actors and crew ready to start the performance.

Preserving the Director's Vision

On opening night, when the director completes an active role in the production process, the stage manager takes over the show and makes sure all the elements of production stay as close as possible to the way the director envisioned them. If a new actor is called in to substitute in a role, the stage manager teaches the part as the director expects it to be played. Attending all rehearsals and production meetings, recording all decisions made about the production, and acting as an assistant to the director enables the stage manager to reliably retain and communicate the director's intentions.

The Production Manager

Some theatres employ a production manager who is in charge of schedules, staffing, and making sure that the information relayed by the stage manager is carried out in a timely manner. The production manager decides the order in which things will be done—for example, when certain set pieces will be moved into the theatre, when lights will be hung, and who will have the performance space at times when there are multiple claims. When not done by the producer, the production manager may make up production budgets and oversee changes in allocations and spending. In theatre companies with large theatres and multiple spaces, the production manager coordinates the scheduling of various productions so that conflicting demands do not arise. To do these jobs effectively, the production manager must have knowledge of all aspects of production and their technical and financial requirements. When there is no production manager, someone must do this job or nothing would ever get done on time. It may be the producer or the managing director. In a small theatre company, it may fall to the director. In college theatre, it may be the job of the department chairperson or a member of the faculty. Sometimes it is the job of the technical director.

The Technical Director

The **technical director**, or TD, is responsible for maintaining the theatre space, ensuring that the theatre is safe, and keeping all equipment and stage machinery in tip-top working order. No one knows more about a theatre and how it works than the technical director, who is in charge of readying the space for performance. The technical director's other major responsibility is executing the set designer's plans. The TD writes technical specifications from the design drawings, costs out and orders the materials needed to build the set, and keeps running inventories of stock supplies for the theatre and scene shop. The TD is part of the design process and may provide reality checks to the set designer's ambitions by suggesting alternative or cheaper construction strategies or noting structural flaws or practical problems in design plans. These are ironed out between the set designer and the TD with the approval of the director. During the construction of the set, the designer may visit the **scene shop**, where the set is constructed, to check on progress or make changes. Sometimes even the director will visit if there is a question about a particular set piece. In small theatres the TD also runs the scene shop and supervises the construction of scenery, making sure everything is done to the designer's specifications. Large theatres may have a shop foreman who oversees the construction crew.

The technical director supervises the load-in of scenery—placing scenic elements according to the designer's plan in the theatre. When there is no master electrician to oversee the hanging and focusing of lights, this job may fall to the TD, as may the job of the sound engineer. The TD supervises technical rehearsals and fixes any technical problems that may arise. In college theatres the TD may be working with inexperienced crews and also be teaching while organizing and coordinating the technical and scenic elements. Often, TDs without staff find themselves building the sets as well. When a production is over, the technical director oversees **strike**, the taking down of the set and lights that follows a show's closing. They create an orderly system for the efficient dismantling of all the scenic elements and then clean and ready the theatre for the next production.

Large commercial productions with complex sets often hire the services of a scenic studio to execute the designs. The designer and technical director hired by the producer will be assigned a project manager who works through the designs with the chief engineer, who along with draftsmen engineers determines the best construction method and materials. On the production floor, various department heads—wood, steel, machine shop, automation, and electrical—take charge of their part of the construction. The producer's technical supervisor is in constant touch with the scenic studio during the construction process, making sure everything is done to the designer's specifications. Most large commercial productions are built at such studios, where the latest technology and computerized systems for changing sets are integrated into the designs.

Photo 16.4
At Hudson Scenic Studios, in the suburb of Yonkers, New York, large sets are built for the Broadway stage and for other theatres in the region and around the country. Sophisticated computerized tools are often used in carpentry. Here welders work to join metal pipes.

The Master Electrician

The master electrician helps execute the lighting designer's plan, supervising the lighting crew as they hang, focus, and filter lights according to the lighting plot. Master electricians set up electrical circuitry that links the instruments to the lighting console, getting the lighting board ready for the adjustment of the lights by the designer and director during technical rehearsals.

The Sound Engineer

The **sound engineer** is responsible for implementing the sound designer's effects. The job includes choosing appropriate microphones and speakers and placing them properly in the theatre or on the actors. The sound engineer also hooks up equipment to amplifiers and speakers so the sound designer and the director can adjust the sound from a sound console.

The Costume Shop Manager

Once costumes have been designed, they are created in a **costume shop** under the oversight of a **costume shop manager**. Every costume shop keeps an inventory of fabric, sewing notions, and most important, old costumes. The manager's job is to know what is available for immediate use and to order supplies, equipment, and repairs. When a shop owns a costume that can be used to fulfill a specific design, the manager tells the designer that a costume can be *pulled* from stock and altered in the shop to fit a particular actor. This is a cost-cutting aid, as building a costume from scratch requires fabric shopping, pattern making, cutting, and sewing that is both expensive and time consuming for financially strapped theatres. Large cities have rental companies where designers can shop for appropriate costumes to rent for a particular production. The Costume Collection in New York receives contributions of used costumes from productions that have closed, which are borrowed by designers from around the country. They are then

Photo 16.5
Designer Louisa Thompson fits an actor for his costume. The sketch from which the costume was fabricated sits on the cutting table so the actor can envision the finished product and use this image to get into character. The rack contains the costumes in progress for the rest of the cast. Each white tab has the actor's name and the role he or she will play marked. Every costume worn by that character in the performance is hung in its place. Costume shops are busy places, filled with supplies, fabric, notions, and trimmings.

brought to the costume shop where the manager and the designer work to make the costume achieve the effect of the original designs. The manager assigns tasks such as cutting, stitching, and dyeing to the costume shop crew, and is present at the costume parade and technical dress rehearsal to take notes from the costume designer. Theatres without costume shops may engage the services of a professional costume shop, which may have individual project managers for various productions.

The Props Manager

The director, stage manager, and designers put together a list of **props**, or **properties**. These are objects that will be used by the actors on stage or that are part of *dressing the set* and complete the scenic design. The props manager is responsible for either procuring or constructing these objects, which are subject to the approval of the director and designers, who may have very specific notions of how a prop will be used and what it should look like.

The Running Crews

When you are in the audience watching a performance, you are often unaware of the crews of people making the performance happen night after night in unseen roles. While the stage manager is running the show from the control booth, that work is supported by many people carrying out various jobs.

Photo 16.6
From the control booth, the stage manager watches a performance and calls the cues to the lighting board and sound console operators. Impeccable timing is required for all involved to support the dramatic moments on the stage.

The stage manager calls the cues in the prompt book to the *lighting board operator*, who must execute lighting effects with split-second accuracy. In the days before computer-operated boards, the operator was also responsible for setting up lighting cue changes and controlling the exact timing of fades and blackouts. Even today, in theatres without computerized equipment, lighting board operators are required to have a sense of the subtleties of the lighting designer's intentions and have exquisite timing. Imagine what would happen if at the height of a dramatic finale, actors had to hold their positions because a blackout was late. Even two seconds can be an eternity on stage and ruin a dramatic moment. The *sound operator* executes the sound designer's effects and follows the cues given by the stage manager. Again, timing is everything. That telephone must ring at exactly the right moment and stop when the phone is answered. Musicals and special effects often require a *follow spot operator*, who moves a spotlight as it follows an actor on stage. The *stagehands* in the *stage crew* also must be ready to change the set on precise cues. The number of stagehands depends on the complexity of the sets and the changes.

After every performance, a *costume crew* collects all the costumes and launders, presses, and repairs any damage that occurred in performance. Costumes are readied and set out in an orderly manner for the actors' next performance. Emergency repairs to tears, replacement of lost buttons, and the like are performed backstage by the costume crew while the show is running. Difficult costumes and rapid costume changes may require the services of a *dresser* to assist the actor. The *prop crew* maintains and repairs props and sets them out on stage. **Personal props**, those carried on stage by actors, are placed on a prop table backstage. No greater panic can ensue for an actor than finding that a prop is missing in performance. Imagine an actor looking for a gun that the prop crew forgot to place in a drawer and trying to figure out how to commit a murder without a weapon, a mishap that actually occurs. Assistant stage managers usually oversee all of these backstage functions and make sure that all the crews are working effectively. They check to make sure the set and props are ready for performance before the house is opened to the public.

The House Manager

Every theatre has a **house manager** who makes sure the theatre is clean and safe and ready to receive the public. They organize and instruct the ticket takers and ushers, resolve any disputes about seats, and clear the theatre and notify the authorities in case of an emergency. They work closely with the **box office manager**, who oversees ticket sales and staff to make sure the audience has a positive experience in the theatre. The stage manager relays information to the house manager at the start of a performance and at intermission about backstage readiness and when the actors are in places so the house manager can signal the audience that the performance is about to begin and secure the house.

Methods of Collaboration

The way people collaborate is a reflection of both cultural values and the kind of theatre they want to create. In the United States, theatre typically consists of a producer and director at the top of a hierarchical structure. Within that structure is a chain of command, and all communication follows that chain. A problem in set construction would be relayed by the crew to the shop foreman, from there to the technical director, then to the set designer, who might alert the stage manager that it is important to discuss solutions with the director. If costs are involved, any changes must then be approved by the producer. Rarely does anyone break this line of communication, which helps avoid misunderstandings.

Although this is the common structure in the professional theatre in Europe and North America, and in theatres modeled on this tradition, many prefer a method of collaboration that challenges the top-down structure. It is possible to work communally, dividing responsibilities among members of a creative team. Designers may write, build, or act. Actors may assemble props or make costumes. The director may be the house manager or lighting board operator. Sometimes this group effort is fostered by financial necessity, but just as often, it is fostered out of belief in a shared commitment to the theatrical process. Even this kind of organization, however, requires that someone be in the position of making final decisions, or nothing would ever be ready. A theatre troupe that stays together over time may choose to rotate positions, so that no one is in a position of absolute authority. Such community-spirited theatrical endeavors provide an alternative model. Much amateur theatre is put together in this way, and many small professional groups work communally out of conviction or necessity.

In some community-based theatres around the world, the audience is also involved in the preparations, readying the playing space, sewing the costumes, making masks, and then taking their places as spectators. South African Township theatre is created for the people and about the people. Stories are often culled from the community and developed into a script based on the conditions of local life by a *playmaker*, who combines the roles of playwright and director. Performances take place in found spaces adapted by adding a few meager props or set pieces. In many traditional Asian performance styles, because every detail of a performance is passed down from generation to generation, and the set and costumes are iconic, long rehearsal periods are unnecessary. As a result, the roles of the director and stage manager are greatly reduced in importance. Theatres in these traditions often organize around the talents of a great actor.

People create methods of theatrical collaboration based on tradition, political, religious, and cultural beliefs, artistic goals, and financial necessity. No one model serves all, and how we create is as diverse as what we create in the theatre.

Closing the Show

At the end of every theatrical creation is the moment when the efforts of so many people end. We have ritualized the moment—*striking the set* marks the end of the creation. The closing night party turns the theatrical event into shared memory. No other art form is so like our common journey through life: launched in hope; realized through hard work, relationships, and travail; struck down; and then immortalized in memory. The collective memory of theatrical productions forms the traditions that guide us in our work, yet all theatre artists dream of yet unimagined possibilities.

■ KEY IDEAS

- People around the world create theatre under a wide variety of conditions and often at great personal risk.
- In many countries theatre is subsidized by the government, often in an effort to preserve traditional forms.
- Theatre festivals offer the opportunity to sample a variety of theatrical experiences in a short period of time.
- Community theatres and community-based theatre can contribute to the culture of a locality and provide a place for shared experiences.
- Theatre in the United States falls broadly into commercial and not-for-profit categories.
- Every production requires someone to function as a producer, who unites a creative team and procures resources for the production.
- All theatrical activity is the result of a team of people working together, many behind the scenes. The audience is often unaware that the performance cannot proceed without their efforts.
- There are many models of collaboration, based on tradition and goals.

Glossary

actor-manager. In the seventeenth through the nineteenth centuries in Europe and America, the head of an acting company who organized the production.

aesthetic distance. The ability to observe a work of art with a degree of detachment and objectivity.

affective memory. *See* emotional memory.

agit-prop. From *agitation* and *propaganda*, a form of political theatre first used by Marxists during the 1920s in Russia that conveys information in a simple and entertaining way to persuade an audience to its point of view.

Alba Emoting. A set vocabulary of emotional expression using breath, facial attitude, and physical position to elicit six primary emotions; developed by Chilean neurophysiologist Susana Bloch.

alienation effect. The emotional distancing of the audience from the dramatic action.

alliteration. The repetition of consonant sounds used to provoke an emotional response in the audience.

antagonist. A character who directly thwarts the desires of the protagonist.

apron. An extension of the proscenium stage protruding past the proscenium arch.

aragoto. The rough style of performance used for superhuman figures in *kabuki* developed by the actor Ichikawa Danjuro (1660–1704). These characters, found in history plays, wear bold makeup called *kumadori* and wild, colorful costumes.

archetypal characters. Characters who embody the essence of particular human traits that enable them to speak across cultures and centuries.

Aristotelian plot. *See* climactic structure.

asides. Short comments that reveal a character's inner thoughts to the audience, often to comic effect.

assonance. The repetition of vowel sounds for emotional effect.

audition. A tryout for a role in a performance at which actors either perform prepared material or read from a play for the director.

auteur. A French term meaning author and originator of a concept; applied to stage directors who conceive a total performance rather than beginning with a play.

autos sacramentales. Christian religious drama developed in Spain circa the sixteenth century.

avant-garde. A French term for the soldiers who march ahead of a military formation; applied to artists and artistic work that rebel against tradition and experiment with new forms.

backlighting. Lights coming from behind the actor that create silhouettes onstage.

balconies. Seating areas that overhang a third to a half of the orchestra or form horseshoe-shaped tiers around the periphery of the auditorium in proscenium theatres.

beat. A unit of dramatic action reflecting a single emotional desire or character objective.

biomechanics. A physical training system for efficient and expressive movement developed in Russia by Vsevolod Meyerhold (1874–1942).

black box theatre. A performance space, usually painted black, that permits the rearrangement of seating and playing areas for every production in a variety of traditional and nontraditional arrangements.

blackface. The derogatory comic black stereotype expressed in makeup consisting of a blackened face with white circles around the eyes and mouth; originated in minstrel shows.

blackout. A rapid and complete dimming of the lights on stage.

blocking. The pattern of actors' movement onstage.

book. The written text of a musical.

book musical. A musical in which the story is told through spoken text, song, and dance.

booth stage. A portable thrust stage used by actors during the Middle Ages.

boxes. Private seating areas in proscenium theatres set in the balcony above the orchestra that once separated the nobility and the wealthy classes from the rest of the theatre-going public.

box office. A booth where theatre tickets are sold.

box office manager. The person who oversees theatre ticket sales and box office staff.

box set. A stage design in which flats form the back and side walls and sometimes even the ceiling of a room.

breeches roles. During the seventeenth to nineteenth centuries, roles in which actresses played young men or characters disguised as men and dressed in short pants or "breeches" revealing their legs.

Broadway. The great concentration of commercial theatres around Times Square in New York City.

bunraku. A Japanese tradition of puppetry that combines the arts of puppet manipulation, ballad singing, and playing the three-stringed *shamisen.* The puppets are three to four feet tall and are operated through direct manipulation by three puppeteers who work together to create a seamless unity of action.

burlesque. A variety entertainment of the early twentieth century that included musical numbers, acrobatic bits, and comedy duos, but was especially known for its bawdy humor and striptease acts.

CAD (computer-assisted drafting). Computer programs that allow theatre designers to draft precise and uniform drawings and to visualize design options.

callback. A second audition for a role that only a few actors are invited to attend.

catharsis. The purging of our aggressive desires through art and enactment; the term was first used by Aristotle in the fourth century B.C.E.

centering. A process of focused relaxation through which an actor integrates breath, movement, feeling, and thought to harness the body's physical, emotional, and intellectual energy for performance.

chariot-and-pole system. A device for accomplishing instantaneous set changes invented by Giacomo Torelli (1608–1678) and consisting of a series of ropes and pulleys attached to a succession of painted flat wings set in grooved tracks on the stage.

cheat out. Turning on an angle on a proscenium stage to allow the audience to see one's face.

cliffhanger. A complicating incident usually placed at the end of an act so the audience is sent off at intermission impatient to find out how this last twist of fate will be resolved.

climactic structure. A tight-knit plot form in which the action builds causally to a moment of high emotional intensity followed by a final resolution.

climax. The point of highest emotional intensity in a drama.

commedia all'improviso. See commedia dell'arte.

commedia dell'arte. A theatre form that emerged in Italy during the sixteenth century, in which masked actors playing stock characters improvised on a scenario using broad physical humor.

commercial theatre. Theatre done for profit in which investors back a production and take a capital return if a show is a success.

complication. Circumstances of a drama building on each other through cause and effect.

concentration of attention. A technique developed by Constantin Stanislavski to keep actors' focus within the stage reality and not on the audience.

concert parties. A form of variety entertainment that developed in Anglophone Africa in the 1920s combining African culture and American and European entertainments.

conflict. Tension between two forces working against each other, creating struggles and obstacles for the characters to overcome.

control board. A computerized system that regulates the execution of light cues.

conventions. *See* theatrical conventions.

costume plot. A chart recording the costume pieces worn by each character in each scene of a play.

costume shop. The workshop where stage costumes are built and assembled.

costume shop manager. The person who oversees costume shop personnel and the process of building and assembling stage costumes.

crisis. The place in the dramatic action where the conflict comes to a head.

cross-dressing. When a man or woman on stage wears clothing traditionally associated with the opposite gender.

cross-fading. Slowly diminishing one lighting cue while adding another to gradually transition from one cue to the next.

curtain. The starting time of a show. Alternate meaning; the end of a show.

cycle plays. Medieval religious drama taken from events in the Old and New Testaments of the Bible.

dada. An artistic movement following the destruction of World War I that projected a world of randomness without the chain of causality found in traditional stories.

dance play. A danced theatre piece without dialogue in which characterization, narrative, and dramatic conflict are expressed in choreography, not words.

deconstruction. The movement in literary criticism that questions the idea of fixed meanings, truths, or assumptions about texts. It is the hallmark of the postmodern aesthetic and has given license to directors to search for new meanings and forms in plays once thought to be confined to particular interpretations and styles.

denouement. A translation of Aristotle's "unknotting," the act of bringing all the parts of the play to a final conclusion.

deus ex machina. Any dramatic device, outside of the main action, used to bring the play to a final resolution. Developed in ancient Greek drama, the "god from a machine" arrived at the end of a play to finalize the fates of the mortal characters on stage.

dimmer board. A board that controls the intensity of stage lights.

dimmers. Instruments that permit the gradual adjustment of the intensity of light.

discovery space. A curtained space at the back of the Elizabethan stage where characters or items could be concealed or revealed.

distancing or distanciation. *See* alienation effect.

dithyrambs. Ancient Greek hymns sung and danced in praise of the god Dionysus, the god of wine and fertility.

docudrama. A performance in which primary sources serve as the play text often addressing pressing issues with theatrical immediacy.

documentary theatre. *See* docudrama.

downstage. The area of the stage closest to the audience.

dramatic structure. The scaffolding on which a playwright plots a tale to frame or shape the action.

dramaturgs. Preproduction aides who work with directors to help explain the text or with playwrights to help define it.

dress parade. A procession of actors in costume offering the director and designer an opportunity to see all the actors together, in costume, under stage lights.

dress rehearsal. A rehearsal at which actors run through the show dressed in their costumes; usually occurs just before opening night.

dressing the set. The addition of final touches to a stage set, which might include upholstery ornaments, small objects for tables and shelves, and pillows and curtains.

drops. Large pieces of painted canvas hung at the back of the stage to set a particular locale or atmosphere.

ekkyklema. A platform on wheels that rolls on stage; first used in the ancient Greek theatre.

ellipsoidal reflector spotlight. A stage lighting instrument that projects a light with a sharp, clearly defined edge.

emotional memory. The recalling of the sensory details around a significant event in an actor's life to evoke an emotional response.

empathy. The capacity of the audience to identify emotionally with the character on stage.

emotional recall. *See* emotional memory.

epic theatre. A proletarian theatre looking to create social change by pioneering new approaches to the stage and stage technology.

existentialism. A philosophic movement after World War II that depicts a senseless, godless world where human beings live in a meaningless void.

exposition. The revelation of events that occurred before the start of the play through dialogue, often employing a device such as a confidant or a soliloquy to enable a character to speak all the necessary information to set up the plot.

expressionism. A style of theatre that projects characters' inner emotional reality onto objects in the external world.

fade. A gradual dimming of the stage lights.

flats. Single units of canvas or other material stretched over a wooden frame that can be painted and connected to each other to create walls or other elements of a stage set.

fly spaces. Very high ceilings behind the proscenium arch of a theatre used to house painted scenery that is literally "flown" up and down on a system of pulleys to change the sets.

follow spots. Stage lights with clearly defined beams that follow an actor in movement across the stage.

footlights. Stage lights placed at the front of the stage.

foreshadowing. Hints about events to come in the dramatic action that can be used to create or break expectations.

fourth wall. The theatrical convention of an invisible wall separating the stage from the audience.

fresnel. Also known as a spherical reflector spotlight, this stage lighting instrument produces a beam of light with a soft edge.

futurism. An artistic movement in the early twentieth century that questioned old authority systems and structures and emphasized the energy, dynamism, and movement of time in modern existence.

gels. Thin colored films inserted in slots in front of lighting instruments to color stage lights.

genres. Categories of drama.

gesamtkunstwerk. Literally "total art work." The union of all of the theatrical elements to create a thematically unified stage work, a concept developed by Richard Wagner (1813–1883).

given circumstances. The physical and emotional conditions that determine the actions of a character.

gobos. Small metal plates with cutout stencil-like patterns that slide in front of a light source to project shapes and patterns or effects on the stage.

green room. A space where actors and audience members can socialize after a performance; first developed during the late seventeenth century in England.

groundlings. The name for lower class spectators in Shakespeare's time who could not afford seats and stood for the duration of the performance in the open pit area in front of the stage.

ground plan. A view of the dimensions of the stage and the placement of set pieces as seen from above.

guerrilla theatre. Political action theatre in the street, so called because it sneaks up on the audience where they least expect it and aggressively exhorts them to engage politically.

half-masks. Masks that cover only the top half of the face, keeping the mouth uncovered so the actor can speak and be heard.

hanamichi. Literally "flower path." A runway in the Japanese *kabuki* theatre that cuts through the audience and leads to the stage on which actors make entrances and exits and perform important poses and speeches.

high-concept productions. Innovative interpretations of plays that express a unique directorial vision and provide illuminating new readings of well-known works.

house. The audience or the area of the theatre allocated to the audience.

house manager. The person who makes sure the theatre is clean and safe and ready to receive the public.

inciting incident. An event that sets the dramatic action into motion.

instrument schedule. A chart that lists each lighting instrument by its number, specific location, purpose, wattage, the color of the gel, and other important information.

interculturalism. Valuing and promoting an exchange and interaction among various cultures that may ignite interest or friction.

lazzi. Set bits of comic stage business all guaranteed to get a laugh used by actors of the *commedia dell'arte*.

light plot. A blueprint of the stage and auditorium with the lighting grid and the location of each light to be used for a production specifically marked.

lighting grid. The metal pipe structure from which the lights are hung.

lines of business. Roles in an acting company that particular actors played designated by types such as young lover, fop, ingenue, or old crone.

literary managers. Dramaturgs attached to theatre companies who are responsible for reading and evaluating plays for the artistic director and helping in other forms of play development such as hosting workshops or play readings.

liturgical drama. Theatrical performance that emerged from the Catholic liturgy during the Middle Ages.

loft. *See* fly spaces.

magic *if*. The ability to act as *if* the imaginary circumstances of a character were real.

master electrician. The person who oversees the hanging, focusing, and filtering of lights.

mēchanē. The large hand-powered crane that hoisted actors above the *skene*, or back wall, of the stage in ancient Greece, usually to portray a god.

meter. The patterns of stressed and unstressed syllables that can draw attention to significant meanings in the text.

mie. Dramatic physical poses executed by *kabuki* actors at climactic moments, underscored by the beats of wooden clappers.

mime. A popular unscripted theatrical performance form in ancient Greece and Rome with stock characters, short improvised comic sketches, broad physical and acrobatic humor, juggling, music, and bawdy jokes. Today the term refers to silent or nearly silent performances and the actors who create them.

minstrel show. A nineteenth-century racist performance style in which whites both appropriated African American culture and music and simultaneously created the denigrating blackface, white-lipped racial stereotype.

miracle plays. Medieval dramas depicting events from the lives of saints.

mobile stages. *See* pageant wagons.

model. A three-dimensional mock-up of the set design that gives the production team and the actors specific information about how the design will actually look and work in the space.

monologues. Passages from a play for a solo actor.

morality plays. Late medieval plays using allegorical characters to depict a moral lesson.

motivated lighting. Light changes specifically indicated in the play text, such as a lamp turning on.

motivated sounds. Sounds with an identifiable source within the context of the play, such as the ring of a telephone.

mudra. Hand gestures used in Indian theatrical traditions.

multiculturalism. A philosophy calling for respect for neighboring cultures living under the same political system.

multifocus theatre. Simultaneous performance in several playing areas during the same event that gives the audience a choice of focus and may require them to move about.

mystery plays. *See* cycle plays.

naturalism. A nineteenth-century movement that sought to paint a scientifically accurate stage picture of life as it is lived.

Natyasastra. A text on Sanskrit drama written sometime between 200 B.C.E. and 200 C.E. containing an encyclopedia of information about theatre from the classical Sanskrit tradition.

naumachiae. Spectacular Roman theatrical events in which flooded arenas permitted naval battles, often resulting in real casualties.

new stagecraft. The expression of highly theatrical trends of European modernism in American stage design.

not-for-profit theatre. A theatrical institution in which the profit is channeled back into the producing organization to defray costs and to fund new projects.

objective. In acting technique, what a character wants at any given moment that drives the action.

Off-Broadway. Smaller New York theatres in and out of the commercial theatre district that are so designated because they have fewer than five hundred seats.

Off-Off Broadway. New York theatres that seek an alternative to the artistic constraints imposed in the commercial theatre.

onnagata. The female role type in *kabuki*; an idealized woman played by male actors in white makeup, black styled wigs, and women's kimono.

onomatopoeia. The use of words that express the feeling of their meaning through sound.

opening night. The show's first full-price public performance.

opera. A dramatic musical form born in the Renaissance in emulation of the heightened emotions of Greek tragedy and written in the tradition of great European art music.

operetta. A mid-nineteenth-century bourgeois entertainment that borrows many features from opera and incorporates dance, farce, and clowning to tell a simple story that always culminates in romance fulfilled.

orchestra. The circular playing space on the ground in front of the *skene* in ancient Greek theatres. Today, the floor-level seating area in front of a proscenium stage.

orchestra pit. The space below the apron of a proscenium stage that houses musicians and often can be elevated to form an extended apron when an orchestra is not required.

Orientalism. A European trend in the early twentieth century that romanticized the Far East and appropriated some of its performance forms. Today the term connotes derisive stereotyping.

pageant masters. In the Middle Ages, those responsible for organizing theatrical events.

pageant wagon. Mobile platform stages on wheels used in the Middle Ages to carry scenery through the town to the location of the performance.

pantomime. In Roman times, a silent storytelling dance. In the eighteenth and nineteenth centuries the term applied to certain popular entertainments in England and France that used *commedia*-type characters. In the twentieth century, a silent storytelling.

paper tech. A walk-through of the technical aspects of the production with the designers and staff and without actors present.

PAR lamps (parabolic aluminated reflectors). Small, cheap, portable lights that can generate different types of beams.

parallel plot. *See* subplot.

parody. The exaggerated imitation of individuals or artistic styles to make them appear ludicrous.

passion plays. Plays depicting events from the passion of Christ.

performance art. An avant-garde form that saw performance as an extension of visual art in time, with more significance accorded to the visual image than the spoken text.

performance studies. An academic field that looks at theatre as one kind of performance on a continuum with other kinds of performance such as ritual and sports events that helps us understand and discuss today's varied theatrical forms.

performance text. A record of all that will happen on stage.

performance traditions. Theatrical forms whose staging, music, dance, characterization, masks, and acting are passed from generation to generation as a totality, preserving the form.

personal props. Objects carried on stage by actors.

picture frame stage. *See* proscenium stage.

pit. In the Elizabethan theatre, the area around the raised stage in which spectators could stand to watch the performance.

plastiques. Difficult physical exercises for actors that were developed by Jerzy Grotowski.

platforms. Raised wooden constructions that can provide playing spaces on different levels.

platform stages. During the Middle Ages, playing areas placed in front of background sets.

play text. A written script containing dialogue spoken by characters that can be interpreted by actors and directors as the basis for action on stage.

plot. The ordering or structuring of the events that actually take place on stage.

point of attack. The point in the story at which the action begins.

postmodernism. A late-twentieth-century concept that replaces absolute values with relativism, opening up the possibility of many new and equally valid forms of artistic expression.

practical. An onstage light such as a lamp or a fire in a fireplace that needs to appear to be controlled from the stage.

presentational. A theatrical style that openly acknowledges the artificiality of a stage performance.

preview. A performance before a production has officially opened that gives the director an opportunity to hone the show in front of a live audience.

processional stage. Moving stages that require the audience to move from place to place to follow the action or to wait for the next wagon stage to appear.

producer. The person who brings together a creative team with the necessary resources to complete a production.

production manager. The person in charge of schedules, staffing, and making sure that the information relayed by the stage manager is carried out in a timely manner.

prompt book. The stage manager's copy of the script on which is recorded blocking and cues.

props or **properties.** Objects that will be used by the actors on stage or that are part of the set.

proscenium arch. A frame constructed over the front of the stage separating the audience from the performance space and forming a frame for the set.

proscenium stage. A configuration of a theatre space in which the audience faces the actors on only one side.

protagonist. The lead role in a drama; from the Greek word *agonistes*, which means both "actor" and "combatant."

psychological characters. Character portraits so rich in detail and interest that spectators feel they can comprehend motivations and desires, and even fabricate a life for them that preexists their appearance in the play.

psychophysical action. Stanislavski's term for physical behavior that reveals the character and the objective.

raked seating. Seating areas on an incline providing solutions to sight line problems for the audience.

rasa. Literally "tastes" or "flavors." A term from Indian theatre that refers to the different moods or feelings expressed in plays and by actors on stage.

realism. The presentation of a stage world as a believable alternate reality where things happen much as they would in life and people behave in seemingly natural ways.

regional theatres. *See* resident theatres.

representational. A theatrical style in which the stage reality attempts to represent real life and the actor seems to be living the part.

resident theatres. Professional not-for-profit theatres around the United States that now provide a permanent theatre presence in almost every major city.

revenge plays. Bloody dramas from the Roman era that influenced Elizabethan theatre.

review. The brief, immediate response to a theatrical event that appears in a newspaper, magazine, or television or radio segment.

revue. A musical form that does not tell a story and moves from number to number.

run-through. Performance of a play from beginning to end without stopping during a rehearsal.

saint plays. *See* miracle plays.

satyr plays. A burlesque of mythic legends that provided comic relief after performances of tragedies in ancient Greece.

scenario. A general plot outline used as the basis for improvisation.

scene house. A curtained area at the back of a platform stage for concealment and costume changes.

scene shop. The workshop where the set is constructed.

scrim. A translucent cloth or gauze that can appear opaque when light shines on it from the front, or transparent when light shines on it from the back, used to create special effects and magical transformations through changes in lighting.

serial structure. A series of scenes that do not follow a continuous story or even include the same characters.

shamans. Priests or priestesses charged with communicating with the spirit world on behalf of the community to bring peace and prosperity to the populace or healing to the sick.

sidelighting. Light coming from the side of the stage that provides accents and highlights that is used often in dance and musical theatre to highlight the dancers' legs.

sides. Actors' individual lines and cues, once copied by a stage manager.

sight lines. Clear vision of the stage action by the audience.

silhouette. The overall shape of a costume.

skene. In the ancient Greek theatre, the stage house behind the area where the main characters performed.

soliloquy. A lengthy solo speech through which a character reveals an interior state of mind.

sound engineer. The person responsible for the functioning of acoustical equipment in a theatre.

sound plot. A chart of all the connections and sound equipment used for a production.

special. A light with a specific and unique dramatic function.

spherical reflector spotlight. *See* fresnel.

spine. A central line of dramatic action that can guide directors in their creative choices.

stage curtain. A curtain contained just inside the proscenium frame that can be raised and lowered to conceal set changes and to reveal the stage action.

stage left. The area to the actor's left when standing center stage facing the audience on a proscenium or thrust stage.

stage manager. The person who works closely with the director in preparing the production and who functions as a liaison between the director and all other members of the creative team, including the actors. The stage manager oversees the accurate execution of the show in performance.

stage right. The area to the actor's right when standing center stage facing the audience on a proscenium or thrust stage.

staged reading. A reading of a play with actors on their feet, scripts in hand, with minimal set pieces.

stock characters. Representatives of a type that are defined by externals such as class, occupation, and marital status, rather than by their individual characteristics.

story. All of the events that happen or are mentioned in the text.

storyboard. A series of sketches showing how the sets or costumes change to tell the story through time.

street theatre. Compelling theatre that uses music, spectacle, masks, costumes, dancing, drumming, or direct audience confrontation to engage with the public in co-opted public spaces.

strike. The orderly dismantling of a production that follows a show's closing; includes taking down the set and lights, readying costumes for storage, and cleaning and preparing the theatre for the next production.

style. The manner in which a performance depicts the world.

subplot. A secondary dramatic action that echoes the main plot of a play through common subjects and themes that reinforce or comment on the central meaning of the drama.

subtext. The meaning of dialogue to the character, which may be different from what is actually said. Literally, the thoughts that lie under the text.

superobjective. The main goal of a play or character that drives the dramatic action.

surrealism. A twentieth-century artistic style inspired by Freudian psychology that mined the unconscious for images that expressed the truth of our hidden desires and the free association of thought.

symbolism. A late-nineteenth-century artistic style that opposed the naturalists' search for meaning in the concrete objects of the world, and felt truth lay in a metaphysical realm.

technical director. The individual responsible for executing the set designer's plans and maintaining the theatre space, including its safety and equipment.

technical dress rehearsal. A rehearsal in which all the elements of the production—costume, sets, lights, sound, and acting—are coordinated to make any final changes before opening night.

technical rehearsal. The first opportunity for the director to work with all the design elements and designers simultaneously in rehearsal.

theatre of the absurd. A term coined by critic Martin Esslin to describe plays that reflected the sense of alienation and meaninglessness of the generation that had lived through the horrific events of World War II.

theatre of cruelty. A name used by Antonin Artaud for a visceral theatre of sounds, movements, and images that assaulted the senses of the audience, opening up new levels of awareness.

theatrical conventions. Rules of conduct and understood communication codes used in the theatre.

upstage. The area of the stage farthest from the audience in proscenium or thrust staging.

upstaged. The claiming of audience attention when one actor walks directly behind another obliging the downstage actor to turn away from the audience to address lines to the actor upstage.

vaudeville. A popular American variety show form toward the end of the nineteenth and the early twentieth centuries that relied heavily on stand-up comedy routines and musical numbers.

verisimilitude. The concept that the theatre should present an idealized reality.

Viewpoints. A system of physical actor training that develops awareness of the basic components of movement—line, rhythm, shape, tempo, and duration.

voms. Aisles for actors' entrances named for the *vomitoria*, or entryways, of the ancient Roman amphitheatres that often run through the audience in an arena theatre.

wagon. A moving platform on wheels that serves as a mobile stage.

warm-up. A series of physical and vocal exercises that prepare the body to act.

wayang kulit. Indonesian leather shadow puppet tradition.

well-made play. A form developed during the nineteenth century that uses a tightly woven plot filled with complications that keep the audience deeply involved in the dramatic action.

West End. London's commercial theatre district.

wings. Areas on the periphery of the playing area that can be masked to hide actors, technicians, props, and scenery.

yūgen. An aesthetic term from the *noh* tradition usually translated as "grace," "suggestive beauty," or "mystery."

Bibliography

General References

Allen, Ralph G., and John Gassner, eds. *Theatre and Drama in the Making: From Antiquity to the Renaissance*. New York: Applause Books, 1992.

Banham, Martin, Errol Hill, and George Woodyard, eds. *Cambridge Guide to African and Caribbean Theatre*. New York: Cambridge University Press, 1994.

Brandon, James R., ed. *The Cambridge Guide to Asian Theatre*. Advisory editor, Martin Banham. New York: Cambridge University Press, 1993.

Brockett, Oscar G., and Franklin J. Hildy. *History of the Theatre*. Boston: Allyn & Bacon, 2003.

Brown, John Russell. *The Oxford Illustrated History of Theatre*. New York: Oxford University Press, 1995.

Esslin, Martin. *Illustrated Encyclopedia of World Theatre*. New York: Thames and Hudson Press, 1981.

Kerr, David. *African Popular Theatre: From Pre-colonial Times to the Present Day*. Portsmouth, NH: Heinemann, 1995.

Meserve, Walter J. *Chronological Outline of World Theatre*. New York: Prospero Press, 1992.

Nagler, A. M., ed. *A Source Book in Theatrical History*. New York: Dover Publications, 1959.

Rubin, Don, ed. *World Encyclopedia of Contemporary Theatre*. 5 vols. New York: Routledge, 1994.

Weiss, Judith A. *Latin American Popular Theatre: The First Five Centuries*. Albuquerque: University of New Mexico Press, 1993.

Wickham, Glynne. *A History of the Theatre*. New York: Cambridge University Press, 1992.

Wilmeth, Don B., and Christopher Bigsby. *The Cambridge History of American Theatre*. 3 vols. New York: Cambridge University Press, 1998–2000.

Chapter 1

Asia Society and Lincoln Center Festival 2002. "Ta'ziyeh: Performing Iran's Living Epic Tradition." Asia Society. http://www.asiasociety.org/arts/taziyeh/.

Auslander, Philip. *Presence and Resistance: Postmodernism and Cultural Politics in Contemporary American Performance*. Ann Arbor: University of Michigan Press, 1992.

Crow, Brian. *An Introduction to Postcolonial Theatre*. With Chris Banfield. New York: Cambridge University Press, 1996.

Darby, Jaye T., and Hanay Geiogamah. *American Indian Theater in Performance: A Reader*. Los Angeles: UCLA American Indian Studies Center, 2000.

Ensler, Eve. *The Vagina Monologues*. New York: Villard, 2001.

Gainor, J. Ellen, ed. *Imperialism and Theatre: Essays on World Theatre, Drama, and Performance*. New York: Routledge, 1995.

Gilbert, Helen, and Joanne Tompkins. *Post-Colonial Drama: Theory, Practice, Politics*. London: Routledge, 1996.

Huerta, Jorge A. *Chicano Drama: Performance, Society, and Myth*. Cambridge: Cambridge University Press, 2000.

Kaye, Nick. *Postmodernism and Performance*. New York: St. Martin's Press, 1994.

Marshall, Herbert, and Mildred Stock. *Ira Aldridge: The Negro Tragedian*. Carbondale: Southern Illinois University Press, 1968.

O'Connor, Garry. *The Mahabharata: Peter Brook's Epic in the Making*. London: Hodder & Stoughton, 1989.

Pavis, Patrice, ed. *The Intercultural Performance Reader*. New York: Routledge, 1996.

Schechner, Richard. *Performance Theory*. 2nd rev. ed. New York: Routledge, 2003.

Soyinka, Wole. *Ake: The Years of Childhood*. Reissue edition. New York: Vintage International, 1989.

———. *Wole Soyinka: Plays*. London: Methuen, 1999.

Van Erven, Eugene. *The Playful Revolution: Theatre and Liberation in Asia*. Bloomington: Indiana University Press, 1992.

Watt, Stephen. *Postmodern/Drama: Reading the Contemporary Stage*. Ann Arbor: University of Michigan Press, 1998.

Chapter 2

Boal, Augusto. *Theatre of the Oppressed*. Translated by Charles A. and Maria-Odilia Leal McBride. New York: Theatre Communications Group, 1985.

Boon, Richard, and Jane Plastow. *Theatre Matters: Performance and Culture on the World Stage*. New York: Cambridge University Press, 1998.

Bradby, David, and John McCormick. *People's Theatre*. Totowa, NJ: Rowman and Littlefield, 1978.

Brecht, Bertolt. *Brecht on Theatre: The Development of an Aesthetic*. Translated by John Willett. London: Methuen, 1964.

Broyles-Gonzalez, Yolanda. *El Teatro Campesino: Theater in the Chicano Movement*. Austin: University of Texas Press, 1994.

Cohen-Cruz, Jan, ed. *Radical Street Performance: An International Anthology*. New York: Routledge, 1998.

Cosgrove, Stuart, Ewan McColl, and Raphael Samuel. *Theatres of the Left, 1880–1935: Worker's Theatre Move-*

ments in Britain and America. Boston: Routledge & Kegan Paul, 1985.

Dodds, E. R. *The Greeks and the Irrational.* Berkeley: University of California Press, 1951.

Doreen G. Fernandez. "Philippine Theatre After Martial Law" *Asian Theatre Journal* 4, no. 1 (1987): 108–114.

Dee, Jonathan. "Reverend Billy's Unholy War." *New York Times Sunday Magazine,* August 22, 2004.

Moody, Richard. *The Astor Place Riot.* Bloomington: Indiana University Press, 1958.

Munk, Erika, et al., eds. Theatre and Social Change. Special issue, *Theatre* 31, no. 3 (2001).

Orenstein, Claudia. *Festive Revolutions: The Politics of Popular Theater and the San Francisco Mime Troupe.* Jackson: University Press of Mississippi, 1998.

Plato. *Republic 10.* Translated by S. Halliwell. Warminsteuk, UK: Aris & Phillips, 1988.

Piscator, Erwin. *The Political Theatre.* Translated by Hugh Rorrison. New York: Avon Books, 1978.

Riantiarno, N. *Time Bomb and Cockroach Opera.* Translated by John McGlynn and Barbara Hatley. Jakarta: Lontar Press, 1992.

Sainer, Arthur. *The New Radical Theatre Notebook.* New York: Applause Books, 1997.

Schechner, Richard. *Environmental Theater (Expanded New Edition).* New York: Applause Books, 1994.

———. *Public Domain: Essays on the Theater.* Indianapolis: Bobbs-Merrill, 1969.

Turner, Victor. *The Anthropology of Performance.* New York: Performing Arts Journal Publications, 1986.

———. *From Ritual to Theatre: The Human Seriousness of Play.* New York: Performing Arts Journal Publications, 1982.

Tytell, John. *The Living Theatre: Art, Exile, and Outrage.* New York: Grove Press. 1995.

Watts, Jerry Gafio. *Amiri Baraka: The Politics and Art of a Black Intellectual.* New York: New York University Press, 2001.

Willett, John. *Brecht in Context: Comparative Approaches.* London: New York: Methuen, 1998.

Chapter 3

Aristotle. *Poetics.* Translated by Gerald F. Else. Ann Arbor: University of Michigan Press, 1967.

Ball, David. *Backwards and Forwards: A Technical Manual for Reading Plays.* Carbondale: Southern Illinois University Press, 1983.

Barranger, Milly. *Understanding Plays As Texts for Performance.* 3rd ed. New York: Allyn & Bacon, 2003.

Bentley, Eric. *The Life of the Drama.* Reissue ed. New York: Applause Books, 1991.

———. *The Playwright as Thinker: A Study of Drama in Modern Times.* New York: Harcourt, 1998.

Brustein, Robert. *The Theatre of Revolt: An Approach to the Modern Drama.* Boston: Little, Brown, 1964.

Clurman, Harold. *Ibsen.* New York: Macmillan, 1977.

Corballis, Richard. *Stoppard: The Mystery and the Clockwork.* New York: Methuen, 1984.

Elam, Harry J. *The Past as Present in the Drama of August Wilson.* Ann Arbor: University of Michigan Press, 2004.

Elam, Harry J., and Alice Rayner, "Body Parts: Between Story and Spectacle in *Venus* by Suzan-Lori Parks." In *Staging Resistance: Essays on Political Theater,* edited by Jeanne Colleran and Jenny S. Spencer, 265–82. Ann Arbor: University of Michigan Press, 1998.

Fletcher, John. *About Beckett: The Playwright and the Work.* London: Faber, 2003.

Fuegi, John. *Bertolt Brecht: Chaos, According to Plan.* New York: Cambridge University Press, 1987.

Greene, Alexis, ed. *Women Who Write Plays: Interviews with American Dramatists.* Lyme, NH: Smith and Kraus, 2001.

Greenwald, Mike, Roger Schultz, and Roberto Dario Pomo, eds. *The Longman Anthology of Drama and Theater: A Global Perspective.* Reprint ed. New York: Longman, 2004.

Hayman, Ronald. *How to Read a Play.* New York: Grove Press, 1999.

Kalb, Jonathan. *The Theater of Heiner Müller.* New York: Cambridge University Press, 1998.

Knowlson, James. *Damned to Fame: The Life of Samuel Beckett.* New York: Simon & Schuster, 1996.

Lamont, Rosette C. *Ionesco's Imperatives: The Politics of Culture.* Ann Arbor: University of Michigan Press, 1993.

Lyons, Charles R. *Samuel Beckett.* London: Macmillan Press, 1983.

McFarlane, James. *The Cambridge Companion to Ibsen.* New York: Cambridge University Press, 1994.

Parks, Suzan-Lori. *The America Play, and Other Works.* New York: Theatre Communications Group, 1995.

Street, Douglas. *David Henry Hwang.* Boise: Boise State University, 1989.

Valency, Maurice. *The End of the World: An Introduction to Contemporary Drama.* New York: Oxford University Press, 1980.

———. *The Flower and the Castle: An Introduction to Modern Drama.* New York: Macmillan, 1963.

Worthen, W. B. *The Wadsworth Anthology of Drama.* 4th ed. Boston: Thomson/Wadsworth, 2004.

Chapter 4

Bermel, Albert. *Farce: A History from Aristophanes to Woody Allen.* New York: Simon & Schuster, 1982.

Corrigan, Robert, W., ed. *Comedy: A Critical Anthology.* Boston: Houghton Mifflin, 1971.

———, ed. *Comedy, Meaning and Form.* San Francisco: Chandler, 1965.

———. *The Theatre in Search of a Fix.* New York: Delacorte Press, 1973.

Easterling, P. E., ed. *The Cambridge Companion to Greek Tragedy.* New York: Cambridge University Press, 1997.

Gerould, Daniel, ed. *American Melodrama.* New York: Performing Arts Journal Publications, 1983.

Grimsted, David. *Melodrama Unveiled: American Theater and Culture, 1800–1850.* Chicago: University of Chicago Press, 1968.

Harris, John Wesley. *Medieval Theatre in Context: An Intro-duction*. New York: Routledge, 1992.

Heilman, Robert Bechtold. *Tragedy and Melodrama: Versions of Experience*. Seattle: University of Washington Press, 1968.

Howarth, William D., ed. *French Theatre in the Neo-Classical Era, 1550–1789*. Cambridge: Cambridge University Press, 1997.

Hrotswitha. *The Plays of Hrotswitha of Gandersheim*. Trans-lated by Larissa Bonfante, with the collaboration of Alexandra Bonfante-Warren. Oak Park, IL: Bolchazy-Carducci, 1986.

Kitto, H. D. F. *Greek Tragedy: A Literary Study*. London: Methuen, 1966.

Kolve, V. A. *The Play Called Corpus Christi*. Stanford, CA: Stanford University Press, 1966.

Miller, Arthur. *The Theatre Essays of Arthur Miller*. New York: Viking Press, 1978.

Millet, Fred B., and Gerald Eades Bentley. *The Art of the Drama*. New York: D. Appleton-Century Company, 1935.

Mulryne, J. R., and Margaret Shewring, eds. *Theatre of the English and Italian Renaissance*. Houndmills, Bas-ingstoke, Hampshire, UK: Macmillan, 1991.

Segal, Erich. *The Death of Comedy*. Cambridge, MA: Har-vard University Press, 2001.

Tiongson, Nicanor G. "Lenten Stage: Sorting Out the His-torical Threads of the Sinakulo." In *Filipino Heritage: The Making of a Nation*. Vol. 6. *The Spanish Colonial Period (18th/19th centuries): Roots of National Identity*, edited by Alfredo R. Roc, 1546–53. Manila: Lahing Pilipino Pub, 1977–78.

Toll, Robert C. *On With the Show: The First Century of Show Business in America*. New York: Oxford University Press, 1976.

Wellworth, George. *The Theatre of Protest and Paradox: De-velopments in the Avant-Garde Drama*. New York: New York University Press, 1964.

Ziomek, Henryk. *The History of Spanish Golden Age Drama*. Lexington: University Press of Kentucky, 1984.

Chapter 5

Adachi, Barbara C. *Backstage at Bunraku: A Behind-the-Scenes Look at Japan's Traditional Puppet Theatre*. 1st ed. New York: Weatherhill, 1985.

Arnoldi, Mary Jo. *Playing with Time: Art and Performance in Central Mali*. Bloomington: Indiana University Press, 1995.

Baird, Bil. *The Art of the Puppet*. New York: Bonanza Books, 1973.

Baumer, Rachel Van M., and James R. Brandon, eds. *Sanskrit Drama in Performance*. Honolulu: University Press of Hawaii, 1981.

Bell, John, ed. *Puppets, Masks, and Performing Objects*. Cam-bridge, MA: MIT Press, 2001.

Brandon, James R., trans. *Kabuki: Five Classic Plays*. Hon-olulu: University of Hawaii Press, 1992.

Brandon, James R., ed. *On Thrones of Gold: Three Javanese Shadow Plays*. Cambridge, MA: Harvard University Press, 1970.

Chikamatsu, Monzaemon. *Four Plays by Chikamatsu*. Trans-lated by Donald Keene. New York: Columbia University Press, 1997.

Commission for Publications of UNIMA (Union Interna-tionale de la Marionnette), ed. *The World of Puppetry*. Translated by Christa Schuenke and Frank Reiter. Berlin: Henschelverlag, 1989.

Crump, J. I. *Chinese Theater in the Days of Kublai Khan*. Ann Arbor: Center for Chinese Studies, University of Michigan, 1990.

Dick, Kay. *Pierrot*. London: Hutchinson, 1960.

Drewal, Margaret Thompson. *Yoruba Ritual: Performers, Play, Agency*. Bloomington: Indiana University Press, 1992.

Duchartre, Pierre-Louis. *The Italian Comedy: The Improvi-sation, Scenarios, Lives, Attributes, Portraits, and Masks of the Illustrious Characters of the Commedia dell'Arte*. Translated by Randolph T. Weaver. New York: Dover Publications, 1966.

Ernst, Earle. *The Kabuki Theatre*. Honolulu: University Press of Hawaii, 1974.

Findlater, Richard. *Grimaldi, King of Clowns*. London: MacGibbon & Kee, 1955.

———. *The Player Kings*. London: Weidenfeld & Nicol-son, 1971.

Gordon, Mel. *Lazzi: The Comic Routine of the Commedia dell'Arte*. New York: Performing Arts Journal Publica-tions, 1983.

Herbert, Mimi. *Voices of the Puppet Masters: The Wayang Golek Theater of Indonesia*. With Nur S. Rahardjo. Hon-olulu: University of Hawaii, 2002.

Keene, Donald, ed. *Twenty Plays of the Noh Theatre*. With the assistance of Royall Tyler. New York: Columbia Uni-versity Press, 1970.

Korean National Commission for UNESCO. *Korean Dance, Theater and Cinema*. Arch Cape, OR: Pace International Research, 1983.

———. *Traditional Performing Arts of Korea*. Seoul: KNCU, 1975.

Lal, P., trans. *Great Sanskrit Plays in Modern Translation*. New York: New Direction Books, 1957.

Leiter, Samuel, ed. *A Kabuki Reader: History and Perfor-mance*. London: M. E. Sharpe, 2002.

———. *The Art of Kabuki Five Famous Plays*. Mineola, NY: Dover, 1999.

———, ed. *Japanese Theater in the World*. New York: Japan Society, 1997.

Mackerras, Colin. *Chinese Theater: From its Origins to the Present Day*. Honolulu: University of Hawaii Press, 1983.

Miller, Barbara Stroller, ed. *The Plays of Kalidasa: Theatre of Memory*. Translated by Edwin Gerow. New Delhi: South Asia Books, 1999.

Oreglia, Giacomo. *The Commedia dell'Arte*. Translated by Lovett F. Edwards. New York: Hill and Wang, 1968.

Orenstein, Claudia. "Dancing on Shifting Ground: The Bali-nese Kecak in Cross-Culture Perspective," *Theatre Sym-posium* VI (August 1998):116–124.

Ortolani, Benito. *The Japanese Theatre: From Shamanistic Ritual to Contemporary Pluralism*. Princeton, NJ: Prince-ton University Press, 1995.

Ortolani, Benito, and Samuel L. Leiter. *Zeami and the Noh Theatre in the World*. New York: Center for Advanced Studies in Theatre Arts, Graduate School and University Center of the City University of New York, 1998.

Richmond, Farley P., Darius L. Swann, and Phillip B. Zarrilli, eds. *Indian Theatre: Traditions of Performance*. Honolulu: University of Hawaii Press, 1990.

Riley, Jo. *Chinese Theatre and the Actor in Performance*. New York: Cambridge University Press, 1997.

Tiongson, Nicanor G. "The Zarzuela From Madrid to Manila" *Solidarity* 116 (January–February 1988): 167–85.

United Nations Educational, Scientific, and Cultural Organization. "Culture Sector Homepage." UNESCO. http://portal.unesco.org/culture/.

Wang-Ngai, Siu. *Chinese Opera Images and Stories*. Vancouver: University of British Columbia Press, 1997.

Chapter 6

Bordman, Gerald. *American Musical Theatre: A Chronicle*. New York: Oxford University Press, 2001.

Blumenthal, Eileen. *Joseph Chaikin: Exploring at the Boundaries of Theater*. New York: Cambridge University Press, 1984.

Bonney, Jo. *Extreme Exposure: An Anthology of Solo Performance Texts from the Twentieth Century*. New York: Theatre Communications Group, 2000.

Carlson, Marvin. *Performance: A Critical Introduction*. 2nd ed. New York: Routledge, 2003.

Champagne, Lenora, ed. *Out from Under: Texts by Women Performance Artists*. New York: Theatre Communications Group, 1990.

Cole, Catherine M. *Ghana's Concert Party Theatre*. Bloomington: Indiana University Press, 2001.

Croyden, Margaret. *Lunatics, Lovers, and Poets: The Contemporary Experimental Theatre*. New York: McGraw-Hill, 1974.

Dance Notation Bureau. Dance Notation Bureau homepage. http://dancenotation.org/DNB/.

Engel, Lehman. *The American Musical Theater*. Rev ed. New York: Macmillan, 1975.

Felner, Mira. *Apostles of Silence: The Modern French Mimes*. London and Cranbury, NJ: Associated University Presses, 1985.

Gilbert, Douglas. *American Vaudeville, Its Life and Times*. New York: Dover Publications, 1963.

Goldberg, RoseLee. *Performance Art: From Futurism to the Present*. New York: Thames & Hudson, 2001.

Huxley, Michael, and Noel Witts, eds. *The Twentieth Century Performance Reader*. New York: Routledge, 1996.

Innes, Christopher. *Avant Garde Theatre, 1892–1992*, London: Routledge, 1993.

Jenkins, Ron. *Acrobats of the Soul: Comedy and Virtuosity in Contemporary American Theatre*. New York: Theatre Communications Group, 1988.

Jones, John Bush. *Our Musicals, Ourselves: A Social History of the American Musical Theater*. Hanover, NH: University Press of New England, 2003.

Kalb, Jonathan. "Documentary Solo Performance: The Politics of the Mirrored Self." *Theatre* 31, no. 3 (2001): 13–29.

Kirby, Michael, and Victoria Nes Kirby. *Futurist Performance*. New York: Performing Arts Journal Publications, 1971.

Lecoq, Jacques. *The Moving Body: Teaching Creative Theatre*. Translated by David Bradby. With a forward by Simon McBurney. Rev ed. London: Methuen, 2002.

Norton, Richard C. *A Chronology of American Musical Theater*. New York: Oxford University Press, 2002.

Riddle, Peter H. *The American Musical: History & Development*. Edited by Gay Riddle. Oakville, Ontario: Mosaic Press, 2003.

Roose-Evans, James. *Experimental Theatre from Stanislavsky to Peter Brook*. New York: Universe Books, 1984.

Smith, Anna Deavere. *Talk to Me: Travels in Media and Politics*. New York: Anchor, 2001.

Watts, Victoria. "The History of Notation." *ballet.co Magazine*, March 1998. http://www.ballet.co.uk/mar98/notation_history.htm.

Chapter 7

Barba, Eugenio, and Nicola Savarese. *Dictionary of Theatre Anthropology: The Secret Art of the Performer*. New York: Routledge, 1991.

Benedetti, Robert. *The Actor at Work*. 9th ed. New York: Allyn & Bacon, 2005.

Benedetti, Jean. *Stanislavski*. London: Routledge, 1988.

Bogart, Anne, and Tina Landau. *A Practical Guide to Viewpoints and Composition*. New York: Theatre Communications Group, 2004.

Carnicke, Sharon M. *Stanislavsky in Focus*. Amsterdam: Harwood Academic Publishers, 1998.

Cole, Toby, and Helen Krich Chinoy, eds. *Actors on Acting*. New York: Crown, 1970.

Copeau, Jacques. *Texts on Theatre*. Edited and translated by John Rudlin and Norman H. Paul. New York: Routledge, 1990.

Dixon, Michael, and Joel A. Smith, eds. *Anne Bogart: Viewpoints*. Lyme, NH: Smith and Kraus, 1995.

Felner, Mira. *Free to Act: An Integrated Approach to Acting*. 2nd ed. New York: Allyn & Bacon, 2004.

Frome, Shelly. *The Actors Studio: A History*. Jefferson, NC: McFarland, 2001.

Garfield, David. *A Player's Place: The Story of the Actors Studio*. New York: Macmillan, 1980.

Grotowski, Jerzy. *Towards a Poor Theatre*. New York: Simon & Schuster, 1968.

Kurtz, Maurice. *Jacques Copeau: Biography of a Theater*. Carbondale: Southern Illinois University Press, 1999.

Linklater, Kristin. *Freeing the Natural Voice*. New York: Drama Book Publishers, 1976.

Meyerhold, Vsevolod. *Meyerhold on Theatre*. Edited and translated by Edward Braun. New York: Hill and Wang, 1969.

Osinski, Zbigniew. *Grotowski and His Laboratory*. Translated and abridged by Lillian Vallee and Robert Findlay. New York: Performing Arts Journal Publications, 1986.

Stanislavski, Constantine. *An Actor Prepares*. Reprint ed. New York: Routledge, 1989.

————. *Building a Character*. Reprint ed. New York: Routledge, 1989.

————. *Creating a Role*. Reprint ed. New York: Routledge, 1989.

Strasberg, Lee. *A Dream of Passion*. Boston: Little, Brown, 1987.

Suzuki, Tadashi. *The Way of Acting*. New York: Theater Communications Group, 2000.

Zarrilli, Phillip B. *Acting (Re)Considered: A Theoretical and Practical Guide*. 2nd ed. London: Routledge, 2002.

————. *Kathakali Dance-Drama: Where Gods and Demons Come to Play*. With translations by V. R. Prabodhachandran Nagar, M. P. Sankaran Namboodiri, and Phillip B. Zarrilli. New York: Routledge, 2000.

Chapter 8

Blumenthal, Eileen, and Julie Taymor. *Julie Taymor: Playing with Fire*. New York: Harry N. Abrams, 1995.

Bogart, Anne. *A Director Prepares: Seven Essays on Art and Theatre*. New York: Routledge, 2001.

Brook, Peter. *The Empty Space*. London: MacGibbon & Kee, 1968.

————. *The Shifting Point: 1946–1987*. New York: Harper & Row, 1987.

Clurman, Harold. *On Directing*. New York: Macmillan, 1972.

Cole, Toby, and Helen Krich Chinoy, eds. *Directors on Directing; A Source Book of the Modern Theater*. Indianapolis: Bobbs-Merrill, 1963.

Foreman, Richard. *Unbalancing Acts: Foundations for a Theater*. Edited by Ken Jordan. New York: Pantheon Books, 1992.

Gorchakov, Nikolai. *Stanislavsky Directs*. Translated by Miriam Goldina. New York: Limelight Editions, 1985.

Jones, David Richard. *Great Directors at Work: Stanislavsky, Brecht, Kazan, Brook*. Berkeley: University of California Press, 1986.

Marranca, Bonnie, ed. *The Theatre of Images*. Baltimore: Johns Hopkins University Press, 1996.

McBurney, Simon, and Complicité. *Complicité Plays: 1: Street of Crocodiles, Mnemonic, Three Lives of Lucie Cabrol*. London: Methuen, 2004.

Whitton, David. *Stage Directors in Modern France*. Manchester: Manchester University Press, 1987.

Chapter 9

Bell, John. "Disney's Times Square: The New American Community Theatre." *TDR: The Drama Review* 42, no. 1 (1998): 26–33.

————. *Landscape and Desire: Bread and Puppet Pageants in the 1990s*. Glover, VT: Bread and Puppet Press, 1997.

Bieber, Margarete. *The History of the Greek and Roman Theater*. Princeton, NJ: Princeton University Press, 1961.

Carlson, Marvin. *Places of Performance: The Semiotics of Theatre Architecture*. Ithaca, NY: Cornell University Press, 1989.

Mackintosh, Ian. *Architecture, Actor, and Audience*. New York: Routledge, 1993.

Morrison, William. *Broadway Theatres: History and Architecture*. New York: Dover Publications, 1999.

Nagler, A. M. *Shakespeare's Stage*. New Haven: Yale University Press, 1981.

Redmond, James. *The Theatrical Space*. New York: Cambridge University Press, 1987.

Schlemmer, Oskar, Laszlo Moholy-Nagy, and Farkas Molnár. *The Theater of the Bauhaus*. Edited by Walter Gropius. Translated by Arthur S. Wensinger. Middletown, CT: Wesleyan University Press, 1971.

Schoenbaum, S. *Shakespeare, The Globe & The World*. New York: Oxford University Press, 1979.

Southern, Richard. *The Seven Ages of the Theatre*. London: Faber and Faber, 1962.

Sussman, Mark. "New York's Facelift." *TDR: The Drama Review* 42, no. 1 (1998): 34–42.

Wiles, David. *Tragedy in Athens: Performance Space and Theatrical Meaning*. New York: Cambridge University Press, 1997.

Chapter 10

Baer, Nancy Van Norman, ed. *Theatre in Revolution: Russian Avant-Garde Stage Design 1913–1935*. San Francisco: Fine Arts Museums of San Francisco, 1991.

Bandem, I Madé, and Fredrik Eugene de Boer. *Balinese Dance in Transition: Kaja and Kelod*. 2nd ed. Kuala Lumpur, Malaysia: Oxford University Press, 1995.

Bernhard Betty, prod. *Bhavai: Folk Theatre of Gujarat*, 23 min. Insight Media Distributors, 1994.

Emigh, John. *Masked Performance: The Play of Self and Other in Ritual and Theatre*. Philadelphia: University of Pennsylvania Press, 1996.

Gorelik, Moredicai. *New Theatres for Old*. New York: Samuel French, 1947.

Jones, Robert Edmond. *The Dramatic Imagination: Reflections and Speculations on the Art of the Theatre*. New York: Theatre Arts Books, 1956.

Shaoshan, Shi. *Make-up Designs in Traditional Chinese Operas*. Beijing: Ke xue chu ban she, 1995.

Slattum, Judy. *Masks of Bali: Spirits of an Ancient Drama*. San Francisco: Chronicle Books, 1992.

Takeda, Sharon Sadako, ed. *Miracles and Mischief: Noh and Kyogen Theatre in Japan*. Los Angeles: Los Angeles County Museum of Art, 2002.

Xiafeng, Pan. *The Stagecraft of Peking Opera: From its Origins to the Present Day*. Beijing: New World Press, 1995.

Chapter 11

Aronson, Arnold. *American Set Design*. New York: Theatre Communications Group, 1985.

Burris-Meyer, Harold, and Edward C. Cole. *Scenery for the Theatre: The Organization, Processes, Materials, and Techniques Used to Set the Stage*. Rev. ed. Boston: Little, Brown, 1971.

Condee, William Faricy. *Theatrical Space: A Guide for Directors and Designers*. Lanham, MD: Scarecrow Press, 2002.

Ingham, Rosemary. *From Page to Stage: How Theatre Designers Make Connections Between Scripts and Images.* Portsmouth, NH: Heinemann, 1998.

Law, Jane Marie. *Puppets of Nostalgia: The Life, Death, and Rebirth of the Japanese Awaji Ningyo Tradition.* Princeton, NJ: Princeton University Press, 1997.

Smith, Ronn. *American Set Design Two.* New York: Theatre Communications Group, 1991.

Chapter 12

Anderson, Barbara, and Cletus Anderson. *Costume Design.* New York: Holt, Rinehart, and Winston, 1984.

Baer, Nancy Van Norman, ed. *The Art of Enchantment: Diaghilev's Ballets Russes, 1909–1929.* New York: Universe Books, 1988.

Boskin, Joseph. *Sambo: The Rise & Demise of an American Jester.* New York: Oxford University Press, 1986.

Corson, Richard. *Stage Makeup.* 9th ed. New York: Allyn & Bacon, 2000.

Cunningham, Rebecca. *The Magic Garment: Principles of Costume Design.* New York: Longman, 1988.

Ingham, Rosemary, and Liz Covey. *The Costume Designer's Handbook.* Portsmouth, NH: Heinemann, 1992.

Pecktal, Lynn. *Costume Design: Techniques of Modern Masters.* New York: Back Stage Books, 1993.

Russell, Douglas A. *Period Style for the Theatre.* Boston: Allyn & Bacon, 1987.

Senelick, Laurence. *The Changing Room: Sex, Drag and Theatre.* New York: Routledge, 2000.

Chapter 13

Appia, Adolphe. *The Work of Living Art: A Theory of the Theatre,* translated by H. D. Albright; and, *Man Is The Measure of All Things,* edited and translated by Barnard Hewitt. Coral Gables: University of Miami Press, 1960.

Lebrecht, James, and Deena Kaye. *Sound and Music for the Theatre: The Art and Technique of Design.* 2nd ed. Oxford: Focal Press, 1999.

Leonard, John A. *Theatre Sound.* New York: Routledge, 2001.

McCandless, Stanely. *A Method of Lighting the Stage.* New York: Theatre Arts Books, 1958.

Pillbrow, Richard. *Stage Lighting Design: The Art, The Craft, The Life.* London: Nick Hern, 1997.

Palmer, Richard H. *The Lighting Art: The Aesthetics of Stage Lighting Design.* Upper Saddle River, NJ: Prentice Hall, 1993.

Reid, Francis. *The Stage Lighting Handbook.* New York: Theatre Art Books, 1996.

Chapter 14

Burian, Jarka. *The Scenography of Josef Svoboda.* Middletown, CT: Wesleyan University Press, 1971.

Butterworth, Phillip. *Theatre of Fire: Special Effects in Early English and Scottish Theatre.* London: The Society for Theatre Research, 1998.

Dixon, Steve. "Metal Performance: Humanizing Robots, Returning to Nature, and Camping About." Special issue, *TDR: The Drama Review* 48, no. 4 (2004): 15–46.

Kaplan, Stephen. "A Puppet Tree: A Model for the Field of Puppet Theatre." *The Drama Review* 43, no. 3 (1999): 28–35.

Marranca, Bonnie. "The Wooster Group: A Dictionary of Ideas." *PAJ: A Journal of Performance and Art* 25, no. 2 (2003): 1–18.

Reid, Francis. *The ABC of Stage Technology.* London: A&C Black, 1995.

Saltz, David. "Performing Arts." In *A Companion to Digital Humanities,* edited by Susan Schreibman, Ray Siemens, and John Unsworth, 121–31. Malden, MA: Blackwell, 2004.

Savran, David. *The Wooster Group: Breaking the Rules.* New York: Theatre Communications Group, 1988.

Svoboda, Josef. *The Secret of Theatrical Space: The Memoirs of Josef Svoboda.* Edited and translated by J. M. Burian. New York: Applause Theatre Books, 1993.

Chapter 15

Artaud, Antonin. *The Theater and Its Double.* Translated by Mary Caroline Richards. New York: Grove Press, 1966.

Brecht, Bertolt. *Brecht on Theatre: The Development of an Aesthetic.* Translated by John Willett. Reissue ed. London: Methuen, 1964.

Carlson, Marvin. *Theories of the Theatre: A Historical and Critical Survey from the Greeks to the Present.* Ithaca, NY: Cornell University Press, 1993.

Dolan, Jill. *The Feminist Spectator as Critic.* Ann Arbor: University of Michigan Press, 1994.

Dukore, Bernard F., ed. *Dramatic Theory and Criticism: Greeks to Grotowski.* New York: Holt, Rinehart, and Winston, 1974.

Esslin, Martin. *The Theatre of the Absurd.* New York: Penguin, 1980.

Goldoni, Carlo. *The Comic Theatre: A Comedy in Three Acts.* Translated by John W. Miller. Lincoln: University of Nebraska Press, 1969.

Kauffmann, Stanley. *Persons of the Drama: Theater Criticism and Comment.* New York: Harper & Row, 1976.

———. *Theater Criticisms.* New York: Performing Arts Journal Publications, 1984.

Kott, Jan. *The Eating of the Gods: An Interpretation of Greek Tragedy.* Translated by Boleslaw Taborski and Edward J. Czerwinski. Reprint ed. Chicago: Northwestern University Press, 1987.

———. *Shakespeare, Our Contemporary.* Translated by Boleslaw Taborski. New York: W. W. Norton, 1974.

Literary Managers and Dramaturgs of the Americas. LMDA homepage. www.lmda.org.

Molière. *Tartuffe And Other Plays.* Translated by Donald L. Frame. New York: Penguin, 1981.

Shaw, Bernard. *Major Critical Essays: The Quintessence of Ibsenism, the Perfect Wagnerite, the Sanity of Art.* Edited by Michael Holroyd. New York: Penguin, 1986.

Zeami. *On the Art of the Noh Drama: The Major Treatises of Zeami.* Translated by J. Thomas Rimer and Masakazu Yamazaki. Princeton, NJ: Princeton University Press, 1984.

Chapter 16

Alexander, Jane. *Command Performance: An Actress in the Theatre of Politics.* New York: Public Affairs, 2000.

Carter, Paul. *Backstage Handbook: An Illustrated Almanac of Technical Information.* New York: Broadway Press, 1988.

Farber, Donald C. *From Option to Opening: A Guide to Producing Plays Off-Broadway.* New York: Limelight Editions, 1997.

Langley, Stephen. *Theatre Management and Production in America: Commercial, Stock, Resident, College, Community, and Presenting Organizations.* New York: Drama Book Publishers, 1990.

Kelly, Thomas. *The Backstage Guide to Stage Management.* 2nd ed. New York: Back Stage Books, 1999.

Shapiro, James. *Oberammergau: The Troubling Story of the World's Most Famous Passion Play.* New York: Pantheon Books, 2000.

Van Erven, Eugene. *Community Theatre: Global Perspectives.* New York: Routledge, 2001.

Volz, Jim. *How to Run a Theatre: A Witty, Practical, and Fun Guide to Arts Management,* New York: Back Stage Books, 2004.

Index

Page numbers in **boldface** followed by a capital letter **B** indicate boxed features.